D1576489

AIRCRAFT IN BRITISH MILITARY SERVICE

Meteor NF(T) Mk 14, Varsity T Mk 1, Dominie T Mk 1

Two generations of navigation trainer are seen in this fine shot of aircraft of 1 ANS at Stradishall photographed in 1966. Meteor NF(T) Mk 14 'F' is in the background while Varsity WF372/A formates with Dominie XS712/A, the type which replaced both earlier aircraft. *(Crown copyright)*

AIRCRAFT IN BRITISH MILITARY SERVICE

BRITISH SERVICE AIRCRAFT SINCE 1946

Vic Flintham

Airlife
England

Acknowledgements

Over the years I have been helped, stimulated and encouraged by a number of writers, editors and enthusiasts who have in common a high degree of generosity in sharing information and material. This book is dedicated to them. I would specifically like to acknowledge help given with photographs by David Gibbings, Peter Green, Bill Hunt, Brian Pickering, Ray Sturtivant and Andy Thomas. Finally, my continuing thanks to Christine, my wife, who has always supported me in an interest which too often intrudes into family life.

Copyright © 1998 Vic Flintham

First published in UK in 1998
by Airlife Publishing Ltd

British Library Cataloguing-in-Publication Data
A catalogue record for this book
is available from the British Library

ISBN 1 85310 891 X

All rights reserved. No part of this book may be reproduced or transmitted in any form or by any means, electronic or mechanical including photocopying, recording or by any information storage and retrieval system, without permission from the Publisher in writing.

Typeset by Phoenix Typesetting, Ilkley, West Yorkshire
Printed in England by Butler & Tanner Ltd,
Frome and London

Airlife Publishing Ltd
101 Longden Road, Shreswbury, SY3 9EB, England

Introduction

This book came about as the result of a boring motorway drive. My mind wandered through the various marks of Meteor fighter and I got stuck at Mark 5. Was there one, and what was it? Indeed, what was the Mark 6? I decided that I knew less than I thought about all marks of aircraft which had flown with, or had been intended for, the Royal Air Force and for my own satisfaction began to compile a computer database. I took as my start date 1946 since post-war aircraft and their use have to some extent been less well documented than those used in the war. Also, I have to admit that my interests, and therefore my references, are in post-war aviation.

I soon realised that for the sake of completeness I would have to include aircraft operated by the other British air arms, since the flow of mark numbers did not respect the user. Thus the Gazelle was operated by four services in four marks.

Soon, what was originally curiosity became an obsession. I expanded the database to include usage. That process in turn led me to learn more about the way in which the services were structured and how aircraft were deployed to meet contemporary needs. It then seemed a shame not to convert what was becoming an extensive *aide-mémoire* into something which others might find useful. Since there was no comprehensive reference available on all post-war aircraft and their users, a book began to write itself.

The most difficult task was to find a shape. Where possible I wanted to relate types to their use over time, but military aircraft do not always lend themselves to easy classification. The Halifax was a bomber, but its post-war use was primarily as a transport. What sort of fighter was the Vampire, or for that matter the Phantom? I decided to use my own judgement and divide the book into sensible chunks, with adequate cross-referencing to ensure easy access to any type. Access to units is essentially by function.

Hard decisions had to be made about where in the chapters to locate certain types. While many may disagree with my classifications, they are to some extent based on my desire to spread material evenly through the chapters and partly on logic. Thus I can justify placing the Tornado with strike aircraft, while its deployment as an air defence fighter is described within the air defence fighter chapter. Similarly, I placed the Phantom in the air defence fighter chapter, while its deployment in the tactical role is described elsewhere.

While I have taken great care to ensure accuracy, constraints of time and money have dictated that this book is the result of much reading and some limited original research. It is essentially a collation and as such it thus draws together primary research undertaken by a number of experts over many years, but any mistakes are mine alone. Over time there have been many disputes about such matters as the precision of production numbers, some of it acrimonious. While there is great merit in searching for the ultimate truth, it needs saying occasionally that unless the reader was there, caution is needed in being too dogmatic; many formal written records in the public domain have been proved to be inaccurate.

Vic Flintham
Bushey, Herts.

How to use this book

I have not attempted to provide a detailed history of the development of each type, neither is the book strong on analysis. I would remind the reader that it really is an *aide-mémoire* concerned solely with post-war usage from January 1946. Against each type I have listed wherever possible the further reading within which much more detail will be found.

I have assumed that the reader will be an enthusiast, broadly familiar with the subject matter. While the book should stand on its own it will prove of much more practical value when read in conjunction with a number of standard reference works, most of which are readily available. There is no point in my locating airfields, for example, when there are excellent books already available and which cover the subject in much greater depth than I could hope to. There is a bibliography which highlights the relevant sources.

There are twelve chapters and each is written to a consistent format. First there is an index of the types covered with a note of those also used in the relevant role but described in other chapters. Then there is a general text which describes the changes over time in the structure and deployment of units. This is supported by a number of tables listing the establishment or orders of battle and showing type, unit and location. The selected dates for the tables vary between chapters to reflect change in relation to key events impacting on the function of aircraft described. It is not necessarily possible, therefore, for the reader to review all units on any given date. Some common dates have been used, however, to enable some comparisons.

The second section of each chapter describes the aircraft. Not all of the aircraft figuring in tables will be described in the relevant chapter. The Tornado, for example, will be listed in the unit tables under air defence fighters, but the type is described in the chapter on strike and bomber types. The reasons for this have already been addressed. The aircraft are described in chronological order and the numbers described in each chapter vary from twelve to thirty. Apart from the contents list at the beginning a full index at the end of the book lists all inclusions by name and manufacturer(s).

For each type, there is a short introduction and then each mark number used post-war is described briefly following which there is a note on usage. In each case squadron usage is given first, followed by training and miscellaneous units. A table then summarises the characteristics of each variant – the tables vary between categories of aircraft to show those features most appropriate for the function. Care needs to be taken with the data tables in that figures for range, for example, depend heavily on load, climatic conditions and the quality of engine maintenance. Wherever possible representative data are given. Finally there is a type-specific reading list.

The book is completed by appendices listing abbreviations, designations, aircraft nicknames, post-war campaigns and operations and weapons systems.

Contents

1 – Trainers

See also: Anson (7.2); Brigand (3.8); Dominie (7.3); Hunter (2.8); Meteor (2.5); Mosquito (3.4); Proctor (7.4); Sea Prince (7.11); Sea Vampire (8.9); Spitfire (2.1); Valetta (6.10); Vampire (3.9)

Tiger Moth T Mk 1

The Tiger Moth was the classic primary trainer on which most wartime aircrew must have cut their teeth. Here, though, the type is seen well after the war in service with 8 EFTS in the form of T-7792/FDRM. *(MAP)*

Throughout the following brief history five terms may be used, while noting that the titles of units have changed over time.

> **Primary** training is the first stage where the student is introduced to flying. Otherwise referred to as elementary, initial or grading.
>
> **Basic** training is the core leading to wings standard. Otherwise referred to as service flying training.
>
> **Advanced** training is the more specific training on the category of aircraft for which the student has been streamed.
>
> Operational or **pre-conversion** training is designed to prepare the student to operate the category of aircraft in role.
>
> **Conversion** training is intended to concentrate on learning to fly and operate a specific type of aircraft.

1946

At the end of the war the structure for training was still the wartime model, although the need for change was urgent as the services prepared for dramatic reduction and de-mobilisation of aircrew. Flying training for all services was managed by Flying Training Command and began as it had before the war with time on the Tiger Moth at an Elementary Flying Training School (EFTS), then switching to a quite separate Service Flying Training School (SFTS) on the Harvard, Anson or Oxford. The student then progressed to an Operational Training Unit (OTU) on a broadly similar type to that which he would fly in service. There was a surplus of piston engine competent pilots, so most new pilot entrants were directed to the new Flying Training Schools in preparation to fly the new generation of jet fighters.

There was a wide range of supplementary specialist schools, generally those which had been set up to address specific problems like beam approach training. Large numbers of surplus aircraft also resulted in schools retaining a range of wartime types on charge. The surplus of pilots resulted in newly qualified aircrew having to wait around nine months for an operational posting. Non-pilot aircrew training was generally managed by Technical Training or Maintenance Commands.

Naval pilots received their initial training with the RAF, as did the Army. The former, however, maintained no fewer than 29 post-basic schools, reflecting, perhaps, the complexity and demands of naval flying. Wartime fighters like the Hellcat and Corsair were much in evidence and the Whitley was still in service for engine handling training.

1947

In the post-war years there was little money available for new equipment for training. The RAF had re-structured and most primary flying, backed by the re-emergence of the University Air Squadrons, was controlled by Reserve Command, created in May 1946. Flying Training Command managed basic flying training and Technical Training Command the range of specialist units. The EFTSs had reduced in numbers and become Reserve

Flying Schools (RFS) with a primary function of keeping the large numbers of VR pilots up to scratch; the SFTSs had become Flying Training Schools (FTS). The Rhodesian Air Training Group remained as the only overseas school while the flying element of the Royal Air Force College had been re-formed from 19 FTS. Operational Training Units or Conversion Units had become Operational Conversion Units.

The Royal Air Force College and its predecessors

The several **Air Gunnery Schools** had merged into the **Central Gunnery School**. The **School of Flying Control** had become the **School of Air Traffic Control** while the **Central Navigation School** had become the **Empire Air Navigation School**. The various instructor units began changing and preparing for eventual merger. The **Empire Central Flying School** had become the **Empire Flying School**. In July 1949 it would merge with the **Empire Air Armament School** to become the **Royal Air Force Flying College** at Manby. Similarly the **Signals Flying Unit** had become the **Radio Experimental Unit** which also in July 1949 was to merge with the **Empire Radio School** and **Empire Armaments School** to become the **Royal Air Force Technical College** at Henlow.

The **Royal Air Force Flying College** became the **College of Air Warfare** in 1962 (including the **School of Refresher Flying** (SRF)) and the **Royal Air Force Technical College** was to merge with the **Royal Air Force College** later in the same year. The **College of Air Warfare** itself disbanded in 1978 with the SRF going to 3 FTS and all other elements into the **Royal Air Force College**.

1950

By now little has changed except for one very important principle: all-through training. Hitherto fledgling pilots had begun their primary flying training at one school and had then moved for basic training to another. Now pilots trained throughout in one FTS moving from the Prentice to the Harvard. With the exception of the Prentice, and the Proctor for use with the Radio Schools, there were no new types in use, although the Chipmunk basic trainer had been ordered.

1952

Reserve Command had become Home Command and the training arm of the RAF had been re-structured and expanded to meet the perceived demands of the Korean War. The Tiger Moth had at last been eclipsed by the Chipmunk which itself was to prove the longest-serving type in the history of the RAF. New Basic Flying Training Schools (BFTS) had been established to train National Service pilots together with Advanced Flying Schools (AFS) which were established to help bridge the gap between the Harvard and the jet types which pilots would find on OCUs. Flying Refresher Schools (FRS) had been set up to enable regular and non-regular aircrew to re-train. There had been parallel changes in navigator and other aircrew training.

1955

The Rhodesian Air Training Group had disbanded in 1953 at the same time that the range of expansion units

Training sequence 1946

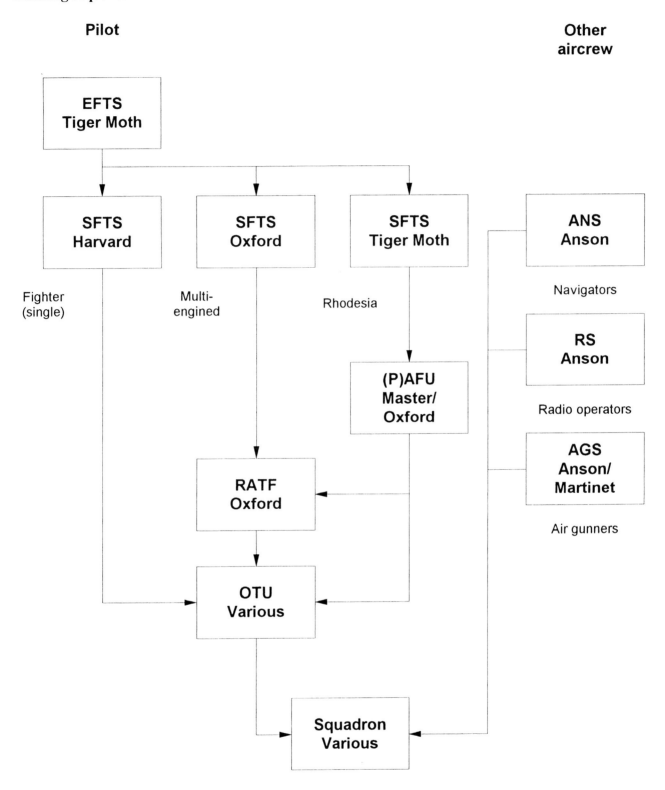

Pilot

Other aircrew

was also closed down. By 1955 there were thirteen FTSs some of which met the need for advanced training. All RFSs had closed. In terms of equipment, the jet age had at last impacted directly on flying training. The Prentice/Harvard all-through training had given way to the much more effective Provost/Vampire T Mk11 combination. During 1955 a remarkable trial took place. 2 FTS employed the new Jet Provost to test all-through jet training, a scheme to be adopted from 1959. Another sign of the times was the Helicopter Development Flight at South Cerney which was soon absorbed into the CFS which thus extended its role of training instructors. In the Navy the first helicopter bought specifically for training, the Hiller HT Mk 1, had joined 705 NAS.

Training sequence 1948

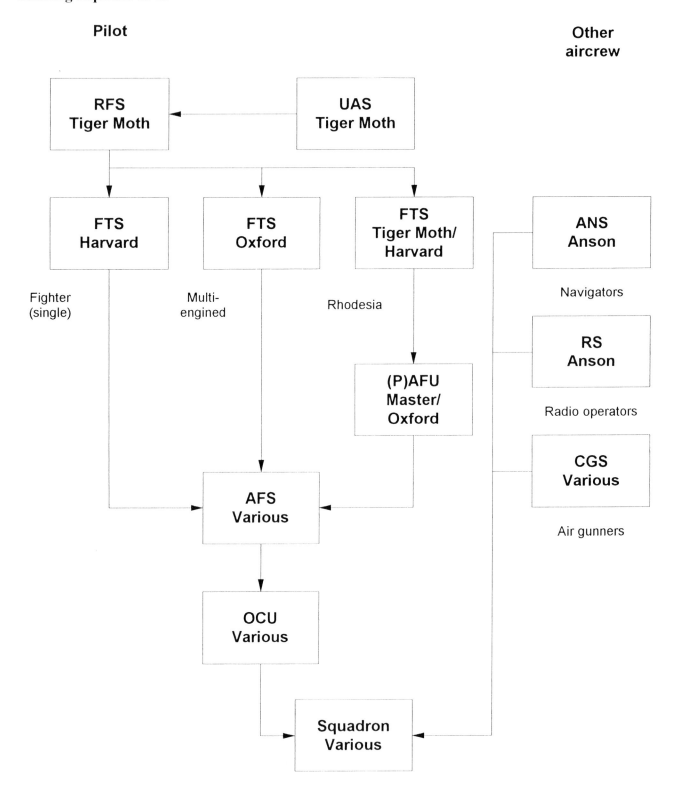

1960

The services had begun anticipating significant reductions and this was reflected in continuing streamlining. Home Command disbanded in 1959 and there were just six FTSs. The Jet Provost T Mk 3 had entered service with 2 FTS at Syerston and the Varsity had been established as the Oxford replacement since 1951. Naval basic training was through 1 FTS and much advanced training was now focused on helicopters.

Training sequence 1953

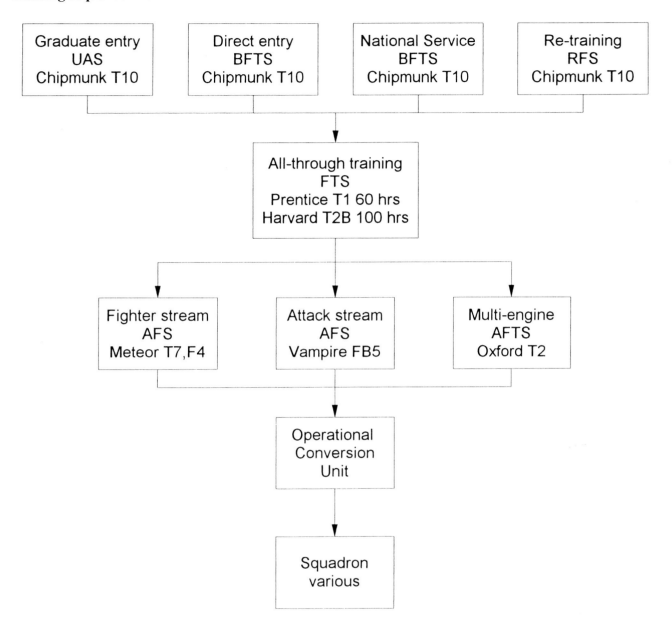

Air experience and the University Air Squadrons

Air experience was by now refined and extensive, operating under direct Flying Training Command control. Many **Combined Cadet Forces** (CCF) had access to their own Grasshopper primary gliders while the **Air Experience Flights** (AEF) had been formed in 1958 with Chipmunks to give experience to Cadets from CCF and **Air Training Corps** (ATC) units. There were 27 **Volunteer Gliding Schools** (VGS) across the country with the Cadet and Sedbergh gliders to provide less expensive flying experience. Finally, the **University Air Squadrons** (UAS) – also equipped with Chipmunks – provided the link into the RAF for potential graduate entrants.

1965

There were now six FTSs all flying the Jet Provost, with the new, pressurised T Mk 5 having just entered service.

Advanced training was conducted on the Gnat and Hunter at 4 FTS for the fast-jet stream and 5 FTS for multi-engine training. This year the Red Arrows formed on the Gnat at Little Rissington as part of the CFS.

1970

In 1968 Training Command had been formed through the merger of Flying Training and Technical Training Commands. Apart from that there were few noticeable changes from 1965 except that significantly the Royal Navy now had no fixed-wing aircraft and thus no need for training fixed-wing pilots. The last Vampire T Mk11 had been retired in 1967 and the Dominie had been introduced in 1965 to replace the Meteor NF(T) Mk 14 as a navigation trainer. Navigator training by 1966 comprised initial training with 2 ANS on the Valetta T Mk 3 (28 hours) then the Varsity T Mk 1 for 82 hours. Students then went

Training sequence 1962

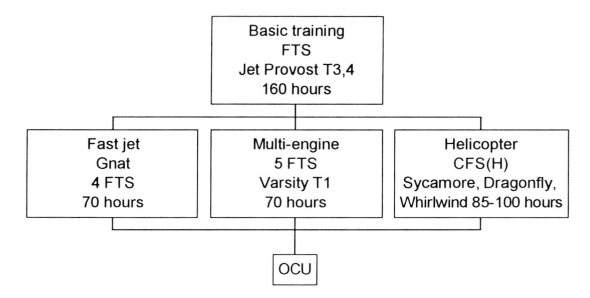

to 1 ANS with the 'slow' stream spending a further four months on the Varsity while those scheduled for fast-jet units trained on the Dominie and Jet Provost.

Other equipment changes included the introduction of the Gazelle HT Mk 3 into the CFS(H). The RAF command structure was further simplified by the merger of Flying and Technical Training Commands into Training Command on 1 June 1968. By 1970 the demand for trained pilots in the RAF was 300 a year who would be trained through four basic FTSs including the RAFC.

1975

Pilot demand was now down to some 160 to 185 a year of whom 50% would be graduate entrants. In 1974 the pattern of training changed to reduce training time without dropping standards. After grading, students were given 100 hours or 75 hours (graduate entrants) on the Jet Provost T Mk 3A or T Mk 5A.

For multi-engine training the Jetstream had replaced the Varsity at 5 FTS, while another equipment change was the introduction of the Bulldog with the CFS and most of the University Air Squadrons. The two Air Navigation Schools had merged into 6 FTS while RN elementary flying training shifted in 1974 from 2 FTS to the RNEFTS within 3 FTS at Leeming. An important development in 1974 was the formation of the Tactical Weapons Unit (TWU) from 229 OCU to help bridge the gap between advanced flying training and conversion to type.

1980

Another structural change had resulted in Training Command being absorbed into Support Command in 1977 with 21 Group having responsibility for flying training. Due to diminishing demand for multi-engine aircrew the Jetstreams of 5 FTS were placed in storage in

1976 and the limited demand met through training with CAT at Hamble. The same year the Hawk entered service with 4 FTS to replace the Gnat. The other new introduction was at the other end of the spectrum – the Venture powered glider for those VGSs where self-launching was feasible. The Jetstreams returned to service with the Multi-Engine Training Squadron (METS) within 3 FTS in 1977, switching to 5 FTS in 1979. Another change in FTS roles was the creation of 2 FTS from the CFS(H) component for helicopter training at Shawbury. The decade ended with the reformation at Church Fenton of 7 FTS with the Jet Provost to meet increased demand.

1985

By now there were only three basic FTSs including the RAFC, and multi-engine training was with the METS within 6 FTS at Finningley; the main role of the latter was navigator training on the Jet Provost and Dominie. The various air experience units continued to develop. New gliders were joining the 27 VGSs which between them used about 150 while 50 Chipmunks served with the thirteen AEFs. Both types of units provided air experience for the cadets of 186 CCF sections (which still operated about 50 Grasshoppers) and 900 ATC squadrons. Significantly the UASs allowed women to join for the first time.

1990

The primary training and grading of pilots remarkably remained with the venerable Chipmunks of the EFTS, while the turboprop Tucano was beginning to replace the Jet Provost, starting with 7 FTS. There were now just three FTSs including 3 FTS which provided the flying element of the RAFC. The TWU had split into two in 1980 and both were equipped with the Hawk. The UAS Bulldogs began a re-equipment programme to improve instrumentation.

Training sequence 1975

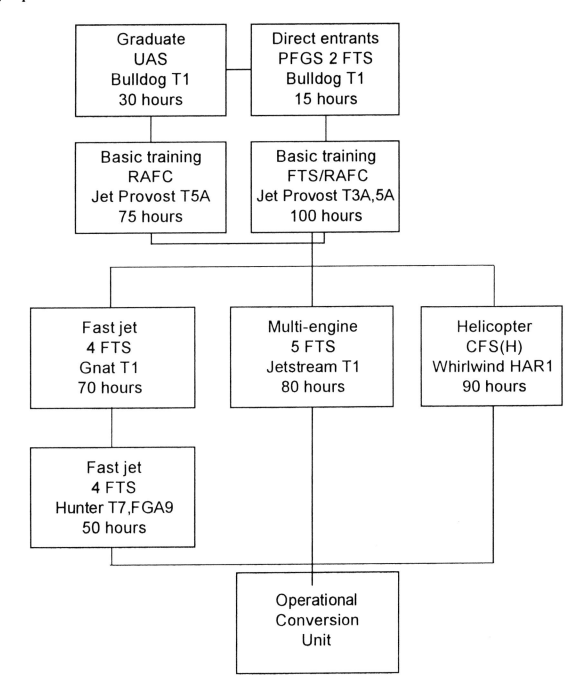

1995

The last Jet Provosts were retired in 1991 and further changes were made as the RAF contracted further as a result of the so-called 'peace dividend' and the search for economy through market testing. Pilots without UAS Bulldog experience got their primary training with the civilian-run JEFTS at Topcliffe on the Slingsby Firefly. (Naval pilots would have first acquired their air experience through the civilian-run Grading Flight at Roborough.) They then went to either 1 or 3 (RAFC) FTS on the Tucano for 110 hours, or 63 hours for those going on to Gazelle then Wessex helicopters at 2 FTS. Multi-engine training was with 6 FTS Jetstreams. Advanced training and weapons training is with 4 FTS on the Hawk. The latter unit assumed the role and equipment of 1 TWU after 7 FTS was disbanded just a year or so after taking over the work of 2 TWU.

Training sequence 1986

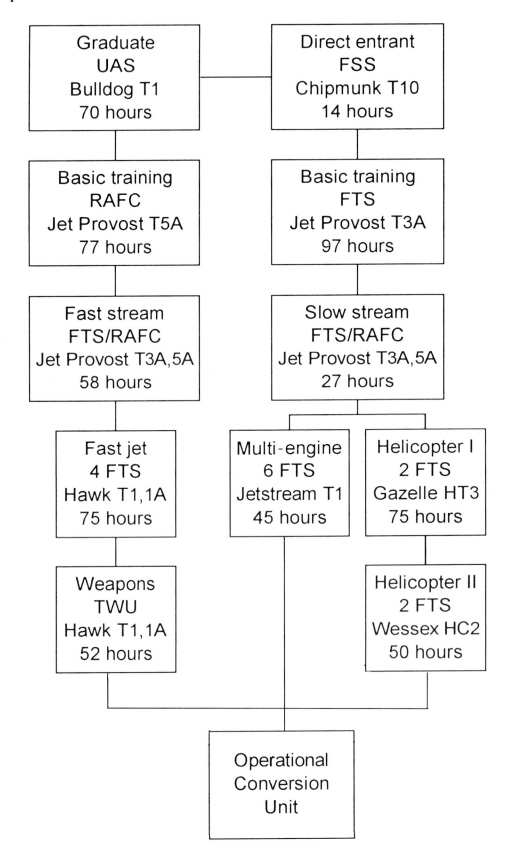

1.A Training at 1 January 1946

Air Ministry

Gliding Schools

Type	Unit	Base
Cadet I	1 GS	Dungavel
	3 GS	Macmerry
	4 GS	Abbotsinch
	5 GS	Fourdoun
	6 GS	Turnhouse
	7 GS	Dalcross
	8 GS	Creetown
Cadet I, II, Kirby Kite	9 GS	Scone
Cadet I	10 GS	Turnberry
	21 GS	Lambton Park
Cadet I, II, Kirby Tutor	22 GS	Kirbymoorside
Cadet I	23 GS	Yeadon
	24 GS	Netherthorpe
	25 GS	Leconfield
Cadet I, II, III, Falcon III, King Kite	26 GS	Durham
Cadet I	27 GS	Woolsington
	28 GS	Middleton St George
	29 GS	Askern
	30 GS	Sherburn-in-Elmet
	31 GS	Usworth
	41 GS	Hockley Heath
	42 GS	Loughborough
	43 GS	Aldridge (Walsall)
	44 GS	Bruntingthorpe
	45 GS	Meir
Cadet I	47 GS	Camphill
	48 GS	Castle Bromwich
	49 GS	Wymeswold
	50 GS	Hereford
	62 GS	Cardiff
	63 GS	Tal-y-Cafn
	65 GS	Rhoose
	68 GS	Stormy Down
	70 GS	Pennard
	72 GS	Newport
	74 GS	Templeton
	81 GS	Yeovil
	82 GS	Roborough
	83 GS	Moreton Valence
	84 GS	Haldon Moor
	87 GS	Locking
	88 GS	Wroughton
	89 GS	Somerford
	92 GS	Charmy Down
	94 GS	Yate
	95 GS	St Eval
	102 GS	Horsham St Faith
	103 GS	Westley
	104 GS	Ipswich
	105 GS	Cambridge
	106 GS	Henlow
	107 GS	Coleby Grange
	108 GS	Desborough
	122 GS	Northwick Park
	123 GS	Bray Court
	124 GS	Elstree
	125 GS	Denham

Slingsby Sedbergh TX Mk 1

Gliders introduced countless future aircrew to their first taste of flight – albeit unpowered – through the Air Training Corps. They remain highly cost-effective as a means of getting off the ground and conveying the basics of flight. This Sedbergh, WG498, is seen with Cranwell Gliding Club in 1975. *(MAP)*

Type	Unit	Base
	126 GS	Booker
	127 GS	Panshanger
	128 GS	Theale
	129 GS	Romney Marsh
	130 GS	Cowley
	141 GS	Gravesend
	142 GS	Stapleford Tawney
	143 GS	Croydon
	144 GS	Heston
	145 GS	Birch (Colchester)
	146 GS	Fairlop
	148 GS	Rochford
	161 GS	Shoreham
	162 GS	? Gatwick
	163 GS	Portsmouth
	166 GS	Hawkinge
	167 GS	Fairoaks
	168 GS	Rochester
	181 GS	Stanley Park
	182 GS	Samlesbury
	183 GS	Woodford
	184 GS	Woodford
	185 GS	Barton
	186 GS	Speke
	187 GS	Stretton
	188 GS	Cark
	189 GS	Kingstown
	190 GS	Cranage
	192 GS	Hooton Park
	201 GS	? Newtonards
	203 GS	Newtonards

Flying Training Command, RAF

Elementary training (50 Group)

Type	Unit	Base
Tiger Moth	1 EFTS	Panshanger
	2 EFTS	Yatesbury
	3 EFTS	Shellingford
	4 EFTS	Brough
	6 EFTS	Sywell
	7 EFTS	Desford
	11 EFTS	Perth
	14 EFTS	Elmdon
	15 EFTS	Carlisle
	16 EFTS	Derby
	18 EFTS	Fair Oaks
	21 EFTS	Booker
	22 EFTS	Cambridge
	24 EFTS	Sealand
	28 EFTS	Wolverhampton
Tiger Moth, Magister	29 EFTS	Clyffe Pypard
Tiger Moth, Magister, Anson I	10 FIS	Woodley

Basic and acclimatisation training

21 Group

Type	Unit	Base
Spitfire II, V, XVI Harvard, Anson I	7 SFTS	Sibson, Sutton Bridge
Spitfire Vc, XVI, Oxford, Master, Harvard	17 SFTS	Harlaxton, Spitalgate
Tiger Moth, Anson, Oxford, Harvard	16 (Polish) FTS	Newton
	19 FTS	Cranwell
	22 SFTS	Calveley
Spitfire XVI, Harvard	5 (P)AFU	Tern Hill
Oxford, Magister, Anson I Spitfire XVI, Harvard	21 (P)AFU	Wheaton Aston

23 Group

Type	Unit	Base
Harvard, Anson	20 FTS	Church Lawford
	21 SFTS	Snitterfield
Oxford, Harvard, Anson I	3 SFTS	South Cerney
Harvard, Anson I, Magister	6 SFTS	Little Rissington
Harvard IIb, Oxford, Spitfire V, IX, XVIII, Magister, Harvard IIb, Tiger Moth, Master II, Mosquito III, Lancaster III,VII	ECFS	Hullavington
Anson, Oxford, Harvard IIb	7 FIS	Upavon
	1537 BATF	Ramsbury
Master, Hotspur, Anson I	1 GTS	Croughton
Master II, Hotspur II, Horsa, Albemarle IV, V	3 GTS	Wellesbourne Mountford

Specialist training (25 Group)

Type	Unit	Base
Anson, Wellington X, Mosquito VI, Spitfire XVI Martinet, Master II, Proctor	CGS	Leconfield
Martinet I, Wellington III, Spitfire Vb	10 AGS	Barrow
Martinet I, Wellington III, Spitfire VII	11 AGS	Andreas
Lancaster	EANS	Shawbury
Anson I, Wellington X, Oxford II, Magister I	5 ANS	Jurby
Anson I, Wellington X, Oxford	7 ANS	Bishops Court
Anson I, Oxford, Magister I	10 ANS	Swanton Morley

Beam approach training (50 Group)

Type	Unit	Base
Oxford	1 BAS	Watchfield
	1547 BATF	Watchfield

Southern Rhodesia – Rhodesia Air Training Group

Type	Unit	Base
Tiger Moth, Harvard	20 SFTS	Cranborne, Salisbury

Technical Training Command (27 Group)

Type	Unit	Base
Dominie, Halifax VI, Proctor, Anson, Oxford	1 RS	Cranwell
Dominie, Proctor, Anson I, Tiger Moth II	2 RS	Yatesbury
Anson I	3 RS	Compton Bassett
Dominie, Proctor, Anson I	4 RS	Madley
? borrowed from 3 RS	5 RS	Compton Bassett
? borrowed from 1 RS	8 RS	Cranwell
? borrowed from 2 RS	9 RS	Yatesbury
Oxford, Anson I, Tiger Moth II	12 RS	St Athan
shared with 12 RS plus Master, Proctor I, II, III	14 RS	St Athan
? borrowed from 2 RS	15 RS	Cosford

Bomber Command

Type	Unit	Base
Spitfire V, Hurricane IIc Martinet II, Oxford	1687 BDTF (1 Group)	Hemswell
Spitfire Vb, Hurricane IIc Martinet I, Wellington X	1688 BDTF (3 Group)	Feltwell

Coastal Command

Type	Unit	Base
Martinet I, Spitfire V, Hurricane IIc	FATU (16 Group)	Langham
Anson	3 SGR (19 Group)	Leuchars

Transport Command (4 Group)

Type	Unit	Base
Oxford	TCAEU	Bramcote
	1511 RATF	Wheaton Aston
	1516 RATF	Snaith
	1521 RATF	Longtown
	1527 RATF	Prestwick
	1528 RATF	Valley
	1529 RATF	St Mawgan
	1552 RATF	Melbourne
	1555 RATF	Fairford
	1556 RATF	Fairford
	1508 AF	Snaith
Anson, Oxford	1510 RATF	Melbourne
Anson	1513 RATF	Bitteswell
Harvard IIB, Buckmaster I	ETPS (46 Group)	Odiham

AHQ Eastern Mediterranean

Type	Unit	Base
Anson I, Oxford, Wellington X	11 FIS	Deversoir
Warwick	MENVTS	Aqir

ACSEA (225 Group (India))

Type	Unit	Base
Harvard, Spitfire VIII, XIV	3 FSTU	Bhopal

Fleet Air Arm

Advanced training

Type	Unit	Base
Barracuda II, Corsair IV, Firefly I Hellcat II	706 *Refresher Flying School*	Nowra (Australia)
Corsair III, IV, Hellcat II, Seafire III	757 *Naval OTU*	Katukurunda (Ceylon)
Anson I, Firefly I, Martinet I	766 *1 Naval OTU*	Inskip
Anson I, Avenger I, II	785 *1 Naval OTU*	Crail
Spitfire Vb, Seafire Ib, IIc, III, Harvard III Wildcat V, VI	748 *10 Naval OTU (refresher training)*	St Merryn
Oxford	798 *Refresher flying ex POWs*	Burscough
Seafire III, XV, Anson I, OxfordI Dominie I,Expeditor II Sea Otter I, Tiger Moth II, Firefly FR1 Harvard III	799 *Refresher flying/various training*	Lee-on-Solent, Gosport, Henstridge
Harvard IIb, Oxford I	702 *Instrument training*	Schofields (Australia)
	729 *Instrument training*	Katukurunda (Ceylon)
Oxford, Harvard IIb, III	758 *Advanced Instrument FS*	Eglinton
Barracuda II	717 *Torpedo Bomber Recce training*	Rattray
Whitley VII	734 *Engine handling*	Hinstock
Beaufort II, Oxford, MosquitoVI	762 *Two-engine CU*	Halesworth
Anson I, Barracuda II,III	735 *Radar training*	Burscough
Anson I, Firefly INF, Hellcat IINF, Harvard III	784 *Night Fighter Training*	Drem
Barracuda II,Corsair III	767 *Deck Landing Training School*	East Haven
Seafire IIc,IIII	768 *Deck Landing Training School*	East Haven
Barracuda III	744 *AS training*	Eglinton, Ballykelly
Anson I, Avenger II, Barracuda II	783 *ASV radar training*	Arbroath
Barracuda II	753 *2 Observer School*	Rattray
Firebrand III	708 *Firebrand advanced training*	Fearn
Hellcat I, Harvard IIb, Seafire XV, 45	709 *Ground Attack School (SNAW)*	St Merryn
Seafire III, F17,46, Harvard III, Firefly FR1	736 *Fighter Combat School (SNAW)*	St Merryn
Oxford, Harvard II, Corsair III Hellcat II, Seafire III, XV	759 *AFS (1 NAFS)*	Zeals
Harvard IIa, Seafire III	760 *AFS (2 NAFS)*	Henstridge
Seafire III, XV, XVII, Harvard III	761 *AFS (2 NAFS)*	Henstridge
Firefly NFI, Corsair III, IV, Harvard IIb, III, Martinet TTI, Seafire III	794 *AFS (3 NAFS)*	Eglinton

Instructor training/trials

Type	Unit	Base
Albacore I, Avenger I, Barracuda II,III Corsair III, Dauntless I, Firebrand III Firefly 1, Fulmar II, Hellcat II, Reliant I Seafire III, XV, Sea Otter I, Walrus II Wildcat IV	700 *Test pilot training*	Middle Wallop
Corsair IV	715 *Fighter Leader Course/Fighter Air Combat Course (SAC)*	St Merryn

1.B Training at 1 July 1947

Reserve Command, RAF

Gliding Schools

61 Group

Type	Unit	Base
Cadet TX1, 2, 3, Dagling Primary Grunau Baby	102 GS	Horsham St Faith
Cadet TX1, 2, Dagling Primary	103 GS	Honington
Cadet TX1, 2, 3	104 GS	Ipswich
Grunau Baby	105 GS	Cambridge
	106 GS	Henlow
Cadet TX1, 2	107 GS	Digby
	108 GS	Desborough
Cadet TX1, 2, Falcon III	141 GS	Gravesend
Grunau Baby	143 GS	Croydon
Cadet TX1, 2	145 GS	Boxted
	148 GS	Rochford
Cadet TX1, 2, Grunau Baby	161 GS	Tangmere
	162 GS	Gatwick
Cadet TX1, Grunau Baby	167 GS	Fairoaks
Cadet TX1, 2, 3, BAC.VII, TX.8/45	168 GS	Rochester

62 Group

Type	Unit	Base
Cadet TX1, Dart Tottenhoe	81 GS	Yeovil
Cadet TX1, 2	82 GS	Roborough
	83 GS	Aston Down
	84 GS	Exeter
Cadet TX1, 2, 3 Grunau Baby	87 GS	Locking
Cadet TX1, 2	88 GS	Wroughton
Cadet TX1, 2, 3 Grunau Baby	89 GS	Christchurch
Cadet TX1, 2, 3, Dart Tottenhoe, Grunau Baby	92 GS	Charmy Down
Cadet TX1, Grunau Baby	94 GS	Yate
	95 GS	St Eval
Cadet TX1, 2, Grunau Baby, Dagling Primary	130 GS	Abingdon
Cadet TX1, 2, Grunau Baby	163 GS	Gosport

63 Group

Type	Unit	Base
Cadet TX1, 2	41 GS	Honiley
Cadet TX1, TX2, King Kite, Grunau Baby	42 GS	Bramcote
Cadet TX1, 2, 3	43 GS	Lichfield
	44 GS	Bruntingthorpe
	45 GS	Meir
Cadet TX1, 2	47 GS	Hucknall
	48 GS	Castle Bromwich
	49 GS	Newton
	50 GS	Pershore
Cadet TX1	62 GS	Cardiff
	63 GS	Valley
Cadet TX1, 2, 3 Falcon III	68 GS	St Athan
Cadet TX1, 2	70 GS	Fairwood Common
Cadet TX1, 2	181 GS	Warton
Cadet TX1, 2, 3, Grunau Baby, Falcon III	183 GS	Woodford
Cadet TX1	185 GS	Barton

Type	Unit	Base
Cadet TX1, 2, 3, Grunau Baby	186 GS	Hooton Park
Cadet TX1, Grunau Baby	187 GS	Stretton
Cadet TX1, 2	188 GS	Barrow
	189 GS	Kingstown
Cadet TX1	190 GS	Woodvale
Cadet TX1, 2, 3, Grunau Baby, Falcon III	192 GS	Sealand

64 Group

Type	Unit	Base
Cadet TX1, Kirby Tutor	22 GS	Kirbymoorside
Cadet TX1, Grunau Baby	23 GS	Yeadon
Cadet TX1	24 GS	Firbeck
	25 GS	Leconfield
	27 GS	Woolsington
Cadet TX1, King Kite, Falcon I, III	28 GS	Middleton St George
Cadet TX1	29 GS	Doncaster
Cadet TX1, Falcon III	31 GS	Usworth

65 Group

Type	Unit	Base
Cadet TX1, 2, 3, Dagling Primary	122 GS	Leavesden
Cadet TX1, 2, Falcon III, King Kite, Grunau Baby, Dagling Primary	123 GS	Bray Court
Cadet TX1, 2	124 GS	Elstree
Cadet TX1, 2 Dagling Primary, Grunau Baby	125 GS	Langley
Cadet TX1, 2,	126 GS	Booker
Grunau Baby	127 GS	Panshanger
Cadet TX1, 2	129 GS	North Weald
Cadet TX1, 2, Dagling Primary	142 GS	North Weald
Cadet TX1, 2	144 GS	Heston
Cadet TX1, 2, 3, Rhonbussard, Dagling Primary, Falcon III, Dagling Primary	146 GS	Hornchurch

66 Group

Type	Unit	Base
Cadet TX1	1 GS	Dungavel
	3 GS	Drem
	4 GS	Abbotsinch
	5 GS	Dyce
Cadet TX1, Grunau Baby	6 GS	Turnhouse
Cadet TX1	7 GS	Dalcross
Cadet TX1, 2, 3	166 GS	Hawkinge
Cadet TX1, 2, 3	203 GS (RAFNI)	Downhill

Air experience – University Air Squadrons

Type	Unit	Base
Tiger Moth	Cambridge (61 Gp)	Cambridge
	Oxford (62 Gp)	Abingdon
	Southampton (62 Gp)	Eastleigh
Tiger Moth, Anson XXI, Prentice T1	Birmingham (63 Gp)	Castle Bromwich
Tiger Moth	Manchester (63 Gp)	Barton
	Durham (64 Group)	Ouston

Type	Unit	Base
	Nottingham (64 Gp)	Newton
	Leeds (64 Gp)	Yeadon
	London (65 Gp)	Biggin Hill
	Aberdeen (66 Gp)	Dyce
	Edinburgh (66 Gp)	Turnhouse
	Glasgow (66 Gp)	Abbotsinch
	St Andrews (66 Gp)	Leuchars
	Queens (RAFNI)	Sydenham

Elementary training and miscellaneous

61 Group

Type	Unit	Base
Tiger Moth, Anson I, Harvard IIb	22 RFS	Cambridge
Tiger Moth, Anson XXI	24 RFS	Rochester
Proctor IV, Spitfire II	OATS	Hornchurch

62 Group

Type	Unit	Base
Tiger Moth, Auster V, Harvard IIb	21 EFTS	Booker
Tiger Moth, Anson XXI	8 RFS	Woodley

63 Group

Type	Unit	Base
Tiger Moth	25 RFS	Wolverhampton
Harvard IIb	ITF	Honiley

64 Group

Type	Unit	Base
Tiger Moth	4 RFS	Brough
	6 RFS	Sywell
	7 RFS	Desford
	16 RFS	Burnaston
Tiger Moth, Anson I, Harvard IIb	11 RFS	Perth

65 Group

Type	Unit	Base
Tiger Moth, Anson I	18 RFS	Fairoaks
Tiger Moth, Anson XXI	1 RFS	Panshanger

Flying Training Command

Type	Unit	Base
Harvard IIb, Tiger Moth, Spitfire XVIII Lancaster III, Mosquito III	CFS	Little Rissington
Tiger Moth, Harvard IIb	RAFC	Cranwell
Harvard IIb, Oxford, Anson XIX, Spitfire IX, XVIII, Mosquito III, Meteor III, Lancastrian I	EFS	Hullavington
Harvard IIb, Spitfire IX, XVIII	RAFFC	Manby

Basic training (21 Group)

Type	Unit	Base
Harvard IIb	1 FTS	Spitalgate
Prentice I, Harvard IIb	20 SFTS	Honiley
Harvard IIb, Anson I	3 FTS	Feltwell
Harvard IIb, Tiger Moth	6 FTS	Tern Hill
Harvard IIb, Oxford	7 FTS	Kirton-in-Lindsey
Harvard IIb, Tiger Moth	22 FTS	Ouston

Advanced training (91 Group)

Type	Unit	Base
Wellington X, Tiger Moth	201 AFS	Swinderby
Wellington X	202 AFS	Finningley
Mosquito III, VI, Tiger Moth	204 AFS	Cottesmore

Advanced training (23 Group)

Type	Unit	Base
Spitfire XVI, Harvard IIb	203 AFS	Keevil
Oxford, Harvard, Spitfire XVI	21 (P)AFU	Moreton-in-Marsh
Oxford II, Proctor IV	1 ITS	Wittering

Miscellaneous (21 Group)

Type	Unit	Base
Lancaster I, Lincoln II, Wellington X, Mosquito VI, Spitfire XVI, Martinet I, Tempest V, Proctor IV, Meteor III,IV, Master II, Harvard IIb	CGS	Leconfield
Anson, Martinet, Spitfire XVI, Harvard IIb	11 AGS	Jurby
Anson I, Wellington X, Lancaster VII	EANS	Shawbury
Wellington X, Anson I	1 ANS	Topcliffe
	2 ANS	Bishop's Court
	10 ANS	Driffield
	SATC	Watchfield

Technical Training Command (27 Group)

Type	Unit	Base
Anson I, XXII, Oxford II, Tiger Moth, Proctor III	ERS	Debden
Proctor III, Tiger Moth, Anson XXII	1 RS	Cranwell
Proctor IV, Anson	2 RS	Yatesbury
Proctor IV, Dominie I, Anson XXI	4 RS	Swanton Morley
Wellington X, Martinet, Spitfire XVI	EAAS	Manby
Wellington X	CVTS	Worksop
Anson	SP	Farnborough

Maintenance Command (41 Group)

Type	Unit	Base
Harvard IIb, Wellington X	1689 FPTF	Aston Down

Southern Rhodesia – Rhodesia Air Training Group

Type	Unit	Base
Tiger Moth, Harvard IIb, Anson I	4 FTS	Heany, Bulawayo
Harvard IIb, Tiger Moth	5 FTS	Thornhill
Anson	3 ANS	Thornhill, Gwalo

Transport Command (17 Group)

Type	Unit	Base
Anson I, Oxford	1510 RATF	Bircham Newton
Oxford	1555 RATF	Bircham Newton
	1559 RATF	Bircham Newton

Fleet Air Arm

Basic

Type	Unit	Base
Tiger Moth II, Harvard II, IIA, III, Oxford I	727 *Air experience*	Gosport

Advanced

Type	Unit	Base
Sea Otter I, Firefly I, Barracuda II, Seafire III, XV, Harvard III	799 *Flying Check and Conversion Training*	Lee-on-Solent
Anson I, Harvard IIb, Seafire III, XV	766 *Pt I Op'l FS*	Lossiemouth
Harvard IIb, III	780 *Naval Instrument Flying School*	Culdrose
Hoverfly I, II	705 *Helicopter training*	Gosport
Barracuda III, Harvard IIb	719 *AS training (JASS)*	Eglinton
Barracuda III, Anson I	744 *AS training (JASS)*	Eglinton
Anson I, Avenger II, Barracuda V	783 *ASV radar training (NASS)*	Lee-on-Solent
Harvard III, Martinet TT1, Seafire XV, XVII, Firefly I	736 *Fighter Combat School (SNAW)*	St Merryn
Firefly I, Seafire III	741 *OFTU*	St Merryn
Oxford, Mosquito III, VI	762 *Heavy Twin CU*	Ford
Seafire XV, Firefly I	767 *Deck Landing Training School*	Milltown

Instructor/trials

Type	Unit	Base
Barracuda III, Firefly I, Harvard III, Seafire, Oxford XV, Sea Otter I	700 *Test pilot training*	Yeovilton

1.C   Training at 1 January 1950

Reserve Command

Air experience – Gliding Schools

61 Group

Type	Unit	Base
Cadet TX1, 2, Sedbergh TX1, Grunau Baby, T.9 King Kite, T.12 Gull, T.14 Gull 2, Rhonbussard	RCGIS	Detling
Cadet TX1, 2, Sedbergh TX1, Grunau Baby	102 GS	Horsham St Faith
Cadet TX1, 2, Sedbergh TX1	104 GS	Martlesham Heath
Cadet TX1, 2, Grunau Baby, T.8 Tutor	105 GS	Cambridge
Cadet TX1, 2, Grunau Baby	106 GS	Henlow
Cadet TX1, Sedbergh TX1, Grunau Baby	141 GS	West Malling
Cadet TX1, 2, Sedbergh TX1, Grunau Baby	143 GS 161 GS	Kenley Tangmere
Cadet TX1, 2, BAC Primary	162 GS	Biggin Hill
Cadet TX1, 2, T.6 Kite, TX.8/45, BAC VII	168 GS	Detling

62 Group

Type	Unit	Base
Cadet TX1, 2	82 GS	Harrowbeer
Cadet TX1, 2, Sedbergh TX1	83 GS	Aston Down
Cadet TX1, Sedbergh TX1	84 GS	Exeter
Cadet TX1, 2, Sedbergh TX1, Grunau Baby	87 GS	Locking
Cadet TX1, 2, Sedbergh TX1	89 GS 92 GS	Christchurch Colerne
Cadet TX1, 2, Grunau Baby	95 GS	St Eval
Cadet TX1, 2, Sedbergh TX1, Grunau Baby	123 GS	White Waltham
Cadet TX1, 2	130 GS	Abingdon

63 Group

Type	Unit	Base
Cadet TX1, 2 Sedbergh TX1	41 GS	Honiley
Cadet TX1, 2	42 GS 43 GS	Cosford Lichfield
Cadet TX1, Sedbergh TX1, T.8 Tutor	44 GS	Desford
Cadet TX1, 2, Sedbergh TX1, T.4 Falcon	45 GS	Meir
Cadet TX1, 2 Sedbergh TX1 T.8 Tutor	48 GS 68 GS	Castle Bromwich St Athan
Cadet TX1, 1, Grunau Baby	182 GS	Samlesbury
Cadet TX1, 2, Sedbergh TX1	183 GS	Woodford
Cadet TX1, 2, Grunau Baby	186 GS	Woodvale
Cadet TX1, 2	188 GS	Barrow
Cadet TX1, 2, Sedbergh TX1	192 GS	Sealand

64 Group

Type	Unit	Base
Cadet TX1, Grunau Baby T.8 Tutor	22 GS	Church Fenton
Cadet TX1, 2, Sedbergh TX1, Grunau Baby, King Kite, Falcon III]	23 GS	Rufforth
Cadet TX1, 2, Sedbergh TX1, T.6 Kite	24 GS	Doncaster
Sedbergh TX1	26 GS	Middleton St George

Type	Unit	Base
Cadet TX1, 2, Sedbergh TX1	27 GS	Ouston
Cadet TX1, 2, Kirby Tutor, King Kite	28 GS	Linton-on-Ouse
Cadet TX1, 2, T.6 Kite	29 GS	Spitalgate
Cadet TX1, 2, Falcon III	31 GS	Usworth
Cadet TX1, 2, Sedbergh TX1	49 GS	Newton

65 Group

Type	Unit	Base
Cadet TX1, 2, 3, Sedbergh TX1	122 GS	Halton
Cadet TX1, 2, Sedbergh TX1, Grunau Baby	126 GS	Booker
Cadet TX1, 2	142 GS	North Weald
Cadet TX1, 2, Sedbergh TX1, Grunau Baby	146 GS	Hornchurch

66 Group

Type	Unit	Base
Cadet TX1, 2, 3,	1 GS	Dungavel
Cadet TX1, 2, Sedbergh TX1, T.6 Kite, T.4 Falcon III	2 GS	Grangemouth
Cadet TX1, 2, Sedbergh TX1	4 GS	Abbotsinch
	5 GS	Dyce
	6 GS	Turnhouse
	7 GS	Dalcross
Cadet TX1, 2, BAC III	166 GS	Hawkinge
Cadet TX1, 2, Sedbergh TX1	203 GS (RAFNI)	Sydenham

Air experience – University Air Squadrons

Type	Unit	Base
Tiger Moth	Cambridge (61 Gp)	Cambridge
	Oxford (62 Gp)	Kidlington
Tiger Moth, Oxford	Southampton (62 Gp)	Hamble
	Manchester (63 Gp)	Barton
Tiger Moth, Anson T21	Birmingham (63 Gp)	Castle Bromwich
Tiger Moth, Harvard T2	Leeds (64 Gp)	Church Fenton
	Durham (64 Group)	Usworth
	Nottingham (64 Gp)	Newton
	London (64 Gp)	Fair Oaks
	Glasgow (66 Gp)	Abbotsinch
	Aberdeen (66 Gp)	Dyce
	St Andrews (66 Gp)	Leuchars
	Edinburgh (66 Gp)	Turnhouse
	Queens (RAFNI)	Sydenham

Elementary training

61 Group

Type	Unit	Base
Tiger Moth, Anson T21	22 RFS	Cambridge
	24 RFS	Rochester

62 Group

Type	Unit	Base
Tiger Moth, Anson T21	8 RFS	Woodley
	10 RFS	Exeter
	12 RFS	Filton
	14 RFS	Hamble

63 Group

Type	Unit	Base
Tiger Moth, Anson T21	2 RFS	Barton
	3 RFS	Cardiff
	5 RFS	West Bromwich
Tiger Moth, Anson T21, Auster AOP5	25 RFS	Wolverhampton
Harvard T2b	ITF	Honiley

64 Group

Type	Unit	Base
Tiger Moth, Anson T21	6 RFS	Sywell
	7 RFS	Desford
	9 RFS	Doncaster
	16 RFS	Derby
	23 RFS	Usworth

65 Group

Type	Unit	Base
Tiger Moth, Anson T21	1 RFS	Panshanger
	15 RFS	Redhill
	18 RFS	Fair Oaks
Tiger Moth, Anson T21, Spitfire 16	17 RFS	Hornchurch

66 Group

Type	Unit	Base
Tiger Moth, Anson T21	11 RFS	Perth

Flying Training Command

Type	Unit	Base
Harvard T2B, Cadet TX1, TX2, Sedbergh TX1	RAFC	Cranwell
Anson, Harvard T2B	RAFFC	Manby
Anson	CFS (23 Gp)	Little Rissington

Basic training (23 Group)

Type	Unit	Base
Prentice T1, Harvard T2B, Tiger Moth	2 FTS	South Cerney
	3 FTS	Feltwell
	6 FTS	Tern Hill
	7 FTS	Cottesmore
	22 FTS	Syerston

Advanced training (21 Group)

Type	Unit	Base
Wellington T10, Tiger Moth	201 AFS	Swinderby
Vampire F3, Meteor F4, T7, Tiger Moth	203 AFS (23 Gp)	Driffield
Mosquito T3, FB6, Tiger Moth	204 AFS	Brize Norton
Oxford T2, Harvard T2b, Spitfire F16, Wellington T10	FRS	Finningley

15

Miscellaneous (21 Group)

Type	Unit	Base
Lancaster B1,	CGS	Leconfield
Lincoln B2,		
Wellington T10,		
Mosquito FB6,		
Spitfire F16,		
Martinet TT1,		
Tempest TT5,		
Proctor C4,		
Meteor F3, F4,		
Master T2,		
Harvard T2b		
Lancaster B7	CNS	Shawbury
Anson T21,	1 ANS	Hullavington
Wellington X	2 ANS	Middleton St George

Technical Training Command (27 Group)

Type	Unit	Base
Proctor C4,	1 RS	Locking
Tiger Moth,		
Anson T21		
Proctor C4, Dominie T1,	4 RS	Swanton Morley
Anson T22		
Cadet TX2, Kranich,	School Flt	Halton
Grunau Baby		

Maintenance Command (41 Group)

Type	Unit	Base
Harvard T2B,	1689 FPTF	Aston Down
Hornet F3,		
Mosquito T3		
Tempest F5, 6,		
Meteor T7,		
Anson C12, C19		

Southern Rhodesia – Rhodesia Air Training Group

Type	Unit	Base
Harvard T2b,	4 FTS	Heany, Bulawayo
Anson C19, T20		
Anson T20	3 ANS	Thornhill, Gwalo

Fleet Air Arm

Basic

Type	Unit	Base
Tiger Moth II,	727	Gosport
Harvard IIA, III,	*Air experience*	
Firefly FR4		

Advanced

Type	Unit	Base
Seafire F15,17,	799	Yeovilton
Firefly FR1, T1,	*Flying Check*	
Firebrand TF5,	*and Conversion*	
Sea Fury FB11,	*Refresher*	
Harvard T2b,3		
Hoverfly I,II,	705	Gosport
Dragonfly HR1	*Helicopter training*	
Firefly FR1,T1,	766	Lossiemouth
Seafire F15,17	*Pt I Op'l FS*	
	Course	
Seafire F115,17,	737	Eglinton
Firefly FR1,T1,2,	*Pt II Op'l FS*	
FR4, AS5	*Course*	
Harvard IIb, III	Shorts	Rochester
	Instrument Flying	
	Course	

Type	Unit	Base
Firefly NF1, Anson I,	792	Culdrose
Sea Hornet NF21	*Night Fighter*	
	Training Unit	
Anson I	AST	Hamble
	ASV radar training	
Seafire F15,	767	Yeovilton
Firefly FR1,T1,	*Deck Landing*	
Harvard T2b,3	*Training School*	
Sea Fury FB11		
Martinet TT1,	736	St Merryn
Seafire F17,	*Fighter Combat*	
Sea Fury FB11	*School (SNAW)*	
Firefly FR1,T1		
Firefly FR1	796	St Merryn
	Aircrewmens	
	School	

Instructor/trials

Type	Unit	Base
Sea Vampire F20,	702	Culdrose
Meteor T7	*Naval Jet*	
	Evaluation and	
	Training Unit	

1.D   Training at 1 July 1952

Home Command

Air experience – Gliding Schools

61 Group

Type	Unit	Base
Cadet TX1, 2,	102 GS	Horsham St Faith
Sedbergh TX1,		
Grunau Baby		
Cadet TX1, 2,	104 GS	Martlesham Heath
Sedbergh TX1		
Cadet TX1, 2,	105 GS	Cambridge
Grunau Baby,		
T.8 Tutor		
Cadet TX1, 2,	106 GS	Henlow
Sedbergh TX1,		
Grunau Baby		
Cadet TX1, 2,	123 GS	White Waltham
Sedbergh TX1,		
Grunau Baby,		
Prefect TX1		
Cadet TX1,	141 GS	Detling
Sedbergh TX1,		
Grunau Baby		
Cadet TX1 2,	143 GS	Kenley
Sedbergh TX1,		
Grunau Baby,		
Prefect TX1		
Cadet TX1, 2,	161 GS	Tangmere
Sedbergh TX1,		
Grunau Baby		
Cadet TX1, 2,	166 GS	Hawkinge
BAC III,		
Sedbergh TX1		
Cadet TX1 2,	168 GS	Detling
TX.8/45,		
Sedbergh TX1		

62 Group

Type	Unit	Base
Cadet TX1, 2,	82 GS	St Merryn
Sedbergh TX1	83 GS	Aston Down
	84 GS	Exeter

Type	Unit	Base
Cadet TX1, 2, Sedbergh TX1, Grunau Baby	87 GS	Locking
Cadet TX1, 2, Sedbergh TX1	89 GS	Christchurch
	92 GS	Colerne
Cadet TX1, 2,	130 GS	Weston-on-the-Green

63 Group

Type	Unit	Base
Cadet TX1, 2, T.6 Kite, Sedbergh TX1	41 GS	Honiley
Cadet TX1, 2, Sedbergh TX1, Prefect TX1	42 GS	Cosford
Cadet TX1, 2, Sedbergh TX1	43 GS	Lichfield
Cadet TX1 Sedbergh TX1, T.8 Tutor	44 GS	Cottesmore
Cadet TX1, 2, Sedbergh TX1, T.4 Falcon	45 GS	Meir
Cadet TX1, 2 Sedbergh TX1, T.8 Tutor	48 GS	Castle Bromwich
Cadet TX1, 2, Sedbergh TX1, T.8 Tutor	68 GS	St Athan
Cadet TX1, 2	180 GS	Warton
Cadet TX1, 2, Sedbergh TX1	183 GS	Woodford
	188 GS	Barrow
	192 GS	Sealand
Cadet TX1, 2, Sedbergh TX1, Grunau Baby	186 GS	Woodvale

64 Group

Type	Unit	Base
Cadet TX1, Grunau Baby, T.8 Tutor, T.6 Kite	22 GS	Kirton-in-Lindsey
Cadet TX1, 2, Sedbergh TX1 Grunau Baby	23 GS	Rufforth
Cadet TX1, 2, Sedbergh TX1, T.6 Kite	24 GS	Lindholme
Cadet TX1, 2, T.8 Tutor Sedbergh TX1	26 GS	Middleton St George
Cadet TX1, 2, Sedbergh TX1	27 GS	Usworth
Cadet TX1, 2, Kirby Kite	29 GS	Spitalgate
Cadet TX1, 2, Sedbergh TX1	31 GS	Usworth
	49 GS	Newton

65 Group

Type	Unit	Base
Cadet TX1, 2, Sedbergh TX1	122 GS	Halton
	125 GS	Langley
Cadet TX1, 2, Sedbergh TX1 Grunau Baby	126 GS	Booker
Cadet TX1, 2	142 GS	Hendon
Cadet TX1, 2, Sedbergh TX1, Grunau Baby	146 GS	Hornchurch

66 Group

Type	Unit	Base
Cadet TX1, 2, Sedbergh TX1	1 GS	Dumfries
Cadet TX1, TX2, Sedbergh TX1, T.6 Kite, T.4 Falcon III, Prefect TX1	2 GS	Grangemouth
Cadet TX1, 2, Sedbergh TX1	5 GS	Dyce
	6 GS	Grangemouth
	7 GS	Dalcross
Cadet TX1, TX2, Sedbergh TX1	203 GS (RAFNI)	Sydenham

Air experience – University Air Squadrons

Type	Unit	Base
Chipmunk T10	Cambridge (61 Gp)	Cambridge
	London (61 Gp)	Booker
Tiger Moth T2	Oxford (62 Gp)	Kidlington
Chipmunk T10	Southampton (62 Gp)	Hamble
Harvard 2b	Bristol (62 Gp)	Filton
Chipmunk T10	Birmingham (63 Gp)	Castle Bromwich
Tiger Moth T2	Manchester (63 Gp)	Barton
Chipmunk T10	Liverpool (63 Gp)	Hooton Park
	Leeds (64 Gp)	Sherburn-in-Elmet
	Durham (64 Gp)	Usworth
	Hull (64 Gp)	Brough
	Nottingham (64 Gp)	Newton
	Edinburgh (66 Gp)	Turnhouse
	Glasgow (66 Gp)	Perth
	St Andrews (66 Gp)	Leuchars
Tiger Moth T2B Harvard T2B	Aberdeen (66 Gp)	Dyce

Elementary flying training

54 Group

Type	Unit	Base
Harvard, Tiger Moth	1 ITS	Jurby
	2 ITS	Kirton-in-Lindsey
	3 ITS	Cranwell
Tiger Moth	5 ITS	Cosford
	1 Grading Unit (Airwork)	Digby
	2 Grading Unit (Airwork)	Kirton-in-Lindsey

61 Group

Type	Unit	Base
Chipmunk T10, Anson 21	1 RFS	Panshanger
	18 RFS	Fairoaks
	24 RFS	Rochester
Tiger Moth T2, Anson T20, T21	17 RFS	Hornchurch
Tiger Moth T2, Chipmunk T10, Anson T21	22 RFS	Cambridge
Tiger Moth T2, Chipmunk T10, Anson T21 Oxford T2	15 RFS	Redhill

Type	Unit	Base
Cadet TX2, Sedbergh TX1, T.6 Kite, TX.8/45, Prefect TX1	HCGIS	Detling

62 Group

Type	Unit	Base
Chipmunk T10	1 BFTS	Booker
Chipmunk T10, Anson 21	8 RFS	Woodley
	10 RFS	Exeter
	12 RFS	Filton
Tiger Moth T2, Anson T21	14 RFS	Hamble
Anson T21	1 BANS	Hamble (AST Ltd)

63 Group

Type	Unit	Base
Chipmunk T10	2 BFTS	Ansty
	5 RFS	Castle Bromwich
Tiger Moth T2	2 RFS	Barton
Chipmunk T10, Anson T21	19 RFS	Woodvale
	3 RFS	Cardiff
	25 RFS	Wolverhampton

64 Group

Type	Unit	Base
Chipmunk T10	3 BFTS	Burnaston
	4 BFTS	Sywell
	5 BFTS	Desford
Tiger Moth, Chipmunk T10, Anson 21	4 RFS	Brough
	23 RFS	Usworth
Chipmunk T10, Anson 21, Prentice T1	6 RFS	Sywell
Tiger Moth T2, Anson T21	7 RFS	Desford
Tiger Moth T2, Prentice T1, Anson T21	9 RFS	Doncaster
	16 RFS	Burnaston
Anson T21	2 BANS	Usworth (Airwork)

66 Group

Type	Unit	Base
Chipmunk T10, Anson 21	11 RFS	Perth

Flying Training Command

Type	Unit	Base
Tiger Moth T2, Prentice T1, Anson T21, Harvard T2B, Prefect TX1	RAFC	Cranwell
Hastings C2, Lincoln B2, Valetta C1, Meteor T7, Anson T21	RAFFC	Manby
Harvard 2b, Meteor T7, Vampire FB5, Prentice T1, Chipmunk T10	CFS (23 Gp)	Little Rissington South Cerney (Basic)

Basic flying training (23 Group)

Type	Unit	Base
Harvard T2b, Prentice T1	1 FTS*	Moreton-in-Marsh
	14 FTS	Holme-on-Spalding Moor

Type	Unit	Base
Prentice T1, Balliol T2, Harvard T2B	7 FTS	Cottesmore
Tiger Moth, Prentice T1, Harvard T2B	3 FTS	Feltwell
	6 FTS	Tern Hill
	22 FTS	Syerston
Oxford T2	8 AFTS	Dalcross
	9 AFTS	Wellesbourne Mountford
	10 AFTS	Pershore

* 21 Group

Advanced flying training (25 Group)

Type	Unit	Base
Varsity T1, Anson T20	201 AFS*	Swinderby
Meteor F4, T7,	203 AFS*	Driffield
	205 AFS	Middleton St George
	207 AFS	Full Sutton
	209 AFS	Weston Zoyland
	215 AFS	Finningley
Meteor F3, T7	206 AFS	Oakington
Vampire F1	208 AFS	Merryfield
Vampire FB5	202 AFS	Valley

* 21 Group

Navigation training and miscellaneous (21 Group)

Type	Unit	Base
Anson T21, Valetta T3	1 ANS	Hullavington
Wellington T10, Anson T21, Valetta T3	2 ANS	Thorney Island
Wellington T10, Anson T21, Valetta T3, Varsity T1	6 ANS	Lichfield
Varsity T1, Anson T21	3 ANS	Bishop's Court
Wellington T10	5 ANS	Lindholme
	CNCS	Shawbury
Meteor F8, Vampire FB5, Lincoln B2	CGS*	Leconfield
Anson T21, T22, Prentice T1	1 ASS*	Swanton Morley
	2 ASS	Halfpenny Green

* 25 Group

Technical Training Command (24 Group)

Type	Unit	Base
Lincoln B2, Spitfire 16, Oxford, Anson T21	RAFTC	Debden
Anson PR1	1 SP	Wellesbourne Mountford

Coastal Command

Type	Unit	Base
Lancaster GR3	SMR	St Mawgan

Fighter Command

Type	Unit	Base
Spitfire LF16, Oxford	CRS (11 Gp)	Middle Wallop
Spitfire F16, Anson, Chipmunk T10, Proctor 4	SLAW (11 Gp)	Old Sarum
Meteor T7, F8, Balliol T2, Tempest TT5, Oxford T1	APS (81 Gp)	Acklington

Transport Command

Type	Unit	Base
Hastings C1	1 PTS	Abingdon
Anson T21	1689 FPTF	Aston Down

Middle East Air Force

Type	Unit	Base
Meteor T7	MEAF ITF	Nicosia (Cyprus)

Rhodesian Air Training Group

Type	Unit	Base
Harvard T2b, Anson T20	4 FTS	Heany
Anson T21	5 FTS	Thornhill

Fleet Air Arm

Advanced

Type	Unit	Base
Seafire F17, Firefly FR1, T1,2, Harvard T2B	799 *Refresher Flying Training*	Macrihanish
Firefly FR1,T2, Seafire F17, Sea Fury T20	766 *Pt I Op'l FS*	Lossiemouth
Firebrand TF5, Sea Hornet F20, PR22 Sea Fury FB11, T20, Vampire T11	759 *1 Op'l FS (NAFS)*	Culdrose
Dragonfly HR1,3, Skeeter 3	705 *Helicopter training*	Gosport
Firefly AS5,6	719 *Naval Air Anti-Submarine School (53 TAG)*	Eglinton
Firefly FR1,T1,2,FR4, AS5	737 *NASS (53 TAG)*	Eglinton
Sea Fury FB11,T20	736,738 *Naval Air Fighter School*	Culdrose
Firefly T1,FR4	767 *Deck Landing School*	Henstridge
Anson I, Barracuda TR3	750 *Observer School Pt II*	St Merryn
Firefly T3,AS6	796 *Observer School Pt II*	St Merryn

Instructor/trials

Type	Unit	Base
Sea Vampire F20, Meteor T7, Vampire T11, 22, Attacker F1	702 *Naval Jet Evaluation and Training Unit*	Culdrose

1.E   Training at 1 January 1955

Home Command

Air experience – Gliding schools

61 Group

Type	Unit	Base
Prefect TX1, Sedbergh TX1	CGIS	Detling
Cadet TX3, Sedbergh TX1	102 GS	Swanton Morley
	104 GS	Martlesham Heath
	105 GS	Cambridge
	106 GS	Henlow
	123 GS	White Waltham

Type	Unit	Base
Cadet TX1, Sedbergh TX1	141 GS	Detling
Cadet TX3, Sedbergh TX1	143 GS	Kenley
	161 GS	Tangmere
Cadet TX1, TX2, Sedbergh TX1, Prefect TX1	166 GS	Hawkinge
Cadet TX3, Sedbergh TX1	168 GS	Detling

62 Group

Type	Unit	Base
Cadet TX3, Prefect TX1	80 GS	Halesland
Cadet TX3,	82 GS	St Merryn
	83 GS	Aston Down
	84 GS	Exeter
Cadet TX3, Prefect TX1	87 GS	Locking
Cadet TX3, Sedbergh TX1	89 GS	Christchurch
	92 GS	Colerne
	130 GS	Weston-on-the-Green

63 Group

Type	Unit	Base
Cadet TX3, Sedbergh TX1	41 GS	Pembrey
	42 GS	Cosford
	43 GS	Lichfield
Cadet TX1, TX2, Sedbergh TX1, Prefect TX1	45 GS	Meir
Cadet TX3, Sedbergh TX1	48 GS	Castle Bromwich
	68 GS	St Athan
	181 GS	Warton
Cadet TX1, 2, Sedbergh TX1	182 GS	Samlesbury
Cadet TX3, Sedbergh TX1	183 GS	Woodford
	186 GS	Hawarden
	188 GS	Barrow

64 Group

Type	Unit	Base
Cadet TX1, T.8 Tutor, T.6 Kite, Prefect TX1	22 GS	Kirton-in-Lindsey
Cadet TX3, Sedbergh TX1	23 GS	Rufforth
	24 GS	Lindholme
	26 GS	Middleton St George
	27 GS	Usworth
Cadet TX1, 2, Kirby Kite	29 GS	Spitalgate
Cadet TX3, Falcon III	31 GS	Usworth
Cadet TX3, Sedbergh TX1	44 GS	Spitalgate
	49 GS	Newton

65 Group

Type	Unit	Base
Cadet TX3, Sedbergh TX1	122 GS	Halton
Cadet TX1, TX2, Sedbergh TX1, Prefect TX1	125 GS	Langley
Cadet TX3, Sedbergh TX1	126 GS	Booker
	142 GS	Hornchurch
	146 GS	Hornchurch

66 Group

Type	Unit	Base
Cadet TX1, 2, 3, Sedbergh TX1	1 GS	Dumfries

Type	Unit	Base
Cadet TX1, TX2, Sedbergh TX1, Prefect TX1	2 GS	Grangemouth
Cadet TX1, 2, 3, Sedbergh TX1	5 GS	Edzell
	7 GS	Dalcross
Cadet TX1, TX2, Sedbergh TX1	203 GS (RAFNI)	Toome

Air experience – University Air Squadrons

Type	Unit	Base
Chipmunk T10	Cambridge (61 Gp)	Cambridge
	London (61 Gp)	Booker
	Oxford (62 Gp)	Kidlington
	Southampton (62 Gp)	Hamble
	Bristol (62 Gp)	Filton
	Birmingham (63 Gp)	Castle Bromwich
	Manchester (63 Gp)	Woodvale
	Liverpool (63 Gp)	Woodvale
	Leeds (64 Gp)	Yeadon
	Durham (64 Gp)	Usworth
	Hull (64 Gp)	Brough
	Nottingham (64 Gp)	Newton
	Edinburgh (66 Gp)	Turnhouse
	Glasgow (66 Gp)	Perth
	St Andrews (66 Gp)	Crail
	Aberdeen (66 Gp)	Dyce
	Queen's	Sydenham

Flying Training Command

Primary training

Type	Unit	Base
Chipmunk T10	1 ITS	Kirton-in-Lindsey

Basic training (23 Group)

Type	Unit	Base
Harvard T2b, Provost T1, Vampire T11	1 FTS	Moreton-in-Marsh
Provost T1, Harvard T2b	3 FTS	Feltwell
	6 FTS	Tern Hill
	22 FTS	Syerston
Provost T1, Chipmunk T10	2 FTS	Hullavington
Balliol T2, Meteor T7, Vampire T11	RAFC	Cranwell

Advanced training (25 Group)

Type	Unit	Base
Meteor T7, F8, Vampire FB5, T11, Provost T1	4 FTS	Middleton St George
	8 FTS	Driffield
Vampire FB5,9,T11 Meteor T7	5 FTS	Oakington
Vampire FB5, 9, T11, Meteor T7	9 FTS	Merryfield

Type	Unit	Base
Vampire T11, Meteor T7	7 FTS*	Valley
Meteor F4, T7	12 FTS inc 3 AWJRS	Weston Zoyland
Varsity T1	11 FTS+	Swinderby
Hastings C2, Lincoln B2, Valetta C1, Meteor T7	RAFFC	Manby
Harvard 2b, Meteor T7, Vampire FB5 Chipmunk T10	CFS#	Little Rissington South Cerney (Basic)
Balliol T2, Chipmunk T10	HCEU	White Waltham
Gull, Cadet TX3, Prefect TX1	HCGIS	Detling

* 23 Group   + 21 Group   #81 Group

Other aircrew training

Type	Unit	Base
Varsity T1, Valetta T3, Vampire NF10, Marathon T11	2 ANS (21 Group)	Thorney Island
Provost T1, Vampire NF10, Varsity T1	CNCS (21 Group)	Shawbury
Anson T21, Prentice	1 ASS (23 Group)	Swanton Morley

Technical Training Command (24 Group)

Type	Unit	Base
Lincoln B2, Varsity T1, Chipmunk T10	RAFTC	Debden
Anson C19, Proctor	1 SP	Wellesbourne Mountford

Coastal Command

Type	Unit	Base
Lancaster GR3	SMR	St Mawgan

Fighter Command

Type	Unit	Base
Meteor T7, F8, Balliol T2, Tempest TT5, Oxford T1	APS (81 Group)	Acklington
Anson, Chipmunk T10	SLAW	Old Sarum
Hunter F4, Venom FB4	FWS	Leconfield

Bomber Command

Type	Unit	Base
Hastings	BCBS	Lindholme

Transport Command

Type	Unit	Base
Hastings C1	1 PTS	Abingdon

Fleet Air Arm

Advanced

Type	Unit	Base
Dragonfly HR3, Hiller HT1, Whirlwind HAS22	705 *Helicopter training*	Gosport
Firefly T7	719 *Naval Air Anti-Submarine School*	Eglinton
Firefly T2, AS5	737 *NASS*	Eglinton

Type	Unit	Base
Sea Vampire T22, Sea Hawk F1, 2, FB3	736 *Advanced Jet Flying School (NAFS)*	Lossiemouth
Sea Vampire T22, Sea Hawk F1	738 *Piston-jet conversion (NAFS)*	Lossiemouth
Sea Hawk F1, 2, Avenger AS4	767 *Landing Signals Officer Training School*	Stretton
Sea Prince T1, Firefly T7	750 *Observer School Pt II*	Culdrose
Firefly T7	796 *Observer School Pt II*	Culdrose

1.F   Training at 1 January 1960

RAF – Flying Training Command

Air experience – Gliding Schools

Type	Unit	Base
Cadet TX3, Sedbergh TX1	613 GS	Halton
	614 GS	Hornchurch
	615 GS	Kenley
	616 GS	Henlow
	617 GS	Hendon
	622 GS	Christchurch
	624 GS	Exeter
	625 GS	South Cerney
	626 GS	St Eval
	632 GS	Meir
	633 GS	Cosford
	634 GS	St Athan
	635 GS	Burtonwood
	641 GS	Ouston
	644 GS	Spitalgate
	645 GS	Middleton St George
	661 GS	Turnhouse
	663 GS	Abbotsinch
	671 GS	Sydenham
Cadet TX3, Sedbergh TX1, Prefect TX1	611 GS	Swanton Morley
	612 GS	Martlesham Heath
	621 GS	Locking
	623 GS	White Waltham
	631 GS	Hawarden
	642 GS	Rufforth
	643 GS	Kirton-in-Lindsey
	662 GS	Arbroath
Cadet TX3, Sedbergh TX1, Prefect TX1 Grasshopper TX1	1 GC	Hawkinge
Cadet TX3, Sedbergh TX1, Prefect TX1	2 GC	Newton
Sedbergh TX1	1 SoTT	Halton

Air experience – Air Experience Flights

Type	Unit	Base
Chipmunk T10	1 AEF	West Malling
	2 AEF	Hamble
	3 AEF	Filton
	4 AEF	Exeter
	5 AEF	Teversham
	6 AEF	White Waltham
	7 AEF	Newton
	8 AEF	Cosford
	9 AEF	Church Fenton
	10 AEF	Woodvale
	11 AEF	Ouston
	12 AEF	Turnhouse
	13 AEF	Sydenham

Air Experience – University Air Squadrons

Type	Unit	Base
Chipmunk T10	Aberdeen	Dyce
	Birmingham	Shawbury
	Bristol	Filton
	Cambridge	Cambridge
	Durham	Usworth
	Edinburgh	Turnhouse
	Hull UAS	Brough
	Leeds	Church Fenton
	Liverpool	Woodvale
	London	Booker
	Manchester	Barton
	Nottingham	Newton
	Oxford	Bicester
	Southampton	Hamble

Basic flying training

Type	Unit	Base
Provost T1	6 FTS	Tern Hill
Provost T1, Vampire T11	1 FTS	Linton-on-Ouse
Jet Provost T3	2 FTS	Syerston
Vampire T11	5 FTS	Oakington
	8 FTS	Swinderby
Vampire T11, Meteor T7, Jet Provost T3, Cadet TX2, Sedbergh TX1, Prefect TX1	RAFC	Cranwell

Other aircrew training

Type	Unit	Base
Varsity T1, Valetta T3, Vampire NF10, T11	1 ANS	Topcliffe
Varsity T1, Meteor NF14(T)	2 ANS	Thorney Island
Varsity T1	1 AES	Hullavington

Advanced flying training

Type	Unit	Base
Swift F7, Javelin	GWTS	Valley
Varsity T1, Vampire NF10	CNCS	Shawbury
Prentice T1, Chipmunk T10, Provost T1, Jet Provost T3, Meteor T7, F8, Hunter F4 Anson 19, Canberra T4, Varsity T1	CFS (Basic)	Little Rissington
Dragonfly, Sycamore, Whirlwind HAR10	CFS (H)	South Cerney
Valetta, Meteor T7, Canberra T4	RAFFC	Manby
Varsity T1, Chipmunk T10	RAFTC	Henlow
SLAW	Old Sarum	

Fleet Air Arm

Basic

Type	Unit	Base
Sea Prince T1, Vampire T22, Dragonfly HR5	727 *Dartmouth Cadet Air Training Sqn*	Brawdy

Advanced

Type	Unit	Base
Dragonfly HR1,5, Hiller HT1, Whirlwind HAR1, 3	705 *Helicopter training*	Culdrose
Whirlwind HAR3, HAS7	737 *AS Op'l FS*	Portland
Sea Hawk FGA6, Scimitar F1	736 *Operational Flying School (NAFSS)*	Lossiemouth
Sea Hawk FGA6, Sea Venom FAW21, Sea Vampire T22	738 *Sea Venom OFS (NAFSS)*	Lossiemouth
Sea Venom FAW21, Sea Vixen FAW1	766 *All Weather Fighter Training*	Yeovilton
Sea Prince T1, Sea Devon C20	750 *Observer School*	Hal Far (Malta)

Instructor/trials

Type	Unit	Base
Gannet AS1,AS4, Meteor TT20, Sea Venom FAW21, Whirlwind HAR1, 3, HAS7	700 *Trials*	Yeovilton
Hunter T8	764 *Air Warfare Instructor training/ Swept wing CU*	Lossiemouth

1.G   Training at 1 January 1965

RAF Flying Training Command

Air experience – Gliding Schools

Type	Unit	Base
Cadet TX1, TX2, Sedbergh TX1	615 GS	Kenley
	617 GS	Bovingdon
	618 GS	West Malling
	621 GS	Locking
	622 GS	Old Sarum
	623 GS	Tangmere
	624 GS	Chivenor
	625 GS	South Cerney
	631 GS	Sealand
	633 GS	Burtonwood
	645 GS	Catterick
	662 GS	Arbroath

Air experience – Air Experience Flights

Type	Unit	Base
Chipmunk T10	1 AEF	Manston
	2 AEF	Hamble
	3 AEF	Filton
	4 AEF	Exeter
	5 AEF	Teversham
	6 AEF	White Waltham
	7 AEF	Newton
	8 AEF	Shawbury
	9 AEF	Church Fenton
	10 AEF	Woodvale
	11 AEF	Ouston
	12 AEF	Turnhouse
	13 AEF	Sydenham

Air experience – University Air Squadrons (25 Group)

Type	Unit	Base
Chipmunk T10	Aberdeen	Dyce
	Birmingham	Shawbury
	Bristol	Filton
	Cambridge	Cambridge

Type	Unit	Base
	Durham	Usworth
	Edinburgh	Turnhouse
	Glasgow/ Strathclyde	Abbotsinch
	Hull	Brough
	Leeds	Church Fenton
	Liverpool	Woodvale
	London	Abingdon
	Manchester	Barton
	Northumbria	Leeming
	Nottingham	Newton
	Oxford	Bicester
	Queen's	Sydenham
	St Andrews	Leuchars
	Southampton	Hamble
	Wales	St Athan

Primary flying instruction (25 Group)

Type	Unit	Base
Chipmunk T10	PFS	South Cerney

Basic flying training (23 Group)

Type	Unit	Base
Jet Provost T3,T4	2 FTS	Syerston
	6 FTS	Acklington
	7 FTS	Church Fenton
	3 FTS	Leeming
Jet Provost T5, Vampire T11	1 FTS	Linton-on-Ouse
Chipmunk T10, Jet Provost T3, T4	RAFC	Cranwell

Advanced flying training (23 Group)

Type	Unit	Base
Gnat T1, Hunter F6, T7	4 FTS	Valley
Varsity T1	5 FTS	Oakington

Navigator training (25 Group)

Type	Unit	Base
Valetta T3, T4, Varsity T1	2 ANS (basic)	Hullavington
Varsity T1, Meteor T7, NF14(T)	1 ANS (advanced)	Stradishall

Miscellaneous

Type	Unit	Base
Provost T1, Vampire T11	CATCS	Shawbury
Chipmunk T10, Jet Provost T3, T4, Varsity T1, Meteor T7, Vampire T11	CFS	Little Rissington
Sioux AH1, Whirlwind HAR10	CFS(H)	Tern Hill
Jet Provost T3, T4, Varsity T1	CAW (inc 1 SRF)	Manby, Strubby

Fleet Air Arm

Type	Unit	Base
Hiller HT2, Whirlwind HAR3, HAS7,	705 *Helicopter training*	Culdrose
Wessex HAS1, Wasp HAS1	706 *Advanced helicopter training*	Portland
Wessex HU5	707 *Commando conversion training*	Culdrose
Wessex HAS1	737 *AS Op'l FS*	Portland

Type	Unit	Base
Scimitar F1	736	Lossiemouth
	Operational	
	Flying School	
	(NAFSS)	
Hunter T8, 8c	759	Brawdy
	AFTC Phase I	
Hunter T8, GA11	738	Brawdy
	AFTC Phase II	
Sea Vixen FAW1	766	Yeovilton
	All Weather	
	Fighter Training	
Sea Prince T1,	750	Hal Far
Sea Vampire T22,	*Observer School*	
Sea Venom FAW22		

Instructor

Type	Unit	Base
Hunter T8,8b,8c,GA11	764	Lossiemouth
	Air Warfare	
	Instructor training	

1.H Training at 1 January 1970

RAF – Training Command

Air experience – gliding schools

Type	Unit	Base
Cadet TX1, TX2,	615 GS	Manston
Sedbergh TX1	617 GS	Bovingdon
	618 GS	West Malling
	621 GS	Locking
	622 GS	Old Sarum
	623 GS	Tangmere
	624 GS	Chivenor
	625 GS	South Cerney
	631 GS	Sealand
	633 GS	Burtonwood
	641 GS	Ouston
	644 GS	Syerston
	645 GS	Catterick
	661 GS	Kirknewton
	662 GS	Arbroath

Air experience – Air Experience Flights

Type	Unit	Base
Chipmunk T10	1 AEF	Manston
	2 AEF	Hamble
	3 AEF	Filton
	4 AEF	Exeter
	5 AEF	Teversham
	6 AEF	White Waltham
	7 AEF	Newton
	8 AEF	Shawbury
	9 AEF	Church Fenton
	10 AEF	Woodvale
	11 AEF	Ouston
	12 AEF	Turnhouse
	13 AEF	Sydenham

Air experience – University Air Squadrons (25 Group)

Type	Unit	Base
Chipmunk T10	Aberdeen	Dyce
	Birmingham	Shawbury
Bristol	Filton	
	Cambridge	Cambridge
	Durham	Usworth
	Edinburgh	Turnhouse
	Glasgow/	Abbotsinch
	Strathclyde	
	Liverpool	Woodvale
	London	Abingdon

Type	Unit	Base
	Manchester	Barton
	Northumbria	Leeming
	Nottingham	Newton
	Oxford	Bicester
	Queen's	Sydenham
	St Andrews	Leuchars
	Southampton	Hamble
	Wales	St Athan
	Yorks	Church Fenton

Primary flying instruction (22 Group)

Type	Unit	Base
Chipmunk T10	PFS	Church Fenton

Basic flying training (23 Group)

Type	Unit	Base
Jet Provost T5	1 FTS	Linton-on-Ouse
Jet Provost T3,T4	2 FTS	Syerston
	inc RNEFTS	
	3 FTS	Leeming
Chipmunk T10,	RAFC	Cranwell
Jet Provost T3, T4		

Advanced flying training (23 Group)

Type	Unit	Base
Gnat T1, Hunter F6, T7	4 FTS	Valley
Varsity T1	5 FTS	Oakington

Navigator training (25 Group)

Type	Unit	Base
Valetta T3, T4,	2 ANS (basic)	Gaydon
Varsity T1		
Varsity T1, Dominie T1	1 ANS	Stradishall
	(advanced)	

Miscellaneous

Type	Unit	Base
Provost T1,	CATCS	Shawbury
Vampire T11		(Marshalls)
Jet Provost T5	CFS	Little Rissington
Gnat T1	CFS	Kemble
	(Red Arrows)	
Gazelle HT3,	CFS(H)	Tern Hill
Whirlwind HAR10		
Jet Provost T3, T4,	CAW	Manby,
Varsity T1	(inc 1 SRF)	Strubby

Fleet Air Arm

Type	Unit	Base
Hiller HT2,	705	Culdrose
Whirlwind HAS7	*Helicopter*	
	training	
Wessex HAS1, 3,	706	Portland
Wasp HAS1,	*Advanced*	
Sea King HAS1	*helicopter*	
	training	
Wessex HU5	707	Culdrose
	Commando	
	conversion training	
Wessex HAS1, 3	737	Portland
	AS Op'l FS	
Buccaneer S1, 2, 2B	736	Lossiemouth
	Jet Strike	
	Training Sqn	
Hunter T8,GA11	738	Brawdy
	Phase II AFTC	
	for ex 759 NAS pupils	
Sea Vixen FAW2	766	Yeovilton
	All Weather	
	Fighter Training	
Phantom FG1	767	Yeovilton
	Phantom CU	
Sea Prince T1,	750	Lossiemouth
Sea Venom FAW22	*Observer School*	

Instructor

Type	Unit	Base
Hunter T8,8b,8c,GA11	764 *Air Warfare Instructor training*	Lossiemouth

1.I Training at 1 January 1975

RAF – Training Command (21 Group)

Air experience – Gliding Schools

Type	Unit	Base
Cadet TX1, TX2, Sedbergh TX1	615 GS	Manston
	617 GS	Manston
	618 GS	West Malling
	621 GS	Locking
	622 GS	Old Sarum
	623 GS	Tangmere
	624 GS	Chivenor
	625 GS	South Cerney
	631 GS	Sealand
	633 GS	Burtonwood
	641 GS	Ouston
	644 GS	Newton
	645 GS	Catterick
	661 GS	Kirknewton
	662 GS	Arbroath
	663 GS	Milltown

Air experience – Air Experience Flights

Type	Unit	Base
Chipmunk T10	1 AEF	Manston
	2 AEF	Hamble
	3 AEF	Filton
	4 AEF	Exeter
	5 AEF	Teversham
	6 AEF	Abingdon
	7 AEF	Newton
	8 AEF	Shawbury
	9 AEF	Church Fenton
	10 AEF	Woodvale
	11 AEF	Ouston
	12 AEF	Turnhouse
	13 AEF	Sydenham

Air experience – University Air Squadrons

Type	Unit	Base
Bulldog T1	Aberdeen	Dyce
	Birmingham	Shawbury
	Bristol	Filton
	Durham	Usworth
	Glasgow/ Strathclyde	Abbotsinch
	Liverpool	Woodvale
	London	Abingdon
	Manchester	Barton
	Northumbria	Leeming
	Queen's	Sydenham
	St Andrews	Leuchars
	Southampton	Hamble
	Wales	St Athan
Chipmunk T10	Cambridge	Cambridge
	Edinburgh	Turnhouse
	Nottingham	Newton
	Oxford	Bicester
	Yorks	Church Fenton

Basic flying training

Type	Unit	Base
Jet Provost T5	6 FTS	Acklington
	1 FTS	Linton-on-Ouse
	RAFC	Cranwell

Type	Unit	Base
Jet Provost T3, T4, Bulldog T1	3 FTS inc SRF and RNEFTS	Leeming

Advanced flying training

Type	Unit	Base
Gnat T1, Hunter F6, T7	4 FTS	Valley

Navigator training

Type	Unit	Base
Jet Provost T3, 4, Varsity T1	6 FTS	Finningley

Miscellaneous

Type	Unit	Base
Jet Provost T4	CATCS	Shawbury (Marshalls)
Jet Provost T5	CFS	Little Rissington
Gnat T1	CFS (Red Arrows)	Kemble
Gazelle HT3, Whirlwind HAR10	CFS(H)	Tern Hill

Fleet Air Arm

Type	Unit	Base
Hiller HT2, Gazelle HT2	705 *Helicopter training*	Culdrose
Wasp HAS1, Sea King HAS1	706 *Advanced helicopter training*	Portland
Wessex HU5	707 *Commando conversion training*	Yeovilton
Wessex HAS1, 3, Sea King HAS1	737 *AS Op'l FS*	Portland
Sea Prince T1	750 *Observer School*	Culdrose
Wessex HAS1	771 *Aircrew training*	Culdrose

1.J Training at 1 January 1980

RAF – Support Command (21 Group)

Air experience – Volunteer Gliding Schools

Type	Unit	Base
Sedbergh TX1	631 VGS	Sealand
	634 VGS	St Athan
Sedbergh TX1, Cadet TX1	614 VGS	Wethersfield
	615 VGS	Kenley
	616 VGS	Henlow
	617 VGS	Manston
	621 VGS	Weston-super-Mare
	622 VGS	Upavon
	625 VGS	South Cerney
	626 VGS	Predannack
	636 VGS	Swansea
	643 VGS	Scampton
	645 VGS	Catterick
	661 VGS	Kirknewton
	662 VGS	Arbroath
	663 VGS	Kinloss
Vanguard TX1	618 VGS	West Malling
Venture TX2	611 VGS	Swanton Morley
	612 VGS	Benson
	613 VGS	Halton
	624 VGS	Chivenor
	632 VGS	Tern Hill
	633 VGS	Cosford
	635 VGS	Samlesbury
	637 VGS	Little Rissington
	642 VGS	Linton-on-Ouse
	644 VGS	Syerston

Air experience – Air Experience Flights

Type	Unit	Base
Chipmunk T10	1 AEF	Manston
	2 AEF	Hurn
	3 AEF	Filton
	4 AEF	Exeter
	6 AEF	Abingdon
	7 AEF	Newton
	8 AEF	Shawbury
	9 AEF	Finningley
	10 AEF	Woodvale
	11 AEF	Leeming
	12 AEF	Turnhouse
Chipmunk T10, Husky	5 AEF	Teversham
Bulldog T1	13 AEF	Sydenham

Air experience – University Air Squadrons

Type	Unit	Base
Bulldog T1	Aberdeen	Leuchars
	Birmingham	Shawbury
	Bristol	Filton
	Cambridge	Teversham
	East Lowlands	Turnhouse
	East Midlands	Newton
	Glasgow	Glasgow
	Liverpool	Woodvale
	London	Abingdon
	Manchester	Woodvale
	Northumbria	Leeming
	Oxford	Abingdon
	Queen's	Sydenham
	Wales	St Athan
	Yorkshire	Finningley

Basic flying training

Type	Unit	Base
Jet Provost T3	7 FTS	Church Fenton
Jet Provost T3A, 5A	1 FTS	Linton-on-Ouse
	RAFC	Cranwell
Jet Provost T3A, 5A, Bulldog	3 FTS inc SRF and RNEFTS	Leeming

Advanced flying training

Type	Unit	Base
Gazelle HT3, Wessex HU5	2 FTS	Shawbury
Hawk T1	4 FTS	Valley
Jet Provost T5, Dominie T1	6 FTS	Finningley
Jetstream T1	METS	Finningley

Miscellaneous

Type	Unit	Base
Jet Provost T4	CATCS	Shawbury (Marshalls)
Jet Provost T5, Bulldog T1	CFS	Leeming
Hawk T1	CFS (Red Arrows)	Kemble
Gazelle HT2, Wessex HC2	CFS(H)	Shawbury

Fleet Air Arm

Type	Unit	Base
Gazelle HT2	705 *Helicopter training*	Culdrose
Lynx HAS3	702 *Advanced Lynx training and OCU*	Portland
Sea King HAS2, 2A, HAR3	706 *Advanced Sea King training and OCU*	Portland
Wessex HU5	707 *Commando conversion training*	Yeovilton
Wessex HAS3	737 *AS aircrew training & Wessex refresher*	Portland
Jetstream T2	750 *Observer School*	Culdrose
Wessex HU5	771 *Aircrew training*	Culdrose

1.K Training at 1 January 1985

RAF – Support Command (21 Group)

Air experience – Volunteer Gliding Schools

Type	Unit	Base
Sedbergh TX1	631 VGS	Sealand
	634 VGS	St Athan
Sedbergh TX1, Cadet TX1	614 VGS	Wethersfield
	615 VGS	Kenley
	616 VGS	Henlow
	617 VGS	Manston
	621 VGS	Weston-super-Mare
	622 VGS	Upavon
	625 VGS	South Cerney
	626 VGS	Predannack
	636 VGS	Swansea
	643 VGS	Scampton
	645 VGS	Catterick
	661 VGS	Kirknewton
	662 VGS	Arbroath
	663 VGS	Kinloss
Vanguard TX1	618 VGS	West Malling
Venture TX2	611 VGS	Swanton Morley
	612 VGS	Benson
	613 VGS	Halton
	624 VGS	Chivenor
	632 VGS	Tern Hill
	633 VGS	Cosford
	635 VGS	Samlesbury
	637 VGS	Little Rissington
	642 VGS	Linton-on-Ouse
	644 VGS	Syerston

Air experience – Air Experience Flights

Type	Unit	Base
Chipmunk T10	1 AEF	Manston
	2 AEF	Hurn
	3 AEF	Filton
	4 AEF	Exeter
	6 AEF	Abingdon
	7 AEF	Newton
	8 AEF	Shawbury
	9 AEF	Finningley
	10 AEF	Woodvale
	11 AEF	Leeming
	12 AEF	Turnhouse
Chipmunk T10, Husky	5 AEF	Teversham
Bulldog T1	13 AEF	Sydenham

Air experience – University Air Squadrons

Type	Unit	Base
Bulldog T1	Aberdeen	Leuchars
	Birmingham	Cosford
	Bristol	Filton
	Cambridge	Teversham
	East Lowlands	Turnhouse
	East Midlands	Newton
	Glasgow	Glasgow

Type	Unit	Base
	Liverpool	Woodvale
	London	Abingdon
	Manchester	Woodvale
	Oxford	Abingdon
	Queen's	Sydenham
	Northumbria	Leeming
	Wales	St Athan
	Yorkshire	Finningley

Basic Training

Type	Unit	Base
Chipmunk T10	FSS	Swinderby
Jet Provost T3A, 5A	1 FTS	Linton-on-Ouse
Bulldog T1	RNEFTS (1 FTS)	Topcliffe
Jet Provost T3A, 5A	7 FTS	Church Fenton
Jet Provost T5	RAFC	Cranwell

Advanced

Type	Unit	Base
Hawk T1, T1A	4 FTS	Valley
Hawk T1	1 TWU (79,234)	Brawdy
	2 TWU (63,151)	Chivenor
Jetstream T1	METS (6 FTS)	Finningley
Gazelle HT3, Wessex HC2	2 FTS	Shawbury

Navigator and specialised aircrew

Type	Unit	Base
Dominie T1, Jet Provost T5A	6 FTS	Finningley
Jet Provost T4	CATCS	Shawbury

Instructor

Type	Unit	Base
Bulldog, Jet Provost T3A, 5A	CFS	Scampton
Hawk T1	Red Arrows (CFS)	Scampton
Gazelle HT3	CFS	Shawbury
Venture TX2, Viking TX1, Vanguard TX1, Valiant TX1, Janus C, Grasshopper TX1	ACCGS	Syerston
As above	CFS EWGS	Syerston

Fleet Air Arm

Type	Unit	Base
Chipmunk T10	FGFlt *Cadet grading*	Roborough
Gazelle HT2	705 *Helicopter training*	Culdrose
Lynx HAS3	702 *Advanced Lynx training and OCU*	Portland
Sea King HAS2A,5	706 *Advanced Sea King training and OCU*	Portland
Sea King HC4, Wessex HU5	707 *Commando conversion training*	Yeovilton
Jetstream T2,3	750 *Observer School*	Culdrose
Wessex HU5, Chipmunk T10, Sea Devon C20	771 *Aircrew training*	Culdrose

Type	Unit	Base
Wessex HU5	772 *Aircrew training*	Portland
Sea Harrier FRS1, T4N, Hunter T8M	899 *Fixed wing pilot training*	Yeovilton

1.L   Training at 1 January 1990

RAF – Support Command (21 Group)

Air experience – Volunteer Gliding Schools

Type	Unit	Base
Viking TX1	611 VGS	Swanton Morley
	614 VGS	Wethersfield
	615 VGS	Kenley
	617 VGS	Manston
	621 VGS	Weston-super-Mare
	622 VGS	Upavon
	625 VGS	South Cerney
	626 VGS	Predannack
	631 VGS	Sealand
	634 VGS	St Athan
	636 VGS	Swansea
	643 VGS	Scampton
	645 VGS	Catterick
	661 VGS	Kirknewton
	662 VGS	Arbroath
Vanguard TX1	618 VGS	West Malling
Venture TX2	612 VGS	Benson
	613 VGS	Halton
	616 VGS	Henlow
	624 VGS	Chivenor
	632 VGS	Tern Hill
	633 VGS	Cosford
	635 VGS	Samlesbury
	637 VGS	Little Rissington
	642 VGS	Linton-on-Ouse
	644 VGS	Syerston
	663 VGS	Kinloss
	664 VGS	Bishop's Court

Air experience – Air Experience Flights

Type	Unit	Base
Chipmunk T10	1 AEF	Manston
	2 AEF	Hurn
	3 AEF	Filton
	4 AEF	Exeter
	5 AEF	Teversham
	6 AEF	Abingdon
	7 AEF	Newton
	8 AEF	Shawbury
	9 AEF	Finningley
	10 AEF	Woodvale
	11 AEF	Leeming
	12 AEF	Turnhouse
Bulldog T1	13 AEF	Sydenham

Air experience – University Air Squadrons

Type	Unit	Base
Bulldog T1	Aberdeen	Leuchars
	Birmingham	Cosford
	Bristol	Filton
	Cambridge	Teversham
	Dundee	Leuchars
	East Lowlands	Turnhouse
	East Midlands	Newton
	Glasgow / Strathclyde	Glasgow
	Liverpool	Woodvale
	London	Abingdon
	Manchester	Woodvale

Type	Unit	Base
	Oxford	Abingdon
	Queen's	Sydenham
	Northumbria	Leeming
	St Andrews	Leuchars
	Southampton	Lee-on-Solent
	Wales	St Athan
	Yorkshire	Finningley

Basic training

Type	Unit	Base
Chipmunk T10	EFTS	Swinderby
Jet Provost T5A	1 FTS	Linton-on-Ouse
Bulldog T1	RNEFTS (1 FTS)	Topcliffe
Tucano T1	7 FTS	Church Fenton
Jet Provost T5A	3 FTS for RAFC	Cranwell
Jetstream T1	METS (6 FTS)	Finningley
Gazelle HT3, Wessex HC2	2 FTS	Shawbury

Advanced

Type	Unit	Base
Hawk T1,T1A	4 FTS	Valley
Hawk T1A	1 TWU (79,234)	Brawdy
	2 TWU (63,151) Chivenor	

Navigator and specialised aircrew

Type	Unit	Base
Dominie T1, Jet Provost T5A	6 FTS	Finningley
Jet Provost T4	CATCS	Shawbury

Instructor

Type	Unit	Base
Bulldog, Jet Provost T3A, 5A, Tucano T1	CFS	Scampton
Hawk T1	Red Arrows (CFS)	Scampton
	CFS	Valley
Gazelle HT3	CFS	Shawbury
Venture TX2, Viking TX1, Vanguard TX1, Valiant TX1, Janus C, Grasshopper TX1	ACCGS	Syerston
As above	CFS EWGS	Syerston

Fleet Air Arm

Type	Unit	Base
Chipmunk T10	FGFlt *Flying grading*	Roborough
Gazelle HT2	705 *Helicopter training*	Culdrose
Lynx HAS3	702 *Advanced Lynx training and OCU*	Portland
Sea King HAS5	706 *Advanced Sea King training and OCU*	Culdrose
Sea King HC4	707 *Commando conversion training*	Yeovilton
Jetstream T2,3	750 *Observer School*	Culdrose
Sea King HAR5	771 *Aircrew training*	Culdrose
Sea King HC4	772 *Aircrew training*	Portland
Sea Harrier FRS1, T4N, Hunter T8M	899 *Fixed wing pilot training*	Yeovilton

1.M   Training at 1 January 1995

RAF – Personnel and Training Command

Air experience – Volunteer Gliding Schools

Type	Unit	Base
Viking TX1	611 VGS	Swanton Morley
	614 VGS	Wethersfield
	615 VGS	Kenley
	617 VGS	Manston
	618 VGS	Challock
	621 VGS	Hullavington
	622 VGS	Upavon
	625 VGS	Hullavington
	626 VGS	Predannack
	631 VGS	Sealand
	634 VGS	St Athan
	636 VGS	Swansea
	645 VGS	Catterick
	661 VGS	Kirknewton
	662 VGS	Arbroath
Vigilant T1	612 VGS	Halton
	613 VGS	Halton
	616 VGS	Henlow
	624 VGS	Chivenor
	632 VGS	Tern Hill
	633 VGS	Cosford
	635 VGS	Samlesbury
	637 VGS	Little Rissington
	642 VGS	Linton-on-Ouse
	663 VGS	Kinloss

Air experience – Air Experience Flights

Type	Unit	Base
Chipmunk T10	1 AEF	Manston
	2 AEF	Hurn
	3 AEF	Colerne
	4 AEF	Exeter
	5 AEF	Teversham
	6 AEF	Benson
	7 AEF	Newton
	8 AEF	Shawbury
	9 AEF	Finningley
	10 AEF	Woodvale
	11 AEF	Leeming
	12 AEF	Turnhouse
Bulldog T1	13 AEF	Aldergrove

Air experience – University Air Squadrons

Type	Unit	Base
Bulldog T1	Aberdeen	Leuchars
	Birmingham	Cosford
	Bristol	Colerne
	Cambridge	Teversham
	Dundee	Leuchars
	East Lowlands	Turnhouse
	East Midlands	Newton
	Glasgow / Strathclyde	Glasgow
	Liverpool	Woodvale
	London	Benson
	Manchester	Woodvale
	Northumbria	Leeming
	Oxford	Benson
	Queen's	Aldergrove
	St Andrews	Leuchars
	Southampton	Boscombe Down
	Wales	St Athan
	Yorkshire	Finningley

Basic training

Type	Unit	Base
T67M-2 Firefly	JEFTS	Topcliffe
Tucano T1	1 FTS	Linton-on-Ouse
	3 FTS (RAFC)	Cranwell
Gazelle HT3, Wessex HC2	2 FTS	Shawbury
Jetstream T1	6 FTS (45R)	Finningley

Advanced

Type	Unit	Base
Hawk T1,T1A (19,74,208R)	4 FTS	Valley

Navigator and specialised aircrew

Type	Unit	Base
Bulldog T1, Dominie T1, Tucano T1, Hawk T1	6 FTS	Finningley

Instructor

Type	Unit	Base
Bulldog T1, Tucano T1, Chipmunk T10	CFS	Scampton
Hawk T1	Red Arrows (CFS)	Scampton
	CFS (19R)	Valley
Gazelle HT3	CFS	Shawbury
Viking TX1, Valiant TX1 Kestrel TX1, Vigilant T1	ACCGS	Syerston
As above	CFS EWGS	Syerston

Fleet Air Arm

Type	Unit	Base
Grob G.115 Heron	FGFlt *Flying grading*	Roborough
Gazelle HT2	705 *Helicopter training*	Culdrose
Sea King HAS5,6	706 *Advanced Sea King training and OCU*	Portland
Sea King HC4	707 *Commando conversion training*	Yeovilton
Jetstream T2	750 *Observer School*	Culdrose
Sea King HAR5	771 *Aircrew training*	Culdrose
Sea King HC4	772 *Aircrew training*	Portland
Sea Harrier F/A2, Harrier T4,4N,8	899 *Fixed wing pilot training*	Yeovilton

BAe Hawk T Mk 1A

The Hawk has been the standard advanced trainer since 1976. Seen here in the relatively new all-black high-visibility finish is XX222/TJ of 74 Sqn/4 FTS over the Irish Sea. *(Crown copyright)*

1.1 de Havilland Tiger Moth (1932–1973)

One of the all-time great light aircraft, the DH 82A Tiger Moth was bought in large numbers by the RAF as a replacement for the venerable Avro 504. Experience with the DH 60 Gipsy Moth led to a re-design with the top wing moved forward to ease egress in an emergency resulting in the need to stagger the wings to regain the centre of gravity. Thirty-five examples of the Mark I were ordered powered by the Gipsy III, but this was prone to overheating so further orders were for the Gipsy Major-powered Mark II.

Mark II/T Mark 2

The DH 82A was initially purchased against specification T.26/33 and a total of 4,668 was ordered in due course, mostly against specification T.7/35. Over 3,000 were built in the Commonwealth, and in the United Kingdom many civilian examples were impressed for use by the elementary flying schools. Early modifications included the fitting of anti-spin strakes on the rear fuselage, plywood fuselage decking and for some aircraft the fitting of a blind-flying hood. The Tiger Moth (in Mark I form) had entered service with the CFS in 1932 and the last of the type in British service retired from the Royal Navy in 1973.

Service (post-1945) Training 1, 2, 3, 4, 6, 7, 11, 14, 15, 16, 18, 21, 22, 24, 28, 29 EFTS; 2, 3, 4, 6, 7, 16, 19, 22 FTS; 1, 2, 3, 5, 6, 7, 8, 9, 10, 11, 12, 15, 16, 17, 18, 22, 23, 24, 25 RFS; 6, 20 SFTS; 201, 203, 204 AFS; CFS; 10 FIS; 3 GTS; 2 ITS; 226 OCU; RAFC; 1 RS; Aberdeen, Birmingham, Cambridge, Edinburgh, Glasgow, Leeds, London, Manchester, Nottingham, Oxford, Queen's, St Andrews, Southampton UAS; 727, 767, 796, 799 NAS; BRNC **Communications** (note: many Tiger Moths were used as hacks with minimal records as to usage. The list here is indicative rather than complete) 663; 12 GCS; 2 TAFCS; 61 GCF; HCMSU; Aldergrove, Ballykelly, Binbrook, Hemswell SF: 701, 721, 781, 1833 NAS; Yeovilton SF.

Specification and production

Mark	Role	Engine	HP	Weight lb	Speed mph	Nos
II	Trainer	Gipsy Major	130	1,770	109	4,668*

* many civilian Tiger Moths were impressed and over 3,000 were built in the Commonwealth

---

Further reading
Tiger Moth Story, The, Bramson, A and Birch, N, Air Review, London, 1971
Tiger Moth, The, Mackay, S, Airlife, Shrewsbury, 1988

1.2 Miles Magister (1937–1946)

The Magister was an all-wood low-wing monoplane faster than the contemporary Tiger Moth but with a slower landing speed. It was built to specification T.40/36 and some 1,293 were constructed starting with L5912. By

de Havilland Tiger Moth T Mk 2

The DH82A Tiger Moth was the most extensively built trainer ever used by the RAF and Empire air forces. Primarily a single variant it remained in service from 1932 to 1973 and many ex-service machines remain on the civil register. Shown are aircraft of Cambridge University Air Squadron over the City in 1947. *(A S Thomas collection)*

Miles Magister Mk I

Well over a thousand of the neat Miles Magister monoplane complemented the Tiger Moth although it was in service only for a year or two after the end of the war. L8277 is marked with a Group Captain's pennant and appears to be based in the Middle East, given the 32 Sqn Spitfire behind. *(MAP)*

the end of the war few remained in service although many were sold on to the civil market.

Mark I

The M.14A was a development of the M.2 Hawk with dual controls in tandem cockpits and with other minor variations. Power was provided by the Gipsy Major I.

Service (post-1945) Trainer ECFS; 29 EFTS; 10 FIS 21 (P)AFU, 6 SFTS

Specification and production

Mark	Role	Engine	HP	Weight lb	Speed mph	Nos
I	Trainer	Gipsy Major	130	1,900	142	1,293

1.3   Airspeed Oxford (1937-55)

The Airspeed AS.10 Oxford was ordered by the RAF before the war to specification T.23/36. This called for a twin-engined trainer incorporating the most modern features and with enough complexity to prepare aircrew for the new generation of monoplane twins then coming into service or on order. In practice the Oxford was relatively unforgiving and as such made an ideal pilot trainer. Like the Mosquito it was of all-wood construction. It entered service in 1937 and after the war remained in use for training until 1954, and in the communications role for a little longer.

Mark I

The AS.10 flew on 19 June 1937 (L4534) and it was intended as a general-purpose trainer with gun turret (one .303-in MG) and bomb-bay. Within four months the first aircraft were being delivered to the Central Flying School. Power was provided by two Cheetah X engines. In the event most of this variant were used for pilot training solely, the majority with turrets removed.

Service (post-1945) Training   1333, 1336 TSCU; 1382 TCU; 1510, 1516, 1521, 1527, 1528, 1529, 1537,

1547, 1552, 1556, 1557 BATF; 15 RFS; 3, 6 SFTS; 26 OTU; 237 OCU; ECFS; EFS; 3 GTS; 1 OFU; 5 (P)AFU; London UAS; 762, 780, 798, 1830, 1841 NAS **Communications** 11, 12, 38, 41, 64, 87 GCF

Mark II

The Mark II was a dual-control version for pilot training; it was built in smaller numbers than the Mark I but continued in use for some time after the war. It differed from the Mark I externally by lacking the turret and bomb-bay, but in practice it was usually indistinguishable. Many post-war operational squadrons flying twin-engined aircraft (typically Meteor or Hornet) had one or two Oxfords on charge for refresher or continuation training.

Service (post-1945) Training   14, 17, 20, 34, 41, 43, 46, 90, 105, 139, 148, 202, 222, 238, 245, 269, 287, 288, 290, 504, 527, 529, 567, 577, 595, 605, 608, 667, 691, 695; 1527 BATF; 1555, 1556 RATF; 1589 HFF; 1689 FPPTF; 226, 228, 233 OCU; 16, 26 OTU; 1665 CU; 8, 9, 10, 14 AFTS; 5, 11, 15, 19, 22 RFS; 7, 17 SFTS; 202, 205 AFS; 1 BAS; BCIS; CFS; CNS; ECFS; EFS; FCCRS; FCITS; 7 FIS; 101, 104 FRS; FRS; 21, 22 HGCU; 1 ITS; 12, 21 (P)AFU; 1 PGTS; 1, 2 PRFU; RAFTC; SFU; Cambridge, Glasgow, Queen's, Southampton UAS **Communications** CCCF; CFE; FCCS; FTCCF; MCS; TCCF; TTCTF; 3, 12, 23, 61, 63, 66 GCF; Aqir, Bassingbourn, Church Fenton, Coltishall, Coningsby, Dishforth, Duxford, Great Dunmow, Hemswell, Hixon, Horsham St Faith, Leuchars, Linton-on-Ouse, North Weald, Waddington, Waterbeach, Wattisham SF **Miscellaneous** BLEU; 1, 3/4 CAACU; ETPS; 1 TTU; TRE: 778 NAS

The Marks III and IV were one-off wartime variants fitted with the Cheetah XV and Gipsy Queen IV engines respectively.

Mark V

Fitted with a Pratt & Whitney Wasp Junior engine with Hamilton Standard propellers which conferred an extra 20mph on the variant. The variant was used in Canada and Southern Rhodesia.

Specification and production

Mark	Role	Engine	HP	Weight lb	Speed mph	Nos
I	Trainer	2xCheetah X	355	7,600	182	6,437
II	Trainer	2xCheetah X	355	7,600	188	1,845
III	Trials	2xCheetah XV	425	7,600	185	1
IV	Trials	2xGipsy Queen IV	375	7,600	170	1
V	Trainer	2xWasp Junior	450	8,000	190	196

Airspeed Oxford Mk II

The Oxford was a twin-engined dual control trainer for multi-engine pilot training. Large numbers were used by operational squadrons for continuation training or as hacks. At Horsham St Faith in 1948 is PH458/4M-C of 695 Sqn. *(A S Thomas collection)*

Further reading

Airspeed Oxford, The (Profile 227) Rawlings, J D R, Profile Publications, Leatherhead, 1971

1.4 Vickers Wellington (1938–1953)

The twin-engined Wellington bomber was designed by Vickers to specification B.9/32 and the protoype (K4049) flew on 15 June 1936 and the Mark I was ordered to B.29/36. The first unit equipped with the type was 99 Sqn in November 1938. The Mark I (Type 285, 415) and Mark II (Type 419) were out of service by the war's end.

Mark III

The Type 417 began life as a bomber powered by the Hercules III. It entered service in 1942 and 1,519 were built. In service it was soon replaced by the four-engined Lancaster and Halifax and the large numbers available were converted for training.

Service (post-1945) Training 10, 17, 21, 26 OTU

The Mark IV (Type 410), Mark V (Type 426), Mark VI (Type 442) were wartime bombers while the Mark VII (Type 416) and Mark VIII (Type 429) were anti-submarine aircraft. All were out of service by 1946. The Mark IX (Type 437) passenger conversion was not in the event produced.

Mark X/T Mark 10

The Type 440 was an improved version of the Mark III with the Hercules XVI engine. It served in large numbers as a bomber and for many years post-war as an advanced multi-engined and navigator trainer until replaced by the Valetta and Varsity. In its latter form the nose turret was faired over.

Service (post-1945) Training 10, 17, 21, 26 OTU; 1380, 1381 TCU; 228 OCU; 1, 2, 5, 6, 7, 10 ANS; 201, 202 AFS; 11 AGS; CNCS; 202 CTU; EAAS; FRS; 101, 104 FRS; 1 PRFU **Other** 527; 38 GCF; APDU; ASWDU; CFE; CGS; CSE; PRDU; SFU; RWE; TFU: 765 NAS

Mark XI

The Type 454 was an anti-submarine variant, retained for training.

Vickers Wellington B Mk X

In the T Mk 10 form the Wellington remained in service as a navigation trainer until replaced by the Varsity in 1953. Shown here at Istres in 1946 is a totally anonymous B Mk X, while parked behind it is a Coastal Command Mk XIV, 'Y' of 38 Sqn. (*Author's collection*)

Specification and production

Mark	Role	Engine	HP	Weight lb	Speed mph	Nos
I	Bomber	2xPegasus XVIII	1,050	28,500	235	2,868
II	Bomber	2xMerlin X	1,145	27,600	247	400
III	Trainer	2xHercules III	1,375	29,500	255	1,519
IV	Bomber	2xTwin Wasp	1,200	31,600	229	220
V	HA bomber	2xHercules III	1,375	32,000	292	2
VI	HA bomber	2xMerlin 60	1,600	31,600	300	64
VII	Bomber	2xMerlin XX	not built			
VIII	GR	2xPegasus XVIII	1,050	25,800	235	394
IX	Transport	not built				
X	Bomber/ Trainer	2xHercules XVI	1,615	29,500	255	3,084
XI	GR	2xHercules VI	1,615	29,500	255	180
XII	GR	2xHercules XVI	1,615	36,500	256	58
XIII	GR	2xHercules XVII	1,725	31,000	250	843
XIV	GR	2xHercules XVII	1,725	31,000	250	841
XV	Transport	2xPegasus XVIII	1,050			*
XVI	Transport	2xPegasus XVIII	1,050			*
XVII	Trainer	2xHercules VI	1,615			~
XVIII	Trainer	2xHercules XVII	1,725			+
XIX	Trainer	2xHercules XVI	1,615	29,500	255	#

* Mark I conversion
~ Mark XI conversion
+ Mark XIII conversion
\# Mark X field conversion

Service (post-1945) Training 765 NAS

The Mark XII (Type 455) was another anti-submarine type out of service by the war's end.

Mark XIII

The Type 466 was a Mark X fitted with the Hercules XVII engine, ASV Mk III radar and torpedoes. The type had been relegated to the training role by 1946.

Service (post-1945) Training 111 OTU; 10 ANS

Mark XIV

The Type 467 was the definitive Coastal Command version similar to the Mark XIII but with Leigh light in addition for night operations. It was the only variant still in front-line service in 1946.

Service (post–1945) Maritime reconnaissance 38, 621 **Training** 111 OTU

The Mark XV and Mark XVI were Mark I transport conversions while the Mark XVII (Type 487) was a short-lived trainer conversion of the XI.

Mark XVIII

The Type 490 was a night fighter crew trainer conversion of the Mark XIII with SCR720 radar in the nose. It was in small-scale use for several years after the war ended.

Service (post-1945) Training 228 OCU; CFE

Mark XIX/T Mark 19

The Type 619 was a Mark X conversion for training. Like the earlier variant it had a faired nose and in most cases the rear turret was also removed.

Service Training 201 AFS

Further reading

Vickers Wellington I and II, The (Profile 125) Andrews, C F, Profile Publications, Leatherhead, 1967

Wellington, Cooksley, P, Patrick Stephens, Cambridge, 1988

Wellington at War, Bowyer, C, Ian Allan, Shepperton, 1983

Wellington Bomber, The, Bowyer, C, William Kimber, London, 1986

1.5   North American Harvard (1938–1957)

The low-wing Harvard was ordered for the RAF before the Second World War and some 400 were delivered by the end of 1940. The type served widely as an advanced trainer and, from 1948, in the light attack role in Malaya and Kenya. The Mark I (NA-49) powered by a single Wasp R-1340 was no longer in service by 1946.

Mark II

The NA-66, -76, -81 incorporated several design refinements including blunt wing-tips and a straight rudder. The construction was of light alloy covered steel tube and the engine was slightly more powerful at 600hp. The variant was the equivalent of the USAAF AT-6 and 519 were delivered, the majority to Canada.

Service (post-1945) Training 20, 22 SFTS Communications 3 ANS

Mark IIa

The NA-88 was equivalent to the AT-6C and it was constructed of low-alloy steel, fabric-covered except the rear fuselage which was ply-covered; 747 were delivered to British services, mainly in South Africa.

Service (post-1945) Training 4, 5 FTS; 727 NAS Communications 43, 213, 249; 3 ANS; 782 NAS; Anthorn SF

Mark IIb

Built by Noorduyn in Canada with a metal stressed skin with fabric-covered control surfaces. Similar to the

North American Harvard T Mk 2B

The American built Harvard served in large numbers across the world and with the DTEO at Boscombe Down remains in service at the time of writing as a photographic and chase aircraft. The type also served in the unarmed reconnaissance and light strike roles as shown here with the RAF in Malaya during the early stages of Operation 'Firedog'. *(Crown copyright)*

USAAF AT-6, it was the most widely used variant (2,557) and the longest serving. At the time of writing one in military markings is still in use with the A&AEE.

Service (post-1945) Training 18 EFTS; 1, 2, 3, 4, 5, 6, 7, 9, 20, 21, 22 FTS; 3, 6, 7, 17, 19, 20, 21, 22 SFTS; 5, 21 (P)AFU; 5, 8, 11, 14, 16, 18, 19, 22, 23, 25 RFS; 203, 207 AFS; 8, 43, 61 OTU; 226, 227, 237 OCU; ATA; BAS; CFE; CFS; CGS; EAAS; EANS; ECFS; EFT; FCITF; 7 FIS; FRS; 101, 102, 103 FRS; FTU; HCEU; HCITF; 1 PGTS; RAFFC; RAFC; RCITF; 1, 2 (P)RFU; Aberdeen, Birmingham, Bristol, Cambridge, Durham, Edinburgh, Glasgow, Hull, Leeds, Liverpool, London, Manchester, Nottingham, Oxford, Queen's, St Andrews, Southampton UAS; 702, 709, 719, 727, 757, 758, 766, 767, 780, 794, 799, 1830, 1831, 1832, 1833, 1834, 1840, 1841 NAS **Communications** 1, 2, 3, 5, 6, 8, 16, 17, 18, 19, 20, 26, 32, 33, 34, 41, 45, 54, 60, 65, 66, 73, 80, 84, 91, 122, 129, 130, 164, 165, 167, 208, 213, 247, 249, 267, 303, 306, 309, 315, 336, 500, 501, 502, 504, 541, 587, 595, 600, 601, 602, 603, 604, 605, 607, 608, 609, 610, 612, 613, 614, 615, 616, 631, 691, 695; 1689, 1315 Flt; AAEE; AFEE; ATDU; BLEU; FCCS; FTCCF; 1 FU; HCCS; OFU; RAE; RCCF/S; 12, 21, 23, 61, 62, 63, 64, 66, 84 GCF; AHQ Malaya CS; BC Air CS; FEAF CF/CS; Biggin Hill, Butterworth, Celle, Church Fenton, Duxford, Feltwell, Halton, Horsham St Faith, Iwakuni, Kai Tak, Manston, Middle Wallop, Northolt, Odiham, Seletar, Sembawang, Tengah, Thorney Island, Wattisham, Wittering SF; 771, 781, 782 NAS; 2, 4 FF; FP; Arbroath, Eglinton, Lossiemouth, Roborough, St Merryn, Syerston SF **Utility** 11 AGS; APS Acklington; 27 APC (Butterworth); ETPS **Light attack** 1340 Flt; HK, KL, Malaya, Penang, Singapore Ftr Sqns

Mark III
Similar in all respects to the Mark II but with a 24, rather than 12, volt electrical system. This variant served almost exclusively with the Fleet Air Arm.

Service (post-1945) Training 718, 727, 729, 736, 748, 758, 759, 760, 761, 766, 767, 780, 784, 794, 799, 1830, 1831, 1832, 1833, 1840, 1841 NAS **Utility** 728, 778, 791 NAS **Communications** 781, 782 NAS; 2 FF; Arbroath, Culdrose, Eglinton, Gosport, Hal Far, Lossiemouth, Rochester SF

Specification and production

Mark	Role	Engine	HP	Weight lb	Speed mph	Nos
I	Trainer	Wasp R-1340	550	5,200	210	400
II	Trainer	Wasp R-1340	600	5,160	206	519
IIa	Trainer	Wasp R-1340	600	5,160	206	747
IIb	Trainer	Wasp R-1340	550	5,250	206	2,557
III	Trainer	Wasp R-1340	600	5,250	206	537

Further reading
Harvard File, The, Hamlin, J F, Air Britain, Tonbridge, 1988
T-6, Smith, P.C., Airlife, Shrewsbury1996.

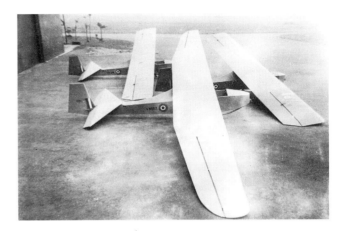

Slingsby Cadet TX Mk 1 and TX Mk 2

This fine shot clearly highlights the difference between the Mk 1 with its straight, plank-like wing, and the Mk 2 with the tapered wing. The very basic construction is also evident. In the background is VM546, while the nearer glider is VM663; both belong to 107 Gliding School and are seen at Digby in 1947. *(P H T Green collection)*

1.6   Slingsby Cadet (1944–1985)

The Cadet started life as the Type 7 Kirby Kadet of 1936. At least 430 were built, probably more since kits were also produced and some were rebuilt after being 'written-off' in accidents. The original type was a single-seat primary glider and its first service-related use was for Air Training Corps air experience from the last year of the war.

TX Mark 1
The Type T.7 was a single-seat glider of which no fewer than 417 were used by the ATC including 36 built from kits or parts or impressed during the war and five rebuilt (in the XE758-762 serial range) from crashed gliders.

Service (post-1945) Training 1, 2, 4, 5, 6, 7, 22, 23, 24, 26, 27, 31, 41, 42, 43, 44, 45, 48, 49, 68, 82, 83, 84, 87, 89, 92, 95, 102, 104, 105, 106, 122, 123, 125, 126, 128, 130, 141, 142, 143, 146, 148, 161, 162, 163, 166, 168, 182, 183, 186, 188, 192, 203, 614, 615, 616, 617, 621, 622, 625, 626, 631, 636, 643, 645, 661, 662, 663 GS

TX Mark 2
The Type T.8 differed from the earlier version in having a tapered wing, small windscreen and landing wheel. Eighty-two were bought, including one for the Royal Navy.

Service Training 1, 2, 4, 5, 6, 7, 23, 24, 26, 27, 31, 41, 42, 43, 45, 48, 49, 68, 82, 83, 87, 89, 92, 95, 102, 104, 105, 106, 122, 123, 125, 126, 128, 130, 142, 143, 146, 148, 161, 162, 163, 166, 168, 182, 183, 186, 188, 192, 203,

TX Mark 3
The Type T.31B was a side-by-side trainer brought into service to support a shift in gliding training policy away from single-seat *ab initio* training.

Slingsby Cadet TX Mk 3

The Slingsby Cadet was an outstanding glider produced in large numbers for Air Training Corps use. Illustrated is a two-seat Mk 3, WT877, probably of 643 Gliding School, and certainly at Kirton-in-Lindsey. *(P H T Green collection)*

Service Training 1, 2 GC; 611, 612, 613, 614, 615, 616, 617, 621, 622, 623, 624, 625, 626, 631, 632, 633, 634, 635, 641, 642, 643, 644, 645, 661, 662, 663, 671; 1 SoTT

Specification and production

Mark	Role	Engine	HP	Weight lb	Speed mph	Nos
TX1	Trainer	none	n/a	513	-	417
TX2	Trainer	none	n/a	520	-	82
TX3	Trainer	none	n/a	640	-	121

Further Reading
Slingsby Sailplanes, Simons, M., Airlife, Shrewsbury, 1996.

1.7   Bristol Buckmaster (1946–1956)

The success of the Mosquito as a light bomber resulted in the Buckingham being abandoned as a Blenheim

Bristol Buckmaster T Mk 1

The Buckmaster was originally intended as a Blenheim bomber replacement but proved surplus to requirements. 110 were fitted with dual controls as an advanced trainer and issued to Brigand units. Aircraft 'O' of 8 Sqn is seen at Aden in February 1953. *(A S Thomas collection)*

successor. The original order was reduced and the type limited to the transport role. However, there was a need for a twin-engined trainer and as the Buckmaster the last 110 were converted to this standard against specification T.13/43.

T Mark 1
The Bristol Type 166 flew on 27 October 1944 (TJ714). It was similar to the Buckingham in most respects except that it was fitted with dual controls. As a fast advanced trainer the type was issued to Brigand units in small numbers and it served both as a pilot and radar navigator trainer with operational conversion units until 1956.

Service Training 8, 17, 36, 45, 84, 254; 6, 132 OTU; 228, 236, 238 OCU; 204 CTU; AIS; CFS; CCFIS; ECFS; EFS; ETPS; FETS; 12 FIS; 1 FU **Communications** HCCS; OFU; SF Chivenor

Specification and Production

Mark	Role	Engine	HP	Weight lb	Speed mph	Nos
T1	Trainer	2xCentaurus VII	2,520	33,700	352	110

1.8   Percival Prentice (1947–1953)

The Prentice was designed as a replacement for the Tiger Moth to specification T.23/43. It was the RAF's first side-by-side trainer and compared to its predecessor was comfortable and well-equipped. It was built as a three-seater, the intention being that a second pupil would observe procedures from a rear third seat; in practice the intention was not pursued.

T Mark 1
The Percival P.40 flew on 31 March 1946 (TV163) and the Prentice entered service with the Empire Flying School in

Percival Prentice T1

A major limitation with the Tiger Moth was the distance between tutor and student in fresh air. Its replacement, the Prentice, was designed as a side-by-side trainer, with enclosed cockpit and with provision for a second student in a rear seat as clearly seen in this photograph of VR227 of the Royal Air Force College. *(MAP)*

1947. It served with a number of flying training schools and latterly in the communications role, finally being replaced by the Provost in 1953.

Service Training 1, 2, 3, 4, 6, 7, 8, 10, 12, 22, 211 FTS; 5, 6, 7, 9, 11, 16, 19, 22, 23, 24, 25 RFS; 203, 205, 211 AFS; 228 OCU; AOPS; CFS; EFS; 1 ITS; PTU; RAFC; RAFFC; Birmingham, Cambridge, Durham, Edinburgh, London, Oxford, Queen's UAS; 1, 2 ASS; 4 RS **Communications** 31; 2, 19, 21, 22, 23, 40, 83, 205, 295 GCF; CCCF; HCCF/S; MECF/S; RAE; 2 TAFCS; TTCCF; WEE; SF Aboukir, Ahlhorn, Akrotiri, Benson, Brüggen, Butzweilerhof, Catterick, Celle, Eindhoven, Fassberg, Gatow, Geilenkirchen, Gütersloh, Ismailia, Jever, Mafraq, Mauripur, Oldenburg, Pembroke Dock, Spitalgate, Wahn, Wildenrath, Wünstorf; AA Paris

T Marks 2 and 3
The Mark 2 was fitted with the Gipsy Queen 51 offering greater power. It was not pursued, the sole example (VR211 a converted T1) being evaluated by the A&AEE. The Mark 3 was an intended version with the Gipsy Queen 70-2, more powerful yet. Although not ordered by the RAF, this variant was built for the Indian Air Force.

Specification and production

Mark	Role	Engine	HP	Weight lb	Speed mph	Nos
T1	Trainer	Gipsy Queen 32	251	4,200	143	370
T2	Trainer	Gipsy Queen 51	296	4,220	150	1*
T3	Trainer	Gipsy Queen 70-2	345	4,220	150	1*

* T1 conversions

1.9 de Havilland Chipmunk (1950–date)

The Chipmunk is a remarkable aircraft in British service history. It was built in Canada by de Havilland Canada as a local replacement for the Tiger Moth and in 1948 offered to the RAF for the same purpose. The initial order was for 200 aircraft at £2,100 each and the subsequent purchase rose to 735. The type has remained in service since initial deliveries in February 1950 and will probably remain in service until into the 21st century – at least 50 years of service and all in a single variant. Further, the Chipmunk is the only fixed-wing type to have served with all four services (including the Royal Marines) and it has almost certainly served with more 'units' than any other type in British military service.

T Mark 10
The Type DHC1 was delivered to specification T.8/48. There were no other mark numbers since the earlier ones were reserved for Canadian production. The prototype (WB549) flew on 22 May 1946 and the Chipmunk entered service with Oxford and Cambridge University Air Squadrons, within two years having re-equipped most University units and Reserve Flying Schools. It was largely replaced by the Bulldog from 1973, but as mentioned above remains in use (with the Battle of Britain Memorial Flight) at the time of writing.

de Havilland Chipmunk T Mk 10

Unique in the history of the RAF is the Chipmunk which remains active in 1997 – just – after 50 years in service. Several generations of aircrew probably got their first taste of flying in the type which equipped air experience flights for decades. One of the last RAF Chipmunks is WK518 which serves with the Battle of Britain Memorial Flight; it is seen on circuits and bumps at Coningsby in July 1996. *(Author)*

Service Training 22 EFTS; 1, 2, 3, 4, 5 BFTS; 9 AFTS; 1, 2, 3, 4, 5, 6, 7, 8 FTS; 1, 2, 3, 5, 6, 8, 9, 10, 11, 12, 14, 15, 16, 17, 18, 19, 22, 23, 24, 25 RFS; 1, 2, 3, 4, 5, 6, 7, 8, 9, 10, 11, 12, 13 AEF; 226, 229, 233, 242 OCU; 1 AES; 1, 2 ANS; ITF Honiley, Honington; 1 ITS; 1, 2, 4 SoTT; AOTS; CFS; CGS; CNCS; FTU; HCEU; HCITF; PFS; PFTS; RAFC; RAFFC; RAFTC; SLAW; SMR; Aberdeen, Birmingham, Bristol, Cambridge, Durham, East Midlands, Edinburgh, Glasgow, Hull, Kent, Leeds, Liverpool, London, Manchester, Northumbria, Nottingham, Oxford, Queen's, St Andrews, Southampton, South Wales, Wales, York UAS: 771, 781 NAS; BRNC: RM Chatham: 651, 652, 657, 661, 662, 663, 664, 666; 1912 Flt; LAS **Training/communications** 8, 31, 51, 100, 111, 147, 202, 228, 257, 275, 288, 613, 622; 1 CAACU; CSE; SF Abingdon, Acklington, Ahlhorn, Andover, Aston Down, Bassingbourn, Benson, Bicester, Biggin Hill, Binbrook, Bircham Newton, Brawdy, Brüggen, Bückeburg, Cardington, Carlisle, Church Fenton, Colerne, Coltishall, Coningsby, Cottesmore, Debden, Detling, Dishforth, Driffield, Duxford, Dyce, Eastleigh, Edzell, Farnborough, Finningley, Gatow, Gaydon, Geilenkirchen, Gütersloh, Halton, Hemswell, Hendon, Henlow, Honiley, Honington, Hornchurch, Horsham St Faith, Hucknall, Jever, Jurby, Kinloss, Laarbruch, Leconfield, Leuchars, Linton-on-Ouse, Litchfield, Little Rissington, Lyneham, Manston, Marham, Middleton St George, Mildenhall, Nicosia, Odiham, Oldenburg, Old Sarum, Ouston, Rufforth, St Athan, St Mawgan, Scampton, Schwechat, Shawbury, South Cerney, Stradishall, Swanton Morley, Ta Kali, Tangmere, Turnhouse, Upavon, Upwood, Waddington, Waterbeach, Wattisham, West Malling, West Raynham, Wildenrath, Wittering, Woodvale, Wünstorf, Wymeswold, Wyton, Yeadon **Communications** BoBMF; BCCF/S; FTCCF/S; HCCF; MCCS; MCS; MPC Valley; MECS; Malta CF/CTTS; 2, 3, 11, 12, 13, 19, 21, 22, 24, 25, 38, 43, 61, 64, 81, 83 GCF; AA Paris, Rome **Internal security** 114

Specification and production

Mark	Role	Engine	HP	Weight lb	Speed mph	Nos
T10	Trainer	Gipsy Major 8	145	2,000	138	735

1.10 Avro Athena (1950–1955)

The Type 701 Athena, like the Balliol, was built to specification T.7/45. This called for a three-seat turbo-prop advanced trainer to replace the Master and Harvard. In the event the specification was before its time and the selected engine, the Mamba, was delayed in development. Like the Balliol the Athena was produced with the Merlin 35.

T Mark 1
The first aircraft flew on 12 June 1948 (VM125) fitted with the Mamba engine. Two Mamba-powered prototypes were built but the specification was changed to require a piston engine.

Avro Athena T Mk 1

The Athena was designed as a Harvard replacement and the original intention was for a turboprop engined type. In the event delays in engine development resulted in the worthy but aged Merlin being used. Only fifteen were built including VR567 used by the Central Flying School. *(MAP)*

T Mark 1A
The T Mk 1A comprised a sole example, VM129 fitted with a Dart 1 engine. Like the Mamba-powered variant it was abandoned.

T Mark 2
The production version equipped with the trusty Merlin engine was constructed to specification T.14/47. The prototype, VW890, flew on 1 August 1948; changed features included moving the mainplane forward 27in to compensate for the heavier engine and a larger fin and rudder of revised shape. Fifteen were built before production ceased in favour of the Balliol.

Service Training AIEU; CFS; RAE; RAFFC

Specification and production

Mark	Role	Engine	HP	Weight lb	Speed mph	Nos
T1	Trainer	Mamba 1	1,010	7,191	291	2
T1A	Trainer	Dart 1	1,400	7,200	295	1
T2	Trainer	Merlin 35	1,280	9,383	293	15

1.11 Slingsby Prefect (1950–1979)

The Prefect was a developed version of the single-seat Grunau Baby, a number of which had served with the Air Training Corps units.

TX Mark 1
The Type T.30 was an intermediate single-seat glider and fifteen were purchased for ATC use. The first, WE979, went to RAF Cranwell in 1950 and the type was withdrawn from the ACCGS in 1979. One was bought for the Royal Navy for carrier wake trials.

Service Training 1, 2, 5, 12, 22, 24, 42, 45, 80, 87, 122, 123, 125, 141, 143, 166, 612, 613, 614, 615, 617, 617, 621, 623, 624, 631, 632, 634, 642, 643, 644, 661, 662 ACCGS; CGIS; 1, 2 GC; HCGS; RAFC: RNGSA **Trials** FAA

Slingsby Prefect TX Mk 1

The Prefect was a development of the Grunau Baby, a number of which was impressed for ATC use during and after the war. It was a single-seat glider and WE980 shown was the second of fifteen bought. It is shown at Detling in 1950 where it served with the Home Command Gliding Instructors School. (*P H T Green collection*)

Specification and production

Mark	Role	Engine	HP	Weight lb	Speed mph	Nos
TX1	Trainer	none	n/a	587	–	16

1.12 Boulton Paul Balliol and Sea Balliol (1952–1958)

The P.108 Balliol was built, like the Avro Athena, to specification T.7/45. It was intended to be fitted with the Mamba engine and thus fitted was the first aircraft in the world to fly with a single turbo-prop. It was originally to have been in widespread production to replace the Harvard, but in the event production was cut back when the decision was taken to move to all-through jet training.

Boulton Paul Balliol T Mk 1

The Balliol was built to the same Harvard replacement specification as the Athena and was the first aircraft in the world to fly with a single turboprop engine. However, like the Athena, it was fitted with the Merlin in production and numbers were limited to 162 (for the RAF) when the decision was taken to introduce all-though jet training. WG178/J was with 288 Sqn in 1957. (*MAP*)

T Mark 1
The prototype (VL892) flew on 24 March 1947 powered, as an interim measure, by the Mercury 30 of just 830hp. The Mamba-powered prototype, VL917, flew on 24 March 1948. The turbo-prop requirement was dropped before production started.

T Mark 2
The definitive variant was built to specification T.14/47 which amended the original requirement by substituting a piston engine for the Mamba. The Merlin 35 was used with some trading of speed for endurance. In 1952 the Balliol entered service with 7 FTS, the only such unit to be primarily equipped with the type. Although the Balliol was very much an interim type, it had some useful characteristics, like hydraulic air brakes, which allowed some simulation of jet-type performance. The Balliol served with the RAF only until 1956.

Service Training 288/FCCRS; 2, 6, 7 FTS; 228, 233, 238 OCU; APS Acklington; 3/4 CAACU; CFE; CFS; CGS; ETPS; FTU; HCEU; RAFC; SFC; Durham UAS **Communications** FTCCS; HCCS; TCCF; 61 GCF; SF Bahrain, Colerne, Upavon **Trials** RAE

T Mark 21
The Sea Balliol was built to Naval requirement N.102D by the simple expedient of fitting an arrester hook to the basic version. The type was used for carrier deck-landing training.

Service Training 702, 727, 796, 1830, 1831, 1832, 1834, 1840, 1843, 1844 NAS; **Communications** 765, 781 NAS; FP Anthorn, Abbotsinch, Culdrose, Lee-on-Solent, Yeovilton. **Trials** 703 NAS; JWE

Specification and production

Mark	Role	Engine	HP	Weight lb	Speed mph	Nos
T1	Trainer	Mamba 1	1,135	7,845	307	2
		Mercury 25	840	7,650	285	1
T2	Trainer	Merlin 35	1,245	8,410	288	162
T21	Trainer	Merlin 35	1,280	8,410	288	30

1.13 Vickers Varsity (1951–1976)

The Varsity was the last of the trio of twin-engined utility types incorporating certain design features from the Wellington. However, unlike the Viking and Valetta it was fitted with a tricycle undercarriage. The type was built to specification T.13/48 which was for a twin-engined pilot and navigation trainer to replace the Wellington T Mk 10 and the prototype, VX828, flew on 17 July 1949.

T Mark 1
The Type 668 was basically similar to the Valetta but, as already noted, it employed a tricycle undercarriage together with a lengthened nose, under-fuselage pannier for bomb-aiming training and extended wings. The first

Vickers Varsity T Mk 1

The Varsity was one of the three Wellington derivatives (the others were the Valetta and Viking) to serve in the RAF. This is 'F' of 6 FTS based at Finningley and seen here at Waterbeach in 1977. *(Author)*

production aircraft (WF324) flew on 21 May 1951 and the type entered service with 201 AFS in October 1951 being finally withdrawn from use in May 1976.

Service Training 42. 204; 4, 5, 6, 8, 11 FTS; 201 AFS; 1, 2, 3 ANS; AES; AEAES; BCBS; CAW; CFS; CNCS; CSDE; ETPS; RAFC; RAFFC; RAFTC; 1 RS; SCBS; 2 SoTT; Ballykelly, Kinloss, St Mawgan **Signals** 51, 97, 115, 116, 151, 192, 527; 1439 Flt; AWRE; BLEU; CSE; EWETU; MRF; RAE; RWE; Debden, Topcliffe, Watton, Weston Zoyland **Communications** 173, 187; FCCS; MCCS; SF Colerne

Specification and production

Mark	Role	Engine	HP	Weight lb	Speed mph	Nos
T1	Trainer	2xHercules 264	1,950	37,500	288	161

1.14 Slingsby Sedbergh (1947–1984)

The Sedbergh was bought as a complement to the basic Cadet and instead of the Type 24 (to specification

Slingsby Sedbergh TX Mk 1

This fine shot shows Slingsby Sedbergh TX Mk 1 WB975. Nearly 100 of the side-by-side trainer were bought to complement the single-seat or tandem Cadet for Air Training Corps use. *(Crown copyright)*

TX.8/45) which after trials was found to be too heavy and too costly for Air Training Corps use.

TX Mark 1

The T.21B flew in 1947 and one of the type, VX275, was bought for 123 Gliding School prior to an order being placed. It remained in use until the 1980s and a total of 95 was supplied.

Service Training 2, 4, 5, 6, 23, 24, 27, 44, 45, 48, 49, 68, 83, 84, 87, 89, 92, 102, 104, 122, 123, 125, 126, 141, 143, 146, 161, 183, 186, 192, 203, 614, 615, 616, 617, 618, 621, 622, 623, 624, 625, 626, 631, 633, 634, 636, 643, 645, 661, 662, 663 GS

Specification and production

Mark	Role	Engine	HP	Weight lb	Speed mph	Nos
TX1	Trainer	none	n/a	1,050	n/a	95

1.15 Percival Provost (1953–1969) and Handley Page HPR.2

The P.56 Provost resulted from an original operational requirement (OR.257) later translated into specification T.16/48 which sought a two-seat, side-by-side, basic trainer capable of operating across the world. Designed to replace the Prentice, the Provost enjoyed considerably superior performance. The first prototype was fitted with the Cheetah 18 engine, but the second and production aircraft employed the Leonides 126. The Provost was a low-wing monoplane of conventional layout with a fixed tailwheel undercarriage. The Handley Page (Reading) HPR.2 is also described here as the unsuccessful contender for the contract.

T Mark 1

The first Provost flew on 24 February 1950 (G-23-1, later WE522) and the sturdy trainer entered service with the

Percival Provost T Mk 1

Specification T.16/48 called for a replacement of the Prentice side-by-side basic trainer. The result was the business-like Provost from which pilots graduated to the Vampire T Mk 11. WW397/NE (G-BKHP) was beautifully preserved and is seen at Fairford in 1990. *(Author)*

Central Flying School in 1953. The Provost was used as the first stage in the Provost/Vampire training sequence and the two types were used by separate, specialised, flying training schools. (In the previous Prentice/Harvard sequence both types had been flown within the same flying training school.) A total of 397 aircraft was delivered. The Provost was withdrawn from service with the CFS in 1969.

Service Training 1, 2, 3, 6, 7, 8, 22 FTS; 5, 11 AEF; CATCS; CAW; CFS; CNCS; ETPS; HCEU; RAFC; RAFFC; Glasgow, London, Manchester, Queen's UAS **Communications** 23, 64 GCF; FTCCF; HCCS

Handley Page HPR.2

The HPR.2 was also built to specification T.16/48. After numerous expressions of interest three protoypes from Handley Page and Percival were ordered. In the event the Percival design, later to become the Provost, won and only two HPR.2s were completed. The first, WE496, was fitted with a Cheetah engine while WE505 was fitted with the Leonides.

Specification and production

Mark	Role	Engine	HP	Weight lb	Speed mph	Nos
T1	Proto-type	Cheetah 18	420	4,400	190	1
T1	Trainer	Leonides 126	550	4,400	200	397

1.16 Hiller HTE-2 (1953–1975)

The small American Hiller training helicopter was delivered to the Royal Navy from 1953 under the Mutual Defence Aid Plan (MDAP). Unlike any other helicopter in British service it was used solely in the training role.

Hiller HTE-2

The compact Hiller was supplied to the Royal Navy by the United States under the Mutual Defence Aid Plan from 1953; it was used solely for training. XS171/41 is an HT Mk 2 with 705 NAS seen here at a Culdrose Air Day. (*A S Thomas collection*)

HT Mark 1

The Type 360 was the equivalent of the US Navy's HTE-2 two-seat trainer. It was fitted with a Franklin engine and was in service from 1953 to 1963.

Service Training 705 NAS

HT Mark 2

The Mark 2 equated to the US Army's OH-23G with a more powerful Lycoming engine and provision for three occupants. Twenty-one were delivered from 1962 and used for training by the Royal Navy.

Service Training 705, 845 NAS

Specification and production

Mark	Role	Engine	HP	Weight lb	Speed mph	Nos
HT1	Trainer	Franklin 6V4-200	200	2,500	84	20
HT2	Trainer	Lycoming VO-540	360	2,750	94	21

1.17 Handley Page (Miles) Marathon (1953–1958)

The Marathon was designed by the Miles company as a medium-range twin-engined feederliner of medium

Miles Marathon T Mk 11

The Marathon was not a success as a civil transport but 30 were bought for navigation training. As such it complemented the Wellington but was soon replaced in service – after just five years – by the Varsity. XA260 served with 2 ANS at Thorney Island. (*Author's collection*)

capacity (22 seats) against a civil transport specification (18/44) issued by the Brabazon Committee. The prototype flew on 19 May 1946, but in 1948 the company was taken over by Handley Page Ltd. The Marathon in military guise featured four engines on a shoulder wing and twin fins; the first military production aircraft, XA249, flew on 28 August 1952.

T Mark 11
The Miles M.60/HPR.5 was bought as a navigation trainer, resulting from a cancelled BEA order. Despite its size, only three crew and two pupils were carried and the aircraft was fitted with Rebecca Mk 4 and Gee. There were two prototypes followed by 28 production aircraft. The Marathon entered service in 1953 and it served with 1 and 2 ANSs until withdrawn from service in 1958.

Service Training 1, 2 ANS; RAFFC

Mark 1A
The second prototype became VX229 at Boscombe Down during acceptance trials. Two further aircraft, both ex-civil machines, were bought for trials use, XJ830 (ex VR-NAS) and XJ831 (ex VR-NAT). Both were sold on to the civil market in 1958.

Service Trials RAE

Mark II
The twin-engined M.69 Marathon II was VX231 when fitted with twin Mamba and later Leonides Major engines.

Specification and production

Mark	Role	Engine	HP	Weight lb	Speed mph	Nos
T11	Trainer	4xGipsy Queen 173	340	18,250	232	28
1A	Trials	4xGipsy Queen 70/4	330	16,500	220	3
II	Trials	2xMamba		16,500	225	1

1.18 Hunting Percival Jet Provost (1955–1994)

By 1952 the standard pilot training sequence was Provost/Vampire and the designers of the Provost identified the scope for all-through jet training. The basic piston Provost design was developed to take a Viper jet engine and the result was the P.84 Jet Provost. In 1953 a first order was placed and the prototype, XD674, flew on 16 June 1954.

T Mark 1
The Jet Provost was built to OR.321 and the first of just ten aircraft was delivered to 2 FTS for comparative trials in through-jet training. The first pupil to solo on the type did so on 17 October 1955.

Service Training 2 FTS; CFS

T Mark 2
The Mark 2 was essentially a developed Mk 1 with an improved canopy design, a lower undercarriage for better airfield performance and larger flaps. Just five were built (first aircraft, XD964, flew 1 September 1955) and delivered to 2 FTS to supplement the original Mk 1s.

Service Training 2 FTS; CFS

T Mark 3
The Mark 3 was the first major production variant, the first machine, XN117, being a company T Mk 2 (G-23-1). No fewer than 201 were delivered, the first to 2 FTS. The T Mk 3 was fitted with a shorter undercarriage, UHF radio, Rebecca Mk 8, ejector seats and wingtip tanks for improved range. The first course on the new type was in 1959.

Service Training 1, 2, 3, 4, 6, 7 FTS; CFE; CFS; RAFC; TWU **Communications** 26; SF St Athan

T Mark 3A
This was a mid-life upgrade of the Mk 3, essentially confined to an avionics upgrade incorporating DME, ILS and VOR. Seventy aircraft were upgraded.

Service Training 1, 7 FTS; CFS

T Mark 4
The Mark 4 was similar to the T Mk 3 but with the much more powerful Viper ASV.11. The T Mk 4 was the nippiest version and it was worked extensively, which accounts for why the relatively under-employed T Mk 3 was upgraded to 3A standard.

Service Training 1, 2, 3, 4, 6, 7, FTS; 1 TWU (79); 3 CAACU; CATCS; CAW; CFS; RAFC; SRF **Trials** JP Trials Unit Forward Air Control 20

T Mark 5
The Hunting 145/BAC 145 was a re-design intended to enable high-level training to 36,700ft. The nose and forward fuselage were lengthened and redesigned to support pressurisation and a completely new cockpit

Hunting Percival Jet Provost T Mk 4

The Jet Provost design was based on that of the piston Provost and it entered service in 1955, being finally withdrawn in 1993. The T Mk 4 was fitted with a more powerful engine than earlier variants and it served in a range of training roles. XP547/03 served as a forward air control (FAC) trainer with the TWU at Brawdy, where it is seen with target towing Meteor F Mk 8 VZ467. (*Crown copyright*)

Hunting Percival Jet Provost T Mk 5A

The Jet Provost was the first purpose-designed trainer intended to support all-through jet training. The Mk 5 was the definitive variant with re-designed forward fuselage to accommodate pressurisation for high level training. XW422 from the 'Poachers' aerobatic team of the RAF College Cranwell is pictured in 1976. *(Crown copyright)*

canopy was incorporated. The wings were also new, with increased internal fuel capacity, and there was provision for tip tanks, although in practice they were not usually carried. The prototype was a converted T Mk 4, XS230, which first flew on 28 February 1967 and first deliveries, in 1969, were to the CFS.

Service Training 1, 3, 6, 7 FTS; CFS; RAFC

T Mark 5A
The Mark 5A was an avionics upgrade to the same standard as the T Mk 3A; 107 of the 110 Mk 5s built were converted.

Service Training 1, 3, 6, 7 FTS; CFS; RAFC

T Mark 5B
The Mark 5B was a T Mk 5A variant used solely for navigator training.

Service Training 6 FTS

Specification and production

Mark	Role	Engine	HP	Weight lb	Speed mph	Nos
T1	Trainer	Viper ASV5	1,750	6,750	330	10
T2	Trainer	Viper 102	1,750	6,850	330	5
T3	Trainer	Viper 102	1,750	7,200	326	201
T3A	Trainer	Viper 102	1,750	7,200	326	70*
T4	Trainer	Viper 200	2,500	7,200	335	185
T5	Trainer	Viper 201	2,500	9,200	440	110
T5A	Trainer	Viper 201	2,500	9,200	440	107+

* T3 conversions
+ T5 conversions

1.19   Folland (Hawker Siddeley) Gnat and Midge (1962–1979)

The Gnat was originally intended as a fighter developed from the Midge lightweight fighter. It was designed by the designer of the English Electric Lightning and in overall shape was reminiscent of a scaled-down Swift with shoulder wings.

Midge
The Fo.139 was an attempt to produce an economic fighter but with high performance. The sole prototype (G-39-1) flew on 11 August 1954 and it was destroyed in a fatal accident a year later after 220 flights with the A&AEE. The aircraft was built around the Armstrong-

Folland Gnat T Mk 1

The Gnat was originally developed as a lightweight fighter based on the diminutive Midge. In its tandem trainer form it replaced the Vampire T Mk 11 with the CFS and 4 Flying Training School at RAF Valley. Illustrated is XP503/03 of the latter unit over Holyhead. *(Folland Aircraft Ltd)*

Siddeley Viper of just 24in diameter and 1,640lb thrust. Notwithstanding the small size and power, the type was flown supersonically in a dive.

F Mark 1

The Fo.140 Gnat was marginally larger than the Midge but fitted with the much more powerful Orpheus engine. The type was built as a private venture and the first (G-39-2) flew on 18 July 1955. Six development aircraft were then ordered by the Ministry of Supply and a further two were built for India and Finland in which countries the type was built and operated. The fighter version was flown only by the A&AEE.

T Mark 1

The Fo.144 was similar in most respects to the fighter but with the obvious addition of a large cockpit area to accommodate instructor and pupil. The engine was of slightly reduced power. The just subsonic Gnat was ordered to replace the Vampire T Mk 11 as an advanced trainer; 105 were built including fourteen pre-production aircraft, and it entered service with the CFS in 1962.

Service Training 4 FTS; CFS; RAFC **Trials** RAE

Specification and production

Mark	Role	Engine	Thrust lb	Weight lb	Speed mph	Nos
Midge	Fighter	Viper 101	1,640	4,500	600	1
Gnat F1	Fighter	Orpheus 2	4,520	8,765	745	6
Gnat T1	Trainer	Orpheus 100	4,230	8,630	740	105

1.20 EoN Eton and Slingsby Grasshopper (1956–1986)

The SG-38 was a German-designed single-seat primary glider – essentially a simple frame fuselage with rigged wing and tailplane. Two 'copies' were used for primary training in the Cadet Forces.

Slingsby Grasshopper TX Mk 1

The very, very, basic Grasshopper was unique in items receiving military aircraft serial numbers in that it was not strictly intended to leave the ground. Rather, it was supplied to Combined Cadet Force and ATC units for rigging and control familiarisation hanging from a frame, although many short hops were made. XP488 seen in 1961 is unusual in belonging to a gliding school, in this case 618 GS. *(MAP)*

Eton TX Mark 1

The EoN (Elliotts of Newbury) Type 7 was a direct copy of the SG-38 fully capable of flight. A total of 90 was built, ten of which were supplied to the RAF and ATC as the Eton, starting from WP262.

Grasshopper TX Mark I

The Slingsby T.38 was broadly based on the SG-38 but utilised redundant T-7 Cadet wings and tailplanes on a new frame fuselage. In this way a much cheaper introduction to gliding was available than the Eton but the Grasshopper was never intended to fly. Rather, it was a vehicle for CCF or ATC cadets to learn rigging and the principles of gliding, although many completed short hops in school playing fields after bungee 'launching'. Some 115 were delivered from 1956 starting with WZ753.

Service Air experience Numerous schools with CCF units and Mobile Glider Servicing Parties

Specification and production

Mark	Role	Engine	Thrust lb	Weight lb	Speed mph	Nos
Eton TX1	Training glider	none	n/a	550	n/a	10
Grass-hopper TX1	Training glider	none	n/a	550	n/a	115

1.21 Hawker Siddeley Dominie (1966–date)

The HS125 Dominie was a military version of what started life as the last de Havilland Hatfield design, the DH125. It was a twin-engined executive jet, originally seating ten over a range of 1,500 miles.

T Mark 1

The Dominie was the HS125 series II model bought as a navigation trainer to replace the Meteor NF(T)14 for

Hawker Siddeley Dominie T Mk 1

The Dominie was a de Havilland design (DH125) which has been extremely successful as an executive jet. Twenty were ordered as navigation trainers and service entry was with 1 ANS in 1966. Thirty years later XS739/F was still operated by successor unit 6 FTS, although aircraft are gradually being modified to T Mk 2 standard. *(Author)*

navigators preparing for fast jets. The crew comprised pilot and assistant plus instructor and two students in rear facing seats. Twenty were ordered, the first (XS709) flying on 30 December 1964, and the Dominie entered service with 1 ANS at Stradishall in 1966.

Service Training 1 ANS; 6 FTS; CAW; RAFC

T Mark 2

The Mark 2 was the result of an upgrade of eleven airframes by Marshall Aerospace with improved avionics. The first conversion was XS728 and eventually all aircraft will go to 6 FTS. The nose profile was changed to accommodate the Super Searchwater radar and new consoles and other internal equipment changes were incorporated.

Service Training 6 FTS

Specification and production

Mark	Role	Engine	HP	Weight lb	Speed mph	Nos
T1	Nav trainer	Viper 520	3,310	20,500	472	20
T2	Nav trainer	Viper 520	3,310	20,500	472	11*

* T1 conversions

1.22 Scottish Aviation Jetstream (1973–date)

In common with many support types the HP137 Jetstream was bought as a variant of a successful commercial type. It was originally designed by Handley Page as an executive type, but when the company went into liquidation production transferred to Scottish Aviation.

Scottish Aviation Jetstream T Mk 1

Designed by Handley Page the Jetstream was secured as a replacement for the Varsity as a navigator trainer. XX476 of 5 FTS is seen banking over the Lincolnshire countryside in October 1973. *(Crown copyright)*

T Mark 1

The Jetstream was originally bought as a Varsity replacement for training navigators; 26 were ordered and the first (XX483) flew on 13 April 1973. Compared with the civil version the military type was fitted with more powerful engines to cater for the extra weight of equipment. Service entry was with 5 FTS in June 1973, but a number was placed in storage as the demand for navigators for multi-engined types diminished with defence reviews.

Service Training   3, 5, 6 FTS (METS); CFS

T Mark 2

The Mark 2 comprised sixteen redundant Mk 1 aircraft modified for naval use. The MEL E.190 radar is fitted in a thimble nose and the variant is used for observer training.

Service Training   750 NAS; TEE; Yeovilton SF

T Mark 3

The Mark 3 is a naval trainer based on the Series 31 – four were delivered fitted with the Garrett TPE 331 engine. The nose profile was as the T Mk 1 but a RACAL ASR360 radar was fitted under the fuselage and the role was the training of observers for the Lynx Mk 8 and Merlin helicopters.

Service Training   750 NAS

Specification and production

Mark	Role	Engine	HP	Weight lb	Speed mph	Nos
T1	Trainer	2xAstazou XVI	940	12,550	285	26
T2	Trainer	2xAstazou XVI	940	12,550	285	16*
T3	Trainer	2xGarrett TPE331	900	12,750	325	4

* T1 conversions

1.23   Scottish Aviation Bulldog (1973–date)

The Bulldog was originally built as a single-engined two-seater lightplane for civilian use by Beagle Aircraft; when the company went into liquidation the type was built by Scottish Aviation. Orders from several foreign air forces prompted an RAF order to replace the Chipmunk as a primary trainer.

T Mark 1

The Type 121 Bulldog was a Series 120 aircraft strengthened to enable aerobatics and fitted with more instruments. The prototype was XX513 which flew on 30 January 1973; 130 were ordered and the first deliveries were just three months later to the CFS.

Service Training   1, 2, 6 FTS; CFS; RNEFTS; 13 AEF; Aberdeen, Birmingham, Bristol, Cambridge, East Lowlands, East Midlands, Glasgow and Strathclyde, Liverpool, London, Manchester, Northumbria,

Scottish Aviation Bulldog T Mk 1

The Bulldog was ordered to replace the Chipmunk as a primary trainer. In addition to serving with various flying training schools it operates with the university air squadrons and air experience flights. XX636/Y is seen at Leeming with Northumbria UAS. *(Author)*

Oxford, Queen's, St Andrews, Southampton, Wales, York UAS

Specification and production

Mark	Role	Engine	HP	Weight lb	Speed mph	Nos
T1	Trainer	Lycoming 360	200	2,350	150	130

1.24   Slingsby Venture (1977–1990)

The Venture was a SF-25C Falke-powered glider licence-built by Slingsby as the T.61. It was the first powered glider bought for the air cadet Volunteer Gliding Schools and it replaced the Sedbergh and Cadet where there were inadequate winch launching facilities.

TX Mark 1

The Mark 1 comprised just one aircraft (XW983) bought for evaluation purposes. The type was metal-framed and powered by a 1,700cc engine.

Slingsby Venture TX Mk 1

The Venture was based on the SF-25C Falke and was the first powered glider bought for the volunteer gliding schools. The idea was to provide gliding facilities for sites where winch launching was difficult. XZ550 was with the Air Cadet Central Gliding School in 1977. *(MAP)*

BAe Hawk T Mk 1A

Exceptionally, the HS1182 Hawk was ordered straight from the drawing board. Conceived as a trainer, it has proved highly successful in that role and as a lightweight fighter for export. XX205/120 of the TWU was used as a development aircraft for the AIM-9L Sidewinder fit as the T Mk 1A in which guise it may provide local air defence. (*British Aerospace*)

Service Trials AAEE; ACCGS

TX Mark 2

The definitive glider differed from the trials aircraft in detail only; 40 were bought and they equipped thirteen schools over time. Their service life was relatively brief, from 1977 to 1990, when they were replaced by glass-reinforced plastic Vigilants.

Service Training/air experience 611, 612, 613, 616, 624, 632, 633, 635, 637, 642, 644, 663, 664 VGS; ACCGS

Specification and production

Mark	Role	Engine	HP	Weight lb	Speed mph	Nos
TX1	Trainer	Limbach SL1700	65	1,435	112	1
TX2	Trainer	Limbach SL1700	65	1,435	112	40

1.25 British Aerospace Hawk (1976–date)

The HS1182 Hawk was unusual in being ordered in quantity from the drawing board – there were no proto-types. The Hawk was designed to replace the Gnat and Hunter as an advanced trainer and the first aircraft to fly was XX154 on 21 August 1974. The first production deliveries were made in November 1976.

T Mark 1

The Hawk first joined 4 FTS at Valley as an advanced trainer. Performance was better than specified (Mach

1.04) and the type could carry 2,000lb of ordnance on wing and fuselage hard-points; 175 were purchased.

Service Training 4 (74, 208, 234), 6, 7 (19, 92) FTS; 1 (79, 234), 2 (63/19, 151/92) TWU; CFS (19), Red Arrows; ETPS **Target facilities** 100: FRADU **Other** IAM; RAE; TEE; St Athan SF

T Mark 1A

The Mark 1A was developed as a standby point defence fighter, capitalising on the Hawk's abilities as a weapons platform. Eighty-eight Mk 1 aircraft were converted to enable them to carry two AIM-9L Sidewinder missiles. They equipped the TWUs and would have been flown by instructors in conjunction with Phantoms and Lightnings in the event of war.

Service Training 4 (74, 208, 234), 6, 7 (19, 92) FTS; 1 (79, 234), 2 (63, 151) TWU; CFS (19) Red Arrows **Target facilities** 100: FRADU

Specification and production

Mark	Role	Engine	Thrust lb	Weight lb	Speed mph	Nos
T1	Trainer	Adour 151	5,200	16,260	647	175
T1A	Trainer	Adour 151	5,430	18,890	662	88*

* T1 conversions

Further reading
Hawk, Braybrook, R, Osprey, London, 1984
BAe Hawk, Reed, A, Ian Allan, Shepperton, 1985

1.26 Sailplanes and gliders (1983–date)

Vanguard TX Mark 1
The Schleicher ASK 21 was a high performance sailplane bought for limited Air Cadet use. Ten were delivered starting with ZD643 on 28 April 1983.

Service Air experience 618, 645 VGS; ACCGS

Valiant TX Mark 1
Five Schleicher ASW 19B gliders were bought for the ACCGS in 1983 starting with ZD657; in service the type was named Valiant.

Kestrel TX Mark 1
Two examples of the German Schempp-Hirth Janus C were bought for the Air Cadet Central Gliding School as the Kestrel to replace two Slingsby Swallow advanced sailplanes. The first was ZD974 which was delivered in July 1983.

Viking TX Mark 1
As the first significant stage in its modernisation programme the RAF ordered 100 Grob G.103 Twin II Acro gliders to replace the Sedbergh and Cadet. In RAF service the type became the Viking and the first, ZE495, was accepted into RAF service on 5 October 1984, going to 631 VGS. The type is used where winch launching is available.

Service Training 611, 614, 615, 617, 621, 622, 625, 626, 631, 634, 636, 643, 645, 661, 662; ACCGS; RAFC

Vigilant TX Mark 1
The second element of the modernisation of Cadet gliding was the introduction of the Grob 109B to replace the Venture. Like the Venture the Grob was also powered by a Limbach engine, but unlike its predecessor it was of glass reinforced plastic. The Vigilant was bought for the Volunteer Gliding Schools where winch launching was available; 54 were bought and the first (ZH115) went to 644 VGS in June 1990.

Service Training 612, 613, 616, 624, 632, 633, 635, 637, 742, 644, 663 VGS; ACCGS

Grob Viking TX Mk 1

The Grob G.103 Twin Acro was bought to replace the Sedbergh and Cadet for ATC use. Gliders appear relatively infrequently at air shows; ZE585 of 614 Volunteer Gliding School is displayed at Mildenhall in May 1991. *(Author)*

Grob Vigilant TX Mk 1

The second element of the Air Cadet modernisation plan was the replacement of the Venture with the Grob 109B. These motorised gliders were used at airfields where winch launching was not available. ZH264 of the Air Cadet Central Gliding School is displayed at Mildenhall in 1991. *(Author)*

Specification and production

Mark	Role	Engine	HP	Weight lb	Speed mph	Nos
Vanguard TX1	Glider	none	n/a	1,323	174	10
Valiant TX1	Glider	none	n/a	1,375	160	5
Kestrel TX1	Sailplane	none	n/a	1,543	155	2
Viking TX1	Glider	none	n/a	1,278	155	100
Vigilant TX1	Glider	Limbach	75	1,874	149	54

1.27 Shorts Tucano (1988–date)

When the Jet Provost basic trainer was approaching 30 years in service the decision was taken to seek a replacement (AST 412) with tandem seats and a turbo-prop powerplant. After intense competition (Pilatus PC-9, Hunting Turbo Firecracker, Westland A-20) the Embraer Tucano was selected to be built by Shorts. Many changes were made over the original design of 1978 including switching from the Pratt & Whitney PT6A engine to the Garrett TPE 331-12B. The eventual design is reported to be 80% British.

T Mark 1
The first anglicised Tucano was flown on 30 December 1986 (ZF135) after Embraer had converted and flown a pattern aircraft nearly a year earlier. Because of the numerous changes demanded for RAF use there were development delays and the type eventually entered service with the CFS in September 1988, a year late. 130 have been supplied.

Service Training 1, 3, 6, 7 FTS; CFS; ETPS; RAFC

Specification and production

Mark	Role	Engine	SHP	Weight lb	Speed mph	Nos
T1	Trainer	Garrett TPE 331	1,100	7,000	310	130

Shorts Tucano T Mk 1

Considerable thought was given to the Jet Provost replacement in terms of performance and economy. The Air Staff Target (412) called for a turboprop type with tandem seating and the Embraer Tucano was the successful contender with manufacture by Shorts. ZF446/446 of 1 FTS is seen in 1996 season display markings. *(Crown copyright)*

1.28 Civil contract types (1993–date)

In the early 1990s the government moved towards market testing for many functions in the public sector. This included elementary flying training and grading and two types are involved, both in civil marks at the time of writing.

Slingsby Firefly

The T-67M Firefly, although ordered for the USAF, is not strictly speaking in service with the British armed forces. Seventeen with civil registrations are operated under contract by Hunting for the Joint Elementary Flying Training School (JEFTS) of 1 FTS.

Grob Heron

As with the Firefly the Grob G.115 is not strictly a service type. Five are operated in civil markings for the Royal Navy's Naval Flying Grading Flight at Roborough by Shorts.

Specification and production

Mark	Role	Engine	HP	Weight lb	Speed mph	Nos
Firefly	Trainer	Lycoming AEIO-320	160	2,100	157	17*
Heron	Trainer	Lycoming O-235	180	1,874	192	5

* some bought used

Slingsby Firefly

Representing the shift to civil contract for second-line tasks is this Slingsby T-67M Firefly G-BUUL operated by Hunting for the Joint Elementary Flying Training School at Barkston Heath. The Firefly was developed from the Fournier RF-6B under licence and has been bought by the USAF as the T-3. *(Author)*

2 – Fighters: air defence

See also: Gnat/Midge (1.19); Mustang (3.5); Thunderbolt (3.6); Tornado (4.14); Vampire (3.9); Venom (3.10)

At the end of the war most fighter units were multi-role in the sense that fighters were sufficiently versatile and pilots sufficiently well-trained to be able to switch from air superiority to ground support, given the nature of the opposition. Through the Cold War, and as the perceived threats changed, units, and indeed types, became dedicated to air defence, and it is these types which are described in this chapter.

January 1946

Within months of the end of the war, many fighter squadrons had disbanded. The aircraft of those which remained were mainly piston-engined types which had seen war service; a hint of the future lay in the Meteor III, newly in service. In the UK there were just thirteen day fighter and seven night fighter squadrons in the air defence role.

At the beginning of 1946 the mainstay of Fighter Command remained the Spitfire, although in the south of England the Meteor Mk III equipped four squadrons with a further squadron in the north-east. Of the Spitfire

Gloster Javelin FAW Mk 9

The Javelin was the first fighter to introduce missile armament to the RAF. FAW Mk 9 XH844/L of 64 Sqn is seen with four Firestreak AAMs while the huge under-fuselage fuel tanks – which led to some uncomplimentary comparisons with Mae West – are also prominent. *(Author)*

units, four operated the Mark IX, two the Mark XVI and two the Mark XXI. In the night fighter role seven English-based squadrons operated the Mosquito.

The Mustang, primarily in the role of escort or close support fighter, equipped eight squadrons in the UK and the units concerned had a secondary air defence role. For a short time early in 1946 two squadrons were equipped with the Tempest Mk II before re-equipping with Vampires.

The distribution of fighter assets was a reflection of the uncertainty of the time. While the Meteor squadrons were spread around the south and east of England, the slightly longer-ranged Spitfires were concentrated in the Midlands, the north and Scotland. The Mosquitos were spread around the country with only one sharing a day fighter base; Scotland appeared undefended at night or in bad weather.

Turning to Germany, the British Air Forces of Occupation confined its fighter elements to day fighter Spitfires, mainly the Griffon-engined Mark XIV. A total of fourteen squadrons was supplemented by four Tempest Mk V units, but as in Scotland night fighters were totally absent.

In the Mediterranean and Middle East, the distribution of fighters was determined in part by the residual demands of occupation and in part by the emergence of post-war insurgency. Yet again the main fighter type was the Spitfire, with the two Greek squadrons operating the Mark V, an Italian-based wing the Mark VIII, while the remaining day fighter units in the theatres used the Mark IX. The total number of Spitfire squadrons was thirteen. The sole night fighter squadron flew the Mosquito XIX, strategically based on Malta.

The occupation squadrons of the Desert Air Force in Italy and Austria were supplemented by a Mustang wing at Lavariano. The troubles in Palestine resulted in the basing there of one Hurricane Mk IV and one Mustang squadron, the former recently transferred from the Greek civil war.

Further afield, in the Far East, the distribution of fighters again reflected the turmoil following the end of the war, which in the region had come just four months earlier. The Spitfire was the primary type, deployed in two versions in nine squadrons. Five squadrons were equipped with the Mark VIII, one of which was in the process of converting to the Mark XIV. Four further squadrons were equipped with the later mark. Two night fighter Mosquito Mark XIX units were based in India and Malaya.

The spread of RAF assets was designed to support the repatriation of prisoners-of-war and to counter civil war or insurrection. One Spitfire unit was temporarily based in French Indo-China, but at the beginning of the year the fighter presence in the Netherlands East Indies was confined to two Thunderbolt squadrons. In this theatre the Thunderbolt equipped eight squadrons until the obligations of lend-lease required their return to the US or destruction.

Fighter Command managed four air defence-related training units. A small number of Meteor Mk III fighters equipped 1335 Conversion Unit. 61 OTU operated a large number of Spitfires of a range of marks and the Mustang Mk III. 80 OTU with the Spitfire Mk IX was responsible for training French pilots, while for night fighter crews the finishing school was 54 OTU with various marks of Mosquito, Beaufighter Mk VI and Mk X, Wellington Mk X and the odd Typhoon.

July 1948

By mid-1948 the first generation of jet fighters was well established in the regular squadrons of the RAF at home with the Meteor the predominant type. Pure fighter versions of the Vampire were also in evidence and the first post-war unit overseas, 3 Sqn in Germany, was equipped with the type. In 12 Group two units were equipped with the agile Hornet piston-engined fighter.

The Royal Auxiliary Air Force units had by now re-formed after their disbandment in 1945 and were generally equipped with potent late-mark Spitfires. The standard night fighter was the Mosquito which served with six regular (NF Mk 36) and five Auxiliary (NF Mk 30) squadrons.

The deployment of units still reflected wartime thinking. Fighters were spread across the country protecting cities and industry from continental threat but relative to the position in 1946 the permanent day and night fighter units were now based, if not operated, as wings. Of day fighters, four wings operated in 11 Group and two in 12 Group, while for night fighters there was one at West Malling (11 Group) and the other at Coltishall (12 Group). By now 13 Group had been merged into 12 Group, but regular units were thinly spread in the east and north of the United Kingdom.

Abroad, the disposition of units related to commitments. In Germany the British Air Forces of Occupation (BAFO) were much reduced from the end of the war although there was normally at least one fighter squadron rotated into Gatow since the Berlin airlift was by now in full swing.

In the Mediterranean, the British had departed Palestine and assets had reduced to just three squadrons, all equipped with the Spitfire. In the Far East, the unrest in Malaya resulted in the two day fighter units in the theatre being based on Singapore. In terms of advanced training the day fighter operational conversion unit was 203 AFS at Chivenor which had assumed the role of 61 OTU. Night fighter conversion was undertaken by 228 OCU at Leeming which had replaced 54 OTU.

January 1950

In the United Kingdom not a lot appears to have changed since 1948 apart from the re-equipment of most of the Auxiliary squadrons in 11 Group with jet types. 12 Group had been strengthened, although four of the regular units were still flying piston-engined Hornets.

In Germany the number of units with the Vampire had increased to three, all at Gütersloh. The balance of the occupation units flew piston-engined types at a time when the MiG-15 was being introduced into the Soviet Air Force.

The RAF in the Middle East had been strengthened with the deployment of a number of units to Egypt and the first jet type, the Vampire, was now operating with 32 and 73 Sqns in the Mediterranean.

The insurrection in Malaya was now full-blown but the location of fighters in the theatre was also determined by the potential threat to Hong Kong as the Chinese Civil War reached a conclusion.

On the advanced training front the new Meteor F Mk 8 had reached 226 OCU (ex 203 AFS) while the Brigand had joined Mosquitos with 228 OCU. Fighter Command was also responsible for the Control and Reporting School at Middle Wallop and perhaps more importantly the Central Fighter Establishment. This latter unit was responsible for developing tactics appropriate to new aircraft types and emerging threats and also for training fighter leaders.

July 1952

The Korean war had by now had some considerable impact in the strength and deployment of the Royal Air Force. New, faster types were on order but not yet in service. The standard day fighter was now the Meteor F Mk 8 supplemented in the United Kingdom by the Vampire F Mk 3 and FB Mk 5. On the night fighter front the Mosquito had given way to the Meteor NF Mk 11 and Vampire NF Mk 10. All piston-engined types had been replaced by jets. The deployment of units through the two Fighter Command groups was still based on a continental threat to cities and centres of industry.

It was in Germany that the response to the perceived threat from the Soviet Union was manifest. Five Vampire day fighter wings and one Meteor NF Mk 11 wing embraced a total of no fewer than eighteen squadrons on six bases. This compared with just four squadrons in 1950, one of which was equipped with Spitfires.

The Middle East Air Force was also fully jet equipped in terms of day fighters, with two Mosquito night fighter units in Egypt. All the aircraft in Egypt – as indeed was the case in Germany – were fighter bombers tasked with defence and ground support roles.

The Hornet had now been relegated to the Far East where the main concern was still the communist terrorist activity in Malaya which had reached its peak at around this time. Jets had reached the area with one squadron in Malaya and one in Hong Kong. Additional OCUs had formed to cope with the great expansion programme. There were now two day fighter and two night fighter units flying a range of contemporary types.

January 1955

Although there was no increase in units there were clear signs of improvement in equipment. Pending delivery of the Hunter, the Sabre was in widespread service, albeit mainly in Germany. In the United Kingdom the Meteor F Mk 8 was still the main type of day fighter in service, but the first Hunters were now in service, significantly based in Scotland. The two UK-based Sabre squadrons were based in the north of England and there was a demonstrable shift in the location of units to respond to attacks from the north-east and north. In the south-east the ill-fated Swift had entered service with 56 Sqn at Waterbeach; within a year the unit was re-equipped with the Hunter.

Another feature of the period was the realignment of night fighter units which began to share bases with day fighters. Equipment was generally upgraded to the Meteor NF Mk 12 or NF Mk 14, which had replaced the short-lived Vampire night fighters. The Venom night fighter had also joined Fighter Command with 23 Sqn at Coltishall.

On mainland Europe the threat posed by the Soviet Union appeared greater than ever. In the light of experience in Korea the western allies were in no doubt as to the quality and numbers of aircraft the enemy could bring to bear in the event of a surprise attack. The number of RAF fighter units within 2 TAF reached its highest level ever with 23 squadrons operating within ten wings now distributed over the same number of airfields. The Sabre was the predominant type complemented by the Venom FB Mk 1 which had joined the RAF in Germany with 11 Sqn several years earlier. Since 1952 two more night fighter units had formed on the Meteor NF Mk 11.

The Venom also featured in the Middle East, where the British were preparing to depart Egypt. In Aden 8 Sqn had re-equipped with the Vampire; the troubles resulted in the type being used in its ground attack role.

The problems in Malaya were by now being brought under control and the Hornet still operated with two squadrons. Hong Kong remained the other focus for air defence as long as there was uncertainty as to the intentions of communist China.

238 OCU had by now disbanded, but an additional day fighter OCU – number 233 – had formed at Pembrey. Although short-lived it was preparing to train the large number of Hunter pilots soon to be required.

June 1957

Compared with just two years previously, the RAF had undergone a number of important changes. The Royal Auxiliary Air Force had ceased to operate any flying units from April, the argument being that modern types were becoming too complex for aircrew to maintain continuously high operational standards.

The Meteor had been completely replaced as a day fighter by the Hunter, the early marks of which had been replaced by the F Mk 4, F Mk 5 and F Mk 6. Two of the Hunter squadrons, 1 and 34 from Tangmere, had seen some limited action in the short Suez campaign of 1956.

The co-location of day and night fighters was firmly established and the heavy Javelin all-weather day and night fighter had entered service, starting with 46 Sqn at Odiham. There were now 33 regular squadrons committed to air defence in the United Kingdom, compared with 29 at the beginning of 1955.

The deployment of units was beginning to reflect a shift to protection of key military targets, especially the bomber bases. More units were committed to 12 Group, which operated from 'new' airfields at Stradishall, Middleton St George, Acklington and Driffield.

The position in Germany had also changed. The stop-gap Sabres had all been replaced by Hunters supplemented by two wings of Venoms (including the newer FB Mk 4) and two wings of Meteor night fighters. The number of units had decreased from 23 to eighteen based on seven airfields.

In the Middle East Air Force three units operated in the Mediterranean and one in Aden, where the troubles had yet to escalate. Apart from the Meteor night fighter squadron, the remainder were, theoretically at least, dual-role units. In this theatre, all units had withdrawn from Egypt in 1955–56 and three Venom squadrons had seen action at Suez in late 1956 in the ground attack role. The Iraq-based units had also been withdrawn.

The Venom was also the sole fighter type in use in the Far East at Hong Kong and Malaya. The anti-terrorist campaign Operation 'Firedog' was drawing to a close.

On the operational training front, 226 and 233 OCUs had disbanded leaving one night fighter (228) and one day fighter (229) conversion units with the Meteor and Hunter respectively.

The Central Fighter Establishment (1945–1966)

The **Central Fighter Establishment** (CFE) was a joint RAF and RN unit formally established on 4 September 1944 but forming on 15 January 1945 at Tangmere where it absorbed the **Night Fighter Development Wing** (NFDW) at Ford, the **Fighter Leader School** (FLS) from Wittering and 787 NAS the **Naval Air Fighting Development Unit** (NAFDU) from Wittering.

The **Night Fighter Development Wing** was formed at Ford on 1 October 1944 from the **Fighter Interception Unit** (FIU) and 746 NAS. The FIU had been formed at Tangmere on 4 April 1940 and moved to Ford, via Shoreham, in January 1941. The FIU then moved to Wittering in May 1944 to make space for aircraft for the forthcoming invasion but returned to Ford in October 1944 with 746 NAS as the Fighter Interception Development Unit (FIDU). No 745 NAS had formed as the **Naval Night Fighter Interception Unit** at Lee-on-Solent in November 1942, moving to Ford shortly after. With the FIU it moved to Wittering in May 1944, returning in October; it became the **Naval Night Fighter Development Squadron** in March 1945. It moved into the CFE at Tangmere between February and July 1945.

The **Fighter Leader School** was formed at Milfield 26 January 1944 with five squadrons. It absorbed **1 Specialised Low Attack Instructors School** (1 SLAIS) which had been part of 59 OTU itself formed at Milfield in 1943. On 27 December 1944 it moved to Wittering as the **Day Fighter Leaders School** (DFLS).

The **Naval Air Fighting Development Unit** was 787 NAS which had formed at Yeovilton in March 1941. In June 1941 it moved to Duxford with the RAF's **Air Fighting Development Unit**. In March 1943 the AFDU moved to Wittering and then via Leconfield on 17 January 1945 to Tangmere to become part of the CFE as the Air Fighting Development Squadron.

The CFE moved to West Raynham in October 1945 to where the NFDW had already moved on 23 August 1945. No 787 NAS/AFDU moved in on 16 November 1945 and absorbed 746 NAS when it disbanded on 30 January 1946. No 787 NAS disbanded on 16 January 1956 having flown a vast range of types. The CFE embraced the day and night tactical development units which changed name as described below, as well as the day and night/all-weather fighter schools. It oversaw the AFDS and AWDS at Coltishall while the DFCS and AWFCS remained at West Raynham. When these latter elements closed the CFE transferred to Binbrook to where the AFDS and AWDS had moved from Coltishall. On 1 February 1966 the CFE disbanded but the AFDS became the FCTU which survived only until 30 June 1967.

The **Night Fighter Development Wing** (NFDW) was renamed **Night Fighter Wing** (NFW) in 1949 and became the **All Weather Wing** (AWW) on 3 July 1950. This became in turn the **All Weather Development Squadron** (AWDS) in February 1956 before being absorbed into the **Air Fighting Development Squadron** (AFDS) in August 1959.

The element of the CFE with the longest history was the **Air Fighting Development Squadron** (AFDS) which began life in 1934 at Northolt as the **Air Fighting Development Establishment** (AFDE). In 1940 it moved to Duxford as the **Air Fighting Development Unit** (AFDU) and with the formation of the CFE it moved to Wittering as the AFDS. The main role of the unit was to develop tactics for new fighter aircraft coming into service including the Meteor, Vampire, Venom, Swift, Sabre,

Hunter, Javelin and Lightning (at Coltishall). It included the **AWDS** in 1959 when it moved to Coltishall to support the introduction of the Lightning. It moved to Binbrook in October 1962 and on 1 February 1966 became the **Fighter Command Training Unit** (FCTU) which disbanded on 30 June 1967.

The **Night Fighter Training Squadron** (NFTS) had formed within the NFDW in 1944 but in 1945 it became the **Night Fighter Leaders School** (NFLS) at West Raynham. The name changed to **All Weather Fighter Leaders School** (AWFLS) in July 1950 and on 15 March 1958, with the DFLS, it became an element of the FCS as the **All Weather Fighter Combat School** (AWFCS). When the DFCS moved to Binbrook AWFCS disbanded with a component becoming the **Javelin Operation Conversion Squadron** (JOCU) at West Raynham with the 219 Sqn shadow designation.

The **Day Fighter Leader School** (DFLS) became the **Day Fighter Combat School** (DFCS) on 15 March 1958 at West Raynham within the **Fighter Combat School** (FCS) formed to embrace both day and night fighter schools. The FCS moved to Binbrook on 13 November 1962 and disbanded on 1 November 1965 just months before the CFE itself disbanded. The **Fighter Command Instrument Training Squadron** (FCITS) became part of the CFE in December 1952 although having moved to West Raynham in February 1950. It was absorbed into the AWFCS.

One final element of the CFE, which it absorbed in mid-life, was **the Fighter Weapons School** (FWS). This had started life as the **Central Gunnery School** (CGS) at Warmwell in 1939 with the task of improving air firing. After the war the CGS moved to Leconfield where on 1 January 1955 it split into the Coastal Command Gunnery School and the FWS. On 2 October 1957 it moved to Driffield and merged into CFE at West Raynham on 15 March 1958.

June 1960

The shape of the Royal Air Force in 1960 was clearly beginning to reflect the intentions of the government set out in the infamous Defence White Paper of 1957. This had signalled the end of manned combat aircraft and a move towards an all-missile force.

The number of units at home and abroad was reducing. While the Hunter was still the mainstay in Fighter Command, the introduction into service of what was intended to be the last manned fighter, the Lightning, was marked by the re-equipment of 74 Sqn with the new type. On the aircraft side the Meteor and Venom night fighters had completely given way to the Javelin and the deployment of units had changed to focus on protecting the V-bomber bases.

Although strictly outside the scope of this book, reference must be made to the long-range surface-to-air (SAM) missile force now established with the Mark 1 Bloodhound. These were now in service with eleven squadrons operating within four tactical control areas. Their deployment was primarily organised to defend the Thor Intermediate Range Ballistic Missile (IRBM) sites.

Contraction had also begun in Germany with a reduction to nine squadrons, now based further west, mainly on the 'clutch' airfields on the German/Dutch border. Again, the force was a mixed Hunter/Javelin one.

Further afield the only dedicated air defence unit was 60 Sqn at Tengah with Meteor night fighters. The Hunters of 8 and 208 Sqns in the Middle East were used in the ground attack role in Aden where the internal troubles were escalating. There was little change in the operational training area, the AFDS at Coltishall helping to ease the Lightning into service.

January 1965

The continued reduction in the Royal Air Force had, *inter alia*, resulted in the merger of 11 and 12 Groups, resulting in the home defence force being Fighter Command. The UK-based fighter squadron strength was at its lowest since the early 1920s, with just six Lightning squadrons on three airfields and one equipped with the longer-legged Javelin. While the Lightning had a phenomenal climb rate, it was a short-range interceptor, not particularly agile by current standards and in the earlier versions only equipped with two Firestreak pursuit-course missiles.

The Mark 1 Bloodhound had followed the short-lived Thor out of service and the Mark 2 version with much improved radar equipped two units. These were based in Lincolnshire to protect the V-bomber bases.

In Germany the sole air defence assets were two Javelin squadrons at Geilenkirchen, but the worsening situation in Aden resulted in an extra Hunter unit, 43 Sqn, being based at Khormaksar. Similarly, the confrontation with Indonesia in Malaysia meant that additional units were deployed in the theatre, both in the air defence and ground attack roles. In addition the first overseas deployment of the Bloodhound was to 65 Sqn at Seletar.

The need to deploy flexibly a range of combat aircraft overseas highlighted the mistaken philosophy around which the 1957 White Paper had been produced. No 228 OCU had disbanded with the reduced need for Javelin crews being met by the JIRS at Leuchars. No 226 OCU had formed in 1961 to convert pilots on the Lightning, while the Hunter conversion unit, 229, was now concentrating on the tactical role.

January 1970

The air defence pattern for the future was now largely established, with only occasional changes in equipment. The Royal Air Force had reorganised and Fighter Command had been absorbed into Strike Command as 11 Group. The Javelin had now been withdrawn from service and the Lightning equipped nine squadrons at home and overseas. In Germany the two Lightning units had had their F Mk 2 aircraft re-worked to F Mk 6 standard.

The Phantom FG Mk 1 had entered service with 43 Sqn at Leuchars mainly in order to utilise redundant naval aircraft; it would be some time before the balance of the Phantom fleet switched from the tactical role to air defence. The British had left Aden and Malta and the sole base in the Middle East was Cyprus, where the Lightning unit, 56 Sqn, was joined by a Bloodhound unit.

In the Far East, one Lightning squadron was supplemented by two Bloodhound units, presumably to deter further aggression from Indonesia, where the confrontation had reached a satisfactory conclusion.

The Hunter conversion unit, shortly to become the Tactical Weapons Unit, now concentrated exclusively in ground attack training.

January 1975

The slow pace of change in equipment and deployment was a reflection of the increasingly long lead times in developing new aircraft and training their crews. The Phantom was being replaced in the tactical role by the Jaguar, thus releasing aircraft for air defence, in which role they began to replace the Lightning with 29 and 111 Sqns.

In Germany the Bloodhound was now deployed, utilising missiles withdrawn from service in the UK and the Far East, from where the British had now withdrawn.

No 228 OCU had re-formed to train Phantom crews, while the diminished demand for Lightning pilots was met by the LTF at Binbrook.

January 1980

In five years there had been some marginal changes in the air defence scene. Two further units had equipped with the Phantom, while the Bloodhound had re-surfaced in the UK after an interlude of a few years. Deployment still resulted from the need to defend military targets and to identify and dissuade the increasing numbers of Soviet intelligence-gathering sorties over the North Sea. The Lightning soldiered on with 5 and 11 Sqns at Binbrook.

The two air defence units in Germany had changed their Lightnings for Phantoms, while the RAF had now withdrawn permanently based combat aircraft from the Middle East while retaining use of the sovereign base at Akrotiri.

January 1985

Two events dictated the shape of air defence by 1985. The Falklands war had stretched the resources of the Royal Air Force and the need to deploy a squadron of Phantoms to Stanley resulted in the purchase of fifteen F-4J aircraft from the United States to compensate for the depletion of home-based fighters. These equipped 74 Sqn at Wattisham. The Tornado fighter variant was about to enter service and the new OCU had already formed with the F Mk 2 version at Coningsby. The radar was proving troublesome, but the task of converting aircrew had already begun.

Perhaps the only other change of note was the formation of a second UK-based Bloodhound unit giving wider coverage in East Anglia and Lincolnshire; the V-bombers had by now retired and had been replaced by Tornado strike aircraft based in East Anglia.

January 1990

The Tornado F Mk 3, with fully automatic wing sweep (and working radar!) was now the mainstay of 11 Group, equipping six squadrons. The long-serving Lightnings had been withdrawn from service in 1987, leaving the RAF without a single-seat interceptor for the first time in its history. Neither the Phantom nor the Tornado were dog-fighters, the Tornado being optimised for long endurance and beyond-visual-range combat.

The Phantom equipped three units at home (in three marks) and two in Germany, from where it would soon be withdrawn following the dramatic changes taking place in Europe. The 23 Sqn detachment to the Falklands had been replaced by a four-aircraft flight.

January 1995

Britain's air defence force now comprised six home-based squadrons and one flight in the Falklands, all equipped with the Tornado FMk3. The Tornado also equipped the sole fighter OCU, now with the shadow designation of 56 Sqn. This was the first time that the air defence of the UK had rested with a single type, although in time of war, the nimble Hawks of 1 TWU, fitted with the AIM-9 AAM and a centreline gun pack, would be available for local defence. The designation of the Hawk in this role is indicative of the need for an agile, close-in, fighter, and the EFA is desperately overdue.

Apart from the commitment to the Falklands there was no permanent overseas basing, all fighter units having departed Germany after nearly 40 years. The Tornados were active in the Middle East, especially during the Gulf War of 1991, and elements of the Leeming Wing were detached to Italy to provide cover for other types involved in operations over Bosnia.

2.A Air defence at 1 January 1946

Fighter Command

11 Group (South, East)

Type	Unit	Base
Meteor III	222, 245	Exeter
	74	Colerne
	124	Bentwaters
Spitfire IX	234	Bentwaters
Tempest II	54, 247	Chilbolton
Mosquito XXX	29	West Malling
	151	Predannack
	85	Tangmere
	25	Castle Camps

12 Group (Midlands, North)

Type	Unit	Base
Meteor III	263	Acklington
Spitfire IX	129	Hutton Cranswick
Spitfire XXI	1	Hutton Cranswick
Spitfire XVI	19	Molesworth
	65	Hethel
Mustang III	306, 309, 315	Coltishall
Mustang III/IV	126	Hethel
Mosquito XXX	219	Acklington
	307	Horsham St Faith
Mosquito XXXVI	264	Church Fenton

13 Group (Scotland)

Type	Unit	Base
Spitfire IX	122	Wick
	164	Turnhouse
Spitfire XXI	91	Dyce
Mustang III	316	Wick
Mustang IV	303	Turnhouse

BAFO (Germany)

2 Group

Type	Unit	Base
Spitfire XIV	16	Celle

83 Group

Type	Unit	Base
Spitfire XIV	41	Lübeck
	412, 416, 443	Utersen
Spitfire XVI	411	Utersen
Tempest V	174	Fassberg
	80	Lübeck

84 Group

Type	Unit	Base
Spitfire XIV	2	Celle
	451	Wünstorf
Spitfire XVI	302, 308, 317	Ahlhorn
	33, 349, 350	Fassberg
Tempest V	3, 56	Fassberg

Mediterranean/Middle East (MED/ME)

Type	Unit	Base
Spitfire V	335, 336	Sedes (Greece)
Spitfire VIII	92, 253	Treviso (Italy)
Spitfire IX	225	Klagenfurt (Austria)
	318	Lavariano (Italy)
	87	Treviso (Italy)
	43, 72, 111	Zeltweg (Austria)
	73	Hal Far (Malta)
	32, 208	Petah Tiqva (Palestine)
Mustang III/IV	112, 250, 237	Lavariano (Italy)
	213	Ramat David (Palestine)
Mosquito XIX	255	Hal Far (Malta)

Far East (ACSEA)

Type	Unit	Base
Spitfire VIII	136	Kuala Lumpur (Mal)
	152, 155	Tengah (Mal)
	273	Tan Son Nhut (Indo-China)
Spitfire VIII/XIV	20	Don Muang (Thai)
Spitfire XIV	132	Kai Tak (HK)
	28	Meiktilla (Burma)
	11, 17	Seletar (Mal)
Mosquito XIX	89	Seletar (Mal)
	176	Baigachi (India)

Training units

11 Group

Type	Unit	Base
Spitfire XVI, Oxford	FCCRS	Rudloe Manor
Spitfire, Tempest II, V, Mustang IV, Mosquito	CFE	West Raynham
Beaufighter X	AICF	Twinwood Farm

12 Group

Type	Unit	Base
Meteor III	1335 CU	Molesworth
Spitfire XVI, X, Mustang III	61 OTU	Keevil (Day fighter OTU)
Spitfire IX, Master I, Martinet II	80 OTU	Ouston (French OTU)
Beaufighter VI, X, Mosquito III, XVI, XXX, Typhoon Ib	54 OTU	East Moor (Night fighter OTU)

2.B Air defence at 1 July 1948

Fighter Command

11 Group (South, East)

Type	Unit	Base
Meteor F3	56	Thorney Island
Meteor F4	63, 222	Thorney Island
	1, 266	Tangmere
	66, 92	Duxford
Vampire F1	54, 247	Odiham
Vampire F3	72	Odiham

Type	Unit	Base
Spitfire F14/F21	615	Biggin Hill
Spitfire F16	501	Filton
	601, 604	Hendon
	614	Llandow
Spitfire F21/F22	600	Biggin Hill
Mosquito NF30	500	West Malling
Mosquito NF36	25,29,85	West Malling

12 Group (Midlands, North, Scotland, Northern Ireland)

Type	Unit	Base
Meteor F3	19	Church Fenton
Meteor F4	74, 245, 257, 263	Horsham St Faith
Hornet F1	65	Linton-on-Ouse
Hornet F3	41	Church Fenton
Spitfire F14	610	Hooton Park
	613	Ringway
Spitfire F14/LF16e	612	Dyce
Spitfire F14/F22	607	Ouston
	611	Hooton Park
Spitfire F21/F22	602	Abbotsinch
Spitfire F22	504	Hucknall
	603	Turnhouse
Mosquito NF30	502	Aldergrove
	605	Honiley
	609	Yeadon
	616	Finningley
Mosquito NF36	23, 141, 264	Coltishall

BAFO (Germany)

Type	Unit	Base
Vampire F1	3	Gütersloh
Tempest F2	16, 26, 33	Gütersloh
Spitfire F24	80	Gatow

Middle East (MED/ME)

Type	Unit	Base
Spitfire FR18	32, 208	Nicosia (Cyprus)
Spitfire F22	73	Ta Kali (Malta)

Far East (ACFE)

Type	Unit	Base
Spitfire FR18	28, 60	Sembawang (Malaya)

Training and development units

Type	Unit	Base
Spitfire F14, Meteor F4	203 AFS	Chivenor
Mosquito T3, FB6, NF36	228 OCU	Leeming
Spitfire F16, Meteor F4	CFE	West Raynham

2.C   Air defence at 1 January 1950

Fighter Command

11 Group (South, East)

Type	Unit	Base
Meteor F3	500	West Malling
Meteor F4	1, 43	Tangmere
	56, 63, 222	Thorney Island
Vampire F1	501	Filton
Vampire F3	54, 72	Odiham
	601, 604	North Weald
Vampire FB5	247	Odiham
Spitfire F21, F22	600, 615	Biggin Hill
Spitfire F22	614	Llandow
Mosquito NF36	25, 29, 85	West Malling

12 Group (Midlands, North, Scotland, Northern Ireland)

Type	Unit	Base
Meteor F3	616	Finningley
Meteor F4	66, 92	Linton-on-Ouse
	74, 245, 257, 263	Horsham St Faith
	504	Wymeswold
Vampire F1	605	Honiley
Hornet F3	19, 41	Church Fenton
	64, 65	Linton-on-Ouse
Spitfire F14, F16	612	Dyce
Spitfire LF16e	609	Yeadon
Spitfire F22	502	Aldergrove
	602	Abbotsinch
	603	Turnhouse
	607	Ouston
	608	Thornaby
	610	Hooton Park
	611	Woodvale
	613	Ringway
Mosquito NF36	23, 141, 264	Coltishall

BAFO (Germany – 2 Group)

Type	Unit	Base
Vampire FB5	3, 16, 26	Gütersloh
Spitfire XIV	2	Wünstorf

Middle East Air Force

Type	Unit	Base
Vampire F3	73	Ta Kali (Malta)

205 Group

Type	Unit	Base
Vampire F3	32	Nicosia (Cyprus)
Tempest F6	6, 213, 249	Deversoir (Egypt)
Spitfire FR18	208	Fayid (Egypt)
Mosquito NF36	39	Fayid (Egypt)

Far East Air Force

Type	Unit	Base
Tempest F2	33	Changi (Malaya)
Spitfire FR18	60	Kuala Lumpur (Malaya)
	28	Kai Tak (Hong Kong)
Spitfire F24	80	Kai Tak (Hong Kong)

Training and development units

11 Group

Type	Unit	Base
Spitfire LF16	FCCRS	Middle Wallop
Spitfire, Anson, Proctor	SLAW	Old Sarum

12 Group

Type	Unit	Base
Meteor F8, Spitfire F16	226 OCU	Stradishall
Brigand B1,T4, Mosquito FB6, NF36, Oxford II	228 OCU	Leeming
Spitfire F9, FR18, Meteor T7, F8, Vampire F1, FB5	CFE	West Raynham

2.D Air defence at 1 July 1952

Fighter Command

11 Group (South, East)

Type	Unit	Base
Meteor F8	1	Tangmere
	41, 600, 615	Biggin Hill
	54, 247	Odiham
	56, 63	Waterbeach
	64, 65	Duxford
	257, 263	Wattisham
	500	West Malling
Vampire F3	601, 604	North Weald
Vampire FB5	72	North Weald
	501	Filton
	614	Llandow
Meteor NF11	29	Tangmere
	85	West Malling
Vampire NF10	25	West Malling

12 Group (Midlands, North, Scotland, Northern Ireland)

Type	Unit	Base
Meteor F8	19, 609	Church Fenton
	43, 222	Leuchars
	66, 92	Linton-on-Ouse
	74, 245	Horsham St Faith
	504	Wymeswold
	610, 611	Hooton Park
	616	Finningley
Vampire F3, FB5	608	Middleton St George
Vampire FB5	502	Aldergrove
	602	Abbotsinch
	603	Turnhouse
	605	Honiley
	607	Ouston
	612	Edzell
	613	Ringway
Meteor NF11	141	Coltishall
	264	Linton-on-Ouse
Vampire NF10	23	Coltishall
	151	Leuchars

1 Wing RCAF

Type	Unit	Base
F-86E	410, 439, 441	North Luffenham

2 TAF (Germany)

Type	Unit	Base
Vampire FB5	3, 67, 71	Wildenrath
	4, 112	Jever
	5, 11	Wünstorf
	14, 98, 118	Fassberg
	16, 93, 94, 145	Celle
Vampire FB5, FB9	26	Wünstorf
Vampire FB9	20	Jever
Meteor NF11	68, 87	Wahn

Middle East Air Force

Type	Unit	Base
Vampire FB5, FB9	185	Hal Far (Malta)
Vampire FB9	6, 73	Nicosia (Cyprus)

205 Group

Type	Unit	Base
Vampire FB5	32, 213, 249	Deversoir (Egypt)
Mosquito NF36	219	Kabrit (Egypt)
	39	Fayid (Egypt)

Far East Air Force

Type	Unit	Base
Vampire FB9	28	Sek Kong (Hong Kong)
	60	Tengah (Malaya)
Hornet F3	33	Kuala Lumpur (Malaya)
	45	Tengah (Malaya)
Hornet F3, F4	80	Kai Tak (Hong Kong)

Training and development units

Type	Unit	Base
Meteor T7, F8, FR9, Mosquito TT35	226 OCU	Stradishall
Vampire FB5, Meteor T7, Oxford T2, Meteor NF11	228 OCU	Leeming
Beaufighter TT10, Mosquito TT35, Tempest TT5	229 OCU	Chivenor
Brigand T4, Buckmaster T1	238 OCU	Colerne
Spitfire LF16	FCCRS	Middle Wallop
Meteor T7, F8, Vampire FB5	CFE	West Raynham

2.E Air defence at 1 January 1955

Fighter Command

11 Group (South, East)

Type	Unit	Base
Swift F1,2	56	Waterbeach
Meteor F8	1, 34	Tangmere
	41, 600, 615	Biggin Hill
	54, 247	Odiham
	63	Waterbeach
	64, 65	Duxford
	111, 601, 604	North Weald
	257, 263	Wattisham
	500	West Malling
Meteor NF11	29	Tangmere
Meteor NF12,14	25, 85	West Malling
	46	Odiham
	152	Wattisham
Vampire FB5	501	Filton
	614	Llandow

12 Group (Midlands, North, Scotland, Northern Ireland)

Type	Unit	Base
Hunter F1	43, 222	Leuchars
Sabre F4	92	Linton-on-Ouse
Meteor F8	19, 72, 609	Church Fenton
	66	Linton-on-Ouse
	74, 245	Horsham St Faith
	504	Wymeswold
	610, 611	Hooton Park
	616	Finningley
Meteor NF11	141	Coltishall
	151	Leuchars
Meteor NF14	264	Linton-on-Ouse
Venom NF2	23	Coltishall
Vampire FB5	602	Abbotsinch
	603	Turnhouse
	605	Honiley
	607	Ouston
	608	Thornaby
	612	Dyce
Vampire FB5,9	502	Aldergrove
	613	Ringway

2 TAF (Germany)

Type	Unit	Base
Sabre 4	3, 234	Geilenkirchen (138 Wing)
	4, 93	Jever (122 Wing)
	20, 26	Oldenburg (124 Wing)
	67, 71	Wildenrath (137 Wing)
	112, 130	Brüggen (135 Wing)
Venom FB1	5, 11, 266	Wünstorf (123 Wing)
	14, 98, 118	Fassberg (121 Wing)
	16, 94, 145	Celle (139 Wing)
Meteor NF11	68, 87	Wahn (148 Wing)
	96, 256	Ahlhorn (125 Wing)

Middle East Air Force

Type	Unit	Base
Venom FB1	6, 73	Habbaniyah (Iraq) (128 Wing)
	32	Kabrit (Egypt)
	249	Amman (Jordan)
Vampire FB9	8	Khormaksar (Aden)
Meteor NF13	39	Kabrit (Egypt)

Far East Air Force

Type	Unit	Base
Vampire FB9	28	Sek Kong (Hong Kong)
	60	Tengah (Malaya)
Hornet F3	33	Butterworth (Malaya)
	45	Tengah (Malaya)
	80	Kai Tak (Hong Kong)

Training and development units

Type	Unit	Base
Vampire F3, Meteor T7, F8, FR9	226 OCU	Stradishall
Meteor NF11, NF14, Valetta T1	228 OCU	Leeming
Vampire FB5,T11, Meteor T7, Sabre F4, Mosquito T35	229 OCU	Chivenor
Vampire FB5, T11, Meteor T7, F8	233 OCU	Pembrey
Vampire FB5, FB9, Meteor T7, F8, FR9, NF11, NF12, NF14, Venom FB1, NF2, FB4, Hunter F1, Sabre F4	CFE	West Raynham

2.F   Air defence at 1 June 1957

Fighter Command

11 Group (South, East)

Type	Unit	Base
Hunter F1	54	Odiham
Hunter F5	1, 34	Tangmere
	41	Biggin Hill
	56	Waterbeach
Hunter F6	63	Waterbeach
	65	Duxford
	111	North Weald
	247	Odiham
	263	Wattisham
Javelin (FAW)1	46	Odiham
Meteor NF12,14	25, 85, 153	West Malling
	152	Wattisham
Meteor NF14	64	Duxford
Venom NF2A	253	Waterbeach

12 Group (Midlands, North, Scotland, Northern Ireland)

Type	Unit	Base
Hunter F4	43, 222	Leuchars
	74	Horsham St Faith
	245	Stradishall
Hunter F6	19	Church Fenton
	66	Linton-on-Ouse
	92	Middleton St George
Javelin (FAW)4	23	Horsham St Faith
	141	Coltishall
Meteor NF11	29	Acklington
Meteor NF12,14	72	Church Fenton
Meteor NF14	264	Middleton St George
Venom NF2	33	Driffield
Venom NF2A	219	Driffield
Venom NF3	89	Stradishall
	151	Leuchars

2 TAF (Germany)

Type	Unit	Base
Hunter F4	3, 234	Geilenkirchen
	26	Oldenburg
	98, 118	Jever
Hunter F6	4, 93	Jever
	14, 20	Oldenburg
Venom FB1	94, 145	Celle
Venom FB4	5, 11, 266	Wünstorf
Meteor NF11	68, 87	Wahn
	96, 256	Ahlhorn

Middle East Air Force

Type	Unit	Base
Venom FB1	8	Khormaksar (Aden)
Venom FB4	6	Akrotiri (Cyprus)
	249	Ta Kali (Malta)
Meteor NF13	39	Luqa (Malta)

Far East Air Force

Type	Unit	Base
Venom FB1	28	Sek Kong (Hong Kong)
	45	Butterworth (Malaya)
Venom FB4	60	Tengah (Malaya)

Training and development units

Type	Unit	Base
Meteor T7,NF14	228 OCU	Leeming
Meteor F8,PR10, Hunter F4	229 OCU	Chivenor
Vampire T11, Meteor T7, F8, Hunter F2 ,F4 , F5, Javelin F(AW)1, F(AW)2	CFE	West Raynham, Wittering

2.G Air defence at 1 June 1960

Fighter Command

11 Group (South, East)

Type	Unit	Base
Hunter F6	56, 111	Wattisham
	65	Duxford
Javelin F(AW) 2	46	Waterbeach
Javelin F(AW) 2, 6	85	West Malling
Javelin F(AW) 7	25	Waterbeach
	64	Duxford

12 Group (Midlands, North, Scotland, Northern Ireland)

Type	Unit	Base
Hunter F6	19	Leconfield
	66	Acklington
	92	Middleton St George
Hunter F6, FGA9	43	Leuchars
Lightning F1	74	Coltishall
Javelin F(AW)4	72	Leconfield
Javelin F(AW)5	151	Leuchars
Javelin F(AW)6	29	Leuchars
Javelin F(AW)7	33	Middleton St George
	23	Coltishall
Javelin FAW8	41	Coltishall

Bloodhound Mk 1 squadrons and tactical control centres

21 Wing Lindholme	94	Misson
	112	Breighton
	247	Carnaby
24 Wing Watton	242	Marham
	263	Watton
	266	Rattlesden
148 Wing North Coates	161	Dunholme Lodge
	222	Woodhall Spa
	264	North Coates
151 Wing North Luffenham	62	Woolfox Lodge
	257	Warboys

2 TAF Germany

Type	Unit	Base
Hunter F4	4	Jever
Hunter F6	14, 20, 26	Gütersloh
	93, 118	Jever
Javelin F(AW)1	87	Brüggen
Javelin F(AW)4	3, 11	Geilenkirchen
Javelin F(AW)5	5	Laarbruch

Middle East Air Force

Hunter FGA9	8	Khormaksar (Aden)
	208	Eastleigh (Kenya)

Far East Air Force

Venom FB4	28	Kai Tak (Hong Kong)
Meteor NF14	60	Tengah (Malaya)

Training and development units

Type	Unit	Base
Meteor T7, NF14, Javelin T3, F(AW)5 Canberra T4,T11	228 OCU (137)	Leeming
Hunter F4, F6, T7	229 OCU (63, 145)	Chivenor
Meteor NF12, NF14, Hunter F6,FGA9, Javelin T3, F(AW)7, F(AW)8, F(AW)9, Lightning F1	CFE	West Raynham, Coltishall

2.H Air defence at 1 January 1965

Fighter Command

Type	Unit	Base
Lightning F1A	56	Wattisham
Lightning F1A, F3	111	Wattisham
Lightning F2	19, 92	Leconfield
Lightning F3	23, 74	Leuchars
Javelin F(AW)9	64	Binbrook
Bloodhound Mk 2	*25*	*North Coates*
	112	*Woodhall Spa*

RAF Germany

Type	Unit	Base
Javelin F(AW)9	5, 11	Geilenkirchen

Middle East Air Force (AFME, NEAF)

Javelin F(AW)9	29	Akrotiri (Cyprus)
Hunter FGA9	43	Khormaksar (Aden)
	208	Muharraq (Oman)
Hunter FGA9,FR10	8	Khormaksar (Aden)

Far East Air Force

Type	Unit	Base
Hunter FGA9	20	Tengah (Malaya)
	28	Kai Tak (Hong Kong)
Javelin F(AW)9	60	Tengah (Malaya)
Bloodhound Mk 2	*65*	*Seletar (Malaya)*

Training and development units

Type	Unit	Base
Lightning F1,F3	226 OCU (65)	Coltishall
Hunter F6,T7,FR10	229 OCU	Chivenor
Javelin T3	JIRS	Leuchars
Lightning F1,F1A,F2,F3	CFE	Coltishall

2.I Air defence at 1 January 1970

Strike Command, 11 Group

Type	Unit	Base
Phantom FG1	43	Leuchars
Lightning F3,F6	29, 111	Wattisham
Lightning F6	5, 11	Binbrook
	23	Leuchars
Bloodhound Mk2	*41*	*West Raynham*

RAF Germany

Type	Unit	Base
Lightning F2A	19, 92	Gütersloh

Near East Air Force

Type	Unit	Base
Lightning F3	56	Akrotiri (Cyprus)
Bloodhound Mk2	*112*	*Paramali (Cyprus)*

Far East Air Force

Type	Unit	Base
Lightning F6	74	Tengah (Malaya)
Bloodhound Mk2	*33*	*Butterworth (Malaya)*
	65	*Seletar (Malaya)*

Training and development units

Type	Unit	Base
Lightning F3, T4	226 OCU (65)	Coltishall
Phantom FGR2	228 OCU (64)	Coningsby
Meteor F8, Hunter F6, T7	229 OCU (63, 79, 234)	Chivenor

2.J Air defence at 1 January 1975

Strike Command, 11 Group

Type	Unit	Base
Phantom FG1	43	Leuchars
Phantom FGR2	29, 111	Coningsby
Lightning F3,F6	5, 11	Binbrook
	23	Leuchars

RAF Germany

Type	Unit	Base
Lightning F2A	19, 92	Gütersloh
Bloodhound Mk 2	*25*	*Brüggen, Laarbruch, Wildenrath*

Near East Air Force

Lightning F3,F6	56	Akrotiri (Cyprus)
Bloodhound Mk 2	*112*	*Paramali (Cyprus)*

Training and development units

Type	Unit	Base
Phantom FGR2	228 OCU (64)	Coningsby
Lightning F3,T4	LTF	Binbrook

2.K Air defence at 1 January 1980

Strike Command, 11 Group

Type	Unit	Base
Phantom FG1	43, 111	Leuchars
Phantom FGR2	23, 56	Wattisham
	29	Coningsby
Lightning F3,F6	5, 11	Binbrook
Bloodhound Mk 2	*85*	*West Raynham, N Coates, Bawdsey*

RAF Germany

Type	Unit	Base
Phantom FGR2	19, 92	Wildenrath
Bloodhound Mk 2	*25*	*Brüggen, Laarbruch Wildenrath*

Training and development units

Type	Unit	Base
Phantom FGR2	228 OCU (64)	Coningsby
Lightning F3,T4	LTF	Binbrook

Bristol Bloodhound Mk 2 SAM

The Defence White Paper of 1957 predicated the end of the manned fighter; aircraft being replaced by missiles. In the event the strategy was reconsidered and the Bloodhound and later the Rapier complemented interceptors. Here, Bloodhound Mk 2 SAMs are on guard at West Raynham in 1976. *(Crown copyright)*

2.L   Air defence at 1 January 1985

Strike Command, 11 Group

Type	Unit	Base
Phantom FG1	43, 111	Leuchars
Phantom FGR2	56	Wattisham
	29	Coningsby
Phantom F3	74	Wattisham
Lightning F3,F6,T5	5, 11	Binbrook
Bloodhound Mk 2	*25*	*Wyton, Barkston Heath, Wattisham*
	85	*West Raynham, N Coates, Bawdsey, Coltishall*

RAF Germany

Type	Unit	Base
Phantom FGR2	19, 92	Wildenrath
Bloodhound Mk 2	*25*	*Brüggen, Laarbruch, Wildenrath*

Falkland Islands

Type	Unit	Base
Phantom FGR2	23	Stanley

Training and development units

Type	Unit	Base
Phantom FGR2	228 OCU (64)	Coningsby
Tornado F2	229 OCU (65)	Coningsby
Lightning F3,T5,F6	LTF	Binbrook
Lightning F6	LAF	Binbrook

2.M   Air defence at 1 January 1990

Strike Command, 11 Group

Type	Unit	Base
Tornado F3	5, 29	Coningsby
	11, 23, 25	Leeming
	43	Leuchars
Phantom FG1	111	Leuchars
Phantom FGR2	56	Wattisham
Phantom F3	74	Wattisham
Bloodhound Mk 2	*85*	*West Raynham, N Coates, Bawdsey, Coltishall, Wyton, Barkston Heath, Wattisham*

RAF Germany

Type	Unit	Base
Phantom FGR2	19, 92	Wildenrath

Falkland Islands

Type	Unit	Base
Phantom FGR2	1435 Flt	Stanley

Training and development units

Type	Unit	Base
Phantom FGR2	228 OCU (64)	Leuchars
Tornado F2	229 OCU (65)	Coningsby

2.N   Air defence at 1 January 1995

Strike Command, 11 Group

Type	Unit	Base
Tornado F3	5, 29	Coningsby
	11, 25	Leeming, det Gioia del Colle (Italy)
	43, 111	Leuchars

Falkland Islands

Type	Unit	Base
Tornado F3	1435 Flt	Port Stanley

Training and development units

Type	Unit	Base
Tornado F3	56(R)	Coningsby

2.1 Supermarine Spitfire (1938–1959)

The Spitfire must surely be the best known of the RAF's fighters of World War Two, but it may not be widely known that later versions were in service with the RAF until 1959.

The Spitfire was designed by R J Mitchell to specification F.37/34 for an eight-gun fighter with a speed of not less than 275mph. The prototype was built in a remarkably short time and first flew on 5 March 1936. The type entered squadron service with 19 Squadron from August 1938 and its Merlin II or III engine conferred a top speed of 362 mph. This brief reference to the initial version is given solely to put the Mark V and later variants which served after the war into some context.

By the end of 1945 the Marks I (Type 300), II (Type 329), IV (Type 353) and VII (Type 351) were out of service completely. Some marks were allocated to second-line units only, but in its Mark IX, XIV and XVI form the Spitfire was the primary day fighter, yet to be eclipsed by the new jet types.

Mark V

The Type 349 was essentially a Mark I or II with fuselage strengthened to accommodate the Merlin 45 engine. Other changes included metal-covered ailerons and numerous minor improvements added in the course of production. The V came in three main versions but the VA with eight machine-gun armament was out of service by September 1945. The VB had an armament of four .303" machine-guns and two 20mm cannon while the VC had the universal wing which would take two or four cannon and four machine-guns. There was provision for the carriage of 500lb of bombs.

Many of each variant of the Mark V were equipped with deep beard tropical filters for service in the Middle East and each variant was also produced with wings clipped from 36'10" to 32'2" for low altitude work. The Mark V was produced in greater numbers than any other version, some 6,487 new-build machines being supplemented by a large number of Mark I and II conversions.

Service (post-1945) ASR/Met 269; 1413, 1414, 1415, 1563, 1564, 1566, 1567 Met Flts; **Calibration** 527 **Training** 203 AFS; 1686, 1687, 1688 BDTF; CCFATU; 61 OTU 17 ASFTS; **Other** 87 GCF

Mark VI

The Type 350 was a high altitude version of the Mark V with wing-span extended to 40'2" and a pressurised cabin. The Merlin 47 drove a four-blade airscrew, which remained the standard until the introduction of five-blade screws on the Griffon-engined Mark XIV.

Service (post-1945) Meteorology 519.

As mentioned above, the photo-reconnaissance Mark VII (Type 351) was out of service by 1946.

Mark VIII

The Type 359 preceded the Mark IX on the drawing board but entered service later. The Mark VII, outside the scope of this book, improved on the Mark VI by the fitting of a Merlin 61 and a retractable tailwheel; later versions had a wider chord rudder. The Mark VIII was the medium-low-altitude version of the Mark VII without pressurisation; a total of 1,658 was built. Armament fit now included provision for one 500lb and two 250lb bombs and top speed was 408 mph compared to 357 mph for the Mark V. All aircraft of this version were fitted with unobtrusive tropical filters in production and by 1946 the Mark VIII equipped units in the Middle and Far East only. The last RAF Mark VIII departed 253 Sqn in December 1947.

Service (post-1945) Fighter 20, 92, 136, 152, 155, 253, 273 **Meteorology** 1563 Met Flt **Training** 3FSTU **Communications** 36 SP

Supermarine Spitfire Mk IX

The Spitfire was still in widespread RAF service well after the end of the War. Merlin-engined Mk IX MK728/GZ-R of 32 Sqn is seen over Palestine in 1946. *(Crown copyright)*

Mark IX

The Type 361 was moved swiftly into production to meet the threat of the FW 190. Whereas the lineage of the Mark VIII was through the VI and VII, the Mark IX was an upgraded Mark V, many of which were production-line or retrospective conversions of the Mark V to the later specification. Engine and performance were similar to those of the Mark VIII, although the tailwheel was fixed.

The Mark IX came in three forms in respect of altitude, the LF with clipped wings, the standard span medium altitude fighter and the HF with standard wingspan but the Merlin 70 engine. By now the eight machine-gun armament had been superseded by combinations of machine-gun and cannon or cannon alone. Variants of the Mark IX were fitted with the B, C and E wing, the latter accommodating two 20mm cannon and two .5" calibre machine-guns. Some later models had the broad-chord rudder, cut-down rear fuselage and tear-drop canopy. Some 5,665 of this popular version of the Spitfire were built from new and its final operational service with the RAF was with 73 Sqn whose last aircraft were withdrawn in May 1948.

Service (post-1945) Fighter 32, 43, 72, 73, 87, 111, 129, 130, 164, 165, 208, 225, 234, 318 **Army Co-operation** 288 **Meteorology** 1401 Met Flt **Training** 61, 80 OTU **Other** 18 APC; CFE; 11, 12 GCF

Mark X

The Type 362, like the Mark VIII, was produced out of sequence. It was a pressurised Mark XI, unarmed for photographic reconnaissance, and fitted with the Merlin 77. It was distinguished by a deeper nose for an enlarged oil cooler. Only sixteen were built.

Service (post-1945) Photo-reconnaissance 541

Mark XI

The Type 365 was the photo-reconnaissance version of the Mark IX with the same engine. Armament was replaced by cameras in three fits. The X fit was two F.8 cameras with 20in lens, the Y fit one F.24 camera with 14in lens and the Z fit one F.52 camera with 36in lens. Production was 471 plus some Mark IX conversions.

Service (post-1945) Photo-reconnaissance 2, 26, 541, 681 **Meteorology** 1401, 1561, 1562 Met Flts **Training** 237 OCU; 8 OTU **Communications** Berlin CF; ADLS; 106 GCF.

The fighter Mark XII (Type 366) and photo-reconnaissance Mark XIII (Type 353) were out of service by 1946.

Mark XIV

The Type 379 was the second of the Griffon-engined Spitfires; the first, the Mark XII was out of service by 1946. For some time it had been intended to fit the more powerful engine and the prototype, built to specification F.4/40, first flew in 1941. The variant was essentially the Mark VIII with the Griffon 65 or 67, with the camshaft and supercharger gear moved forward in order to keep overall length broadly the same as in the Merlin-engined versions. Notwithstanding the modification to the engine, the Mark XIV was longer than the Mark IX by 1½ ft. The five-blade airscrew had a larger spinner and the added

length was compensated for by a larger fin and rudder. The fuselage contours changed on the nose with fairings on either side to accommodate the cylinder blocks.

As with later models of the Mark IX, for better all-round vision the rear fuselage was cut down and a tear-drop canopy fitted, albeit at the expense of slight deterioration in directional stability. Some aircraft had the clipped wing for low-altitude work, including a number of the FR variant which were equipped with an obliquely mounted F.24 camera. Apart from the four 20mm Hispano cannon there was provision for one 500lb bomb or Mark IX rocket projectiles.

Service (post-1945) Fighter/FR 2, 11, 16, 17, 20, 26, 28, 41, 132, 411, 412, 416, 443, 451, 600, 602, 607, 610, 611, 612, 613, 615 **Training** 203 AFS; 3 FSTU 226 OCU; 61 OTU **Other** CGS; 1 FP

Mark XVI

The Mark XVI Type 380 was the next Spitfire variant; the Mark XV was a Seafire. This final Merlin version of the Spitfire was similar in all essential features to the Mark IX but fitted with a US-build Packard Merlin 266. At one stage the production line was delivering both marks depending on which engine was to hand. Like some late model Mark IXs some XVIs had the cut-down rear fuselage and rear-view canopy. The last Merlin-engined Spitfire XVIs in RAF front-line service were withdrawn from 63 Sqn in May 1948 but the type continued in service with the RAuxAF until June 1951 (612 Sqn) and well into the mid-fifties with second-line or training units.

Service (post-1945) Fighter 19, 63, 65, 126, 164, 302, 308, 317, 349, 350, 443, 501, 601, 603, 604, 609, 612, 614; AAC 5, 17, 20, 21, 287, 567, 577, 587, 595, 631, 691, 695 **Communications** 31; Berlin CFFCCRS; FCCS; 11; 12, 13, 21 GCF; HCCS; MCS; MCCS; RCCS **Training** 202, 203 AFS; 1689 FPTF; 101, 102, 103 FRS; 226, 236 OCU; 6, 10, 17, 61, 111 OTU; 5, 21 (P)AFU 7, 17 SFTS; 1380 TSCU **Other** 11 AGS; 2 APS; BCIS; 1, 2, 3, 4, 5 CAACU; CBE; CFS; CGS; CRS; EAAS; EANS; 1 OFU; 1 PRFU; SLAW; 1353 TTF

Mark XVIII

The Type 394 was the next Spitfire variant, the XVII being allocated to the Seafire. This Mark was a XIV but with a new wing with increased fuel capacity. All had

Supermarine Spitfire F Mk 18

Installation of the Griffon engine changed the nose profile of the Spitfire and also resulted in a changed fin and rudder to counter the increased torque. F Mk 18 TP448/GZ-? of 32 Sqn clearly demonstrates the purposeful lines of the type. *(Crown copyright)*

clear-view canopies and 300 were built of which 200 were fighter-reconnaissance variants fitted with one oblique and two vertical F.24 cameras. Production was barely underway before the war ended. In the Far East, with 60 Sqn, the FR Mk 18 flew the last RAF Spitfire fighter sortie on 1 January 1951 with an attack on a terrorist hideout in Johore.

Service (post-1945) **Fighter** 11, 28, 32, 60, 81, 208 **Training** 203 AFS; 1335 CU; 226 OCU; 61 OTU **Other** CFE; ECFS; FECS; 2, 4 FP; FCCRS

Mark XIX

The Type 389 was a Griffon-engined hybrid for unarmed photographic reconnaissance tasks. It was built around a Mark XIV fuselage with the Mark Vc wing; engine was a Griffon 66. The Mark XIX, of which 225 were built, entered service with 541 Sqn in June 1944 and was finally withdrawn from front-line units in June 1951 (2 Sqn). The version was the last Spitfire mark to fly in British military markings when the remaining three aircraft of the Temperature and HUMidity (THUM) Flight at Woodvale were withdrawn in June 1957. All three are now operated by the RAF Battle of Britain Memorial Flight.

Service (post-1945) **Photo-reconnaissance** 2, 31, 34, 81, 82, 541, 681 **Meteorology** THUM Flt **Training** 226, 237 OCU

F Mark 21

The Type 368 (the Mark XX was the Mark IV renumbered and not built) introduced a new strengthened wing of subtly different planform with the span increased by 1". The original fuselage profile and canopy was retained and armament fixed at four 20mm cannon. Powerplant was the Griffon 61 or 64, although some later aircraft were fitted with the Mark 85 driving contra-rotating propellers. Late production aircraft were also fitted with a 24-volt electrical system. The undercarriage was strengthened to cope with a greater all-up weight. The F Mk 21 entered service just as the war in Europe was ending.

Service (post-1945) **Fighter** 1, 41, 91, 122, 600, 602, 615 **Army co-operation** 595 **Training** 226 OCU **Other** AFDU; 3 CAACU; FLS; 2 FP; HCCS; TFU

F Mark 22

The Type 356 was similar to the F Mk 21 but with a cutdown rear-fuselage and tear-drop canopy. Some later models were fitted with a larger fin and rudder, similar to that fitted to the Spiteful; as with the F Mk 21, some were fitted with the Griffon 85 driving contra-rotating propellers. Some 278 were built compared with 122 of the preceding version.

Service **Fighter** 73, 500, 502, 504, 600, 602, 603, 607, 608, 610, 611, 613, 614, 615 **Training** 2 ANS; 102 FRS; 226 OCU; 4 RS **Other** CBE; CFE; 1 FU; IAM; MCCF; 1 OFU.

The F Mark 23 (Type 372) was a project only, designed as an F Mk 22 with an improved wing section. One aircraft, a converted Mark VIII, flew with the new wing section.

F Mark 24

The Type 356 was the definitive Spitfire. Powered by the Griffon 61 driving a five-blade airscrew it carried extra fuel tanks in the fuselage and had the enlarged elliptical fin and rudder of the Spiteful. Twenty-seven F Mk 22s were partially converted while 54 new-build aircraft were fitted with four Hispano Mk V 20mm cannon and zero-length underwing rocket launchers. The F Mk 24 served only with 80 Sqn which exchanged them for the Hornet in December 1951.

Service **Fighter** 80

		Specification and production				
Mark	Role	Engine	HP	Weight lbs	Speed mph	Nos
I	Fighter	Merlin II, III	1,030	6,200	362	1,583
II	Fighter	Merlin XII	1,175	6,275	370	920
III	Fighter	Merlin XX	1,390	7,110	360	2
IV	PR	Merlin 45	1,470	6,850	365	229
V	Fighter	Merlin 45	1,470	6,750	369	6,487
VI	HA fighter	Merlin 47	1,415	6,797	364	100
VII	HA fighter	Merlin 61	1,565	7,875	408	140
VIII	Fighter	Merlin 63, 66	1,650 (63)	7,767	408	1,658
IX	Fighter	Merlin 61	1,565	7,500	408	5,665
X	PR	Merlin 64	1,710	7,900	422	16
XI	PR	Merlin 61	1,565	7,900	422	471
XII	Fighter	Griffon III	1,735	7,280	393	100
XIII	PR	Merlin 32	1,645	6,750	348	18
XIV	Fighter/ FR	Griffon 65, 67	2,035 (65)	8,375	439	957
XV	SEAFIRE					
XVI	Fighter	Merlin 266	1,580	7,500	408	1,054
XVII	SEAFIRE					
XVIII	Fighter/ FR	Griffon 65, 67	2,035 (65)	9,300	439	300
XIX	PR	Griffon 66	2,035	9,202	446	225
XX	Exp	Griffon IIb	1,735			1
F21	Fighter	Griffon 61, 64	2,035 (61)	9,900	450	122
F22	Fighter	Griffon 61, 64	2,375 (64)	9,900	451	278
F23	Project	Griffon 61	2,035			1
F24	Fighter	Griffon 61	2,035	9,900	451	54

Further reading
Calling all Spitfires – a Scale Modeller's Guide, Beaman, J R, Privately published, 1973
Sigh for a Merlin, Henshaw, A, John Murray, London, 1979
Spitfire (Classic Aircraft No 1) Cross, R, and Scarborough, G. PSL, London, 1971
Spitfire – A Documentary History, Price, A, Macdonald and Janes, London, 1977
Spitfire at War, Price, A, Ian Allan, London
Spitfire at War 2, Price, A, Ian Allan, London
Spitfire in Action, Scutts, J, Squadron/Signal, Carrollton
Spitfire Story, The, Price, A, Janes, London, 1979
Spitfire: The, Morgan, E, and Shacklady, E. Key Publishing, Stamford, 1987
Spitfire – The Story of a Famous Fighter, Robertson, B, Harleyford, Letchworth, 1960

Supermarine Spitfire, Moss, P, Ducimus, London, 1970

Supermarine Spitfire V Series, (Profile 166) Hooton, E, Profile Publications, Leatherhead, 1965

Supermarine Spitfire Mk I-XVI, (Aircam 4) Hooton, E, Osprey, Canterbury

Supermarine Spitfire Mk IX, (Profile 206) Moss, P and Bachelor, L J, Profile Publications, Windsor, 1969

Supermarine Spitfire Mk XII-24, (Aircam 8) Hooton, E, Osprey, Canterbury

Supermarine Spitfire Mks XIV and XVIII, (Profile 246) Bachelor, L J, Profile Publications, Windsor, 1972

2.2 Hawker Tempest (1945–1955)

The Tempest was a natural development of the Typhoon built to specification F.10/41 and originally named Typhoon Mark II. The main differences were in the wing which was to a new elliptical plan and much thinner, and the fuselage which was longer to accommodate the fuel no longer carried in wing tanks. A dorsal fillet was also incorporated. Because of problems with the early Sabre engines prototypes were ordered to be fitted with a variety of engines – Mark I Sabre IV, Mark II Centaurus IV, Mark III Griffon IIB, Mark IV Griffon 61 and Mark V Sabre II.

In the event the Mark V flew first, followed by the Mark I (HM599) on 24 February 1943. The Mark III and Mark IV were never flown due to a shortage of Griffons while the Mark II was last on the scene. The Mark I was clean cowled and had wing leading edge radiators, but

Hawker Tempest Mark VI

The later (but earlier in service) Tempest Mk V and VI employed the Napier Sabre engine with the distinctive chin radiator originally seen on the Typhoon. Although in use with first-line units for some time they were latterly converted to target-tugs, as seen here with TT Mk 5 SN260/WH17 of APS Acklington *(R C Sturtivant)*

due to problems with the Sabre IV the version was abandoned.

Mark II

The Mark II first flew on 28 June 1943 powered by the Centaurus V but engine teething troubles resulted in delayed introduction into service. The Tempest was armed with four 20mm cannon and it could carry two

Hawker Tempest Mk II

The sleek but functional lines of the radial-engined Tempest Mk II are clearly shown-off in this shot of early production aircraft PR533, which later went on to serve with 33 Sqn after trials with A&AEE. *(Hawker Siddeley)*

500lb or 1,000lb bombs under the wings or eight rocket projectiles. The fighter was optimised for the war in the Far East with long range and heavy armament. The prototype (LA602) flew on 28 June 1943 but it did not enter service (with 183 Sqn) until June 1945.

Service (post-1945) Fighter 5, 16, 20, 26, 30, 33, 54, 152, 247 **Training** 226 OCU; 13 OTU **Communications** BAFO CW; 1, 3 FP; 16 FU; Bückeburg SF **Other** CFE; ETPS

Mark V

The Mark V was the first variant to fly. Unlike the later radial-engined Mark II the Mark V shared the distinctive deep chin radiator of the Typhoon. In other respects it was similar to the Mark II but was 5mph slower. The prototype (HM595) flew on 2 September 1942 and the first squadron equipped with the type was 486. Post-war the Mark V served in Europe while the Mark II was used additionally in the Far East.

Service (post-1945) Fighter 3, 16, 26, 33, 41, 56, 80, 174, 287 **Training** 226, 233 OCU; 56 OTU **Communications** 1689 Flt; 84 GCS **Other** CFE

TT Mark 5

In the target-towing conversion of redundant Mark Vs the armament was removed and a Malcolm G type winch fitted under the port wing. The first conversion was SN329 which first flew in October 1947.

Service Target-towing AMSDU; APS Acklington, Sylt; CGS; 226, 229, 233 OCU

Mark VI

The Mark 6 was a tropicalised version similar in most respects to the Mark V; indeed the prototype was HM595 flying in this guise on 9 May 1944. However, it was powered by the Sabre V and had the air intakes moved from the radiator to the wing. The version served exclusively in the Middle East and India (one squadron), joining 6 and 249 Sqns concurrently in December 1946. Two aircraft were stripped of armament and fitted with underwing winches as the TT Mark 6.

Service Fighter 6, 8, 39, 213, 249

Specification and production

Mark	Role	Engine	HP	Weight lb	Speed mph	Nos
I	Fighter	Sabre IV	2,500	11,300	466	1
II	Fighter	Centaurus V	2,526	11,400	440	472
III	Fighter	Griffon IIB	1,735			
IV	Fighter	Griffon 61	2,375			
V	Fighter	Sabre II	2,180	13,540	435	800
TT5	Target tug	Sabre II	2,180	11,500	435	81*
VI	Fighter	Sabre V	2,340	13,700	438	142
TT6	Target tug	Sabre V	2,340	12,000	438	2+

* Mark V conversions
+ Mark VI conversions

Further reading

Hawker Tempest 1-VI, The, (Profile 197) Mason, F K, Profile Publications, Leatherhead, 1965
Typhoon and Tempest Story, The, Thomas, C, and Shores, C, Arms and Armour Press, London, 1991

2.3 Supermarine Spiteful (1944–1947)

Supermarine was engaged in developing a new, laminar flow, wing for the Spitfire, where the thickest part of the wing would be much further from the leading edge than in the original wing. The design of a new fighter to incorporate the wing was undertaken against specification F.1/43.

The new aircraft was sufficiently different from the Spitfire as to merit a new name; Victor, proposed for the Griffon-engined Spitfires, was rejected in favour of Spiteful. The first prototype was a converted Mark XIV, NN660, which in common with the second prototype retained the Spitfire tail unit. The first true prototype, NN664, flew in June 1944. Aircraft built to production standard featured the new wing, an inward-retracting undercarriage and a fin and rudder and tailplane of increased area to improve directional stability.

The early aircraft displayed a number of problems, none of which would have been insurmountable, although the type was probably taking piston-engine design to the limits. Some 373 were ordered from a revised Spitfire F21 contract, but production was cancelled with the war's end and with the introduction into service of the new jet types, the Meteor and Vampire.

Mark XIV

The Type 371 was fitted with the Griffon 69 driving a five-blade airscrew. Top speed was 475mph and eleven were built, one or two reportedly spending some time with the CFE.

Mark XV

The Mark XV employed the Griffon 89 or 90 driving two contra-rotating three-blade propellers; five were built to

Supermarine Spiteful Mk XIV

When Supermarine developed a new laminar flow wing for the Spitfire the change in shape was such that at last a new name was called for – the Spiteful. A large order, replacing a Spitfire Mk 21 purchase, was cancelled since jet types offered better performance. RB520 was fitted with an arrester hook in support of Seafang development. (MAP)

this standard. It had a shorter wing-span and a top speed of 483mph.

Mark XVI

The Mark XVI, of which only one was completed, was similar to the Mark XIV but was fitted with the Griffon 101 conferring a top speed of 494mph.

Specification and production

Mark	Role	Engine	HP	Weight lb	Speed mph	Nos
XIV	Fighter	Griffon 69	2,375	9,950	475	11
XV	Fighter	Griffon 89	2,350	10,200	483	5
XVI	Fighter	Griffon 101	2,420	9,950	494	1

2.4 Hawker Fury (1944–1947)

The Fury was developed as a lightweight Tempest, designed to confer relatively low wing loading on a powerful fighter. Originally designed to specification F.6/42, later refined in F.2/43, the prototype, NX798, first flew on 1 September 1944. Its relationship to the Tempest II was clear but the aircraft featured a revised fin and rudder. It was hoped that the Fury would more than match the manoeuvrability of the Japanese fighters then in production, but before problems with the Centaurus engine could be resolved the war had ended. With a surplus of piston-engined fighters now available and the the introduction of jet types an order for 200 was cancelled, although in naval form the type served with the Royal Navy for some years as the Sea Fury.

Four prototypes were constructed. NX798 had the Centaurus XII, rigid mounted and driving a four-blade airscrew. LA610 was first fitted with a Griffon 85 driving three-blade contra-rotating propellers. It was later fitted with the Sabre VII with which it attained a top speed of 485mph. NX802 employed the Centaurus XV on a dynamic mounting. The fourth, and final, Fury, VP207, also flew with the Sabre VII.

Hawker Fury

The Fury was a wartime design based on a lightweight Tempest and intended to out-manoeuvre contemporary Japanese fighters. It never entered RAF service, but did perform outstandingly with the Fleet Air Arm. LA610 is seen here with the Sabre engine with which it achieved 485 mph. (*MAP*)

Specification and production

Mark	Role	Engine	HP	Weight lb	Speed mph	Nos
	Fighter	Centaurus XII	2,520	11,990	460	1
	Fighter	Griffon 85	2,340	12,000	450	1
	Fighter	Centaurus XV	2,550	11,990	460	1
	Fighter	Sabre VII	2,340	12,000	485	1

Further reading
Hawker Sea Fury, The (Profile 126) Mason, F K, Profile Publications, Leatherhead, 1965

2.5 Gloster Meteor (1944–1965)

The Gloster Aircraft Company was responsible for building Britain's first jet aircraft, the G.40 built to specification E.28/39. First flight of the prototype, W4041, was from Cranwell on 15 May 1941. Before this date specification F.9/40 was issued calling for a twin-engined jet fighter. The specification was written around Gloster experience with the low-powered G.40 (one W.I engine of 860lb thrust) and the company proceeded with development. An order for twelve aircraft (DG202-213) was received in February 1941. First flight was by the fifth, Halford H.1 engined, prototype DG206 at Cranwell on 5 March 1943.

Gradually more prototypes were brought into the flight test programme and as problems were identified, so great effort was made to address them. The first aircraft built to the Mark I (Type G.41) standard, DG210, flew on 12 January 1944. Twenty production machines, commencing EE210, were produced, twelve being issued to 616 Squadron at Culmhead in July. Armament was four 20mm Hispano Mk 5 cannon in the nose and the engine was the Welland series 1 of 1,700lb thrust. The type was used to counter the V1 flying bombs, 616 Sqn moving to Manston for 'Diver' patrols. The first V1 was brought down on 4 August 1944. One flight was moved into Nijmegen in January 1945, although the Meteor was not to be flown over enemy territory. The Mark I was withdrawn at the end of January.

The Mark II was intended to be the first production

Gloster Meteor F Mk 4

The Meteor was Britain's first jet fighter and was in front-line service from 1945 to 1960. F Mk 4 RA444/B of 257 Sqn was based at Horsham St Faith when pictured in 1950. (*Crown copyright*)

aircraft, given prospective delivery problems with the W.2B/Welland engines of the Mark I. In the event the Halford H.1B Goblin was to be earmarked for the Vampire and the version flew in prototype form only.

Mark III/F Mark 3

The Mark III was generally similar to the Mark I but it incorporated numerous refinements, including a sliding canopy, increased fuel capacity and airframe strengthening. The first fifteen were fitted with the Welland, while the remainder of the total of 210 had the improved Derwent I of 2,000lb thrust. A ventral fuel tank was fitted. The Mark III began coming off the production lines in early 1945 and the first were issued to 616 Sqn then 504 Sqn. Both units were disbanded in August 1945 in common with all Auxiliary Air Force squadrons, although 616 was to be re-equipped with the F Mk 3 in 1949, after re-formation. On 7 September 1946 Gp Capt E M Donaldson raised the world air speed record to 615.78mph in specially modified EE549.

Service (post-1945) Fighter 1, 56, 63, 66, 74, 91, 92, 124, 222, 234, 245, 257, 263, 266, 500, 616 **Training** 205, 206, 208, 210 AFS; 1335 CU; 226, 229 OCU; 61 OTU **Communications** FCCS **Other** 541; CFE; CGS; CRD; ECFS; ETPS; RAE: 703 NAS

Mark IV/F Mark 4

This variant evolved through the special Mark III designed to secure the world air speed record. The Mark IV employed the Derwent 5 of 3,500lb thrust with extended engine nacelles and in later models wings clipped from 43' to 37' 2". Top speed at sea level increased from 420 to 585mph. The first squadron to equip with the Mark IV was No 92 and some aircraft of 245 Sqn were modified with probes for in-flight refuelling trials.

Service Fighter 1, 19, 41, 43, 56, 63, 64, 65, 66, 74, 92, 111, 222, 245, 257, 263, 266, 500, 504, 600, 609, 610, 611, 615, 616 **Training** 203, 205, 206, 207, 208, 209, 210, 215 AFS; 1335 CU; 101 FRS; 4, 8, 12 FTS; 226 OCU; RAFFC **Communications** 1, 12 GCF; FCCS; 2 FP; 2 FU **Other** 29, 85, 141, 264; AFDS; AIEU; 5 CAACU; CBE; CFE; CGS; CPE; DFLS; ECFS; EFS; ETPS; JCF; JCU; NGTE; RAE; RRE; TFU; TRE; WEE

FR Mark 5

The Mark 5 was built to capitalise on trials with camera installations on Mark III and IV aircraft. The prototype VT347 broke up in the air on its maiden flight, killing the pilot.

F Mark 6

The Mark 6 progressed no further than the drawing board. It was described as being the forerunner of the F Mk 8 with a tail assembly similar to that of the E.1/44.

T Mark 7

The next version of the Meteor was designed in response to the obvious need for a trainer variant, especially given the significant overseas orders now being received. There was no official requirement and the prototype, G-AIDC (later G-AKPK), flew on 19 March 1948, nearly four years after the single-seat fighter entered service. There was immediate official interest and specification T.1/47

was issued to cover the type. The trainer was based on the Mark IV but with the fuselage extended by 30 inches to accommodate the second seat. An extra fuel tank was fitted replacing ballast and there was also provision for underwing tanks. The canopy was heavily framed. The longer nose conferred added directional stability which was to have an impact on the design of later variants. Later production models were fitted with the Derwent 8 and the square-cut tail unit of the F Mk 8.

Service Trainer 202, 203, 205, 206, 207, 208, 209, 210, 211, 215 AFS; 1, 2 ANS; CFS; ECFS; 1689 FPPTF; 3, 4, 5, 8, 9, 10, 12, 211 FTS; 101, 102, 103, 105 FRS; 226, 228, 229, 231, 233, 237, 238 OCU; AWOCU; 32 OTU; RAFC; RAFFC *All Meteor and some other squadrons had one or two T7s on charge including* 1, 2, 3, 4, 5, 6, 8, 9, 11, 13, 14, 16, 19, 20, 23, 24, 25, 26, 28, 29, 32, 33, 34, 39, 41, 43, 45, 46, 54, 56, 60, 63, 64, 65, 66, 67, 68. 71, 72, 73, 74, 78, 79, 81, 85, 87, 89, 92, 93, 94, 96, 98, 111, 112, 118, 125, 130, 141, 145, 151, 152, 153, 185, 208, 213, 216, 219, 222, 234, 245, 247, 249, 256, 257, 263, 264, 266, 500, 501, 502, 504, 527, 540; 541, 600, 601, 602, 603, 604, 605, 607, 608, 609, 610, 611, 612, 613, 614, 615, 616 **Communications** 1, 2, 3, 11, 12, 13, 14, 25, 64, 81, 83, 205 GCF; 2 TAFCS; 41 GTPP; BCCF; BCCS; CCCF; FCCS; FECS; Levant CF; MECS; PCCS Aden **Other** AFDS; AMSDU; APS Acklington, Sylt; AWDS; BLEU; 3, 3/4, 5 CAACU; CAW; CFE; CGS; EAAS; ETPS; FETS; FTU; FWS; GWDS; IAM; ITF Nicosia, Shallufa, Tangmere, West Raynham, JCF; JCU; JTF; NGTE; 1 OFU; RAE; SCU; TAFC; TTF Nicosia; Seletar; 1574 TFF; TWU; 1 TWU **Royal Navy** 700Z, 702, 703, 728, 736, 759, 767, 771, 781, 806, 813

F Mark 8

The Mark 8 was the result of increasing the nose of the Mark IV by 30 inches to improve directional stability and add fuel capacity. Unfortunately expenditure of the ammunition, which was also moved forward, resulted in some loss of stability so a new tail unit was fitted. Further improvements included a retractable gunsight and Martin Baker ejection seat. Some 1,079 were built, making this the most popular version of Gloster's now ageing fighter. The last F Mk 8s in front-line service were withdrawn from 245 Sqn in April 1957; the unit had been equipped with Meteor fighters continuously since August 1945.

Service Fighter 1, 19, 34, 41, 43, 54, 56, 63, 64, 65, 66, 72, 74, 92, 111, 222, 245, 247, 257, 263, 500, 504, 600, 601, 604, 609, 610, 611, 615, 616 **Training** 203, 206, 209, 211 AFS; CFS; 4, 5, 8, 211 FTS; 226, 229, 233, 238 OCU; RAFFC *Some non-F8 equipped fighter squadrons also had on charge one or two F8s, including* 12, 23, 33, 45, 60, 79, 85, 89, 125, 141, 151, 152, 153, 208, 219, 501, 605, 608, 613 **Communications** FCCS; FECS; 11, 12, 13 GCF; Levant CF; AA Paris **Other** AFDS; AOS; 2 APS; AWDS; 5 CAACU; CAW; CFE; CGS; CSDE; CSE; DFLS; ETPS; FETS; FWS; NGTE; OFU; RAE; RRE; THUM Flt; TRE; TWU; 1 TWU

F(TT) Mark 8

This was a simple conversion of the F Mk 8 with a towing lug fitted on the ventral tank. The arrangement was first tried on VZ438 and many F Mk 8s were subsequently converted.

Service Target-towing 1, 29, 85; 26 APC Nicosia; APS Acklington, Sylt; 5 CAACU; 229 OCU (79); 1 TWU; 1574 TTF (Changi); Gibraltar TTF; Malta TTS; Biggin Hill, Church Fenton, Coltishall, Duxford, Geilenkirchen, Horsham St Faith, Leuchars, Linton-on-Ouse, North Weald, Odiham, Ouston, Stradishall, Tangmere, Waterbeach, Wattisham, West Malling, Wymeswold SFs

T Mark 8 and FB Mark 8

The T designation was apparently applied to a number of F Mk 8s which were modified as advanced trainers. The FB designation was informally applied to F Mk 8s equipped to carry two 1,000lb bombs underwing.

FR Mark 9

To provide a tactical reconnaissance platform the Mark 9 was based on the F Mk 8 but with a new nose retaining the four cannon of the fighter but incorporating glazed panels either side of the nose and with a remotely controlled F.24 camera. Heating was provided by hot air bled from the starboard engine. The prototype flew on 22 March 1950 and 126 were produced, serving with the RAF from 1951 to 1957.

Service Fighter reconnaissance 2, 79, 208, 541; FR Flt Aden Training 226, 237 OCU **Communications** 187; 2 GCF **Other** 8; CFE; CSDE; RAE

PR Mark 10

The Mark 10 was designed to replace the Spitfire IX and XIX. In relation to earlier Meteors the design was a hybrid utilising the long wing-span of the earlier Mark III (for high-altitude work), the F Mk 8 fuselage mated to a Mark IV tail unit and with the FR Mk 9 nose. Armament was deleted and two additional cameras located in the rear fuselage. The type was a contemporary of the FR Mk 9 and the two versions were complementary although both types served with 541 Sqn.

Service Photo-reconnaissance 2, 13, 81, 541 **Training** 231, 237 OCU; RAFFC **Communications** 2 GCF **Other** CSDE; NGTE; RAE

NF Mark 11

The Type G.47 Mark 11 was the first night fighter version of the Meteor and was designed to specification F.24/48 for a two-seat, twin-engined night fighter capable of intercepting contemporary bombers. Armstrong Whitworth, who had built a number of Meteors under sub-contract, were contracted to design and develop the new version, experiments at the TRE having confirmed that the Meteor airframe would suit the purpose. The prototype was a converted T Mk 7, VW413, but the first true NF Mk 11 built as such was WA546 which first flew on 31 May 1950. The lengthened nose contained an AI Mark 10 (SCR 720) radar and the four 20mm cannon were rehoused in the wing just outboard of the engine nacelles. The version retained the heavily framed canopy of the T Mk 7. The Meteor NF Mk 11 entered service with 29 Sqn at Tangmere in May 1951 and finally departed front-line service when 5 Sqn became operational on the Javelin in June 1960.

Service Night fighter 5, 11, 29, 46; 68, 85, 87, 96, 125, 141, 151, 219, 256, 264 **Training** 226, 228 OCU; RAFFC

Armstrong Whitworth Meteor NF Mk 11

The Armstrong Whitworth Company was contracted to design the night-fighter variants of the Meteor. The change in nose profile is evident on NF Mk 11 WD597 of 29 Sqn, which was based at Tangmere in 1952. *(Hawker Siddeley)*

Calibration 527 **Communications** 81 GCS; 83 GCF; 2 TAFCS **Other** AFEE; AWDS; CFE; CSDE; ETPS; 6 JSTU; RAE; RRE; TRE

NF Mark 12

The Mark 12 was a development of the NF Mk 11 with an American APS 21 radar which necessitated an increase in fuselage length of 17in. To counter the extra length the fin was faired at the junction with the tailplane.

Service Night fighter 25, 29, 46, 64, 72, 85, 152, 153 **Training** 228, 238 OCU; AWOCU **Other** CFE; CSE; FWS

NF Mark 13

This was a tropicalised version of the NF Mk 11, 40 being built for use in the Middle East. The NF Mk 13 had larger engine nacelles, a cold air unit and modified radio.

Service Night fighter 39, 219 **Other** 213; CSE; RAFFC; RRE

NF Mark 14

The Mark 14 was the final night-fighter variant. It differed from the NF Mk 12 in having a completely transparent, electrically operated, cockpit canopy. In common with the other nocturnal Meteors no ejection seats were fitted.

Service Night fighter 25, 33, 46, 60, 64, 72, 85, 96, 152, 153, 213, 264 **Training** 228, 238 OCU; AWOCU; 2 ANS; RAFFC **Calibration** 527 **Communications** FCCS; 12, 13 GCF; 2 TAFCS **Other** CFE; NAWCU; NFLS; TRE

NF(T) Mark 14

The designation was applied when redundant aircraft had their radars removed and replaced by UHF radio for navigation training.

Service Training 1, 2 ANS

U Mark 15

The drone designation was applied to conversions of redundant F Mk 4 aircraft. The work was undertaken by Flight Refuelling Ltd and some 92 airframes were converted starting with RA421, which first flew in its new guise on 11 March 1955.

Service Target drone RAE: 728B NAS

U Mark 16

The Mark 16 was the conversion of F Mk 8 aircraft to drone configuration, also undertaken by FRL. Some 150 airframes were converted. The designation was later changed to **D Mark 16** to avoid confusion with the utility designation.

Service Target drone RAE: 728B NAS.

The designations U Mark 17, U Mark 18 and U Mark 19 may have been reserved for intended drone conversions of the NF Mk 11, Mk 12 and Mk 14. However, there would have been a gap to the Mark 20 since that version was initially intended for Naval use and given a high designation accordingly. The designation T Mark 17 has been informally applied to the two modified T Mk 7s flown by Martin Baker on ejection seat research.

TT Mark 20

This was yet another conversion, this time of the NF11 for target-towing duties. The radar was removed to compensate for the weight of an ML Aviation G type winch above the port wing, between the fuselage and the engine nacelle. VHF radio was replaced by a UHF set. Forty-nine conversions were completed by ML Aviation and the type served with the RAF and Royal Navy.

Service Target-towing 3, 3/4, 5 CAACU; 1574 TTF; TTF Seletar, Kai Tak: 700, 728 NAS

U Mark 21

This was the final Meteor variant apart from numerous trials aircraft. (The Meteor proved to be a remarkably robust aeroplane used for a wide range of development work.) Eight F Mk 8 airframes were prepared by FRL as drones and shipped to Australia for re-assembly by Fairey Aviation. Further kits were supplied for local production and 22 F Mk 8s were converted. The type differed from the U Mk 16 in detail only.

Service Target drone WRE

Specification and production

Mark	Role	Engine	Thrust lb	Weight lb	Speed mph	Nos
I	Fighter	2xWelland	1,700	11,755	420	20
II	Fighter	2xGoblin	2,700	11,755	?	1
III	Fighter	2xDerwent I	3,500	14,460	520	210
IV	Fighter	2xDerwent 5	3,500	14,460	585	465
FR5	FR	2xDerwent 5	3,500	14,460	?	1
F6	Fighter	2xDerwent 7				
T7	Trainer	2xDerwent 8	3,500	17,600	585	642
F8	Fighter	2xDerwent 8	3,500	19,065	592	1079
T8	Adv trainer	2xDerwent 8	3,500	19,065	592	

Mark	Role	Engine	Thrust lb	Weight lb	Speed mph	Nos
F(TT)8	Target tug	2xDerwent 8	3,500	19,065	590	
FR9	FR	2xDerwent 8	3,500	15,770	592	126
PR10	PR	2xDerwent 8	3,500	15,400	541	59
NF11	Night fighter	2xDerwent 8	3,700	19,790	541	338
NF12	Night fighter	2xDerwent 9	3,800	20,380	541	100
NF13	Night fighter	2xDerwent 8	3,700	20,490	541	40
NF14	Night fighter	2xDerwent 8	3,700	20,444	576	100
NF(T)14	Nav trainer	2xDerwent 8	3,700	20,000	576	
U15	Target drone	2xDerwent 5	3,500	14,250	585	92*
U16	Target drone	2xDerwent 8	3,500	19,000	590	150+
D16	Target drone	U16 redesignated				
T17	Ej seat test	2xDerwent 8	3,500			2#
TT20	Target tug	2xDerwent 8	3,700	19,750	541	49~
U21	Target drone	2xDerwent 8	3,500			22+

* F4 conversions
\+ F8 conversions
\# T7 conversions
\~ NF11 conversions

Further reading

Gloster Meteor, Bowyer, C, Ian Allan, Shepperton, 1985

Gloster Meteor, The, Shacklady, E, Macdonald, London, 1962

Gloster Meteor F.IV, The (Profile 78) Partridge, J J, Profile Publications, Leatherhead, 1966

Gloster Meteor F.8, The (Profile 12) Andrews, C F, Profile Publications, Leatherhead, 1966

Meteor Philpott, B, Patrick Stephens, Wellingborough, 1986

2.6 North American Sabre (1953–1956)

The Korean war demonstrated the potency of contemporary Soviet aircraft, especially the MiG-15. At the time the current day fighter was the Meteor which was outclassed by the MiG type and the Hunter was not due in service in Germany until 1955. As a stop-gap the RAF took on charge Canadian-built Sabres, a type which had shown its superiority to the MiG-15 in combat. The aircraft were supplied by the United States under the Mutual Defence Aid Plan.

The Mark 1 was built in prototype form only in Canada. The F Mark 2 was equivalent to the American F-86E and three of this version were delivered to the United Kingdom. Armament was six .50" calibre machine-guns. The Mark 3 was another Canadian prototype fitted with an Orenda engine.

F Mark 4

The Mark 4 was the standard variant for the RAF, some 427 being delivered. It differed from the F Mk 2 only in

North American Sabre F Mk 4

The Canadair-built F-86E was bought in large numbers for the RAF to counter the Soviet threat and pending introduction of the (inferior) Hunter. The Sabre served, between 1953 and 1956 only, in thirteen squadrons, mainly in Germany. XB933/W was operated by 130 Sqn at Brüggen. *(2 Sqn records via A S Thomas)*

having a changed compass and canopy release. It was first to serve with 26 Sqn from May 1953 and was finally replaced by the Hunter in May 1956. All but two of the units operating the Sabre (66 and 92 Sqns) were based in Germany. On withdrawal from RAF service the aircraft were notionally returned to the USAF, but in fact overhauled in the UK and passed on to various NATO air forces.

Service Fighter 3, 4, 20, 26, 66, 67, 71, 92, 93, 112, 130, 147, 234 **Training** FTU; 229 OCU; SCF **Other** AFDS; CFE; CGS; FWS; 1 OFU; RAE

Specification and production

Mark	Role	Engine	Thrust lb	Weight lb	Speed mph	Nos
F2	Fighter	J-47 GE-13	5,200	16,500	670	3
F4	Fighter	J-47 GE-13	5,200	16,500	670	427

Further reading
Canadair Sabre, The, Milberry, L, CANAV, 1986
Canadair Sabre, The, (Profile 186) Joos, G, Profile Publications, Leatherhead, 1967
North American F-86A – L Sabre (Aircam 17) McDowell, E R, Osprey, Canterbury, 1967
North American F-86A Sabre, The (Profile 20) Shacklady, E, Profile Publications, Leatherhead, 1965
North American Sabre, The, Wagner, R, Macdonald, London, 1963

2.7 Supermarine Swift (1954–1961)

The Swift was developed to specification F.105, the contract being raised as a fall-back in the event of there being problems with the Hunter. The first stage in the evolution of the Swift was the **Supermarine 510** (VV106) which was intended as a high-speed fighter built to specification E.38/46; it flew on 29 December 1948. It had swept wings and tail combined with an Attacker fuselage and incorporated the latter's tailwheel undercarriage. In due course it was fitted with an arrester hook and as the

Supermarine 517 made carrier deck landings on HMS *Illustrious*. The second prototype (VV119) was designated **Supermarine 528**. It was later fitted with an afterburning Nene engine, a lengthened nose and tricycle undercarriage as the **Supermarine 535**. Via the Supermarine types 510 and 535, the Swift evolved from the straight-wing Attacker; 100 were ordered in 1950 and another 100 from Short and Harland in 1952. Performance problems led to cancellation of many of the fighters although the type served for some years in the fighter-reconnaissance role.

F Mark 1
The Type 541 flew first in production form on 25 August 1952 (WK194). It was fitted with two 30mm Aden cannon, had a fixed tailplane and an Avon 108 without reheat. Development problems delayed entry into service with 56 Sqn until February 1954. Twenty were built, several being used as prototypes for later variants.

Service Fighter 56 **Other** AFDS

F Mark 2
The Mark 2 first flew in December 1952 and sixteen were built. The version differed from the F Mk 1 in having four cannon and a cranked wing and like the earlier version it also served with 56 Sqn. Serviceability of the Swift was generally poor and it lasted just over one year in service before being replaced by the Hunter.

Service Fighter 56 **Other** AFDS

F Mark 3
The Mark 3, of which 25 were built, was similar to the F Mk 2 but with reheated engines. This version was to have formed a second Swift squadron but in the event none was issued to operational units, most serving as instructional airframes.

F Mark 4
The Type 546 was to have comprised the balance of the 100 initial order. Of the intended 39, although most were built, only eight were flown, the balance being converted to the FR Mk 5. The sole refinement added to the F Mk 4 was a variable incidence tailplane.

Supermarine Swift FR Mk 5

The Swift was ordered as a fall-back in the event of the Hunter not meeting expectations. Fortunately the Hunter worked out, for the Swift had a brief career as a fighter, being ultimately developed as a useful photo-reconnaissance platform. FR Mk 5 XD962/J was in service with 2 Sqn when this photo was taken in September 1960. *(Author)*

FR Mark 5

The Type 549 represented an attempt to salvage something from the Swift programme. The first aircraft of the new variant, XD903, flew on 25 May 1955 and the type entered service with the RAF in February 1956, being replaced by the Hunter FR Mk 10 in 1960. The FR Mk 5 featured a longer nose with three F.95 cameras and it was armed with two Aden cannon. A 220-gallon ventral fuel tank was fitted as standard and the wing incorporated a saw-tooth leading edge.

Service Fighter-reconnaissance 2, 4 **Other** AFDS; CFE; FTU

PR Mark 6

The Type 550 was an intended unarmed strategic reconnaissance aircraft but problems with reheat on the Avon at altitude led to the project being still-born.

F Mark 7

The Type 552 Mark 7 was the final Swift version built in small numbers (twelve) for guided weapons trials. Cannon armament was deleted and the wing-span increased by three feet. The engine was the more powerful Avon 716.

Service Trials 1 GWDS; GWTS; ETPS

Specification and production

Mark	Role	Engine	Thrust lb	Weight lb	Speed mph	Nos
F1	Fighter	Avon 108	7,500	15,800	660	20
F2	Fighter	Avon 108	7,500	15,800	660	16
F3	Fighter	Avon 114	7,500	15,800	660	25
F4	Fighter	Avon 114	7,500	15,800	660	8
FR5	Fighter-recce	Avon 114	7,175	21,673	713	94*
PR6	Photo-recce	Not built				
F7	Fighter	Avon 716	9,950	21,500	700	12

* including 31 F4 conversions

2.8 Hawker Hunter (1950–1993)

If the Spitfire was the classic piston-engined design, the Hawker Type P.1067 Hunter must surely have been the most beautiful jet aeroplane ever built. Like the Spitfire it had a reputation as a pilot's aircraft. After a failure to meet two specifications for a Meteor replacement (F.43/46 and F.44/46) a new specification, F.3/48, was issued against which the P.1067 was tendered. Outline design began in 1946 around the Rolls-Royce A.J.65 engine (later the Avon) and all flying surfaces were swept. Armament was to be two Aden cannon.

The design evolved from the **P.1040** (Sea Hawk) through the swept wing (straight tail assembly) **P.1052** and the fully swept **P.1081**. Three prototypes were ordered, one with the Sapphire engine. The first, WB188, flew from Boscombe Down on 20 July 1950 by which time 400 Hunters had been ordered, 200 with the Avon, the balance with the Sapphire. The second prototype was

Hawker Hunter F Mk 4

The Hunter was slow to enter service as an interceptor and was outclassed when it did. However, it was perhaps the most graceful of jet fighters and its lines are well shown in this classic photograph of F Mk 4 WV272/L of 74 Sqn seen at readiness at Horsham St Faith in 1957. (*Author's collection*)

equipped with four Aden cannon and gun-ranging radar in the nose.

F Mark 1

The first production variant was fitted with the Avon 113 engine. The type entered squadron service with 43 Sqn at Leuchars in July 1954 after development delays while the airbrake position was tested for optimum performance. The F Mk 1 suffered problems with the engine surging when the guns were fired at altitude.

Service Fighter 43, 54, 222 **Training** 229, 233 OCU **Other** CFE (AFDS, DFLS); ETPS; FWS; NGTE; RAE; RRE

F Mark 2

The Mark 2 was similar to the F Mk 1 but was fitted with the Sapphire 101 engine. Forty-five were manufactured by Armstrong-Whitworth Aircraft and went into service with just two units, 257 and 263 Squadrons at Wattisham.

Service Fighter 257, 263 **Other** 1; CFE (AFDS); RAE

F Mark 3

The designation was applied to the first prototype F Mk 1 fitted with an Avon RA7R engine delivering 9,600lb thrust in reheat. Other modifications included a pointed nose. The aircraft was used to set a new world air speed record of 727.6mph on 7 September 1953, flown by Sqn Ldr Neville Duke.

F Mark 4

The Mark 4 was the first significant Hunter variant. Earlier versions had limited fuel capacity and after tests on early production aircraft pylons for drop tanks were fitted. Internal fuel was also increased and the changes were incorporated on the production line. Later the Avon 115 was fitted, which cured the engine surging problem when gun-firing. The new engine was retrospectively fitted to most earlier aircraft.

Service Fighter 3, 4, 14, 20, 26, 43, 54, 66, 67, 71, 74, 92, 93, 98, 111, 112, 118, 130, 208, 222, 234, 245, 247 **Training** 12, 208; 229, 233, 237 OCU; RAFFC; CFS **Other** 167; APS Sylt; 3/4 CAACU; CFE (AFDS, DFLS); ETPS; FWS; RAE; RRE

F Mark 5

The Mark 5 brought to the F Mk 2 the same developments that the F Mk 4 incorporated from the Avon-engined F Mk 1. The version entered service in 1955 and was withdrawn from front-line units by 1958.

Service Fighter 1, 34, 41, 56, 257, 263 **Other** CFE (AFDS); RAE

F Mark 6

The P.1099 featured the Avon 200 series engine of 10,500lb thrust. The version was fitted for underwing stores and a wing leading edge extension to avoid pitch-up at high altitude under high g-loading. Faired link-collectors were fitted as standard to avoid damage to underwing tanks by spent shell casings. Numerous F Mk 6s were used for trials and two were converted to the Type P.1109 which had an extended nose radome and two Firestreak missiles on the outer wing pylons.

Service Fighter 1, 4, 14, 19, 20, 26, 34, 43, 54, 56, 63, 65, 66, 74, 92, 93, 111, 208, 247, 263 **Training** 4 FTS; 12, 216; 229 (63, 79, 145), 237 OCU; TWU **Other** CFE (AFDS, DFLS); CFCS; DFCS; FCS; FWS; RAE

F Mark 6A

This designation was applied to a number of F Mk 6 aircraft brought up to FGA Mk 9 standard.

Service Training TWU; 1 TWU (79); 2 TWU

T Mark 7

The P.1101 was a two-seat side-by-side trainer, initially developed as a private venture and ordered to specification T.157D. The first prototype, based on the F Mk 4, flew on 8 July 1955. A single Aden cannon was retained on the starboard side. Forty-five aircraft were built from new, while a further 28 were F Mk 4 conversions. Eventually the type served with most Hunter squadrons as well as with training units.

Service Training 1, 2, 4, 8, 14, 15, 16, 19, 20, 28, 43, 45, 54, 56, 58, 65, 66, 74, 92, 93, 111, 208, 216; 1417 Flt; 3/4 CAACU; CFS; DFCS; ETPS; FCIRS; FCS; 4 FTS;

Hawker Hunter FGA Mk 9

Ever a pilot's aircraft the Hunter came into its own in the ground-attack role. Well after it had been superseded by the Lightning as an interceptor it operated as an advanced weapons trainer as illustrated in this photograph of nine aircraft of 229 OCU (79 and 234 Sqns) in formation over the Devon coastline. *(BAe)*

IAM; 229, 237, 238 OCU; RAE; TMTS Scampton; TWU; 1, 2 TWU

T Mark 7A
The Mark 7A comprised T Mk 7s adapted to accommodate TACAN. The first aircraft to be modified was XF289.

Service Training 5, 12, 15, 16, 19, 23, 43, 45, 56, 74, 111, 208; 237 OCU; 1 TWU; WTS Sylt

T Mark 8
The Mark 8 was essentially similar to the T Mk 7 but was fitted with an arrester hook for naval use with airfield arrester gear. A total of 41 was built including 31 F Mk 4 conversions.

Service Training 111, 208; 237 OCU; 700B, 700X, 736, 738, 759, 764, 776, 800, 899 NAS; ADS; FRU; FRADU

T Mark 8B
This was the T Mk 8 with full TACAN provision. Four airframes were converted from the standard T Mk 8.

Service Training 759, 764, 800 NAS

T Mark 8C
The Mark 8C comprised eleven F Mk 4 or T Mk 8 conversions with partial TACAN.

Service Training 16; 237 OCU: 759 NAS; FRADU

T Mark 8M
The Mark 8M was specially developed to support the Royal Navy Sea Harrier programme. It was fitted with the Blue Fox radar in a redesigned nose.

Service Training 899 NAS

FGA Mark 9
The Mark 9 was an F Mk 6 conversion originally built to replace Venoms in the Middle East after competition with the Gnat. Braking parachutes were fitted and the aircraft was equipped with large, 230-gallon drop tanks and cockpit ventilation and refrigeration. The Avon 207 engine was selected but pending deliveries the 203 was fitted in an interim version; all aircraft were retrospectively fitted with the later engine. The Hunter FGA Mk 9 entered service with 1 and 8 Sqns in January 1960 and the type remained in front-line service until 1968. A total of 126 conversions was built.

Service Ground attack 1, 8, 20, 28, 43, 45, 54, 58, 208 **Training** HCT; 229 OCU; TWU; 1, 2 TWU **Other** RAE

FR Mark 10
The Mark 10 was yet another F Mk 6 conversion originally designed to specification FR.164D. The first of 33 conversions, XF429, flew on 7 November 1958. Two ex Swift units were equipped with the type and several were flown by 8 Sqn in Aden.

Service Fighter reconnaissance 2, 4, 8; 1417 Flt **Training** 229 OCU

GA Mark 11
The Mark 11 was built for the Royal Navy to serve in the Fleet Requirements and Air Direction roles in support of naval vessels. Forty were built as F Mk 4 conversions fitted with TACAN and an arrester hook.

Service Training 738, 764, 776; FRU; FRADU

PR Mark 11
This was the designation applied to the GA Mk 11 fitted with an interchangeable camera nose.

Service Fleet Requirements FRADU

Mark 12
The Mark 12 designation was applied to a sole Hunter F Mk 6 conversion, XE531, fitted with two seats and head-up display (HUD) for TSR2 trials.

Service Trials RAE

Specification and production

Mark	Role	Engine	Thrust lb	Weight lb	Speed mph	Nos
F1	Fighter	Avon 107/113	7,550	16,200	675	139
F2	Fighter	Sapphire 101	8,000	16,200	680	45
F3	Experimental	Avon RA7R	7,500	16,000	721	1
F4	Fighter	Avon 115/121	7,550	17,100	675	365
F5	Fighter	Sapphire 101	8,000	17,100	680	105
F6	Fighter	Avon 203	10,150	17,910	715	139
F6A	Trainer	Avon 207	10,150	18,000	710	25*
T7	Trainer	Avon 122	8,000	17,200	690	45$
T8	Trainer	Avon 122	8,000	17,200	690	10+
T8B	Trainer	Avon 122	8,000	17,200	690	4#
T8C	Trainer	Avon 122	8,000	17,200	690	11#
T8M	Trainer	Avon 122	8,000	17,200	690	10#
FGA9	Ground attack	Avon 207	10,150	18,000	71	126*
FR10	Fighter recce	Avon 207	10,150	18,090	710	33*
GA11	Trainer	Avon 122	7,550	17,100	700	40^
PR11	Trainer	Avon 122	7,550	17,100	700	
Mk 12	Research	Avon 208	10,150	17,600	690	1*

* F6 conversions
$ plus 28 F4 conversions
+ plus 31 F4 conversions
# T8 conversions
^ F4 conversions

Further reading
Hawker Hunter, Hardy, M J, Winchmore Publishing Service, 1986
Hawker Hunter, Jackson, R, Ian Allan, Shepperton, 1983
Hawker Hunter, Mason, F K, Patrick Stephens, Wellingborough, 1981
Hawker Hunter F6, The (Profile 4) Mason, F K, Profile Publications, Leatherhead, 1965
Hawker Hunter Two-Seaters, The (Profile 167) Mason, F K, Profile Publications, Leatherhead, 1967
Hunter Squadrons, Ward, R L, Linewrights, Essex, 1986

2.9 Gloster Javelin (1951–1968)

The Gloster Type GA.5 Javelin was designed by Glosters to specification F.4/48 for an all-weather fighter capable of a maximum speed of 600mph at 40,000ft. The solution was a large, twin-engined delta, the first of its kind in the world. The Javelin was also the first fighter to introduce guided weapon armament into the RAF.

The first prototype (WD804) flew from Moreton Valence on 26 November 1951; it was followed by four further prototypes. The type was evaluated by an American delegation and the Javelin was ordered in quantity applying much of the £37m funding from the US under the Mutual Defence Aid Plan. The aircraft replaced the Meteor NF Mks 11/12 and Venom NF Mk 3 in service. Its top speed was some 45mph better than that of the Meteor and its ceiling 12,500ft higher at 52,500ft.

F(AW) Mark 1
The Mark 1 was powered by the Sapphire Sa6 and equipped with the AI17 radar. Armament was four 30mm Aden cannon in the outer wing. A total of 40 was built and it joined 46 Sqn in February 1956.

Service Fighter 46, 87 **Other** CFE

F(AW) Mark 2
The Mark 2 was similar to the F(AW) Mk 1 but equipped with US AI22 (APQ-43) radar in an enlarged radome. It entered service in June 1957 with 46 Sqn.

Service Fighter 46, 85, 89 **Other** CFE (AWDS)

T Mark 3
The trainer variant was built to specification T118D calling for a machine with dual control. The cockpit was redesigned to allow for the rear seat to be raised and an enlarged canopy fitted. External periscopes on the fuselage side assisted the instructor (in the rear seat) to view gun-aiming.

Service Training 3, 5, 11, 23, 25, 29, 33, 41, 46, 60, 64, 72, 85, 87, 151; JIRS; 226, 228 OCU **Other** FCIRS

F(AW) Mark 4
The Mark 4 was similar to the F(AW) Mk 1 but with an all-moving tailplane fitted. Fifty were built and the version served with eight squadrons.

Service Fighter 3, 11, 23, 41, 72, 87, 96, 141 **Other** CFE (AWDS)

F(AW) Mark 5
This variant improved on the range of the F(AW) Mk 4 by introducing a new wing with internal tanks for an additional 250 gallons of fuel.

Service Fighter 5, 11, 41, 72, 87, 151 **Training** 228 OCU Other IAM

F(AW) Mark 6
The Mark 6 incorporated all the developments of the F(AW) Mk 5 but reverted to the US radar of the F(AW) Mk 2. The type, of which 33 were constructed, was issued to four squadrons including those using the F(AW) Mk 2, which employed both versions concurrently.

Gloster Javelin F Mk 2

The Javelin was the first RAF aircraft to employ a delta wing planform and was also the first to introduce guided weapon armament. F Mk 2s XA812/B and XA733/S of 46 Sqn make a rapid departure from Odiham in 1958. *(Author's collection)*

Service Fighter 29, 46, 85, 89 **Other** CFE (AFDS); FTU; IAM

F(AW) Mark 7

The Mark 7 was the most numerous of all versions of the Javelin. It was fitted with the Sapphire Sa7 delivering an extra 3,000lb static thrust (11,000lb) over the Sa6. The fuselage was lengthened to accommodate the engines and revised nozzles were incorporated. Armament was extended to include four wing-mounted Firestreak air-to-air missiles. It had been intended to reduce the cannon armament to two, but delays in Firestreak development led to the retention of the original four guns in many aircraft. The F(AW) Mk 7 entered service with 33 Sqn in July 1958 and with full Firestreak armament with 25 Sqn in December of that year.

Service Fighter 23, 25, 33, 64 **Training** 228 OCU **Other** CFE (AFDS, AWDS); 1 GWTS; NGTE; RAE

F(AW) Mark 8

The Mark 8 was the final production version of the Javelin. It employed the Sa7R Sapphire with partial reheat which enabled it to outclimb and out-turn the Hunter. It used the US radar coupled to a Sperry autopilot. The version also had a revised wing with a slightly drooped leading edge and double rows of vortex generators. Other improvements included simpler engine starting and better windscreen rain dispersal.

Service Fighter 41, 85 **Other** CFE (AFDS)

F(AW) Mark 9

The Mark 9 was the definitive version of the Javelin although there were no new-build aircraft; all (116) were conversions of the F(AW) Mk 7. They differed from the Mark 7 by incorporating the reheated Sapphire and the wing of the F(AW) Mk 8. Numerous minor improvements were included, although they did not alter the external appearance.

Service Fighter 5, 11, 23, 25, 29, 33, 64, **Training** 228 OCU **Other** CFE(AFDS); 12 GFU RAE;

F(AW) Mark 9R

This was the Mark 9 with extended range (R). As the RAF lost staging posts between the UK and the Far East in the 1960s, it became important to fit the Javelin with in-flight refuelling. Large probes were fitted to the starboard fuselage and canted underwing pylons accommodated four 230-gallon tanks. Twenty-two aircraft were converted. The Javelin was withdrawn from service when 60 Sqn disbanded at Singapore on 30 April 1968.

Service Fighter 23, 29, 60, 64

Specification and Production

Mark	Role	Engine	Thrust lb	Weight lb	Speed mph	Nos
F(AW)1	AW fighter	2xSapphire Sa6	8,000	36,690	710	40
F(AW)2	AW fighter	2xSapphire Sa6	8,000	37,200	710	30
T3	Trainer	2xSapphire Sa6	8,000	42,000	640	22
F(AW)4	AW fighter	2xSapphire Sa6	8,000	37,480	702	50
F(AW)5	AW fighter	2xSapphire Sa6	8,000	39,370	705	64
F(AW)6	AW fighter	2xSapphire Sa6	8,000	40,600	705	33
F(AW)7	AW fighter	2xSapphire Sa7	11,000	40,270	710	142
F(AW)8	AW fighter	2xSapphire Sa7R	11,000	42,510	702	47
F(AW)9	AW fighter	2xSapphire Sa7R	11,000	43,165	702	116*
F(AW)9R	AW fighter	2xSapphire Sa7R	11,000	43,165	702	41$

* conversions from F(AW)7
$ conversions from F(AW)9

Further reading

Gloster Javelin, Allward, M, Ian Allan, London, 1983
Gloster Javelin 1-6 (Profile 179) Partridge, J, Profile Publications, Leatherhead, 1967
Gloster Javelin Marks 1 to 6, Lindsay, R, Privately published, Stockton-on-Tees, 1976
Gloster Javelin Marks 7 to 9R, Lindsay, R, Privately published, Stockton-on-Tees

2.10   English Electric Lightning (1954–1988)

Where the Hunter was ultimately shapely, its successor was the epitome of functionality; the Lightning's curves were confined to the fuselage cross-section.

The original design study was in response to a research specification ER.103 of 1947. Both English Electric and Fairey Aviation submitted designs. That from the latter company was a pure research design, the FD.2, whereas the English Electric design, the P.1, had operational potential built in. As a result specification F.23/49 was issued which extended the P.1 concept to include operational fighter equipment.

The original design incorporated highly swept wings and a low-set tailplane, about which characteristics there was some official concern. Apart from investment in a new wind tunnel by English Electric, it was also decided to build a flying model to test wing sweep and tailplane setting, especially at low speeds. The **Short SB5** (WG768) with fixed undercarriage and powered by a Derwent engine flew on 2 December 1952. The wings could be swept (on the ground) to 50°, 60° and 69° and the tailplane position could be moved from fin-tip to lower fuselage.

As a result of tests on the SB5 the design was set with 60° wing sweep and with a low-set tailplane. Three prototype P.1A aircraft were ordered and the first (WG760) flew on 4 August 1954. No operational equipment was built in and the power was provided by two Sapphire Sa5 engines of 8,100lb thrust. The engines were mounted one above the other, but staggered to reduce frontal area. On its third flight on 11 August WG760 became the first British aircraft to exceed Mach 1 in level flight.

The research design was then developed into the proto-

English Electric Lightning F Mk 6

The Lightning was the match of any aircraft and although short-legged and unforgiving was a superb interceptor. Four F Mk 6 aircraft of 23 Sqn (Leuchars) formate in their element. Through the 1960s the Lightning force operated in bare metal finish, often with colourful unit markings. Nearest is XR754/M which displays an enlarged version of the squadron's eagle crest. *(Crown copyright)*

type fighter as the P.1B designed to accommodate missiles and Ferranti AI23 Airpass radar in the nose shock cone. The first of three, XA847, flew on 4 April 1957 and on 25 November 1958 the aircraft flew at Mach 2 for the first time. The P.1B had two Avon engines of 11,250lb thrust (14,350lb with reheat) and the fuselage was re-designed to take the larger engine.

In October 1958 the type was named Lightning and 50 were ordered, the first 20 to be pre-production machines for a wide range of development work. Several of the later of these aircraft served with the AFDS.

The Lightning was almost certainly the last single-seat fighter to be designed and built in Britain. On its entry into service it represented a spectacular advance over the Hunter, with its top speed in excess of Mach 2 and a ceiling of 60,000ft which it could reach in little over a minute. It remained in front-line service from 1960 to 1987.

F Mark 1
The designation was applied to the balance of the first order of 30 production aircraft. During development

work with the pre-production machines the fin height was increased but in other respects the design was unchanged. Armament was fixed at two Firestreak air-to-air missiles and two 30mm Aden cannon in the nose. The Lightning entered service with 74 Sqn in June 1960.

Service Fighter 74 **Training** LCU; LTF; 226 OCU **Target Facilities** 5, 23, 111; Binbrook, Leconfield, Leuchars, Wattisham TFFs **Other** CFE (AFDS)

F Mark 1A
This differed from the F Mk 1 in several respects. Provision was made for in-flight refuelling through a detachable probe fitted under the port wing and the radio fit was changed from VHF to UHF. Wiring changes to the missile pylons resulted in external ducts along the fuselage side. The engine was the Avon 210R with a four-position reheat control.

Service Fighter 56, 111 **Target Facilities** 5, 11, 23 **Other** FCTU

F Mark 2

The Mark 2 was externally virtually similar to the F Mk 1A but it incorporated several internal changes. These included improved navigation equipment, a steerable nosewheel, offset TACAN, liquid oxygen breathing and variable nozzle reheat. The only external difference was a small intake scoop on the fuselage spine for a DC standby generator. The first F Mk 2 (XN723) flew on 11 July 1961 and the version entered service with 19 Sqn at Leconfield in December 1962.

Service Fighter 19, 92 **Other** CFE (AFDS)

F Mark 2A

This was the F Mk 2 rebuilt to incorporate some F Mk 6 features; 31 of the original 44 F Mk 2s were converted from 1968. The engines fitted were the Avon RA211R but the F Mk 2 armament fit was retained. External features were the most noticeable, comprising the cambered wing, square-cut fin and much enlarged ventral tank of the F Mk 6.

Service Fighter 19,92 **Other** RAE

F Mark 3

The Mark 3 employed the Avon 301R and was the fastest of the Lightnings having a superb power to weight ratio of nearly 1:1. Armament was changed to the Red Top collision course missile (two carried) mated to the revised AI23B radar; the Aden cannon were omitted. The fin was enlarged by 15% and given a square-cut tip to maintain stability with the new missile. The F Mk 3 retained the original small ventral tank and range was limited. Cockpit instrumentation was brought up to full OR946 Integrated Flight System standard. The F Mk 3 joined the RAF with 23 Sqn in August 1964.

Service Fighter 23, 29, 56, 74, 111 **Training** 5, 11; 226 OCU; LTF **Target Facilities** Leuchars, Wattisham TFFs **Other** CFE (AFDS); FCTU

F Mark 3A

This was the designation applied to the F Mk 3 developed primarily to extend range. The designation was changed to F Mark 6 before entry into service.

T Mark 4

This was the first of the two-seat trainer versions of the potent fighter, based on the F Mk 1A. The upper forward fuselage was widened to accommodate side-by-side seats and the cannon armament deleted.

Service Training 19, 23, 56, 74, 111; LCS; 226 OCU **Other** RAE

T Mark 5

The Mark 5 was the second trainer version based on the F Mk 3 with provision for either Firestreak or Red Top missiles. The variant was fully operational.

Service Training 5, 11, 23, 29, 56, 74, 111; 226 OCU; LTF **Target Facilities** Wattisham TDFF

F Mark 6

The Mark 6 was the ultimate Lightning, developed from the F Mk 3. The prototype was F Mk 3 XP697 which flew in its new guise on 17 April 1964. The aircraft featured a new cambered wing which reduced drag and improved range at subsonic speeds. The wing also incorporated a revised spar which enabled the carriage of jettisonable overwing tanks. Range was further extended by a new ventral tank, with twin strakes, carefully designed to reduce drag and increasing the external fuel from 250 gals to 600 gals. From 1970 a number of F Mk 6s were fitted with two 30mm Aden cannon in the forward section of the ventral tank since the missile-only armament did not confer sufficient flexibility in handling Soviet North Sea reconnaissance flights.

Service Fighter 5, 11, 23, 56, 74, 111 **Training** 226 OCU; LTF

English Electric Lightning F Mk 6

Fine judgement indeed! Flt/Lt Chris Allan of 11 Sqn pushes Lightning F Mk 6 XS929/BG to Mach 0.98 almost on the deck. The occasion was a very watery final Binbrook display on 22 August 1987. *(Author)*

Specification and production

Mark	Role	Engine	Thrust lb	Weight lb	Speed	Nos
F1	Fighter	2xAvon 200R	11,250	25,753	M2.1	19
F1A	Fighter	2xAvon 210R	11,250	25,737	M2.1	28
F2	Fighter	2xAvon 210R	11,250	27,000	M2.1	44
F2A	Fighter	2xAvon 211R	11,250	27,500	M2.1	31*
F3	Fighter	2xAvon 301R	12,690	26,905	M2.2	70
F3A	Fighter	2xAvon 301R	12,690	28,041	M2.2	16
T4	Trainer	2xAvon 210R	11,250	27,000	M2.1	20
T5	Trainer	2xAvon 301R	13,200	27,000	M2.2	22
F6	Fighter	2xAvon 301R	13,200	28,041	M2.2	38+

* F2 conversions
+ plus 9 F3 conversions

Further reading

BAC Lightning, Jackson, P A, Alan Hall Pubs, Amersham, 1977

BAC Lightning, The (Air Extra 14) Cornwell, E L (ed), Ian Allan, Shepperton, 1978

English Electric (BAC) Lightning (Aircam 37) Levy, R, Osprey, Canterbury, 1972

English Electric/BAC Lightning, Philpott, B, Patrick Stephens, Wellingborough, 1984

English Electric Lightning, Beamont, R, Ian Allan, Shepperton, 1985

English Electric Lightning, Halpenny, B B, Osprey, London, 1984

English Electric P1 and Lightning 1 (Profile 114) James, H G, Profile Publications, Leatherhead, 1966

Lightning, Black, I, Airlife, Shrewsbury, 1988

Lightning, Lindsay, R, Ian Allan, Shepperton, 1989

Lightning, Reed, A, Ian Allan, London, 1984

Lightning: The Operational History, Darling, K, Airlife, Shrewsbury, 1996

Lightnings Live On! Trevor, H (ed), Lightning Preservation Group, Bruntingthorpe, 1996

2.11   McDonnell Phantom (1968–1992)

The McDonnell Phantom rates as one of the most successful warplanes of all time. It was developed by the company which had produced the F2H Banshee and F3H Demon shipboard fighters as an air defence fighter for the United States Navy. First flight of the F4H-1, as the new aircraft was initially designated, was on 27 May 1958. The first F4H-1 Phantoms entered USN service with VF74 in July 1961. The new comprehensive designation system introduced in 1962 resulted in the F4H becoming the F-4. Before that time the F4H had been selected by the USAF as a tactical fighter designated F-110. Subsequently the Phantom served with distinction in a range of roles with US air arms and further afield.

Selection of the Phantom for British services was the result of strong but inappropriate government policy between 1957 and 1965 when the TSR.2 was cancelled. The Hunter ground attack replacement was due to be the Hawker P.1154, a type which the Royal Navy was encouraged to buy as a Sea Vixen replacement. The operational requirements were so dissimilar that both users had to accept compromise which eventually led to the Navy looking instead to the Phantom which had been vigorously marketed. When the TSR.2 was cancelled, the initial replacement was the F-111K which in turn was cancelled in favour of the Phantom and Buccaneer.

McDonnell Douglas Phantom FGR Mk 2

The Phantom started its RAF service as a Canberra replacement following cancellation of the TSR.2 and F-111K order. When the Jaguar entered service the Phantom switched to the interceptor role in the United Kingdom and Germany. FGR Mk 2 XV485/P of 23 Sqn thunders away from Wattisham in March 1982 with full reheat. *(Author)*

From 1962 McDonnell had been studying F-4 and Rolls-Royce Spey compatibility and orders for the type for both British air arms specified the Spey engine. In addition British avionics were specified although the Westinghouse AWG-10 radar was retained, albeit built in the UK under licence. The Royal Navy's requirement was subsequently reduced in size when the government in 1968 decided to scrap the carrier force. Phantoms in British service (except the F-4J) were easily distinguished from other variants. The Spey installation resulted in a 20% larger air intake and quite different, drooping jetpipes. From 1976 the distinctive Marconi ARI18228 RWR was added to the fin-tip.

FG Mark 1

The Mark 1 was the senior service's version of the Phantom, the original order for which was 140. The type was based on the F-4J and designated F-4K. The nose cone was hinged to allow use of British carrier lifts and the nosewheel leg increased in height to 40in to increase the angle of attack at launch. Other devices to ease operation from small carriers included a strengthened undercarriage and arrester hook, drooped ailerons and enlarged leading edge flaps.

The Phantom was not built with internal armament and the naval aircraft were not fitted for the SUU-23A under-fuselage gunpack. In the air defence role armament options were four AIM-9 Sidewinders and four AIM-7 Sparrow air-to-air missiles. In the ground attack or strike roles there was provision for the carriage of up to 16,000lb of stores on eight underwing and one fuselage hardpoints. A wide range of stores could be carried and on British aircraft the wing points were capable of taking 1,000lb bombs. In the air defence role the eight missile fit would typically be complemented by two 370-gallon wing tanks and one 600-gallon centreline tank. In the attack roles stores would normally be confined to around 6,000lb plus fuel tanks. The FG Mk 1 entered naval service with 700P NAS in April 1968 and with the decision to reduce the naval requirement, some went direct to the RAF (43 Sqn) from September 1969.

Service Air defence 43, 111 **Fighter, ground attack** 892 NAS **Training** 700P, 767 NAS; PTF

FGR Mark 2

The Mark 2 was the RAF version of the Phantom, the F-4M. It was similar to the FG Mk 1 but lacked the extendable nose leg and had a standard stabilator. The version was also fitted for the SUU-23A gun-pod and some were wired for the EMI reconnaissance pod carried on the centreline. The RWR was also fitted from 1976 and some aircraft were equipped with dual controls. The FGR Mk 2 began its operational RAF career with 6 Sqn in January 1969 and it was used primarily in the tactical role until replaced by Jaguars. The last tactical operator was 41 Sqn which replaced its aircraft in September 1977. Two units, 2 and 41 Sqns, had a primary reconnaissance role. From 1974 the FGR Mk 2 was switched to the air defence role; the last was withdrawn from UK service with 56 Sqn in June 1992, while 1435 Flt in the Falklands converted to the Tornado two months later.

Service Air defence 19, 23, 29, 43, 56, 74, 92, 111; 1435 Flt **Tactical** 2, 6, 14, 17, 31, 41, 54; **Training** 228 OCU (64)

F Mark 3/F-4J

F Mk 3 was the initial designation applied to fifteen F-4J aircraft (F-4JUK) purchased to address the reduction in air defence capability when one unit had to be based in the Falklands. The designation was soon withdrawn in favour of the F-4J label in order to avoid confusion with the Tornado F Mk 3. The aircraft retained their American engines and equipment and were thus physically very different from the Spey-engined variants; in addition the grey paint scheme, applied in the States, had a pink sheen. The F-4J was operated by one unit, 74 Sqn at Wattisham, from July 1984 to early 1991.

Service Air defence 74

Specification and production

Mark	Role	Engine	Thrust lb	Weight lb	Speed mph	Nos
FG1	Fighter	2xSpey 203	20,515*	58,000	M1.9	50
FGR2	Fighter	2xSpey 202	20,515*	58,000	M1.9	116
F4JUK	Fighter	2xJ79-GE-10	17,900*	61,795	M2.1	15

* with reheat

Further reading

Many books have been written about the Phantom. Listed below are those which relate in whole or in part to British use.

F4 Phantom; A Pilot's Story, Prest, R, Cassell, London, 1979
F-4 Phantom, Gunston, W, Ian Allan, Shepperton, 1977
F-4 Phantom (Air Extra 40) Horseman, M (ed), Ian Allan, Shepperton, 1983
McDonnell Douglas F-4 Phantom (Profile 208) Turner, P, St J, Profile Publications, Windsor, 1973
McDonnell Douglas F-4K and F-4M Phantom II, Burns, M, Osprey, London, 1984
McDonnell F-4 Phantom; Spirit in the Skies, Lake, J (ed), Aerospace Publishing, London, 1993
Phantom: A Legend in its Own Time, Mason, K, Patrick Stephens, Cambridge, 1984
RAF Phantom Foster, P R, Ian Allan, Shepperton, 1989
The Phantom Story, Thornborough, A M, Arms and Armour, London, 1994

2.12 British Aerospace EAP (1986) and Eurofighter 2000

In 1982 the partners in the Tornado aircraft, Panavia, agreed to cooperate on the design and manufacture of a new agile fighter to meet NATO staff requirements. The type was intended to secure and maintain air superiority in combat and at long range and would have to be capable of short field performance in all weathers. Shortly afterwards the German and Italian parties withdrew from the programme but British Aerospace continued with development of the Experimental Aircraft Programme (EAP). The first and only example of the aircraft (ZF534) flew on 8 August 1986. Powered by two RB.199 Mk 104D turbofans, it embraced many advanced features.

The fact that BAe kept the project alive through the

Eurofighter 2000

The Eurofighter is, as its name implies, a multinational
programme involving Germany, Italy, Spain and the
United Kingdom. British single-seat prototype
DA-2 ZH588 shows off the clean lines of the
intended multi-role fighter. *(BAe)*

demonstrator probably ensured that the specification was resurrected as revised ESR-D. Now the Panavia partners were to be joined by CASA in Spain; in 1988 two main development contracts were signed calling for seven development aircraft known in the short term as the European Fighter Aircraft (EFA). The first of these, DA-1 98+29, powered by two RB.199-22 engines, flew on 27 March 1994 while the British prototype, DA-2 ZH588, flew on 6 April of the same year. DA-3 (Italy) flew on 4 June 1995 and the first two-seater (Spain DA-6) on 31 August 1996. With a British commitment to production made in September 1996 the future of the type looks secure and it should enter service in 2002.

Specification and production

Mark	Role	Engine	Thrust lb	Weight lb	Speed	Nos
EAP	Fighter	2xRB.199 104D	17,000*	32,000	M2.0+	1
EF 2000	Fighter	2xEJ200	20,000*	37,000	M2.0+	7

* with reheat

3 – Fighters: ground attack, close support, light strike

SEPECAT Jaguar GR Mk 1

For over twenty years the Jaguar provided the backbone of the RAF's ground attack and tactical reconnaissance force, serving in the Gulf and Bosnia. In this fine shot XZ104/24 of 2 Sqn is seen over Mt Stromboli off the north coast of Sicily in November 1982. Normally based at Laarbruch in Germany, the unit was detached to Decimomannu in Sardinia for weapons-firing practice. *(Crown copyright)*

See also: Hunter (2.8); Phantom (2.11); Spitfire (2.1); Tempest (2.2)

The types included in this chapter are those that were used, in the main, for ground attack, close support of ground troops or light, tactical, bombing. Inevitably, many units operating in the ground attack role had a secondary air defence capability while some units operating in the air defence role had a reciprocal close support role, albeit with gun rather than rocket or bomb armament. For some time fighters which did not meet expectations in the air defence role – mainly in respect of climb rate or performance at height – were relegated to ground attack where a steady, robust, low-level platform was more important than speed alone. In this way aircraft like the Typhoon, Beaufighter and Hornet were all used operationally in the close support role.

Similarly as jets like the Vampire and Hunter were superseded in their air defence roles they continued in use as ground attack platforms. In the post-war years it was only aircraft like the Jaguar and Harrier which were designed for the tactical strike or close support roles from the outset. While the Tornado is a sound interdictor and long-range interceptor it is not a genuine multi-role aircraft, but for the future the EFA is intended to meet the air defence and close support roles equally effectively and without compromising either.

January 1946

In the UK there remained a number of tactical fighter Mustang units, most of which were due to disband shortly. In addition there was a Tempest II wing in the south. In Bomber Command there were three Mosquito light bomber squadrons with a further two strike squadrons within Coastal Command. The Mosquito equipped ten units in Germany which also hosted four Tempest units.

In the Mediterranean theatre three Mustang units were based in Italy waiting to disband while a Beaufighter squadron was in Greece following the civil war there with a Mustang and Hurricane unit in Palestine where there was also civil unrest. In the Far East the Mosquito (six squadrons) was supplemented by eight Thunderbolt units and 27 Sqn flying Beaufighters primarily in the search and rescue role. Distribution of units to some extent reflected actual or potential trouble spots – the Netherlands East Indies, Malaya and Indo-China.

The training units used contemporary fighters, with the Typhoon soldiering on with 56 OTU.

July 1948

Within the space of two and a half years the number of close support/light bomber units had diminished considerably. There were no ground attack fighters in the UK but the light bomber units comprised two Mosquito squadrons. There were a further four Mosquito units in Germany which also had three Tempest squadrons. Britain had withdrawn from Greece and Palestine and the Tempest equipped five squadrons across the region. The two Beaufighter squadrons in the Far East were shortly to become embroiled in the insurrection in Malaya.

January 1950

Although the Mosquito still equipped two units in the UK and four in Germany new types were now in evidence. The Vampire in ground attack form served with three Germany-based squadrons and one in the UK while the Brigand light bomber had succeeded the Beaufighter in the Middle East and Far East. There was a Wing of Tempest F Mk 6s in Egypt and Operation 'Firedog' in Malaya had seen the transfer of 33 Sqn with the Tempest Mk II from Germany to Changi.

Fighter Weapons School, Land/Air Warfare and Control & Reporting

By early 1946 there were still two **Air Gunnery Schools**, numbers 10 and 11, at Barrow and Andreas respectively. The former closed in June 1946, while 11 AGS soldiered on at Jurby until 15 October 1947. In addition there was the **Central Gunnery School** which had formed in November 1939 at Warmwell and which had moved to Leconfield in November 1945. The function of the gunnery schools was initially to provide advanced training to bomber air gunners and in due course to fighter pilots. The task included the firing of rockets. In 1955 the CGS was renamed the **Fighter Weapons School** (FWS) which in October 1957 moved to Driffield where it remained until March 1958 when it merged into the **Central Fighter Establishment** (CFE).

The CGS operated in close collaboration with the **Empire Air Armament School** (EAAS) at Manby. The School became part of the **Royal Air Force Flying College** (RAFFC) on 31 July 1949 and the RAFFC in due course became the **College of Air Warfare** (CAW) in 1962.

The **School of Air Support** (SAS) was formed in 70 Group at Old Sarum on 5 November 1944 to coordinate all training in air support for ground units including tactical reconnaissance and forward air control. In July 1945 it transferred to 11 Group Fighter Command and on 1 May it was renamed the **School of Land/Air Warfare** (SL/AW). The School disbanded into the **Joint Warfare Establishment** (JWE) on 31 March 1963. The JWE was formed at Old Sarum from SL/AW and the Amphibious Warfare School (AWS) and it quickly transferred to Transport Command concentrating on helicopter tactics. It disbanded on 22 July 1976.

A miscellany of units supported the control of aircraft, including fighters, in the air and for convenience these are listed together in this section.

The Army air observation post squadrons in Italy had pioneered Forward Air Control with Austers, reporting targets to their batteries where RAF liaison officers took the references and called in close support fighters. After the war the technique appears to have been taught haphazardly but from mid 1975 C Flight of 79 Sqn, 1 Tactical Weapons Unit operated three Jet Provost T Mk 4 trainers as the **Joint Forward Air Controllers Standards and Training Unit** (JFACSTU). In March 1989 the role transferred to 6 Flying Training School at Finningley with the Hawk T Mk 1 and then on 1 October 1995 to 100 Sqn at Leeming.

The **Fighter Command Control and Reporting School** (FCCRS) was formed on 19 December 1945 at Rudloe Manor, Box. It absorbed the **SCR.584 Training Unit** which had formed 25 January 1945 at Drem to train controllers to support aircraft using the AI Mk X. The Flying element with the Spitfire XIV and F Mk 16 was at Middle Wallop to where FCCRS moved on 12 January 1948. From 16 March 1953, 288 Sqn provided Balliol aircraft for the School. CRS then became the **School of Fighter Control** (SFC) on 9 September 1957 in 11 Group at Hope Cove, moving on 31 October 1958 to Sopley; by 18 April 1960 the aircraft element had gone.

The School was re-formed on 1 October 1968 from the **RAF School of Flying Control** as the **RAF School of Control and**

Reporting at Bawdsey, moving on 31 October 1974 to West Drayton and then in June 1990 to Boulmer. On the disbanding of the CRS in September 1957 the **School of Fighter Plotting** (SFP) formed at Middle Wallop in 81 Group with the Balliol until it disbanded on 1 March 1958.

The **Empire Air Navigation School** (EANS) at Shawbury became the **Central Navigation School** (CNS) on 31 July 1949. This in turn was re-designated the **Central Navigation and Control School** (CNCS) in 21 Group on 10 February 1950. In a separate strand, the **School of Flying Control** (SFC) at Watchfield had become the **School of Air Traffic Control** (SATC) on 1 November 1946 in 50 Group, switching on 21 April 1947 to 25 Group. When CNCS was formed in 1950 it absorbed SATC, transferring into 25 Group in February 1955. It was redesignated **Central Air Traffic Control School** (CATCS), still at Shawbury, on 11 February 1963. Although extant, the School lost its own aircraft from 4 July 1989.

July 1952

By now the Vampire fighter-bomber was in widespread use, primarily with the auxiliary squadrons, while the Mosquito was about to be replaced by the Canberra. With the RAF at its post-war peak there were sixteen Vampire squadrons in Germany, six in the Middle East and two in the Far East. No 8 Sqn was based in Aden with the Brigand anticipating the strife to come. The war in Malaya continued and the sole Brigand unit there was complemented by two Hornet squadrons with a third in Hong Kong.

Training arrangements had changed with the onset of the Korean War and increasing tension through the Cold War. A number of advanced flying schools had been established including one for ground attack training and two operational conversion units prepared aircrew for combat.

January 1955

There were no regular close support units in the UK but ten auxiliary squadrons continued flying with the Vampire FB Mk 5. Things were different in Germany where the new Venom served with nine units in three Wings with the Vampire replaced by the potent air-superiority Sabre. The Venom also held sway in the Middle East except in Aden where the Vampire had replaced the Brigand. In the Far East the Vampire and Hornet served in five squadrons in Hong Kong and Malaya where the communist terrorists were being defeated.

July 1957

The Hunter had been introduced from 1954 in the air defence role but it had a secondary ground attack capability. By 1957 it was in widespread use having also replaced the short-lived Sabre stop-gap fighter in Germany, where two Wings of Venoms were based. Two interdictor variants of the Canberra were also in service with three squadrons in Germany. In the Middle East the Venom served with three squadrons, having played a part in the Suez operation and operating against rebels in Aden. In the Far East the Venom remained with three squadrons, two of which were involved in the final stages of Operation 'Firedog'.

July 1960

Perhaps the most important development at this time was the introduction of the ground attack version of the Hunter, the FGA Mk 9, which equipped three units in the UK and one each in Aden and Kenya. In Germany there were no longer close support fighters, but four Canberra interdictor units. The insurrection in Malaya had been defeated and the sole close support unit in the Far East was 28 Sqn in Hong Kong.

January 1965

The Hunter FGA Mk 9 was the standard close support fighter with two units in the UK, four in Aden and Oman and two in the Far East, one of which was heavily engaged in the confrontation in Borneo. In Germany there remained the Canberra light bombers which also equipped a large tactical, nuclear capable, wing in Cyprus with a further squadron in Malaya.

January 1970

Two very different aircraft had just entered service, both with extraordinary performance. The most significant from a close support standpoint was the Harrier, the world's first operational short/vertical take-off and landing aircraft which appropriately entered service with 1 Sqn. The other introduction was the potent Phantom which served with two ground attack squadrons pending the introduction of the Jaguar. Tactical capability in the Middle East was confined to one Hunter squadron at Muharraq. In the Far East the long-serving Hong Kong unit, No 28 Sqn, had given up an offensive role having converted to helicopters, while single squadrons of the Canberra and Hunter were based in Malaya.

January 1975

Re-equipment of the RAF had continued with the introduction of the Jaguar and Buccaneer into service, the former in the UK and the latter in Germany. To provide a means of keeping ground attack pilots current, two Hunter FGA Mk 9 squadrons had formed at Wittering pending the delivery of sufficient Jaguars. The Jaguar situation also resulted in the temporary equipment of close support squadrons in Germany with the Phantom but there were now also three Harrier squadrons with RAF Germany. Britain had withdrawn from the Far East and in the Middle East no close support units remained.

January 1980

The Jaguar now operated with seven units at home and in Germany while the Harrier force had been reduced to three squadrons with a further flight based in Belize. An important training development was the establishment of the Tactical Weapons Unit at Brawdy intended to provide the transition between advanced fast jet flying and conversion to type with the operational conversion units. Like the OCUs the TWU carried shadow squadron numbers and in time of conflict the instructors would have provided a local air defence capability.

Within a few months the Harrier would demonstrate its versatility and potential during the Falklands war when aircraft of 1 Sqn operated from HMS *Hermes*, each having made an epic flight from the UK to Ascension of some 9¼ hrs.

January 1985

In Strike Command the Jaguar and Harrier equipped four squadrons while two flights of Harriers were located at Belize and on the Falklands. In Germany the Jaguar was being replaced by the potent Tornado which served with five squadrons. The TWU had split into two units, both fully equipped with the Hawk, reflecting the importance placed on weapons training, especially in close support operations.

January 1990

The Harriers had been withdrawn from the Falklands but still served in Belize. The more powerful and night capable new Harrier was in service in the form of the interim GR Mk 5 and there were seven Tornado squadrons in Germany. However, the Cold War had by now ended and the inevitable rundown of forces was being planned. Fortunately there were still sufficient units for the RAF to be able to make a significant contribution to the second Gulf War with German-based Tornado squadrons operating from Saudi Arabia along with Jaguars and Buccaneers detached from the UK.

January 1995

British commitments in relation to peacekeeping in the Middle East and the Balkans resulted in Jaguar detachments in Italy, Harriers to Turkey and Tornados to Saudi Arabia. In respect of ground attack the RAF now possessed in total six Tornado squadrons, three of Harriers (now the GR Mk 7) and three of Jaguars. To keep squadron numbers alive the OCUs were renamed and given reserve status.

3.A Ground attack/close support/light strike at 1 January 1946

Fighter Command

11 Group (South, East)

Type	Unit	Base
Tempest II	54, 247	Chilbolton
Mustang III, IV	64	Horsham St Faith
Mustang III	118	Horsham St Faith

12 Group (Midlands, North)

Type	Unit	Base
Mustang III	306, 309, 315	Coltishall
Mustang III/IV	126	Hethel

13 Group (Scotland)

Type	Unit	Base
Mustang III	316	Wick
Mustang IV	303	Turnhouse

Bomber Command

1 Group

Type	Unit	Base
Mosquito XVI	109	Hemswell

3 Group

Type	Unit	Base
Mosquito IX, XVI	105, 139	Upwood

Coastal Command

16 Group

Type	Unit	Base
Beaufighter X	254	Langham

19 Group

Type	Unit	Base
Mosquito VI	248	Chivenor

de Havilland Venom FB Mk 4

The ground attack Venom variants saw action in South Arabia, Suez and Malaya. FB Mk 4 WR444 of 249 Sqn is seen at Akrotiri in November 1956 in the distinctive yellow/black identification stripes carried during the Suez campaign. *(Bruce Robertson)*

BAFO (Germany)

2 Group

Type	Unit	Base
Mosquito XVI	98, 128, 180	Melsbroek (139 Wing)
Mosquito VI	305	Melsbroek (139 Wing)
	69, 268	Cambrai
	4, 21, 107	Gütersloh (140 Wing)
	14	Wahn

83 Group

Type	Unit	Base
Tempest V	174	Fassberg
	80	Lübeck

84 Group

Type	Unit	Base
Tempest V	3, 56	Fassberg

Mediterranean/Middle East (MED/ME)

Type	Unit	Base
Mustang III/IV	112, 237, 250	Lavariano (Italy)
Beaufighter X	252	Araxos (Greece)
Mustang III/IV	213	Ramat David (Palestine)
Hurricane IV	6	Ramat David

Far East (ACSEA)

225 Group (India)

Type	Unit	Base
Thunderbolt II	5, 30	Baigachi
Mosquito VI	45, 82	St Thomas Mount

AHQ Burma

Type	Unit	Base
Mosquito VI	47	Hmawbi
	47 (det)	Meiktila
Thunderbolt II	42, 79	Meiktila
Beaufighter X, Auster V, Sentinel	27	Mingaladon

AHQ Malaya

Type	Unit	Base
Thunderbolt II	131, 258	Kuala Lumpur
Mosquito VI	84, 110	Seletar

RAF Siam

Type	Unit	Base
Mosquito VI	211	Bangkok

AHQ RAF Netherlands East Indies

Type	Unit	Base
Thunderbolt II	60, 81	Kemajoran

Training units

12 Group Fighter Command

Typhoon, Tempest	56 OTU	Milfield (Ground attack TU)
Spitfire XVI, X, Mustang III	61 OTU	Keevil (Day fighter TU)

91 Group Bomber Command

Type	Unit	Base
Mosquito III, XVI	16 OTU	Upper Heyford

18 Group Coastal Command

Type	Unit	Base
Mosquito III/VI	132 OTU	East Fortune
Beaufighter X	1 TTU	Tain

3.B Ground attack/close support/light strike at 1 July 1948

Bomber Command (1 Group)

Type	Unit	Base
Mosquito FB16, B35	109, 139	Coningsby

BAFO (Germany)

Type	Unit	Base
Tempest II	16, 33	Gütersloh
	26	Lübeck
Mosquito FB6	107	Gatow
Type	*Unit*	*Base*
	4	Wahn
Mosquito FB16, B35	14, 98	Wahn

Mediterranean/Middle East (MED/ME)

Type	Unit	Base
Tempest F6	6	Fayid (Egypt)
	249	Habbaniyah (Iraq)
	8	Khormaksar (Aden)
	39, 213	Khartoum (Sudan)

Far East (ACFE)

Type	Unit	Base
Beaufighter X	45	Negombo (Ceylon)
	84	Tengah (Malaya)

3.C Ground attack/close support/ light strike at 1 January 1950

Fighter Command (11 Group)

Type	Unit	Base
Vampire FB5	247	Odiham

Bomber Command (1 Group)

Type	Unit	Base
Mosquito B35	109, 139	Coningsby

BAFO (Germany – 2 Group)

Type	Unit	Base
Mosquito FB6	4, 11	Celle
Mosquito B35	14, 98	Celle
Vampire FB5	3, 16, 26	Gütersloh

Mediterranean/Middle East

Air HQ RAF Iraq

Type	Unit	Base
Brigand B1	84	Habbaniyah

HQ BF Aden

Type	Unit	Base
Brigand B1	8	Khormaksar

205 Group

Type	Unit	Base
Tempest F6	6, 213, 249	Deversoir (Egypt)

Far East (FEAF)

Type	Unit	Base
Tempest F2	33	Changi (Malaya)
Brigand B1	45	Tengah (Malaya)

3.D   Ground attack/close support/light strike at 1 July 1952

Fighter Command

11 Group

Type	Unit	Base
Vampire FB5	72	North Weald
	501	Filton
	614	Llandow

12 Group

Type	Unit	Base
Vampire F3, FB5	608	Middleton St George
Vampire FB5	502	Aldergrove
	602	Renfrew
	603	Turnhouse
	605	Honiley
	607	Ouston
	612	Edzell
	613	Ringway

Bomber Command (1 Group)

Type	Unit	Base
Mosquito B35	109, 139	Hemswell

2 TAF (Germany)

Type	Unit	Base
Vampire FB5	3, 67, 71	Wildenrath
	4, 112	Jever
	5, 11	Wünstorf
	14, 98, 118	Fassberg
	16, 93, 94, 145	Celle
Vampire FB5, FB9	26	Wünstorf
Vampire FB9	20	Jever

Middle East Air Force

Type	Unit	Base
Vampire FB5	32, 213, 249	Deversoir (Egypt)
Vampire FB5, FB9	185	Ta Kali (Malta)
Vampire FB9	6, 73	Nicosia (Cyprus)

Aden Command

Type	Unit	Base
Brigand B1	8	Khormaksar

Far East (FEAF)

Type	Unit	Base
Vampire FB9	28	Sek Kong (Hong Kong)
	60	Tengah (Malaya)
Hornet F3	33	Kuala Lumpur (Malaya)
	45	Tengah (Malaya)
Hornet F3, F4	80	Kai Tak (Hong Kong)
Brigand B1	84	Tengah (Malaya)

Training

Fighter Command

Type	Unit	Base
Vampire FB5, Meteor T7, Oxford T2, Beaufighter TT10, Mosquito TT35, Tempest TT5	229 OCU	Chivenor
Brigand T4, Buckmaster T1	228 OCU	Colerne

Flying Training Command

Type	Unit	Base
Vampire FB5	202 AFS	Valley

3.E   Ground attack/close support/light strike at 1 January 1955

Fighter Command

11 Group

Type	Unit	Base
Vampire FB5	501	Filton
	614	Llandow

12 Group

Type	Unit	Base
Vampire FB5	602	Abbotsinch
	603	Turnhouse
	605	Honiley
	607	Ouston
	608	Thornaby
	612	Dyce
Vampire FB5, 9	502	Aldergrove
	613	Ringway

2 TAF (Germany)

Type	Unit	Base
Venom FB1	5, 11, 266	Wünstorf
	14, 98, 118	Fassberg
	16, 94, 145	Celle

Middle East Air Force

Type	Unit	Base
Venom FB1	6, 73	Habbaniyah (Iraq)
	32	Kabrit (Egypt)
	249	Amman (Jordan)
Vampire FB9	8	Khormaksar (Aden)

Far East (FEAF)

Type	Unit	Base
Vampire FB9	28	Sek Kong (Hong Kong)
	60	Tengah (Malaya)
Hornet F3	33	Butterworth (Malaya)
	45	Tengah (Malaya)
	80	Kai Tak (Hong Kong)

Training

Type	Unit	Base
Vampire FB5, T11, Meteor T7, F8	233 OCU	Pembrey

3.F   Ground attack/close support/light strike at 1 July 1957

Fighter Command

11 Group

Type	Unit	Base
Hunter F5	1, 34	Tangmere
	41	Biggin Hill
	56	Waterbeach
Hunter F6	63	Waterbeach
	65	Duxford
	111	North Weald
	247	Odiham
	263	Wattisham

12 Group

Type	Unit	Base
Hunter F4	43, 222	Leuchars
	74	Horsham St Faith
	245	Stradishall
Hunter F6	19	Church Fenton
	66	Linton-on-Ouse
	92	Middleton St George

2 TAF (Germany)

Type	Unit	Base
Hunter F4	3, 234	Geilenkirchen
	26	Oldenburg
	98, 118	Jever
Hunter F6	4, 93	Jever
	14, 20	Oldenburg
Venom FB1	94, 145	Celle
Venom FB4	5, 11, 266	Wünstorf
Canberra B(I)6	213	Ahlhorn
Canberra B(I)8	59	Gütersloh
	88	Wildenrath

Middle East Air Force

Type	Unit	Base
Venom FB1	8	Khormaksar (Aden)
Venom FB4	6	Akrotiri (Cyprus)
	249	Ta Kali (Malta)

Far East (FEAF)

Type	Unit	Base
Venom FB1	28	Sek Kong (Hong Kong)
	45	Butterworth (Malaya)
Venom FB4	60	Tengah (Malaya)

3.G Ground attack/close support/light strike at 1 July 1960

Fighter Command

11 Group

Type	Unit	Base
Hunter F6	56, 111	Wattisham
	65	Duxford
Hunter FGA9	1, 54	Stradishall

12 Group

Type	Unit	Base
Hunter F6	19	Leconfield
	66	Acklington
	92	Middleton St George
Hunter F6,FGA9	43	Leuchars

RAF Germany

Type	Unit	Base
Hunter F6	4, 93, 118	Jever
	14, 20, 26	Gütersloh
Canberra B(I)6	213	Brüggen
Canberra B(I)8	16	Laarbruch
	59	Geilenkirchen
	88	Wildenrath

Middle East Air Force

Type	Unit	Base
Hunter FGA9	8	Khormaksar (Aden)
	208	Eastleigh (Kenya)
Canberra B(I)6	249	Akrotiri (Cyprus)

Far East Air Force

Type	Unit	Base
Venom FB4	28	Kai Tak (Hong Kong)

Training

Type	Unit	Base
Hunter F4,F6,T7	229 OCU (63, 145)	Chivenor

3.H Ground attack/close support/light strike at 1 January 1965

Fighter Command

Type	Unit	Base
Hunter FGA9	1	Stradishall
	54	West Raynham

RAF Germany

Type	Unit	Base
Canberra B(I)6	213	Brüggen
Canberra B(I)8	3	Geilenkirchen
	14	Wildenrath
	16	Laarbruch

Air Forces Middle East

Type	Unit	Base
Canberra B15	32, 73	Akrotiri (Cyprus)
Canberra B16	6, 249	Akrotiri "
Hunter FGA9,FR10	8, 43	Khormaksar (Aden)
	208	Muharraq (Oman)
Hunter FR10, T7	1417 Flt	Khormaksar

Far East Air Force

Type	Unit	Base
Hunter FGA9	20	Tengah (Malaya)
	28	Kai Tak (Hong Kong)
Canberra B15	45	Tengah (Malaya)

Training

Type	Unit	Base
Hunter F6,T7,FR10	229 OCU (63)	Chivenor

3.I Ground attack/close support/light strike at 1 January 1970

Air Support Command (38 Group)

Type	Unit	Base
Harrier GR1	1	Wittering
Hunter FGA9 (pending Harrier)	4	West Raynham
Phantom FGR2	6, 54	Coningsby

RAF Germany

Type	Unit	Base
Canberra B(I)8	3, 16	Laarbruch
	14	Wildenrath

Near East Air Force

Type	Unit	Base
Hunter FGA9	208	Muharraq

Far East Air Force

Type	Unit	Base
Hunter FGA9	20	Tengah (Malaya)
Canberra B15	45	Tengah

Training

Type	Unit	Base
Phantom FG1, FGR2	228 OCU (64)	Coningsby
Meteor F8,	229 OCU	Chivenor
Hunter F6, T7	(63,79,234)	

3.J Ground attack/close support/light strike at 1 January 1975

Strike Command (38 Group)

Type	Unit	Base
Harrier GR3	1	Wittering
Jaguar GR1	6, 54	Coltishall
Hunter FGA9	45, 58	Wittering

RAF Germany

Type	Unit	Base
Harrier GR3	3, 4, 20	Wildenrath
Phantom FGR2	14, 17, 31	Brüggen
Buccaneer S2	15, 16	Laarbruch

Training

Type	Unit	Base
Jaguar GR1, T2	226 OCU	Lossiemouth
Phantom FG1, FGR2	228 OCU (64)	Coningsby
Hunter F6, T7, FGA9	TWU	Chivenor
	(63,79,234)	
Harrier GR1, T2A	233 OCU	Wittering

3.K Ground attack/close support/light strike at 1 January 1980

Strike Command (38 Group)

Type	Unit	Base
Harrier GR3	1	Wittering
	1417 Flt	Belize
Jaguar GR1	6, 41, 54	Coltishall

RAF Germany

Type	Unit	Base
Harrier GR3	3, 4	Gütersloh
Jaguar GR1	14, 17, 20, 31	Brüggen
Buccaneer S2	15, 16	Laarbruch

Training

Type	Unit	Base
Jaguar GR1, T2	226 OCU	Lossiemouth
Harrier GR3, T4, 4A	233 OCU	Wittering
Hunter T7, FGA9,	1 TWU	Brawdy
Hawk T1	(79, 234)	
	2 TWU	Lossiemouth
	(63, 151)	

3.L Ground attack/close support/light strike at 1 January 1985

Strike Command (1 Group)

Type	Unit	Base
Harrier GR3	1	Wittering
	1417 Flt	Belize
	1453 Flt	Stanley (Falklands)
Jaguar GR1, T2	6, 41	Coltishall
Jaguar GR1A, T2A	54	Coltishall

RAF Germany

Type	Unit	Base
Harrier GR3	3, 4	Gütersloh
Tornado GR1	15, 16, 20	Laarbruch
	17, 31	Brüggen
Jaguar GR1A. T2A	14	Brüggen

Training

Type	Unit	Base
Jaguar GR1, T2	226 OCU	Lossiemouth
Harrier GR3, T4, 4A	233 OCU	Wittering
Hawk T1, T1A,	1 TWU	Brawdy
Jet Provost T4	(79, 234)	
Hawk T1, T1A	2 TWU	Chivenor
	(63, 151)	
Tornado GR1, GR1T	TWCU (45)	Honington

3.M Ground attack/close support/light strike at 1 January 1990

Strike Command (1 Group)

Type	Unit	Base
Harrier GR5	1	Wittering
Jaguar GR1A, T2A	6, 41, 54	Coltishall
Harrier GR3	1417 Flt	Belize

RAF Germany

Type	Unit	Base
Harrier GR3	4	Gütersloh
Harrier T4	SF	Gütersloh
Harrier GR5	3	Gütersloh
Tornado GR1	15, 16, 20	Laarbruch
	9, 14, 17, 31	Brüggen

Training

Type	Unit	Base
Jaguar GR1A, T2A	226 OCU	Lossiemouth
Harrier GR3, T4, 4A,	233 OCU	Wittering
GR5		
Hawk T1, T1A	1 TWU	Brawdy
	(79, 234)	
Hawk T1, T1A	2 TWU	Chivenor
	(63, 151)	
Tornado GR1, GR1T	TWCU (45)	Honington

3.N Ground attack/close support/light strike at 1 January 1995

Strike Command

1 Group

Type	Unit	Base
Harrier GR7	1	Wittering
Jaguar GR1A,	6, 41, 54	Coltishall
GR1B, T2A	Operation	det Gioia del Colle
	Grapple	(Italy)
Tornado GR1,GR1B	12, 617	Lossiemouth

2 Group (Germany)

Type	Unit	Base
Harrier GR7	3, 4	Laarbruch
	Operation	det Incirlik (Turkey)
	Warden	
Tornado GR1	9, 14, 17, 31	Brüggen
	Operation	det Dharhan (Saudi
	Jural	Arabia)

Training

Type	Unit	Base
Tornado GR1, GR1T	15(R)	Lossiemouth
Jaguar GR1A, T2A	16(R)	Lossiemouth
Harrier GR3, T4, 4A, GR5	20(R)	Wittering
Hawk T1, T1A	19(R); 74(R); 208(R); (4 FTS)	Valley
Harrier GR7,T4, Jaguar T2A, Tornado GR1, GR1A, GR1B	SAOEU	Boscombe Down

BAe Harrier GR Mk 7

The Harrier has served with great effect since 1970 and is here seen in its latest form as the GR Mk 7. The type will shortly be withdrawn from Germany where the RAF has maintained a presence since the end of the War; here ZG511/CD of 4 Sqn makes a fast (and clean!) exit from a stretch of road near its base at Laarbruch. *(BAe)*

3.1 Hawker Hurricane (1937–1947)

Although not as long-serving as its Battle of Britain partner, the Spitfire, the Hurricane did remain in service at the end of the war for about eighteen months, albeit with only one front-line unit. Both aircraft were powered by the Rolls-Royce Merlin and were initially armed with eight .303in Browning machine-guns. But while the Hurricane was robust and manoeuvrable it lacked the Spitfire's overall potential for development.

Like the Spitfire, the Hurricane was built to specification F.36/34 calling for an eight-gun monoplane fighter. In due course the specification for the Hurricane evolved as F.15/36 and the first prototype, K5083, was flown on 6 November 1935. The first squadron to operate the type was No 111 at Northolt from November 1937. By the outbreak of war nearly 500 had been completed and they equipped eighteen squadrons. The Mark I was out of service by the war's end.

Mark II

The Mark II employed the Merlin XX and the prototype, P3269, flew on 11 June 1940. This version was about 20mph faster than the Mark I and in due course it came in four sub-types mainly indicated by armament fit. The IIA retained the eight-gun fit while the IIB had no fewer than twelve machine-guns all in the wings. The IIA entered service with No 111 Sqn in September 1940. The IIC was the most commonly used, mainly in the ground attack role where its four 20mm cannon could cause maximum impact. The IID was used in limited numbers as a tank-buster fitted with a 40mm Vickers 'S' gun under each wing. Over time the Mark II was fitted to carry two 250lb or two 500lb bombs under the wings and from 1942 eight three-inch rocket projectiles. By 1946 the Mark IIB, C and D remained in service with a number of second-line units.

Service (post-1945) Meteorology 1301, 1302, 1303, 1402, 1415, 1565, 1569 Flt **Communications** Eastleigh SF

Hawker Hurricane Mk IV

The Hurricane remained in service for only a year or two after the War's end and then only with one front-line unit, No 6 Sqn. One of the squadron's aircraft is seen fully armed with an asymmetric load of four 3in rockets and one 500lb bomb in the Middle East. *(Crown copyright)*

Training BCIS; 1686, 1687, 1688 BDTF; FATU; 10, 17, 21, 26 OTU; 5 (P)AFU.

The Mark III was to have used the Packard Merlin 28 but in the event sufficient British engines were available although the Packard was used on the Canadian-built Marks X, XI and XII. These variants were equivalent to the Mark I (X) and II (XI and XII).

Mark IV

The penultimate variant was fitted with the Merlin 24, 27 or 32 and it differed from the Mark II primarily in having a universal wing and additional armour protection. The prototype Mark IV, KX405, flew on 14 March 1943 and it was introduced into the production line between Mark IIs. The variant was used extensively in the Middle and Far East towards the closing stages of the war with great effect.

Service (post-1945) **Ground attack** 6 **Meteorology** 520, 521 **Communications** 48 GCF; 36 SP **Training** CCFIS The Mark V was a developed Mark IV with a Merlin 32 (1,700hp) driving a four-bladed propeller; prototype was KZ193. Development was not pursued after engine maintenance problems.

Specification and production

Mark	Role	Engine	HP	Weight lb	Speed mph	Nos
I	Fighter	Merlin II	1,030	6,447	316	3,844
II	Fighter	Merlin XX	1,260	7,544	339	8,287
III	Fighter	Packard Merlin 28	1,260	not built		
IV	Fighter	Merlin 24, 27, 32	1,620	8,462	330	580
V	Fighter	Merlin 32	1,700	8,500	330	1*

* Mk IV conversion

Further reading

Classic Aircraft No 4; Their History and How to Model Them – Hawker Hurricane, Robertson, B, and Scarborough, G, PSL, Cambridge, 1974
Hawker Hurricane I (Profile 111) Mason, F K, Profile Publications, Leatherhead, 1965
Hawker Hurricane IIC (Profile 24) Mason, F K, Profile Publications, Leatherhead, 1963
Hawker Hurricane, The, Jackson, R, Arms and Armour Press, London, 1988
Hawker Hurricane, The, Mason, F K, Macdonald, London 1962
Hawker Hurricane Mk II/IV in RAF and Foreign Service Shores, C F and Ward, R, Osprey, London, 1971
Hurricane, Bishop, E, Airlife, Shrewsbury,1986
Hurricane at War, Franks, N, Ian Allan, Shepperton,

3.2 Bristol Beaufighter (1940–1960)

The Bristol Type 156 Beaufighter was a private-venture, fast, long-range fighter which attracted interest in the form of specification F.17/39. The prototype, R2052, with the Hercules powerplant first flew on 17 July 1939 and as the Fighter Command Mark IF night fighter version joined 25 Sqn in September 1940. With additional radio and navigational aids the Mark IC was the Coastal Command variant. The Mark IIF was powered by the Merlin XX. The Mark III (Type 158) was to have had a slimmer fuselage while the Mark IV was to have been powered by the Griffon engine; in the event neither variant was produced. The Mark V was fitted with a four-gun turret behind the cockpit but the variant was not successful.

Mark VI

The Mark VI reverted to the Hercules, now the more powerful Mark VI or XVI. Again the Beaufighter came in VIF and VIC variants, the latter employing a single Vickers machine-gun in the navigator's cockpit and in due course fitted to fire eight 90lb rockets and two 250lb bombs. In common with the Mark I the VIF had four 20mm nose cannon and six .303in machine-guns in the wings. Fifty Mark VIC were fitted with dive brakes and provision for carrying a torpedo; they were designated **Mark VI (ITF)** (interim torpedo fighter). Apart from the engines the most obvious change against earlier versions was the introduction of dihedral on the tailplane.

Service (post-1945) Training AICF; 1653 CU; 54 OTU

TF Mark X

The Mark X was the next variant in service (the Mark VII, Mark VIII and Mark IX designations were provided for Australian production and not used). It was essentially similar to the Mark VI (ITF) being optimised as an anti-shipping strike fighter powered by the Hercules XVII and in due course with ASV Mark VIII radar. Later, the additional weight of armament and radar changes caused some deterioration of handling and a dorsal fin was introduced, retrospectively fitted on earlier aircraft and some Mark VIs.

Service (post-1945) Strike fighter 27, 42, 45, 84, 252, 254 **Training** 236 OCU; 132 OTU; PAU **Communications** 6, 684; Hong Kong CS; Malta CTTF; Tengah SF; 109 MU; 59 SP **Other** ASWDU; TFU

TT Mark 10

The designation was applied to 35 Mark Xs equipped for target towing post-war. All armament and the radar was removed and a winch fitted in the rear fuselage.

Service Target-towing 5, 17, 20, 34, 577, 695; 26, 27 APC; 1, 2, 3, 4, 5 CAACU; Malta CTTF; FETS; 226, 229 OCU; 17 RFS; Kai Tak, Seletar SF; Nicosia, Shallufa TTF **Trials** AFEE; RAE. To complete the record, the Mark XI was similar to the X but without the torpedo fit while the Mark 21 was an Australian variant with armament changes. The former was out of service by 1946 while the latter was never in RAF service.

Specification and production

Mark	Role	Engine	HP	Weight lb	Speed mph	Nos
I	Fighter	2xHercules III	1,400	21,000	330	910
II	Fighter	2xMerlin XX	1,280	21,000	330	450
III	Fighter	2xMerlin	Not built			
IV	Fighter	2xGriffon	Not built			
V	Fighter	2xMerlin XX	1,280	21,000	330	2*
VI	Fighter	2xHercules VI,XVI	1,670	21,600	333	1,832
VII	Fighter	2xDouble Cyclone				1+
VIII	Fighter	2xDouble Cyclone	Not built			
IX	Fighter	2xDouble Cyclone	Not built			
TF X	Torpedo fighter	2xHercules XVII	1,770	25,200	323	2,205
TT 10	Target tug	2xHercules XVII	1,770	23,000	330	61#
XI	Fighter	2xHercules XVII	1,770	25,200	323	2,205

* Mk II conversions
\+ Mk 1 conversion for possible Australian build
\# rebuilt Mark X

Further reading
Beaufighter, Bowyer, C, William Kimber, London, 1987

3.3   Hawker Typhoon (1941–1946)

The Typhoon was designed as a natural successor to the Hurricane and bore a considerable resemblance in plan. It was built to specification F.18/37 which called for interceptors to be fitted with the developing 2,000hp engines. The unsuccessful Tornado, employing the Vulture, flew in October 1939 but it did not enter service. The Sabre-powered Typhoon, which as a result of experience with the Tornado had the distinctive chin radiator, flew on 24 February 1940 (P5212). The type joined 56 Sqn in September 1941.

After numerous teething problems the Typhoon's outstanding low-level performance resulted in the type serving as a close support fighter coming into its own in support of the Normandy invasion. The first variant, the Mark IA, was fitted with the Sabre I and twelve .303in

Bristol Beaufighter Mk X

The pugnacious lines of the Beaufighter are shown in this post-war photo of X8079, then serving with 272 Sqn in Italy. The type served for several years post-war with strike units, especially in the Far East, and many were converted for target-towing in which role they served until 1960. *(Crown copyright)*

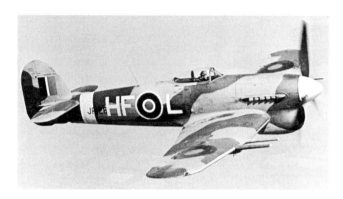

Hawker Typhoon Mk IB

In service until the end of the War, the Typhoon was soon eclipsed, except with 56 OTU and Acklington. This photo shows JR128/HF-L of 183 Sqn which used the type until July 1945. *(MAP)*

de Havilland Mosquito NF Mk 36

Typifying the Mosquito in post-war service is the NF Mk 36 model, of which 236 were built from 1945. RL148 wears the distinctive hexagon marking of 85 Sqn as it sits on a damp hardstanding at West Malling in 1951. *(P H T Green collection)*

Browning machine-gun armament – hardly adequate for a fighter bomber, and the version was soon withdrawn from service.

Mark IB

The second variant was powered by the Sabre II and four 20mm Hispano cannon replaced the ineffectual machine guns. In addition the rugged Typhoon could carry a 2,000lb bomb load or eight 3in (60lb) rockets. By the end of the war the Typhoon was being withdrawn from front-line service after just four years.

Service (post-1945) Training CCFIS; 56 OTU **Communications** Acklington SF

Specification and production

Mark	Role	Engine	HP	Weight lb	Speed mph	Nos
IB	Fighter	Sabre II	2,260	13,250	412	3,330

Further reading

Hawker Typhoon, The (Profile 81) Mason, F K, Profile Publications, Leatherhead, 1963
Hawker Typhoon and Tempest, The, Mason, F K, Aston, Bourne End, 1988
Typhoon and Tempest Story, The, Thomas, C, and Shores, C, Arms and Armour Press, London, 1988

3.4   de Havilland Mosquito (1941–1955)

The DH 98 Mosquito was remarkable both in terms of performance and construction. It was designed as a private venture in 1938 and constructed mainly of wood. As a bomber it was to be unarmed and when it entered service in 1941 it was (and remained to 1944) the fastest aircraft operated by the RAF. In its bomber and reconnaissance forms it flew with no defensive armament. On 1 March 1940 specification B.1/40 was issued to cover development of the bomber variant, while specification

F.21/40 covered the simultaneous development of the design as a fighter.

The Mark I prototype W4050 flew in the manufacturer's markings E-0234 on 25 November 1940 from Hatfield. The first aircraft of nine designated for the unarmed reconnaissance role (W4051) flew on 10 June 1941 and the type entered service with the Photographic Development Unit. In common with the NF Mark II the variant was no longer in service by 1946.

The NF Mark II was similar to the reconnaissance version except for the addition of four 20mm cannon and four .303in machine-guns in the nose. In service the Mosquito night fighter was also fitted with the AI Mk IV radar. The prototype, W4052, flew on 25 May 1941 and like the other early machines it was powered by the Merlin 21. Some 466 were built and it entered service with 157 Sqn in January 1942.

T Mark III

The Mark III was a dual control variant without armament. The prototype was a converted NF Mk II which flew on 30 January 1942 and first deliveries were to the Mosquito Training Unit in September 1942. The T Mk III remained in service until 1955.

Service (post-1945) Training 6, 13, 16, 54, 132 OTU; 226, 228, 231, 237 OCU; 204 AFS; 21 (P)AFU; BCIS; CFS; EFS; FCITS; 4 FP; 1689 Flt; 13, 19, 23, 25, 29, 33, 39, 41, 45, 58, 64, 81, 98, 107, 109, 114, 138, 199, 219, 264, 266, 500, 502, 504, 605, 608, 609, 616 Sqns; 728, 762, 780 NAS **Communications** FCCS; FETS; FTU; 1 FU; HCCS; HCEU; IAM; Acklington, Lübeck, Sylt APS; 1, 3, 3/4 CAACU; Coltishall, Hahn, Hemswell, Leuchars, Linton-on-Ouse, Tangmere, West Malling, Wittering SFs; FRU

B Mark IV

This was the first bomber version to go into service and the protoype (W4072) flew on 8 September 1941. Unarmed, it carried one 1,000lb bomb and two 500lb bombs for 1,200 miles at 380mph. The first nine aircraft were Series 1 while the balance of 300 series 2 machines had extended engine nacelles. Service entry was with 105 Sqn in May 1942.

Service (post-1945) Training 16 OTU.
The PR Mark IV were converted B Mk IV (27 aircraft) to take cameras. The B Mark V was a proposed development of the Mk IV with underwing pylons for 500lb bombs. It was not pursued. Neither was the PR Mark V variant.

FB Mark VI
The Mark VI was developed from the NF Mk II but with provision for four 250lb bombs (series 1) in addition to the eight-gun armament or four 500lb bombs (Series 2). Alternatively extra fuel could be carried. Series 2 aircraft also featured the Merlin 25 engine. The prototype was HJ662, a converted NF Mk II (DZ434/G) which first flew on 1 June 1942. First unit equipped with the FB Mk VI was 418 Sqn from May 1943 and the variant remained in service as the light bomber mainstay in occupied Germany until 1950.

Service (post-1945) Fighter-bomber 4, 8, 11, 14, 18, 21, 36, 39, 45, 47, 69, 82, 84, 107, 110, 114, 211, 248, 268, 305 Training 201, 204 AFS; CFS; CGS; EAAS; EAS; 228, 231, 237 OCU; 6, 13, 16, 51, 54, 132 OTU; RAFFC: 700, 703, 751, 762, 771, 773, 780, 787, 790 NAS Communications APC Acklington, Sylt; BAFOCS; FCTTS; 3 FP; 1, 12, 16 FU; 2 GpCS; 216 GpCF; NEICS; OFU; 2 APS; 59 SP Bückeburg, Northolt, North Creake, Pershore SFs: 811 NAS Other 1300 Met Flt; AFDS; ASWDU; ATDU; BSDU; CFE; ETPS; RWE; TFU

The B Mark VII was the Canadian version of the B Mark IV with a Packard Merlin 31. The PR Mark VIII was similar to the PR Mk IV but with the Merlin 61. Five were built. The PR Mark IX was similar to the PR Mk VIII but with Merlin 72 engines and with much higher flying capability. The prototype (DZ570) flew on 24 March 1943 and the version joined 540 Sqn in April 1943. The NF Mark X was an intended NF Mk II development with the Merlin 61 engine, while the FB Mark X was an intended FB Mk VI development with the Merlin 101 engine. Neither was produced. The FB Mark XI was an intended development of the FB Mk VI with the Merlin 61.

NF Mark XII
The Mark XII was similar to the NF Mk II but with the machine-guns removed and with AI radar Mk VIII. Prototype was DD715 (August 1942) and 97 were built.

Service (post-1945) Miscellaneous CFE.
The NF Mark XIII was similar to the NH Mk XII but with auxiliary underwing tanks. The NF Mark XIV was an intended development of the NF Mk XIII but with the Merlin 67. The NF Mark XV was a specialised high-altitude conversion of the NF Mk XIII with the Merlin 61. The five built served with 85 Sqn during the war, operating at heights up to 44,600ft.

B Mark XVI
This was a pressurised high-altitude bomber version of the PR Mk IX. The armament was confined to one 4,000lb bomb or six 500lb bombs in a bulged bomb bay in addition to two 100-gallon drop tanks. Some 400 were built and it remained in widespread service for some time after 1946.

Service (post-1945) Light bomber 14, 69, 98, 105, 109, 114, 128, 139, 180, 256 Training EANS; 231 OCU;

13, 16, 54 OTU Other 680, 684 Sqns; 1409 Flt; CBE; CSE; RWE

PR Mark XVI
The Mark XVI was similar to the PR Mk IX but with a pressurised cockpit. Prototype MM258 flew in July 1943 and 499 were built of which 79 were supplied to the USAAF.

Service (post-1945) Photo-reconnaissance 13; 1340 Flt Training 703, 728, 772, 772, 790 NAS; FRDU.
The NF Mark XVII was a NF Mk II conversion fitted with US AI radar. The FB Mark XVIII was a development of the FB Mk VI with a 57mm Molins gun in the fuselage replacing the four cannon. Twenty-seven FB Mk VI conversions were completed.

NF Mark XIX
The Mark XIX was similar to the NF Mk XIII but with US AI Mk 10 radar fitted in a more bulbous nose. Prototype was DZ659 (April 1944) and 220 were built; it entered service with 157 Sqn in May 1944.

Service (post-1945) Night fighter 89, 255, 256, 500 Training 1653, 1660, 1668 HCU; 230 OCU; 54 OTU Communications 176

B Mark XX
This was a Canadian version of the B Mk IV fitted with the Packard Merlin 31/33.

Service (post-1945) Training 16 OTU Communications 162; ADLSS Other TFU.
The FB Mark 21 was the Canadian equivalent of the FB Mk VI fitted with the Packard Merlin 31/33. Only three were built. The T Mark 22 was an FB Mk 21 dual control conversion. The B Mark 23 was an intended Canadian equivalent of the B Mk IX. The FB Mark 24 was an intended high-altitude version of the FB Mk 21.

B Mark 25
The Mark 25 was another Canadian variant, this time a B Mk XX with Merlin 225 engines delivering 1,620 hp. Of the 400 built, the majority were delivered to the RAF.

Service (post-1945) Light bomber 139, 502 Training EANS; 16 OTU:: 700, 728, 762, 771, 772 Communications 162 Other CFE; NFRU

FB Mark 26
The Mark 26 was similar to the FB Mk 21 but with the Packard Merlin 225 engine. Most of the 337 built were used by the RAF in the Middle East.

Service (post-1945) Fighter-bomber 55, 249 Communications 39; 1 FU Other CBE.
The T Mark 27 was similar to the T Mk 22 but with the Packard Merlin 225. The Mark 28 was an unused Canadian mark number.

T Mark 29
The Mark 29 was a dual control version of the FB Mk 26.

Service (post-1945) Training 64, 65, 151, 264; 3 FP Communications Linton-on-Ouse SF

NF Mark 30

This was a development of the NF Mk XIX but with two-stage Merlin 72 and, later, Merlin 76 and 113 engines. It was an unpressurised night fighter with AI Mk 8 or 10 radar the prototype of which (MM686) first flew in March 1944; it served for some years post-war.

Service (post-1945) **Night fighter** 23, 25, 29, 39, 85, 151, 219, 255, 264, 307, 500, 502, 504, 605, 608, 609, 616 **Training** CFE; 228 OCU; 8, 54 OTU **Other** CSE; RAE; RWE; TFU.

The NF Mark 31 was an intended Packard Merlin 69 variant of the NF Mk 30. The PR Mark 32 was a high altitude lighter version of the PR Mk XVI with extended wing-tips. Five were built, all flying with 540 Sqn until November 1945.

TR Mark 33

The Mark 33 was the first specialised naval version built as a carrier-borne torpedo reconnaissance aircraft. It was a variant of the FB Mk VI designed to specification N.15/44 and it was fitted with tail hook, folding wings, four-blade propellers, provision for JATO and thimble radome to take ASH radar. The prototype (LR359), a partly converted FB Mk VI, flew on 25 March 1944 while the first of 50 production aircraft, TW227, flew on 10 November 1945.

Service **Anti-shipping** 811 NAS **Training** 739, 751, 762, 771, 790 NAS **Trials** 703, 778, 787 NAS **Other** 771 NAS

PR Mark 34

The war in the Far East called for a long-range version of the Mosquito and resulted in the PR Mk XVI with extra fuel in a bulged fuselage and wing drop tanks; range was 3,600 miles. The first production aircraft flew on 4 December 1944. Equipment included four F.52 vertical and one F.24 oblique cameras.

Service **Photo-reconnaissance** 13, 58, 81, 540, 541, 680, 681, 684 **Training** 231, 237 OCU; 8 OTU **Electronic warfare** 192; CSE **Trials** APDU; Met Res Flt (RAE); RWE: 751 NAS **Communications** 1 FU; OFU **Other** 771, 772 NAS

PR Mark 34A

A number of PR Mk 34 were converted with modified Gee and the Merlin 114A engine with slightly more power. This variant was the last in RAF front-line service, the final flight being made on 15 December 1955 by RG314 of 81 Sqn.

Service **Photo-reconnaissance** 58, 81, 540 **Electronic warfare** 192; CSE **Training** 230, 231, 237 OCU **Other** FEFU

B Mark 35

The last bomber variant was an improved B Mk XVI with the Merlin 113/114; 276 were built, mostly post-war, and it entered service in 1946 with 109 and 139 Sqns.

Service **Bomber** 14, 98, 109, 139, 142 **Training** CGS; EANS; LBS; 230, 231 OCU; RAFFC **Communications** Coningsby SF **Trials** AFEE; APDU; BBU; CBE; CSE; PRDU; RWE **Other** 527; 1409 Flt; 5 CAACU

TT Mark 35

The target towing conversion of the Bomber Mk 35 was fitted with a ML type G wind-driven winch under the forward fuselage. Several were further modified for meteorological work as the **Met Mark 35**.

Service **Target towing** APS Sylt; 1, 2, 3, 4, 3/4, 5 CAACU; 223, 226, 228, 229, 233, 236, 238 OCU; SIU; Gibraltar, St Eval TTFs **Other** 4 FP; 2 TAFCS; THUM Flt; Schleswigland SF

PR Mark 35

Ten B Mk 35 aircraft were converted for flashlight photography.

Service **Photo-reconnaissance** 58; CPE

NF Mark 36

The Mark 36 was similar to the NF Mk 30 but with the Merlin 113, handed propellers and US AI radar. The engines were 9in longer than the earlier Merlins and to compensate extra weights were added to the elevators.

Service **Night fighter** 23, 25, 29, 39, 85, 141, 199, 219, 264 **Training** NFLS; 228 OCU; 8 OTU **Trials** CFE; CSE; RWE

TR Mark 37

Used exclusively for training the Mark 37 was similar to the TR Mk 33 but with British AI radar in an enlarged nose.

Service **Training** 703, 771 NAS

NF Mark 38

The Mark 38 was similar to the NF Mk 36 but with British Mk IX AI radar and a lengthened cockpit enclosure. Most were sold to the Yugoslav Air Force.

Service **Trials** CFE

TT Mark 39

With an extended and heavily glazed nose the Mark 39 was a singular Mosquito. It was a B Mk XVI conversion (26 airframes) built for the Royal Navy to specification Q.19/45 for target towing.

Service **Fleet requirements** 728, 771 NAS **Trials** 703 NAS.

The remaining Mosquito marks were reserved for Australian types, none of which served with British services. They included the FB Mk 40, PR Mk 40, PR Mk 41, FB Mk 42 and T Mk 43.

Specification and Production

Mark	Role	Engine	HP	Weight lb	Speed mph	Nos
I	PR	2xMerlin 21	1,480	20,000	356	9
II	Night fighter	2xMerlin 21	1,480	20,000	356	28
III	Trainer	2xMerlin 21/23	1,460	20,319	384	358
IV	Bomber	2xMerlin 21/23	1,480	22,380	380	309
IV	PR	2xMerlin 21/23	1,480	22,000	385	27*

Mark Nos	Role	Engine	HP	Weight lb	Speed mph	
V	Bomber	2xMerlin 21	1,480	Not built		
VI	Fighter-bomber	2xMerlin 21/23	1,460	22,258	378	2,292
VII	Bomber	2xP-Merlin 31	1,460	22.000	360	25
VIII	PR	2xMerlin 61	1,565	22,500	380	5
IX	PR	2xMerlin 72	1,680	23,000	408	90
X	Night fighter	2xMerlin 61	1,565	Not built		
X	Fighter-bomber	2xMerlin 101	2,420	Not built		
XI	Fighter-bomber	2xMerlin 61	1,565	Not built		
XII	Night fighter	2xMerlin 21/23	1,460	19,700	370	97
XIII	Night fighter	2xMerlin 21/23	1,460	19,700	370	5
XIV	Night fighter	2xMerlin 67	2,375	Not built		
XV	Night fighter	2xMerlin 61	1,565	19,500	370	5
XVI	Bomber	2xMerlin 72/73	1,680	25,917	408	400
XVI	PR	2xMerlin 73	1,680	22,350	415	499
XVII	Night fighter	2xMerlin 21	1,480	20,500	365	100#
XVIII	Fighter-bomber	2xMerlin 21/23	1,480	22,400	380	27~
XIX	Night fighter	2xMerlin 25	1,635	20,500	370	220
XX	Bomber	2xP Merlin 31	1,460	22,380	380	245
FB21	Fighter-bomber	2xP-Merlin 31	1,460	22,250	380	3
T22	Trainer	2xP-Merlin 31	1,460	22,250	370	4
B23	Bomber	2xP-Merlin 31	1,460	Not built		
FB24	Fighter-bomber	2xP-Merlin 31	1,460	Not built		
B25	Bomber	2xP-Merlin 225	1,680	22,380	380	400
FB26	Fighter-bomber	2xP-Merlin 225	1,680	22,250	380	337
T27	Trainer	2xP-Merlin 225	1,680	22,250	380	21
28	Canadian	unused mark number				
T29	Trainer	2xP-Merlin 225	1,680	22,250	380	61+
NF30	Night fighter	2xMerlin 72, 76	1,690	21,600	407	530
NF31	Night fighter	2xP-Merlin 69	2,375	Not built		
PR32	PR	2xMerlin 73	1,680	22,350	415	5
TR33	Torpedo recce	2xMerlin 66	1,705	23,850	376	376
PR34	PR	2xMerlin 114	1,690	22,100	425	425
PR-34A	PR	2xMerlin 114A	1,710	22,100	425	37^
B35	Bomber	2xMerlin 113	1,690	23,000	415	276
TT35	Target tug	2xMerlin 113	1,690	23,000	405	105$
PR35	PR	2xMerlin 113	1,690	23,000	415	10$
Met35	Meteorology	2xMerlin 113	1,690	23,000	415	c5$
NF36	Night fighter	2xMerlin 113	1,690	21,600	405	236
TR37	Torpedo-recce	2xMerlin 25	1,635	23,850	375	14
NF38	Night fighter	2xMerlin 114	1,690	21,400	404	101
TT39	Target tug	2xMerlin 77	1,710	23,000	299	26@

40-43 Australian versions; not used by British services

```
*   BIV conversions
#   NFII conversions
~   FBVI conversions
+   1 new build, 60 FB26 conversions
^   PR34 conversions
$   B35 conversions
@   BXVI conversions
```

Further reading

de Havilland Mosquito, The, Hardy, M J, David and Charles, Newton Abbot. 1977
de Havilland Mosquito Mks I-IV, The (Profile 52) Moyes, P J R, Profile Publications, Leatherhead, 1964
Mosquito, Bowyer, M J F and Philpott, B, Patrick Stephens, Cambridge, 1980
Mosquito, Sharp, C M and Bowyer, M J F, Faber and Faber, London, 1968
Mosquito, Sweetman, W, Janes, London, 1981
Mosquito – A Pictorial History of the DH98, Birtles, P J, Janes, London, 1981
Mosquito at War, Bowyer, M J F, Ian Allan, London
Mosquito Squadrons of the RAF, Bowyer, C, Ian Allan, Shepperton, 1984
Wooden Wonder, The, Bishop, E, Max Parrish, London, 1959

3.5 North American Mustang (1942–1947)

The highly successful Mustang was built in the United States to a British requirement and when first flown in September 1940 was faster, at 390mph, than any contemporary American fighter. The NA-73 Mark I, Mark IA (four 20mm cannon armament) and Mark II were all powered by the Allison V-1710 engine but through relatively poor high-level performance the type was confined to low-level operations. All the earlier versions were out of service by 1946.

Mark III
The NA-102 Mark III was similar to the P-51B and -C with original cockpit canopy and a Packard Merlin engine. Armament was four .50in guns and there was provision for a 1,000lb bomb load. A key feature of the

North American Mustang Mk IV

The graceful Mustang was built to a British specification and operated in large numbers by the RAF and USAAF during the War. Like so many American types it was withdrawn from use soon after the war, although serving for a short time with fighter units in the United Kingdom and Middle East. KM348/AK-V was with 213 Sqn at Nicosia in 1946.
(A S Thomas collection)

Mustang was its great range which made it an ideal escort fighter, and it entered RAF service with 65 Sqn in December 1943.

Service (post-1945) **Fighter** 64, 118, 126, 213, 237, 250, 303, 306, 309, 315, 316 **Reconnaissance** 541 **Other** CFE

Mark IV
The NA-104 was similar to the USAAF P-51D and had a slightly more powerful version of the Packard Merlin and, more importantly, a tear-drop canopy. To improve longitudinal stability a dorsal fin was fitted at an early stage in production and the armament was changed to six .50in guns in the wing. The Mark IV (and Mark IVA) joined units operating the earlier Mark III as aircraft became available; some units operated both versions.

Service (post-1945) **Fighter** 19, 65, 126, 213, 303

Mark IVA
The NA-111 Mark IVA differed from the Mark IV only in having an Aero-products propeller unit as opposed to the Hamilton Standard type. In US service it was the P-51K.

Service (post-1945) **Fighter** 19, 64, 65, 93, 112, 118, 126, 213, 303 **Training** AST; 1330, 1331 CU; 71 OTU; 5 RFU **Communications** 4, 12, 15 FU; 17, 36 SP Fairwood Common, Horsham St Faith SF **Other** AFDU; AFEE; CFE; TWDU

Republic Thunderbolt Mk II

The Thunderbolt operated with the RAF almost exclusively in the Far East and was used heavily in the Netherlands East Indies in the campaign against nationalists after the Japanese defeat. Aircraft of 60 Sqn armed with 250lb bombs taxi out at Kemajoran for a strike in early 1946. *(Crown copyright)*

fighters in the Far East where, apart from an operational training unit in the Middle East, it served exclusively. The Mark I was equivalent to the USAAF P-47B or early -D models and was no longer in service by 1946.

Mark II
Featuring a tear-drop canopy and R-2800-59 Double Wasp engine the Mark II was equivalent to the American P-47D-25. It joined 146 and 261 Sqns in India in September 1944. The armament comprised eight .50in guns in the wings and there was provision for the carriage of two 1,000lb bombs. After service in support of British troops in the Netherlands East Indies the Thunderbolt was withdrawn from service in December 1946.

Service (post-1945) **Fighter** 5, 30, 42, 60, 79, 81, 131, 258 **Communications** 36, 202 SP

Specification and production

Mark	Role	Engine	HP	Weight lb	Speed mph	Nos
I	Fighter	Allison V-1710-39	1,150	8,600	390	612
II	Fighter	Allison V-1 1710-8	1,120	8,600	390	50
III	Fighter	P Merlin V-1650-3	1,680	11,800	442	900
IV	Fighter	P Merlin V-1650-7	1,680	11,600	437	30
IVA	Fighter	P Merlin V-1650-7	1,680	11,600	437	844

Specification and production

Mark	Role	Engine	HP	Weight lb	Speed mph	Nos
I	Fighter	D Wasp R-2800-59	2,300	14,600	427	239
II	Fighter	D Wasp R-2800-59	2,300	14,600	427	590

Further reading
Camouflage and Markings: RAF Northern Europe: N A Mustang, Ducimus, London, 1968
Mustang: The Story of the P-51 Fighter, Gruenhagen, R W, Arco, 1981
North American P-51B and C Mustang (Profile 100) Atkins, R, Profile Publications, Leatherhead, 1968
North American P-51D Mustang, The (Profile 8) Shacklady, E, Profile Publications, Leatherhead, 1965
P-51 Mustang, Cross, R & Scarborough, G, PSL, London, 1973

Further reading
Royal Air Force Thunderbolts, Thomas, G, Air Research Publications, Surbiton, 1987

3.7 de Havilland Hornet (1945–1955)

The DH.103 Hornet was designed as a private-venture lightweight twin-engined fighter, optimised for use in the war against Japan. Specification F.12/43 was written around the type which first flew (RR915) on 28 July 1944. In design it resembled a scaled-down Mosquito and like its forebear it was remarkably fast: the prototype exceeded 485mph. The Hornet equipped Fighter Command day fighter units in the UK and later was used with success as a strike fighter in Malaya. It was the fastest piston-engined fighter in Royal Air Force service.

3.6 Republic Thunderbolt (1944–1946)

The heavy Thunderbolt single-engined fighter was taken into RAF service to supplement the limited number of

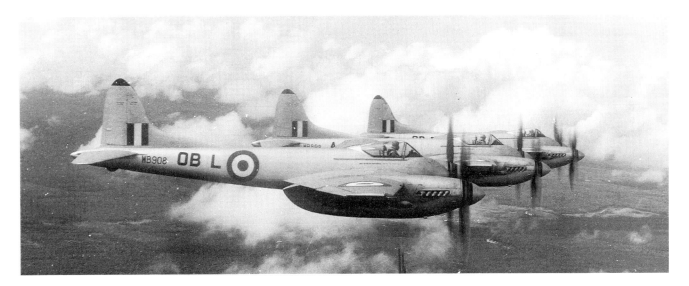

de Havilland Hornet F Mk 3

Capable of 485mph the Hornet was the fastest piston-engined fighter in RAF service and after operating in the United Kingdom as a day fighter it flew with three units in the light strike role in Operation 'Firedog' in Malaya. These rocket-armed aircraft, with WB908/OB-L nearest camera, are from 45 Sqn and are seen over the Malayan coastal plain in 1954. *(Crown copyright)*

F Mark 1

The first Hornet was armed with four 20mm cannon and it entered service with 64 Sqn in May 1946. Like all variants it was powered by the Merlin 130/131 driving handed four-blade propeller units. First production machine was PX210 which flew on 1 March 1945 and the Mark 1 served only in the UK, lacking the range of later variants.

Service Fighter 19, 41, 64, 65 **Training** 1335 CU; 226 OCU; CFS; ECFS **Communications** FCCS; 12 GCF; 1 OFU; Horsham St Faith SF **Other** CFE (AFDS); CGS; PRDU; RAE; TRE

PR Mark 2

The Mark 2 was designed as an unarmed reconnaissance vehicle for use in the Far East. An early production F Mk 1 (PX216) served as the prototype and five were built before the end of the war resulted in the decision to abandon the type.

Service Trials PRDU; RAE

F Mark 3

The main fighter variant was provided with increased internal tankage (from 360 to 540 gals) plus a further 400 gals in underwing tanks. To improve lateral stability a dorsal fillet was introduced and provision was made for two 1,000lb bombs or eight 60lb RPs under the wings. It entered service with 19 Sqn in March 1948 and when replaced by jet types in the UK this variant, together with the FR Mk 4, served in Malaya and Hong Kong.

Service Fighter 19, 33, 41, 45, 64, 65, 80 **Training** FETS; Hornet CU; RAFC **Communications** 1689 Flt; 12 GCF; 10 MU; 1 OFU; Linton-on-Ouse SF **Other** CFE

FR Mark 4

The Mark 4 was the last of the Hornets and it was used exclusively in the Far East. It was basically an F Mk 3

equipped for photo-reconnaissance with an F.52 camera displacing 21 gals of fuel. Some were built on the production line while others were F Mk 3 conversions.

Service Fighter reconnaissance 33, 45, 80

Specification and production

Mark	Role	Engine	HP	Weight lb	Speed mph	Nos
F1	Fighter	2xMerlin 130/131	1,770	14,100	472	60
PR2	Photo-recce	2xMerlin 130/131	1,770	15,000	472	5
F3	Fighter	2xMerlin 130/131	1,770	19,550	472	121
FR4	Fighter recce	2xMerlin 130/131	1,770	19,550	472	23*

* 12 new aircraft, 11 rebuilt from F3

Further reading
de Havilland Hornet, The (Profile 174) Birtles, P, Profile Publications, Leatherhead, 1968
Hornet File, The, Cooper, L G, Air Britain, Tonbridge, 1992

3.8 Bristol Brigand (1949–1958)

The Type 164 Brigand was originally designed as a torpedo bomber successor to the Beaufighter to specification H.7/42. It was intended that it would be powered by two Hercules engines, but as the latter were not adequate for the task the aircraft eventually flew with the Centaurus. By the time the type was in production there had been changes in the torpedo fighter role, which transferred to ship-based fighters.

Bristol Brigand B Mk 1

The Brigand was originally designed as a torpedo-bomber but when the role requirement changed it was developed as a light bomber. It carried a 2,000lb load externally as seen is this shot of RH826/R of 84 Sqn with sixteen 60lb rockets and 500lb bombs at Tengah in 1952 at the height of Operation 'Firedog'. *(Crown copyright)*

TF Mark I
The first Brigand first flew on 27 October 1944 (MX988); first production machine was RH742. It was intended for 36 and 42 Sqns at Thorney Island and notionally allocated to the units between 1 and 15 October, at which date they were disbanded. Armament comprised four 20mm cannon and a .5in machine-gun in the rear cockpit and provision for a single torpedo.

Service Trials ASWDU; ATDU; ECFS

B Mark 1
The bomber variant was a successful attempt to salvage something from the programme, given the change in the torpedo fighter role. The Brigand was now intended to replace the Mosquito in the Far East and it differed from the TF Mk 1 in the deletion of the rear machine gun and a weapons load which comprised four 500lb bombs or rocket projectiles. It joined 84 Sqn in Iraq in June 1949.

Service Light bomber 8, 45, 84 **Training** 228 OCU; CFS **Trials** ASWDU; ATDU; 51/TRE **Communications** Iraq CF; 1 FU

T Mark 2
The Type 165 was an intended trainer variant which was not pursued.

Met Mark 3
This was a variant built expressly for meteorological tasks. Armament was deleted and weather recording equipment and a radio altimeter fitted; most were new-build aircraft.

Service Meteorology 45; 1301 Flt; Acklington SF

T Mark 4
The Mark 4 was a radar navigator trainer for the Meteor NF Mk 11. Most were B Mk 1 conversions.

Service Training AIS; 228, 238 OCU

T Mark 5
The second trainer variant was a T Mk 4 conversion with revised nose to take the Meteor NF Mk 12/14 radar for navigator training.

Service Training 238 OCU

T Mark 6
The Mark 6 was an intended Javelin radar operator trainer.

Specification and production

Mark	Role	Engine	HP	Weight lb	Speed mph	Nos
TF1	Torpedo fighter	2xCentaurus 57	2,470	39,100	350	14
B1	Torpedo fighter	2xCentaurus 57	2,470	39,000	358	107
T2	Trainer	2xCentaurus 57	not built			-
Met3	Meteorology	2xCentaurus 57	2,470	37,000	360	17*
T4	Trainer	2xCentaurus 57	2,470	39,100	335	49+
T5	Trainer	2xCentaurus 57	2,470	39,100	335	21~
T6	Trainer	2xCentaurus 57	not built			-

* 16 new, l Bl conversion
\+ 9 new, 40 Bl conversions
~ T4 conversions

3.9 de Havilland Vampire (1946–1969)
While much energy was expended on the first British jet fighter, the Meteor, a second and smaller type was being built by de Havilland as the DH.100 to specification E.6/41. Originally and unofficially named Spidercrab, the new fighter was eventually produced as the Vampire. The first prototype, LZ548/G, flew on 20 September 1943, some six months later than the Meteor. It was designed around a single H1 engine, later to become the Goblin; power was limited and a lightweight twin-boom configuration was employed. Armament was to be four 20mm cannon.

F Mark I
The Mark I first flew (TG274) on 20 April 1945 with a square-cut tail fin after modifications to the prototype to establish the best fin and rudder configuration. The first aircraft went to 247 Sqn from March 1946 and as production progressed improvements were introduced on the line. From the 40th aircraft the Goblin 2 of 3,100lb thrust was introduced together with auxiliary underwing fuel tanks, and from the 51st machine the type had a pressurised cockpit and bubble canopy.

Service Fighter 3, 20, 54, 72, 130, 247, 501, 600, 605, 608, 613 **Anti-aircraft co-operation** 595, 631 **Training** 1689 Flt; 202, 203, 208 AFS; CFS; 19 FTS; 102, 103 FRS; 226 OCU; RAFC **Communications** FCCS; 12 GCF; Acklington APS; **Other** AFDS; CFE; ETPS; NGTE; WEE

Mark II
The next variant comprised four F Mk 1 aircraft fitted with the Nene I of 4,500lb thrust. Built to specification

de Havilland Vampire FB Mk 9

The Vampire joined the RAF after the war and although it equipped numerous fighter squadrons it would have been no match for contemporary Soviet aircraft. Later versions were used effectively in the ground attack role. This line-up of 60 Sqn FB Mk 9 aircraft is at Tengah in 1955 prior to re-equipment with the Venom; the two nearest machines are WL514/X and WG878/A. *(Crown copyright)*

F.11/45 the version featured two small additional intakes mounted just behind the cockpit. The fourth conversion, with revised main intakes, served as the prototype for the Australian-built **Mk 30**.

F Mark 3

The short range of the early aircraft was addressed in the Mark 3 which was built to specification F.3/47 and carried more fuel in wing tanks resulting in extended range (730 to 1,145 miles). The tanks caused stability problems which were cured by lowering the tailplane, extending its chord and changing the shape of the fin and rudder. The prototype was TG275 which flew on 4 November 1945 and the type joined 54 Sqn in April 1948.

Service Fighter 5, 20, 32, 54, 72, 73, 247, 502, 601, 604, 605, 608, 614 **Training** CFS **Communications** 25, 602, 603; Chivenor, Odiham, Thorney Island SFs; **Other** AMSDU; 1, 4, 5 CAACU; CFE; 1 OFU; TEU Khartoum; TFU

Mark IV

This was an intended Nene-powered version of the F Mk 3.

FB Mark 5

The Mark 5 resulted from capitalising on the Vampire's sound handling qualities as a ground attack platform. The wings were clipped and strengthened to enable the carriage of two 1,000lb bombs or eight rockets. To compensate for the additional wing loading a longer stroke undercarriage was fitted. TG444, a converted F Mk 1, flew on 29 June 1948 and the first production aircraft followed a year later. The first aircraft were delivered to 54 Sqn. Some aircraft operated by OCUs were informally designated **FB(T) Mk 5**.

Service Fighter/close support 3, 4, 5, 6, 11, 14, 16, 20, 26, 28, 32, 54, 60, 67, 71, 72, 73, 93, 94, 98, 112, 118, 130, 145, 185, 213, 234, 247, 249, 266, 501, 502, 602, 603, 605, 607,

608, 609, 612, 613, 614 **Training** 45, 111, 151; 226, 229, 233, 236 OCU; 202, 203, 206, 208, 210 AFS; CFS; CNCS; CNS; FETS; 1, 4, 5, 6, 7, 8, 9, 10 FTS; 102, 103 FRS; FTU; RAFFC **Communications** 2, 12, 43, 63, 81, 83 GCF; FCCS; MCCS; MECF; 2 TAFCS; 2 FP; Abu Sueir, Aldergrove, Filton, Gütersloh, Habbaniyah, Honiley, Kinloss, North Weald, Odiham, Ouston, St Eval, Tangmere, Thornaby, West Raynham SFs **Other** APS Acklington, Sylt; AFDS; ATDU; 2, 3, 3/4, 4, 5 CAACU; CCGS; DFLS; ETPS; FWS; IAM; 1 OFU; SLAW; TRE; VFE

FB Mark 6

A single test aircraft (TG433) was fitted with the Goblin Mk 3 as the Mark 6 prior to a Swiss Air Force order where, unusually, the British designation was retained.

Mark 7

Like the Mark 6 the Mark 7 was intended for the Goblin 3 but in the event it was not produced as such, being developed into the export FB Mark 50.

FB Mark 8

The Mark 8 was the precursor to the Type 112 Venom. A single F Mk 1 conversion, TG278, was fitted with the Ghost engine while retaining the Vampire wing.

FB Mark 9

The need for improved pilot comfort in the tropics resulted in the Mark 9. The basic FB Mk 5 was fitted with air conditioning which resulted in an eight-inch increase in the starboard wing root fillet.

Service Fighter/close support 4, 5, 6, 8, 11, 20, 26, 28, 32, 45, 60, 73, 93, 185, 213, 234, 249, 501, 502, 603, 607, 608, 613, 614 **Training** 203, 208 AFS; 1, 4, 5, 7, 8 FTS; FETS; 233 OCU; RAFC **Communications** 147; 1 OFU; Aden CF; Butterworth APC; Iraq, Malta CS; MECF **Other** 1, 3 CAACU

NF Mark 10

The DH.113 was originally built as a private-venture night fighter equipped with the AI Mark 10 radar. The fuselage was widened and lengthened to accommodate pilot and navigator and the tailplane was extended beyond the fins and rudders to compensate. The prototype, as G-5-2, flew on 28 August 1949 and pending the delivery of the Meteor night fighters the type served with three UK-based units, starting with 25 Sqn in July 1951.

Service **Night fighter** 23, 25, 151 **Other** CSE

NF(T) Mark 10

The sub-variant was a conversion of the NF Mk 10 for navigator training. The radar was removed and replaced with Rebecca 3 and Gee 3 navigational aids. The canopy was replaced with the type fitted to the Venom NF Mk 2A.

Service **Training** 1, 2 ANS; CNCS; RAFFC

T Mark 11

The DH.115 was also built as a private venture trainer to which specification T.111 was issued. The configuration was similar to that of the NF Mk 10 but the fin was extended by a fillet; radar and armament was deleted and dual controls fitted. The prototype (G-5-7/WW456) flew on 15 November 1950 and a total of 530 was delivered. Most operational units employed one or two, but the type was notable for introducing jet training before qualification.

Service **Training** 1, 3, 4, 5, 6, 8, 11, 14, 16, 19, 20, 23, 25, 28, 32, 33, 34, 41, 43, 45, 54, 56, 60, 63, 65, 66, 67, 71, 73, 74, 79, 80, 89, 92, 93, 94, 97, 98, 111, 112, 118, 125, 130, 141, 142, 145, 151, 167, 213, 219, 222, 234, 245, 247, 249, 253, 257, 263, 266, 500, 502, 602, 603, 608; 1, 3, 4, 5, 7, 8, 9, 10, 11, 211 FTS; 202, 205, 206, 208 AFS; 226, 228, 229, 233 OCU; 1, 2 ANS; 1 RS; AWOCU; CATCS; CFS; CGS; CNCS; FCS; FLS; FETS; FTU; FWS; IRS; ITS; RAFC **Communications** Ahlhorn, Brüggen, Butterworth, Celle, Church Fenton, Coltishall, Driffield, Duxford, Fassberg, Geilenkirchen, Gütersloh, Horsham St Faith, Jever, Laarbruch, Leuchars, Linton-on-Ouse, Middleton St George, Nicosia, Odiham, Oldenburg, Swinderby, Tengah, Waterbeach, Wattisham, Wünstorf SF; APC Butterworth; APS Sylt; 2TAF CS; 23, 25, 83 GCF; Levant CF; FECS; MCCS; MCS **Other** ETPS; RRE; SLAW

Specification and production

Mark	Role	Engine	Thrust lb	Weight lb	Speed	Nos
F1	Fighter	Goblin	2,700	10,480	540	170
II	Trials	Nene	4,500	11,000	570	3*
F3	Fighter	Goblin 2	3,100	11,970	531	117
IV	Trials	Nene I	4,500	11,000	570	1*
FB5	Fighter-bomber	Goblin 2	3,100	12,360	535	473
FB6	Fighter-bomber	Goblin 3	3,300	12,390	548	1
7	Fighter-bomber	Goblin 3	3,300	not built		
FB8	Fighter-bomber	Ghost 2	4,400	13,000	570	1
FB9	Fighter-bomber	Goblin 3	3,350	12,390	548	275
NF10	Night fighter	Goblin 3	3,350	13,100	538	78
NF (T)10	Trainer	Goblin 3	3,350	13,100	538	37+
T11	Trainer	Goblin 35	3,500	11,150	538	530

* F1 conversions
+ NF 10 conversions

Further reading

de Havilland Vampire F1-T55 Levy, R and Ward, R, Osprey, 1973

de Havilland Vampire Mk 5 & 9, The (Profile 48) Mason, F K, Profile Publications, Leatherhead, 1965

de Havilland Vampire, Venom and Sea Vixen Birtles, P J, Ian Allan, Shepperton, 1986

3.10   de Havilland Venom (1952–1962)

The DH.112 Venom was designed as a natural successor to the Vampire to specification F.15/49. It was generally similar in layout but the wing was re-designed with thinner section and straight trailing edge and new tanks were fitted to the wing-tips. The engine was the Ghost, first fitted to the Vampire FB Mk 8 TG278, which served as the development aircraft first flying on 8 May 1947. The Venom served extensively in Germany, the Middle and Far East.

FB Mark 1

The prototype, VV612, first flew on 2 September 1949. Performance was much improved over the Vampire due to the engine/wing combination. Armament was four 20mm guns (150 rounds each) with provision for 2,000lb of bombs or eight RPs; as in the Vampire no ejection seat was fitted. Service entry was with 11 Sqn in Germany in August 1952.

Service **Fighter/close support** 5, 6, 8, 11,14, 16, 28, 32, 45, 60, 73, 94, 98, 118, 145, 249, 266 **Communications** 147, 187 **Other** AFDS; CFE; CFS; CGS; RAE

de Havilland Venom FB Mk 4

The Venom had a successful but largely unsung operational life as a ground attack fighter. An anonymous FB Mk 4 of 8 Sqn is seen taxiing out at Sharjah during operations in Oman in 1958. *(A S Thomas collection)*

NF Mark 2

The night fighter variant was built with side by side seating for pilot and navigator and equipped with AI Mark 10 radar. The prototype (G-5-3/WP227) flew on 22 August 1950 only a year after the Vampire NF Mk 10 which it superseded.

Service Night fighter 23, 33, 219, 253 **Training** 141 **Other** CFE; RRE

NF Mark 2A

Many NF Mk 2 aircraft were converted to Mk 2A standard to counter stability problems. The fin and rudder shape was changed and the dorsal fillet of the Vampire T Mk 11 was added; in addition a clear-view canopy was incorporated.

Service Night fighter 33, 219, 253

NF Mark 3

The Mark 3 was an upgraded night fighter equipped with powered ailerons, ejection seats and a more bulbous nose to accommodate the American AI Mk 21 (APS-57) radar. Power was provided by the slightly more powerful Ghost 104 and the tailplane extension beyond the fin and rudders was deleted.

Service Night fighter 23, 89, 125, 141, 151 **Communications** 173; Coltishall, Stradishall SF **Other** CFE; RAE; RRE

FB Mark 4

The Mark 4 was an improved single-seat fighter similar to the FB Mk 1 but with the Ghost 104, powered ailerons, ejection seat and revised fin and rudder. The FB Mk 4 entered service with 123 Wing, Wünstorf, in July 1955.

Service Fighter/close support 5, 6, 8, 11, 28, 60, 73, 94, 142, 208, 249, 266 **Other** FWS

Specification and production

Mark	Role	Engine	Thrust lb	Weight lb	Speed mph	Nos
FB1	Fighter-bomber	Ghost 103	4,850	15,400	597	363
NF2	Night fighter	Ghost 103	4,850	15,800	590	90
NF2A	Night fighter	Ghost 103	4,850	15,800	590	*
NF3	Night fighter	Ghost 104	4,950	15,800	595	129
FB4	Fighter-bomber	Ghost 103	4,850	15,400	597	150

* Most NF2 were converted but no record of exact numbers

Further reading

de Havilland Vampire: The Complete History, Watkins, D, 1996

de Havilland Vampire, Venom and Sea Vixen, Birtles, P J, Ian Allan, Shepperton, 1988

de Havilland Venom, Lindsay, R, Lindsay, Stockton on Tees, 1974

3.11 Hawker P.1127 and Kestrel (1960–1966)

In the short history of powered flight there are no more than a dozen or so major milestones. One has to be the P.1127 development aircraft leading via the Kestrel to the vertical take-off and landing (VTOL) Harrier. There were two schools of thought in relation to VTOL. Rolls-Royce, among others, developed high thrust to weight ratio engines for fixed vertical installation for lift with separate engines for horizontal flight. The format was abandoned in the West but employed on the Yak-36, albeit with a main vectored thrust engine.

The **P.1127** design began in 1957 of an airframe to be built around the revolutionary BE53 vectored thrust engine. By 1960 the Ministry of Supply issued ER.204D funding two prototypes, the first of which (XP831) flew on 21 October 1960. The installed engine delivered 11,300lb of thrust and weight was reduced to just 10,000lb for the first tethered 'flight'. The first conventional take-off was on 13 March 1961 and transition from vertical to horizontal flight in September of the same year. The aircraft went supersonic in a dive on 12 December 1961. By now a second prototype (XP836) had joined the first and in the light of experience numerous design changes were incorporated in subsequent prototypes (XP972, 976, 980, 984).

Engines were improved and replaced frequently. In 1959 the BE53 produced only 9,000lb thrust; as the Pegasus 2 (11,300lb) it powered the prototype; and as the 3 (14,000lb) it saw the aircraft into transition. The Pegasus 4 (15,500lb) powered the last prototype.

From the outset the P.1127 was intended to act as a prototype for an operational aircraft rather than simply being a research machine. As solutions to problems were identified they were incorporated in airframes. By 1963 there was interest from Germany and the United States in the project and an agreement reached to build nine trials aircraft to examine every aspect of VTOL operations.

Hawker P.1127

Although not an operational aircraft the P.1127 undertook pioneering work leading to service entry – via the Kestrel – of the world's first operational VTOL aircraft the Harrier. The fifth prototype, XP980, was fitted with the Pegasus 3 engine of 13,500lbs thrust and is seen here on trials at Dunsfold.
(Hawker Aircraft Ltd)

Kestrel F(GA) Mark 1

The Kestrel was the response to the agreement and in effect the prototype was the last P.1127 development aircraft. It was produced to requirement GOR.345. Compared to the earlier P.1127s it had the Pegasus 5 of 15,500lb thrust, inflatable intake lips, a swept wing, longer fuselage and a tailplane of increased span. Nine Kestrels were constructed (starting XS688) and the Tripartite Evaluation Squadron was formed at West Raynham in March 1965 within the Central Fighter Establishment. The unit flew the Kestrel intensively for nine months during which 930 sorties covering 600 hours were flown. The type was never more than an interim vehicle and from January 1965, at which time the intended supersonic P.1154 was cancelled, the subsonic fully operational P.1127/Kestrel derivative was ordered. Those trials aircraft transferred to the US were given the designation XV-6A.

Service **Trials** Tripartite Trials Squadron; CFE

Specification and production

Mark	Role	Engine	Thrust lb	Weight lb	Speed mph	Nos
P.1127	Prototype	Pegasus 1	11,300	10,000	-	2*
P.1127	Prototype	Pegasus 2	12,500	12,000	-	1+
P.1127	Prototype	Pegasus 3	13,500	12,000	700	3~
P.1127	Prototype	Pegasus 4	15,500	13,000	700	1#
Kestrel	Trials	Pegasus 4	15,500	15,000	660	9

* XP831, 836
+ XP972
~ XP831, 976, 980
# XP984

Further reading

British Aerospace Harrier and Sea Harrier, Braybrook, R, Osprey, London, 1984
Harrier, Calvert, D J, Ian Allan, London, 1990
Harrier, Gunston, W, Ian Allan, Shepperton, 1984
Harrier, Mason, F K, Patrick Stephens, 1986
Hawker P.1127 and Kestrel (Profile 198) Mason, F K, Profile Publications, Leatherhead, 1969

3.12 Hawker Harrier (1969–date)

Following the success of the P.1127/Kestrel in demonstrating the viability of VTOL for a close support combat aircraft the type was ordered into production in mid-

---

Hawker Harrier GR Mk 1

The Harrier introduced unprecedented versatility in its ability to operate close to the front-line in support of ground forces. GR Mk 1 'N' of 3 Sqn normally based at Wildenrath is seen during Exercise 'Oak Stroll' in Germany in 1974. *(Crown copyright)*

1966. Six development and 60 production aircraft were ordered. Whereas the Kestrel embodied about 50% of the structure of the P.1127, the Harrier was in many respects a new aircraft re-engineered around the more powerful Pegasus 101 engine.

GR Mark 1

The P.1127/7 first flew on 31 August 1966 (XV276) and the first six development batch machines went to the manufacturer and Boscombe Down for intensive trials, development and weapons work. The first production aircraft (XV738) flew on 28 December 1967 and in January 1969 the Harrier Conversion Team was formed which in turn became the Conversion Unit at Wittering. It was there that the first VTOL squadron in the world, appropriately No 1, was formed in July 1969. The GR Mk 1 was fitted with four underwing and one fuselage pylons to accommodate a total of 5,000lbs of bombs or rockets. In addition a pair of Aden 30mm cannon could be carried in detachable under-fuselage pods.

Service Close support 1, 3, 4, 20 **Training** HCT/HCU; 233 OCU

GR Mark 1A

Numerous GR Mk 1 aircraft were retro-fitted with the Pegasus 102 of 20,500lb thrust as the Mark 1A.

Service Close support 1, 3, 4, 20 **Training** 233 OCU

T Mark 2

The trainer was a two-seat tandem variant with nose and tail extensions of 47in and 33in respectively. It was fitted with an extended under-fuselage strake and later in the service life was given a taller fin. The engine was the Pegasus 101 of the GR Mk 1. The prototype (XW174) flew on 24 April 1969 and the type was issued to squadrons as well as the OCU.

Service Training 1, 3, 4; 233 OCU

T Mark 2A

The Mark 2A designation was applied to eleven examples of the T Mk 2 fitted with the Pegasus 102 engine. Most were fitted with the taller fin.

Service Training 1, 3, 4; 233 OCU

GR Mark 3

The Mark 3 was developed from the GR Mk 1. As additional aircraft were ordered to cope with attrition the number of changes from the original was sufficient to merit a new designation. The more powerful Pegasus 103 of 21,500lb thrust was fitted and other differences were connected with sensors. The Ferranti LRMTS target seeker and marker was installed in a revised nose and a passive warning receiver on the fin. Forty new-build aircraft were constructed but most were GR Mk 1/1A aircraft upgraded as they required major servicing.

Service Close support 1, 3, 4, 20; 1351, 1417, 1453 Flts; 1 HarDet

T Mark 4

Like the GR Mk 3, the Mark 4 was a re-designation given the number of changes to an earlier version, in this case the T Mk 2. The changes were similar to those embodied on the GR Mk 3 but the T Mk 4 reverted to the original, lower, fin of the early Mk 2. Like the Mk 2 the T Mk 4 was fully combat capable.

Service Training 1, 3, 4; 233 OCU; Gütersloh SF

T Mark 4A

The Mark 4A was similar to the T Mk 4 but without the laser nose. The equipment was deleted to save weight, allowing increased range.

Service Training 233 OCU; RAE: 899 NAS

T Mark 4N

The Mark 4N was built for the Royal Navy and was similar to the T Mk 4A but with the Pegasus 104 engine.

Service Training 899 NAS

GR Mark 5

The next variant was a major re-design sufficient to justify a new name let alone a new designation. The new type was the result of USMC pressure for a more capable aircraft, building on experience with the early Harrier (AV-8A); McDonnell Douglas was contracted to work on the new type in 1978. The RAF also required a developed aircraft and BAe designed the machine with a larger wing to specification ASR409. In the event in 1981 agreement was reached for a common type to become the AV-8B/GR-5.

The GR Mk 5 was built around the Pegasus 105 engine with the new composite wing of much larger area and a revised forward fuselage and cockpit with much better visibility. Eight underwing and one under-fuselage hardpoints allow the carriage of up to 9,200lb of stores plus two 25mm cannon. The avionics includes a Litton ASN 130 inertial navigation system, Hughes Angle Rate Bombing Set using both TV and laser trackers, and Ferranti moving map display. The prototype (ZD318) flew on 30 April 1985 and the new version entered service with 1 Sqn in 1988. There were several problems in introduction into service and in the event the GR Mk 5 was an interim type pending the GR Mk 7.

Service Interdiction 1, 3, 4 **Training** 233 OCU **Other** SAOEU

GR Mark 5A

The Mark 5A was similar to the GR Mk 5 but with fitments to GR Mk 7 standard. The airframes (nos 42-60) were placed in storage for full conversion later; the first was ZD432.

T Mark 6

The Mark 6 was a proposal to bring the T Mk 4 to GR Mk 7 standard with night attack avionics; it was not pursued.

GR Mark 7

The definitive 'new Harrier' is similar in nearly all respects to the GR Mk 5 but with night attack capability. This

Hawker Harrier GR Mk 7

The developed Harrier, with a completely new wing and forward fuselage, bears an obvious family relationship to the earlier versions but is a completely new aircraft. Relative to the GR Mk 1 engine power increased from 19,500lst to 21,750lst while weapons load improved from 5,000lb to 9,200lb. GR Mk 7 ZD378/A belongs to the Harrier Operational Conversion Unit at Wittering which carries the markings of 20 (reserve) Sqn. *(Author)*

results in a slight change in the nose profile to accommodate FLIR in a fairing above the nose, while two smaller bulges below the nose house the forward Zeus ECM antennae. The aircraft is effective at night through the provision of night vision goggle (NVG) compatible instruments. Nine aircraft have been wired for the Vinten camera pod used on the GR Mk 3 but with camera changes. Armament remains as on the GR Mk 5 but with the Aden cannon still not operational at December 1994.

Service Interdiction 1, 3, 4; SAOEU/AWC **Training** HOCU (20)

T Mark 8

The Mark 8 is the designation for two T Mk 4 trainers transferred to the Royal Navy when the T Mk 10 became available to the RAF.

Service Training 899 NAS

GR Mark 9

This is the intended designation for the GR Mk 7 mid-life update with the Pegasus 11-61 (flown in ZD402 in 1989), terrain referenced navigation system and provision for the AIM-120.

T Mark 10

The Mark 10 is a tandem trainer built to match the GR Mk 7. The variant is fully combat capable, unlike the American TAV-8B, and the prototype, ZH563, flew on 7 April 1994.

Service Training 1, 3, 4; HOCU (20) **Trials** DTEO

Specification and production

Mark	Role	Engine	Thrust lb	Weight lb	Speed mph	Nos
GR1	Close support	Pegasus 101	19,500	23,500	730	84
GR1A	Close support	Pegasus 102	20,500	23,500	730	*
T2	Trainer	Pegasus 101	19,500	26,200	720	16
T2A	Trainer	Pegasus 102	20,500	26,200	720	11+
GR3	Close support	Pegasus 103	21,500	25,000	730	102~
T4	Trainer	Pegasus 103	21,500	26,200	720	25#
T4A	Trainer	Pegasus 103	21,500	26,200	720	5$
T4N	Trainer	Pegasus 104	21,500	26,200	720	3
GR5	Inter-diction	Pegasus 105	21,750	31,000	720	43
GR5A	Inter-diction	Pegasus 105	21,750	31,000	720	19
T6	Trainer	not pursued				
GR7	Inter-diction	Pegasus 105	21,750	31,000	720	83@
T8	Trainer	Pegasus 104	21,500	26,200	720	1^
GR9	Inter-diction	Pegasus 11-61	23,800	31,500	GR7 MLU	
T10	Trainer	Pegasus 105	21,500	32,000	720	13

* Most GR1s retrofitted to GR1A
\+ T2 conversions
\~ Including 62 GR1/1A conversions
\# Including 14 T2/T2A conversions
$ Including 4 T4 conversions
@ Including 49 GR5/5A conversions
^ T4N conversion

Further reading
British Aerospace Harrier and Sea Harrier, Braybrook, R, Osprey, London, 1984
Harrier, World Air Power Journal Vol 6, Aerospace Publishing, London, 1991
Harrier, Calvert, D J, Ian Allan, London 1990
Harrier, Gunston, W, Ian Allan, Shepperton, 1984
Harrier, Mason, F K, Patrick Stephens, Cambridge, 1986
Harrier GR3, Shaw, M, Ian Allan, 1988
Harrier Story, The (Air Extra) Gunston, W, Ian Allan, London, 1979
Hawker P.1127 and Kestrel, The (Profile 198) Mason, F, K Profile Publications, Leatherhead, 1967

3.13 SEPECAT Jaguar (1973–date)

The Jaguar is the first warplane produced on a collaborative basis by two partners in different countries. The design of the aircraft had its distant origins in the Breguet Taon which in 1957 won a NATO light fighter competition, in the event not progressed. The French and Royal Air Forces both had a requirement for a fast trainer and Breguet/Dassault and the British Aircraft Corporation (BAC) collaborated in the production both of training and attack versions – in the case of the UK the fighter version was required to compensate for the cancellation of the P.1154 and the intended Anglo-French Variable Geometry (AFVG) aircraft, which later re-surfaced as the Tornado. Agreement was reached in 1966 for joint development and manufacture, in the UK to AST362. During the course of early development the aircraft was fitted

SEPECAT Jaguar GR Mk 1

The Jaguar was a joint Anglo-French aircraft which replaced the Canberra and (interim) Phantom in the RAF light strike, interdiction and reconnaissance roles. A total of 203, including 38 fully operational trainers, was delivered. XZ118/Y is seen in Gulf War finish and configuration with a single 264-gal centre-line fuel tank, overwing AIM-9L AAMs and an ALQ-101 ECM pod; bombs were carried on the inner wing pylons. *(Crown copyright)*

with a taller fin and larger nosewheel door. The single-seat fighter replaced the Phantom in Germany and the UK where the latter type was an interim solution to replacement of the Canberra.

GR Mark 1

The Jaguar first flew in French two-seat (E) form in September 1968 and the first British prototype, XW560, a single-seater, flew on 12 October 1969. The Jaguar was intended as a low-level strike aircraft capable of Mach 1.6 but operating from simple strips and carrying a powerful external weapons load of up to 10,500lb on five hardpoints. In addition there are two fixed 30mm Aden cannon. The RAF attack version differs from the French in having a digital inertial navigation system, and from 1974 external changes included a revised nose to accommodate the Ferranti Laser Ranger and Marked Target Seeker (LRMTS) and a radar warning receiver on the fin. The changes were retro-fitted to all surviving aircraft. Service introduction was with the Jaguar OCU in September 1973 and the first squadron was 54 from March 1974.

Service Ground attack 6, 14, 17, 20, 31, 54 **Reconnaissance** 2, 41 **Training** JOCU/226 OCU

GR Mark 1A

The Mark 1A was a GR Mk 1 conversion with the improved FIN 1064 INS which gave unprecedented

accuracy and which was fitted from 1983. From 1978 the engines had been upgraded to the Adour 104, while from 1982 a range of defensive and offensive equipment changes was incorporated, partly to meet operational requirements of the Gulf War and operations in Bosnia.

Service Ground attack 6, 14, 17, 20, 31, 54 **Reconnaissance** 2, 41 **Training** 226 OCU; 16(R) **Trials** RAE/DRA

T Mark 2

The Mark 2 was designed from the outset as a fully operational two-seat tandem trainer. The prototype, XW566, first flew on 30 August 1971 and the 38 ordered were split between operational squadrons and the OCU.

Service Training 2, 6, 14, 17, 20, 31, 41, 54; JOCU/226 OCU **Other** ETPS; RAE

T Mark 2A

This designation was applied at that stage in Jaguar development when the INS was replaced with the FIN 1064, by which time the engine had been uprated to the Adour 104. Only fourteen conversions were completed.

Service Training 2, 6, 41, 54; 226 OCU; 16(R) **Trials** DRA; SAOEU

Specification and production

Mark	Role	Engine	Thrust lb	Weight lb	Speed mph	Nos
GR1	Ground attack	Adour 102	8,040	33,500	M1.6	165
GR1A	Ground attack	Adour 104	8,400	34,170	M1.6	75*
T2	Trainer	Adour 102	8,040	34,000	M1.6	38
T2A	Trainer	Adour 104	8,400	34,000	M1.6	14+

* GR1 conversions
+ T2 conversions

Further reading
Jaguar, World Air Power Journal Vol 11, Aerospace Publishing, London, 1992
SEPECAT Jaguar, Reed, A, Ian Allan, Shepperton, 1982

4 – Bombers

See also: Liberator (5.6)

During the war the classification of bombers, and the units which flew them, was usually clear, although the multi-role Mosquito blurred the definition. After the war the traditions of the heavy bomber were maintained with the Lincoln, supplemented by the Washington, succeeding the Lancaster in service. The first jet bomber was the Canberra, a worthy successor to the Mosquito and still in service at the time of writing after some 44 years. During the height of the Cold War the Valiant, Vulcan and Victor bombers were, in theory at least, complemented by 60 Thor missiles which were in reality under US control.

After the demise of the V-bombers the vehicles for delivering the strategic deterrent switched to Royal Navy submarines, but air delivery of nuclear strike weapons remained with types like the Buccaneer, Phantom and Tornado. Inevitably, in describing the units involved in flying 'bombers' there is some overlap with those flying in the ground attack and reconnaissance roles.

January 1946

The equipment and deployment of bomber units in early 1946 was very much a reflection of the situation at the war's end but on a smaller scale. Heavy bomber squadrons, of which there were 24, were all equipped with the Lancaster, while three pathfinder units employed the Mosquito. Seven light bomber units with Mosquitos were based in Germany with BAFO while another five Mosquito squadrons were deployed in the Far East. In the Middle East and Africa there was a total of seven medium bomber units mainly equipped with war-weary American types; these included four squadrons flying operationally in Greece.

The training situation was such that there was a surplus of units relative to the demand for aircrew with no fewer than five OTUs, generally equipped with Wellingtons, and three Lancaster conversion units. Ageing bomber types still in second-line service included the Beaufort, Whitley, Baltimore, Boston, Marauder and Mitchell.

For the future, the Air Staff had identified a need for jet-powered bombers to carry the new nuclear weapons and had issued a specification met in due course by the relatively conventional Valiant and the more advanced Victor and Vulcan.

July 1948

Within two and a half years the situation had changed dramatically to a much slimmer bomber force, at least overseas. The Lincoln had entered service and equipped fourteen squadrons, while the Lancaster remained in service with eight squadrons in 3 Group. This was just two fewer squadrons than had been deployed in 1946, but they were located on seven airfields compared with fifteen. Two Mosquito pathfinder units remained in 1 Group, while four light bomber squadrons, also equipped with the Mosquito, were based in Germany. Perhaps the most marked change was the disbanding of all the OTUs and CUs, leaving just one OCU with the Lincoln and Mosquito at Scampton.

January 1950

By now the Lancaster had been withdrawn from service with Bomber Command and, significantly, the new Canberra light bomber, built to a 1945 specification, had flown. The threat from the Soviet Union was now explicit and the number of heavy bomber squadrons remained at 22, still with two Mosquito pathfinder units and four light bomber squadrons in Germany. But there was an urgent need for new equipment capable of holding its own against the MiG-15.

English Electric Canberra PR Mk 9

The Canberra, although designed as a bomber, was quickly taken into service as a photo-reconnaissance platform due to its ceiling. Allegedly the RAF undertook overflights of the Soviet Union in 1953 and 1954 using the Canberra. The definitive reconnaissance variant was the PR Mk 9 exemplified by XH136 which entered service with 58 Sqn in 1960. The extended wing chord inboard of the much more powerful Avon 206 engines conferred a ceiling of at least 70,000ft. *(Crown copyright)*

April 1953

Total number of units had increased to 25 and equipment changes were now evident. Pending full introduction of the Canberra, arrangements had been made for the transfer of 88 B-29 bombers from the US, known as the Washington in British service. In fact the Washington was of Lincoln vintage, so it should be seen as supplementing the latter, rather than replacing it. Thus there were seven Washington and nine Lincoln squadrons. It needs to be noted, though, that serviceability on the Washingtons was very poor.

The most important change was with the introduction of the Canberra with 101 Sqn in January 1951 fewer than two years after the first flight. Nine squadrons were operational within 1 Group, having replaced the Mosquito, and the type now equipped the sole OCU. There were now no bomber units in Germany or further afield but anticipating the Canberra in Germany was the Tactical Development Unit (TDU). Signs of further changes were in the wings. New bombers had flown in 1951 in the shape of the Sperrin (not proceeded with) and the Valiant, and in late 1952 the other V-bombers, the Victor and Vulcan, had flown in prototype form.

A characteristic of a number of RAF commands at this time was the dual numbering of many units in order to preserve the identities of famous squadrons. Nowhere was this short-lived practice more evident than in Bomber Command.

January 1955

Within just two years the Canberra was much in evidence and a further landmark had been the introduction of the first of the V-bombers, the Valiant. The RAF was preparing to assume responsibility for managing the United Kingdom's deterrent force, and the second Valiant unit was 1321 Flight which was preparing for the nuclear weapon tests in Australia. Twenty-three Canberra squadrons were operational in the UK with a further four within 2 TAF. The Lincoln equipped five units and as noted above the Valiant was in service. In total, then, there were no fewer than 33 squadrons, the largest number since the end of the war

While the primary purpose of the bomber force was deterrence against Soviet attack on the West, Lincoln units were rotated through Aden, Kenya and Malaya in support of campaigns in those countries against terrorists or dissidents. This was a process begun in 1948 and which continued through into the 1960s.

Bomber trials units

The **Bomber Command Development Unit** (BCDU) originated at Boscombe Down in 1940. On 24 July 1954 it reformed at Wittering and then moved to Finningley on 1 March 1960 with the Canberra, Valiant and Victor. It became the **Strike Command Development Unit** (SCDU) before disbandment on 31 December 1968.

The **Bombing Trials Unit** (BTU) was formed on 1 August 1942 at West Freugh in Scotland for trials with weapons, spending the period June 1947 to May 1948 at Wigtown. The BTU was re-designated **Air Armament Trials Establishment** (AATE) in 64 Group on 1 January 1957 and it was disbanded into the RAE on 10 June 1959. The unit remains at West Freugh at the time of writing.

The **Bomb Ballistics Unit** (BBU) was formed on 22 May 1944 at Woodbridge where it was concerned with trials of the 'Tallboy' and 'Grand Slam' bombs. The **Blind Landing Experimental Unit** (BLEU) was formed at Woodbridge as an outstation of the RAE in October 1945 and both merged on 1 November 1949; both units had moved to Martlesham Heath in 1946. The new unit became the **Bomb Ballistics and Blind Landing Experimental Establishment** (BBBLEE). Within BBBLEE the BBU became the **Armament and Instrument Experimental Unit** (AIEU) on 1 May 1950 using a variety of types. The BBBLEE was absorbed into the RAE at Bedford on 30 June 1957.

The **Bomber Command Instructors' School** (BCIS) was formed at Finningley on 5 December 1944 with Lancasters, Halifaxes, Wellingtons and Spitfires to train instructors in bomber and fighter tactics. On 22 January 1947 BCIS moved to Scampton and on 5 June became the **Bomber Command Instrument Rating and Examining Flight** (BCIREF) disbanding on 10 March 1952.

The **Bombing Development Unit** (BDU) formed at Gransden Lodge in July 1942 and developed bombing aids and techniques. It eventually moved to Feltwell and late in 1945 was absorbed into the **Central Bomber Establishment** (CBE) equipped with Lancasters to train bombing and gunnery leaders. The CBE had formed at Marham on 25 September 1945 with Mosquitoes and Lancasters and it was later equipped with the Lincoln. The CBE undertook much overseas work including tests against reinforced concrete installations in France. In April 1949 the CBE moved to Lindholme where it disbanded on 21 December of that year.

The **Bomber Command Bombing School** (BCBS) was formed at Lindholme on 15 October 1952 in 1 Group equipped with the Lincoln. In 1968, by now equipped with the Hastings T5, BCBS was renamed **Strike Command Bombing School** (SCBS) and on 1 September 1972 it moved to Scampton where it operated the Vulcan before disbanding on 1 January 1974. The Hastings continued to serve in the **Hastings Radar Flight** (HRF) at Scampton until July 1977.

July 1957

At this time the Canberra force was reducing fast, the Valiant fleet was complete and the newer V-bombers were just entering service. The British and French had embarked on the Suez intervention in late 1956, success in which, it had been assumed, would rely heavily on the deployment and operation of British bombers. During the campaign five Canberra B Mk 6 and four Valiant squadrons were deployed to Malta while seven Canberra B Mk 2 units were based on Cyprus. During this period bombs were dropped in anger on Egypt by both types. There were one Vulcan and eight Valiant squadrons and thirteen Canberra squadrons in the UK with three Canberra interdictor units in Germany and two squadrons based in Cyprus, although within a few months these latter would re-equip with the Venom.

June 1960

At the very time when every component of the V-force nuclear deterrent was in place the vulnerability of the high-flying bomber was vividly demonstrated. On 1 May 1960 a U-2 reconnaissance aircraft, flying at around 65,000ft, was shot down over Sverdlovsk in the Soviet Union. All of the V-bombers were now in service in two groups comprising in total three squadrons each of Victor B Mk 1 and Vulcan B Mk 1 and seven Valiant squadrons. In addition there were three Canberra squadrons in the

UK, four in the Middle East and one in the Far East. In Germany four squadrons were equipped with interdictor variants of the Canberra.

In addition to the manned aircraft of Bomber Command there were also deployed some 60 American Thor IRBMs in four clusters each of five squadrons with three missiles each. They were slow to react, vulnerable, contributed little of value and given the dual control arrangements a cynic might argue that the British taxpayer subsidised forward-basing of American missiles. They were gone by 1963 in the aftermath of the Cuban missile crisis. Finally, it is perhaps worth pointing out that eighteen day and night fighter squadrons were backed by eleven Bloodhound units in protecting the bomber and missile bases.

January 1965

Following the U-2 incident there was urgent re-thinking about tactics and strategy and these were developed so that the bombers would fly at low level. This created a number of problems. By 1965 the Valiant was about to depart service, the stresses of low-level flying having caused fatigue problems. The nuclear weapons were clearly not intended for low-level delivery and Yellow Sun and the new WE-177 were developed for medium-level or toss-bombing delivery. This was only an interim solution and the Blue Steel stand-off bomb introduced into service in 1963 was capable of flying 100 miles at low level and delivering a one megaton warhead.

While five Valiant units were notionally still operational the V-force comprised three Vulcan B Mk 1 and six B Mk 2 squadrons, three of the latter at Scampton equipped with Blue Steel. There were also two Victor B Mk 1 and two Blue Steel-equipped B Mk 2 squadrons (100 and 139 Sqns based at Wittering). The Canberra had gone in Bomber Command but remained in Germany (four interdictor units) and in a nuclear-equipped strike wing of four squadrons on Akrotiri. The Canberra replacement, the BAC TSR.2, had flown in 1964 but there were signs that the programme was in political difficulty.

January 1970

Responsibility for the nuclear deterrent had transferred to the Royal Navy Polaris missile fleet on 1 July 1969 leaving the RAF with an essentially tactical role. Bomber Command had been absorbed into a new Strike Command as 1 Group and five Vulcan B Mk 2 squadrons were based in the UK with another two on Cyprus. The only unit properly equipped for a tactical role was 12 Sqn with the Buccaneer S Mk 2 while the Canberra remained in service in Germany and the Far East. The TSR.2 Canberra replacement had indeed been cancelled and after a succession of false starts through the Anglo-French Variable Geometry (AFVG) aircraft and the F-111K the RAF was forced to settle for ex Royal Navy and additional new-build Buccaneers and as an interim measure the Phantom FGR Mk 2. In the event the Buccaneer was to serve the RAF well for over twenty years.

January 1975

The British had withdrawn from the Far East with the exception of the Hong Kong garrison and a small detachment in Brunei. In Strike Command the Vulcan B Mk 2/SR Mk 2 equipped five squadrons in the UK- and two in Cyprus. The Buccaneer formed the equipment of two UK and two German-based units while there was a three-squadron wing with the Phantom FGR Mk 2 at Brüggen. The first Multi-Role Combat Aircraft (MRCA) had flown in 1974 and as the Tornado it was due to replace the Vulcan, and eventually the Buccaneer.

January 1980

The Vulcan remained in seven squadrons, now all UK-based as the withdrawal from the Middle East had been completed. The only other strike assets were five squadrons of the Buccaneer S Mk 2. The Vulcans were due to be phased out of service as the Tornado joined the RAF from 1982.

January 1985

No 1 Group Strike Command comprised just three Tornado squadrons, the last Vulcans having departed in 1984 but not before having undertaken the task for which they were originally designed. During the Falklands war in 1982 several aircraft from 44, 50 and 101 Sqns had attacked installations at Port Stanley from Ascension in seven sorties, each of which involved a flight of nearly fifteen hours and no fewer than eighteen in-flight refuellings. The Buccaneers now served only in the maritime strike role in two units based at Lossiemouth, while the Tornado also equipped five strike squadrons in RAF Germany.

January 1990

As in 1985 the strike force was confined to the Buccaneer (12 and 208 Sqns) and the Tornado which equipped two strike units in the UK and seven in Germany. In addition a new reconnaissance variant had entered service with 2 and 13 Sqns.

January 1995

For perhaps the first time in its history the RAF's attack potential (and indeed its air defence) was confined to just one type. While the Tornado is undoubtedly a fine aircraft, it had proved vulnerable to ground defences when operating in Arabia during the Second Gulf War in 1990/91. Of about 50 aircraft deployed four were lost in accidents but six RAF and one Italian aircraft were brought down, mostly while attacking airfields at low level – a task for which the aircraft and weapons combination were allegedly optimised. However, this was in the context of around 1,600 sorties flown, but it serves to demonstrate that the theoretical success rate of strike aircraft is much greater than the reality. New equipment and new tactics had to be introduced rapidly (as ten years earlier during the Falklands campaign) and it is a tribute to the RAF and British industry that so much was achieved. Particularly noteworthy was the swansong of the Buccaneer which was deployed at short notice to target mark for the Tornadoes.

These comments describe the context within which it has to be noted that the RAF has just four strike units at Brüggen, two maritime strike squadrons at Lossiemouth and two optimised for tactical reconnaissance at Marham. The quality of the aircraft and the competence of its crews cannot compensate for the paucity of numbers even allowing for the Conversion Unit being given a reserve squadron number (45 then 15).

4.A   Bombers at 1 January 1946

Bomber Command

1 Group

Type	Unit	Base
Lancaster I, III	12, 101	Binbrook
	83, 97	Coningsby
	300	Faldingworth
	427, 429	Leeming
	106	Metheringham
	57*, 100	Scampton
	50, 61	Sturgate
Lancaster VII	9, 617	Waddington
Mosquito XVI	109	Hemswell

3 Group

Type	Unit	Base
Lancaster I, III	35, 115	Graveley
	15, 44*	Mildenhall
	149, 207	Methwold
	90, 138	Tuddenham
	7, 49	Mepal
Mosquito IX, XVI	105, 139	Upwood

* converting to the Lincoln

BAFO (2 Group)

Type	Unit	Base
Mosquito VI	305	Melsbroek
	69, 268	Cambrai
	4, 21, 107	Gütersloh
	14	Wahn

Middle East Air Force

Type	Unit	Base
Marauder III	39	Khartoum

AHQ Greece

Type	Unit	Base
Wellington	13 Hellenic	Hassani
Boston V	13, 18, 55	Hassani

AHQ East Africa

Type	Unit	Base
Baltimore IV, V	249	Eastleigh

HQ British Forces Aden

Type	Unit	Base
Boston IV, V	114	Khormaksar

Allied Command South East Asia

AHQ Malaya

Type	Unit	Base
Mosquito VI	84, 110	Seletar

AHQ French Indo-China

Type	Unit	Base
Mosquito VI	211	Bangkok

225 Group

Type	Unit	Base
Mosquito VI	45, 82	St Thomas Mount

Training and Development

3 Group

Type	Unit	Base
Lancaster III, Lincoln I, Mosquito	CBE	Feltwell

91 Group

Type	Unit	Base
Wellington X, Anson	10 OTU	Abingdon
Wellington III, X, Anson	17 OTU	Turweston
	21 OTU	Moreton-in-Marsh
Wellington III, X, Hurricane, Anson, Master	26 OTU	Wing
Mosquito III, XVI, Oxford, Anson	16 OTU	Upper Heyford
Lancaster I, III	1660 CU	Swinderby
Lancaster I, III, Mosquito XIX	1668 CU	Cottesmore
Lancaster I, III, Mosquito XIX, Beaufighter VI	1653 CU	North Luffenham
Lancaster I, III, Lincoln BII, Oxford	BCIS	Finningley
Lancaster I	BTU	West Freugh
Mosquito VI, Halifax, Lancaster	BBU	Martlesham Heath

4.B   Bombers (and strike) at 1 July 1948

Bomber Command

1 Group

Type	Unit	Base
Mosquito B16, 35	105, 139	Coningsby
Lincoln B2	9, 12, 101, 617	Binbrook
	50, 57, 61	Waddington
	83, 97, 100	Hemswell

3 Group

Type	Unit	Base
Lancaster I, I(FE), III	7, 49, 148, 214	Upwood
	35, 115, 149, 207	Stradishall
Lincoln II	15, 44, 90, 138	Wyton

BAFO

Type	Unit	Base
Mosquito FB6	4	Wahn
Mosquito B16, 35	14, 98	Wahn
Mosquito FB6	107	Gatow

Training and development

Type	Unit	Base
Lincoln II, Mosquito B35, Anson	230 OCU	Scampton
Lincoln II	BCIRE	Scampton
Lincoln II, Mosquito	BTU	West Freugh
Lancaster	BBU	Martlesham Heath
Lancaster, Lincoln II	CBE	Marham

4.C Bombers (and strike) at 1 January 1950

Bomber Command

1 Group

Type	Unit	Base
Mosquito B35	105, 139	Coningsby
Lincoln B2	9, 12, 101, 617	Binbrook
	50, 57, 61	Waddington
	83, 97, 100	Hemswell

3 Group

Type	Unit	Base
Lincoln II	7, 49, 148, 214	Upwood
	15, 44, 90, 138	Wyton
Type	Unit	Base
	35, 115, 149, 207	Mildenhall

BAFO

Type	Unit	Base
Mosquito FB6	4	Wahn
Mosquito B16, 35	14, 98	Wahn
Mosquito FB6	107	Gatow

Training and development

Type	Unit	Base
Lincoln II, Mosquito B35, Anson, Oxford	230 OCU	Scampton
Lincoln II	BCIRE	Scampton
Lincoln II, Mosquito	BTU	West Freugh
Lancaster	BBU	Martlesham Heath

4.D Bombers (and strike) at 1 April 1953

Bomber Command

1 Group

Type	Unit	Base
Canberra B2	9, 12, 50/103, 101, 617	Binbrook
	10	Scampton
	105/109, 139	Hemswell
	44/55	Coningsby
Washington B1	15/21, 57/104, 149	Coningsby
Lincoln B2	83/150, 97	Hemswell
	49/102, 44/61, 100	Waddington
Lincoln B2, Canberra B2	199	Hemswell

3 Group

Type	Unit	Base
Washington B1	35, 90, 115/218, 207	Marham
Lincoln B2	7/76, 148, 214	Upwood

2nd TAF

Type	Unit	Base
Canberra B2	TDU	Ahlhorn

Training and development

Type	Unit	Base
Meteor T7, Canberra B2, T4	231 OCU	Bassingbourn
Washington B1	WCU	Marham
Canberra B2	AIEU	Martlesham Heath
Canberra B2	BCIRE	Scampton
Lincoln II, Canberra B2	BTU	West Freugh

4.E Bombers (and strike) at 1 January 1955

Bomber Command

1 Group

Type	Unit	Base
Canberra B2	9, 12, 50, 617	Binbrook
	10, 18, 21, 27	Scampton
	15	Coningsby
	139, 199	Hemswell
Canberra B6	101	Binbrook
	109	Hemswell
Lincoln B2	7, 49, 148	Upwood
	83, 97	Hemswell

3 Group

Type	Unit	Base
Valiant B1	138	Gaydon
	1321 Flt	Wittering
Canberra B2	35, 90, 115, 207	Marham
	40, 61, 76, 100	Wittering
	44, 57	Cottesmore

2nd TAF

Type	Unit	Base
Canberra B2	102, 103, 104, 149	Gütersloh

Training and development

Type	Unit	Base
Valiant B1	232 OCU	Gaydon
Canberra B2, T4, Meteor T7	231 OCU	Bassingbourn
Lincoln B2	AIEU	Martlesham Heath
Canberra B2, Hastings	BCBS	Lindholme
Canberra B2, Valiant B1	BCDU	Wittering
Canberra B2	BTU	West Freugh

4.F Bombers (and strike) at 1 July 1957

Bomber Command

1 Group

Type	Unit	Base
Valiant B1	199	Hemswell
Vulcan 1	83	Waddington
Canberra 6	9, 12, 139	Binbrook
	76	Hemswell
Canberra 2	21, 27	Waddington
	57	Coningsby
	542	Hemswell

3 Group

Type	Unit	Base
Valiant B1, BK1, B(PR)K1	7, 90	Honington
Valiant B1, BK1	49, 138	Wittering
	149, 207, 214	Marham
Canberra B2	35, 50, 61	Upwood
	44	Honington
Canberra B2, 6, T4	100	Wittering

2 TAF

Type	Unit	Base
Canberra B(I)6	213	Ahlhorn
Canberra B(I)8	59	Gütersloh
	88	Wildenrath

Middle East Air Force (Cyprus)

Type	Unit	Base
Canberra 2	32	Nicosia
	73	Akrotiri

Training and development

Type	Unit	Base
Vulcan B1, Canberra T4	230 OCU	Waddington
Canberra B2, T4, Meteor T7	231 OCU	Bassingbourn
Valiant B1, Canberra T4	232 OCU	Gaydon
Hastings	BCBS	Lindholme
Valiant B1, Canberra B2, T4	BCDU	Wittering
Canberra B6	BTU	West Freugh

4.G   Bombers (and strike) at 1 July 1960

Bomber Command

1 Group

Type	Unit	Base
Vulcan B1	83	Waddington
	101	Finningley
	617	Scampton
Valiant B1	18	Finningley
Canberra B2	35	Upwood
Canberra B6	9, 12	Coningsby
Thor SSM	*98**	*Driffield*
	102	*Full Sutton*
	150	*Carnaby*
	226	*Catfoss*
	240	*Breighton*
Thor SSM	*97**	*Hemswell*
	104	*Ludford Magna*
	106	*Bardney*
	142	*Coleby Grange*
	269	*Caistor*

3 Group

Type	Unit	Base
Victor B1	10, 15	Cottesmore
	57	Honington
Valiant B1, BK1, BPR1	49, 138	Wittering
	90	Honington
	148, 207, 214	Marham
Thor SSM	*77**	*Feltwell*
	82	*Shepherd's Grove*
	107	*Tuddenham*
	113	*Mepal*
	220	*North Pickenham*
Thor SSM		
	144*	*North Luffenham*
	130	*Polebrook*
	218	*Harrington*
	223	*Folkingham*
	254	*Melton Mowbray*

* HQ squadrons. Each Thor wing comprised five squadrons with three missiles based on an HQ unit with four satellites.

RAF Germany

Type	Unit	Base
Canberra B6	213	Brüggen
Canberra B(I)8	16	Laarbruch
	59	Geilenkirchen
	88	Wildenrath

Middle East Air Force (Cyprus)

Type	Unit	Base
Canberra B2	32, 73	Akrotiri
Canberra B6	6, 249	Akrotiri

Far East Air Force (Malaya)

Type	Unit	Base
Canberra B2	45	Tengah

Training and development

Type	Unit	Base
Vulcan B1, Canberra T4	230 OCU	Waddington
Canberra B2, T4, Meteor T7	231 OCU	Bassingbourn
Victor B1	232 OCU	Gaydon
Hastings T5	BCBS	Lindholme
Canberra B6, Valiant B1, Victor B1	BCDU	Finningley
Canberra B6	BTU	West Freugh

4.H   Bombers (and strike) at 1 January 1965

Bomber Command

1 Group

Type	Unit	Base
Vulcan B1	44, 50, 101	Waddington
Vulcan B2	27, 83, 617	Scampton

3 Group

Type	Unit	Base
Victor B1	55, 57	Honington
Victor B2	100, 139	Wittering
Vulcan B2	9, 12, 35	Cottesmore
Valiant BK1, BPRK1	49, 148, 207, 214	Marham
	90	Honington

RAF Germany

Type	Unit	Base
Canberra B(I)6	213	Brüggen
Canberra B(I)8	3	Geilenkirchen
	14	Wildenrath
	16	Laarbruch

Near East Air Force

Type	Unit	Base
Canberra B15	32, 73	Akrotiri
Canberra B16	6, 249	Akrotiri

Far East Air Force

Type	Unit	Base
Canberra B15	45	Tengah

Training and development

Type	Unit	Base
Vulcan B2	230 OCU	Waddington
Canberra B2, T4, Meteor T7	231 OCU	Bassingbourn
Victor B1	VTF	Wittering
Hastings T5	BCBS	Lindholme
Victor B1, Vulcan, Canberra	BCDU	Finningley
Canberra B6	BTU	West Freugh

4.I   Bombers (and strike) at 1 January 1970

Bomber Command

1 Group Strike Command

Type	Unit	Base
Vulcan B2	27, 617	Scampton
	44, 50, 101	Waddington
Buccaneer S2	12	Honington

RAF Germany

Type	Unit	Base
Canberra B(I)8	3, 16	Laarbruch
	14	Wildenrath

Near East Air Force (Cyprus)

Type	Unit	Base
Vulcan B2	9, 35	Akrotiri

Far East Air Force (Malaya)

Type	Unit	Base
Canberra B15	45	Tengah

Training and development

Type	Unit	Base
Vulcan B2	230 OCU	Scampton
Canberra B2, T4, Meteor T7	231 OCU	Cottesmore
Victor K1	232 OCU	Marham
Hastings C1A, T5	SCBS	Lindholme
Vulcan B2	BCDU	Scampton

4.J   Bombers (and strike) at 1 January 1975

1 Group Strike Command

Type	Unit	Base
Vulcan SR2	27	Scampton
Vulcan B2	617	Scampton
	44, 50, 101	Waddington
Buccaneer S2	12, 208	Honington

RAF Germany

Type	Unit	Base
Phantom FGR2	14, 17, 31	Brüggen
Buccaneer S2	15, 16	Laarbruch

Near East Air Force

Type	Unit	Base
Vulcan B2	9, 35	Akrotiri

Training and development

Type	Unit	Base
Vulcan B2	230 OCU	Scampton
Canberra B2, T4	231 OCU	Cottesmore
Victor K1	232 OCU	Marham
Vulcan B2	Giant Voice Flt	Waddington
Hastings T5	SCBS	Scampton

4.K   Bombers (and strike) at 1 January 1980

1 Group Strike Command

Type	Unit	Base
Vulcan B2	9, 27, 35, 617	Scampton
	44, 50, 101	Waddington
Buccaneer S2	12, 208, 216	Honington

RAF Germany

Type	Unit	Base
Buccaneer S2	15, 16	Laarbruch

Training and development

Type	Unit	Base
Canberra B2, T4	231 OCU	Cottesmore
Victor K1, K2	232 OCU	Marham
Buccaneer S2C, Hunter T7	237 OCU	Honington
Vulcan B2	Giant Voice Flt	Waddington

4.L   Bombers (strike) at 1 January 1985

1 Group Strike Command

Type	Unit	Base
Tornado GR1	9	Honington
	27, 617	Marham

18 Group Strike Command

Type	Unit	Base
Buccaneer S2, Hunter T7	12, 208	Lossiemouth

RAF Germany

Type	Unit	Base
Tornado GR1	15, 16, 20	Laarbruch
	17, 31	Brüggen

Training and development

Type	Unit	Base
Tornado GR1, GR1T	TTTE	Cottesmore
Tornado GR1, GR1T	TWCU(45)	Honington
Canberra B2, T4	231 OCU	Wyton
Victor K2	232 OCU	Marham
Buccaneer S2C, Hunter T7	237 OCU	Lossiemouth

4.M   Bombers (strike) at 1 January 1990

1 Group Strike Command

Type	Unit	Base
Tornado GR1	27, 617	Marham
Tornado GR1A	13	Honington

18 Group Strike Command

Type	Unit	Base
Buccaneer S2B, Hunter T7	12, 208	Lossiemouth

RAF Germany

Type	Unit	Base
Tornado GR1	15, 16, 20	Laarbruch
	9, 14, 17, 31	Brüggen
Tornado GR1A	2	Laarbruch

Training and development

Type	Unit	Base
Tornado GR1, GR1T	TTTE	Cottesmore
Tornado GR1, GR1T	TWCU(45)	Honington
Canberra B2, T4	231 OCU	Wyton
Buccaneer S2C, Hunter T7	237 OCU	Lossiemouth

4.N   Bombers (strike) at 1 January 1995

Strike Command

Type	Unit	Base
Tornado GR1, GR1A	2, 13	Marham
Tornado GR1, GR1B	12, 617	Lossiemouth
Tornado GR1	9, 14, 17, 31	Brüggen

Training and development

Type	Unit	Base
Tornado GR1, GR1T	TTTE	Cottesmore
Tornado GR1, GR1T	TWCU(15)	Lossiemouth

4.1 Bristol Beaufort (1939–1946)

The Bristol Type 152 Beaufort was designed to a requirement for a torpedo-bomber in specification G.10/36. The prototype flew on 15 October 1938 and the type served throughout the war primarily in Coastal Command. The Mk I was powered by two Taurus VI engines of 1,130hp but it was no longer in service by 1946.

Mk II

The Mark II differed from the earlier version by being fitted with Twin Wasp engines. The Beaufort had a 1,500lb bomb load with two .303in guns each in the nose and dorsal turret. However, the variant in use at the end of the war was a trainer conversion with the rear turret deleted and twin controls fitted. Some were so built on the production line while others were converted.

Service (post-1945) Training 17 STTS: 762 NAS

Specification and production

Mark	Role	Engine	HP	Speed mph	Range miles	Nos
I	Torpedo bomber	2xTaurus VI	1,130	265	1,600	1,013
II	Torpedo bomber	2xTwin Wasp	1,200	265	1,450	415
II	Trainer	2xTwin Wasp	1,200	265	1,450	*

* limited number of Mk II conversions

4.2 Douglas Boston and Havoc (1940–1946)

The Douglas A-20 was a light attack bomber bought by foreign air forces before the USAAF placed a first order. The RAF took over unfulfilled French orders and the type entered second-line service in 1940 (Mk I). The Mark II (DB-7B) was used in service as the **Havoc**, which itself came in two versions. Both were intruder variants, and the Mk II had twelve .303in guns in the nose compared to eight in the Mk I. The Boston Mk III (DB-7) was the first

Douglas Boston Mk V

The Boston continued to operate with the RAF for some months into 1946; indeed, the type played an active role in the Greek campaign. This flight of aircraft of 13 Sqn, based at Hassani during the campaign, includes BZ611/Z nearest the camera. (*Crown copyright*)

version to be used in the light bomber role; all were out of service by 1946.

Mark IV

The DB-7B was similar to the American A-20J with two Cyclone engines and a power-operated dorsal turret. Bomb load was 2,000lb and armament included six .50in calibre guns in the nose and two each in the ventral and dorsal turrets.

Service (post-1945) Light bomber 55, 114, 249

Mark V

The Mark V differed from the Mark IV in having a clear 'bombardier' nose and a more powerful engine.

Service (post-1945) Light bomber 13, 18, 55, 114

Specification and production

Mark	Role	Engine	HP	Speed mph	Range miles	Nos
I	Bomber	2xR-1830-S3C4	1,200	293	462	20
II	Intruder	2xR-1830-S3C4	1,200	295	1,000	280
III	Bomber	2xGR-2600-A5B	1,600	304	1,020	980
IV	Bomber	2xGR-2600-A5B	1,600	304	1,020	-
V	Bomber	2xR-2600-29	1,700	339	1,090	259*

* combined Mk IV and V deliveries

Further reading
Douglas A-20 (7A to Boston III) (Profile 202) Gann, H, Profile Publications, Leatherhead, 1972

4.3 Avro Lancaster (1941–1956)

The Type 683 Lancaster was Bomber Command's most successful bomber of the Second World War. It derived

Avro Lancaster GR Mk 3

The Lancaster was the RAF's main bomber pending introduction of the Lincoln. It also continued as the mainstay of Coastal Command's long-range maritime patrol fleet until replaced by the Shackleton from 1954. SW336/V of 38 Sqn shows to advantage the ASV radar and rear flare chute. (*A S Thomas collection*)

from the flawed twin-engined Manchester and remained in RAF service to 1956. The bomb load eventually stretched to 22,000lb and the wartime exploits of Lancaster units and crews, while beyond the scope of the present volume, are well documented elsewhere.

B Mark I

The Lancaster was built to specification P.13/37 and was originally the Manchester III. The prototype (BT308) flew on 9 January 1941, the first production aircraft flying just nine months later. The Lancaster joined 44 Sqn in December 1941 with first operations in March 1942. Standard bomb-load was 7,000lb and guns included two .303in guns in nose and dorsal turrets and four in the tail.

Service (post-1945) Bomber 7, 8, 12, 15, 35, 44, 49, 50, 57, 61, 83, 90, 97, 100, 101, 106, 115, 138, 149, 207, 214, 300, 427, 429 **Training** 82; BCIS; 1653, 1660, 1667, 1668 CU; 230 OCU **Trials** APDU; BBU; BTU; CPE; RWE **Communications** Scampton SF.

The B Mark I (Special) was adapted for the carriage of large bombs in the range 8–22,000lb. The H2S radar was removed and Merlin 22 engines were fitted.

B Mark I (FE)

The variant was a conversion of the basic model for use in the Far East as the war in Europe was drawing to a close. The changes included fitting the Merlin 24 engine plus a 400gal fuel tank in the bomb-bay. The mid-upper turret was removed and the radio and radar changed for long-range flights.

Service (post-1945) Bomber 7, 9, 35, 70, 115, 148, 214, 617 **Training** BCIS; CGS; 1653, 1660, 1668 CU; EFS; 230 OCU; RAFFC **Trials** ASWDU; CBE; RWE

PR Mark 1

After the war the Lancaster was adapted for photo-reconnaissance with the nose turret faired over and cameras fitted. Finish was invariably silver overall.

Service Photo-reconnaissance 82, 541, 683.

The B Mark II was fitted with the Hercules VI engine to cover the prospect of shortages of Merlins, which in the event was not a problem. The type was no longer in service by 1946.

B Mark III

The Mark III was similar to the Mk I but with marginally more powerful Packard Merlin engines.

Service (post-1945) Bomber 9, 101, 101, 115, 138, 149, 207, 300 **Training** 37; BCIS; EFS; 1653, 1660, 1668 CU; 6 OTU; RAFFC **Transport** 178; 1, 16 FU **Trials** CBE

The Mark III (FE) was a conversion for Far East use similar in every respect to the Mk I (FE). Service use post-war is not distinguishable and is shown above under the Mk I (FE).

ASR Mark 3

The rescue variant was fitted with ASV and adapted by Cunliffe-Owen to carry an airborne lifeboat.

Service Air-sea rescue 38, 179, 210, 279, 621; 1348 Flt **Training** 236 OCU **Trials** ASWDU; JASS

GR/MR Mark 3

In its Mark III form the Lancaster was converted for maritime reconnaissance and developed to replace the Liberator when lend-lease ended. The mid-upper turret was removed, ASV radar fitted together with fuselage windows towards the tail. This variant was the last to see service with the RAF being replaced by the Neptune and Shackleton.

Service Maritime reconnaissance 18, 37, 38, 120, 160, 203, 210, 224, 279, 621 **Training** 236 OCU; 6 OTU; SMR **Trials** ASWDU; JASS.

The Mark IV and Mark V (Type 694) became the Lincoln B Mk 1 and 2 respectively.

Mark VI

The Mark VI was a limited version developed for radar jamming. Merlin 85/102 engines were fitted driving four-bladed propellers. Just ten Mk III aircraft were converted.

Service (post-1945) Trials RAE

Mark VII

The Mark VII was built by Austin Motors and differed from the Mk I in having a Glenn Martin dorsal turret located further forward along the fuselage.

Service (post-1945) Bomber 9, 40, 104, 617 **Training** 37; 1689 Flt; CNCS; CNS; EANS; EFS; 16 FU; RAFFC

The B Mark VII (FE) was the third mark converted for Far East use; it was similar in every respect to the Mk I (FE). Service use post-war is not distinguishable and is shown above under the Mk I (FE). The Mark X was the Canadian-built Mark III.

Specification and production

Mark	Role	Engine	HP	Speed mph	Range miles	Nos
I	Bomber	4xMerlin XX	1,280	287	2,530	3,425
I Spec	Bomber	4xMerlin 22/24	1,280	280	1,550	*
I (FE)	Bomber	4xMerlin 24	1,620	287	2,530	#
PR1	Photo-recce	4xMerlin XX	1,280	287	2,500	*
II	Bomber	4xHercules VI	1,650	270	1,100	300
III	Bomber	4xP Merlin 28	1,300	287	2,530	2,990
GR3	Maritime recce	4xP Merlin 28	1,300	280	2,500	+
ASR3	Rescue	4xP Merlin 28	1,300	280	2,500	+
IV	Bomber; Lincoln I					
V	Bomber; Lincoln II					
VI	EW	4xMerlin 85/102	1,750			10*
VII	Bomber	4xMerlin XX	1,280	287	2,530	180
X	Bomber	4xP Merlin	1,300	280	2,500	430~

* Mk I or III conversions
# Mk I, III or VII conversions
+ Mk III conversions
~ Canadian built

Further reading
Avro Lancaster, The, Mason, F K, 1989
Avro Lancaster I (Profile 65) Garbett, M, and Goulding, B, Profile Publications, Leatherhead, 1967

Lancaster, Franklin, N, and Scarborough, G, Patrick Stephens, 1979 (inc Lancastrian and York)

Lancaster at War, Garbett, M and Goulding, B, Ian Allan, London (4 vols)

Lancaster in Action, Mackay, R S G, Squadron/Signal, Carrollton, 1982

Avro Lancaster – The Definitive Record, Holmes, Harry, Airlife, 1997

4.4 Lend-lease aircraft (1942–1946)

A very large number and variety of American aircraft was made available to supplement indigenous types prior to the United States' entry into the war. They were provided under an ingenious scheme whereby the equipment was provided on a temporary basis for return at the war's end.

Martin Baltimore Mk V

Used exclusively in the Middle East, the Baltimore soldiered on into 1946 with 249 Sqn. Here FW811, an aircraft of the Malta Communications Flight, looks set for a long stay at a damp El Adem, Libya, in 1946. *(A S Thomas collection)*

The **Martin Baltimore** (Model 187) was a more powerful development of the Maryland designed to a British requirement. The type first flew on 14 June 1941 and it entered service with 223 Sqn in January 1942. It was used exclusively in the Mediterranean theatre. The Mark I and Mark II differed from each other only in having a single and twin Vickers K gun in the mid-upper position respectively. The Mark III had a twin-gun Boulton Paul dorsal turret. All these early variants were out of service by 1946.

The **Mark IV** used a Martin turret but was otherwise similar to earlier variants. It was powered by two GR-2600-A5B engines. The **Mark V** was similar to the Mk IV but with slightly more powerful engines. Armament comprised four .50in guns in the wings, two in the dorsal turret and one under the fuselage. Bomb load was 2,000lb. The Mark VI was equipped for general reconnaissance duties but was not introduced into service.

Service (post-1945) Bomber 249

The **Martin Marauder** (Model 179) was built for the USAAF as a medium bomber where it served with the designation B-26. Like the Baltimore it served solely in the Mediterranean area from October 1942. The Mark I was powered by the Double Wasp of 2,000hp and equated to the USAAF B-26A while the Mark IA (B-26B) differed in the tail gun fittings. The Mark II was similar to the B-26C and enjoyed a greater wing-span to decrease

Martin Marauder Mk III

Like the Baltimore the Marauder was confined to the Mediterranean theatre and never in large numbers – perhaps as well given its fearful reputation as a difficult aircraft to fly. No 39 Sqn flew from Khartoum until disbanded in September 1946. *(39 Sqn via P H T Green)*

wing-loading and thus improve handling. All were out of service by 1946.

The **Mark III** was equivalent to the USAAF B-26F/G and had the wing incidence angle increased to improve take-off performance. Eleven .50in guns were fitted in nose, dorsal and tail turrets and in packs on the forward fuselage and bomb-load was 4,000lb.

Service (post-1945) Bomber 39

The **North American Mitchell** (Type NA-62B) was built for the USAAF as a light day bomber with the designation B-25. It served extensively in Europe and the Far East and was used in relatively small numbers by the RAF as one of the types covered by the lend-lease scheme. The Mark I equated to the B-25B and entered RAF service in 1942. Armament comprised two .50in guns in the nose, ventral and dorsal turrets. Bomb load was 3,000lb. The Mark II (NA-82) was similar to the B-25C/D which differed from the earlier version in having an auto-pilot

North American Mitchell Mk III

This view of restored Mitchell (N88972 masquerading as KL161/VO-B of 98 Sqn) shows off to advantage the lines of the Mitchell. One example served for some years after the war with the AFEE at Beaulieu. *(Author)*

and external racks for up to eight 250lb bombs. Both initial variants were quickly out of service at the end of the war.

The **Mark III** (NA-82) had the dorsal turret well forward plus four guns in packs on the sides of the forward fuselage. In addition a tail turret was fitted and bomb load increased.

Service (post-1945) Trials AFEE

Specification and production

Mark	Role	Engine	HP	Speed mph	Range miles	Nos
Baltimore I	Bomber	2xGR-2600-A5B	1,600	305	950	
Baltimore II	Bomber	2xGR-2600-A5B	1,600	305	950	150*
Baltimore III	Bomber	2xGR-2600-A5B	1,600	305	950	
Baltimore IV	Bomber	2xGR-2600-A5B	1,600	305	950	
Baltimore V	Bomber	2xGR-2600-A5B5	1,700	305	950	
Baltimore VI	Bomber	2xGR-2600-A5B	1,600	305	950	1,323#
Marauder I	Bomber	2xR-2800-5	1,850	315	1,000	52
Marauder IA	Bomber	2xR-2800-41	2,000	317	1,150	19
Marauder II	Bomber	2xR-2800-43	1,920	282	1,150	100
Marauder III	Bomber	2xR-2800-43	2,000	305	1,200	330
Mitchell I	Bomber	2xR-2600-9	1,700	315	1,350	23
Mitchell II	Bomber	2xR-2600-13	1,700	284	1,500	500+
Mitchell III	Bomber	2xR-2600-92	1,700	272	1,350	314

* Mks I and II combined
# Mks III, IV, V and VI combined
+ many diverted to SAAF

Further reading
North American Mitchell B-25A to G (Profile 59) Wagner, R, Profile Publications, Leatherhead, 1966

4.5 Avro Lincoln (1945–1963)

The Type 694 Lincoln was designed to specification B.14/43 as an improved Lancaster for use in the Pacific theatre. Better overall performance, heavier armament and longer range were conferred through wider span high aspect ratio wings and Merlin 85 engines. There were two versions of the Lincoln, originally designated Lancaster IV and V, similar in most respects but fitted with different powerplants. Although too late to see service in the Second World War the type flew in three campaigns – Aden, Kenya and Malaya.

B Mark 1
The Mark I was fitted with the Merlin 85, 85A or 66 engine. Armament was two .50in guns each in nose, dorsal

Avro Lincoln B Mk 2

The Lincoln was a natural successor to the Lancaster from which it was derived. It served with the RAF between 1946 and 1955, until fully replaced by the Canberra, and flew offensive operations in Kenya, Malaya and South Arabia. RF555 of 61 Sqn is pictured over Kenya in May 1954. *(Crown copyright)*

and tail turrets and bomb load was 14,000lb. The type entered service with 57 Sqn in September 1945.

Service (post-1945) Bomber 44, 57 **Training** BCIS; ETPS **Trials** AFEE; AIEU; ATDU; AWA; BBU; BCIRE; CBE; LRWE; RAE; RWE; SIU; TFU

B Mark 2
In this version several changes were made including the fitting of the Packard-built Merlin 68, 68A or 300 with the same power rating as the British equivalents. A ventral gun was added and the nose guns remotely controlled by the bomb aimer. This was the main variant in use, being finally replaced by the Canberra in 1955, but remaining in second-line use until 1963. Two sub-variants were operated, distinguished by the H2S radar version used, either IIIG or IVA. The B Mk 2 optimised for meteorological work was given the type number 712.

Service (post-1945) Bomber 7, 9, 12, 15, 35, 44, 49, 50, 57, 61, 75, 83, 90, 97, 100, 101, 115, 138, 148, 149, 207, 214, 617; 1321, 1426 Flts **Signals** 116, 151, 192, 199, 527 **Survey** 58 **Training** 230 OCU; AIEU; BCBS; BCIS; CGS; CNCS; EAAS; EANS; ECFS; ERS; RAFFC; RAFTC **Trials** AFEE; ARDU; AST; BBU; BDU; BTU; CBE; CSE; FTU; NGTE; RAE; RRF; RWE; TFU; TRE; WEE **Other** 1689 Flt.

The ASR Mark 3 (Type 696) was an air-sea rescue project which became the Shackleton. The B Mark 4 was the designation formally applied to the B Mk 2 re-engined with the Merlin 85. The U Mark 5 was applied to two CGS aircraft converted to target drone configuration.

Specification and production

Mark	Role	Engine	HP	Speed mph	Range miles	Nos
B1	Bomber	4xMerlin 85	1,750	295	3,570	85
B2	Bomber	4xP Merlin 68	1,750	295	3,570	459*
ASR3	ASR	became Shackleton				
B4	Bomber	4xMerlin 85	1,750	295	3,570	n/k+
U5	Drone	4xMerlin 85	1,750	295	3,570	2+

* includes 12 Mk 1 conversions
+ Mk 2 conversions

Further reading
Lincoln at War 1944–1966, Garbett, M & Goulding, B,
  Ian Allan, Shepperton, 1979

4.6   Boeing Washington (1950–1958)

By 1950 the Lincoln was five years old and the new jet
bombers were still some way off service entry. Thus the
Boeing Model 345 Superfortress (B-29) came to be
supplied to the RAF from the US under the Mutual
Defence Aid Plan. In fact the type was of Lincoln vintage
(first flight 1942) and broad performance so it should be
seen as supplementing the Lincoln rather than replacing
it. In RAF service the B-29 became the Washington.

B Mark 1
The Washington entered RAF service with 115 Sqn in
March 1950 and within months the type was in service
with eight front-line squadrons at Marham and
Coningsby. The Washington carried ten .50in machine
guns in five turrets (upper and lower forward fuselage,
dorsal, ventral and tail) and carried a bomb load of
17,500lb over 1,000 miles. It was replaced by the Canberra
by 1954 and the last were in service with 90 Group for
ELINT work until 1958.

Service **Bomber** 15, 35, 44, 57, 90, 115, 149, 207 **Training**
WCU (35) **Trials** ARDU **Elint** 192 **Other** SF Marham

Specification and production						
Mark	Role	Engine	HP	Speed mph	Range miles	Nos
B1	Bomber	4XCyclone R-3350-23	2,200	350	2,850	88

Further reading

Boeing Washington B Mk 1

Delays with the introduction of the first jet bombers led to the
introduction of the Washington, provided by the US under the
Mutual Defence Aid Plan, to supplement the Lincoln force. 88
aircraft equipped eight bomber squadrons between 1950 and
1953. WF557 is an aircraft of 57 Sqn. *(N Oakden via A S
Thomas)*

The Washington File, Fopp, M A, Air Britain, Tonbridge,
  1983

4.7   English Electric Canberra (1951–date)

The Canberra is one of the all-time great military aircraft
– a worthy successor to the Mosquito which in many
respects it succeeded, and the RAF's first jet bomber. The
type had its origins in specification B.3/45 which called for
a medium-range unarmed bomber with a crew of two. As
the design evolved the specification changed (B.5/47) to
accommodate a crew of three with visual bomb-aiming
rather than the original radar bombing requirement.

The Canberra was produced in large numbers in the
United Kingdom and the United States (B-57) and it
served with fifteen nations in many variants. The
Canberra/B-57 played an active role in numerous
conflicts including Malaya, Suez, Vietnam,
India/Pakistan and the Falklands. At the time of writing
the type remains in service with the RAF (1 PRU) 45 years
after service entry.

B Mark 1
The English Electric A.1 was built to the original two-
crew specification and four prototypes only were built.
The first, VN799, flew on 13 May 1949 and just four were
built.

Service **Trials** RAE; TRE/RRE

B Mark 2
The Mark 2 (A.3) was the first production variant and no
fewer than 416 were built for RAF or trials use. The bomb
load was six 1,000lb bombs carried internally. The
Canberra joined the RAF with 101 Sqn in January 1951,
just nine months after the sole prototype (VX165) flew on
21 April 1950.

Service **Bomber** 6, 9, 10, 12, 15, 18, 21, 27, 32, 35, 40, 45,
50, 57, 59, 61, 73, 76, 88, 90, 100, 101, 102, 103, 104, 109,
139, 149, 199, 202, 207, 213, 249, 617 **Elint** 51, 192
Calibration 97, 98, 115, 245 **Training** 13, 58, 360, 527, 540,
542; 228, 230, 231 OCU; BCHU; CAW; CFS; ETPS; JCU
Hemswell; RAFFC; 1 RS **Target facilities** 7, 56, 85;
FRADU **Air sampling** 76; 1323 Flt **Trials** 151; 1321 Flt;
ARDU; ATDU; BCDU; CFE; CSDE/CSE; IAM;
NGTE; RAE; Swifter Flt; 2 TAF TDU; TRE/

English Electric Canberra B Mk 6

One of the truly great postwar military aircraft, the Canberra
remains in service at the time of writing nearly fifty years after
the first flight of prototype VN799. The definitive light
bomber version, a worthy successor to the Mosquito, was the
B Mk 6, an example of which is depicted here in Cyprus
during the Suez campaign while serving with 27 Sqn. *(27 Sqn)*

RRE/RSRE; WRE (4, 12 JSTU) **Communications** MECS; NECS; Binbrook, Honington, Khormaksar, Upwood, Waddington, West Raynham, Wittering SF

B(TT) Mark 2
This was an unofficial designation applied to seven B Mk 2 aircraft converted to near TT Mk 18 standard.

Service **Target facilities** RAE Llanbedr

PR Mark 3
The A.2 was, as its manufacturer's type number suggests, the second version in production and the prototype, VX181, flew on 19 March 1950, before that of the B Mk 2. There was an urgent need for a high-flying replacement for the Mosquito to specification PR.31/46 and compared to the bomber the PR Mk 3 was fitted with a solid, slightly longer nose. Seven cameras were carried together with extra fuel and flares were carried in a reduced-size bomb-bay. The first formal unit to receive the variant was 540 Sqn in December 1952, but first operational use, possibly over Eastern Europe, was probably earlier from RAF Watton.

Service **Photo-reconnaissance** 17, 39, 58, 69, 82, 540, 541 **Training** 16; 231, 237 OCU **Trials** RAE; TRE/RRE **Communications** Upwood SF

T Mark 4
The A.4 was a dual control version with solid nose ordered against specification T.2/49. The prototype, WN467, flew on 6 June 1952 and service entry was with 231 OCU in 1954. Examples of the trainer served with most operational squadrons as well as many second-line units and its service life was 40 years.

Service **Training** 3, 7, 13, 14, 15, 16, 17, 31, 32, 39, 45, 51, 56, 58, 59, 69, 73, 76, 80, 81, 85, 88, 97, 98, 100, 102, 103, 104, 149, 151, 213, 245, 249, 360, 527; AIEU; BCHU; CAW; CFS; ETPS; FTU; 228, 230, 231, 232, 237 OCU; PRU; RAFFC; TFS West Raynham **Trials** BLEU; RAE; RRE **Communications** FECS; 1 GCF; Ahlhorn, Akrotiri, Binbrook, Brüggen, Coningsby, Cottesmore, Finningley, Gaydon, Geilenkirchen, Gütersloh, Hemswell, Honington, Laarbruch, Marham, Scampton, Upwood, Waddington, Wahn, Weston Zoyland, Wildenrath, Wittering, Wyton SF

B Mark 5
The A.6 was an intended pathfinder variant to specification B.22/48 with an extended solid blind-bombing nose. Only the prototype, VX185, a B Mk 2 conversion, flew before the project was cancelled. The design did, however, feature integral wing fuel tanks and later the Avon RA.7, both of which features were fitted to the B Mk 6.

B Mark 6
The Mark 6 was essentially similar to the B Mk 2 but with extra fuel in integral wing tanks (900 gals) and the more powerful Avon RA.7 (109) engine. Both of these features had been built into the B Mk 5. By the time of service entry the Canberra bombers were fitted with wing-tip tanks each taking 250 gals, although speed was then limited to 420mph. The first aircraft went to 101 Sqn in June 1954 and in operational service the last Canberra bombers in

Bomber Command were replaced by V-bombers in September 1961. Twenty-five aircraft were converted to **B Mk 6(BS)** standard with Blue Shadow radar navigation aid; these were distinguished by a strake along the starboard forward fuselage.

Service **Bomber** 6, 9, 12, 21, 45, 76, 100, 101, 109, 139, 249, 617 **Elint** 51, 192 **Calibration** 97 **Training** 58, 360, 542 **Trials** 151; TFE308; BCDU; CSE; IAM; RAE; RRE/RRF/RSRE; WRE **Communications** Binbrook, Coningsby, Hemswell, Upwood SF

B(I) Mark 6
This was a conversion of the B Mk 6 as an interim interdictor pending introduction of the B(I) Mk 8. First conversion was WT307 which flew on 31 May 1955. An under-fuselage gun pack with four 20mm cannon was fitted under the rear part of the bomb-bay, which still took three 1,000lb bombs. The weapons fit was further changed with two underwing pylons each taking a single 1,000lb bomb.

Service **Intruder** 213 **Trials** BCDU; CFE; RAE; RRE **Communications** Brüggen, Laarbruch, Wildenrath SF

B Mark 6 (Mod)
The designation was applied to two different versions of the B Mk 6 modified for ELINT tasks. Three were fitted with a T Mk 11 nose and used by 192 Sqn, while four later modifications with an extended radar nose and ESM 'dustbin' behind the cockpit were used by the successor 51 Sqn.

Service **ELINT** 51, 192 **Trials** RAE; RRE

PR Mark 7
The Mark 7 was the photo-reconnaissance version of the B Mk 6 with a similar camera fit to the PR Mk 3 but more powerful engines. The first aircraft was WH773 which flew on 16 August 1953.

Service **Photo-reconnaissance** 13, 17, 31, 39, 58, 80, 81, 82, 527, 540, 542; 1 PRU **Training** 100; RAFFC **Trials** CFE; RAE; RRE **Communications** Wyton SF

B(I) Mark 8
The interdictor introduced a fundamental change in profile with a new nose and offset fighter-type canopy. A crew of two was carried and like the interim B(I) Mk 6 armament comprised a four-gun (20mm cannon) under-fuselage pack and five 1,000lb bombs, two on underwing pylons. The prototype was the B Mk 5 aircraft which flew in its new configuration on 23 July 1954 and the first unit to operate the interdictor was 88 Sqn in 1956. Many of the 82 produced were delivered direct to the Indian Air Force.

Service **Intruder** 3, 14, 16, 59, 88 **Trials** BCDU; RAE **Communications** Brüggen, Geilenkirchen, Laarbruch, Wildenrath SF **Miscellaneous** 100

PR Mark 9
The third photo-reconnaissance variant had a broadly similar fuselage profile to the B(I) Mk 8, but there the similarity ended. A crew of three was carried, the navigator entering through the hinged nose. The Mark 9 had

a much larger wing with 4ft extra span and greater chord inboard of the engines. The latter were Avon 206s of 10,050lb thrust which with the greater wing area gave a much higher ceiling of at least 70,000ft. The prototype was a PR Mk 7 (WH793) converted by Shorts and flying on 8 July 1955. Service entry was with 58 Sqn in 1960. One aircraft, XH132, was converted as the **SC.9** for Red Top missile trials and later operated by the RRE.

Service Photo-reconnaissance 13, 39, 58; 1 PRU **Trials** RAE; RRE

U Mark 10

The Mark 10 (later **D Mk 10**) comprised eighteen B Mk 2 unmanned target drone conversions for use in guided weapons trials in Australia.

Service Trials LRWE/WRE (1 ATU); RAE

T Mark 11

The Mark 11 was another B Mk 2 conversion with a new nose containing a Mk 17 AI radar for Javelin navigator training. Later the aircraft were use for AI interception training as targets.

Service Training 228 OCU **Target facilities** 7, 85, 100; TFS West Raynham B(I) Mk 8 aircraft built for the RNZAF and SAAF were given the **B(I) Mark 12** desig-

nation while the **T Mark 13** designation applied to the T Mk 4 built for the RNZAF.

U Mark 14

The Mark 14 (later **D Mk 14**) was similar to the U Mk 10 but with hydraulic servo controls. Most were B Mk 2 conversions, although one was a U Mk 10. The first conversion, the Shorts SC.6 WH921, flew on 28 March 1961 and the main user was 728B NAS for Seacat and Seaslug SAM trials.

Service Trials RAE Llanbedr: 728B NAS

B Mark 15

The Mark 15 was a conversion of the B Mk 6 for tactical nuclear bombing. Additional radar and navigation equipment was installed, with three cameras rather than one and underwing pylons fitted for rockets or the AS.30 ASM. The first aircraft was WH961 which flew on 4 October 1960 and first deliveries were to the Akrotiri Strike Wing (32 Sqn) in July 1961. In front-line service the aircraft also flew with 45 Sqn in the Far East.

Service Tactical bomber 6, 32, 45, 73, 249 **Training** 98

E Mark 15

Radio and radar calibration needs led to the conversion of the B Mk 15 with various electronic equipment fitted.

English Electric Canberra TT Mk 18

When redundant in the original bomber role many bomber versions were converted for a wide range of research and second-line duties. Typical is this TT Mk 18, WJ721 of 7 Sqn, which started life as a B Mk 2, serving with 40 and 50 squadrons before conversion to a target tug. The Rushton winch is clearly visible as the aircraft banks over the north Cornwall coast. *(Author's collection)*

Service Calibration 98, 100, 360

B Mark 16

This was similar in every respect to the B Mk 15 but with Blue Shadow radar fitted.

Service Tactical bomber 6, 32, 249

T Mark 17

The Mark 17 was an electronic warfare training variant based on converted B Mk 2 aircraft. The nose profile was changed significantly to accommodate various aerials. The first conversion was WJ977 which flew on 9 September 1965; the type was operated solely by the unique joint services 360 Sqn.

Service EW training 360

T Mark 17A

Six T Mk 17 aircraft were fitted with upgraded avionics and jammers. They were distinguished by additional underwing aerials and a hemp camouflage finish.

Service EW training 360

TT Mark 18

The Mark 18 was a target tug conversion of the B Mk 2 with Rushton winches under each wing capable of handling Rushton Mk 2 targets or sleeve targets. The first conversion, by Flight Refuelling Ltd, was WJ632 which flew on 21 March 1966.

Service Target facilities 7, 100. RAE Llanbedr: 776; FRU/FRADU

T Mark 19

Eight of the remaining T Mk 11 aircraft were upgraded with various equipment changes made for interception training. The radar was removed.

Service Training 7, 85, 100.

The **B Mark 20** was the Australian version of the B Mk 2/6 while the **T Mark 21** was a trainer conversion of the B Mk 20 for the RAAF.

T Mark 22

The Mark 21 was the final British Canberra variant. Seven PR Mk 7 aircraft, starting WT510 which first flew in its new form on 28 June 1973, were converted with a pointed radar nose for Fleet Air Arm air direction training.

Service Training FRADU

Further reading

English Electric Canberra, Delve, K, Green, P H T, Clemons, J, Midland Counties Publications, Leicester, 1992

The English Electric Canberra Mk1&IV (Profile 54) Munson, K, Profile Publications, Leatherhead, 1965

Specification and production

Mark	Role	Engine	Thrust lb	Speed mph	Range miles	Nos
B1	Bomber	2xAvon RA.2	6,500	570	2,660	4
B2	Bomber	2xAvon RA.3	6,500	570	2,656	416
B(TT)2	Target tug	2xAvon RA.3	6,500	570	2,000	7+
PR3	Photo-recce	2xAvon RA.3	6,500	570	3,580	35
T4	Trainer	2xAvon RA.3	6,500	570	3,110	92*
B5	Pathfinder	2xAvon RA.3	6,500	570	3,000	1+
B6	Bomber	2xAvon RA.7	7,500	605	2,750	96
B(I)6	Intruder	2xAvon RA.7	7,500	580	2,500	22~
B6(mod)	ELINT	2xAvon RA.7	7,500	590	3,000	7~
PR7	Photo-recce	2xAvon RA.7	7,500	580	4,340	74
B(I)8	Intruder	2xAvon RA.7	7,500	541	805	82
PR9	Photo-recce	2xAvon 206	10,050	547	5,075	23
U10	Drone	2xAvon RA.3	6,500	570	2,600	18+
T11	Trainer	2xAvon RA.3	6,500	550	2,750	8+
B(I)12	Intruder	2xAvon RA.7	7,500	541	805	11
T13	Trainer	2xAvon RA.3	6,500	570	3,110	2
U14	Drone	2xAvon RA.3	6,500	570	2,600	7#
B15	Bomber	2xAvon RA.7	7,500	605	2,750	39~
E15	Calibration	2xAvon RA.7	7,500	605	2,750	8^
B16	Bomber	2xAvon RA.7	7,500	605	2,750	20~
T17	EW trainer	2xAvon RA.3	6,500	570	2,656	24+
T17A	EW trainer	2xAvon RA.3	6,500	570	2,656	6>
TT18	Target tug	2xAvon RA.3	6,500	570	2,656	23+
T19	Trainer	2xAvon RA.3	6,500	550	2,750	8<
B20	Bomber	2xAvon RA.7	7,500	605	2,750	48
T21	Trainer	2xAvon RA.7	7,500	605	2,750	7%
T22	Trainer	2xAvon RA.7	7,500	580	4,000	7$

* Includes 17 B2 conversions
+ B2 conversion(s)
~ B6 conversions
# 6 B2 conversions, 1 U10 conversion
^ B15 conversions
> T17 conversions
< T11 conversions
% B20 conversions
$ PR7 conversions

4.8 Short Sperrin (1951)

The SA.4 Sperrin was built to specification B.14/46. It was a four-jet bomber to a relatively conventional design with straight wings and the engines mounted in vertical pairs in wing nacelles. It was intended as a stop-gap in the event of problems with the more advanced swept-wing V-bombers. The Sperrin was unarmed and would have carried a 16,000lb bomb load, but in the event the Valiant was on time and the type served for some time as an engine test-bed. Two prototypes were built, the first, VX158, flying on 10 August 1951.

Service Trials RAE

Short Sperrin

The Sperrin was a conventional design intended as a stop-gap in the event of problems with the introduction of the more advanced V-bombers. Two were built and the first, VX158, was used as a test-bed for the Gyron engine as seen in this shot. *(MAP)*

Specification and production

Mark	Role	Engine	Thrust lb	Speed mph	Range miles	Nos
SA.4	Bomber	4xAvon RA.3	6,500	514	3,860	2

4.9   Vickers Valiant (1954–1965)

The Valiant was the first of the new bombers designed to requirement OR.229 (specification B.35/46) capable of delivering a 10,000lb nuclear weapon over a range of 3,600 miles. The prototype (Type 660) was built to specification B.9/48 and as WB210 it flew on 18 May 1951. The second prototype (Type 667) was followed by five pre-production aircraft (Type 674). The Valiant was flown operationally during the Suez campaign and with 49 Sqn dropped the first British nuclear and thermonuclear weapons at Maralinga, Australia and Christmas Island respectively.

Vickers Valiant B PR(K) Mk 1

The first of the three V-bombers designed to carry a 10,000lb nuclear bomb, the Valiant was also the most conventional. It was produced in four sub-variants, all of which were capable of the primary bombing role, but which also enabled tanking and/or photo-reconnaissance. WZ391 was a PR version with tanking capability and it is seen here on short finals when in service with 543 Sqn in 1960. The camera ports are under the centre fuselage. *(Author)*

The Valiant was built in four sub-variants and in service most units were issued with two or more of these versions at any time.

B Mark 1

The Type 706 was built as a medium-range unarmed bomber with a pressurised cabin, a crew of five and a bomb-load of 10,000lb. The first aircraft were delivered to 232 OCU in 1954 with the first squadron, 138, forming on the type in February 1955. Developments in air defence meant that the Valiant was soon incapable of flying high enough to evade interception and in 1960 its role changed to low-level bomber. The stresses of low-level flying took their toll and in early 1965, after cracks were found in the wing main spar, the type was scrapped.

Service Bomber 7, 49, 138, 148, 207, 214 **ECM** 18, 199 **Training** 232 OCU **Trials** BCDU

B(PR) Mark 1

The photo-reconnaissance Type 710 was similar to the B Mk 1 but with an extensive camera fit for strategic reconnaissance.

Service Reconnaissance 543 **Bomber** 7, 49, 90, 138, 148, 207, 214 **Training** 232 OCU **Trials** RAE

B(K) Mark 1

To extend range and flexibility the Type 758 tanker was built; it was similar to the B Mk 1 but with a nose probe and single point refuelling.

Service Tanker 90, 214 Bomber 7, 49, 138, 148, 207 **Reconnaissance** 543 **Training** 232 OCU **Trials** BCDU

B PR(K) Mark 1

The Type 733 was a hybrid bomber/tanker with features of the PR and K variants of the basic bomber.

Service Bomber 7, 138, 148 **Tanker** 90, 214 **Reconnaissance** 543

B Mark 2

The Type 673 was a night pathfinder version optimised for low-level flying. The forward fuselage was extended and rear wing pods accommodated a revised four-wheel undercarriage. The prototype, WJ954, flew on 4 September 1954, but the variant was not developed.

Specification and production

Mark	Role	Engine	Thrust lb	Speed mph	Range miles	Nos
B1	Bomber	4xAvon RA.28	10,050	567	4,500	29
B(PR)1	Photo-recce	4xAvon RA.28	10,050	567	4,500	11
B(K)1	Bomber/tanker	4xAvon RA.28	10,050	567	4,500	45
BPR(K)1	Bomber	4xAvon RA.28	10,050	567	4,500	14
B2	Pathfinder	4xAvon RA.7	7,500	550	3,000	1

Further reading
The Vickers Valiant (Profile 66) Andrews, C F, Profile
    Publications, Leatherhead, 1966
V-Bombers, Jackson, R, Ian Allan, Shepperton, 1981
V-Force – The History of Britain's Airborne Deterrent
    Brookes, A, Janes, London, 1983

4.10   Avro Vulcan (1956–1984)

The Avro 698 Vulcan was the second of the new V-
bombers built to specification B.35/46 to fly. Because of
the revolutionary design several 'models' were produced
in the form of the Avro 707, a total of four of which was
eventually flown (Chapter 12.2). The prototype Avro 698,
VX770, flew on 30 August 1952 powered by four Avon
RA.3 engines each of 6,500lb thrust. The wing was a
simple delta of 99ft span, changed early in production to
a compound shape to reduce outer wing fatigue. The
prototypes were later fitted with the Sapphire of 8,000lb
thrust. Fortunately the Vulcan was never required to
perform the ultimate task for which it was produced, but
it was used operationally for the only time in 1982 in the
Falklands war just prior to withdrawal from service.

B Mark 1
The first production aircraft flew on 4 February 1955
(XA889) and the type entered service with 230 OCU in
May 1956. First operational unit was 83 Sqn formed on
the Vulcan at Waddington in July 1957. The Vulcan had
a crew of five, was unarmed with an H2S Mk 9 radar and
a weapons load of 21 1,000lb bombs carried internally.
The engine was the Olympus 102 which almost doubled
the power of the aircraft from the original prototype.

Service Bomber 44, 50, 83, 101, 617 **Training** 230 OCU
Trials BCDU; BLEU; RAE

B Mark 1A
Thirty B Mk 1 aircraft were rebuilt as the Mark 1A with
ECM sensors in an extended tailcone and an aerial plate
between the starboard jetpipes. The first conversion was
XA8995 in 1958.

Service Bomber 44, 50, 101, 617 **Trials** BCDU

B Mark 2
The Mark 2 employed a significantly larger wing than the
B Mk 1 together with the much more powerful Olympus
201 engine. The Vulcan was equipped to carry the WE-
177 or Yellow Sun nuclear weapons. 230 OCU
re-equipped in 1960 followed by 83 Sqn in October of that
year. In bomber form the Vulcan finally left RAF service
in December 1982 (44 Sqn). Some Vulcans were wired for
the AGM-87A Skybolt stand-off missile, ordered from
the United States but cancelled. Six of these aircraft were
hastily adapted to carry four Shrike ARM missiles and
the AN/ALQ-101 jamming pod under the wings for use
in the Falklands campaign.

Service Bomber 9, 12, 27, 35, 44, 50, 83, 101, 617
Training 230 OCU **Trials** BCDU

B Mark 2A
As the Mk 2A the Vulcan was adapted to carry a single
Blue Steel stand-off bomb semi-recessed in the bomb-bay.
It came in two sub-variants. Some were fitted with the
Olympus 301 of 20,000lb thrust (Coningsby Wing – 9, 12,
35 Sqns) but only the Scampton Wing (27, 83, 617 Sqns)
was supplied with the weapon.

Service Bomber 9, 12, 27, 35, 83, 617

Avro Vulcan B Mk 2

The delta-wing Vulcan was an awesome sight, especially climbing out on a four-aircraft scramble. In this photograph an
anonymous B Mk 2 aircraft of 617 Sqn appears to be taking its time to retract the undercarriage at the start of a training sortie in
1975. *(Crown copyright)*

SR Mark 2

This was a B Mk 2 conversion fitted with LORAN for maritime reconnaissance. Nine aircraft equipped 27 Sqn which flew in the role between January 1973 and 1983.

Service Strategic reconnaissance 27

K Mark 2

The tanker variant was the result of a stop-gap measure to increase the RAF tanker force during the Falklands war. Six aircraft were converted from B Mk 2 with tankage in the bomb-bay and a single Mk 17B HDU was carried in the redundant ECM tailcone. The first conversion, XH561, flew on 18 June 1982 and the version was the last in RAF service, finally departing on 31 March 1984.

Service Tanker 50

Specification and production

Mark	Role	Engine	Thrust	Speed mph	Range miles	Nos
B1	Bomber	4xOlympus 102	12,000	625	3,450	45
B1A	Bomber	4xOlympus 102	12,000	625	3,450	30*
B2	Bomber	4xOlympus 201	17,000	645	4,600	89
B2A	Bomber	4xOlympus 301	20,000	645	4,200	~
SR2	Strat recce	4xOlympus 201	17,000	645	4,600	9~
K2	Tanker	4xOlympus 201	17,000	645	4,600	6~

* B1 conversions
~ B2 conversions

Further reading

Avro Vulcan, Jackson, R, Patrick Stephens, Wellingborough, 1984

V-Bombers, Jackson, R, Ian Allan, Shepperton, 1981

V-Force – The History of Britain's Airborne Deterrent Brookes, A, Janes, London, 1983

Vulcan, Chesneau, R and Rimmell, R, Linewrights, Essex, 1984

4.11 Handley Page Victor (1958–1993)

The Victor was Handley Page's response to specification B.35/46 and with the Vulcan it maintained the Avro/Handley Page (Lancaster/Halifax) partnership. It

Handley Page Victor B Mk 2

The unique crescent-winged Victor was the last of the V-bombers to enter service and then only in small numbers. As manned bombers became more vulnerable the Victor was adapted to carry the 'Blue Steel' stand-off bomb, seen here under XL190 of 100 Sqn in 1965. *(Author)*

incorporated a wing of unusual, crescent-shaped compound sweep design. The design was first tested in the wind tunnel from 1947 and then on a 40% scale model, the HP.88 which was based on the Attacker fuselage and built by Blackburn to specification E.6/48 (Chapter 12.3). It flew on 21 June 1951 and broke up shortly after but the prototype Victor (WB771) was almost complete, flying for the first time on Christmas Eve 1952.

The HP.80 Victor was the last of the V-bombers to enter service and its operational life was longer than that of the Valiant and Vulcan. However, although the most potent, it did not drop bombs in anger, but served with distinction as a tanker in the Falklands and second Gulf wars.

B Mark 1

The first production aircraft (XA917) flew on 1 February 1956 and was 40in longer than the prototypes. Compared to the Vulcan, the Victor had much greater load-carrying capability, being able to carry 35 1,000lb bombs. In fact the bomb-bay was designed to accommodate four nuclear weapons but the early Blue Danube bomb was so large that only one could be carried. The aircraft was unarmed and had H2S radar. It entered service with 232 OCU, joining 10 Sqn in April 1958. Four aircraft were fitted at an early stage with Yellow Aster radar for reconnaissance tasks

Service Bomber 10, 15, 55, 57 **Reconnaissance** RRF **Training** 232 OCU **Trials** RAE

B Mark 1A

Twenty-four B Mk 1 aircraft were fitted with a blunter tail cone incorporating ECM equipment as the Mark 1A.

Service Bomber 10, 15, 55, 57 **Training** 232 OCU

B(K) Mark 1A

This was a two-point tanker conversion of the B Mk 1A undertaken with some urgency when the Valiant tankers were withdrawn from service at short notice in 1965. No 55 Sqn converted to the tanker role in June 1965.

Service Tanker 55, TTF

K Mark 1

The second tanker variant was a three-point conversion of the B Mk 1 while the **K Mark 1A** was the B Mk 1A conversion.

Service Tanker 55, 57, 214

B Mark 2

The Mark 2 was a completely new model employing the Conway engine and with increased wing-span. Further changes to the wing included revised intakes, Küchemann wing fairings and large, fixed, underwing fuel tanks. This variant was adapted to carry the Blue Steel stand-off bomb and entered service with 139 Sqn in February 1962, but production was limited, despite superior performance to the Vulcan.

Service Bomber 100, 139 **Training** VTF

B Mark 2R

The Mk 2R was a retrofit of some 21 B Mk 2 airframes with the Conway 201 of 20,600lb thrust with an increase in take-off weight to 223,000lb. In addition was installed Red Steer ECM equipment. When high flying bombers became vulnerable to SAM defences and the role shifted to low level, the Victor was soon retired in favour of the Vulcan which had better fatigue resistance; the Victor remained in service only to 1968 as a bomber.

Service Bomber 100, 139

B(SR) Mark 2

The B Mk 2 conversion for strategic reconnaissance was designed to replace the Valiant in the role. Various camera fits were enabled, including the F49 Mk 4, F89 Mk 3 and F96 Mk 2 and Red Neck reconnaissance radar was fitted.

Service Reconnaissance 543

K Mark 2

The tanker was the final Victor variant and it remained in service to 1993 with 55 Sqn. Twenty-four B Mk 2, B Mk 2R or B(SR) Mk 2 aircraft were converted to three-point tankers with the wing-span reduced from 120ft to 113ft to extend fatigue life.

Service Tanker 55, 57

Specification and production

Mark	Role	Engine	Thrust lb	Speed mph	Range miles	No
B1	Bomber	4xSapphire ASSa.7	11,050	627	6,000	50
B1A	Bomber	4xSapphire ASSa.7	11,050	627	6,000	24*
B(K)1A	Tanker	4xSapphire ASSa.7	11,050	627	6,000	6~
K1	Tanker	4xSapphire ASSa.7	11,050	627	6,000	11*
K1A	Bomber	4xSapphire ASSa.7	11,050	627	6,000	14~
B2	Bomber	4xConway 200	17,250	647	6,000	34
B2R	Bomber	4xConway 201	20,600	647	6,000	21#
B(SR)2	Recce	4xConway 200	17,250	647	3,600	9#
K2	Tanker	4xConway 201	20,600	647	3,600	24+

* B1 conversions
~ B1A conversions
\# B2 conversions
\+ B2/B2R/B(SR)2 conversions

Further reading

Handley Page Victor, Brookes, A, Ian Allan, London, 1988

V-Bombers, Jackson, R, Ian Allan, Shepperton, 1981

V-Force – The History of Britain's Airborne Deterrent Brookes, A, Janes, London, 1983

Handley Page Victor BK Mk 2

After a short service life as a bomber the Victor was converted to fulfil the tanker requirement in which role it operated from 1965 to 1993. It proved its worth during the Falklands and Second Gulf wars. XL163 of 57 Sqn in hemp finish refuels Tornado GR Mk 1 ZA609/02 of 27 Sqn. *(Author's collection)*

4.12 Blackburn Buccaneer (1962–1994)

The B.103 Buccaneer was originally designed against a naval operational requirement (N.R/A.39) which called for a fast carrier-borne strike aircraft capable of flying close to the speed of sound at very low level. To cope with the inevitable stresses involved, the structure was constructed in new ways to confer high strength. Twenty prototype and development aircraft were ordered and the first, XK486, flew on 30 April 1958.

S Mark 1

The Mark 1 was a solely naval variant fitted with two Gyron Junior engines of 7,100lb thrust. Weapons included 4,000lb in the internal rotating bomb-bay and in theory up to 12,000lb on wing pylons. In fact the power was inadequate for the size and the variant had to be catapulted light and refuelled in flight in order to fulfil its function. The Buccaneer joined the Fleet Air Arm with 801 NAS in July 1962 and was replaced in service with the S Mark 2 by November 1966.

Service **Strike** 800, 801, 803, 809 **Training** 736 **Trials** 700Z

S Mark 2

In Mark 2 form the Buccaneer was powered by the Spey turbofan to overcome the performance limitations of the initial version. The tenth development aircraft, XK526, was the first to be fitted with the new engine and the first production aircraft, XN974, flew on 6 June 1964. Radar was the Ferranti Blue Parrot. The first naval unit to be re-equipped was 801 NAS in October 1965. Within several years the naval fixed-wing force was being phased out, but co-incident was the urgent need for the RAF to make good cancellation both of the TSR.2 and the interim intended replacement, the American F-111K. Sixty-seven ex FAA aircraft were transferred to the RAF and 26 new aircraft were ordered but in practice most of the S Mk 2 variant were either delivered as, or converted to, sub-marks.

Service **Strike** 800, 801, 803, 809 **Training** 736

S Mark 2A

The A suffix was applied to 46 ex FAA airframes with the Martel ASM fit. The first RAF unit with the type was 12 Sqn.

Blackburn Buccaneer S Mk 2B

The Buccaneer was designed for naval strike. Scrapping of the TSR.2 and cancellation of the intended F-111K order coincided with the loss of the Fleet Air Arm carrier force and the RAF took over the now redundant Buccaneers in addition to securing new-build aircraft. In the event the type was an excellent low-level weapons platform, being sent to the Gulf to provide target marking for Tornados. Unusually configured XX893/H of 15 Sqn flies along the Mosel valley with Pave Spike ESM on the port wing and a Sidewinder AAM and 250 gal fuel tank under the starboard wing. *(Crown copyright)*

Service Strike 12, 15, 16, 208 **Training** 237 OCU

S Mark 2B
The Mark 2B was the main RAF variant. The major change was the addition of a 425gal fuel tank under the bomb-bay; 32 were later equipped to operate the Sea Eagle ASM and a number were fitted with the ALQ-119 Pave Spike designator. These latter aircraft flew in the Second Gulf war, target marking for Tornados.

Service Strike 12, 15, 16, 208, 216 **Training** 237 OCU
Trials RAE

S Mark 2C
The C sub-type comprised four S Mk 2 examples fitted with Mk 20 AAR pods for buddy in-flight refuelling and operated by the FAA.

Service Strike/tanker 809

S Mark 2D
The Mark 2D was the first variant with the extended fuel tank and Martel fit. Twelve aircraft, all S Mk 2 conversions, were flown by the FAA and then the RAF.

Service Strike 12: 809

BAC TSR.2

Sadly but appropriately seen grounded (preserved at Duxford) is XR222 the fourth prototype of the TSR.2. The type was scrapped in April 1965 just six months after the first flight although development had been promising. *(Author)*

Specification and production

Mark	Role	Engine	Thrust lb	Speed mph	Range miles	Nos
S1	Strike	2xGyron Junior	7,100	654	2,300	60*
S2	Strike	2xSpey 101	11,100	645	1,250	84
S2A	Strike	2xSpey 101	11,100	645	1,250	46+
S2B	Strike	2xSpey 101	11,100	645	1,250	79~
S2C	Tanker	2xSpey 101	11,100	645	1,250	4+
S2D	Strike	2xSpey 101	11,100	645	1,250	12+

* Includes 20 development aircraft
\+ S2 conversions
\~ 49 new build, 21 ex FAA S2, 9 S2A conversions

Further reading
Buccaneer, Allward, M, Ian Allan, London, 1981

4.13 BAC TSR.2 (1964)

The operational requirement for the Canberra replacement, OR.339, was issued in 1956. It called for an aircraft capable of operating from small airfields at supersonic speeds and at all levels, especially close down; by now the threat to high flying aircraft was appreciated. The complexity of the requirement was such that no single aerospace company, except possibly Hawker Siddeley, was capable of designing and producing a solution. Thus Bristol, English Electric and Vickers merged to form British Aircraft Corporation in 1960.

The accepted Vickers design, built to the revised GOR.343, was nearly 90ft long with a shoulder wing and two Olympus engines each delivering 30,610lb thrust. Intended performance was Mach 2.25 at above 36,000ft and Mach 1.1 at sea level with a tactical operating radius of around 800 miles. Maximum weapons load would have been 6,000lb internally and 4,000lb on underwing pylons.

The aircraft was constructed at Weybridge and transported to Boscombe Down for the first flight (XR219) on 27 September 1964. For a variety of reasons, political and military, the TSR.2 was cancelled in April 1965 by which time over thirteen hours of flight had been achieved in 24 sorties. Five airframes were complete, four were nearly completed and eleven pre-production aircraft and 30 production aircraft were on the production line. Replacement of the programme was determined in the form of the AFVG (Chapter 4.14), and as an interim measure 50 F-111K (Chapter 12.9). The AFVG was abandoned in 1966 and the F-111 order cancelled in 1968.

Specification and production

Mark	Role	Engine	Thrust lb	Speed mph	Range miles	Nos
–	Strike	2xOlympus 320	30,610	1,485	2,000	5

Further reading
Phoenix Into Ashes, Beamont, R J, William Kimber, London, 197?
The Murder of the TSR.2, Hastings, S, Macdonald, London, 197?

4.14 Panavia Tornado (1980–date)

The origins of the Tornado lie with Dr Barnes Wallis of geodetic structures and dam-busting bomb fame. From 1944, working with Vickers at Weybridge, he had explored the feasibility of a wing which changed shape critically by sweeping. Models were flown in the form of the Wild Goose and then Swallow on behalf of Vickers and the RAE at Predannack between 1952 and 1954 (Chapter 12.3). In 1963 BAC undertook a private-venture study of a military variable geometry aircraft and when the TSR.2 was abandoned the government decided to pursue two collaborative programmes with France, one to become the Jaguar and the other the so-called AFVG (Anglo-French Variable Geometry). Intended for conflicting roles the latter stood little chance of being built and indeed the French pulled out in late 1966.

The design principles were kept alive and after various false starts Britain, Germany and Italy agreed, in 1968, to move ahead on what was initially described as the Multi-Role Combat Aircraft (MRCA). The prototype (01) was flown in Germany on 14 August 1974 and the first British aircraft, XX946, flew on 10 October the same year.

GR Mark 1

The first version was built for all three participating countries. All armament, apart from the two 27mm Mauser cannon, was carried externally and stores included typically eight 1,000lb bombs under fuselage, two 330gal tanks on inner and pylons and generally a BOZ-107 chaff/flare dispenser and Sky Shadow jamming pod on outer pylons. There is provision for in-flight refuelling on the starboard side of the forward fuselage but the probe

needs to be fitted semi-recessed as needed. The first production aircraft was ZA319 which flew on 10 July 1979 and service entry was with the unique Tri-National Tornado Training Establishment (TTTE) at Cottesmore in July 1980. The first operational unit to form on the Tornado was 9 Sqn early in 1982.

Service **Tactical strike** 2, 9, 13, 14, 15, 16, 17, 20, 27, 31, 617 **Training** TTTE; TWU (45) **Trials** DRA; SAOEU; TOEU

GR Mark 1(T)

The 'two-stick' aircraft was similar to the GR Mk 1 but with dual controls for training. The variant was fully operational and served with all GR Mk 1 units.

GR Mark 1A

The Mark 1A is a dedicated reconnaissance variant with the gun armament deleted and three Vinten Linescan infra-red sensors fitted in the space released. The GR Mk 1A is capable of flying offensive sorties with a full range

Panavia Tornado GR Mk 1

Not for nothing is the Tornado nicknamed 'the fin'! The type introduced variable wing-sweep into the RAF and its useful 10,000lb weapons load is all carried externally under the wings and fuselage. Gulf War veteran ZD747/AL of 9 Sqn retains 29 mission symbols and is seen with 'Sky Shadow' jamming pod, 330-gal tanks and underfuselage Alarm anti-radiation missiles. *(BAe)*

of external weapons. Service entry was with 2 Sqn in January 1989 and the variant was used during the Second Gulf War at which time the Thermal Imaging and Laser Designator (TIALD) equipment was pressed into operational use.

Service **Photo-reconnaissance** 2, 13 **Trials** SAOEU

GR Mark 1B
The Mark 1B is optimised for the maritime strike role and in service has replaced the Buccaneer, although the two dedicated units retain an overland role. The variant is equipped to operate the Sea Eagle ASM (two missiles) and at least 21 had been converted by April 1995.

Service **Maritime strike** 12, 17 **Trials** SAOEU

F Mark 2
The Mark 2 was very much an interim fighter version of which only ten were built. The Tornado fighter was intended as a long-range interceptor optimised for

defending against Warsaw Pact bomber attacks on the United Kingdom. Its Skyflash AAM armament enables contact at 25 miles range in hostile weather and ECM environments. The type was never intended as a dogfighter and it is not especially agile. The Air Defence Variant (ADV) was not required by the other partners and the prototype (ZA254) flew on 27 October 1979. Problems with the Foxhunter radar resulted in ballast being installed in the nose but service entry with 229 OCU enabled a start to be made on training from November 1984.

Service **Training** 229 OCU

F Mk 2T
The Mark 2T comprised eight of the first ADV batch of eighteen aircraft fitted with dual controls.

Service **Training** 229 OCU

Panavia Tornado F Mk 3T

When Britain alone ordered the long-range interceptor variant (ADV) the assumed threat was from Soviet long-range bombers. In the role the Tornado is effective but it is no dogfighter and there is an urgent need for a highly manoeuvreable fighter to complement it. ZH559/AO of the OCU (56(R) Sqn) is fully armed with AIM-9 Sidewinders and four Skyflash AAMs and shows off the wings fully swept. *(BAe)*

F Mark 3

The Mark 3 was the fully operational fighter variant of the Tornado. The engine was slightly more powerful and fully automatic wing sweep was incorporated. Additional fuel was carried in larger (495gal) drop tanks and 200 gals internally. In addition there is provision for inflight refuelling with a fully recessed probe on the port side of the fuselage. Armament comprises a sole 27mm Mauser cannon, four Skyflash and four AIM-9 Sidewinders. Prototype was ZA267 and the first production aircraft, ZE154, flew on 20 November 1985. Service entry was with 29 Sqn in July 1987. Upgrades in the light of experience in Bosnia include underwing Phimat chaff pods and Tracor ALE-40 chaff and flare dispensers under the rear fuselage.

Service Fighter 5, 11, 23, 25, 29, 43, 111; 1435 Flt **Trainer** 229 (65, 56) OCU

F Mark 3(T)

The two-stick trainer comprised 31 airframes incorporating dual control and minimum flight instruments in the rear cockpit.

Service Fighter/training 5, 11, 23, 25, 29, 43, 111; 229 (65, 56) OCU

GR Mark 4

The Mark 4 will comprise a mid-life update of the GR Mk 1/1A/1B. Up to 150 aircraft are being upgraded between 1996 and 2000. Improvements include TIALD, improved control, armament control and computing systems, Global Positioning System (GPS) and Forward-Looking Infra-Red (FLIR). The development aircraft was ZD708.

Specification and production

Mark	Role	Engine	Thrust lb	Speed mph	Range miles	Nos
GR1	Tac strike	2xRB199 Mk 103	15,800	1,460	1,600	192
GR1(T)	Tac strike/ trainer	as above				36
GR1A	Recce	as above				28*
GR1B	Maritime strike	as above				21~
F2	Fighter	2xRB199 Mk 103	15,800	1,460	1,700	10
F2(T)	Fighter/ trainer	as above				8
F3	Fighter	2xRB199 Mk 104	16,250	1,480	1,800	121
F3(T)	Fighter/ trainer	as above				31
GR4	Strike	2xRB199 Mk 103	15,800	1,460	1,600	150~

* 12 GR1 conversions, 16 new build
~ GR1 conversions

Further reading
Panavia Tornado, Gunston, W, Ian Allan, Shepperton, 1980
Panavia Tornado, Price, A, Ian Allan, London, 1988
Tornado IDS (Aeroguide 24) Linewrights, Ongar, 1988
Tornado (Warbirds 42) Gething, M J, Arms and Armour, London, 1987

5 – Maritime, photo-reconnaissance, and control

See also: B-45 (12.8) Canberra (4.7); Gannet (9.11); Hornet (3.7); Hunter (2.8); Jaguar (3.13); Lancaster (4.3); Meteor (2.5); Mosquito (3.4); Phantom (2.11); Sea King (9.14) Skyraider (9.9); Spitfire (2.1); Swift (2.7); Tornado (4.14); Valiant (4.9); Victor (4.11); Vulcan (4.10); Wellington (1.4)

Short Sunderland GR Mk 5

Mainstay of Coastal Command through the war years was the Sunderland, which went on to serve in the maritime reconnaissance role until 1959. DP198/W of 209 Sqn is seen taxying in the Far East during Operation 'Firedog' in Malaya where the Sunderland was involved in dropping bombs on terrorist strongholds. *(Crown copyright)*

A range of aircraft was used to collect 'intelligence' of one sort or another, primarily for the RAF. At the war's end most of the effort was connected with maritime patrol, photo-reconnaissance and weather reporting. Fifty years on weather assessment is carried out remotely while electronic intelligence gathering has assumed the importance it had during the war with the work of 100 Group.

January 1946

In the United Kingdom the anti-submarine warfare squadrons were quickly reduced at the end of the war, with a diminished presence in the Middle East but more assets in the Far East. The Sunderland flying boat equipped five squadrons at home and abroad, while the Liberator served with just two prior to being scrapped or returned to the United States. Most Liberator units had switched to Transport Command to meet the much increased demand for intra-theatre supplies movement and for moving men and materiel back to the United Kingdom.

Photo-reconnaissance units were equipped with the Spitfire XI and XIX or Mosquito XVI and PRMk34 with two home-based squadrons, one in the Middle East and two in the Far East. The iron curtain had not yet dropped across Europe and the disposition of reconnaissance units did not extend to Germany.

In respect of electronic intelligence gathering (Elint), 100 Group, which had been accountable for electronic countermeasures – essentially jamming – and for gathering data on enemy signals, had disbanded. Its wide range of functions was assumed by the Radio Warfare Establishment (RWE), newly moved to RAF Watton.

The extensive weather reporting network developed during the war remained largely intact at its end. Long-range types comprised the Halifax, Fortress and Warwick working out into the Atlantic and North Sea. Across the Mediterranean, the Middle East, Africa and the Far East locally based flights of short-range types – usually Spitfire and Hurricane – were deployed to check local weather in climates where rapid changes were common.

Maritime operational training was still being carried out by three Operational Training Units (OTUs) including 302 FTU which operated the RAF's last Catalinas. The latter and 111 OTU were to disband within a few months while 4 OTU became 235 Operational Conversion Unit (OCU) in 1947. A miscellany of types was on the strength of various specialised training units while the Air-Sea Warfare Development Unit operated both Air Force and Royal Navy types (within 703 NAS) at Thorney Island. Photo-reconnaissance training was centred at Benson with 8 OTU, which became 237 OCU in 1947.

July 1948

In the United Kingdom Coastal Command had been reduced to two groups, 18 Group in the north and 19 Group in the south. Land-based patrol was carried out exclusively by the Lancaster GR Mk 3 with two home-based and three Far East-based Sunderland squadrons.

Photo-reconnaissance was still the preserve of the Mosquito PR Mk 34 and Spitfire PR Mk 19 and growing tension in the world dictated the need for an increase in the number of units committed.

The RWE at Watton had expanded and become the Central Signals Establishment (CSE) which co-operated closely with the Telecommunications Flying Unit at Defford. With the borders across Europe closing there was a growing need to collect data on potential enemy radars and radio usage. The change of name and accountability within Transport Command were no doubt intended to disguise the true function of the unit.

The local meteorology flights across the world had disbanded. Two long-range met squadrons, both equipped with Halifaxes, were based at Aldergrove with permament detachments at Gibraltar.

Operational training was conducted by 235 and 236 OCUs with Sunderlands and Lancasters respectively with PR training conducted by 237 OCU at Benson. The ASWDU had moved to Ballykelly in Northern Ireland, where it was co-located with the Joint Anti-Submarine School (JASS).

January 1950

Little had changed in the disposition and equipment of most types of units within this section. In terms of maritime patrol two squadrons of Sunderlands were based in Malaya to help cope with the insurrection there. The only new type (operated by 1301 Flt on met duties) was the Brigand.

Photo-reconnaissance had also stood still, although military developments in the Soviet Union suggested a need for types capable of overflights. From having been a self-contained unit within Transport Command, the CSE operated within 90 (Signals) Group. Training arrangements were also little changed with no new equipment on charge. No 237 OCU had moved temporarily to Leuchars to allow space at Benson for the Air Photographic Development Unit (APDU).

July 1952

In common with other branches of the services, Coastal Command and the reconnaissance units had expanded to reach their post-war peak. The most important change to have taken place was the introduction of the Shackleton MR1 which within two years had supplanted the Lancaster in most units. The Neptune was also in service with 217 Sqn pending sufficient Shackletons being available. The Sunderland remained in service and the total number of home-based units had doubled in the period. The Halifax had been replaced by the Hastings for Atlantic meteorological duties with 224 Sqn in Northern Ireland.

In the tactical reconnaissance role the Spitfire had been replaced, except in Malaya, by the jet-powered Meteor and the number of such units in Germany had increased from one to three. The need for better signals intelligence had resulted in the creation of 192 Sqn within 90 Group.

January 1955

While the Sunderland soldiered on at home and in Malaya the Shackleton equipped no fewer than eleven squadrons in the UK and the Middle East, with the improved MR Mk 2 coming into service. The Neptune equipped four home-based units, primarily covering the North Sea. Remarkably, the Lancaster remained in service with the School of Maritime Reconnaissance at St Mawgan.

In the photo-reconnaissance role, the Canberra had entered service for strategic work, serving with five squadrons. The main PR base was now Wyton, leaving Benson as the OCU base. Modified variants of the Canberra B Mk 2 and B Mk 6 also served with 192 Sqn on ELINT duties. In the Far East, the Spitfire had finally succumbed to old age and had been replaced by the Meteor with 81 Sqn. The Central Signals Establishment and 192 Sqn, both at Watton, continued to receive new types, with the latter operating the Varsity and Washington in addition to Canberras.

Perhaps one of the most interesting developments was the establishment of 1453 Flt at Topcliffe in the airborne early warning role equipped with four modified Neptunes. Shortly the RAF relinquished the role until the Royal Navy lost its capacity in 1970; then another maritime type, the Shackleton, took over the reins.

Reconnaissance and anti-submarine development units

The **School of General Reconnaissance** (SGR) trained observers and was formed at Leuchars on 1 March 1946 from 3 SGR. It disbanded on 5 September 1947. In due course its function was taken over by the **School of Maritime Reconnaissance** (SMR) which formed in April 1951 at St Mawgan. The SMR was disbanded into the **Maritime Operational Training Unit** (MOTU) in September 1956 which also assumed the tasks of 236 OCU. The **Air-Sea Warfare Development Unit** (ASWDU) was formed on 1 January 1945 from the **Coastal Command Development Unit** (CCDU) in 16 Group at Thorney Island moving to Ballykelly in May 1948 equipped with the Lancaster, Anson and Sunderland. It transferred to St Mawgan from May 1951 to September 1958 in 19 Group, where it included 744 NAS from 1952 to 1956, and it disbanded at Ballykelly in 18 Group on 1 April 1970.

The **Joint Anti-Submarine School** (JASS) was formed at Ballykelly on 19 November 1945 with Lancasters and Warwicks and in due course it operated the Neptune and Shackleton. Its purpose was to train aircrew from the Fleet Air Arm and RAF in techniques of anti-submarine warfare including detection and attack. The FAA element was 719 and 737 NAS based at Eglinton. It became the **Joint Maritime Operational Training School** (JMOTS) by March 1970.

The **Central Photographic Establishment** (CPE) was formed at Benson on 15 August 1946 from 106 Group. The **Photographic Reconnaissance Development Unit** (PRDU) had formed in 1943 at Benson where it was re-designated the **Air Photography Development Unit** (APDU) in August 1947 within the CPE until both disbanded on 1 March 1950.

The **Central Reconnaissance Establishment** (CRE) was formed at Brampton on 12 January 1957 to control the UK-based photo-reconnaissance squadrons. It disbanded on 1 October 1970.

June 1957

Coastal Command was beginning to contract from the 1955 peak. The Shackleton was now the sole maritime reconnaissance type, the mutual aid Neptunes having been passed on to various foreign air arms. St Eval was in the process of closing with its squadrons moving several miles down the road to St Mawgan.

In the strategic reconnaissance role the Canberra

squadrons had been re-numbered and more were by now based in Germany. Also in Germany the Swift FR Mk 5 had entered service with two squadrons for tactical reconnaissance. In the UK 543 Sqn had taken on charge the new Valiant in B(PR) form; several of this variant also equipped a number of primarily bomber units. The British nuclear tests in the Pacific had resulted in the establishment of several specialised Canberra squadrons for weather reconnaissance and monitoring. All MR training was now concentrated within 18 Group and the OCUs had been absorbed into the Maritime Operational Training Unit at Kinloss.

June 1960

The Shackleton MR Mk 3 had supplanted the MR Mk 1, which itself had finally replaced the Sunderland in Malaya. In the photo-reconnaissance role the improved Canberra PR Mk 9 had joined 58 Sqn in the UK while earlier versions equipped six squadrons overseas.

192 Sqn had been re-numbered as 51 Sqn, still based at Watton but now equipped with modified Comets, in addition to Canberras, for long-range signals intelligence. To reflect the importance of the role Signals Command had been formed on 3 November 1958. No 237 OCU had disbanded and PR crews were now being trained by the bomber OCUs.

January 1965

In five years there were no significant changes in equipment or basing of the maritime reconnaissance squadrons. For tactical reconnaissance the Swift had now been replaced by the Hunter FR Mk 10 in Germany and the Canberra PR Mk 9 equipped the MEAF PR units.

January 1970

Coastal Command had been absorbed into Strike Command on 27 November 1969. The Shackleton units had reduced by one and with one exception were based within 18 Group in Northern Ireland or Scotland. No 543 Sqn, engaged in strategic reconnaissance, had lost its Valiants which had been replaced by the Victor B Mk 2(SR). The reduction of forces in Germany had seen just one Hunter and one Canberra PR squadrons there.

As a foretaste of things to come the MOTU had received its first Nimrod MR Mk 1 in September 1969 and first crews were in training.

Radar development units

The **Telecommunications Research Establishment** (TRE) was based at Malvern and became the **Radar Research Establishment** (RRE) in 1953. Its purpose was to develop new equipment and test it in an operational setting. Within TRE was the **Telecommunications Flying Unit** (TFU) based at Defford. This was re-named the **Radar Research Flying Unit** (RRFU) on 1 November 1955, still at Defford until September 1957 when it moved to nearby Pershore. In 1977 Pershore closed with the transfer of the RRFU to the **Radar Research Squadron** (RRS) within the **Royal Aircraft Establishment** (RAE) at Bedford until 1988. In the meantime the RRE had become the **Royal Signals and Radar Establishment** (RS&RE) in March 1976.

The **Signals Flying Unit** (SFU) formed at Honiley in July 1944 and stayed to September 1946. In 1946 Watton was the home to the **Radio Warfare Establishment** (RWE) and when the SFU transferred to Watton the RWE became the **Central Signals Establishment** (CSE). Its function was to provide aircraft and equipment for calibration and electronic warfare within 90 (Signals) Group. For calibration duties in August 1952 'N' Sqn became 116 then 115 Sqn while 'R' Sqn became 527 then 245 then 98 Sqn, which eventually disbanded into 100 Sqn.

Electronic intelligence gathering (ELINT) was handled centrally by CSE until July 1951 when 192 Sqn was formed, becoming 51 Sqn in August 1958. At the same time 199 Sqn was formed for jamming tasks with the Lincoln and Mosquito, transferring to Hemswell in 1952 where it was re-equipped with Canberras then Valiants. When the unit disbanded in 1958 its Lincolns had already formed 1321 Flt while the Valiants were absorbed into 18 Sqn. General development tasks transferred from the **Signals Development Sqn** into 151 Sqn in January 1962 which in 1963 became 97 Sqn until disbandment in January 1967. The Fleet Air Arm also had a presence at Watton; 751 NAS was based there for EW tasks between 1951 and 1957 while 831 NAS was based there for ECM work from 1963 to 1966 when crews were transferred to the joint services 360 Sqn.

The **Radar Reconnaissance Flight** (RRF) was formed on 2 October 1951 from 58 Sqn, which was confined to photo-reconnaissance at Benson. It moved to Upwood in March 1952 then on to Wyton in October 1955 where it was equipped with Canberras. It then moved on to Gaydon in September 1961 where it disbanded on 1 November 1963.

January 1975

The piston-engined Shackleton had at last been replaced in service by the jet-engined Nimrod, starting from late 1970. The new type provided the equipment for just four squadrons in the UK and one in the Mediterranean. The Nimrod force was supplemented by 27 Sqn with the Vulcan B Mk 2(MRR). In the tactical reconnaissance role the Hunter had given way to the Phantom FGR Mk 2 with one squadron each in the UK and Germany. PR Canberras equipped one unit at home and one in the Mediterranean and 81 Sqn had disbanded with British withdrawal from the Far East.

On the signals front 90 Signals Group had been absorbed into 1 Group, Strike Command. Four squadrons operated a range of types on SIGINT, ELINT, calibration and training duties; in the latter role 360 Sqn had formed with the bulbous Canberra T Mk 17 at Cottesmore to provide EW training for the RAF and Royal Navy. 51 Sqn now had three special Nimrod R Mk 1 on charge to replace the Comets.

As the Shackleton had been replaced in 18 Group, a small number was converted to AEW Mk 2 configuration and equipped 8 Sqn at Lossiemouth to provide essential airborne radar cover of the Northern Approaches.

MOTU had moved to St Mawgan and in the process been re-named as 236 OTU. The ASWDU had been disbanded with the closure of Ballykelly.

January 1980

The Nimrod units were by now reduced to four with the withdrawal from the Mediterranean. For tactical PR the interim Phantom had been replaced by the Jaguar with 41 Sqn (UK) and 2 Sqn (Germany) and for the first time for some years there were two Canberra PR units at Wyton including 13 Sqn which had withdrawn from Malta

January 1985

The maritime reconnaissance units were now all equipped with Nimrod MR Mk 2 conversions, many being fitted for in-flight refuelling following the Falklands campaign. The type had also been fitted with Sidewinder missiles for protection and the Harpoon ASM. The Canberra served on with 1 PRU and 360 Sqn which between them relied on 231 OCU for trained crews. The Shackleton crews of 8 Sqn were looking forward to the promised re-equipment with the Nimrod AEW Mk 3.

January 1990

In five years there were few changes, with the notable exception of the establishment of 13 Sqn with the Tornado GR Mk 1A in the tactical reconnaissance role. Several units continued to operate the Canberra which had by now been in service for approaching 40 years. The Nimrod AEW Mk 3 had been cancelled against the Boeing E-3D and the Shackletons thus soldiered on with 8 Sqn.

January 1995

All maritime reconnaissance assets were by now based at Kinloss in Scotland. Wyton was in the process of closing with the few remaining Canberra PR Mk 9s of 39 Sqn (1 PRU) moving to Marham. Tactical reconnaissance was handled by two Tornado GR Mk 1A units, both also based at Marham. No 51 Sqn Nimrods were due to transfer to Waddington. Also based at Waddington since service entry in 1991 with 8 Sqn was the Sentry, which allowed the much overdue retirement of the Shackleton.

5.A   Maritime and photo-reconnaissance at 1 January 1946

Maritime reconnaissance

Coastal Command (19 Group)

Type	Unit	Base
Sunderland V	201	Pembroke Dock
Warwick V	179	St Eval
Liberator V,VI,VIII	224	St Eval

Coastal Command (247 Group)

Type	Unit	Base
Liberator V,VI,VIII	224 (det)	Azores

Mediterranean and Middle East Air Force (AHQ Malta)

Type	Unit	Base
Wellington XIV,	38	Luqa (Malta)
Warwick I	38 (det)	Elmas (Sardinia)

Allied Command South East Asia

HQ RAF Hong Kong

Type	Unit	Base
Sunderland V	209, 1430 Flt	Kai Tak

AHQ Ceylon

Type	Unit	Base
Sunderland V	230, 240	Red Hills Lake (India)
	240 (det)	Bally (Ceylon)
	205	Koggala (Ceylon)
Liberator VI	203	Kankesanturai (Ceylon)

Photo-reconnaissance

Bomber Command (106 (PR) Group)

Type	Unit	Base
Mosquito XIV, PR34	540	Benson
Spitfire X, XI, XIX, Mustang	541	Benson

Mediterranean and Middle East Air Force

AHQ Eastern Mediterranean

Type	Unit	Base
Mosquito XVI	680	Deversoir (Egypt)

AHQ Levant

Type	Unit	Base
Mosquito XVI	680 (det)	Aleppo (Syria)
	680 (det)	Aqir (Palestine)

AHQ Iraq and Persia

Type	Unit	Base
Mosquito XVI	680 (det)	Habbaniya (Iraq)

Allied Command South East Asia

HQ RAF Hong Kong

Type	Unit	Base
Spitfire XI,XIX	681	Kai Tak

AHQ French Indo-China

Type	Unit	Base
Mosquito XVI	684	Tan Son Nhut (Indo-China)

AHQ Malaya

Type	Unit	Base
Mosquito XVI`	684 (det)	Seletar (Malaya)

Elint

Type	Unit	Base
Mosquito XVI	RWE	Watton

Meteorology

RAF Northern Ireland

Type	Unit	Base
Halifax II	518	Aldergrove

Coastal Command (16 Group)

Type	Unit	Base
Hurricane IIc	521 (det), 1402 Flt	Langham
Spitfire XI	1561, 1562 Flts	Langham

Coastal Command (18 Group)

Type	Unit	Base
Fortress II/IIA, Spitfire VI	519	Leuchars
Halifax III/V	518 (det)	Tain

Coastal Command (19 Group)

Type	Unit	Base
Fortress II/IIA	521	Chivenor
Halifax III/V	517	Chivenor

Transport Command (47 Group)

Type	Unit	Base
Mosquito IX,XVI	1409 Flt	Lyneham

Coastal Command (247 Group)

Type	Unit	Base
Spitfire V, Martinet, Warwick I	269	Azores

BAFO (Germany)

Type	Unit	Base
Spitfire IX,XI	1401 Flt	Celle

Mediterranean and Middle East Air Force

AHQ Cairo

Type	Unit	Base
Spitfire Vb	1412 Flt	Khartoum (Sudan)
Spitfire Vc	1567 Flt	El Genina (Egypt)

AHQ Eastern Mediterranean

Type	Unit	Base
Spitfire Vb, Vc,VIII	1563 Flt	Benina (Libya)
Spitfire Vb, Vc	1564 Flt	Castel Benito (Libya)
Spitfire Vb, Vc, Hurricane IIb, IIc	1565 Flt	Nicosia (Cyprus)

AHQ Levant

Type	Unit	Base
Spitfire Vb, Vc	1413 Flt	Lydda (Palestine)

AHQ Iraq and Persia

Type	Unit	Base
Spitfire Vc, Hurricane IIc	1415 Flt	Habbaniya (Iraq)

AHQ East Africa

Type	Unit	Base
Hurricane IIb, IIc	1569 Flt	Diego Suarez (Madagascar)
Spitfire Vc, Anson	1414 Flt	Eastleigh (Kenya)

HQ British Forces Aden

Type	Unit	Base
Spitfire Vc	1566 Flt	Khormaksar (Aden)

AHQ West Africa

Type	Unit	Base
Spitfire XI	1561 Flt	Ikeja (Nigeria)
	1562 Flt	Waterloo (Sierra Leone)

Allied Command South East Asia

AHQ Ceylon

Type	Unit	Base
Hurricane IIc,IId	1303 Flt	Ratmalana (Ceylon)

225 Group

Type	Unit	Base
Hurricane IIc, IId	1302 Flt	St Thomas Mount (India)

227 Group

Type	Unit	Base
Hurricane IIc, IId, Harvard IIb	1301 Flt	Nagpur (India)

228 Group

Type	Unit	Base
Spitfire XI	1300 Flt	Alipore (India)

Training and development units

Coastal Command (16 Group)

Type	Unit	Base
Martinet I, Spitfire	CCFATU	Langham
Sea Otter II,	ASWDU	Thorney Island
Beaufighter X,	(inc 703 NAS)	
Mosquito VI,		
Spitfire V, IX,		
Walrus II, Anson I,		
Liberator VI Warwick I,		
Lancaster III, Wellington XIV,		
Sunderland V,		
Barracuda, Avenger		
Wellington,	ATDU	Gosport
Beaufighter X		

Coastal Command (18 Group)

Type	Unit	Base
Sunderland V	4 OTU	Alness, Tain
Warwick I, II	6 OTU	Kinloss
Wellington XIII, XIV,	111 OTU	Lossiemouth
Liberator VIII		
Catalina III,	302 FTU	Alness
Sunderland V		
Anson I, Mosquito	3 SGR	Leuchars
Liberator, VI,VII,	CCFIS	Tain
Master II,		
Hurricane IV,		
Typhoon IB		
Beaufighter X,	1 TTU	Tain
Oxford II		

Coastal Command (19 Group)

Type	Unit	Base
Sea Otter II, Warwick I	SRTU	Calshot

Bomber Command (106 Group)

Type	Unit	Base
Spitfire XIX,	8 (PR) OTU	Benson
Mosquito XXXIV		

5.B Maritime and photo-reconnaissance at 1 July 1948

Maritime reconnaissance

Coastal Command (18 Group)

Type	Unit	Base
Lancaster GR3	120	Leuchars

Coastal Command (19 Group)

Type	Unit	Base
Lancaster GR3	203	St Eval
Sunderland GR5	201	Pembroke Dock
	230	Calshot

MEAF

Type	Unit	Base
Lancaster GR3	37, 38	Luqa (Malta)

FEAF

Type	Unit	Base
Sunderland GR5	88	Kai Tak (Hong Kong)
	205	Koggala (Ceylon)
	209	Seletar (Malaya)

Photo-reconnaissance

Bomber Command

Type	Unit	Base
Mosquito PR34,	58	Benson
Anson C19		
Mosquito PR34	540	Benson
Spitfire PR19	541	Benson
Lancaster PR1	82	Benson

BAFO (Germany)

Type	Unit	Base
Spitfire PR19	2	Wahn

MEAF

Type	Unit	Base
Mosquito PR34	13	Fayid (Egypt)

FEAF

Type	Unit	Base
Mosquito PR34,	81	Tengah (Malaya)
Spitfire PR19		

ELINT

Type	Unit	Base
Lincoln B2, Oxford T2,	CSE	Watton
Mosquito B16, PR34,		
Proctor C3, Anson C10,		
19, Lancaster B1		

Meteorology

Coastal Command

Type	Unit	Base
Halifax GR6,A9	202, 224	Aldergrove

Training and development units

Type	Unit	Base
Sunderland V	235 OCU	Calshot
Lancaster GR3, ASR3,	236 OCU	Kinloss
Spitfire F16,		
Proctor C3		
Spitfire F9, PR19,	237 OCU	Benson
Harvard T2,		
Mosquito T3, FB6,		
PR34, Oxford T2		
Lancaster GR3,	ASWDU	Ballykelly
Lincoln B2,		
Anson 19		
Lancaster GR3	JASS	Ballykelly

5.C Maritime and photo-reconnaissance at 1 January 1950

Maritime reconnaissance

Coastal Command (18 Group)

Type	Unit	Base
Lancaster GR3	120	Leuchars

Coastal Command (19 Group)

Type	Unit	Base
Lancaster GR3	203, 210	St Eval
Sunderland GR5	201, 230	Pembroke Dock

MEAF – AHQ Malta

Type	Unit	Base
Lancaster GR3	37, 38	Luqa (Malta)

FEAF

AHQ Hong Kong

Type	Unit	Base
Sunderland GR5	88	Kai Tak (HK)

AHQ Malaya

Type	Unit	Base
Sunderland GR5	205, 209	Seletar (Malaya)

Photo-reconnaissance

Bomber Command (Central Photographic Establishment)

Type	Unit	Base
Mosquito PR34, Anson C19	58	Benson
Mosquito PR34	540	Benson
Spitfire PR19, Harvard T2	541	Benson
Lancaster PR1, Dakota	82	Benson

BAFO (Germany)

Type	Unit	Base
Spitfire PR19	2	Wünstorf

MEAF

Type	Unit	Base
Mosquito PR34	13	Fayid (Egypt)

FEAF

Type	Unit	Base
Mosquito PR34, Spitfire PR19	81	Tengah (Malaya)

ELINT

Transport Command (90 Signals Group)

Type	Unit	Base
Lincoln B2, Mosquito 30, B35, 36	CSE	Watton

Meteorology

Coastal Command (RAF Northern Ireland)

Type	Unit	Base
Halifax GR6, A9	202	Aldergrove

Coastal Command (RAF Gibraltar)

Type	Unit	Base
Halifax Met6	224	Gibraltar

FEAF – AHQ Ceylon

Type	Unit	Base
Brigand Met1	1301 Flt	Negombo (Ceylon)

Training and development units

Coastal Command (18 Group)

Type	Unit	Base
Lancaster GR3, Oxford	236 OCU	Kinloss
Spitfire PR19, Mosquito PR34	237 OCU	Leuchars

Coastal Command (19 Group)

Type	Unit	Base
Sunderland GR5	235 OCU	Calshot

Coastal Command (RAF Northern Ireland)

Type	Unit	Base
Lancaster GR3, Anson C12, 19, Sunderland GR5	ASWDU	Ballykelly
Lancaster GR3	JASS	Ballykelly

Bomber Command (CPE)

Type	Unit	Base
Mosquito PR34, Spitfire PR19, Lancaster PR1	APDU	Benson

5.D Maritime and photo-reconnaissance at 1 July 1952

Maritime reconnaissance

Coastal Command (18 Group)

Type	Unit	Base
Shackleton MR1	120	Aldergrove
	240, 269	Ballykelly
Neptune MR1	217	Kinloss

Coastal Command (19 Group)

Type	Unit	Base
Shackleton MR1	42, 220	St Eval
Lancaster MR3, ASR3	203/36, 210	St Eval
Sunderland GR5	201, 230	Pembroke Dock

Coastal Command (RAF Gibraltar)

Type	Unit	Base
Shackleton MR1	224	Gibraltar

MEAF – AHQ Malta

Type	Unit	Base
Lancaster MR3	37, 38	Luqa (Malta)

FEAF (230 Group)

Type	Unit	Base
Sunderland GR5	88, 205, 209	Seletar (Malaya)

Photo-reconnaissance

Bomber Command (3 Group)

Type	Unit	Base
Mosquito T3, PR34, Anson C19	58	Benson
Mosquito PR34	540	Benson
Lancaster PR1	82	Eastleigh (Kenya)

2 TAF (Germany)

Type	Unit	Base
Meteor FR9	2, 79, 541	Gütersloh

MEAF

Type	Unit	Base
Meteor FR9	208	Abu Sueir (Egypt)
Meteor PR10	13	Fayid (Egypt)

AHQ Iraq

Type	Unit	Base
Lancaster PR1, Valetta C1	683	Habbaniyah (Iraq)

FEAF (230 Group)

Type	Unit	Base
Mosquito PR34, Spitfire PR19	81	Seletar (Malaya)

ELINT

Maintenance Command (90 Signals Group)

Type	Unit	Base
Lincoln B2	RRF	Upwood
Lincoln B2, Hastings C1, Anson C19	CSE	Watton
Lincoln B2, Mosquito PR34	192	Watton

Meteorology

RAF Northern Ireland (18 Group)

Type	Unit	Base
Hastings Met1	202	Aldergrove

Training and development units

Coastal Command (18 Group)

Type	Unit	Base
Shackleton MR1	236 OCU	Kinloss
Spitfire PR19, Mosquito PR34	237 OCU	Leuchars
Lancaster GR3, Anson C12,19, Sunderland GR5	ASWDU	Ballykelly
Lancaster GR3	JASS	Ballykelly

Coastal Command (19 Group)

Type	Unit	Base
Lancaster MR3	SMR	St Mawgan
Shackleton MR1, Sycamore HC12	ASWDU	St Mawgan
Sunderland MR5	235 OCU	Calshot

Bomber Command (CPE)

Type	Unit	Base
Mosquito PR34, Spitfire PR19, Lancaster PR1	APDU	Benson

5.E Maritime and photo-reconnaissance at 1 January 1955

Maritime reconnaissance

Coastal Command (18 Group)

Type	Unit	Base
Shackleton MR1	120	Aldergrove
	240, 269	Ballykelly
Shackleton MR2	204	Ballykelly
Neptune MR1	36, 203, 210	Topcliffe
	217	Kinloss

Coastal Command (19 Group)

Type	Unit	Base
Shackleton MR1	220	St Eval
Shackleton MR1A	206	St Eval
Shackleton MR2	42, 228	St Eval
Sunderland GR5	201, 230	Pembroke Dock

Coastal Command (RAF Gibraltar)

Type	Unit	Base
Shackleton MR2	224	Gibraltar

MEAF

Type	Unit	Base
Shackleton MR2	37, 38	Luqa (Malta)

FEAF

Type	Unit	Base
Sunderland GR5	205	Seletar (Malaya)

Photo-reconnaissance

Bomber Command

Type	Unit	Base
Canberra PR3	58	Wyton
Canberra PR3, PR7	82	Wyton
Canberra PR7	540, 542	Wyton

2 TAF (Germany)

Type	Unit	Base
Meteor FR9	2	Wahn
	79	Laarbruch
Canberra PR3	69	Laarbruch
Meteor PR10	541	Laarbruch

MEAF

Type	Unit	Base
Meteor FR9	208	Abu Sueir (Egypt)
Meteor PR10	13	Fayid (Egypt)
Lancaster PR1, Valetta C1	683	Habbaniyah (Iraq)

FEAF

Type	Unit	Base
Meteor PR10	81	Seletar (Malaya)

ELINT

Transport Command (90 (Signals) Group)

Type	Unit	Base
Lincoln B2, Hastings C1, CSE Anson C19		Watton
Washington B1, Varsity T1, Canberra B2, B6	192	Watton

Airborne Early Warning

Type	Unit	Base
Neptune MR1	1453 Flt	Topcliffe

Meteorology

Fighter Command (12 Group)

Type	Unit	Base
Spitfire PR19	THUM Flt	Woodvale

Coastal Command (RAF Northern Ireland)

Type	Unit	Base
Hastings Met1	202	Aldergrove

Training and development units

Coastal Command (18 Group)

Type	Unit	Base
Shackelton MR1, 1A, Neptune MR1	236 OCU	Kinloss
Shackleton MR	ASWDU	Ballykelly
Shackleton	JASS	Ballykelly

Coastal Command (19 Group)

Type	Unit	Base
Sunderland GR5	235 OCU	Pembroke Dock
Lancaster GR3	SMR	St Mawgan
Meteor T7, FR9, PR10, Canberra PR3, T4	237 OCU	Benson

5.F Maritime and photo-reconnaissance at 1 June 1957

Maritime reconnaissance

Coastal Command (18 Group)

Type	Unit	Base
Shackleton MR1	240, 269	Ballykelly
Shackleton MR2	120	Aldergrove
	204	Ballykelly

Coastal Command (19 Group)

Type	Unit	Base
Shackleton MR1A	206	St Eval
Shackleton MR1, MR2	220	St Mawgan
Shackleton MR2	42	St Eval
	228	St Mawgan

Coastal Command (RAF Gibraltar)

Type	Unit	Base
Shackleton MR2	224	Gibraltar

MEAF

Type	Unit	Base
Shackleton MR2	37, 38	Luqa (Malta)

FEAF

Type	Unit	Base
Sunderland GR5	205	Seletar (Malaya)

Photo-reconnaissance

Bomber Command (3 Group)

Type	Unit	Base
Valiant B1, B(PR)1	7, 90	Honington
Valiant B1, B(PR)1, B(PR)K1	138	Wittering
Valiant B(PR)1, B(K)1	207	Marham
Valiant B1, B(K)1, B(PR)1, B(PR)K1	214	Marham
Valiant B(PR)1, B(PR)K1	543	Wyton
Canberra PR7	58	Wyton

2 TAF (Germany)

Type	Unit	Base
Swift FR5	2	Geilenkirchen
	79	Gütersloh
Canberra PR7	17	Wildenrath
	31, 80	Laarbruch
Canberra PR3	69	Laarbruch
Meteor PR10	541	Wünstorf

MEAF

Type	Unit	Base
Meteor FR9	208	Ta Kali (Malta)
Canberra PR7	13	Akrotiri (Cyprus)

FEAF

Type	Unit	Base
Meteor PR10, Pembroke C(PR)1	81	Seletar (Malaya)

ELINT

Transport Command (90 (Signals) Group)

Type	Unit	Base
Lincoln B2, Hastings C1, Anson C19	CSE	Watton
Washington B1, Canberra B2, B6	192	Watton

Meteorology and nuclear monitoring

Bomber Command (1 Group)

Type	Unit	Base
Canberra B2, B6	76	Hemswell
	det	Christmas Island
	542	Hemswell

Bomber Command (3 Group)

Type	Unit	Base
Canberra B2, B6, PR7	100	Wittering
	det	Christmas Island

Coastal Command (18 Group)

Type	Unit	Base
Hastings Met1	202	Aldergrove

Training and development units

Coastal Command (18 Group)

Type	Unit	Base
Shackleton	MOTU	Kinloss
Shackleton, Sycamore	ASWDU	Ballykelly
Shackleton	JASS	Ballykelly

Coastal Command (19 Group)

Type	Unit	Base
Meteor T7, FR9, PR10, Canberra PR3, T4	237 OCU	Merryfield

5.G Maritime and photo-reconnaissance at 1 June 1960

Maritime reconnaissance

Coastal Command (18 Group)

Type	Unit	Base
Shackleton MR2	210	Ballykelly
Shackleton MR2C	204	Ballykelly
Shackleton MR3	120	Kinloss
	203	Ballykelly

Coastal Command (19 Group)

Type	Unit	Base
Shackleton MR2	42	St Mawgan
Shackleton MR3	201, 206	St Mawgan

Coastal Command (RAF Gibraltar)

Type	Unit	Base
Shackleton MR2	224	Gibraltar

MEAF

Type	Unit	Base
Shackleton MR2	37	Khormaksar (Aden)
	38	Luqa (Malta)

FEAF

Type	Unit	Base
Shackleton MR1A	205	Changi (Malaya)

Photo-reconnaissance

Bomber Command (3 Group)

Type	Unit	Base
Valiant B1, B(PR)1	7, 90	Honington
Valiant B1, B(PR)1, B(PR)K1, B(K)1	138	Wittering
Valiant B(PR)1, B(K)1	207	Marham
Valiant B1, B(K)1, B(PR)1, B(PR)K1	214	Marham

Type	Unit	Base
Valiant B(PR)1, B(PR)K1	543	Wyton
Canberra PR7, PR9	58	Wyton

2 TAF (Germany)

Type	Unit	Base
Swift FR5	2	Jever
	79	Gütersloh
Canberra PR7	17	Wildenrath
	31	Laarbruch
	80	Brüggen

MEAF

Type	Unit	Base
Canberra PR3	39	Luqa (Malta)
Canberra PR7	13	Akrotiri (Cyprus)
Meteor FR9, Hunter FR10	APRF	Khormaksar (Aden)

FEAF

Type	Unit	Base
Canberra PR7	81	Tengah (Malaya)

ELINT

Signals Command (90 (Signals) Group)

Type	Unit	Base
Lincoln B2, Hastings C1, Anson C19	CSE	Watton
Canberra B6, Comet C2(R)	51	Watton
Canberra B2, Victor B1	RRF	Wyton

Meteorology and nuclear monitoring

Bomber Command (3 Group)

Type	Unit	Base
Canberra B6	76	Upwood
	det	Christmas Island

Coastal Command (18 Group)

Type	Unit	Base
Hastings Met 1	202	Aldergrove

Training and development units

Coastal Command (18 Group)

Type	Unit	Base
Shackleton MR2, MR3	MOTU	Kinloss
Shackleton MR2, MR3	ASWDU	Ballykelly
Shackleton MR2, MR3	JASS	Ballykelly

5.H   Maritime and photo-reconnaissance at 1 January 1965

Maritime reconnaissance

Coastal Command (18 Group)

Type	Unit	Base
Shackleton MR2	203, 210	Ballykelly
Shackleton MR2C	204	Ballykelly
Shackleton MR3	120	Kinloss

Coastal Command (19 Group)

Type	Unit	Base
Shackleton MR2	42	St Mawgan
Shackleton MR3	201, 206	St Mawgan

Coastal Command (RAF Gibraltar)

Type	Unit	Base
Shackleton MR2	224	Gibraltar

MEAF

Type	Unit	Base
Shackleton MR2	37	Khormaksar (Aden)
	38	Luqa (Malta)

FEAF

Type	Unit	Base
Shackleton MR2C	205	Changi (Malaya)

Photo-reconnaissance

Bomber Command (3 Group)

Type	Unit	Base
Valiant B(PR)1, B(PR)K1	543	Wyton
Canberra PR7	58	Wyton

2 TAF (Germany)

Type	Unit	Base
Hunter FR10	2, 4, 79	Gütersloh
Canberra PR7	17	Wildenrath
	31	Laarbruch
	80	Brüggen

MEAF

Type	Unit	Base
Canberra PR9	39	Luqa (Malta)
Canberra PR9	13	Akrotiri (Cyprus)

FEAF

Type	Unit	Base
Canberra PR7	81	Tengah (Malaya)

ELINT

Signals Command (90 (Signals) Group)

Type	Unit	Base
Lincoln B2, Hastings C1	CSE	Watton
Canberra B6, Comet C2(R), Hastings C1	51	Wyton

Training and development units

Coastal Command (18 Group)

Type	Unit	Base
Shackleton MR3	MOTU (220)	Kinloss
Shackleton MR3	ASWDU	Ballykelly

5.I   Maritime and photo-reconnaissance at 1 January 1970

Maritime reconnaissance

Strike Command (18 Group)

Type	Unit	Base
Shackleton MR2	210	Ballykelly
Shackleton MR2C	204	Ballykelly
Shackleton MR3	120, 201, 206	Kinloss
	42	St Mawgan

MEAF

Type	Unit	Base
Shackleton MR3	203	Luqa (Malta)

FEAF

Type	Unit	Base
Shackleton MR2C	205	Changi (Malaya)

Photo-reconnaissance

Strike Command (1 Group)

Type	Unit	Base
Victor B2(SR)	543	Wyton
Canberra PR7	58	Wyton

RAF Germany

Type	Unit	Base
Hunter FR10	2	Gütersloh
Canberra PR7	31	Laarbruch

MEAF

Type	Unit	Base
Canberra PR9	13, 39	Luqa (Malta)

FEAF

Type	Unit	Base
Canberra PR7	81	Tengah (Malaya)

ELINT

Strike Command (90 (Signals) Group)

Type	Unit	Base
Canberra B6, Comet C2(R)	51	Wyton

Training and development units

Strike Command (18 Group)

Type	Unit	Base
Shackleton MR3, Nimrod MR1	MOTU (220)	Kinloss
Shackleton MR3	ASWDU	Ballykelly

5.J   Maritime and photo-reconnaissance at 1 January 1975

Maritime reconnaissance

Strike Command (18 Group)

Type	Unit	Base
Nimrod MR1	120, 201, 206	Kinloss
	42	St Mawgan

MEAF

Type	Unit	Base
Nimrod MR1	203	Luqa (Malta)

Photo-reconnaissance

Strike Command (38 Group)

Type	Unit	Base
Phantom FGR2	41	Coningsby

Strike Command (1 Group)

Type	Unit	Base
Vulcan B2(MRR)	27	Scampton
Canberra PR7, PR9	39	Wyton

RAF Germany

Type	Unit	Base
Phantom FGR2	2	Laarbruch

MEAF

Type	Unit	Base
Canberra PR7, PR9	13	Luqa (Malta)

ELINT

Support Command (90 (Signals) Group)

Type	Unit	Base
Canberra B6, Comet C2(R), Nimrod R1	51	Wyton

Airborne Early Warning

Strike Command (11 Group)

Type	Unit	Base
Shackleton AEW2	8	Lossiemouth

Training and development units

Strike Command (18 Group)

Type	Unit	Base
Nimrod MR1	236 OCU	St Mawgan

5.K   Maritime and photo-reconnaissance at 1 January 1980

Maritime reconnaissance

Strike Command (18 Group)

Type	Unit	Base
Nimrod MR1	120, 201, 206	Kinloss
	42	St Mawgan

Photo-reconnaissance

Strike Command (38 Group)

Type	Unit	Base
Jaguar GR1	41	Coltishall

Strike Command (1 Group)

Type	Unit	Base
Vulcan B2(MRR)	27	Scampton
Canberra PR7	13	Wyton
Canberra PR9	39	Wyton

RAF Germany

Type	Unit	Base
Jaguar GR1	2	Laarbruch

Electronic Warfare

Strike Command (1 Group)

Type	Unit	Base
Nimrod R1	51	Wyton

Airborne Early Warning

Strike Command (11 Group)

Type	Unit	Base
Shackleton AEW2	8	Lossiemouth

Training and development units

Strike Command (18 Group)

Type	Unit	Base
Nimrod MR1	236 OCU	St Mawgan

5.L Maritime and photo-reconnaissance at 1 January 1985

Maritime reconnaissance

Strike Command (18 Group)

Type	Unit	Base
Nimrod MR2, MR2P	120, 201, 206	Kinloss
	42	St Mawgan

Photo-reconnaissance

Strike Command (1 Group)

Type	Unit	Base
Jaguar GR1, GR1A, T2, T2A	41	Coltishall

Strike Command (18 Group)

Type	Unit	Base
Canberra PR9	1 PRU	Wyton

RAF Germany

Type	Unit	Base
Jaguar GR1, GR1A, T2, T2A	2	Laarbruch

ELINT

Strike Command (18 Group)

Type	Unit	Base
Nimrod R1, Andover C1	51	Wyton

Airborne Early Warning

Strike Command (11 Group)

Type	Unit	Base
Shackleton AEW2	8	Lossiemouth

Training and development units

Strike Command (18 Group)

Type	Unit	Base
Canberra B2, T4	231 OCU	Wyton
Nimrod MR2	236 OCU (38)	St Mawgan

5.M Maritime and photo-reconnaissance at 1 January 1990

Maritime reconnaissance

Strike Command (18 Group)

Type	Unit	Base
Nimrod MR2, MR2P	120, 201, 206	Kinloss
	42	St Mawgan

Photo-reconnaissance

Strike Command (1 Group)

Type	Unit	Base
Jaguar GR1, GR1A, T2, T2A	41	Coltishall
Tornado GR1A	13	Honington

Avro Shackleton MR Mk 1

The Shackleton was a development of the Lincoln – itself a Lancaster derivative – to succeed the Sunderland and Lancaster in the maritime reconnaissance role. In its earliest form as seen here it had the ASV radar in a chin radome, removed later after bird-strike problems. MR Mk1 WB831 was with 220 Sqn in early 1956 when photographed at Aden. *(R B Trevett via A S Thomas)*

Strike Command (18 Group)

Type	Unit	Base
Canberra PR9	1 PRU	Wyton

RAF Germany

Type	Unit	Base
Jaguar GR1, GR1A, T2, T2A	2	Laarbruch

ELINT

Strike Command (18 Group)

Type	Unit	Base
Nimrod R1P, Andover C1	51	Wyton

Airborne Early Warning

Strike Command (11 Group)

Type	Unit	Base
Shackleton AEW2	8	Lossiemouth

Training and development units

Strike Command (18 Group)

Type	Unit	Base
Canberra B2, T4	231 OCU	Wyton
Nimrod MR2	236 OCU (38)	St Mawgan

5.N   Maritime and photo-reconnaissance at 1 January 1995

Maritime reconnaissance

Strike Command (18 group)

Type	Unit	Base
Nimrod MR2, MR2P	120, 201, 206	Kinloss

Photo-reconnaissance

Strike Command (1 Group)

Type	Unit	Base
Tornado GR1A	2, 13	Marham

Strike Command (18 Group)

Type	Unit	Base
Canberra PR7, PR9, T4	39 (1 PRU)	Marham

ELINT

Strike Command (18 Group)

Type	Unit	Base
Nimrod R1P, Andover C1	51	Wyton

Airborne Early Warning

Strike Command (11 Group)

Type	Unit	Base
Sentry AEW1	8	Waddington
	dets	Aviano, Trapani

Training and development units

Strike Command (18 Group)

Type	Unit	Base
Canberra B2, T4	231 OCU	Wyton
Nimrod MR2	42(R)	Kinloss

5.1 Supermarine Walrus (1936 – 1947)

The Type 315 Walrus light general observation flying boat had its origins in the Seagull design of 1922. With a single Pegasus engine and pusher propeller it was the first British amphibian; of metal construction it was stressed for catapult launching. Ordered against specification 37/36 it served with the Fleet Air Arm and as an air-sea rescue aircraft with the RAF throughout the war, although from 1944 it was supplanted by the Sea Otter.

The type carried a crew of four and was armed with two .303in machine-guns mounted on Scarff rings in open cockpits. A light load of bombs or depth charges could be carried. By 1946 the Walrus still served with two RAF rescue squadrons abroad and with the FAA in the Far East both in the rescue (733 NAS) and bomber-reconnaissance roles.

Mark I

The Mark I was built by Supermarine and featured a metal hull. The prototype, K4797, first flew on 21 June 1933 and the first production aircraft, K5772, on 18 March 1936. The single 775hp Pegasus conferred a top speed of 135mph, with a range of 600 miles at a cruising speed of 90mph; 556 were built.

Service (post-1945) ASR 293: 733 NAS

Mark II

The Mark II was similar in every respect to the Mark I except that it was built by Saro and featured a wooden hull which conferred smoother and quieter landing runs. The first of 190, W2780, flew on 2 February 1940.

Supermarine Walrus Mk I

The Walrus joined the RAF as a light reconnaissance aircraft in 1936, although throughout the War it was used widely for search and rescue. Postwar use was mainly confined to rescue and it was soon superseded by the Sea Otter. These aircraft of 624 Sqn were used for mine-spotting in Greek waters during the early stages of the Greek civil war. *(A S Thomas collection)*

Service (post-1945) ASR 294 **General reconnaissance** 1700 NAS

Specification and production

Mark	Role	Engine	HP	Weight lb	Range miles	Nos
I	Gen recce	Pegasus II	775	7,200	600	556
II	ASR	Pegasus VI	775	7,200	600	190

Supermarine Sea Otter ABR Mk I

The Sea Otter was a natural successor to the Walrus and was broadly similar apart from the Mercury engine which drove a tractor propeller. As well as limited postwar RAF use the Sea Otter served as a general duties type in the Fleet Air Arm until at least 1952. JM946/983MF was with the St Merryn Station Flight; of note are what appear to be underwing bomb racks. *(A S Thomas collection)*

5.2 Supermarine Sea Otter (1944–1952) and Seagull (1948)

The Type 309 Sea Otter was built as a Walrus successor to specification S.12/40. Of mixed metal and wood construction, the type featured a conventional tractor propeller driven by a Bristol Mercury engine. The prototype, K8854 (designed to spec S.7/38), flew in August 1938 but the Sea Otter did not enter service until 1944. A total of 290 of both versions was built.

Sea Otter ABR Mark I
The initial version was designed as a general reconnaissance/rescue type for the Fleet Air Arm. Armament comprised Vickers machine guns in the nose and aft positions with provision for four 250lb bombs. The first production aircraft, JM738, flew on 7 January 1943 and service entry was with 1700 NAS in November 1944.

Service (post-1945) General reconnaissance 810, 1700, 1701, 1702 NAS; **Communications** Eastleigh SF; NEICF **Training** 728, 733, 772

Sea Otter ASR Mark II
The Mark II was the air-sea rescue variant built for the RAF. Armament was deleted and there were minor modifications over the Mark I, the most noticeable being grab lines along the fuselage.

Service (post-1945) ASR 270; SRTU **Communications** 19 GCF: 781 NAS; Eglinton, Kai Tak, Lossiemouth SF

Seagull ASR Mark I
The Type 381 Seagull was designed to specification S.14/44 to replace the Walrus and Sea Otter as a short-range ASR flying boat. It was powered by a Griffon 29 and employed a variable-incidence wing. The prototype (PA143) flew on 14 July 1948 and three were built. The type did not enter service, its role being assumed by helicopters.

Specification and production

Mark	Role	Engine	HP	Weight lb	Range miles	Nos
Sea Otter I	Gen recce	Mercury XXX	855	10,000	725	} 290
Sea Otter II	Gen recce	Mercury XXX	855	10,000	725	
Seagull ASR1	ASR	Griffon 29	1,815	14,500	1,230	3

5.3 Lockheed Hudson (1940–1946)

The Hudson was both the first American-built combat aircraft to serve with the RAF in the second war and also the first type in Coastal Command to be fitted with ASV radar. The twin-engined maritime reconnaissance type was acquired in great numbers through direct purchase and lend-lease. By the end of the war they were relegated to second-line duties and most were swiftly scrapped or returned to the United States.

Lockheed Hudson Mk V

Evocative shot of Hudson Mk V AM586/4 of the ATA landing at White Waltham on a bright summer's day. Apart from such use the Hudson operated with 520 Sqn on meteorological tasks into 1946. *(P H T Green collection)*

Armament comprised twin fixed forward-firing .303in guns, twin .303in guns in a dorsal turret (often removed on later marks in second-line service) and one gun in the ventral position. The Mark I was powered by the R-1280-G102A of 1,100hp while the Mark II had a different propeller unit; both were out of service by 1946.

Mark III
The Type L-414-56 was powered by the Wright Cyclone GR-1820 and was similar to the USAAF A-29. The Mark III flew at 235mph with a 750lb bomb load, but in the ASR role was the first aircraft to fly with an airborne lifeboat.

Service (post-1945) Meteorology 520. The Mark IV designation was applied to RAAF aircraft.

Supermarine Seagull ASR Mk 1

Helicopters offered more flexibility as short-range search and rescue vehicles, so that the Seagull – a Walrus/Sea Otter replacement – was not put into production. Prototype PA143 shows off the type's clean lines. *(MAP)*

Mark V

The Mark V was fitted with the Double Wasp and was 1,000lb lighter than the Mark III. Top speed was increased to 284mph.

Service (post-1945) **Communications** EACF **Training** CNS

Mark VI

The Mark VI was the equivalent of the USAAF A-29A and like the Mark V was also fitted with two Double Wasps. The bomb load was increased to 1,000lb.

Service (post-1945) **Meteorology** 520

Specification and production

Mark	Role	Engine	HP	Weight lb	Range miles	Nos
I	Maritime recce	2xCyclone GR-1820	1,100	17,500	1,700	350
II	Maritime recce	2xCyclone GR-1820	1,200	18,500	2,000	20
III	Maritime recce	2xCyclone GR-1820	1,200	19,500	2,160	382
IV	Maritime recce	2xCyclone GR-1830	1,050	18,500	1,800	23
V	Maritime recce	2xDouble Wasp R-1830	1,200	18,500	2,160	309
VI	Maritime recce	2xDouble Wasp R-1830	1,200	18,500	2,160	450

Further reading
Lockheed Hudson Mks I to VI, Shores, C F, Profile Publications, Windsor, 1973

5.4   Consolidated Catalina (1941–1946)

The long-range Catalina flying boat entered RAF service with 240 Sqn in 1941 and a total of 570 was supplied. They were highly successful in the war against U-boats but by the end of the war only a handful remained in service in the training role.

Mark III

The Type 28-5A was the amphibian version of which twelve only were supplied; it was equivalent to the USN PBY-5A. Armament comprised four .303in guns and a useful 2,000lb bomb load.

Service (post-1945) **Training** 302 FTU

Specification and production

Mark	Role	Engine	HP	Weight lb	Range miles	Nos
III	Maritime recce	2xDouble Wasp R-1830	1200	34,000	4,000	12

Further reading
Consolidated PBY Catalina, The (Profile 183) Cassagneres, E, Profile Publications, Leatherhead, 1968
Flying Cats: The Catalina Aircraft in World War II, Hendrie, A, Airlife, Shrewsbury, 1988

5.5   Boeing Fortress (1941–1946)

The Royal Air Force employed the Fortress I (B-17C) from early in 1941 and as a result of experience numerous improvements were made to the type which were of particular benefit to the USAAF when the United States deployed the type in Europe. The RAF also used over 200 later versions in Coastal Command and with 100 Group on radio countermeasures work. Like most US types they were returned to the United States or scrapped soon after the end of the war.

Mark II

The Type 299-P was the same as the USAAF B-17F. It was powered by four Wright Cyclone R-1820-97 engines delivering 1,200hp each and weighed rather less than the earlier (later in RAF mark numbers) B-17E. Externally it differed from the Mark IIA in having an extended Plexiglass nose, paddle-blade airscrews and a slightly revised engine cowling. Fuel load was increased from 2,550 to 3,630 US gals.

Consolidated Catalina Mk III

Although in theory only operated by 302 FTU for training purposes after 1945, this rogue Catalina – unit and identity unknown – is seen flying over 107 MU at Kasfareet in Egypt early in 1946. As a lend-lease type the seaplane was soon returned to the US or scrapped. *(R Collison via A S Thomas)*

Boeing Fortress Mk III

The RAF used the Fortress for long-range maritime reconnaissance and electronic warfare as well as meteorology. This Mk III, HB792/AD-D, served with the short-lived 251 Sqn and is seen here at Prestwick prior to return to the US. *(A S Thomas collection)*

Service (post-1945) Meteorology 521

Mark IIA

The Type 299-O was the equivalent of the B-17E which used the R-1820-65 engine. The defensive armament was a total of two .303in guns in the nose and ten .50in guns in the forward fuselage, dorsal turret, ventral turret, tail turret and waist. Bomb load was a maximum of 9,600lb, but in practice much lower loads were traded for range.

Service (post-1945) Meteorology 521

Mark III

The Mark III equated to the B-17G and had defensive armament further improved through the use of a chin turret with two .50in guns.

Service (post-1945) Meteorology 521

Specification and production

Mark	Role	Engine	HP	Weight lb	Range miles	Nos
I	Heavy bomber	4xCyclone R-1820-65	1,200	42,600	1,400	20
II	Heavy bomber	4xCyclone R-1820-97	1,200	40,260	1,850	19
IIA	Heavy bomber	4xCyclone R-1820-65	1,200	54,000	1,850	45
III	Heavy bomber	4xCyclone R-1820-97	1,200	55,000	1,850	85

Further reading

B-17 Flying Fortress (Warbirds 41) Ethell, J, Arms and Armour, London, 1986
Boeing B-17E & F Flying Fortress (Profile 77) Thompson, C D, Profile Publications, Leatherhead, 1964

5.6   Consolidated Liberator (1941 – 1946)

The Type 32 Liberator heavy bomber was used in great numbers by the RAF, as a bomber, transport and for

Consolidated Liberator C Mk VI

The Liberator was used mainly by Coastal Command but after 1945 many were transferred for transport use given the need to move vast numbers of troops and stores and repatriate PoWs. Mk VI EV828/PQ-Y of 206 Sqn is seen under a heavy coating of snow at Oakington in 1946 just prior to disbandment. *(A S Thomas collection)*

maritime reconnaissance. Compared with its contemporary, the Fortress, it had greater range/bomb load. Early versions used by the RAF were unarmed transports. As with the Fortress, American designers incorporated improvements in the light of British experience, especially in respect of armour and defensive weapons. All versions were powered by four 1,200hp Double Wasp engines. While early variants were purchased, those still in use at the end of the war were supplied under lend-lease; they were thus withdrawn from service by early 1946.

Confusingly, the RAF attributed mark numbers across USAAF type numbers, depending primarily on the use to which they were to be put and apparently to some extent the theatre in which they were received. At the end of the war many bomber and coastal units transferred to Transport Command; the type was used as a transport in all theatres, sometimes with the turrets faired over, mainly to move passengers, of whom it could carry 24. The Mark I (maritime reconnaissance), Mark II (B-24C bomber, Middle East), Mark III (B-24D maritime reconnaissance) and Mark IV (B-24E maritime reconnaissance) were all out of service by 1946.

Mark V

The Mark V was similar to the USAAF B-24G which had three guns in the Plexiglass nose. In addition the B-24 employed twin .50in guns in dorsal and tail turrets and one each in a ventral turret and two waist positions. Maximum bomb load was 12,800lb.

Service (post-1945) Maritime reconnaissance 224

Mark VI

The Mark VI equated to the B-24H and J although some G versions were included in the designation. The main difference for the H model onwards was the provision of a nose turret with two .50in guns. They were used by bomber and coastal squadrons but their range/payload made them ideal aircraft for long-range supply dropping.

Service (post-1945) Maritime reconnaissance 203, 224, 321 Bomber 37, 40, 70, 148, 214 Transport 53, 59, 86, 102, 104, 178, 206, 220, 311 Training CCIS

Mark VII

The Mark VII was designed as a transport and in USAAF service was the C-87. The nose was faired and armament removed and accommodation was provided for 20 passengers.

Service (post-1945) Training 1332 TCU; TCDU

Mark VIII

The Mark VIII was similar to the Mark VI but with detail differences of equipment; USAAF equivalent was the B-24J and L model. In Coastal Command service a number were fitted with Leigh lights and a range of radars for long-range maritime patrol.

Service (post-1945) Maritime reconnaissance 160, 224 Transport 53, 59, 86, 102, 159, 206, 220, 232, 355 Training 111 OTU

Mark IX

Although a sole Liberator II was modified with a single fin the Mark IX, equivalent to the USAAF C-87C, was the first of the type built with a faired nose and single fin and rudder. It served with SEAC until early 1946 on Pacific routes.

Service (post-1945) Transport 231

Specification and production

Mark	Role	Engine	HP	Weight lb	Range miles	Nos
I	Maritime recce	4xR-1830-43	1,200	60,000	1,700	26
II	Bomber	4xR-1830-43	1,200	60,000	1,700	165
III	Maritime recce	4xR-1830-43	1,200	60,000	1,700	156
IV	Not taken up					
V	Maritime recce/bomber	4xR-1830-43	1,200	62,000	1,700	236
VI	Maritime recce/bomber	4xR-1830-43	1,200	62,000	1,700	1157
VII	Transport	4xR-1830-94	1,200	62,000	1,550	24
VIII	Maritime recce/bomber	4xR-1830-43	1,200	62,000	1,700	300*
IX	Transport	4xR-1830-65	1,300	62,000	3,000	27+

* approx
+ not all delivered

Further reading

Consolidated B-24J Liberator, The (Profile 19) Freeman, R A, Profile Publications, Leatherhead, 1963
Liberator at War, Freeman, R A, Ian Allan, Shepperton, 1983

5.7 Vickers Warwick (1942–1946)

The Warwick was built as a heavy contemporary of the Wellington and was of similar appearance, although

Vickers Warwick GR Mk V

The Warwick was built as a heavier development of the Wellington bomber; it was obsolescent when available and was thus used for long-range air-sea rescue. This GR Mk V belongs to 621 Sqn based at Aqir in Palestine in 1946. *(A S Thomas collection)*

roughly 12% larger overall. Designed to specification B.1/35, the prototype (K8178) first flew on 13 August 1938 but for a variety of reasons, mainly to do with engine problems, the first production aircraft did not fly until May 1942. The Warwick was then obsolescent and the type was relegated to the air-sea rescue role, where it supplanted Ansons. Later Warwicks were built as general reconnaissance and transport aircraft. They were quickly replaced in service by more appropriate types.

ASR Mark I

The Type 462 had been intended to be powered by the Centaurus engine, but shortages led to the installation of the Double Wasp. Some 275 were converted for air-sea rescue duties although many did not see service; fitted with airborne lifeboats they served mainly in Europe and the Middle East. Armament was twin .303in machine-guns in nose and dorsal turrets and four similar guns in a tail turret.

Service (post-1945) Air-sea rescue 38, 269, 279, 280, 283, 293, 520 **Training** 6, 26 OTU; SRTU **Other** ASWDU

GR Mark II

The Type 469, of which 133 were built, was fitted with the Centaurus engine. It was a general reconnaissance type with some being used for meteorology. In the latter case the nose armament was deleted and replaced with a wider window.

Service (post-1945) Air-sea rescue 280 **Training** 6 OTU; MENVTS **Other** 16 FU

C Mark III

The Type 460 was in effect a development of the Warwick I, some of which had been converted to transports. Fitted with the Double Wasp the type could carry 24 to 30 troops and freight. The nose and tail turret were faired over and additional stores were carried in an under-fuselage pannier.

Service (post-1945) Transport 167, 301, 304.
The Type 438 C Mark IV utilised the Centaurus, but the type was not put into production.

GR Mark V

The Type 474 was an improved maritime reconnaissance aircraft fitted with the more powerful Centaurus VII. Two beam guns were fitted in place of the dorsal turret and the aircraft was fitted with a Leigh light. The nose profile was modified to take a radar scanner. The Warwick had always suffered from stability problems and later models were fitted with a fin strake. Of the total production of 210 relatively few were issued to operational units.

Service (post-1945) Maritime reconnaissance 179 **Air-sea rescue** 294, 621 **Training** 6 OTU **Other** ASWDU; ECFS; JASS; TFU; TRE.

The Type 485 ASR Mark VI was a further Double Wasp engined variant but of the 94 produced only several saw service before the war in the Pacific – for which theatre they had been intended – came to a close.

Specification and production

Mark	Role	Engine	HP	Weight lb	Range miles	Nos
ASR I	ASR	2xDouble Wasp	1,850	44,764	2,300	275
GR II	Maritime recce	2xCentaurus VI	2,500	51,250	3,050	133
C III	Transport	2xDouble Wasp	1,850	46,000	2,150	100
C IV	Transport	2xCentaurus VI	2,500	50,000	3,000	-
GR V	Maritime recce	2xCentaurus VII	2,500	50,000	3,050	210
ASR VI	ASR	2xDouble Wasp	1,850	46,000	2,200	94

5.8 Short Sunderland/Seaford (1937–1959) and Shetland (1944–1946)

The S.25 Sunderland was one of the longest-serving and most robust flying boats; it was still in service some 20 years after first joining 230 Sqn in 1938. Originally designed to specification R.22/36 the Sunderland was intended to replace the Singapore as a long-range maritime reconnaissance aircraft. The prototype Mark I (K4774) with four 1,010hp Pegasus XXII engines first flew on 16 October 1937 and the type was in service just eight months later. The Sunderland had a distinguished war serving in fourteen squadrons in the United Kingdom, the Middle and Far East and Africa.

The Mark II was fitted with Pegasus XVIII of 1,065hp and a power-operated dorsal turret and entered service in 1941 while the Mark III was similar to the Mark II but with an improved planing hull. All three early marks were out of service by the end of 1945.

Mark IV
The Mark IV was fitted with the much more powerful Hercules engine in order to improve speed. The hull was

Short Sunderland GR Mk 5

The Sunderland had a very long range and was a very successful submarine hunter throughout the War. Later it served as a transport and bomber (in Malaya) as well as remaining in the maritime reconnaissance role well after the Shackleton had entered service. Aircraft 'P' of 230 Sqn was involved in repatriation of allied prisoners-of-war and internees from the Netherlands East Indies in 1945 and 1946. (*Crown copyright*)

lengthened by 3ft and the fin and rudder area was increased. The differences were sufficient to justify a new type number and the S.45 Mark IV was re-named **Seaford**. The first prototype (MZ269) flew on 30 October 1944 and after protracted development only eight of the 30 ordered were completed. They entered service briefly with 210 Sqn in early 1946 but offered no improvement over the Sunderland V.

Service Maritime reconnaissance 210

GR Mark V/MR Mark V
The Mark V was the result of an Australian suggestion that the type would benefit from being re-engined with the Pratt & Whitney Double Wasp. The arrangement was first tried on a Mark III ML839 and the first of 150 production aircraft was ML765. A new radar, the ASV Mk VIC, was fitted in split scanners under the outer wings. Armament was four .303in guns both in nose and tail turrets and two in the dorsal turret plus two .5in manually operated guns in the beam position. Bomb load was 2,000lb. The last Mark V retired from RAF service with 205 Sqn in the Far East in 1959.

Service (post-1945) Maritime reconnaissance 88, 201, 205, 209, 230, 240 **Training** 302 FTU; 4(C)OTU; 235 OCU; FBTS **Other** ASWDU; TRE; BTU; Koggala SF

Shetland Mark I
The Type S.35 Shetland was built as a long-range patrol flying boat to specification R.14/40. The prototype (DX166) did not fly until 14 December 1944 and only two were built. The need for the Shetland diminished with the end of the war and although the type was tested at the MAEE it did not enter production.

Specification and production

Mark	Role	Engine	HP	Weight lb	Range miles	Nos
Sunderland I	Maritime recce	4xPegasus XXII	1,010	44,600	1,780	90
Sunderland II	Maritime recce	4xPegasus XVIII	1,065	44,750	1,780	43
Sunderland III	Maritime recce	4xPegasus XVIII	1,065	44,750	1,780	462
Sunderland IV*	Maritime recce	4xHercules 19	1,800	75,000	2,800	8
Sunderland V	Maritime recce	4xDouble Wasp	1,200	65,000	2,980	242+
Shetland I	Maritime recce	4x Centaurus XI	2,500	120,000	3,000	2

* Seaford
+ includes 88 Mk III conversions

Further reading
Short Sunderland, The (Profile 189) Norris, G, Profile Publications, Leatherhead, 1968
Sunderland at War, Bowyer, C, Ian Allan, Shepperton, 1973
Short Sunderland in World War II, Hendrie, A., Airlife, Shrewsbury, 1994

5.9   Avro Shackleton (1949–1991)

The Type 696 Shackleton was the first British post-war type designed specifically as a land-based long-range maritime reconnaissance aircraft. The need for such a type was confirmed by the success of the Liberator and Lancaster in the role and the Shackleton was to replace the latter type in service. It was originally to have been the Lincoln III and used the Lincoln's wing and under-carriage but with a re-designed fuselage and with Griffon engines.

The Shackleton was designed to specification R.5/46 and the prototype (VW126) flew on 9 March 1949; the type finally retired from RAF service in 1991.

MR Mark 1

The Mark I differed slightly from the prototypes in having twin 20mm cannon in nose and dorsal and turrets and twin .5in guns in the tail. Maximum weapons load was 15,000lb. The first version, which entered service with 120 Sqn in 1951, carried its radar in a glazed chin mounting, which suffered somewhat from bird strikes.

MR Mark 1A

In the Mark 1 the outer and inner engines were not inter-changeable, whereas in the Mark IA they were. The change was introduced on the production line after 27 of the total of 77 had been built; most Mark 1s were subsequently brought up to the later standard.

Service **Maritime reconnaissance** 42, 120, 203, 204, 205, 206, 210, 220, 224, 240, 269 **Training** 236 OCU; MOTU **Other** ASWDU; JASS; RAFFC; TFU

MR Mark 2

The Mark 2 incorporated a revised nose profile with the radar moved to a retractable 'dustbin' under the rear fuse-lage. The prototype (WB833) flew on 17 June 1952 and the first production aircraft several months later. It was slightly heavier than the Mark 1 and was progressively upgraded over the years. Armament was twin .5in guns in the nose and dorsal turret, although the latter was removed on some later aircraft.

Service **Maritime reconnaissance** 37, 38, 42, 120, 204, 206, 210, 220, 224, 228, 240, 269 **Training** 8 **Other** ASWDU; JASS; RAE; RAFFC; Eastleigh SF

Avro Shackleton MR Mk 2

Shackleton in its element. MR Mk 2 Phase II WR952/B of 205 Sqn is seen off Singapore around 1965 during the Borneo campaign. The Shackleton maintained the long-range maritime reconnaissance role and carried a useful 15,000lb weapons load over 2,000 miles. *(Crown copyright)*

MR Mark 2 Phase I

The Phase I aircraft incorporated some changes from the subsequently introduced MR Mk 3 including plotting table and ASV Mk 21 radar. The variant was also known as the MR Mk 2C and of the total of 70 Mark 2 aircraft, 52 were updated.

Service Maritime reconnaissance 37, 38, 42, 204, 210, 224 **Other** ASWDU

MR Mark 2 Phase II

This represented yet another upgrade of the basic Mark 2 to incorporate Mark 3 features, in this case a new ECM and radio fit; 54 aircraft were updated.

Service Maritime reconnaissance 37, 38, 42, 203, 204, 205, 210, 224 **Other** ASWDU

MR Mark 2 Phase III

The final Mark 2 update was to MR Mk 3 Phase III standard enabling the aircraft to carry the Mark 10 nuclear depth charge. In addition Griffon 58 engines were fitted with a change in the oil feed system. Most of the Phase II aircraft were updated.

Service Maritime reconnaissance 42, 204, 205, 210 **Other** ASWDU

T Mark 2

The trainer variant was a conversion of ten MR Mk 2 Phase III aircraft for operator training. Bunks in the operational version were replaced by additional consoles.

Service Training 8, 204, 205, 210; 236 OCU; MOTU

AEW Mark 2

The airborne warning aircraft was a significant conversion of the Mark 2 Phase II version designed to Mod 1493.

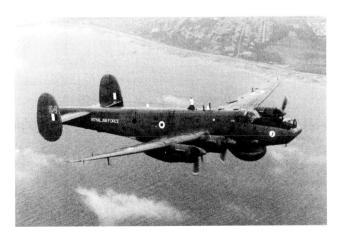

Avro Shackleton AEW Mk 2

When the last of the Gannet airborne warning aircraft was withdrawn at the demise of the carrier force the United Kingdom was without flexible airborne radar pickets. The Shackleton MR Mk 2 was a vehicle for the third-hand AN/APS 20 radar since the aircraft had lower airframe hours – and less structural stress – than the Mk 3. The radome is obvious in this 1976 photograph of WL754/54 'Paul' of 8 Sqn (the unit's aircraft were all named after *Magic Roundabout* characters). *(Crown copyright)*

With the intended demise of the aircraft carrier there was an urgent need for high-level radar surveillance to supplement ground-based radars in detecting low-flying intruders. Until 1971 the role was fulfilled by carrier-based Gannet aircraft. The older Mark 2 was chosen for conversion because of the availability of aircraft with low airframe hours and which had not been subjected to the stresses imposed on the later Mark 3 by heavier landing weights. The large AN/APS 20 radars from the Gannet were installed under the forward fuselage of the twelve aircraft converted.

Service Airborne early warning 8

MR Mark 3

The Type 716 Mark 3 incorporated a number of improvements and although retaining the same overall shape as the MR Mk 2 a tricycle undercarriage was fitted to help cope with the higher all-up weight resulting from increased fuel capacity. The cockpit glazing was also improved and the dorsal turret of the Mark 2 deleted; weapons load was 14,000lb, carried in an internal bomb-bay, including mines, depth charges, sonobuoys, and 500lb or 1,000lb GP bombs. Thirty-four Mark 3 aircraft were built for the Royal Air Force and they were successively updated as anti-submarine warfare evolved to take account of new tactics and technology.

Service Maritime reconnaissance 120, 201, 203, 206, 220

MR Mark 3 Phase I

The Phase I was introduced on the production line with six aircraft built as such and a further 22 converted. The changes included the ASV Mk 21 radar, ILS and VHF radio homer.

Service Maritime reconnaissance 120, 201, 203, 206

MR Mark 3 Phase II

These aircraft incorporated ECM equipment (Orange Harvest), the Mk 1c sonics plotting table, UHF radio, TACAN and an improved radio compass; 29 aircraft were updated.

Service Maritime reconnaissance 120, 201, 203, 206

MR Mark 3 Phase III

The ultimate Shackleton, to which standard 27 aircraft were upgraded, introduced the ability to carry and use the Mk 10 'Lulu' depth charge. The necessary equipment brought the all-up weight to a level where the safe take-off limit had to be traded for range, and it was decided to add two supplementary Viper turbojet engines of 2,500lb thrust in the rear nacelles of the outer engines.

Service Maritime reconnaissance 42, 120, 201, 203, 206 **Other** ASWDU

T Mark 4

The second trainer variant was a conversion of the Mark 1. All armament was deleted and additional radar positions installed for pupils and instructors. Seventeen aircraft were converted.

Service Training 236 OCU; SMR; MOTU

Specification and production

Mark	Role	Engine	HP/ thrust	Weight lb	Range miles	Nos
MR1	Maritime recce	4xGriffon 57	1,960	82,000	2,160	29
MR1A	Maritime recce	4xGriffon 57/A	1,960	82,000	2,160	47
MR2	Maritime recce	4xGriffon 57/	1,960	84,000	1,720	70
MR2/I	Maritime recce	4xGriffon 57/	1,960	84,000	1,720	52+
MR2/II	Maritime recce	4xGriffon 57/	1,960	84,000	1,800	54+
MR2/III	Maritime recce	4xGriffon 57/	1,960	89,000	1,980	33+
T2	Trainer	4xGriffon 57	1,960	84,000	1,720	10+
AEW2	AEW	4xGriffon 58	1,960	89,000	1,800	12+
MR3	Maritime recce	4xGriffon 57A	1,960	85,000	2,300	34
MR3/I	Maritime recce	4xGriffon 57A	1,960	85,000	2,300	28~
MR3/II	Maritime recce	4xGriffon 57A	1,960	85,000	2,300	29#
MR3/III	Maritime recce	4xGriffon 57A + 2xViper 203	1,960 2,500	89,000	1,800	27#
T4	Trainer	4xGriffon 57	1,960	86,000	2,160	17*

* MR1 conversions
+ MR2 conversions
~ 22 MR3 conversions, 6 new build
# MR3 conversions

Further reading

Avro Shackleton, Chartres, J, Ian Allan, Shepperton, 1985
Avro Shackleton Mks 1 to 4 (Profile 243) Howard, P J, Profile Publications, Leatherhead, 1972
Shackleton, The, Ashworth, C, Aston, Bourne End, 1990

5.10 Lockheed Neptune (1952–1957)

As tensions increased between NATO and the Warsaw Pact signatories in the early 1950s Britain's maritime commitments were extended. With the Shackleton still due to come into service, the United States supplied 52 Neptunes under the Mutual Defence Aid Plan (MDAP).

MR Mark 1

The RAF Neptune equated to the P2V-5 in USN service. Designed in the light of Lockheed's experience with earlier land-based patrol aircraft, the Neptune was intended to have long range, slow landing speed and a good weapons load. First flown in May 1945, the type was powered by two Wright Cyclone piston engines and had a range of 4,200 miles. Armament comprised two .5in guns in the nose and dorsal turrets and twin 20mm guns in the tail. The total stores load was 8,000lb. Compared to earlier models the P2V-5 had enlarged wing-tip tanks incorporating searchlight (starboard) and radar (port); 27 of the total supplied were later brought towards P2V-7 standard with a Plexiglass nose and magnetic anomaly

Lockheed Neptune MR Mk 1

The Neptune was supplied under the MDAP at a time of great perceived growth in Soviet capability in submarine development. It was a robust aircraft and served between 1952 and 1957 easing the introduction of the Shackleton. This aircraft of 36 Sqn from Topcliffe, modified to P2V-7 standard, is seen loosing-off a salvo of rockets. *(K J Ripley via A S Thomas)*

detector (MAD) rear fuselage extension – airframes so modified were not given any change of designation. The Neptune entered service with 217 Sqn at St Eval in January 1952 and the last were replaced by Shackletons in 1957.

Service **Maritime reconnaissance** 36, 203, 210, 217 **Training** 236 OCU; MOTU **Other** JASS

MR Mark 1 mod

The modified aircraft were four examples of the basic MR Mk 1 adapted for use by Fighter Command for airborne early warning. The ASV radar was used with various detailed equipment modifications to enable the aircraft to work in conjunction with contemporary ground-based radars. Early examples of the Neptune were used by 'Vanguard Flight' from November 1952 which, based at Topcliffe, became 1453 Flt on 1 June 1953.

Service **Airborne early warning** Vanguard/1453 Flt

Specification and production

Mark	Role	Engine	HP	Weight lb	Range miles	Nos
MR1	Maritime recce	2xR-3350 -30W	3,250	72,000	4,200	52*

* including four MR1 mod with same characteristics

Further reading

Lockheed P2V Neptune, The (Profile 204) Anderson, H G, Profile Publications, Leatherhead, 1968
Lockheed Neptune in RAF Service, The, Howard, P J, Air Pictorial, Windsor, August/September 1972

5.11 Short Seamew (1953)

The SB.6 Seamew was a remarkable aircraft designed to a naval specification but also intended for land-based use by the RAF. The type was intended to be a robust and simple anti-submarine aircraft for use on small carriers, with a crew of two, good range and capable of carrying and operating the latest radars. The Mamba ASM.6 turboprop was able to run on virtually any fuel and the tailwheel undercarriage was fixed. After a number of development machines were built and tested – stated to be up to ten flown – the Seamew was scrapped in 1957.

AS Mark 1
The Seamew Mark 1 was the intended naval version with arrester and catapult hooks and manual wing-folding. It could carry up to 1,100lb of munitions. The prototype, XA209, first flew on 13 August 1953 and at least two were built and flown.

Service **Trials** ATDU: 700 NAS

MR Mark 2
The Mark 2 was similar in every respect to the AS Mk 1 except that it was optimised for land-based use from hastily prepared airstrips. It thus had oversize tyres and was slightly heavier than the naval version; although naval equipment was deleted it was cleared to carry a higher weapons load. Two were built including XA213 but it was not put into service before being cancelled.

Specification and production

Mark	Role	Engine	HP	Weight lb	Range miles	Nos
AS1	Anti--submarine	Mamba ASM.6	1,590	14,400	750	2+
MR2	Maritime	Mamba ASM.6	1,590	15,100	750	2+

Short Seamew AS Mk 1

The basic, cheap and ungainly Seamew was conceived as a short range and lightweight maritime reconnaissance aircraft designed for naval or land-based operations. Up to ten were completed before the project was abandoned. The third naval prototype, XE169, is seen on a test flight, possibly with 700 NAS. *(Author's collection)*

5.12 Hawker Siddeley Nimrod (1967–date)

The maritime patrol HS 801 Nimrod was developed from the commercial Comet 4 airliner to meet Air Staff Requirement ASR381 in 1964. The prototype, XV148, was built around the penultimate Comet 4c airframe with a large unpressurised lower fuselage 'bubble' to accommodate the 48ft weapons bay. Other major changes included four Spey engines and a revised fin and rudder with fin-mounted radome. First flight of the prototype was on 23 May 1967. From the outset the Nimrod was intended to be flown with the two inboard engines only while on patrol and all systems are driven by these engines.

MR Mark 1
The Nimrod entered service with the RAF (MOTU) in 1969. It was equipped with ASV21D radar, similar to that fitted to the Shackleton, and was capable of carrying nine Mk 44 or Mk 46 homing torpedoes, nuclear depth charges or conventional 1,000lb bombs. Provision was made for the underwing carriage of two Martel or AS.12 missiles. The crew comprised eleven, including two pilots and a flight engineer. A range of contemporary navigation and weapons management systems was built in including an Elliot 920 digital computer. A 70 million candlepower searchlight was fitted in the starboard wing pod; 46 were built.

Service **Maritime reconnaissance** 42, 120, 201, 203, 206 **Training** MOTU; 236 OTU **Other** RRE/RSRE (XV148)

R Mark 1
The ELINT version, three of which were built, differed considerably from the patrol aircraft but in order not to draw attention to the type no new mark number was applied. Externally it differed in having a shorter tail boom, an extended port wing pod and various fuselage aerials. In service it replaced the Comet R Mk 2 with 51 Sqn. The **R Mark 1P** was the R1 fitted with a refuelling probe mounted over the cockpit. The R Mk 1 was subject to regular upgrading including the fitting of finlets on the tailplane and ESM Loral pods on the wing-tips. A fourth aircraft was converted from MR Mk 2 stock to replace one lost in 1995.

Service **Electronic intelligence gathering** 51

MR Mark 2
The Mark 2 was in effect a mid-life update of the MR Mk 1. Thirty-five airframes were converted and the first conversion, XV236, flew on 13 February 1979, although several airframes had earlier been fitted with new systems. The main external differences were the fitting of Loral ESM pods on the wing-tips and an additional air intake below the fin for air cooling. Internal changes included replacement of the earlier radar with the much improved EMI Searchwater and a new twin Marconi AQS 901 acoustics system. The other major change was a new central tactical system. The new equipment increased all-up weight by 6,000lb and the crew was increased to twelve.

Service **Maritime reconnaissance** 42, 120, 201, 206 **Training** 236 OTU (38)

Hawker Siddeley Nimrod MR Mk 1

The Nimrod was developed from the Comet airliner, with a large unpressurised lower fuselage accommodating a 48ft weapons bay. Service entry was in 1969; ten years later a midlife update resulted in the MR Mk 2. XV244 of 120 Sqn from Kinloss is seen 100 miles north of Scotland investigating a Soviet ocean-going 'tug' in 1978. *(Crown copyright)*

MR Mark 2P

The -P variant was the post-Falklands fit with an inflight refuelling probe above the cockpit. Auxiliary fins were added to the tailplanes to help improve stability during the physically tiring task of refuelling. Another recent change has been the introduction of the Harpoon anti-ship missile, carried in the weapons bay. The Nimrod was fitted with two Sidewinder AAMs during the Falklands war and this underwing fit was developed into a four-missile system from 1983. Some aircraft involved in the Second Gulf War were modified to carry an underwing FLIR turret and BOZ chaff/flare dispenser and a towed radar decoy, informally designated **MR Mark 2P(GM)**.

Service **Maritime reconnaissance** 42, 120, 201, 206 **Training** 236 OTU (38)

AEW Mark 3

The Mark 3 was an intended airborne early warning replacement for the Shackleton AEW Mk 2. In fact an airline-surplus Comet 4c had been bought and fitted with a nose radar in 1969 but the project was cancelled before first flight. Subsequently the aircraft was completed with a forward-looking radar and flew on 28 June 1977. The Nimrod AEW was intended to have radars in the nose and tail, each with 180° coverage. The first MR Mk 1 conversion, XZ286, flew on 17 July 1980; eleven MR Mk 1 airframes were set aside for conversion. Sadly continuing development problems and escalating cost resulted in cancellation in December 1986 by which time all eleven aircraft had been converted, five of which were operated by the Joint Trials Unit at Waddington. XV263 was the sole aircraft to be fitted for inflight refuelling as the Nimrod **AEW Mark 3P**.

Service **Trials** Joint Trials Unit

MRA Mark 4

The Nimrod replacement to ASR420 will comprise 21 Mark 2 aircraft re-manufactured with new wings incorporating the Rolls-Royce BR710 turbofan and new electronics and avionics including a new tactical sytem, Searchwater 2000MR radar, better acoustics and advanced instrumentation. Service entry is intended to be in 2002.

BAe Nimrod MRA Mark 4

After service entry in 1969 some 21 Nimrod airframes are being completely rebuilt around existing fuselages with new wings and engines and, of course, developed avionics. This artist's impression of the new variant shows it releasing a Sea Eagle missile. *(BAe)*

Specification and production

Mark	Role	Engine	Thrust lb	Weight lb	Range miles	Nos
MR1	Maritime recce	4xSpey 250	12,160	177,500	5,180	46
R1	Elint/sigint	4xSpey 250	12,160	185,000	5,000	3
R1P	Elint/sigint	4xSpey 250	12,160	190,000	5,000	4*
MR2	Maritime recce	4xSpey 250	12,160	184,000	5,200	35+
MR2P	Maritime recce	4xSpey 250	12,160	192,000	5,200	27#
AEW3	AEW	4xSpey 250	12,160	195,000	5,000	11+
MRA4	Maritime recce	4xBMW/RR BR710	15,000	n/a	n/a	21#

* R1 conversions plus one MR2 conversion
+ MR1 conversions
# MR2 conversions

Further reading
BAe Nimrod (Modern Combat Aircraft 24) Chartres, J, Ian Allan, London, 1986

5.13 Boeing Sentry (1991–date)

The United States' solution to the need for airborne warning and control was to fit large 360° radars on the upper rear fuselage of several types, the largest of which was the Boeing 707 airframe. As the E-3A Airborne Warning And Control System (AWACS) the type entered service with the USAF in 1977 and with the unique NATO AEWF in 1983. When the Nimrod AEW Mk 3 was finally abandoned in 1986, an improved version of the E-3 was ordered to make good the loss.

Sentry AEW Mark 1
The Sentry entered RAF service with 8 Sqn at RAF Waddington in 1991. Seven were ordered and the first, ZH101, was handed over to the RAF on 26 March 1991.

The RAF variant, the E-3D, was fitted with GE/SNECMA CFM-56 turbofans and was also distinguished by having wing-tip Loral ESM pods. Other changes from the earlier variants include dual inflight refuelling receivers, improved radar and communications fit.

Service Airborne Early Warning 8 Training 23

Specification and production

Mark	Role	Engine	Thrust lb	Weight lb	Range miles	Nos
AEW1	Airborne warning and control	4xCFM-56	24,000	332,500	5,000	7

Further reading
Boeing KC-135 Stratotanker (Modern Combat Aircraft 27) Dorr, R F, Ian Allan, London, 1987

Boeing Sentry AEW Mk 1

After lengthy attempts to develop a Nimrod airborne early warning variant were abandoned the Government had little choice but to look to Boeing for a version of the E-3. As the Sentry the E-3D entered service with 8 Sqn at Waddington in 1991 and aircraft are regularly detached to Italy in support of UN forces in Bosnia including ZH103/03 seen here. *(Author)*

6 – Transport

Vickers VC-10 C Mk 1

An important acquisition for the long-range trooping routes and for VIP duties was the VC-10. Fourteen of the passenger/freight C Mk 1 variant were bought including XV109/109 of 10 Sqn seen here. It was brought up to C(K) Mk 1 standard to extend the refuelling fleet when the Victor tankers were withdrawn from service. *(Crown copyright)*

157

See also: Coronado (7.5); Ju 52/3M (7.8); Liberator (5.6); SM.82 (7.8); Twin Pioneer (7.15); Warwick (5.7); Sea King (9.14); Whirlwind (11.11)

January 1946

While numerous fighter and bomber units had disbanded within months of the end of the war, in contrast the transport squadrons of the RAF were as busy as ever. They were committed across Europe, the Middle and Far East to a wide range of tasks, not least those of repatriating prisoners-of-war and of returning home millions of servicemen and women.

Predictably much of the transport fleet comprised lend-lease aircraft or either bomber conversions or developments. In the former category were the Dakota and Liberator and such exotic types (at least for the RAF) as the Coronado and Skymaster. Among the bomber variants were the Stirling and Halifax. The transport squadrons were complemented by bomber units, typically using Lancasters, to return Allied soldiers to the United Kingdom. The only indigenous transport type in service was the York, itself a derivative of the Lancaster, whereas the Lancastrian was a civil conversion of the bomber type.

All transport squadrons were under the control of Transport Command which had been formed in 1943 from Ferry Command. The Command assumed responsibility for local transport as well as the trunk routes across the Empire. By March 1946, however, the units had reverted to local control apart from those flying the long-distance routes. Four groups managed a total of 30 squadrons and one flight in the UK; in addition 4 group managed ten training units. The operational groups tended to operate a limited number of types within defined geography with the shorter-range Dakotas, for example, being based in the south-east.

In the Middle East there were two groups with eleven squadrons and one heavy freight flight mainly based in Egypt and supporting low-level conflict in Greece and Palestine. In the Far East there was a total of eighteen squadrons and one heavy freight flight plus two glider squadrons yet to be disbanded. Most of the units flew the Dakota and 31 Sqn was in Singapore pending supporting British forces in the Netherlands East Indies. Further afield there were two Dakota units in Australia and 231 Sqn with the Liberator and Coronado in Canada.

Conversion training was mainly in the hands of 4 Group. The importance still placed on assault gliders was reflected in the fact that no fewer than five conversion, development or experimental units were equipped with gliders; two of these units were within Training Command. There were also conversion units in the Middle and Far East and one experimental flight, 1577, flew borrowed USAAF C-46 Commandos.

July 1948

By now the Liberators had returned to the United States, the Stirlings and Lancastrians had gone and Transport Command had consolidated on three types. The Dakota operated within 38 Group in East Anglia while 46 Group operated Yorks and a Halifax wing in the south. Thirty squadrons had reduced to twenty in two and a half years.

In the Middle East five Dakota units were based in Egypt in the aftermath of the Greek Civil War and the

independence of Israel. In the Far East all Indian and Burmese-based units had gone leaving just three Dakota squadrons in Malaya where they would soon be put to use in the insurrection there.

Two operational conversion units were based in the north of England and there was still a heavy investment in trials both by the TCDU and the AFEE, now a part of Maintenance Command

January 1949

This period was remarkably busy for the RAF transport units since in partnership with the Americans and French they were committed to the supply of Berlin by air. The surface routes had been cut by the Russians in June 1948 and were not to re-open until May 1949. The new Hastings, broadly a derivative of the Halifax, had entered service and was operated by two squadrons and the OCU.

All European RAF units were committed to supply and most were temporarily detached to West German airfields. In addition to the transport squadrons, two Sunderland units flew into Lake Havel until December 1948 when they withdrew with the onset of winter and ice.

January 1950

Most of the thirteen squadrons in the UK were still equipped with the relatively short-range Dakota as were three of the five units in Egypt and the three in the Far East. The only newly introduced equipment in the five years since the end of the war were the Valettas of 114 and 204 Sqns with much shorter range than the Dakota but the ability to carry 34 troops.

July 1952

While the RAF was at its post-war peak the transport units were still steadily reducing in numbers. European re-supply would have been by ship and road in the event of war while the long-range routes remained the preserve of the Hastings although most trooping was by sea. Of the seven UK units two now operated the Valetta including the sole, and short-lived, RAuxAF transport squadron, No 622. The Valetta also served universally overseas where there had been little change in basing; duties in the Far East, however, were much concerned with re-supply of troops in Malaya fighting the insurrection.

January 1955

There was still a gentle reduction in units and no change in equipment. By now a certain amount of overseas trooping, especially to the Middle East, was conducted by charter flights.

A significant development was the formation of two units in Malaya to cope with the need for supply and casualty evacuation into and from small strips and clearings. The first RAF transport helicopter unit, 155 Sqn, had been formed with Whirlwinds in September 1954 while 267 Sqn flew a miscellany of types including the STOL Pioneer. Also in the Malayan theatre was 848 NAS with the Whirlwind HAR Mk 1 and HAR Mk 21 establishing what was to become a commando transport role. No 845 NAS in Malta, while ostensibly equipped for anti-submarine duties, was also shortly to become a short-range troop transport unit.

Transport trials units

The **Airborne Forces Experimental Establishment** (AFEE) had its origins in the **Central Landing School** (CLS), later **Central Landing Establishment** (CLE), at Ringway which became the AFEE in January 1942. It moved into Sherburn-in-Elmet in July 1942 then to Beaulieu in January 1945. Its purpose was to test new aircraft types and equipment, including gliders and parachutes, which were vital to supporting airborne forces. A Flight was responsible for glider-towing, target-towing and pick-up trials. B Flight comprised Hoverflys and part of its task included the training of the Army's first helicopter pilots. C Flight was engaged in parachute-dropping trials. In September 1950 AFEE was absorbed into D Flight of the A&AEE at Boscombe Down.

No 1 Parachute Training School (1 PTS) formed Ringway in 1942 to train parachutists, having split from the CLE when the AFEE was formed. It moved to Upper Heyford in March 1946 equipped with Dakotas and was re-designated **No 1 Parachute and Glider Training School** (1 P&GTS) on 3 December 1947. It moved on to Abingdon in 1950 by which time Valettas were on charge, with a name change in June 1950 to **1 Parachute School** (1 PS). On 1 November 1953 the unit was further re-named **1 Parachute Training School** (1 PTS) and became simply the **Parachute Training School** (PTS) using aircraft from other units. It moved to Brize Norton on 1 January 1976.

The **Transport Command Development Unit** (TCDU) was formed at Netheravon from the **Air Transport Tactical Development Unit** (ATTDU) in the summer of 1945 to carry out trials on the use of transport aircraft. On 1 September 1945 it moved to Harwell for just a few months before moving on to Brize Norton. In 1946 its equipment included Buckingham, Lancaster, Stirling, Dakota, York, Hoverfly, Halifax, Liberator, Lancastrian, Horsa and Hadrian. Hastings and Valettas were received during 1948 and in June 1949 the unit moved to Abingdon where it remained until in 1971 it became the **Joint Air Transport Establishment** (JATE) which moved to Brize Norton in December 1975.

The **Joint Experimental Helicopter Unit** (JEHU) was formed at Middle Wallop as a joint Army/RAF unit to test the use of helicopters in support of Army mobility. It was equipped with the Sycamore HC Mk 14 and Whirlwind HAR Mk 2. After a series of successful trials the unit was embarked on HMS *Ocean* for the Suez campaign in October 1956, being re-titled as JHU with the 'Experimental' dropped. The JEHU title was restored after the Suez affair and trials continued until the Whirlwinds were despatched to Cyprus for internal security late in 1958, returning to the UK in March 1959. The unit disbanded into 225 Sqn on 31 December 1959.

July 1957

At last significant new types were entering service with Transport Command. To complement the ageing Hastings, Comet C Mk 2 jet transports had equipped 216 Sqn on the longer routes while the Beverley replaced the Valetta in the UK.

The British withdrawal from Egypt had resulted in a reduction of Middle East units and their dispersal to Cyprus and Aden. In the latter area, where dissidents were becoming consistently more troublesome, a Pioneer unit, 78 Sqn, had formed in 1956. Much further afield 1325 Flt operated Dakotas in Australia in support of the British nuclear tests.

Within months the transport units would be sorely tested in the Suez campaign. There were far too few aircraft capable of dropping paratroopers – just three Valetta and three Hastings squadrons – and Shackletons had to be pressed into service as troop transports from the UK carrying up to 33 troops in considerable discomfort. This was not the first time that Shackletons had been used in this way: when there was an outburst of violence in Cyprus in January 1956, 28 Shackletons and sixteen Hastings shifted 1,200 paratroopers and their heavy equipment to the Island in Operation 'Encompass'.

July 1960

Another strategic introduction was the Britannia, like the Comet a commercial type, which equipped two squadrons. The distribution of tactical units in the Middle East and East Africa was dictated by the need for in-theatre support for troops in Aden, Oman and Kenya. The Beverley was now operating in both the Middle and Far East. With the end of Operation 'Firedog' in Malaya 110 Sqn had been disbanded while the helicopter unit, 155 Sqn, had merged with 194 Sqn (rescue Sycamores) to form a new 110 Sqn. 848 NAS in Malaya had re-equipped with the Whirlwind HAS Mk 7.

A significant development was the formation of the first dedicated tanker unit, 214 Sqn, equipped with the Valiant BK Mk 1. Most other Valiant squadrons had a few tankers on charge for mutual support, but since 1958 214 had gradually been proving the technique.

January 1965

The early sixties were an important time of growth and re-equipment for the RAF transport fleet. The Comet C Mk 2 of 216 Sqn were complemented by five of the larger C Mk 4 variants for long-range tasks. With British forces involved in limited wars in Cyprus, Aden, Dhofar, East Africa, Borneo and British Guiana there was a growing emphasis on tactical and short-range types. 38 Group had been re-formed and new equipment had entered service in the form of the Argosy medium-range transport (four squadrons in the UK) and the Belvedere medium-lift helicopter (two squadrons, one in Borneo). Another newcomer was the Twin Pioneer STOL transport. In Borneo 845 NAS was busy, now equipped with the Wessex HAS Mk 1.

The Wessex had also begun its RAF career with, for the first time, a German-based unit. No fewer than five units were equipped with the Whirlwind including three in Borneo and a mixed flight (with the Twin Pioneer) in British Guiana. On the tanker front there was cause for great concern. The Valiant had just been grounded through wing-spar failure and with a reduced need for bombers, the decision was taken to scrap the survivors.

January 1970

In the space of just five years there had been significant changes in types and structure. Air Support Command had been formed, embracing Transport Command, and all transport units were incorporated in 38 Group. Four important new types had entered service with the transport fleet, perhaps at its most powerful at any time since the end of the war, given that Britain still, just, maintained a presence in the Far East and Middle East.

For long-range tasks the VC-10 equipped 10 Sqn, a disbanded Victor unit. For heavy-lift tasks the Belfast had joined 53 Sqn, also at Brize Norton which had been brought into RAF commission to accommodate the new large aircraft. To complement (and quickly replace) the short-lived Argosy, the RAF had the Hercules in service with four units and the OCU. Finally for short-range operations in rugged terrain, the Andover had entered service in the UK and Middle East. Four naval squadrons now operated the Wessex HU Mk 5 in the commando transport role, three based at Culdrose but ready to embark on carriers at short notice, while the fourth was in Malaya.

The hiatus created by the loss of the sole dedicated Valiant tanker unit was soon repaired by the formation of three squadrons, all based at Marham, with tanker variants of the Victor Mark 1. The bombers were now redundant with the nuclear deterrent role having transferred to the Royal Navy submarine fleet.

January 1975

A further re-structuring left all RAF operational units within one organisation, Strike Command, but in two groups. No 38 Group comprised the tactical helicopters based in the UK while the balance of the fleet, primarily long-range, fell within 46 Group. By now all the Hercules had been delivered and they equipped six squadrons including No 70 in Cyprus which was in the process of converting from the Argosy.

The only new type to have joined the transport units in the period was the Puma helicopter which now equipped two squadrons. Such was the importance of medium-lift helicopters that conversion was now the task of a full OCU based at Odiham.

No 18 Sqn with the Wessex had returned to Germany while further afield the RAF had withdrawn from the Gulf area and now had transport elements concentrated on Cyprus. In preparation for the withdrawal from the Far East just two helicopter units remained in the theatre. The tanker fleet remained based at Marham with Victors in three squadrons.

January 1980

With Britain's overseas commitments apparently reduced to a handful of far-flung interests the RAF had been reduced to just one long-range and four tactical transport squadrons with the VC-10 and Hercules respectively. The Britannias, Comets and Belfasts had all been scrapped or sold privately (in the case of the Belfast to be chartered back!) and the Andover was confined to non-transport duties.

Apart from the five fixed-wing squadrons the transport assets were all helicopter units flying either the Whirlwind, Wessex or Puma. Four squadrons were based in Europe, one in Cyprus on behalf of the UN and one in Hong Kong. Chinook helicopters were on order, but the RAF was ill-equipped to address the needs of the Falklands war of 1982, especially in respect of long-range transports and tankers; the three tanker units had been reduced to two. The Navy retained two commando helicopter units, one of which, 846 NAS, was re-equipping with the Sea King.

January 1985

The Falklands war had highlighted the limitations of the RAF's transport and tanker resources. Too late to take any part in the conflict was the TriStar which was intended to double as a transport and tanker; it entered service with 216 Sqn in 1983. Some Hercules had by now been stretched, although the longer Mark 3 was not tactical in the sense that it needed good runways. In a further re-structuring the transport units were now part of 1 Group, Strike Command.

The Chinook had joined the RAF in 1982 and four had been sent to the Falklands although three were lost when the *Atlantic Conveyor* was sunk. The survivor performed admirably and by 1985 one unit each in the UK and Germany was equipped with the type. To support the military in the island there remained a flight of Chinooks and one of Hercules, all of the transports equipped for tanking. The continuing problems in Northern Ireland had resulted in the permanent deployment of 72 Sqn with the Wessex to the province. To help counter the perceived threat to Belize from Guatemala a flight of Puma helicopters was based in the country. In Cyprus and Hong Kong the Whirlwind had made way for the Wessex.

The tanker fleet was to enjoy the most significant changes. As the Victor had been withdrawn from service in the strategic bomber role the Mark 2 had replaced the earlier Mark 1 with 55 and 57 Sqns. In an endeavour to supplement the Victor force some Vulcans and Hercules were rapidly converted to the tanker role while aircraft of many types were fitted for inflight refuelling. A second VC-10 squadron had also been formed in the tanker role flying the Mark 2 and 3.

January 1990

The preceding five years had seen virtually no changes to the organisation, deployment or establishment of the transport units. There were two exceptions. In the Falklands 1310 Flight had joined with the resident Sea King flight to form 78 Sqn. In the UK one of the two remaining Victor tanker squadrons, 57, had disbanded.

January 1995

Additional TriStars were on charge with 216 Sqn and additional tankers were available in the form of the VC-10 K Mk 4 with 101 Sqn and the converted C Mk 1K with 10 Sqn. This extension of the tanker fleet was essential given the demise of the Victor. At the tactical level 230 Sqn had moved from Germany to Northern Ireland while 60 Sqn had formed with the Wessex to complement 72 Sqn, also committed to the province. In respect of training the Victor OCU had disbanded and the remaining OCUs had been re-titled with reserve squadron numbers; in fact only the helicopter unit, 27(R) Sqn, had its own aircraft. Consideration was now being given to replacement of the Hercules fleet, which at the time of writing appears to have been determined at a mix of C-130J Hercules and the European Future Large Aircraft (FLA).

6.A Transport at 1 January 1946

Transport Command

38 Group

Type	Unit	Base
Halifax III	296, 297	Earls Colne
Halifax VIII	295, 570	Rivenhall
Stirling IV, V	196, 299	Shepherds Grove

46 Group

Type	Unit	Base
Warwick CIII	301, 304	Chedburgh
	167	Blackbushe
Dakota	435, 436	Down Ampney
	437	Odiham
Dakota IV	147	Croydon
Liberator	311	Prague (Czechoslovakia)

47 Group

Type	Unit	Base
Dakota	512, 575	Blakehill Farm
	271	Broadwell
	187, 525	Membury
Liberator	53	Merryfield
Stirling V	46, 242	Stoney Cross
York C1	246	Holmsley South
	511	Lyneham
York C1, Lancastrian C2, Dakota 3, 4, Anson, Dominie	1359 Flt	Lyneham

48 Group

Type	Unit	Base
Liberator VI, VIII	102	Bassingbourn
	86, 206	Oakington
	426	Tempsford
	59, 220	Waterbeach
Stirling V	51	Stradishall

Middle East (MED/ME)

205 Group (Egypt)

Type	Unit	Base
Liberator VI	40, 104	Abu Sueir
	37, 70	Shallufa
	214	Fayid
	148	Gianaclis
Liberator IV, Lancaster III	178	Fayid

216 Group

Type	Unit	Base
Dakota	78, 216	Almaza (Egypt)
	512	Gianaclis (Egypt)
	216 Det	Habbaniyah (Iraq)
	78 det	Maison Blanche (Algeria)
Halifax VII, Dakota 3, Stirling V	1589 HFF	Cairo West (Egypt)

Far East (Air Command South East Asia)

299 Transport Command Group (India)

Type	Unit	Base
Dakota	52	Dum Dum
	77	Mauripur
	10	Poona
	76	Tilda
	353	Palam
Liberator VIII, Skymaster	232	Palam
Halifax VIII	298	Raipur
Horsa	670	Fatehjang
Hadrian	672	Kargi Road
Stirling V	1588 HFF	Santa Cruz

AHQ Burma

Type	Unit	Base
Liberator VIII	159, 355	Salbani (India)

232 Group (Burma)

Type	Unit	Base
Dakota	96, 117	Hmawbi
	62, 194, 267	Mingaladon
	48	Patenga
	31	Kallang (Singapore)
	233	Tulihal (India)

AHQ Malaya

Type	Unit	Base
Dakota	215	Singapore

Australia

Type	Unit	Base
Dakota	238	Parafield
Dakota, Anson	243	Camden

Canada (45 Group)

Type	Unit	Base
Liberator II, IX	231	Dorval
Coronado I	231	Boucherville

Training and development units

4 Group

Type	Unit	Base
Dakota, Oxford	1333 TSCU	Syerston
Dakota, Oxford, Horsa II	1336 TSCU	Welford
Dakota	1381 CU	Desborough
Dakota, Anson, Oxford	1382 CU	Wymeswold
	1383 CU	Crosby-on-Eden
York, Lancastrian, Dakota	1384 HTCU	Ossington
Dakota	1 PTS	Ringway
Liberator VII, York	1332 HTCU	Dishforth
Wellington X, Anson, Spitfire	1380 TSCU	Tilstock
Halifax III, VIII, Stirling III	1665 HTCU	Linton-on-Ouse

38 Group

Type	Unit	Base
Halifax III, Stirling V, Albemarle, Horsa, Tiger Moth	ORTU	Wethersfield
Halifax VII, Stirling V, Liberator VII, Lancaster III, Horsa II, Hamilcar I	TCDU	Harwell
Horsa, Hamilcar	1 HGSU	Netheravon

23 Group

Type	Unit	Base
Halifax VII, Albemarle, Whitley, Dakota, Hamilcar, Horsa II, Hadrian	21 HGCU	Elsham Wolds
Stirling V, Halifax III, VII, Lancaster III, York C1, Dakota, Hadrian, Hamilcar, Hotspur II, CG-13	AFEE	Beaulieu

216 Group (Middle East)

Type	Unit	Base
Dakota	1330 CU	Bilbeis (Egypt)

299 Group (India)

Type	Unit	Base
Dakota, Halifax	1331 HCU	Risalpur
Dakota	1334 CU	Baroda
Dakota III, C-46	1577 AEF	Dhamial

6.B Transport at 1 July 1948

Transport Command

38 Group

Type	Unit	Base
Dakota	10, 27, 30, 46, 238	Oakington
	18, 53, 62, 77	Waterbeach
York C1	24	Bassingbourn

46 Group

Type	Unit	Base
	40, 51, 59, 242	Abingdon
	99, 206, 511	Lyneham
Halifax A9	47, 295, 297	Fairford

Middle East (MED/ME) 205 Group

Type	Unit	Base
Dakota	70, 78, 114, 204, 216	Kabrit (Egypt)

Far East (ACFE)

Type	Unit	Base
Dakota	48, 52, 110	Changi (Malaya)

Training and development

38 Group

Type	Unit	Base
Halifax, Anson, Dakota	240 OCU	North Luffenham
York	241 OCU	Dishforth

47 Group

Type	Unit	Base
Dakota, Halifax, Hamilcar, Horsa, York	TCDU	Abingdon

41 Group Maintenance Command

Type	Unit	Base
Dakota C3, Halifax A7, A9, Anson C10, Valetta C1, Firefly I, Monitor II, Martinet GT1, Auster AOP5, Seafire III, Hamilcar I, X, Horsa II, GAL 55, Hoverfly I, II, Proctor C3,	AFEE	Beaulieu

6.C Transport at 1 January 1949 (during the Berlin Airlift)

Transport Command

38 Group

Type	Unit	Base
Dakota IV	10, 18	Lübeck
	53, 62, 77	Waterbeach
York C1	24	Bassingbourn
	27	Oakington

Type	Unit	Base
	30	Wünstorf
	46	Lübeck
Hastings	240 OCU	North Luffenham

46 Group

Type	Unit	Base
York C1	40, 99, 206, 242	Wünstorf
	51, 59	Abingdon
	511	Lyneham
	241 OCU	Dishforth
Hastings C1	47, 297	Schleswigland

6.D Transport at 1 January 1950

Transport Command

38 Group

Type	Unit	Base
York C1	40, 51, 59	Bassingbourn
Hastings C1	47, 53, 297	Topcliffe

46 Group

Type	Unit	Base
Dakota C4	10, 27, 30, 46	Oakington
	18, 206	Waterbeach
Dakota C4, York C1	24	Waterbeach

Middle East (MEAF) 205 Group

Type	Unit	Base
Valetta C1	114, 204	Kabrit (Egypt)
Dakota C4	70, 78, 216	Kabrit

Far East (FEAF)

Type	Unit	Base
Dakota C4	48, 52	Changi (Malaya)
	110	Kuala Lumpur (Malaya)
	110 det	Negombo (Ceylon)

Training and development

38 Group

Type	Unit	Base
York C1, Hastings C1	241 OCU	Dishforth
Dakota, York	TCDU	Abingdon
Dakota	1333 TSTU	Netheravon
Dakota	1 PGTS	Upper Heyford

46 Group

Type	Unit	Base
Dakota, Anson, Oxford	240 OCU	North Luffenham

41 Group (Maintenance Command)

Type	Unit	Base
Hastings C1, Valetta C1, Dakota C4, Halifax A7, A9 Proctor C3	AFEE	Beaulieu

6.E Transport at 1 July 1952

Transport Command (38 Group)

Type	Unit	Base
Hastings C1,C2	24, 47	Topcliffe
	53, 99, 511	Lyneham
	30	Benson

Home Command (62 Group)

Type	Unit	Base
Valetta C1, C2	622	Blackbushe

Middle East (MEAF)

Type	Unit	Base
Valetta C1	78, 204, 216	Fayid (Egypt)
	70, 114	Kabrit (Egypt)

Far East (FEAF)

Type	Unit	Base
Valetta C1	48, 110	Changi (Malaya)
	52	Kuala Lumpur (Malaya)

Training and development 38 Group

Type	Unit	Base
Hastings	1 PTS	Abingdon
Hastings C1, Valetta C1, C2	242 OCU	Dishforth
Hastings C2, Valetta C1, Anson C12	TCDU	Abingdon

6.F Transport at 1 January 1955

Transport Command

Type	Unit	Base
Hastings C1, C2, C4	24, 47	Abingdon
	53, 99, 511	Lyneham
Valetta C1, C2	30	Dishforth

Middle East (MEAF)

Type	Unit	Base
Valetta C1	70, 84, 114, 216	Fayid (Egypt)

Far East (FEAF)

Type	Unit	Base
Valetta C1	48, 52, 110	Changi (Malaya)
Whirlwind HAR2, HAR4	155	Kuala Lumpur (Malaya)
Dakota C4, Pembroke C1, Pioneer CC1, Auster AOP6, Harvard 2b	267	Kuala Lumpur (Malaya)

Fleet Air Arm

Type	Unit	Base
Whirlwind HAS22	845	Hal Far (Malta)
Whirlwind HAR1, 21	848	Sembawang (Malaya)

Training and development

Type	Unit	Base
Hastings C1, Valetta C1	242 OCU	Dishforth
York C1, Hastings C1, Valetta C1	TCDU	Brize Norton

6.G Transport at 1 June 1957

Transport Command

Type	Unit	Base
Hastings C1,C2,C4	24, 511	Colerne
	99	Lyneham
Comet C2	216	Lyneham
Beverley C1	30	Dishforth
	47, 53	Abingdon
Pioneer CC1	215	Dishforth

Middle East (MEAF)

Type	Unit	Base
Valetta C1	70, 114	Nicosia (Cyprus)
Valetta C1, Pembroke C1	84	Khormaksar (Aden)
Pioneer CC1	78	Khormaksar (Aden)

Far East (FEAF)

Type	Unit	Base
Valetta C1	52, 110	Changi (Malaya)
Valetta C1, Hastings C1, C2	48	Changi (Malaya)
Whirlwind HAR2, HAR4	155	Kuala Lumpur (Malaya)
Dakota C4, Pembroke C1, Pioneer CC1, Auster AOP6,	267	Kuala Lumpur (Malaya)

Australia

Type	Unit	Base
Dakota C4	1325 Flt	South Australia

Fleet Air Arm

Type	Unit	Base
Whirlwind HAS22, HAR3, 7	845	Lee-on-Solent

Training and development

Type	Unit	Base
Hastings C1, Valetta C1, Beverley C1	242 OCU	Dishforth
York C1, Anson C19, Hastings C1, Valetta C1	TCDF	Benson

6.H Transport and refuelling at 1 July 1960

Transport

Transport Command

Type	Unit	Base
Hastings C1,C2,C4	24, 36, 114	Colerne
Britannia C1, C2	99, 511	Lyneham
Beverley C1	47, 53	Abingdon
Comet C2	216	Lyneham
Twin Pioneer CC1, Pioneer CC1	230	Odiham

Middle East (MEAF)

Type	Unit	Base
Hastings C1, C2	70	Nicosia (Cyprus)
Twin Pioneer CC1	78	Khormaksar (Aden)
Valetta C1, Beverley C1	84	Khormaksar (Aden)
Twin Pioneer CC1, Pembroke C1	152	Muharraq
Beverley C1	30	Eastleigh (Kenya)
Twin Pioneer CC1	21	Eastleigh

Far East (FEAF)

Type	Unit	Base
Valetta C1, Dakota C4	52	Changi (Malaya)
Hastings C1,C2, Beverley C1	48	Changi (Malaya)
Twin Pioneer CC1, Pioneer CC1	209	Seletar (Malaya)
Whirlwind HAR4, Sycamore HR14	110	Butterworth (Malaya) dets Labuan, Brunei, Situ

Fleet Air Arm

Type	Unit	Base
Whirlwind HAS7	848	Sembawang (Malaya)

Tanker

Type	Unit	Base
Valiant BK1	214	Marham

Training and development

Type	Unit	Base
Hastings C1, Beverley C1	242 OCU	Dishforth
Hastings C1, Valetta C1	TCDF	Benson

6.I   Transport and refuelling at 1 January 1965

Transport

Transport Command (38 Group)

Type	Unit	Base
Britannia C1, C2	99, 511	Lyneham
Comet C2, C4	216	Lyneham
Hastings C1,C2,C4	24, 36	Colerne
Beverley C1	47, 53	Abingdon
Argosy C1	105, 114, 215, 267	Benson
Belvedere HC1	26	Odiham
Wessex HC2	72	Odiham
Whirlwind HC10	230	Odiham

Germany (RAFG)

Type	Unit	Base
Wessex HC2	18	Gütersloh

Middle East (MEAF)

Type	Unit	Base
Twin Pioneer CC1	21	Eastleigh (Kenya)
Beverley C1	30	Muharraq
	84	Khormaksar (Aden)
Hastings C1, C2	70	Nicosia (Cyprus)
Twin Pioneer CC1, CC2, Pembroke C1	152	Muharraq

Far East (FEAF)

Type	Unit	Base
Beverley C1	34	Seletar (Malaya)
Hastings C1,C2	48	Changi (Malaya)
Valetta C1	52	Butterworth (Malaya)
Twin Pioneer CC1, Pioneer CC1	209	Seletar
Belvedere HC1	66	Seletar
Whirlwind HC10	103, 110	Seletar
	225	Kuching (Borneo)

Central America

Type	Unit	Base
Twin Pioneer CC2, Whirlwind HC10	1310 Flt	Atkinson Field (Br Guiana)

Fleet Air Arm

Type	Unit	Base
Whirlwind HAS7, Wessex HAS1	845	Sibu (Borneo)

Tanker

Type	Unit	Base
Valiant BK1	214	Marham

Training and development

Type	Unit	Base
Argosy C1, Beverley C1	242 OCU	Thorney Island

6.J   Transport and refuelling at 1 January 1970

Transport

Air Support Command (38 Group)

Type	Unit	Base
VC-10 C1	10	Brize Norton
Belfast C1	53	Brize Norton
Britannia C1, C2	99, 511	Lyneham
Comet C4	216	Lyneham
Hercules C1	24, 36	Lyneham
	30, 47	Fairford
Argosy C1	114, 267	Benson
Andover C1	46	Abingdon
Wessex HC2	18, 72	Odiham
Whirlwind HC10	230	Wittering

Middle East

NEAF

Type	Unit	Base
Argosy C1	70	Akrotiri (Cyprus)

Air Force Gulf

Type	Unit	Base
Andover C1	84	Sharjah
Wessex HC2	78	Sharjah

Far East (FEAF)

Type	Unit	Base
Hercules C1	48	Changi (Malaya)
Whirlwind HC10	103, 110	Changi
	28	Kai Tak (Hong Kong)

Fleet Air Arm

Type	Unit	Base
Wasp HAS1, Wessex HU5	845	Culdrose
Wessex HU5	846, 848	Culdrose
	847	Sembawang (Malaya)

Tanker

Strike Command (1 Group)

Type	Unit	Base
Victor K1, K1A	55, 57, 214	Marham

Training and development

Type	Unit	Base
Argosy C1, Andover C1, Hercules C1	242 OCU	Thorney Island
Wessex HC2	HOCU	Odiham

6.K   Transport (and refuelling) at 1 January 1975

Transport

Strike Command

46 Group

Type	Unit	Base
VC-10 C1	10	Brize Norton
Belfast C1	53	Brize Norton
Britannia C1, C2	99, 511	Lyneham
Comet C4	216	Lyneham
Hercules C1	24, 30, 36, 47, 48	Lyneham
Andover C1	46	Thorney Island

38 Group

Type	Unit	Base
Puma HC1	33, 230	Odiham
Wessex HC2	72	Odiham

Germany (RAFG)

Type	Unit	Base
Wessex HC2	18	Gütersloh

Middle East (NEAF)

Type	Unit	Base
Argosy C1, Hercules C1	70	Akrotiri (Cyprus)
Whirlwind HC10	84	Akrotiri

Far East

Type	Unit	Base
Whirlwind HC10	28	Kai Tak (Hong Kong)
Wessex HC2	103	Tengah (Malaya)

Fleet Air Arm

Type	Unit	Base
Wessex HU5	845	Yeovilton, RFA *Sir Galahad*
	846, 848	Yeovilton

Tanker

Strike Command (1 Group)

Type	Unit	Base
Victor K1, K1A	55, 57, 214	Marham

Training and development

38 Group

Type	Unit	Base
Wessex HC2, Puma HC1	240 OCU	Odiham

46 Group

Type	Unit	Base
Andover C1, Hercules C1	242 OCU	Thorney Island

6.L   Transport and refuelling at 1 January 1980

Transport

Strike Command (38 Group)

Type	Unit	Base
VC-10 C1	10	Brize Norton
Hercules C1	24, 30, 47, 70	Lyneham
Puma HC1	33, 230	Odiham
Wessex HC2	72	Odiham

Germany (RAFG)

Type	Unit	Base
Wessex HC2	18	Gütersloh

Middle East (NEAF)

Type	Unit	Base
Whirlwind HC10	84	Akrotiri

Far East

Type	Unit	Base
Whirlwind HC10	28	Sek Kong

Fleet Air Arm

Type	Unit	Base
Wessex HU5	845	Yeovilton
Wessex HU5, Sea King HC4	846	Yeovilton

Tanker

Strike Command (1 Group)

Type	Unit	Base
Victor K1, K1A	55, 57	Marham

Training and development

38 Group

Type	Unit	Base
Puma HC1	240 OCU	Odiham
Hercules C1	242 OCU	Lyneham

6.M   Transport and refuelling at 1 January 1985

Transport

Strike Command (1 Group)

Type	Unit	Base
TriStar C1	216	Brize Norton
VC-10 C1	10	Brize Norton
Hercules C1, C1K, C1P, C3	24, 30, 47, 70	Lyneham
Chinook HC1	7	Odiham
Puma HC1	33	Odiham
Wessex HC2	72	Aldergrove

Germany (RAFG)

Type	Unit	Base
Chinook HC1	18	Gütersloh
Puma HC1	230	Gütersloh

Middle East (RAF Cyprus)

Type	Unit	Base
Wessex HC2, HU5C	84	Akrotiri

Far East (RAF Hong Kong)

Type	Unit	Base
Wessex HC2	28	Sek Kong

Central America

Type	Unit	Base
Puma HC1	1563 Flt	Belize

Falkland Islands

Type	Unit	Base
Chinook HC1	1310 Flt	Kelly's Garden
Hercules C1K	1312 Flt	Stanley

Fleet Air Arm

Type	Unit	Base
Wessex HU5	845	Yeovilton
Sea King HC4	846	Yeovilton

Tanker

Strike Command (1 Group)

Type	Unit	Base
VC-10 K2, K3	101	Brize Norton
Victor K2	55, 57	Marham

Training and development

Type	Unit	Base
Chinook HC1, Puma HC1	240 OCU	Odiham
VC-10C1, TriStar C1, BAe146	241 OCU	Brize Norton
Hercules C1	242 OCU	Lyneham
Victor K2	232 OCU	Marham

6.N Transport and refuelling at 1 January 1990

Transport

Strike Command (1 Group)

Type	Unit	Base
TriStar C1, KC1	216	Brize Norton
VC-10 C1	10	Brize Norton
Hercules C1, C1K, C1P, C3	24, 30, 47, 70	Lyneham
Chinook HC1	7	Odiham
Puma HC1	33	Odiham
Wessex HC2	72	Aldergrove

Germany (RAFG)

Type	Unit	Base
Chinook HC1	18	Gütersloh
Puma HC1	230	Gütersloh

Middle East (RAF Cyprus)

Type	Unit	Base
Wessex HU5C	84	Akrotiri

Far East (RAF Hong Kong)

Type	Unit	Base
Wessex HC2	28	Sek Kong

Central America

Type	Unit	Base
Puma HC1	1563 Flt	Belize

Falkland Islands

Type	Unit	Base
Chinook HC1, Sea King HAR3	78	Mount Pleasant
Hercules C1K	1312 Flt	Mount Pleasant

Fleet Air Arm

Type	Unit	Base
Sea King HC4	845, 846	Yeovilton

Tanker

Strike Command (1 Group)

Type	Unit	Base
VC-10 K2, K3	101	Brize Norton
Victor K2	55	Marham

Training and development

Type	Unit	Base
Chinook HC1, Puma HC1	240 OCU	Odiham
VC-10C1, TriStar C1, BAe146 CC2	241 OCU	Brize Norton Benson
Hercules C1, C1K, C1P, C3, C3P	242 OCU	Lyneham
Victor K2	232 OCU	Marham

6.O Transport and refuelling at 1 January 1995

Transport

Strike Command (1 Group)

Type	Unit	Base
TriStar K1, KC1, C2, C2A	216	Brize Norton
VC-10 C1, C1K	10	Brize Norton
Hercules C1, C1K, C1P, C3	24, 30, 47, 70	Lyneham
Chinook HC2, Gazelle HT1	7	Odiham
Puma HC1	33	Odiham
	230	Aldergrove
Wessex HC2	60	Benson
	72	Aldergrove

Germany (RAFG)

Type	Unit	Base
Chinook HC2, Puma HC1	18	Laarbruch

Middle East (RAF Cyprus)

Type	Unit	Base
Wessex HU5C	84	Akrotiri

Far East (RAF Hong Kong)

Type	Unit	Base
Wessex HC2	28	Sek Kong

Falkland Islands

Type	Unit	Base
Chinook HC2, Sea King HAR3	78	Mount Pleasant
Hercules C1K	1312 Flt	Mount Pleasant

Fleet Air Arm

Type	Unit	Base
Sea King HC4	845, 846	Yeovilton

Tanker

Strike Command (1 Group)

Type	Unit	Base
VC-10 K2, K3, K4	101	Brize Norton
see also 10, 216 above		

Training and development

Type	Unit	Base
Chinook HC2, Puma HC1	27(R)	Odiham
VC-10C1, C1K, K2, K3 TriStar K1, KC1, C2, C2A	55(R)	Brize Norton
Hercules C1, C1K, C1P, C3, C3P	57(R)	Lyneham

6.1 Short Stirling (1940–1946)

The S.29 Stirling was designed as a bomber against specification B.12/36. The prototype flew in 1939 and in its bomber form the type entered service with 7 Sqn in 1940. By the end of the war the Stirling was obsolescent, having been superseded by the Lancaster and Halifax, and the Mark I was no longer in service. (The Mark II was not built.) However, the shortage of aircraft for transport work and heavy machine training led to the Stirling soldiering on in support roles for several years after the war.

Mark III
The Mark III was fitted with four Hercules XVI engines and carried a load of 6,000lb over 1,600 miles. The armament of two .303-in guns in nose and dorsal turrets and four in the tail turret was generally retained in training service.

Service (post-1945) **Training** 1665 HCU; ORTU; TCDU

Mark IV
The next variant was similar to the Mark III except that the nose and dorsal turrets were deleted and provision was made for glider towing. The Stirling tugs played an important part in the D-Day invasion and four squadrons were still operating this variant in early 1946.

Service (post-1945) **Transport** 196, 295, 299, 570

Mark V
Some 160 of the dedicated transport variant were constructed on the production line as such. All turrets were deleted and the nose extended. The load of 10,000lb or 40 troops was carried for up to 3,000 miles. In the build-up for the defeat of Japan the Stirlings were used extensively between Europe and India, but with the sudden end to the war remained in service only for a few months into 1946.

Service (post-1945) **Transport** 46, 51, 196, 242, 299; 1588, 1589 HFFs **Training** ORTU **Other** AFEE; ATTDU; 16 FU; SFU; TCDU

Short Stirling Mk V

Obsolescent as a bomber by the end of the War, the Stirling was later built as a glider tug and transport. In the Mk V 40 troops or 10,000lb of freight could be carried for up to 3,000 miles. PK178 of 1588 Heavy Freight Flight is seen at Santa Cruz in the Spring of 1946. *(A J B Harding via A S Thomas)*

6.2 Handley Page Halifax (1940–1952)

Like the Stirling the Halifax started life as a bomber in which role it was highly successful. It was designed to a specification calling originally for a twin-engined bomber some 10,000lb lighter than the Stirling. The HP 57 Mark I was out of service as was the more heavily armed HP 63 Mark V. (The Mark IV was not built.) By the war's end the Halifax in its bomber form remained in service with training units but it was to last for many years as a transport and for meteorological work.

B Mark II
The HP 59 was powered by four Merlin XX engines. It carried a maximum 13,000lb bomb load and defensive armament included .303-in guns in nose, dorsal and tail turrets. By the war's end it was in use in training units.

Service (post-1945) **Training** 1 BDU; CCDU; 1 FU

Mark III
The HP 61 was fitted with the Hercules XVI radial engine and was capable of carrying a heavier load. The C Mark III was a conversion of the B Mark III with the armament,

Handley Page Halifax Mk III

The Halifax served with great success through the strategic bomber offensive against Germany but later versions were built for transport tasks. The example illustrated, however, was a converted B Mk III (PP285) used by two transport squadrons post-war; the freight pannier is clearly visible. *(MAP)*

Specification and production

Mark	Role	Engine	HP	Load lb/men	Range miles	Nos
I	Bomber	4xHercules II	1,400	n/a	2,010	716
II	Bomber	Prototype only				1
III	Bomber	4xHercules XVI	1,650	6,000/-	1,600	6,187
IV	Glider tug	4xHercules XVI	1,650	6,000/-	1,600	450
V	Transport	4xHercules XVI	1,650	10,000/ 40	3,000	160

Further reading
The Stirling File, Gomersall, B, Air Britain, Tonbridge, 1979

mid upper turret and H2S scanner removed; the conversion carried 24 troops up to 2,230 miles. The **Met Mark III** retained the armament but had minor changes in internal equipment.

Service (post-1945) Transport (CIII) 296, 297 **Meteorology** (CIII,MetIII) 202, 204, 517, 518, 519, 520 **Training** (CIII) 1 GTS; 1665 HCU; 21 HGCU; 1385 HTSCU (MetIII) 111 OTU **Other** (CIII) 16 FU; (BIII) AFTDU; ASWDU; CGS; EANS; RWE; 1577 TF

Mark VI

The Mark VI (HP 61) employed the more powerful Hercules 100 and was the final bomber variant. Additional fuel in the wings conferred extended range. Some were converted for meteorological use.

Service (post-1945) Meteorology 202, 224, 269, 518, 521; RAE(MRF) **Training** BCIS; EANS; ERS; 1665 HCU; PTF; 1,2 RS

A Mark VII

The Mark VII (HP 61) was similar to the Mark VI but with Hercules XVI through shortages of the 100 model. No dorsal turret or radar scanner was fitted and the type was fitted with a glider towing hook; 333 were built.

Service (post-1945) Transport 47, 296, 297, 298, 620, 644 **Training** 21 HGCU; 1331, 1332, 1665 HTCU; 1385 HTSCU; ORTU; 1383 TSCU; 1333 TSTU **Other** 16 FU; TCDU

C Mark VIII

The HP 70 was purpose-built as a transport with no upper or rear turrets and dual control; the prototype was PP225. The variant was designed to carry a detachable freight pannier and up to eleven passengers. Many were later converted for civilian use as the Halton.

Service Transport 113, 301, 304 **Training** 1332, 1665 HTCU **Other** 1361 Met Flt; AFTDU; TCDU

A Mark IX

The HP 71 was built as an airborne forces variant, designed to carry sixteen fully equipped paratroopers. The prototype, RT758, first flew in October 1945.

Service Transport 47, 113, 202, 297, 620 **Training** EANS; 1 GTS; 1 PTS; 1 RS; PTU; 1333 TCU **Other** AFEE; TCDU; TCSF.

The **A Mark X** was a planned version of the A Mark IX with Hercules 100 engines; it was not built.

Specification and production

Mark	Role	Engine	HP	Load lb/men	Range miles	Nos
BI	Bomber	4xMerlin X	1,130	n/a	1,552	84
BII	Bomber	4xMerlin XX	1,220	10,000/-	1,885	1,966
CIII	Transport	4xHercules XVI	1,675	-/24	2,230	2,238
BV	Bomber	4xMerlin XX	1,220	n/a	2,200	904
BVI	Bomber	4xHercules 100	1,680	8,000/-	2,280	557
AVII	Transport	4xHercules XVI	1,675	-/18	2,050	333
CVIII	Transport	4xHercules 100	1,800	8,000/11	2,420	160
AIX	Transport	4xHercules XVI	1,675	-/16	2,050	145

Further reading

Halifax at War, Rapier, B J, Ian Allan, 1987
Halifax File, The, Roberts, R N, Air Britain, Hornchurch, 1982
Halifax in Action, Scutts, J, Squadron/Signal, Carrollton, 1984
Halifax Special, Robertson, B, Ian Allan, London
Handley Page Halifax, The, Merrick, K A, Aston, Bourne End, 1990
Handley Page Halifax B.III, VI, VII (Profile 11) Moyes, P J R, Profile Publications, Leatherhead, 1964

6.3 Douglas Dakota (1943–1970)

Surely the most famous of all transports, the Douglas Dakota was similar to the Douglas Commercial 3 (DC-3) of 1935. Some 10,926 were built of which over 1,900 were supplied to the RAF; in USAAF service the DC-3 was designated C-53 and C-47. The type served in every theatre during the war and for many years after.

C Mark I

The Mark I was similar to the USAAF C-47 and entered RAF service in limited numbers. It carried 28 men or 10,000lb of freight.

Service (post-1945) Training 1330 CU.

The **C Mark II** equated to the C-53 fitted with seats only and a single door. It was no longer in service by the end of the war.

C Mark III

The Mark III was similar to the C-47A, with a 24-volt electrical system rather than the 12-volt of the original model. The range was extended to 1,600 miles. It joined 31 Sqn in the Far East in early 1943 and served in all war theatres.

Douglas Dakota C Mk IV

The most famous transport of all time and still in service in large numbers across the world the Dakota (or DC-3 or C-47) operated with the RAF in all theatres until well after the War. Aircraft "US" of 31 Sqn was involved in the repatriation of prisoners-of-war from the Netherlands East Indies in 1946. *(Crown copyright)*

Service (post-1945) Transport 10, 18, 24, 31, 48, 52, 53, 62, 76, 77, 78, 96, 117, 147, 187, 194, 215, 216, 233, 238, 243, 267, 271, 353, 435, 436, 437, 512, 525, 575; 1359 Flt **Training** 21 HGCU; 1384 HTCU; 240 OCU; 1 PTS; 1331, 1332, 1336, 1381, 1383 TCU; 1333, 1382 TSCU **Communications** EACF; 16 FU; 12, 18 GCF **Other** AIEU; TCDU; TCEU

C Mark IV

The Mark IV was the equivalent of the C-47B with high-altitude blowers and extra fuel to confer a higher operational ceiling.

Service (post-1945) Transport 21, 27, 30, 46, 70, 110, 114, 204, 209, 231; 1325, 1359 Flts **Training** 1381 TCU; 1382 TSCU **Photo-recce** 82 **Communications** Aden CF; BAFO CS; FTCCF; Iwakuni SF; Malta CF; MECS; QF; Seletar TTF.

Many units were equipped with both Marks III and IV without distinction; below are listed units which were equipped with unspecified, or both, marks.

Transport 113, 167, 206, 620; 1315, 1680 Flts **Training** CFE; 242 OCU; 3 PTS; 1381 TCU **Communications** AA Delhi; ACSEA CS; AFNE Oslo; AHQ India CS; BCOF Japan; CCCF; Burma, Gibraltar, Iraq CF; MCS; RAE; Accra, Changi, Gatow, Kabrit, Kasfareet, Mauripur, Northolt, Palam, St Eval SFs; 46 GCF **Other** AFEE; ATDU; RAE

Specification and production

Mark	Role	Engine	HP	Load lb/men	Range miles	Nos
I	Transport	2xDouble Wasp R-1830-92	1,200	10,000/28	1,500	52
II	Transport	2xDouble Wasp R-1830-92	1,200	10,000/28	1,600	8
III	Transport	2xDouble Wasp R-1830-92	1,200	10,000/28	1,600	963
IV	Transport	2xDouble Wasp R-1830-92	1,200	10,000/27	1,600	895

Further reading

Dakota at War, Pearcey, A, Ian Allan, Shepperton, 1982
Douglas DC-3 Survivors, Volume One, Pearcey, A, Aston, Bourne End, 1987
Douglas DC-3 Survivors, Volume Two, Pearcey, A, Aston, Bourne End, 1988

6.4   Avro York (1943–1957)

The Avro Type 585 York was first flown in 1942 (LV626 first flight 5 July 1942) but it was not in significant RAF service during the war. Due in large part to American constraints on British development and production of transport aircraft as just one condition of lend-lease the type was based on the Lancaster, utilising the bomber's wings, undercarriage and engines but with a new, box-section fuselage and tail unit. It was built to specification C.1/42 to carry 24 passengers or 6,400lb of freight.

Avro York C Mk I

Utilising the Lancaster's wings, engines and undercarriage, the York transport had a new box-section fuselage. It joined 24 Sqn in 1943 and this anonymous aircraft of 246 Sqn is seen at Istres in 1946 en route to India. In the background can be seen a Warwick C MK III of 167 Sqn. *(Author's collection)*

C Mark I

The basic York was powered by four Merlin T.24 engines which gave it a top speed of 298mph at 21,000ft. It served with ten squadrons, and played a significant part in the Berlin Airlift, being replaced by the Hastings in due course. The York was fitted either as a freighter or passenger transport or in a combined form; it was finally withdrawn from service in 1957.

Service Transport 24, 40, 48, 51, 59, 99, 206, 242, 246, 511; 1310, 1359 Flts ACSEA CS; FECS; MCS **Training** 1332 CU; EANS; 1384 HTCU; 241 OCU **Other** AFEE, ATTDU; CRD; ITCE; RAE; TCDU; TCEU; TRE

C Mark II

The Mark II utilised the Hercules VI engine but only one (the CI prototype LV626) was produced.

Service Communications FEAF CS

Specification and production

Mark	Role	Engine	HP	Load lb/men	Range miles	Nos
I	Transport	4xMerlin T.24	1,620	6,400/24	2,700	208
II	Transport	4xHercules VI	1,650	6,400/24	2,700	1*

*   Mk I prototype converted

Further reading

Avro York (Profile 168) Hannah, D, Profile Publications, Leatherhead, 1968
Lancaster Franklin, N and Scarborough, G, Patrick Stephens, 1979 (includes York)

6.5   Douglas Skymaster (1944–1946) and Curtiss Commando (1944–1946)

The **Douglas DC-4 Skymaster** was another commercial type, like the DC-3/C-47/Dakota, put into service with the USAAF and then with the RAF. In the case of the four-engined C-54 the RAF received only small numbers for use on the Far East routes.

Douglas Skymaster C-54

Some 23 C-54 Skymasters were supplied to the RAF for use on the Far East routes. They were all operated by 232 Sqn based at Palam in India, including KL977 seen here. (*A S Thomas collection*)

Avro Lancastrian C Mk II

The Lancastrian was a short-term Lancaster conversion originally built for civil use. In the event 33 were built for RAF use and the modified fuselage is evident in this photograph of FGA-L of the Empire Air Armament School. (*P H T Green collection*)

The type apparently did not merit a mark number and 23 were acquired in 1944. The Skymaster was powered by four Pratt & Whitney R-2000 and carried up to 50 passengers.

Service (post-1945) Transport 232.

The Curtiss **C-46 Commando** served extensively in the USAAF, but only one or two were lent to the RAF where they undertook trials work in India.

Service (post-1945) Trials 1577 AEF

Specification and production

Mark	Role	Engine	HP	Load lb/men	Range miles	Nos
Skymaster	Transport	4xPW R-2000	1,350	-/50	3,800	23
Commando	Transport	2xPW R-2800	2,000	16,250/40	1,700	*

* several on loan from USAAF

6.6 Avro Lancastrian (1946–1949)

Whereas the York was a new design utilising some Lancaster components, the Type 691 Lancastrian was very much a short-term Lancaster conversion. It was built to specification C.16/44 with a completely revised fuselage with turrets removed and faired and windows added.

The Mark I was a civilian conversion for Trans Canada Airlines, the first of which was Lancaster R5727 which flew in late 1942. Six were converted plus a further 21 changed on the production line for BOAC.

Mark II

The military version was similar to the Mark I but with only nine seats; 33 were built for the RAF.

Service Transport 24, 231, 232, 511; 1359 VIP Flt; 1699 Flt Training EANS; ECFS; 1384 HTCU.

The Mark III was the second civilian version, equipped to seat thirteen but with a shorter range than the Mark I. The Mark IV (Type 691) was intended to be the RAF equivalent of the Mark III. Eight were constructed (from TX283) but delivered direct to civilian operators.

Specification and production

Mark	Role	Engine	HP	Load lb/men	Range miles	Nos
I	Transport	4xMerlin T24	1,250	14,000/10	4,150	*
II	Transport	4xMerlin T24	1,250	14,000/9	4,150	33
III	Transport	4xMerlin T24	1,250	/13	2,820	*
IV	Transport	4xMerlin T24	1,250	-/13	2,820	8

* None RAF

Further reading
Lancaster, Franklin, N and Scarborough, G, Patrick Stephens, 1979 (including Lancastrian)

6.7 Transport gliders (1942–1949)

During the war several types of glider had been built for use by airborne forces. They had proved their worth during operations during the liberation of Europe and a number remained in service with the RAF after the war, although flown by the Army.

The **Airspeed AS 51 Horsa** was the first glider designed and built for the RAF for carrying troops. It was designed to specification X.26/40 and the prototype DG597 first flew on 12 September 1941. Production was mainly of wood and most of the 3,655 built were constructed by furniture manufacturers. The Horsa was widely operated in Sicily, Normandy, at Arnhem and on the Rhine crossings. Two of the Mark I, which was out of service by 1946, were used in the ill-fated assault on the Norwegian heavy water plant in November 1942.

Mark II

The Mark II was similar to the Mark I in that it had a crew of two and carried between 20 and 25 troops subject to equipment. The difference was that the later version had a hinged nose as well as the (slow to operate) un-boltable rear fuselage.

Service (post-1945) Training 46, 53, 77, 238, 644, 670; 1385 CU; 21 HGCU/HGTS; 7 GSE; 38 GpORTU; 1 HGSU 1333, 1336 TSCU Other AFEE; ATDC(India); GPEU; TCDU

Airspeed Horsa Mk II

The Horsa was built in large numbers and the Mk II, seen here, was distinguished in having a hinged nose for ease of loading. This anonymous example is seen at AFEE in 1949, probably at Beaulieu. *(MAP)*

The **General Aircraft Hamilcar** was built to complement the smaller Horsa as the vehicle for bringing in heavy freight to limited landing sites. It met specification X.27/40 and the first flight of prototype DP206 took place on 27 March 1942. Maximum load was 17,500 lb.

Mark I
The GAL 49 was a high-wing glider with fixed-wheel undercarriage; 412 were built and it was used operationally in Normandy and Arnhem. By 1946 the type remained in training and development roles.

Service (post-1945) Training 21 HGCU; 1 HGSU
Other AFEE; TCDU

Mark X
The GAL 58 was a powered version of the Mark I with two Bristol Mercury engines. It was intended for use in the Far East in hot and high conditions. Some 20 conversions were completed before the war drew to an end.

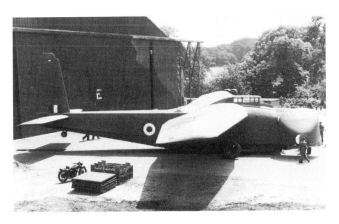

General Aircraft Hamilcar

The Hamilcar was built to complement the Horsa as a heavy freight carrier with a maximum load of 17,500lb. As with the Horsa, this shot is of an AFEE aircraft at Beaulieu in 1950 where the figures provide scale. *(MAP)*

Waco Hadrian

The Hadrian was an American design of which 695 were supplied to the British. Some were used in Italy in 1943 and the balance supplied to units in the Far East. This example, complete with American serial 274521, is with the AFEE in 1949. *(MAP)*

Service (post-1945) Other AFEE; ASWDU; CFE; TCDU; TFU/TRE

The American **Waco Hadrian** was of mixed construction and in US service was the CG-4A Haig. Carrying capacity was less than that of the indigenous Horsa and after use in Sicily in 1943 the Hadrian was supplied to six units in the Far East pending a possible invasion of Japan.

Service (post-1945) Training 22 HGCU **Other** AFEE; TCDU

Specification and production

Mark	Role	Engine	HP	Load lb/men	Range miles	Nos
Horsa I/II	Troop glider	none	n/a	7,500/25	n/a	3,655*
Hamilcar I	Freight glider	none	n/a	17,500/-	n/a	412
Hamilcar X	Freight glider	2x Mercury 31	965	15,500	705	20+
Hadrian I	Transport glider	none	n/a	3,800/15	n/a	695

* both Marks I and II
+ Mark I conversions

6.8 Handley Page Hastings (1948–1977)

Unlike the York, which it superseded, the HP 67 Hastings owed less to earlier designs apart from experience with the Halifax. The type was built to specification C.3/44 which called for a four-engined transport and the prototype, TE580, first flew on 7 May 1946. The Hastings entered service after the war but in time to see service through the Berlin Airlift, Suez and in support of British troops in brushfire wars throughout the 1950s.

C Mark 1
The Mark I had a relatively high-set tailplane of short span. The first production aircraft was TG499 and it equipped initially No 47 Squadron from September 1948. It carried 50 equipped troops and power was provided by four Bristol Hercules 101 engines.

Service Transport 24, 36, 47, 48, 51, 53, 70, 99, 114, 242, 297, 511; 1312 Flt; FECS **Meteorology** 202 **Calibration** 116, 151; CSE **Training** BCBS; 241, 242 OCUs; 1 PTS; RAFFC **Other** AAEE; AFEE; ETPS; MRF(RAE); PTU; RRF/RRE; TCDU; TCASF; TCEU; WEE

C Mark 1A
The designation applied to some 50 C Mk 1 models brought up to C Mk 2 standard and fitted with the Hercules 216. Extra fuel was carried in wing tanks, however, rather than in the wings as in the later variant.

Service Transport 48, 70

Met Mark 1
The met variant was a conversion of the C Mk 1 for meteorological work with the seating replaced by crew positions and specialised equipment. First conversion was TG620 which flew on 27 September 1950.

Service Meteorology 202 **Training** 242 OCU **Other** 70; AAEE; RRE

C Mark 2
The Mark 2 was fitted with more powerful Hercules 106 engines and a wider, lower-set tailplane to improve stability. Increased fuel capacity in internal wing tanks

Handley Page Hastings C Mk 1

Apart from the York the RAF relied in the immediate post-war period on bomber conversions or US-supplied aircraft. The Hastings was significant in being a purpose-built transport which went on to serve in the Berlin airlift, Malaya and Suez as well as numerous minor affairs. TG577/577 of 511 Sqn is pictured at Luqa, Malta, in 1956. (*Author's collection*)

extended the range by some 40%. The prototype was TG502 which first flew on 23 October 1948 and the first production aircraft was WD475 to specification C.19/49.

Service Transport 24, 36, 47, 48, 53, 70, 99, 114, 511; 1312 Flt; FECS **Signals** 97, 115, 151; CSE **Training** 1 PTS; RAFFC **Other** CSDS; RAE; RRE; TCASF; TCDF/TCDU.

The C Mark 3 (HP 95) was as the C Mk 2 but built for the Royal New Zealand Air Force; four were delivered.

C Mark 4

The HP 94 was a VIP version seating up to 20, four of which were built to specification C.115/P; original designation was Mark 2A. The first, WD500, flew on 22 September 1951.

Service Transport 24, 70; FECS; MECS

T Mark 5

The Mark 5 was a conversion of the C Mk 1 with a ventral radome for bomber navigator/aimer training. Eight aircraft were converted and the variant was not retired until June 1977.

Service Training BCBS/SCBS; 230 OCU

Specification and production

Mark	Role	Engine	HP	Load lb/men	Range miles	Nos
C1	Transport	4xHercules 101	1,615	16,600/50	1,025	100
C1A	Transport	4xHercules 216	1,675	16,600/50	1,500	50*
Met 1	Meteorology	4xHercules 101	1,615	–	1,300	19*
C2	Transport	4xHercules 106	1,675	16,600/50	1,690	43
C3	Transport	4xHercules 737	1,675	16,600/50	1,690	4
C4	VIP transport	4xHercules 130	1,675	-/20	4,250	4
T5	Trainer	4xHercules 101	1,615	-	1,700	8*

* C1 conversions

6.9 Vickers Viking (1946 – 1957)

The Viking was built to specification 17/44 as a twin-engined civil airliner. Its design relied heavily on that of the Wellington bomber whose wings it shared. The Viking was operated by various trials units and by the RAF only in the King's (later Queen's) Flight.

C Mark 1A

The Types 495, 496 and 498 were the original 27-seat airliner in its early forms. The aircraft was powered by two Hercules 634 engines and the prototype Type 491 G-AGOK first flew on 22 June 1945.

Service Trials RAE (2nd proto G-AGOL Type 495 as VX238; 1st prod G-AGON Type 498 as VX214); BLE

Vickers Viking C Mk 2

The Viking was the first twin-engined post-war British airliner and it was used in small numbers by the RAF. Eight C Mk 2 aircraft were used in the VIP role as typified by this example, VL246 of the King's Flight, seen here at Lübeck in May 1947 bringing HRH the Duke of Gloucester on an official visit. *(P H T Green collection)*

(3rd proto G-AGOM Type 496 as VX141); ETPS (2nd prod G-AGRM Type 498 as VW215)

C Mark 2

The Mark 2 was produced in several forms, primarily to equip or support the King's Flight. The VIP six-seater was the Type 621 of which eight were built, the first being VL245. In addition the Types 623 (2), 624 (1) and 626 (1) were supplied plus the Type 618 Nene-powered variant (VX856).

Service Communications KF/QF; LRWE **Other** ETPS; RAE

Specification and production

Mark	Role	Engine	HP	Load lb/men	Range miles	Nos
C1A	Trials	2xHercules 634	1,690	-/27	1,620	4*
C2	VIP transport	2xHercules 634	1,690	-/6+	1,620	8
C2	Communication	2xHercules 634	1,690	-/27	1,620	4
	Testbed	2xNene	4,500			1

* plus many for civil use

6.10 Vickers Valetta (1949–1968)

The Valetta (Type 607) was the military version of the Viking transport, designed and built to specification C.9/46. At first glance it was virtually indistinguishable from the civil type apart from a blunt tail cone but compared to the Viking it had a strengthened floor, large loading doors on the port side and a revised undercarriage. The Valetta was equipped for troop transport, freight, air-dropping, paratrooping and air ambulance and it entered service with 204 Sqn in Egypt in 1949. The Valetta operated in every RAF Command and supported operations in Malaya and at Suez.

C Mark 1

The Mark 1 (Type 637, 651) carried 34 passengers or up to 8,000lb of freight. The prototype, VL249, flew on 30

Vickers Valetta C Mk 1

The Valetta was intended to replace the Dakota, which it did to some extent in the RAF but not more widely. It was a tactical transport capable of carrying 34 troops over a range of around 350 miles. Apart from use at Suez, it served in Malaya for some years as exemplified by WJ497/U of 52 Sqn on a leaflet-dropping sortie in 1956. *(Crown copyright)*

June 1947 and within two years the type was in service. The powerplant was the Hercules 230, a more powerful version of the engine installed in the Viking. The C Mk 1 was unique in that it equipped the sole Royal Auxiliary Air Force transport unit, No 622 Sqn.

Service Transport 30, 48, 52, 70, 78, 84, 110, 114, 167, 204, 205, 216, 233, 622; 1312 Flt; APCS; EACF; FECS; MCS; OFU; SCS; TCASF; 2 TAFCS; Aden, Malta, Iraq CF; Benson, Eastleigh, Labuan, Seletar SFs **Signals** 115 **Training** CATCS; CFS; CNCS; 228, 238, 240, 241, 242 OCUs; 1 PTS; RAFFC **Other** 683; AES; AFEE; FSS; FTF/FTU; RAE; RRE; TCDF/TCDU; TCEU; TRE; WEE

C Mark 2
The Type 659 was similar to the C Mk 1 except that it was fitted as a VIP transport. It was distinguishable externally by having a pointed tail cone and extra fuel provided a greater range than the C Mk 1. Ten were built.

Service Transport/communications 24, 30, 70, 114, 233; BAFOCS; CCCF; MCS; MECS; RAFFC; RAFGCS; SCS; 2 TAFCS; Aden, Malta, Nicosia CF/CS; Gibraltar, Khormaksar SF

T Mark 3
The Type 664 was designed to specification T.1/49 as a flying classroom navigation trainer; the first (VX564) flew on 31 August 1950. The main differences were to the internal fittings and the addition of five astrodomes along the top of the fuselage.

Service Training 201 AFS; 1, 2, 3, 5, 6 ANS; CNCS; 228, 238 OCU; RAFFC **Other** 70, 84, 215; AES; CSDE; ETPS; FECS; MECS; Malta CTTS; RRE

T Mark 4
The Type 743 was a conversion of the T Mk 3 for navigator training. The nose was extended to incorporate a radar scanner and the type was used by the air navigation schools and to train Javelin navigators.

Service Training 1, 2 ANS; 228 OCU

Specification and production

Mark	Role	Engine	HP	Load lb/men	Range miles	Nos
C1	Transport	2xHercules 230	1,975	8,000/34	360	212
C2	VIP transport	2xHercules 230	1,975	-/15	650	10
T3	Trainer	2xHercules 230	1,975	-	650	40
T4	Trainer	2xHercules 230	1,975	-	650	16*

* T3 conversions

6.11 Blackburn Beverley (1956–1967)

The B.101 Beverley was a developed version of the General Aircraft Company's Universal transport which had been designed in 1946 (specification C.3/46) and flew in 1950 powered by the ubiquitous Hercules engine. The military variant, the Beverley, first flew (WZ889) on 17 June 1953 with the engines changed to the more powerful Centaurus.

The Beverley was the largest freighter aircraft to have been built in Britain and it was to serve the RAF from 1956 to 1967 in most theatres. It came into its own in the Aden campaign with its excellent short field capability.

Blackburn Beverley C Mk 1

For carrying awkward loads over short distances the Beverley was unsurpassed in RAF service. It had excellent short-field performance and was especially valuable in South Arabia, where it coped well with short desert strips. XM104 is pictured in the Far East. *(Crown copyright)*

C Mark 1
The Mark 1 was the basic and only version to enter service. The Beverley was designed for dropping heavy equipment through the rear detachable doors and featured a fixed undercarriage. The total load was 45,000lb which could be flown over a range of 450 miles.

Service Transport 30, 34, 47, 48, 53, 84 **Training** 242 OCU **Other** FETS; RAE

Specification and production

Mark	Role	Engine	HP	Load lb/men	Range miles	Nos
C1	Transport	4xCentaurus 273	2,850	45,000/94	450	47

Further reading
Blackburn Beverley, Hobson, C, Aviation News, Berkhamsted, 1988
Blackburn Beverley, Overton, W, 1990

6.12 de Havilland Comet (1956–1975)

The DH106 Comet was produced to specification 22/46 as the first jet passenger aircraft in the world and the Series 1 entered service with BOAC in 1952. The prototype, G-ALVG, flew on 27 July 1949 from Hatfield. It was powered by four Ghost 50 engines and accommodated 36 passengers. After two BOAC machines had crashed with considerable loss of life the type was grounded; detailed examination of the wreckage and structural testing confirmed failure of the fuselage around a window. The Comet was withdrawn from service and the Series 2 aircraft on the production line were strengthened. Two RCAF 1As were re-built to the standard as the 1XB.

The **Series 1** did not serve with the RAF but 1A

de Havilland Comet C Mk 2

The World's first jet airliner ran into difficulties in BOAC service when structural failure caused several major accidents with large loss of life. When the problem was identified and rectified, the Comet went on to perform well for many years with 216 Sqn. XK671/671 is one of ten of the original Comets, which were later replaced by the much larger Mk 4. *(Crown copyright)*

(XM823) and 1XB (XM829) both served as trials aircraft. The **Series 2** was as the Series 1 but with a re-built fuselage as described above. Two 2E aircraft served as trials machines, XN453 (RAE) and XV144 (BLEU).

C Mark 2
The Mark 2 was delivered to the RAF in 1956 when the type went into service with 216 Sqn. This version seated 44 being powered by the Avon 117/118 and it remained in service until May 1967.

Service Transport 216 **Signals** 51

T Mark 2
The trainer was a dual control version of which two were built. They were fully operational aircraft and formed part of the establishment of 216 Sqn.

Service Transport/trainer 216

R Mark 2
This was the designation for three airframes converted for special ELINT work by Marshalls of Cambridge. The Comet remained in service with 51 Sqn until replaced by special Nimrods in 1971.

Service ELINT 51, 192

The **Series 3** (Type 106) was an interim type with a stretched fuselage seating 78 and with Avon 502 engines. A single example was produced, but it led to the Series 4. It was later re-engined with the Avon 523, becoming the 3B in which guise it served the BLEU as XP915. The **Series 4** (Type 106) was based on the 3 with increased fuel and between 60 and 101 passengers. It was primarily built for BOAC on the Atlantic route engined with the Avon 524. Four wore military markings as XS235 (BLEU/AAEE), XV814 (RAE), XW262 (AAEE and Nimrod aerodynamic prototype) and XX944 (RAE). Two further aircraft were used as Nimrod prototypes, XV147 and XV148.

C Mark 4
The military Mark 4 was the 4C and was the natural successor to the C Mk 2 on the RAF's trunk routes. It carried 94 passengers in rear-facing seats and was powered by the Avon 350. Five were operated between 1962 and 1975.

Service Transport 216

Specification and production

Mark	Role	Engine	Thrust lb	Load lb/men	Range miles	Nos new
1	Airliner	4xGhost 50.1	4,450	-/36	1,500	*
1A	Airliner	4xGhost 50.2	5,000	-/44	1,770	*
C2/T2	Transport	4xAvon 117	7,350	—/44	2,200	10
R2	ELINT	4xAvon 117	7,350	-	2,200	3
3	Airliner	4xAvon 502	10,000	-/78	2,700	*
4	Airliner	4xAvon 524	10,000	-/81	3,225	*
C4	Transport	4xAvon 350	10,500	-/94	2,500	5

* None for RAF

Further reading
Comet, Classic Civil Aircraft, Ian Allan, London
de Havilland Comet Series 1-4, (The Profile 108) Birtles, P J, Profile Publications, Leatherhead, 1966
DH Comet: The World's First Jet Airliner, Cowell, J G, Airline Publications, 1976

6.13 Bristol Britannia (1959–1976)

The Type 175 Britannia airliner was built to specification 2/47 calling for a medium-range airliner for the Empire routes. The original design was for a 36-seat aircraft powered by the Centaurus piston engine. The design was developed to accommodate the Proteus engine and the prototype, G-ALBO (notionally VX447), flew on 16 August 1952. Capacity of the early production aircraft was 90 passengers.

In a significantly revised form the Britannia provided the basis for the Canadair Argus maritime reconnaissance aircraft. The Britannia entered RAF service in March 1959 and was withdrawn in early 1976 as an economy measure.

C Mark 1
The Britannia series 253 was ordered for the RAF as a mixed-traffic transport to support rapid deployment of the strategic reserve to the Far and Middle East, Africa and the West Indies. The series 253 was powered by the Proteus 255 and featured a strengthened floor with tie-down points and a large cargo door; first production aircraft was XL635 which flew on 29 December 1958. The Britannia joined 99 Sqn in 1959.

Service Transport 99, 511

C Mark 2
The Mark 2 was the designation applied to three series 252 Britannias originally ordered by the Ministry of Supply for leasing to charter companies charged for

Bristol Britannia C Mk 2

Surely one of the most elegant of propeller driven aircraft, the Britannia was originally designed as a mere 36-seat aircraft for the Empire routes. In the event the design developed to accommodate the Proteus turboprop engine. It enjoyed commercial success and operated with 99 and 511 Sqns from 1959 until 1976 when the fleet was sold off on economy grounds. XN392/392 was named *Acrux*, one of three Mk 2 aircraft. *(Author)*

trooping contracts. In the event policy changed and the aircraft were delivered to the RAF. They were similar in all important respects to the series 253.

Service Transport 99, 511

Specification and production

Mark	Role	Engine	HP	Load lb/men	Range miles	Nos
C1	Transport	4xProteus 255	4,400	37,400/113	4,270	20
C2	Transport	4xProteus 255	4,445	37,400/113	4,270	3

Further reading
Bristol 170, Britannia, Air Britain, Essex, 1977

6.14 Bristol (Westland) Belvedere (1961–1969)

The twin-engined, twin-rotor, Type 192 Belvedere helicopter was the first in Britain to be designed from the outset as a troop carrier to meet a range of needs for army support including supply dropping and casualty evacuation. The design was based on that of the Type 173 which first flew in January 1952 (Chapter 12.5).

HC Mark 1
The Belvedere was built to carry eighteen fully equipped troops and both rotors were synchronised through a shaft enabling single engine performance through either powerplant in the event of an emergency. The first production aircraft, XG447, flew on 5 July 1958 and the Belvedere joined 66 Sqn in 1961. It saw service in Europe, Africa, South Arabia and Borneo.

Service Transport 26, 66, 72 **Training** BTU

Bristol Belvedere HC Mk 1

The Belvedere was designed originally for naval use and adapted as a troop carrier capable of lifting eighteen troops. Although suffering from engine starter problems it served operationally in the United Kingdom, Borneo and the Radfan. A 26 Sqn aircraft, XG461/G of 26 Sqn is seen at Aden lifting a 25pdr gun in 1964. *(J Manton via A S Thomas)*

Specification and production

Mark	Role	Engine	HP	Load lb/men	Range miles	Nos
HC1	Helicopter	2xGazelle NGa.2	1,650	6,000/18	445	26

6.15 Armstrong Whitworth (Hawker Siddeley) Argosy (1962–1978)

The Type 660 Argosy was a military development of the AW.650 civil transport which first flew in 1958. Built to OR 351 the military version differed from the original design in having split 'crocodile-jaw' rear doors for easy and fast loading and off-loading of bulky freight. It had excellent short and rough landing characteristics, and although flight refuelling trials were completed before introduction into service, the technique was not used operationally.

C Mark 1
The Mark 1 was powered by four Dart 101 engines and carried 69 troops or 29,000lb of freight 345 miles; the maximum useful range (20,000lb load) was 1,070 miles. First aircraft, XN814, flew on 4 March 1961. The Argosy joined 114 Sqn in 1962 and was initially complemented by the Hercules from 1967 and finally supplanted by it in 1974.

Service Transport 70, 105, 114, 215, 267; SF Benson **Training** AOCU; 6 FTS; 240, 242 OCUs **Other** 115; AAEE; AEAES; ETPS; Cottesmore Trials Flt

E Mark 1
The designation applied to C Mk 1 conversions operated by 115 Sqn in the radar and navigational aids calibration role. They replaced Varsitys from 1968 and were withdrawn from use in early 1978.

Service Calibration 115

T Mark 1
The designation is believed to have applied to two C Mk 1s (XP411 and XR107) made available for use by 6 FTS in preparation for the intended T Mk 2 trainers.

T Mark 2
The Mark 2 was an intended navigation trainer for use by 6 FTS; it featured an enlarged radome. At least six were earmarked for conversion from C Mk 1 status and the first of two completed was XP442 which flew on 30 October 1975. The project was abandoned shortly thereafter.

Specification and production

Mark	Role	Engine	HP	Load lb/men	Range miles	Nos
C1	Transport	4xDart 101	2,680	29,000/69	345	56
E1	Calibration	4xDart 101	2,680	-	1,200	11*
T1	Trainer	4xDart 101	2,680	-	750	2*
T2	Trainer	4xDart 101	2,680	-	1,200	2*#

* C1 conversions
\# 14 intended, 6 begun, 2 completed

Armstrong Whitworth Argosy C Mk 1

The thimble-shaped radar nose conferred on the Argosy the disrespectful 'flying tit' epithet while the shape and powerplant resulted in the slightly more appropriate 'whistling wheelbarrow' nickname. The Argosy was a medium range tactical transport with good short-field performance and was a useful paratroop vehicle as evidenced here with XR107/107 of 70 Sqn dropping parachutists over Cyprus. *(Author's collection)*

6.16   Short Belfast (1965–1976)

The SC.5/10 Belfast was designed from the outset as a strategic transport and was the first in the world to employ a fully automatic landing system. The design was broadly based on that of the Britannia and similarity in the wings and tail unit are obvious.

C Mark 1
The Belfast was built to specification C.203 and the first aircraft (XR362) – there were no prototypes – flew on 5 January 1964, five years after being ordered. All ten

Short Belfast C Mk 1

The Belfast strategic transport was broadly based on the Britannia but with a more capacious fuselage with rear uplift for ease of loading. XR364/364 of 53 Sqn is seen at Farnborough in 1964 making a pass at a height rather lower than that permitted nowadays at air displays. *(Author)*

aircraft had been delivered to 53 Sqn by 1966. The Belfast was essentially a large freighter with a 10,000 cubic feet hold but it could be equipped to carry up to 150 troops. The type was withdrawn from service in 1976 in the light of defence cuts; the Ministry of Defence had to charter the aircraft from their subsequent owner, Heavylift, to support the Falkland operations in 1982.

Service Transport 53

Specification and production

Mark	Role	Engine	HP	Load lb/men	Range miles	Nos
C1	Transport	4xTyne Ty.12	5,730	80,000/150	3,600	10

6.17   Vickers VC-10 (1967–date)

The Vickers VC-10 went into service with BOAC in April 1964 just six years after design work began and only two years from the flight of the prototype G-ARTA (29 June 1962). The type was ordered by the RAF to specification C.239/60 for VIP duties and on the Far East routes. As a transport the VC-10 carried up to 150 passengers while later versions were used for air-to-air refuelling.

C Mark 1
The Type 1106 was similar to the Type 1103 for British United Airways with cargo door and floor. Fuel tanks

were also fitted in the fin. The first VC-10 was XR806 (first flight 26 November 1965) and the type entered service with 10 Sqn in 1967. In addition to the fourteen delivered for transport duties, one Type 1101 (ZD493 ex G-ARVJ) was used by RAF Brize Norton for ground training and one Type 1103 (XX914 ex G-ATDJ) by the RAE.

Service **Transport** 10 **Training** 241 OCU **Trials** RAE

C(K) Mark 1
The Type 1106 was the designation applied to the original aircraft converted from 1992 for supplementary air-to-air refuelling with FR Mk 32 refuelling pods under each wing. The passenger configuration is retained and no extra fuel is carried. By December 1995 all thirteen intended conversions had been made; first conversion was XV103.

Service **Transport/refuelling** 10 **Training** 242 OCU

K Mark 2
The Type 1112 were conversions of the civil Type 1101 bought from Gulf Air and fitted for air refuelling with two underwing pods and one under the rear fuselage. Total transferable fuel load is 70,000 gals.

Service **Refuelling** 101

K Mark 3
The Type 1154 was the first Super VC-10 variant used by the RAF, being conversions of Type 1153 aircraft ex East African Airways. Like the K Mk 2 the stretched aircraft featured three refuelling points but fuel load was extended to 80,000 gals.

Service **Refuelling** 101

VC-10 K Mark 4
The Type 1151 is the second Super VC-10 conversion. Some fourteen ex BA aircraft had been bought and stored

Vickers VC-10 K Mk 2

When it entered civil service with BOAC in 1964 the VC-10 was unique in having its four engines astride the rear fuselage. The type joined 10 Sqn in 1967 and thirty years later the fleet has been joined by a number of second-hand aircraft completely refitted for the tanker role. Seen here are two three-point tankers of 101 Sqn, ZA143 leading in hemp finish and refuelling ZA141. *(BAe)*

at RAF Abingdon for many years. Five were selected for conversion as mixed freight/refuellers against ASR 415 and the first joined 101 Sqn in 1993. Fuel load is 66 tonnes.

Service Refuelling/freight 101

Specification and production

Mark	Role	Engine	Thrust lb	Load lb/men	Range miles	Nos
C1	Transport	4xConway 301	22,500	59,000/150	3,700	14
C(K)1	Transport/ AAR	4xConway 301	22,500	59,000/150	3,700	6*
K2	Refuelling	4xConway 550	22,500		3,900	5
K3	Refuelling	4xConway 550	22,500		3,900	4
K4	Freight/ AAR	4xConway 550	22,500	60,500/?	3,900	5

* C1 conversions

6.18 Hawker Siddeley Andover (1966–1995)

The Type 780 Andover was based on the Avro 748 twin-engined civil transport which first flew in 1960. The military requirement was for a multi-purpose transport capable of working from short, ill-prepared strips in a range of environments. The type would be used for trooping, paratrooping, ambulance work, aerial supply and general utility transport. Compared with the civil type the Andover had more powerful Dart 12 Mk 201C engines driving larger propellers. The fuselage was lengthened and revised with a rear ramp; access was facilitated by an unusual kneeling undercarriage.

Hawker Siddeley Andover C Mk 1

The Andover C Mk 1 was based on the commercial Avro 748 but with modifications to the rear fuelage with a rear ramp and an unusual 'kneeling' undercarriage to ease access. This aircraft of 46 Sqn, based at Thorney Island, is seen on an exercise in Scotland in 1967. It is finished in the brown/stone over, black under, camouflage scheme also worn for a short time by the Argosy and Hercules. *(Crown copyright)*

C Mark 1

The Mark 1 entered service with 46 Sqn in December 1966; the prototype, XS594, had flown on 9 July 1965. Thirty-one were built and in its original transport roles it served with three squadrons in the UK, Far East and Middle East where it replaced Beverleys with 84 Sqn. Compared with many types the Andover was short-lived, being finally withdrawn from service in the UK in August 1975. It also served in various communicatons and development units.

Service Transport 46, 52, 84 **Communications** 21, 32, 60; MECS; Abingdon, Brize Norton SFs; Oslo CAFN **Calibration** 115 **Training** AOCU; 242 OCU **Other** ETPS; EWAU; RAE

C Mark 1 (PR)

The (PR) variant comprised two Mark 1 aircraft fitted with cameras and flown by 60 Sqn; the first was XS596. The designation also apparently applied to an aircraft used to monitor the Open Skies policy after the end of the Cold War.

Service Reconnaissance 60

CC Mark 2

The designation was applied to six original Avro 748 aircraft supplied for communications duties. Two served with the Queen's Flight while the remainder circulated through a number of units.

Service Communications 21, 32, 48, 60, 152; FEAF VIP Flt; MCS; MECCF; MECS; QF; Abingdon, Brize Norton SFs

E Mark 3

The Mark 3 was a conversion of the C Mk 1 designed for radar calibration work. Seven aircraft were converted and the variant served with 115 Sqn from November 1976, taking over from the Argosy.

Service Calibration 115

E Mark 3A

The Mark 3A was an upgrade of the E Mk 3; three machines were fitted with improved electronics.

Service Calibration 115

Specification and production

Mark	Role	Engine	HP	Load lb/men	Range miles	Nos
C1	Tractical transport	2xDart 12	3,245	14,000/44	374	31
C1(PR)	Photo recce	2xDart 12	3,245	na	550	2*
CC2	Comm-- unication	2xDart 7	2,230	-/16	850	6
E3	Calibra- tion	2xDart 12	3,245	na	550	7*
E3A	Calibra- tion	2xDart 12	3,245	na	550	3#

* C1 conversions
\# E3 conversions

6.19 Lockheed Hercules (1967–date)

The Lockheed C-130 Hercules originated from a USAF design requirement issued in 1951 (during the Korean War) and intended to secure improvements over the contemporary C-46, C-47 and C-119. The prototype YC-130A first flew on 23 August 1954 just three years after the initial order. The Hercules must be the most successful transport type ever produced, having been in constant production for over forty years and serving with over fifty air forces. With the cancellation of the indigenous jet-propelled HS681 it was inevitable that the RAF would order the proven Hercules.

The full story of the Hercules is outside the scope of the present work, but major developments are summarised. The -A and -B versions were essentially tactical transports, the -C was not built and the -D was ski-equipped. The -E was designed for longer-range work with the more powerful Allison T56-A-7 engine and an extra 3,730 gals of fuel. The -F and -G were naval -B and -E respectively. The -H was similar to the -E but with de-rated engines and a re-designed airframe to improve service life. The -J was not built in sequence and the -K was the version ordered for the RAF. It was essentially a C-130H but with British instrumentation.

C Mark 1

The Type 382-19B first flew on 19 October 1966 (XV176) and the first of 66 ordered was delivered to 242 OCU in April 1967. The first squadron to receive the type was 36 Sqn then based at Thorney Island. The Hercules served with distinction through numerous relief operations and critically during and after the fight to re-take the Falklands. The latter campaign prompted several important developments. All surviving C Mk 1s have been converted to C1P, C1K or C3 standard.

Service Transport 24, 30, 36, 47, 48, 70, LTW **Training** 242 OCU

C Mark 1 LR2 and LR4

These were temporary designations applied to long-range aircraft fitted with extra fuel tanks in the forward fuselage, albeit at the expense of payload. Two (LR2) or four (LR4) 850gal tanks were fitted and at least sixteen LR2 and four LR4 conversions were completed by the Lyneham Engineering Wing. Sixteen LR2s were later fitted with refuelling probes becoming, temporarily, the **PLR2**. The LR4 became the basis of the C Mark 1K.

Service Transport LTW **Trials** JATE

C Mark 1P

The Mark 1P comprised 25 C Mk 1 aircraft fitted with probes above the cockpit for inflight refuelling (Mod 5308) and the CMA 771 Omega navigation fit (Mod 5309). The first conversion was XV200. At least one aircraft, XV206, was fitted (April 1984) with the Racal Orange Blossom ESM pods under each wing-tip; the aircraft is believed to support special operations. Subsequently aircraft of this version have been fitted with AN/ALQ 157 IR jamming equipment and chaff and flare dispensers.

Service Transport LTW **Training** 242 OCU **Trials** JATE

C Mark 1K

The Mark 1K also originated in the Falklands War with the need for additional tanker aircraft. Six aircraft with the extended internal fuel cells, starting with XV296 (first flight 5 July 1982), were fitted with a single Mk 17B HDU (Mod 5310) and they initially served on the Falklands

Lockheed Hercules C Mk 1

Another great aircraft, the ubiquitous Hercules was nearing the end of its service life with the RAF when the replacement was announced as – the Hercules! Seen in this shot is C Mk 1 XV178 of the Lyneham Wing (whose aircraft are pooled between 24, 30, 47 and 70 sqns) dropping food aid during Operation 'Bushell' in November 1984. In total 3,594 sorties were flown. *(Crown copyright)*

with 1312 Flt. Three C Mk 1Ks were equipped with the Racal Orange Blossom ESM for use in support of a supplementary maritime reconnaissance role in the Falklands.

Service Tanker 1312 Flt, LTW

W Mark 2

The Mark 2 designation was applied to one aircraft, XV208, modified by Marshalls for the Meteorological Research Flight of the RAE. A long instrumented nose boom resulted in the radar scanner being relocated above the cockpit.

Service Research MRF (RAE)

C Mark 3

The Mark 3 is a C Mark 1 conversion with extended fuselage. Starting with XV223, which first flew as such on 10 January 1980, some 30 aircraft were converted. The fuselage was extended by fifteen feet with extensions fore and aft of the wings. The larger aircraft are mainly used on longer routes and for paratrooping but are not ideally suited for rough field performance.

Service Transport LTW **Training** 242 OCU

C Mark 3P

The P variant is the C Mk 3 retro-fitted with in-flight refuelling probe above the cockpit. All 30 aircraft were converted.

Service Transport LTW **Training** 242 OCU

C Mark 4 and C Mark 5

In 1994 the MoD made an interim decision in relation to replacement of its ageing Hercules. Pending the development and production of a European Future Large Aircraft (FLA) an order was placed for the C-130J Hercules II. This was for 25 aircraft with options on a further five and these are due to be delivered in two versions. Some will be stretched C-130J-30 aircraft apparently to be designated C Mk 4 while the balance will be standard fuselage aircraft as the C Mk 5. The first C Mk 4, ZH865 (US serial 93-3026), was rolled out in October 1995 and service entry is delayed into 1998. The main differences include Allison AE 2100 turboprops driving six-bladed propellers, a new cockpit, composite flaps and wing leading edges and no external fuel tanks. There is provision for a refuelling probe.

Specification and production

Mark	Role	Engine	HP	Load lb/men	Range miles	Nos
C1	Transport	4xAllison T-56-A-15	4,910	45,900/92	2,430	66
C1P	Transport	4xAllison T-56-A-15	4,910	45,900/92	2,430	25*
C1K	Tanker	4xAllison T-56-A-15	4,910	10,000	2,430	6+
W2	Research	4xAllison T-56-A-15	4,910	n/a	2,430	1*
C3	Transport	4xAllison T-56-A-15	4,910	45,900/128	2,490	30*

Mark	Role	Engine	HP	Load lb/men	Range miles	Nos
C3P	Transport	4xAllison T-56-A-15	4,910	45,900/92	2,430	30#
C4	Transport	4xAllison AE 2100	6,000	45,000/128	2,400	15~
C5	Transport	4xAllison AE 2100	6,000	45,000/92	2,400	10~

* C1 conversion
\+ C1P conversion
\# C3 conversion
~ Tentative balance of order

Further reading

C-130 Hercules in Action, Drendel, L, Squadron Signal, Carrollton, 1981
C-130 Hercules: Tactical Airlift Missions 1956–1975 McGowan, S, Airlife, Shrewsbury 1988
Hercules: The RAF Workhorse, Muniandy, A, Muniandy, Swindon 1993
Lockheed Hercules, Mason, F K, PSL, Wellingborough, 1984
Lockheed Hercules Production List 1954–1994 (11th Edition) Olausson, L, Olausson, Satenas, 1994

6.20 Westland/Aérospatiale Puma (1971–date)

The Puma was one of the three Anglo-French helicopters involved in the 1968 manufacturing agreement (the others were the Lynx and Gazelle). It was the largest and was intended to fulfil a number of roles including troop transport, casualty evacuation, freighter and even gunship. A sole French-manufactured SA.330, XW241, was supplied and in due course it served as a trials aircraft with the RAE/DRA. The Puma has operated widely with the RAF including Belize, Northern Ireland, the Gulf and Bosnia.

Westland/Aérospatiale Puma HC Mk 1

The versatile medium-lift Puma has been operational with the RAF since 1971 and from 1995 42 of the original fleet of 48 were upgraded with provision for full night operations. XW218/DT of 230 Sqn is seen over German ranges in January 1985. (*Crown copyright*)

HC Mark 1

The Puma entered service with 33 Sqn in June 1971. It carried a crew of two and up to sixteen troops or ten casualties over 390 miles at up to 174mph. In gunship mode two 7.62 GPMG are carried. A total of 48 was built and of these 42 were upgraded in 1995 under operational requirement SR(A)1107. The upgrade included provision for night operations and improved avionics; no new designation was applied.

Service Transport helicopter 18, 33, 230; 1653 Flt **Training** 27(R); 240 OCU **Trials** RAE/DRA

Specification and production

Mark	Role	Engine	HP	Load lb/men	Range miles	Nos
HC1	Heli transport	2xTurmo 111C4	1,320	4,000/16	390	49*

* includes one SA330

6.21 Boeing-Vertol Chinook (1981–date)

The RAF had had a long-standing need for a medium-lift helicopter to replace the Belvedere when the American Boeing-Vertol 114 CH-47 Chinook was ordered in 1978. The version supplied was equivalent to an improved CH-47C with better flight control systems and a triple cargo hook; it also operated at a higher weight limit than the basic type. Thirty-three were ordered and deliveries started with ZA670 which first flew on 23 March 1980.

Boeing-Vertol Chinook HC Mk 1

Some camouflage just doesn't work! Clearly seen in sharp contrast to the background foliage is Chinook ZA670/BN of 18 Sqn in Germany. The Chinook routinely carries 44 troops, although the sole Falklands machine often took considerably more. Eight new Chinooks are on order for Special Forces use. *(Crown copyright)*

Four were sent to the Falklands in 1982 of which three were lost with the sinking of *Atlantic Conveyor*; replacements were ordered together with a supplementary batch of five and the eventual delivery was thus 41. In addition one Argentinian CH-47C was captured and brought to the UK where it has remained in store as ZH257.

HC Mark 1

The Chinook entered service with 240 OCU in January 1981 and subsequently served in the UK, Germany and the Falklands. The first fifteen aircraft had metal rotor blades and the balance composite ones. The crew of four included two pilots and two crewmen but no navigator.

Service Transport helicopter 7, 18, 78; 1310 Flt **Training** 240 OCU

HC Mark 2

The Mark 2 was a major upgrade of the HC Mk 1 to CH-47D standards with new dynamic parts and instruments, improved self-defence, including provision for machine gun mountings and a long-range fuel system. All remaining HC Mk 1 aircraft were due for conversion and this eventually totalled 30 of which one was written off in a crash. The first conversion, ZA718, flew in the UK on 20 May 1993. A further six new aircraft have been ordered.

Service Transport helicopter 7, 18, 78 **Training** 27(R); 240 OCU

HC Mark 3

Eight HC Mk 3 Chinooks were ordered primarily for special services support, the version being the equivalent of the MH-47E. Changes to the earlier versions include provision for night vision goggles, terrain-following radar, advanced ESM and a refuelling probe. Serial range is ZH897-904 and service entry will be in 1998.

Specification and production

Mark	Role	Engine	HP	Load lb/men	Range miles	Nos
HC1	Heli transport	2xT-55-L-11	3,750	22,000/44	215	41
HC2	Heli transport	2xT-55-L-712	4,500	21,000/44	160	37*
HC3	Heli transport	2xT-55-L-712	4,500	22,500/44	300	8

* 31 HC1 conversions, 6 new order

6.22 Lockheed TriStar (1983–date)

Having reduced the tanker and long-range transport fleet, the RAF was in need of a complement to the Victor during the Falklands war. A decision was made to purchase second-hand L-1011-500 TriStars to meet the need. Six ex British Airways and three ex Pan American aircraft were bought and modified by Marshalls to three different configurations. All variants have twin hose drum units mounted under the rear fuselage. Unlike other

RAF strategic transports the TriStar is unique in having forward-facing passenger seats.

K Mark 1

The K variant comprised two ex BA machines which were tanker/passenger configured. In common with the KC Mk 1 a total of 313,300lb of fuel was carried. The Tristar entered RAF service in 1983.

Service **Tanker/transport** 216

KC Mark 1

The KC variant referred to the remaining four ex BA machines which were fitted with larger cargo doors and reinforced floors and designed as tanker/cargo aircraft.

Service **Tanker/transport** 216

C Mark 2

The passenger variant is a long-term interim version pending fitting of the HDUs to two of the ex Pan American aircraft to bring them into the tanker role. It carries 10,000lb less fuel, is not fitted with a refuelling probe and has different avionics. The **C Mark 2A** is similar to the C Mk 2 but with full military avionics fit.

Service **Transport** 216

Specification and production

Mark	Role	Engine	Thrust lb	Load lb/men	Range miles	Nos
K1	Tanker/ passenger	3xRB-211-524	50,000	98,110/204	4,310	2
KC1	Tanker/ cargo	3xRB-211-524	50,000	98,110/196	4,310	4
C2	Transport	3xRB-211-524	50,000	-/267	4,310	2
C2A	Transport	3xRB-211-524	50,000	-/267	4,310	1

Further reading
Lockheed TriStar, Birtles, P, Ian Allan, London

Lockheed TriStar C Mk 2

In the wake of the Falklands campaign which highlighted deficiencies in the tanker force it was decided to purchase second-hand TriStars which were then re-modelled to three configurations. ZE704 of 216 Sqn is actually a passenger variant without in-flight refuelling capability. *(Author)*

7 – Communications

See also: Andover (6.18); Auster (10.1); Balliol (1.12); Bird Dog (10.3); Chipmunk (1.9); Dakota (6.3); Dragonfly (11.10); Gazelle (10.10); Hastings (6.8); Harvard (1.5); Hirondu (10.12); Hoverfly (10.2); Lynx (10.11); Meteor (2.5); Mosquito (3.4); Oxford (1.3); Prentice (1.8); Provost (1.15); Tempest (2.2); Tiger Moth (1.1); Valetta (6.10); Vampire (3.9); Wessex (9.12); Whirlwind (11.11); York (6.4)

Pilatus Britten-Norman Islander AL Mk 1

Although first flying in 1966 and being used by a number of air forces world-wide the Islander (also referred to as the Defender) was slow to enter British service. In 1989 the Army bought the type to replace the Beaver, especially for service in Northern Ireland. Seen in this shot is ZG846 of 1 Flt AAC.

In many respects communications aircraft and units are the poor relations of air forces and in the case of British services this has generally been true. Most aircraft used for liaison and transporting small numbers of people have been conversions or types that have passed their original usefulness and in some cases were 'tired'. Most of the aircraft described in this chapter fitted into this category, although there were exceptions like the highly successful Hawker Siddeley 125.

There is no clear distinction between communications and transport aircraft except at the extremes. As an example the York and Valetta transports were both used in the communications roles while helicopters like the Whirlwind formed the equipment of light transport units. There is of necessity some overlap between aircraft and units featured in the present chapter and those described in Chapter 6.

In preparing the lists of units space has been saved by omitting the station flights, which between them operated vast numbers of aircraft as hacks up to the mid-1950s after which the practice diminished considerably. Many squadrons also had their own hacks, at least for a year or two after the war, and in some cases perhaps semi-officially for some time after. In some instances the types flown would have been those designated as liaison aircraft while many two-seat trainer versions of fighter aircraft were flown in the communications role. It follows, therefore, that many types have been used to enable staff to attend to a multiplicity of duties away from base.

This chapter also needs to be used alongside Chapter 10 on Army types and units. Many Army units assumed a secondary or even primary liaison role from around 1947 and the number of such units developed to an extent where there is no point in duplicating the orders of battle by including them in the present chapter.

January 1946

The distribution of units gives the clearest possible impression of the spread of British military interests some months after the war had ended. Quite apart from station flights each group had its own communications flight usually equipped with some permutation of Proctor, Dominie and Anson. A number of units seem to have justified hanging on to Spitfires, Tempests, Mosquitoes and even in one case a Hurricane for speedy communications including the Air Delivery Letter Service based at Northolt.

In Germany the need for staff transport was such that the groups operated squadrons equipped in many instances with captured enemy aircraft. The practice of using such machines was terminated a few months into 1946 through a combination of spares and maintenance problems and the availability of standard service types. In the Middle East and Far East the distances involved resulted in a number of units being equipped with the Dakota, while in Indo-China the RAF supervised a Task Force of Japanese types flown by Japanese crews until the French regained control.

The Fleet Air Arm operated a number of exotic models including lend-lease types like the Reliant or the Expeditor which was to remain in Naval service until 1955.

January 1950

The Dominie was now largely out of service except with the Fleet Air Arm and the standard communications type was the Anson C Mk 12 or C Mk 19 supplemented by the Proctor. Although groups retained their flights there were now also command level squadrons or flights based close to command headquarters and providing services for staff officers. The King's Flight had re-formed and was equipped with the new Viking airliner and the Metropolitan Communications Squadron was now 31 Sqn which had taken over the mantle from 24 Sqn at Hendon. This unit was responsible for the movement of, among others, politicians hence the varied equipment which included the first Devons. Also based at Hendon was the Antarctic Flight equipped with the Auster AOP Mk 6.

The number of units in Germany and the Middle East had diminished considerably and 2 Group Communications Flight was one of several units which managed to justify retaining Spitfires on charge. In the Far East the only communications unit employed the sole York C Mk 2 fitted with the Hercules engine.

July 1952

Notable changes, through a period of growth, were the addition of fighter types – the Meteor and Vampire – to a number of command communications flights or squadrons and the widespread distribution of the Anson C Mk 20 and C Mk 21. One completely new type, the Valetta, was in use in the Middle and Far East.

January 1955

Trainers like the Balliol, Provost and Chipmunk were in use alongside the reliable Anson and a miscellany of operational types. The Pembroke had entered service with 1417 Flt in the Middle East and the short take-off and landing Pioneer operated in Malaya with 267 Sqn as described below. There were no significant changes in the number, nature and distribution of units except in the Far East. There the 1st Commonwealth Light Liaison Flight had moved from Korea to Japan and Operation 'Firedog' dictated the need for a utility squadron, 267, equipped with five types to support the Army.

January 1960

Again the main changes were in equipment, although the location of units reflected British commitments and troubles abroad. The most significant new types were the helicopters, the Sycamore and Whirlwind, which were in widespread use in Britain and Aden. The Whirlwind equipped the Queen's Flight, although it was not the first rotary-wing type to be involved. The Hoverfly had been used to carry mail between Aberdeen and Balmoral and the Dragonfly had been used in a supporting role from 1954. No 225 Sqn had formed from the Joint Experimental Helicopter Unit as a light troop transport unit. The Heron had replaced the Viking in the Queen's Flight, but for long-distance travel the royal family had to rely on the Comets of Transport Command.

The Twin Pioneer had joined its smaller brother, the Pioneer, in service and was especially valuable in the Middle East where, operating from unprepared strips, it supported the campaigns in Aden and Oman. It also served in Malaya with 209 Sqn. The Fleet Air Arm was using the Sea Prince and Sea Devon in the communications role.

January 1965

There had been structural change with the disbanding of group and command communications flights and the establishment of a geographical structure of squadrons within Transport Command. In fact the units still retained some relationship with the command from which they had originally derived. The Anson remained in service although largely replaced by the Pembroke and Devon. A new addition to the Queen's Flight was the Andover CC Mk 2.

There was relatively little change in the Middle East, but a utility helicopter flight had formed to provide general support for military exercises in Libya. The Canberra served as a high-speed communications aircraft with the Middle and Far East Communications Squadrons. British presence in British Guiana included 1310 Flt with the Whirlwind and Twin Pioneer which also operated in a general utility role. In the Fleet Air Arm the Sea Heron had joined 781 NAS which also included on charge such diverse types as the Tiger Moth and Sea Hawk.

January 1970

The Basset had entered service as a V-bomber crew transport and the Wessex had joined the Queen's Flight as the first helicopter for royal transport. The communications squadrons had been numbered in order to sustain several famous squadrons: Metropolitan became 32, Southern 207, Western 21, Northern 26 and RAF Germany 60 Sqn.

January 1975

The HS125 had joined 32 Sqn in 1971 as a VIP transport and in successive variants it was to serve to the time of writing. The short-lived Basset, which could not achieve its specified performance, was about to be retired and the three types providing fixed-wing support remained the Andover, Devon and Pembroke. A small number of the latter had been re-sparred in 1970 to extend their working lives. Withdrawal from the Far East and Middle East resulted in the need for communications flying being confined to Western Europe.

January 1980

In the UK communications services were centred on Northolt and Lee-on-Solent with 60 Sqn in Germany the sole residual user of the Pembroke. A new light transport aircraft specification, ASR 408, had been issued for eighteen small turboprop twins to be delivered by March 1981 to replace the Devon and Pembroke. The Jetstream or Super King Air were considered but in the event the need was never met.

January 1985

No 32 Sqn now met all UK needs except those of the royal family. In the former unit all models of the HS125 were now in service offering a balance of size, speed, range and comfort while the Queen's Flight had taken on two BAe146 CC Mk 2 aircraft after successful trials with the Mk 1.

January 1990; January 1995

Little had changed to 1990 apart from the re-equipment of 60 Sqn in Germany with the Andover. By 1995, though, force reductions in Germany had resulted in 60 Sqn being disbanded while the Queen's Flight had been absorbed into 32 Sqn at Northolt as an economy measure with the clumsy title '32 (The Royal) Squadron'. Shortly after, the Wessex were replaced by two leased Twin Squirrel helicopters, while the Navy used civil contract Dauphins, perhaps presaging a shift to civil contract for all service and government communications.

7.A   Communications at 1 January 1946

Bomber Command

Type	Unit	Base
Anson XII, Proctor III, IV	1 GCF	Finningley
Dominie II, Oxford II, Anson XII, Proctor III, IV Master II	3 GCF	Snailwell
Anson XII, Proctor III, IV, Tutor I	91 GCF	Abingdon

Fighter Command

Type	Unit	Base
Mosquito VI, Spitfire IX, XVI	11 GCF	Northolt
Auster V, Oxford I, II, Proctor III Spitfire IX, XVI	12 GCF	Hucknall
Dominie II, Spitfire XVI, Anson XII	13 GCF	Dalcross

Coastal Command

Type	Unit	Base
Proctor, Dominie, Oxford	16 GCF	Rochester
Dominie, Anson I, X, XII, Proctor IV, Dakota III	18 GCF	Leuchars, Scatsa
Dominie, Anson XII, Proctor III, Auster V	19 GCF	Roborough
Anson II, XII, Spitfire XI, Oxford	106 GCF	Benson

Transport Command

Type	Unit	Base
Anson, Proctor, York, Dakota	24	Hendon
Mosquito IV, XX, XXV	162	Blackbushe
Coronado I	231	Boucherville (Canada)
Liberator	231	Dorval (Canada)
Anson XII, Proctor III	MCS	Hendon
Dakota	1316 Flt	Croydon
Anson X	1680 Flt	Prestwick
Mosquito XX, Anson X Spitfire XI, Proctor III	ADLS	Northolt, Fuhlsbüttel (B.168)
Dominie, Proctor, Anson I	4 GCF	Full Sutton

Type	Unit	Base
Oxford II, Proctor, Anson XII	38 GCF	Earls Colne
Oxford II	44 GCF	Staverton
Martinet TT1, Hurricane IV, Anson, Proctor III	48 GCF	Tempsford
Spitfire Vb, Argus II Anson I, XII, Proctor	87 GCF	Le Bourget
Anson I, Harvard IIB, Dominie, Mosquito III, VI Spitfire XXII	1 FU	Pershore
Dominie, Mosquito VI, Halifax, Dakota III, Warwick II	16 FU	Dunkeswell

Flying Training Command

Type	Unit	Base
Auster III, Anson X, XII, Master, Martinet	FTCCF	Woodley
Harvard IIb, Oxford, Proctor	21 GCF	Cranwell
Anson I, Oxford, Proctor	22 GCF	Tern Hill
Proctor, Oxford, Harvard IIb, Anson I, XII	23 GCF	South Cerney
Proctor, Anson I, XI shared with 22 GCF	24 GCF	Halton
	25 GCF	Tern Hill
Anson I, Tiger Moth and aircraft from FTCCF	50 GCF	Woodley
Anson I, Tiger Moth Proctor IV	54 GCF	Fair Oaks

Technical Training Command

Type	Unit	Base
Anson I, Oxford II, Dominie, Messenger	TTCCF	Wyton
Anson I, XII, Dominie Proctor, Master	27 GCF	Southrop
Wellington X, Tiger Moth	60 GCF	Wing

Maintenance Command

Type	Unit	Base
Oxford I, Proctor	41 GCF	Andover
Anson XII, Reliant, Proctor	43 GCF	Henlow
Anson I, Tempest II, Auster V, Spitfire XIV	1 FP	White Waltham
Anson I, Harvard IIB, Spitfire XVIII, XXI	2 FP	Aston Down
Anson I, Mosquito VI, Tempest II, Auster V	3 FP	Lichfield
Harvard IIB, Proctor II, Spitfire XVIII, Oxford	4 FP	Hawarden
Anson I, Dominie, Mosquito XVI	5 FP	Silloth

BAFO Germany

Type	Unit	Base
Anson I, XI, Mosquito VI, Dakota IV, Auster V, DC-2, Bf 108, Bu 181, Fi 156, Si 204	BAFO CW	Hannover Langenhagen
Anson XII	ADCS	Gatwick
Anson XI, Spitfire XI, XVI, Dominie	Berlin CF	Gatow

Type	Unit	Base
Auster V, Mosqito VI, Anson I, XII, Spitfire XVI Bu 181, Bf 108, Fi 156	2 GCS	Melsbroek (B.58)
Anson, Proctor, Auster V, Messenger Bf 108, Bu 181, Fi 156, Ju 52/3m	83 GCS	Schleswigland (B.164)
Bu 181, Fi 156, Si 204, SM 82, Spitfire II Anson, Messenger	84 GCS	Celle (B.118)
Anson I, XI, XII, Auster III, IV, Oxford, Mosquito XIII, Spitfire IX	85 GCF	Northolt
Si 204, Ju 52/3m	EASSU	Fuhlsbüttel (B.168)
Fi 156, Anson II	Denmark CS	Copenhagen

MEDME

Type	Unit	Base
Anson XII	MEDME CS	Heliopolis (Egypt)
Proctor III	AHQ Eastern Mediterranean CF	Mariut (Egypt)
Dominie	206 GCF	Heliopolis (Egypt)
Dakota IV, Anson XII Mosquito VI	216 GCF	Heliopolis (Egypt)
Spitfire Vc, Anson XII Proctor III	219 GCF	Mariut (Egypt) Anson I
Vengeance, Warwick	5 FU	Cairo West (Egypt)
Baltimore III, Anson XII, Wellington X	218 GCF	Mason Blanche (Algeria)
Anson, Argus II, Warwick	3 FU	Blida (N Africa)
?	Desert Air Force CF	Campoformido (Italy)
Proctor III, IV, Spitfire IX, Anson XII	205 GCF	Foggia Main (Italy)
Auster V	AHQ Italy CF	Marcianese (Italy)
Expeditor II, Argus II, Anson	4 FU	Capodichino (Italy)
Auster V, Anson XII	HQ RAF Austria CF	Klagenfurt (Austria)
Anson XII	AHQ Malta CF	Hal Far (Malta)
Anson I, Magister	AHQ Levant CF	Lydda, Beirut
Anson XII	HQ British Forces in Aden CF	Khormaksar (Aden)
Dakota, Anson XII Dominie	W Africa TCS	Accra (Gold Coast)

ACSEA

Type	Unit	Base
Dakota III, Expeditor II, Argus II	HQ ACSEA CS	Palam (India)
Harvard IIb, Anson I, Proctor I?	ACSEA Internal Air Service Sqn	Yelahanka (India)
Dakota III, Harvard IIb, Argus II, Thunderbolt II	AHQ Burma CS	Mingaladon (Burma)
Expeditor, Harvard IIb Vengeance, Oxford	1(Indian) GCF	Peshawar (India)
Oxford, Proctor III, Vengeance IV, Anson I	225 GCF	Yelahanka (India)

Type	Unit	Base
Expeditor II, Harvard IIb, Argus II	232 GCF	Mingaladon (Burma)
Auster III, IV, Dakota, Expeditor II	AHQ Malaya CS	Kuala Lumpur
Anson I, Argus, Oxford Vengeance	226 GCF	Chakeri (India)
Expeditor, Anson I Argus, Anson I	227 GCF	Agra (India)
Expeditor, Argus, Harvard, Vengeance	228 GCF	Barrackpore (India)
Expeditor II, Proctor III	229 GCF	Palam (India)
Auster V, Dakota IV	BCAF	Iwakuni (Japan)
Ki-21, Ki-57	'Gremlin' Task Force*	Saigon

* Captured Japanese aircraft flown by Japanese pilots under RAF supervision

Staging posts

Throughout the war numerous staging posts were established to support aircraft in transit. Some retained their own aircraft for ferry tasks well after the end of the war.

Type	Unit	Base
Mustang IV	17 SP	Castel Benito (Libya)
Siebel 204	18 SP	Valkenberg (B.93) (N'lands)
Anson I	19 SP	Gatow (Berlin)
Thunderbolt II, Hurricane IV, Dakota, Spitfire VIII Mustang IV	36 SP	Allahabad (India)
Hurricane IIc, Harvard IIb, Argus	47 SP	Lahore (India)
Expediter II	49 SP	Helen Hill (Marianas)
Expediter II, Mosquito VI, Beaufighter X	59 SP	Palam (India)
Dakota, Argus	61 SP	Campoformido (Italy)
Anson XI, Auster III	103 SP	Istres (France)
Argus II	146 SP	Milan (Italy)
Auster V	160 SP	Wormingford
Thunderbolt I, Tiger Moth	202 SP	Drigh Road (India)

Fleet Air Arm

Type	Unit	Base
Oxford, Tiger Moth II	701	Heston
Oxford I, Tiger Moth II, Dominie, Expediter II, Hudson IV, Firefly I	782	Lee-on-Solent, Eglinton
Anson I, Dakota IV, Expediter II, Oxford, Dominie	X Flt 799	Wünstorf (Germany)
Wellington X, XI	765	Hal Far (Malta)
Expediter II, Anson I	724	Bankstown (Australia)
Baltimore IV, V	Malta CF	Ta Kali (Malta)
Anson I, Reliant I	FP	Culham
Traveller, Sea Otter, Martinet I, Hellcat II, Wildcat VI, Corsair III, IV, Anson I, Barracuda III	5 FP	Stretton
Leopard Moth, Anson I	6 FP	Worthy Down
Anson I, Dominie	5 FS	Donibristle

7.B Communications at 1 January 1950

Bomber Command

Type	Unit	Base
Anson C19	BCCS	Booker
Anson C12, Proctor C3,4	1 GCF	Lindholme
Anson C12, Proctor C3,4	3 GCF	Mildenhall

Fighter Command

Type	Unit	Base
Anson C12	FCCS	Bovingdon
Anson, Proctor C3	12 GCF	Newton

Coastal Command

Type	Unit	Base
Anson C12, 19, Sea Otter, Dominie	RAFNICF	Aldergrove
Anson C12, Dakota C3, Proctor C4	18 GCF	Leuchars
Anson C12, 21, Sea Otter	19 GCF	St Eval

Transport Command

Type	Unit	Base
Viking	King's Flight	Benson
Anson C12, Dakota IV	46 GCF	Abingdon
Anson C21, Oxford 1, Proctor C4	38 GCF	Upavon
Anson C12, 19, Proctor, Spitfire 16, 19, Devon C1	31	Hendon
Spitfire 16, 22, Harvard IIB, Mosquito T3, Dakota IV	OFU	Manston

Flying Training Command

Type	Unit	Base
Anson C19, Harvard IIB, Dakota C4	FTCCF	Woodley
Harvard IIB, Proctor, Anson	21 GCF	Swinderby

Technical Training Command

Type	Unit	Base
Anson C19	TTCCF	Wyton
Anson C12	22 GCF	Tern Hill
Anson C12, Proctor C3	27 GCF	Colerne
Auster AOP6	Antarctic Flt	Hendon

Reserve Command

Type	Unit	Base
Anson C12, 19, Spitfire 16, Harvard IIB	RCCS	White Waltham
Dominie, Harvard IIB, Anson C12, 19	61 GCF	Kenley
Anson C12, 19, Harvard IIB, Auster AOP6	62 GCF	Colerne
Anson C12, 19, Harvard IIB, Oxford II	63 GCF	Hawarden
Anson C12, 19, Harvard IIB, Oxford I	64 GCF	Linton-on-Ouse
Anson C12, 19, Harvard IIB, Oxford II	66 GCF	Turnhouse

Maintenance Command

Type	Unit	Base
Anson C12, 19, Spitfire 16, 22	MCCS	Andover

Type	Unit	Base
Anson C12, Dakota C4	43 GCF	Hucknall
Anson C12, 19, Spitfire 18	2 FP	Aston Down
Anson C19, Spitfire 18	4 FP	Hawarden
Anson I, Dominie	5 FP	Silloth
Hornet F3, Harvard IIB, Tempest F5, 6 Mosquito T3, Spitfire 16, Vampire FB5	1689 FPTF	Aston Down

BAFO Germany

Type	Unit	Base
Anson C12, Dakota C4, Auster AOP5	BAFO CS	Bückeburg
Anson C12, Mosquito FB6, Spitfire 16	2 GCF	Gütersloh
Anson C12, 19, Proctor C3	85 GCF	Ütersen

MEAF

Type	Unit	Base
Dakota C4, Proctor C4	MEAFCF	Ismailia, Kabrit
Anson C19	RAF Deleg Greece CF	Ellenikon
Dominie	Malta CF	Luqa
Anson C19	Iraq CF	Habbaniyah
Anson C19, Proctor C4	EACF	Eastleigh
Anson C19, Auster AOP6	ACF	Khormaksar

FEAF

Type	Unit	Base
York C2, Harvard IIB	FEAF CS	Changi

Fleet Air Arm

Type	Unit	Base
Expediter C2, Sea Otter, Dominie I, Oxford I Seafire F15, Auster AOP1, Firefly FR1 Harvard T2B, Sea Fury F10	781	Lee-on-Solent
Oxford I, Expediter C2, Firefly FR1, 4, Sea Fury FB11 Dominie I	782	Donibristle
Dominie, Firefly AS5	1 FF	Culham
Harvard T2B	2 FF	Stretton
Dominie	3 FF	Anthorn
Seafire F15	4 FF	Arbroath
Dominie, Harvard T2B	FP	Anthorn

7.C   Communications at 1 July 1952

Bomber Command

Type	Unit	Base
Anson C19	BCCS	Booker
Meteor F4, T7, Anson C12	1 GCF	Finningley
Anson C12, 20, 21, Proctor C4	3 GCF	Mildenhall

Fighter Command

Type	Unit	Base
Anson C12, Meteor F8, Vampire FB5	FCCS	Bovingdon
Anson C20, C21, Meteor T7, F8, Vampire FB5	12 GCF	Newton

Coastal Command

Type	Unit	Base
Anson C12, C19, Meteor T7	CCCS	Bovingdon
Anson C12, C21, Proctor C4	18 GCF	Leuchars
Anson C12, C21, Auster AOP6	19 GCF	Roborough

Transport Command

Type	Unit	Base
Viking C2, Valetta C1	King's Flight	Benson
Anson C12, C19, Proctor C4, Devon	31	Hendon
Meteor T7, F8, Valetta T1, Vampire FB5	OFU	Abingdon
Anson C19	2 HFU	Aston Down
Anson C19, Oxford	4 HFU	Hawarden
Meteor T7, Lincoln B2, Anson C12	1689 FPTF	Aston Down

Flying Training Command

Type	Unit	Base
Anson C19, Harvard T2B	FTCCF	Woodley
Anson C19, 20	21 GCF	Swinderby
Anson C20, C21	23 GCF	Cranfield
Meteor T7, Anson C19 Chipmunk T10	25 GCF	Manby

Technical Training Command

Type	Unit	Base
Anson C19, C21, C22	TTCCF	Wyton
Anson C12, C21, Chipmunk T10	22 GCF	Tern Hill

Home Command

Type	Unit	Base
Anson C12, C19	HCCS	White Waltham
Anson C19, C20	61 GCF	Kenley
Anson C20, C21	62 GCF	Colerne
Anson C19, C21, Vampire FB5	63 GCF	Hawarden
Anson C19, C20, C21, Meteor T7, Chipmunk T10	64 GCF	Rufforth
Anson C19, C20, C21	66 GCF	Turnhouse
Anson C19, C20	67 GCF	Aldergrove

Maintenance Command

Type	Unit	Base
Anson C19	MCCF	Andover
Anson C12, Chipmunk T10	43 GCF	Hucknall

BAFO Germany

Type	Unit	Base
Anson C12, Dakota C4, Auster AOP5	BAFO CS	Bückeburg
Anson C12, Mosquito FB6, Spitfire 16	2 GCF	Gütersloh
Anson C12, 19, Dakota C4	High Commissioner's Flt	Wahn

MEAF

AHQ Ismailia

Type	Unit	Base
Dakota C4, Proctor C4	MEAFCF	Ismailia, Kabrit

205 Group

Type	Unit	Base
Anson C12, 19, Valetta C2	Special Comms Sqn	Fayid
Anson C12, 19, Meteor T7	205 GCF	Fayid

AHQ Malta

Type	Unit	Base
Dominie	Malta CF	Ta Kali

AHQ Iraq

Type	Unit	Base
Valetta C1	Iraq CF	Habbaniyah

HQBF Aden

Type	Unit	Base
Anson C19, Dakota C4, Proctor C4	EACF	Eastleigh
Anson C19, Auster AOP6	APSF	Khormaksar

FEAF

Type	Unit	Base
Valetta C1	FEAF CS	Changi

Fleet Air Arm

Type	Unit	Base
Expediter C2, Sea Otter, Dominie I, Oxford I, Firefly FR1, T1, T2, Harvard T2B	781	Lee-on-Solent
Oxford I, Expediter C2, Firefly FR1, T2, FR4, AS6 Domine I	782	Donibristle
Dominie, Harvard T2B	FP	Anthorn

7.D   Communications at 1 January 1955

Bomber Command

Type	Unit	Base
Anson C19,C21	BCCS	Booker
Anson C12, Meteor F4, T7, Canberra T4	1 GCF	Finningley

Type	Unit	Base
Anson C12,C20,C21, Meteor T7, Chipmunk T10	3 GCF	Mildenhall

Fighter Command

Type	Unit	Base
Anson C12,C19, Meteor F8, Vampire FB5	FCCS	Bovingdon
Anson C20, C21, Meteor T7, F8, Vampire FB5	12 GCF	Newton

Coastal Command

Type	Unit	Base
Anson C19, Meteor T7	CCCS	Bovingdon
Anson C12,C21, Proctor C4	18 GCF	Leuchars
Anson C12,C21, Chipmunk T10	19 GCF	Roborough

Transport Command

Type	Unit	Base
Viking C2, Dragonfly	Queen's Flight	Benson
Anson C12,C19, Devon C1, Chipmunk T10	31	Hendon

Flying Training Command

Type	Unit	Base
Anson C19, Chipmunk T10, Balliol T1	FTCCF	White Waltham
Anson C20,C21, Vampire T11	23 GCF	Cranfield

Technical Training Command

Type	Unit	Base
Anson C19,C21,C22, Devon C1	TTCCF	Wyton
Anson C12,C21, Chipmunk T10	22 GCF	Tern Hill
Auster AOP6, T7	Antarctic Flt	Hendon

Home Command

Type	Unit	Base
Anson C12,C19, Balliol T1, Provost T1	HCCS	White Waltham
Anson C19,C20, Balliol T1	61 GCF	Kenley
Anson C20,C21	62 GCF	Middle Wallop
Anson C19,C21, Vampire FB5	63 GCF	Hooton Park
Anson C19,C20,C21, Meteor T7, Chipmunk T10	64 GCF	Linton-on-Ouse
Anson C19,C20,C21	66 GCF	Turnhouse

Maintenance Command

Type	Unit	Base
Anson C19,C21, Devon C1	MCCF	Andover
Anson C12, Vampire FB5, Chipmunk T10	43 GCF	Hucknall
Vampire FB9, Venom FB1	147	Benson
Valetta C1	167	Benson
Anson C19, Venom NF3	173	Hawarden
Anson C19, Meteor FR9, Venom FB1	187	Aston Down

2 TAF Germany

Type	Unit	Base
Anson C19,C21, Valetta C2, Devon C1, Vampire FB5, T11, Prentice	2TAF CS	Wildenrath
Anson C12, Vampire FB5, Meteor T7, FR9	2 GCF	Gütersloh
Anson C12,C19,C21, Vampire FB5, T11	83 GCF	Wahn

MEAF

Type	Unit	Base
Anson C12, Pembroke C1	1417 Flt	Muharraq
Valetta C1, Proctor C4	MEAF CF	Kabrit
Valetta C1, Vampire FB9, Chipmunk T10	Malta CF	Luqa
Pembroke C1, Meteor F8	Levant CF	Nicosia (Cyprus)
Valetta C1,C2, Brigand B1, Vampire FB9	Iraq CF	Habbaniyah (Iraq)
Valetta C1	EACF	Eastleigh (Kenya)
Anson C19, Auster AOP6	APSF	Khormaksar (Aden)

FEAF

Type	Unit	Base
Dakota C4, Auster AOP6, Pioneer CC1, Pembroke C1, Harvard T2B	267	Kuala Lumpur
Valetta C1, Meteor T7, F8	FEAF CS	Changi
Auster AOP6	1st Comm LLF	Iwakuni (Japan)

Fleet Air Arm

Type	Unit	Base
Expediter C2, Dominie I, Firefly T2, Sea Fury FB11, Sea Vampire T22, Sea Balliol T21	781	Lee-on-Solent
Dominie,	NCS (Airwork)	Donibristle
Dominie	SFF	Rochester

7.E Communications at 1 January 1960

Bomber Command

Type	Unit	Base
Anson C19,C21, Pembroke C1, Chipmunk T10, Meteor T7	BCCF	Booker
Canberra T4, Meteor T7, Chipmunk T10	1 GCF	Finningley
Meteor T7, Chipmunk T10	3 GCF	Mildenhall

Fighter Command

Type	Unit	Base
Anson C12,C19, Meteor F8, Varsity T1	FCCS	Bovingdon
Anson C21, Meteor T7,F8, Chipmunk T10	11 GCF	Leconfield
Anson C21, Meteor T7, F8, NF14, Chipmunk T10	12 GCF	Horsham St Faith

Coastal Command

Type	Unit	Base
Anson C19, Meteor T7, Valetta C2	CCCS	Bovingdon
Anson C21, Dakota C4	18 GCF	Turnhouse

Transport Command

Type	Unit	Base
Anson C19,C21, Devon C1, Chipmunk T10, Sycamore HR14	TCCF	Upavon
Devon C1, Pembroke C1, Valetta C2, Sycamore HR14	MCS	Northolt
Anson C21, Devon C1, Chipmunk T10	38 GCF	Odiham
Heron CC3, Whirlwind HCC8	Queen's Flight	Benson
Sycamore HC14, Whirlwind HC2,HC4	225	Odiham

Flying Training Command

Type	Unit	Base
Anson C20,C21, Chipmunk T10, Pembroke C1	FTCCF	White Waltham
Anson C20, C21, Provost T1	23 GCF	Dishforth

Technical Training Command

Type	Unit	Base
Anson C21, 22, Devon C1, Chipmunk T10	TTCCF	Wyton
Anson C12, 21, Chipmunk T10	22 GCF	Stoke Heath
Anson C12	24 GCF	Colerne

Maintenance Command

Type	Unit	Base
Anson C19, 21, Chipmunk T10, Devon C1	MCCF	Andover
Anson	FS	Benson

RAF Germany

Type	Unit	Base
Pembroke C1, Meteor T7	RAFG CS	Wildenrath

MEAF

Type	Unit	Base
Twin Pioneer CC1, Wessex HC2	78	Khormaksar (Aden)
Pembroke C1, Twin Pioneer CC2	152	Muharraq
Twin Pioneer CC1	21	Eastleigh (Kenya)
Canberra T4, Valetta C2, Hastings C1	MECS	Khormaksar
Sycamore HC14, Whirlwind HC2	Aden Heli Flt	Khormaksar
Devon C1, Meteor F8, Valetta C2	CCF	Ta Kali (Malta)

FEAF

Type	Unit	Base
Pioneer CC1, Twin Pioneer CC1	209	Seletar
Meteor T7,F8, Canberra T4, Valetta C1, C3	FECS	Changi
Meteor F8, Pembroke C1	224 GCF	Seletar

Fleet Air Arm

Type	Unit	Base
Sea Vampire T22, Sea Devon C20, Sea Prince C1,C2, Whirlwind HAS22	781	Lee-on-Solent
Sea Prince T1	SFF	Rochester

7.F Communications at 1 January 1965

Transport Command

Type	Unit	Base
Pembroke C1, Devon C1, Sycamore HR14	MCS	Northolt
Anson C19,C21	SCS	Bovingdon
Anson C19	NCS	Wyton
Pembroke C1	WCS	Andover

Type	Unit	Base
Heron CC2,CC3, Whirlwind HCC8, 12, Andover CC2	QF	Benson

RAF Germany

Type	Unit	Base
Pembroke C1	RAFG CS	Wildenrath

MEAF

Type	Unit	Base
Twin Pioneer CC1	21	Eastleigh (Kenya)
Pembroke C1, Twin Pioneer CC1, CC2	152	Muharraq

Type	Unit	Base
Canberra T4, Valetta C2, Hastings C1	MECS	Khormaksar (Aden)
Devon C1, Meteor F8, Valetta C2	CCF	Ta Kali (Malta)
Sycamore HC14, Whirlwind HC10	1564 Flt	El Adem (Libya)

FEAF

Type	Unit	Base
Meteor T7,F8, Canberra T4, Valetta C1, C3	FECS	Changi (Malaya)
Pioneer CC1, Twin Pioneer CC1	209	Seletar (Malaya)

Caribbean

Type	Unit	Base
Whirlwind HC10, Twin Pioneer CC2	1310 Flt	Atkinson Field (Br Guiana)

Fleet Air Arm

Type	Unit	Base
Sea Devon C20, Sea Heron C20, Sea Prince C1, Sea Hawk FGA6, Whirlwind HAS22, Tiger Moth T1	781	Lee-on-Solent

7.G Communications at 1 January 1970

Air Support Command

Type	Unit	Base
Pembroke C1, Sycamore HR14, Basset CC1, Andover CC2	32	Northolt
Basset CC1, Pembroke C1, Devon C2	207	Northolt
Basset CC1, Devon C2	26	Wyton
Pembroke C1, Devon C2	21	Andover
Andover CC2, Wessex HCC4, Basset CC1	QF	Benson

RAF Germany

Type	Unit	Base
Pembroke C1, Heron C4	60	Wildenrath

MEAF

Type	Unit	Base
Canberra T4, Valetta C2, Hastings C1	MECS	Khormaksar

Type	Unit	Base
Devon C1, Meteor F8, Valetta C2	CCF	Ta Kali (Malta)

FEAF

Type	Unit	Base
Meteor T7, F8, Canberra T4, Valetta C1, 3	FECS	Changi

Fleet Air Arm

Type	Unit	Base
Sea Devon C20, Sea Heron C20, Heron C4, Wessex HU5, Whirlwind HAS22, Tiger Moth T1	781	Lee-on-Solent

7.H Communications at 1 January 1975

Support Command

Type	Unit	Base
Andover CC2, HS125 CC1, 2, Whirlwind HCC12	32	Northolt
Pembroke C1, Devon C2	207	Northolt
Basset CC1, Devon C2	26	Wyton
Pembroke C1, Devon C2	21	Andover
Andover CC2, Wessex HCC4	QF	Benson

RAF Germany

Type	Unit	Base
Pembroke C1, Andover CC2	60	Wildenrath

Fleet Air Arm

Type	Unit	Base
Sea Devon C20, Sea Heron C20, Heron CC4, Wessex HU5, Chipmunk T10	781	Lee-on-Solent

7.I Communications at 1 January 1980

Support Command

Type	Unit	Base
Andover C1, CC2, HS125 CC1, 2, Gazelle HCC4	32	Northolt
Devon C2	207	Northolt det Turnhouse
Andover CC2, Wessex HCC4	QF	Benson

RAF Germany

Type	Unit	Base
Pembroke C1	60	Wildenrath

Fleet Air Arm

Type	Unit	Base
Sea Devon C20, Sea Heron C20, Heron CC4, Wessex HU5, Chipmunk T10	781	Lee-on-Solent

7.J Communications at 1 January 1985

Strike Command (1 Group)

Type	Unit	Base
Andover C1, CC2, HS125 CC1, 2, 3,	32	Northolt
Gazelle HT3, HCC4 Andover CC2, BAe 146 CC2, Wessex HCC4	QF	Benson

RAF Germany

Type	Unit	Base
Pembroke C1	60	Wildenrath

7.K Communications at 1 January 1990

Strike Command (1 Group)

Type	Unit	Base
Andover C1,CC2, HS125 CC1, CC2, CC3, Gazelle HT3,HCC4	32	Northolt
Andover CC2, BAe 146 CC2, Wessex HCC4	QF	Benson

RAF Germany

Type	Unit	Base
Andover C1, CC2	60	Wildenrath

7.L Communications at 1 January 1995

Strike Command (38 Group)

Type	Unit	Base
HS125 CC2, BAe 125 CC3, BAe 146 CC2 Gazelle HT3, HCC4, Wessex HCC4	32	Northolt

7.1 Avro Tutor (1933–1946)

Mark I
The Avro 621 Tutor was built as a trainer to specification 18/31 and 394 were built. In its original role it was out of service by the beginning of the war but it soldiered on as a hack, with one example still in service at 1946.

Service Communications 91 GCF

Specification and production

Mark	Role	Engine	HP	Speed mph	Crew/passengers	Nos
I	Trainer	Lynx IVC	240	122	1/1	394

Avro Tutor Mk I

The Tutor started life as a trainer before the war and a sole example appears to have operated as a general runabout for 91 Group Communications Flight in 1946. K3215 is a preserved example with the Shuttleworth Trust. *(MAP)*

7.2 Avro Anson (1936–1962)

The Anson originated as the Avro 652 six-seat commercial aircraft. In 1934 Avro tendered a design for a coastal reconnaissance aircraft and specification 18/35 was issued to cover an initial purchase; the prototype, K4771, had flown on 24 March 1935. The Type 652A Anson entered service with 48 Sqn at Manston in March 1936. Although built for reconnaissance the Anson served extensively as a trainer and in the communications role.

Mark I/C Mark 1
The first variant was powered by two Cheetah IX engines and was characterised by extensive continuous glazing extending back along the fuselage from the cockpit. For self-defence the Anson was fitted with a mid upper gun turret with one .303in machine-gun; a second gun was fixed forward. By the end of the war the Anson was confined to communications and training pilots, navigators, wireless and radar operators and gunners. Some had their turrets removed.

Service (post-1945) Training ACS; 1, 2, 7, 10 ANS; 1, 2 BANS; BAS; CFS; EANS; ERS; 4, 5 FTS; 2 OAPU; 240 OCU; 13, 16, 54 OTU; 21 (P)AFU; 3, 12, 17, 18 RFS; 14

RS; SATC; SFC; SGR; 1, 2 SGR; SP: 720, 735, 750, 766, 783, 784, 791 NAS; RNASS **Communications** AHQInCF; BAFOCF; CSE; EACF; 1, 2, 3, 5 FP; 1 FP (ATA); FTCCS; 1 FU; 2, 18, 25, 61, 62, 63, 64, 66, 83, 84, 85, 87, 225 GCF; Iraq & Persia, Levant CF; MCCS; MCS; RAE Defford; RWE; SFU; TTCCF; VISTRE; Aldergrove, Bircham Newton, Church Fenton, Halton, Heston, Honiley, Hooton Park, Kenley, Kinloss, Lagens, Northolt, Sealand, Ternhill, Thornaby, Thorney Island, Watchfield SF: 771 NAS; Anthorn, Belfast (Sydenham), Bramcote, Brawdy, Crail, Culdrose, Culham, Dale, Ford, Gosport, Lee-on-Solent, Lossiemouth, St Merryn, Stretton SF.

The Marks II, III, IV, V and VI were all Canadian-built trainers, while Marks VII, VIII and IX were reserved for Canadian variants but not taken up.

Mark X/C Mark 10
The Mark X was considered an interim model for light transport duties. The prototype was NK753. It had a strengthened floor and weight increased accordingly. The series I retained the Cheetah IX engine while the series II employed the Cheetah XIX and a hydraulically operated undercarriage.

Service (post-1945) Communications 84 GCF; MCCS

Mark XI/C Mark 11
This mark also had smooth-cowled Cheetah XIXs, hydraulically operated undercarriage and flaps and a higher roof with greater headroom. Three square windows replaced the 'glasshouse'. It was built to OR.141 calling for a light ambulance aircraft for use after D-Day. Like the Mark X it was used widely for transport and communications work.

Service (post-1945) Communications 58; BAFOCF/W; CBE; CSE; 106 GCF; 103 SP RAF Mission Denmark; Benson, Dishforth, Gatow, Northolt SF.

Mark XII/C Mark 12
The Mark 12 was similar to the Mark XI but with more powerful Cheetah XV engines fitted with spinners. Prototype was NL152 which flew on 5 September 1944; some Mark 1 aircraft were converted to this standard.

Avro Anson C Mk 19

The pre-war Anson served extensively as a trainer and communications 'hack' until 1968. C Mk 19 VL339 belonged to the Aden Communications Flight and it is seen at Khormaksar in 1955 *(A S Thomas collection)*

Service (post-1945) Training CFS; CNCS; EFS; HCEU; 231 OCU **Communications** 31, 173; 2 TAFCF/S; ASWDU; Austria CF; BAFOCF/W; CCCS; EACF; FCCS; 1, 2, 3, 12, 18, 19, 22, 61, 62, 63, 64, 66, 67, 81, 83, 84, 85, 87, 106, 205, 216 GCF; HCCS; MCCS; MCS; MECS; MEDMECS; RAF deleg France CF; RAF mission NZ; RAFNICF; RCCF; TCCS; TCEU; WACS; Abingdon, Acklington, Akrotiri, Aston Down, Ballykelly, Benson, Church Fenton, Colerne, Coningsby, Finningley, Gatow, Gibraltar, Halton, Hemswell, Jurby, Leconfield, Marham, North Coates, Ramat David, St Eval, Schwechat, Spitalgate, Sylt, Turnhouse, Wattisham, West Malling, Wyton SF.

The Marks XIII, XIV, XV and XVI were all intended specialised trainers while the designation XVII was never allocated and the Mark 18 was a modified Mark 19 sold to Afghanistan.

Mark XIX/C Mark 19

Based on the post-war Avro 19 which accounts for the jump in type number. It was similar to the Mark XII but with superior internal fittings, five oval windows and a lowered port side entry door with window. The series I employed wooden wings and tailplanes while the series II had metal planes. Some earlier aircraft were brought up to series II standards.

Service Training 1 ASS; CFS; CNCS; 236 OCU; 1, 4 RS **Communications** 31, 58, 116, 173, 187, 202, 216, 224, 228, 527; 1315, 1417 Flt; 2 ATAFCS; ACF/S; ACSEACS; AHQInCF; AHQItCF; AHQMCF; APSF; BAFOCF/W; BCCF/S; BTU; 1 CAACU; CCCS; CSE; EACF; FCCS; FECS; 2, 4 FP; FTCCS; 1, 2, 3, 11, 12, 13, 18, 19, 21, 22, 23, 24, 25, 27, 38, 43, 47, 61, 63, 64, 66, 67, 81, 83, 84, 85, 205 GCF; HCCS; 2, 4 (H)FU; JASS; LRWE Woomera; MCCS; MCS; MECS; MEDMECS; NCS; 230, 231, 240, 241 OCU; RAE Bedford, Llanbedr; RAFC; RAF deleg France CF; RAF deleg Greece CF; RAFNICF; RATG; RCCF; RWE; SCS; SLAW; TCCS; TCDU; TRE; TTCCF; WCS; Abingdon, Acklington, Aldergrove, Amman, Andover, Bahrein, Ballykelly, Bassingbourn, Benson, Bovingdon, Church Fenton, Colerne, Coningsby, Cottesmore, Dishforth, Eastleigh, El Adem, Fayid, Finningley, Gaydon, Gibraltar, Gütersloh, Habbaniyah, Halton, Hassani, Hemswell, Hendon, Henlow, Honington, Hornchurch, Ismailia, Jever, Kabrit, Khartoum, Kinloss, Kuala Lumpur, Laarbruch, Leconfield, Leuchars, Lyneham, Manston, Marham, Negombo, Nicosia, North Coates, Old Sarum, St Eval, St Mawgan, Scampton, Schwechat, Shaibah, Spitalgate, Sylt, Turnhouse, Upavon, Waddington, West Raynham, Wittering, Wyton SF.

T Mark 20

The Mark 20 was a specialised navigation trainer built to specification T.24/46. It was tropicalised for use in Southern Rhodesia, had a transparent nose and was fitted to carry sixteen 8.5lb practice bombs. Many returned to the United Kingdom.

Service Training 201 AFS; 2, 3, 5, 6 ANS; CFS; 4, 5 FTS; HCEU; 1 ITS **Communications** AMSDU; ECFS; FCCF; FCU Benson; FTCCF; 3, 5, 12, 23, 25, 61, 62, 64, 66, 67 GCF; 226, 231 OCU; RATGCF; 2 TAFCS; Bassingbourn, Merryfield, Duxford, Stradishall, Tangmere, Turnhouse, West Raynham SF

T Mark 21

The Mark 21 was ordered to specification T.25/46 also as a navigation trainer, but for use in the United Kingdom.

Service Training 1, 2, 3, 5, 6 ANS; 2 ASS; 1, 2 BANS; 1 BNS; CFS; CNCS; CNS; EANS; 1 ITS; RAFC; RAFFC; 1, 2, 5, 6, 7, 8, 9, 10, 11, 12, 13, 14, 15, 16, 17, 18, 19, 22, 23, 24, 25 RFS; SATC **Communications** 42, 206, 220, 228, 275, 288; AAEE; AAFCE; AIEU; AWOCU; BCCS; 1, 2, 3/4, 5 CAACU; CCCF/S; 1, 2 CFCCU; CFE; ETPS; FCCS; FTCCF; 2 FTS; 3, 12, 13, 18, 21, 22, 23, 25, 38, 61, 62, 63, 64, 67, 83 GCF; HCCS; JCC; LAS; MCCS; MCS; OCTU; 229 OCU; RAE Bedford, Llanbedr; SCS; SFC; SLAW; 2 TAFCS; TCCF/S; TTCCF; Birmingham, Cambridge, Durham, Glasgow, Manchester, Queen's UAS; Aldergrove, Ballykelly, Benson, Biggin Hill, Binbrook, Booker, Chatham, Church Fenton, Cluntoe, Colerne, Coltishall, Cottesmore, Driffield, Duxford, Gaydon, Hemswell, Hornchurch, Horsham St Faith, Laarbruch, Leconfield, Leuchars, Linton-on-Ouse, Marham, Middleton St George, North Coates, North Weald, Odiham, Old Sarum, St Eval, Scampton, Stradishall, Tangmere, Thorney Island, Upwood, Waddington, Waterbeach, Wattisham, West Malling, Weston Zoyland, Wittering, Wymeswold, Wyton SF.

C Mark 21

This variant was a simple conversion of the T Mark 21 with training equipment removed and nine seats installed.

Service Communications 31; AAEE; BCCF/S; EEC; FCCF; FTCCS; 2, 3, 11, 13, 12, 18, 19, 61 GCF; HCCS; MCCS; MCS; RAE; 2 TAFCS; TCCS; Colerne, Finningley, Gütersloh, Lindholme, Mildenhall, Wyton SF.

T Mark 22

The ultimate variant was a radio trainer built to specification T.26/46. In all significant respects it was similar to the T Mark 21.

Service Training 1 AES; 1, 2 ASS; ERS; 229, 231 OCU; 11 RFS; 1, 2, 4, 6 RS; RAFFC; RAFTC **Communications** BCCF; FTCCS; 62, 81 GCF; HCCS; Bassingbourn, Colerne SF.

Specification and production

Mark	Role	Engine	HP	Crew/ passengers	Speed mph	Nos
I	Trainer	2xCheetah IX or 2xCheetah XIX	335 395	2/9	188	6,870
X	Comms	2xCheetah IX or 2xCheetah XIX	350 395	2/9	175	103
XI	Comms	2xCheetah XIX	395	2/9	185	90
XII	Comms	2xCheetah XV	425	2/9	190	246
C19	Comms	2xCheetah XV	425	2/9	190	264
T20	Trainer	2xCheetah XV	425	3/3	171	59
T21	Trainer	2xCheetah XV	425	3/3	171	252
C21	Comms	2xCheetah XV	425	2/9	171	*
T22	Trainer	2xCheetah XV	425	3/3	171	54

* Unknown number of T21 conversions

Further reading
Anson File, The, Sturtivant, R, Air Britain, Tonbridge, 1988

7.3 de Havilland Dominie (1938–1963)

The highly successful and graceful de Havilland 89 Dragon Rapide twin-engined biplane passenger aircraft was widely used throughout the UK by the outbreak of war. It was originally proposed to the RAF to meet specification G.18/35 for a coastal reconnaissance type, but the need was met by the Anson. After one was evaluated by the A&AEE and then passed on to the Metropolitan Communications Squadron (24 Sqn) the RAF ordered a number of radio trainers against specification T.29/38 for delivery in 1939. These were designated Mark I. Soon after the outbreak of war a number of civil aircraft was requisitioned for use in the communications role for use by the National Air Communications organisation. Finally, a large order was placed for the standard aircraft for use as communications aircraft which became the Mark II. The name Dominie was not applied until 1941.

The differences between the variants were marginal and many of the earlier version were converted for light transport use, not necessarily with a change of number. There is some confusion about the total production, especially given the number of impressed aircraft and those built towards the end of the war and made available for immediate civilian acquisition. Furthermore, it is impossible to be clear in all cases which versions served with which units.

Mark I
As mentioned above the DH89B Mk I was ordered to T.29/38 as a radio trainer. It was distinguished by a d/f loop above the forward fuselage and seated five students, and instructor and pilot. It was 300lb heavier than the passenger variant.

Service (post-1945) Training 1, 2, 4 RS; 2, 4 SS: 799 NAS

Mark II
The DH89A Mk II comprised a number of the passenger aircraft either impressed, built as such for the armed services or converted from the Mark I. Remarkably the type remained in service (with the Royal Navy) until 1963. In the communications role the Dominie carried up to ten passengers.

Service (post-1945) Communications 271, 527; 1680 Flt; ATDU; CCCF; CSE; 21 EFTS; FCCF; 1, 12, 16 FU; 3, 4, 13, 15, 16, 18, 19, 21, 22, 23, 25, 27, 61, 62, 63, 64, 66, 85, 87 GCF; MCS; NGTE; 56, 58, 61 OTU; 1 PGTS; RAE; RAFNICF; RCCS; RWE; SCCF; SHAEFCF; SLAW; TTCCF; WACS; Alconbury, Church Fenton, Exeter, Grimsetter, Halton, Hawarden, Leuchars, Old Sarum, Pershore, Prestwick, Redhill, St Eval, St Mawgan, Sealand, Staverton, Valley, Yatesbury SFs: 700, 701, 703, 739, 744, 767, 778, 781, 782, 790, 799, 1832, 1844 NAS; Abbotsinch, Anthorn, Arbroath, Bramcote, Brawdy, Crail, Culdrose, Culham, Donibristle, Evanton, Ford, Gosport, Lee-on-Solent, Lossiemouth, Machrihanish, Stretton, Yeovilton SFs

Specification and production

Mark	Role	Engine	HP	Speed mph	Crew/ passengers	Nos
I/T1	Trainer	2xGipsy Queen	200	157	1/6	
II/C2	Comms	2xGipsy Queen	200	157	1/10	508*

* both marks

7.4 Percival Proctor (1940–1955)

The Proctor was a development of the Percival Vega Gull, fifteen of which had been bought by the RAF for communications duties before the war. The new type was built to specification 20/38 as a three-seat communications and training aircraft.

The Mark I (P 28) was a dual control aircraft, the prototype of which, P5998, flew on 8 October 1939; 190 were built but it was out of service by 1946. The Mark II (P 30) was externally similar to the Mark I but it was built as a radio trainer and although some were converted to

de Havilland Dominie Mk II

The delicate Dominie was the military version of the civil Dragon Rapide and remarkably it remained in service with the Royal Navy until 1963. The example shown is actually a preserved aircraft G-AGTM painted as NF875/603CH of 1 Ferry Flight at NAS Culham. *(Author)*

Percival Proctor C Mk 4

The Proctor succeeded the Vega Gull which had been bought for communications pre-war. Many were originally built for training and later converted as three-seat transports. NP193/3V-D served with Bomber Command's 1 Group Communications Flight. *(MAP)*

Mark III standard, this variant also was out of service soon after the war's end.

Mark III
The P 34 was also a radio trainer but with the radio equipment re-distributed internally on a cradle alongside the pilot and a crew of just two.

Service (post-1945) Training ERS; 1, 2, 3 RS **Communications** AHQ EMCF; 1, 3, 12, 19, 48, 91 GCF; MCS

Mark IV
The P 31 was a revised design radio trainer built to specification T.9/41 with a longer and deeper fuselage accommodating four. It also had a large window behind the cabin. The prototype was LA586 which flew in 1943. Of the 256 built many were converted to dual control as communications aircraft, a role in which they served for many years.

Service (post-1945) Training 1 ASS; 1 ITS; 1 OATS; 2, 4 RS **Communications** 24, 31; CGS; CNS; EAAS; EACF; 18 EFTS; FCCS; 16 FU; 1, 2, 3, 12, 16, 18, 21, 25, 46, 54, 83, 205 GCF; HCCS; MCCS; MCS; RCCS; 2 TAF CW; TTCCF; Benina, Debden, Ismailia, Locking, Northolt, St Athan SF

Mark V
The P 31 was essentially a civil version of the Mark IV. Four were bought after the war for communications duties with air attachés in Europe.

Service Communications AA Brussels, Hague, Rome

Specification and production

Mark	Role	Engine	HP	Speed mph	Crew/ passengers	Nos
I	Comms	Gipsy Queen II	210	160	1/2	190
II	Trainer	Gipsy Queen II	210	160	1/2	54
III	Trainer/ Comms	Gipsy Queen II	210	160	1/1	192*+
IV	Trainer/ Comms	Gipsy Queen II	210	157	1/3	256+
V	Comms	Gipsy Queen II	210	160	1/2	4

* includes 16 Mk II conversions
+ many converted for communications

7.5 Lend-lease aircraft (1943–1955)

A very large number and variety of American aircraft was made available to supplement indigenous types from before the United States entered the war. They were supplied under an ingenious scheme whereby the equipment was provided on a temporary basis for return at the war's end. With peace most were soon either scrapped, passed on to other air forces or returned to the US.

Fairchild Argus
The Argus was an adaptation of the 1932 Model 24 supplied to the RAF as a light military transport. The

Fairchild Argus Mk II

Several of the 832 Argus utilities supplied under lend-lease were still in service in 1946. Mk II FZ782 is pictured at Istres in early 1946. Behind it is a Dakota of 1333 TCU coded CM and in the background is a Baltimore. *(Author's collection)*

Mark I (Model 24W-41; USAAF C-61A Forwarder) was powered by a Super Scarab radial engine of 145hp. Like the Model 24R Mark III (in-line 200hp Ranger; USAAF UC-61K) it was out of service by 1946. The **Mark II** (Model 24W-41A) equated to the USAAF UC-61A four-seat utility aircraft. Several remained in service early in 1946.

Service (post-1945) Communications 216, 680; MECS; 47, 61, 146 SP

Stinson Reliant
The Stinson V-77 was the AT-19 in US service and under lend-lease served mainly with the Royal Navy. The **Mark I** was a 4/5-seat transport, the Mark II a navigation trainer, the Mark III observation and survey and the Mark IV a light freighter. After the war some Mark I aircraft remained in service for a few months as a general hack.

Service (post-1945) Communications 700; Belfast, Culham SF

Beech Traveller
The Beech D-17S was used by the USN as the GB-1 and US Army as the UC-43; 105 were supplied mainly for the

Stinson Reliant Mk I

The Reliant served mainly with the Royal Navy and several escaped the lend-lease return requirement into 1946. The example seen here is coded 63. *(MAP)*

Royal Navy and several remained in service at the beginning of 1946.

Service (post-1945) Communications Stretton Ferry Pool

Beech Expediter

The Beech B-18S was a twin-engined light transport supplied in large numbers to the RAF and Royal Navy during the war. The Mark I equated to the US C-45B/JRB-3 and was out of service by 1946. The **Mark II** was the C-45F/JRB-4 with a changed interior and seats for seven passengers resulting in a slightly longer nose; it remained in service with 781 NAS until 1955.

Service (post-1945) Communications 49, 59, SP: 781, 782; Hal Far, Ronaldsay, Trincomalee, Yeovilton SF

Beech Expediter Mk II

Another lend-lease type was the Beech 18 Expediter of which 430 were supplied, mainly for use in the Far East. Unlike most aircraft supplied from the US in this way a number of Expediters remained in service with the Fleet Air Arm until 1955. HB245 was from Air Forces South East Asia Communications Squadron but it is seen here at Tunisia in 1946. *(A S Thomas collection)*

Consolidated Coronado

The Coronado was built as a patrol bomber in which guise ten were supplied under lend-lease for possible Coastal Command use. In the event they went to Transport Command eventually being used for long-range communications work. The **Mark I** (Model 29) was a four-engined flying boat known as the PB2Y-3 in USN service. They were in use with 231 Sqn between Canada and Bermuda but by early 1946 they were withdrawn from service.

Service (post-1945) Communications 231

Stinson Sentinel

A relatively small number of the Stinson Model 76 was supplied to the RAF for ambulance and related duties in Burma. The Mark I was equivalent to the USAAF L-5 and seated two in tandem; of limited value it served in the liaison role but was out of service by 1946. The **Mark II** (Model 76) was similar to the L-5B and was fitted with a large hatch behind the fuselage door to accommodate a stretcher case. Several remained in service for a few months into 1946.

Service (post-1945) Ambulance 27

Specification and production

Mark	Role	Engine	HP	Speed mph	Crew/ passengers	Nos
Argus I	Comms	S Scarab	145	108	1/3	118
Argus II	Comms	S Scarab	165	108	1/3	407
Argus III	Comms	Ranger L-440	200	112	1/3	307
Reliant I	Comms	R-680-13	290	141	1/4	500
Traveller	Comms	R-985	450	195	1/3	105
Expediter	Comms	2xR-985	450	225	2/7	430
Coronado I	Comms	4xR-1830-88	1,200	200	5/44	10
Sentinel I	Liaison	Lycoming O-435	185	129	1/1	40
Sentinel II	Liaison	Lycoming O-435	185	129	1/1	60

7.6 Miles Messenger (1943–1947)

Mark I

The Miles M38 was based on the unsuccessful Miles M28 design. It was a low-wing single-engined monoplane with three fins and fixed undercarriage. A small number was ordered for communications duties against specification 17/43 and the prototype, RG327, flew on 12 September 1942. They served for several years post-war.

Service (post-1945) Communications BAFO CW; BCCF; 21 EFTS; 47, 48, 83, 84 GCS; RAE; TTCCF

Specification and production

Mark	Role	Engine	HP	Speed mph	Crew/ passengers	Nos
I	Comms	Gipsy Major	140	115	1/3	23

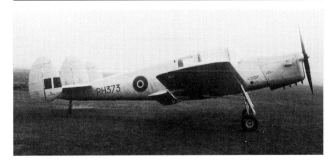

Miles Messenger

A small number of the four-seat Messenger was bought, one of which became famous as Field Marshal Montgomery's personal transport. RH373 in bare metal finish operated with 84 GCS; the keen-eyed may notice the unusual style of the '3's in the serial presentation. *(Crown copyright via P H T Green)*

7.7 Bristol Buckingham (1945–1946)

The Type 163 Buckingham had a complex gestation initially as a bomber built to an updated specification

Bristol Buckingham Mk I

The Buckingham started life as a bomber, was eclipsed by the Mosquito in the role, then converted on the production line to the Buckmaster trainer, but with some aircraft produced as a four-seat transport. DX255 is an early production aircraft seen here in bomber configuration. *(MAP)*

B.2/41 as a twin-engined torpedo bomber. In the event the Mosquito went into service with Coastal Command. The prototype, DX249, flew on 4 February 1943 but in August that year a start was made to convert some production aircraft on the line to the trainer Buckmaster. It was still intended to produce a much smaller number of Buckingham bombers for use in the Middle East, but after 54 had been produced as bombers, the remainder of the order of 119 was produced as a four-seat transport.

Mark I

The Buckingham was intended as a fast but small transport primarily to cut losses in developing the bomber type

which did not – and probably could not – meet service needs as such. In the event only several of the 65 produced saw any service.

Service (post-1945) Communications MEDMECS; TCDU **Trials** ATDU; RAE

Specification and production

Mark	Role	Engine	HP	Speed mph	Crew/ passengers	Nos
I	Transport	2xCentaurus VII	2,520	330	3/4	65

7.8 Captured enemy aircraft (1939–1946)

Throughout the war German, Italian and Japanese aircraft had been captured and evaluated and in some cases impressed into service locally, especially in the Western Desert. At the end of the war a large number of enemy aircraft became available and for a short period were used in the communications role in Germany. Although the numbers given British serials is known it is not clear how many actually flew in service. In addition, in Indo-China the 'Gremlin' Task Force operated Japanese aircraft flown by Japanese pilots under RAF supervision until April 1946 when the French assumed responsibility in the theatre.

The use of captured aircraft stopped in April 1946 when serviceability, although not a serious problem, was such

Fieseler Fi 156C Storch

Among a number of captured types operated by the RAF post-war the Storch was the longest-lived. This example was captured at Flensburg, allocated the Air Ministry number AM101 and flown to Farnborough where it was given the serial VP546 and used for a range of purposes until about 1953. The wing slots and flaps of the STOL aircraft are clear in this view. *(A S Thomas collection)*

that it became more cost-effective to use Allied types for which there were large and accessible spares holdings. The exceptions were in respect of gliders and sailplanes (Chapter 12.10), which continued in service use for many years, and the Ju 52/3m, many of which were placed on the civil register. The large number of captured types flown by the RAE or other research and development establishments are not listed in this book except those still in use after 1945 (Chapter 12.1, 12.5, 12.8). The following types are those known to have been in significant use; it is possible that odd examples of other types were in 'informal' use by British services around the globe.

Bucker Bu 181 Bestmann
The Bestmann was a single-engined low-wing fixed-undercarriage trainer, many of which were recovered intact.

Service (post-1945) Communications BAFO CW; 2, 83, 84 GCS

Fieseler Fi 156C Storch
The Storch was a single-engined high-wing monoplane with extremely good low-speed (under 30mph) and short take-off and landing characteristics. Many were used informally by the Allies during the war and after short-term service with BAFO the type was evaluated extensively for many years, influencing designs like the Auster Type S and Prestwick Pioneer.

Service (post-1945) Communications BAFO CW; 2, 83, 84 GCS; Denmark CS

Junkers Ju 52/3m
The Ju 52 was a three-engined transport with excellent rough-field performance. After limited RAF use a large number was used for a short time by BEA.

Service (post-1945) Communications/transport 83 GCS; EASSU

Messerschmitt Bf 108 Taifun
The Bf 108 (Aldon in British service) had flown with the

Messerschmitt Bf 108 Taifun

Four Bf 108 monoplanes were impressed from 1939 including the German Ambassador's aircraft. Although a German machine D-IMTT gives a good impression of the lines of this neat aircraft. (*Author's collection*)

RAF since 1939 as four of the type had been impressed in the UK. In addition a number of this single-engined type, easily confused with the Bf 109, was operated in Germany.

Service (post-1945) Communications BAFO CW; 2, 83 GCS

Savoia Marchetti SM.82 Cangaru
The SM.82 was a large three-engined transport capable of carrying up to 40 armed troops.

Service (post-1945) Communications/transport 84 GCS

Siebel Si 204D
The Si 204 was in service from 1942 as a trainer and communications type carrying a crew of two and five passengers. It was powered by two Argus AS411 engines.

Service (post-1945) Communications BAFO CW; 84 GCS; EASSU; 18 SP

Mitsubishi Ki-21 'Sally'
The Ki-21 was a twin-engined bomber which was virtually obsolete by the war's end. It was used as a freighter in Japanese use and in Indo-China after the war.

Service (post-1945) Communications/transport 'Gremlin' Task Force

Mitsubishi Ki-57 'Topsy'
The Ki-57 was a neat twin-engined aircraft similar in overall layout to the DC-2. Four were used in Indo-China.

Service (post-1945) Communications/transport 'Gremlin' Task Force

---

Specification and production

Mark	Role	Engine	HP	Speed mph	Crew/ passengers	Nos
Bf 108	Comms	Argus AS 10	270	196	1/3	20
Bu 181	Trainer	Hirth HM504	105	133	1/1	62
Fi 156C	Comms	Argus AS10	270	109	1/2	45
Ju 52/3m	Transport	3xBMW 132A	830	165	2/18	104
Si 204D	Comms	2xArgus AS411	600	230	2/5	54
SM 82	Transport	3xAlfa Romeo 128	900	205	3/40	2
Ki-21	Transport	2xMitsubishi Ha-6	825	300	3/-	4
Ki-57	Transport	2xMitsubishi 97	850	266	4/20	4

Further reading
Junkers Ju 52, Nowarra, H, Foulis, London, 1987
War Prizes, Butler, P, Midland Counties Publications, Hinckley, 1994

de Havilland Devon C Mk 2

The elegant Dove was designed as a successor to the Dragon Rapide for civil use and it was bought for military communications duties as the Devon (and Sea Devon). Forty were bought for the RAF of which 25 were converted to Mk 2 standard with more powerful engines. VP971 is one such aircraft of 207 Sqn Northolt, seen here in 1981. *(Author)*

7.9   de Havilland Devon/Sea Devon (1948–1984)

The civil DH104 Dove was designed as a successor to the DH89A Dragon Rapide with a similar internal layout and basically the same engines, although more powerful models. It was natural that the new type would be ordered by the RAF (as the **Devon**) to meet specification C.13/46 as a communications type to replace the Dominie.

C Mark 1
The Devon seated seven passengers and a crew of two and enjoyed a range of 500 miles; it was similar to the civil Mk 2B. It was widely used by communications squadrons and flights and was also provided for the use of British air attachés, often sporting civil registrations in such use. The initial order for 30 was supplemented by a further six after which four more were purchased from the civil register to meet specific needs.

Service Communications 21, 31, 60, 207, 267; AAFCE; AFWE; BCCS; BLEU; CCCF/S; CPE; ETPS; FCCF/S; FECS; FTCCF/S; 11, 12, 13, 18, 19, 38 GCF; HCCS; MCCF/S; MCS; MECF/S; MFCE; NATO CF; NEAFCF; NCS; 240 OCU; RAE; RAFGCS; RCCF; RRE; SCS; 2 TAFCF/S; TCCF; TCDF; TRE; TTCCF;

WCS; Fontainbleu, Idris, Iraq, Malta CF; Andover, Coltishall, Gibraltar, Hendon, Odiham, Upavon, Wahn, White Waltham, Wildenrath, Woodvale, Wyton SFs; Ankara, Baghdad, Bangkok, Belgrade, Caracas, Djakarta, Mexico City, Paris, Pretoria, Rangoon, Saigon, Teheran AAs

C Mark 2
The Mark 2 comprised some 25 C Mk 1 conversions with the more powerful Gipsy Queen 70 Mk 3 engines giving 400hp for improved performance. They were distinguished by oil cooler intakes above the nacelle. A smaller but unrecorded number of conversions was completed to full civil Mk 8 standard as the **C Mark 2/2** with an enlarged and covered cockpit canopy giving better headroom and changed instrument layout.

Service Communications 21, 26, 60, 207; AAFCE; NCS; RAE; SCCS; SCS; Northolt SF; Bangkok, Saigon, Teheran AAs

C Mark 20
The Mk 20 designation was applied to the **Sea Devon**, the name applied to the Dove as bought for the Royal Navy. Thirteen were bought from storage from 1955 and used until 1981 for communications duties in the UK and Malta.

Service Communications 750, 765, 771, 781; Culdrose SF

Specification and production

Mark	Role	Engine	HP	Speed mph	Crew/ passengers	Nos
C1	Comms	2xGipsy Queen 70-4	340	210	2/7	40
C2	Comms	2xGipsy Queen 70 Mk3	400	235	2/7	25*
C20	Comms	2xGipsy Queen 70-4	340	210	2/7	13

*   C Mk 1 conversions

7.10   Bristol Sycamore (1949–1972)

The Bristol Aeroplane Company had bought a stake in the A.R.III autogiro and its developer, Raoul Hafner. At the end of the war, as Bristol's chief helicopter designer, he designed the Type 171 as a single piston-engined, four-seat aircraft, the first of which flew on 27 July 1947. This was Mk 1 VL958 built to specification E.20/45 powered by the Pratt & Whitney Wasp engine since the intended Leonides was not ready. The first Mk 2 aircraft, powered by the Leonides, flew on 3 September 1949 to specification 35/46. Six Mk 3 aircraft flew in military markings (one in HR Mk 14 configuration), but only one was to fly within the military designation range (as the HC Mk 10). The remainder were used for evaluation and tropical and Arctic trials.

HC Mark 10

The Sycamore was ordered to specification A.9/49. It equated to the Company's Mk 3 and carried five people in a slightly re-designed shorter nose. The sole example, WA578, was modified to carry casualty evacuation equipment and undertook trials in Malaya.

Service Trials RAE

Bristol Sycamore HC Mk 12

The Sycamore was the first helicopter of indigenous design in British military service, with trials aircraft joining the Army in 1951. HC Mk 12 WV783 seen in this photograph joined Coastal Command for trials with the Air/Sea Warfare Development Unit; the winch is evident above and behind the cabin door. The Sycamore went on to serve in Cyprus, Malaya and Suez. *(Author)*

HC Mark 11

The Mk 11 was developed for Army use to specification A.106P. It was not ideal as an air observation type, but was used mainly for VIP transport.

Service Air Observation 651, 656 **Communications** 1906 Flt; MCS **Trials** *JEHU*

HR Mark 12

The Mk 12 was the first aircraft for RAF operational use but the four delivered were used for trials and latterly training.

Service Trials ASWDU; HDU **Training** CFS

HR Mark 13

The Mk 13 was similar to the Mk 50 built for the Royal Australian Navy and it employed a longer-stroke undercarriage giving better ground clearance.

Service Search and Rescue 275

HR Mark 14

The Mk 14 was the definitive version and was to all intents similar to the HR Mk 13 but with four doors. It served widely in the search and rescue role and latterly as a communications aircraft in which role it was designated **HC Mark 14** but with no discernible external changes. Those operated in the VIP role by 32 Sqn had fixed external steps and an improved interior.

Service Search and Rescue 103, 110, 118, 194, 228, 275, 284; 1563, 1564 Flts; Aden SAR Flt; APS Sylt **Transport** 225 **Communications** 32; MCS; TCCF; Levant CF; Eastleigh, El Adem, Khormaksar, Kuala Lumpur, Nicosia, Seletar SF **Trials** JEHU; 1 ATU LRWE; RAE **Training** CFS

Specification and production

Mark	Role	Engine	HP	Speed mph	Crew/ passengers	Nos
HC10	Utility	Leonides 73	550	127	1/3	5*
HC11	Utility	Leonides 73	550	127	1/3	4
HR12	Utility	Leonides 73	550	127	1/3	4
HR13	SAR	Leonides 73	550	127	1/4	2
HR14	Utility	Leonides 73	550	127	1/4	87

*   four of these were Company Mk 3 aircraft for trials

7.11   Percival Sea Prince (1953–1979)

The Hunting P.50 Prince was designed as a twin-engined eight-seat feeder-liner and the prototype, G-23-1 (later G-ALCM), flew on 13 May 1948. The type was ordered for the Fleet Air Arm, both for communications and training purposes.

C Mark 1

The P.66 was similar in most respects to the Prince series II and three were bought against specification C.18/49, the first, WF136, flying on 24 March 1950. It was fitted with eight seats plus toilet and had a crew of two. Power

Percival Sea Prince T Mk 1

The Fleet Air Arm needed a flying classroom to train observers and to replace the Barracuda in the role. The Sea Prince was chosen, three of the type having been bought for communications tasks in 1950. WM735/578CU is a trainer from 750 NAS at Culdrose. (*R C B Ashworth via P H T Green*)

was provided by two Leonides 125 engines and the range was 1,320 miles. The Sea Prince was replaced in service by the Sea Devon from 1965.

Service Communications 781; Joint Services Mission Washington

T Mark 1
The P.57 was ordered to specification T.17/49 as a flying classroom in which role it operated from 1953 to 1979. It replaced the Barracuda for observer training and 41 were bought. Accommodation was provided for an instructor and three pupils plus crew and the T Mk 1 differed from the communications version in having a longer radar nose, twin-wheel main undercarriage and longer engine nacelles.

Service Training 702, 727, 744, 750, 1830, 19440, 1841, 1844 **Communications** 781 **Trials** 831

C Mark 2
The C Mk 2 was a communications version of the T Mk 2 with the two-wheel main undercarriage, radar and extended nose. Four were used by 781 NAS between 1953 and 1970.

Service Communications 781

Specification and production

Mark	Role	Engine	HP	Speed mph	Crew/ passengers	Nos
C1	Comms	2xLeonides 125	550	223	2/8	3
T1	Trainer	2xLeonides 125	550	223	2/4	41
C2	Comms	2xLeonides 125	550	223	2/8	4

7.12 Hunting Percival Pembroke (1953–88)

The P.66 Pembroke, like the Sea Prince, was developed from the civil Prince twin-engined feeder-liner, but in the

Hunting Percival Pembroke C Mk 1

The RAF's Pembroke was similar to the Sea Prince but with extended wing span of 64½ feet. Fifty-seven were bought as Anson replacements and the type was in service from 1953 to 1988. WV701 was with 60 Sqn at Wildenrath in February 1983. (*Crown copyright*)

case of the Pembroke the differences were more noticeable since the wing-span was increased from 56 to 64.5ft.

C Mark 1
The Mk 1 was bought in significant numbers as a staff transport to replace the Anson. Like its civil counterpart it accommodated a crew of two and eight passengers in rear-facing seats over a range of 1,150 miles. The Pembroke entered service with the Middle East Air Force in 1953. From 1970 a small number was re-sparred to extend airframe life and the last of the type was withdrawn from 60 Sqn in Germany in 1988.

Service Communications 21, 32, 60, 70, 78, 81, 84, 152, 207, 209, 267; 1417 Flt; AAFCECS; APCS; BCCF/S; FCCS; FECSMCS; Ferry Sqn; FTCCS; 18, 205 GCF; MCCS; MECS; NCS; RAFGCS; SCCS; SCS; 2 TAFCS; TCCF; TCEU; WCS; Amman, Gulf, Levant, Malta, Seletar, Wildenrath CF; Abu Sueir, Bahrain, Ballykelly, Eastleigh, El Adem, Gibraltar, Habbaniyah, Khormaksar, Labuan, Muharraq, Negombo, Nicosia, Wyton SFs

C (PR) Mark 1
The photo-reconnaissance variant was similar in most respects to the communications variant except that sideways and oblique-facing cameras were fitted for survey tasks, a requirement in the Far East.

Service Survey 81; 209, 267 **Communications** 60, 207; AAFCE; 18 GCF; MCS; NCS; RAFGCS; 2 TAFCS; WCS; St Mawgan SF

Specification and production

Mark	Role	Engine	HP	Speed mph	Crew/ passengers	Nos
C1	Comms	2xLeonides 127	550	224	2/8	51
C(PR)1	Survey	2xLeonides 127	550	224	2/8	6

Scottish Aviation Pioneer CC Mk 1

The Pioneer originated as a response to specification A.4/45 as a short take-off and landing Army utility. The design was influenced by that of the Fieseler Storch as evidenced in this photo of XE512 prior to delivery to 1311 Flt in Malaya. *(Author's collection)*

7.13   Scottish Aviation Pioneer (1953–1969)

The Pioneer short take-off and landing utility first flew in May 1950 (VL515) initially powered by a single 240hp Gipsy Queen. Built to specification A.4/45 the influence of the Fieseler Storch was evident but the newer type was under powered. A civil version followed and when its potential was appreciated the Pioneer was ordered for RAF duties.

CC Mk 1
The Pioneer was a five-seat utility aircraft with quite remarkable short-field performance: take-off was in 75yds and landing in only 65yds. Stalling speed was just 43 mph. The Pioneer joined 1311 Flt in Malaya in September 1953 and it remained in service until 1969, serving latterly in Borneo in the Forward Air Control (FAC) role with 20 Sqn supporting its Hunters.

Service Communications 78, 209, 215, 230, 267; 1311 Flt; Benson, Muscat, Seletar SF **Forward Air Control** 20

Specification and production

Mark	Role	Engine	HP	Speed mph	Crew/ passengers	Nos
CC1	Comms	Leonides 502	520	145	1/4	40

Further reading
Scottish Aviation Pioneer CC Mk 1, Hobson, C, Aviation News, Berkhamstead

7.14   de Havilland Heron/Sea Heron (1955–1989)

The DH114 Heron was built as an economical and simple short-to-medium-stage transport utilising many Dove components. The series 1 aircraft had the well tried Gipsy Queen 30 and a fixed undercarriage which resulted in easy maintenance and good rough-field performance.

CC Mark 2
The first variant in military marks was a series 2 aircraft two of which (XG603 and XH373) were bought for the British Joint Services Mission in Washington from 1955 to 1960. The series 2 differed from the first version in having a retractable undercarriage; presumably the CC Mk 2 designation was used to accord with the manufacturer's series number. A further aircraft, XL961, was given military marks briefly for the royal tour of Africa in 1956.

Service Communications JSM Washington; QF

CC Mark 3
The Mk 3 equated to the series 3 aircraft which was externally similar to the series 2; they were fitted internally to VVIP standard. Two were bought for the Queen's Flight and later transferred to RAF Germany and the Royal Navy.

Service Communications 60; QF; RAFGCS: FONAC

CC Mark 4
The Mk 4 designation was applied to a further series 3 aircraft (XR391) which was bought for the Queen's Flight and which had a different internal fit from earlier aircraft.

Service Communications 60; QF

C Mark 20
The Sea Heron is sometimes quoted as the C Mark 1 but the order was after the first RAF purchase. The Royal Navy bought five (XR441-5) to complement the Sea Devon in service between 1961 and 1989. One of the CC Mk 3 aircraft was also used by the Fleet Air Arm.

Service Communications 781; Culdrose, Yeovilton SF

de Havilland Sea Heron C Mk 20

The Heron utilised Dove components and served in small numbers with the RAF and FAA for medium range communications carrying fourteen passengers or six in VIP configuration. XR443 of Yeovilton Station Flight is displayed at Yeovilton in August 1984. *(Author)*

Specification and production

Mark	Role	Engine	HP	Speed mph	Crew/ passengers	Nos
CC2	Comms	4xGipsy Queen 30	250	183	2/14	3
CC3	Comms	4xGipsy Queen 30	250	183	3/6	2
CC4	Comms	4xGipsy Queen 30	250	183	3/6	1
C20	Comms	4xGipsy Queen 30	250	183	2/14	5

7.15 Scottish Aviation Twin Pioneer (1958–1968)

The Twin Pioneer built on the success of the single-engine STOL utility Pioneer and first flew as a sixteen-seat civil transport in 1955. The type, which used two of the same Leonides engine, was bought for the RAF to complement the Pioneer.

CC Mark 1

The Twin Pioneer first flew in military form (XL966) on 29 August 1957 and after A&AEE evaluation it joined 78 Sqn in Aden in October 1958. The Twin Pioneer could be armed with bombs on the undercarriage struts and a movable Bren gun in the rear door. Range was in the order of 400 miles loaded and it could operate comfortably from 1,000ft strips.

Service **Light transport** 21, 78, 152, 209, 225, 230; FSS; 224 Gp Supp Flt; SRCU; Katunayake, Odiham SF

CC Mark 2

The Mk 2 was similar in all respects to the CC Mk 1 but with many machined and fabricated components replaced by forgings and castings. The final seven aircraft were built to this standard. The last three aircraft were fitted with the more powerful Leonides 531 engine which was later retro-fitted to earlier machines.

Service **Light transport** 209, 230; 1310 Flt; Odiham SF

Specification and production

Mark	Role	Engine	HP	Speed mph	Crew/ passengers	Nos
CC1	Transport	2xLeonides 514	550	165	3/11	32
CC2	Transport	2xLeonides 531	640	165	3/11	7

Scottish Aviation Twin Pioneer CC Mk 1

No 78 Sqn in Aden was the first recipient of the Twin Pioneer in 1958 and two of the unit's aircraft, XL992 and XL991/W, are seen in this official – and, one suspects, posed – photograph. Although designated as a communications type, the 'Twin Pin' was a light transport with excellent short-field performance. *(Crown copyright)*

7.16   Beagle Basset (1964–1974)

The Beagle Aircraft Company was formed to compete in the international light aircraft market and the first twin-engined product was the five-seat B.206 which first flew in 1961.

Beagle Basset CC Mk 1

In its intended role of placing V-bomber crews the Basset was a failure and it was short-lived, the task placing an extra load on the Devon. It entered service in 1965 and was withdrawn in 1974. XS771 is from 26 Sqn at Wyton, previously the Northern Communications Sqn. *(26 Sqn via A S Thomas)*

B.206Z

The B.206Z was the first of the type ordered for the Ministry of Aviation for evaluation and two were bought for trials by A&AEE prior to a definitive purchase; the first, XS742, flew on 24 January 1964. The B.206Z was larger than the prototype and seated up to eight; the second was converted for use as a variable stability demonstrator by the ETPS.

Service Trials AAEE; ETPS

CC Mark 1

The B.206R was the definitive Basset which was intended to match the operational requirement for an Anson replacement which would carry a V-bomber crew of five plus ground-crew chief and kit, all over 400nm. In the event the Basset could not meet the requirement and the Devon remained the primary communications type of the period. The CC Mk 1 had a wider-span tailplane and changed hatches relative to the B.206Z. The first production aircraft, XS765, flew on 28 December 1964 and it entered service with the Northern Communications Sqn at Topcliffe in June 1965. It was withdrawn from service in May 1974.

Service Communications 26, 32, 207; BCCS; MCS; NCS; QF; SCCS; SCS; TCCS; WCS

Specification and production

Mark	Role	Engine	HP	Speed mph	Crew/ passengers	Nos
206Z	Trials	2xG10-470-A	310	220	2/6	2
CC1	Comms	2xG10-470-A	310	220	2/6	20

7.17 Hawker Siddeley 125 (1971–date)

The 125 began life as the de Havilland 125 executive jet which flew in 1961 and which in one form or another has remained in continuous production ever since. It became the first jet-powered communications type operated by the RAF.

A sole **125 series 1** aircraft, XW930 (G-ATPC), was used by Hawker Siddeley at Dunsfold for trials associated with the Sea Harrier.

CC Mk 1
The 125-400B was powered by two Viper 301 turbojets with a range of 1,750 miles. Six of this variant (XW788-91;XX505-6) were bought for 32 Sqn, which it joined in 1971, and all were subsequently re-engined with the Garrett TFE731.

Service Communications 32

CC Mark 2
The 125-600 was powered by the more powerful Viper 601-22 and seated six passengers in a VIP fit. Two were bought and like the CC Mk 1 aircraft they were later re-engined with the Garrett. A further machine, ZF130, was used by BAe at Dunsfold in connection with Sea Harrier development.

Service Communications 32 Trials BAe/RN

CC Mark 3
The 125-700 was originally powered by the Viper but quickly re-engined with the Garrett TFE731 which was a much quieter and cleaner engine. Seven passengers were carried over a range of up to 2,000 miles and the aircraft was fitted with MIRTS infra-red countermeasures.

Hawker Siddeley 125 CC Mk 3

With the HS125 RAF communications entered the jet age. Although in civil form the 125 first flew in 1961 it did not join 32 Sqn until 1971 in Mk 1 form with the Viper engine. ZD704 of 32 Sqn is a Mk 3 aircraft with the Garrett TFE731 which was more powerful, quieter and cleaner than the Viper. *(Author)*

Service Communications 32

Specification and production

Mark	Role	Engine	Thrust lb	Speed mph	Crew/ passengers	Nos
Sers 1	Trials	2xViper 521	3,120	490	n/a	1
CC1	Comms	2xViper 301	3,000	505	2/8	6
CC2	Comms	2xViper 601-22	3,700	570	2/6	3
CC3	Comms	2xTFE371	3,700	533	2/7	6

7.18 BAe 146 (1983–date)

Design of the BAe 146 quiet transport was begun by Hawker Siddeley in 1973 but delays caused by the state of the national economy resulted in first flight of the prototype (G-SSSH) taking place on 3 September 1981. First commercial deliveries of the high-wing, four-jet aircraft were made in 1983.

CC Mark 1
The 146-100 comprised two aircraft (ZD695-6) operated for the Queen's Flight by 10 Sqn from 1983 to 1985. The aircraft were in effect being evaluated and were later returned to the manufacturers.

Service Communications 10; QF; 241 OCU

CC Mark 2
The 146-200 was the definitive variant for VIP transport, being larger than the CC Mk 1 and fitted for up to 19 passengers. Range is nearly 2,000 miles and three were bought (ZE700-2) joining the Queen's Flight in 1985. All are fitted with Loral Matador IR jamming.

Service Communications 32; QF

Specification and production

Mark	Role	Engine	Thrust lb	Speed mph	Crew/ passengers	Nos
CC1	Comms	4xAvco ALF502R-5	6,790	440	2/82	2
CC2	Comms	4xAvco ALF502R-5	6,790	440	6/19	3

7.19 Britten-Norman Islander (1982–date)

The twin-engined Islander was built as an unsophisticated and therefore inexpensive light STOL transport for use especially in under-developed areas. The first flight of the BN2 took place on the Isle of Wight in August 1966 and commercial deliveries began in 1967. At several stages in its British military career the Islander has been referred to as the Defender.

A single **BN2A** (G-DIVE) was given military marks (ZB503) in 1982 for parachute training. It accommodated eight. Three turbine-powered **BN2T** aircraft were also used by the services for training and trials. G-

BAe 146 CC Mk 1

After a long gestation the BAe 146 flew in 1981 and was quickly a commercial success. Two 146-100 series aircraft, ZD696 and 696, were evaluated at Brize Norton for the Queen's Flight between 1983 and 1985. ZD696 of 241 OCU is here displayed at Greenham Common in 1983. *(Author)*

WOTG/ZF444 was used for parachute training at Weston-on-the-Green from 1987 to 1994. G-SRAY/ZF573 was used for Stingray torpedo trials from 1987 to 1994 when it was converted to communications configuration. G-DLRA was flown from 1984 in relation to Airborne STand-off Radar (ASTOR) trials. In 1990, equipped with the Thorn-EMI Skymaster radar, it acquired the serial ZG989 being flown for several years from Boscombe Down.

AL Mark 1
The Mk 1 designation was applied to the BN2T when

Pilatus Britten-Norman Islander

The Army has seven Islander light transports which replaced a rather larger fleet of Beavers. The RAF also uses two at RAF Northolt and in addition several examples have flown on trials tasks including ZG989 (ex G-DLRA) equipped with Thorn-EMI Skymaster radar. The extended fin strake to counter the changed nose profile is evident in this shot of the aircraft as exhibited at Farnborough in 1990. *(Author)*

purchased for Army use to replace the Beaver in the light transport and liaison role. It was to be used primarily in Northern Ireland and entered service with 1 Flt in 1989.

Service Liaison 1 Flt; AAC/Islander Training Flt

CC Mark 2
The Mk 2 was similar in all respects to the Army variant apart from detailed fitments and a single ex-civil example (ZH536) was used by 32 Sqn from 1991. The Stingray trials aircraft ZF573 was converted to **CC Mark 2A** standard in 1994 with minor differences.

Service Communications 32; Northolt SF

Specification and production

Mark	Role	Engine	HP	Speed mph	Crew/ passengers	Nos
BN2A	Para training	2xLycoming O-540-E4B5	260	160	1/8	1
BN2T	Various	2xAllison 250-B17C	320	165	1/9	3
AL1	Liaison	2xAllison 250-B17C	320	165	1/9	7
CC2/A	Comms	2xAllison 250-B17C	320	165	1/9	2*

* including one BN2T conversion

7.20 Aérospatiale AS355 Twin Squirrel and AS350 Squirrel (1996–date)

Twin Squirrel

HC Mark 1

The Mk 1 comprised two aircraft leased for use by 32 Sqn to replace the ageing Wessex and the single-engined Gazelle. The Twin Squirrel, as its name implies, is twin-engined and it carries up to three passengers in a compact (compared with the Wessex) fuselage over a range of 437 miles.

Service Communications 32

Aérospatiale Twin Squirrel HC Mk 1

Two twin-engined Squirrel helicopters are leased by 32 Sqn for royal duties, the type having taken over from the Wessex. While more comfortable than the latter, the Squirrel hardly leaves room for privacy. ZJ140 illustrates the adaptation of the civil colour scheme for its RAF role. *(A S Thomas collection)*

Squirrel

The AS350 Squirrel was one of the two types ordered for the civilian managed Defence Helicopter Flying School (DHFS) based at Shawbury and Middle Wallop. The type replaces the Gazelle in the training role and it is in service in two variants, although both are basically the AS350BA model.

HT Mk1

A total of 38 Squirrels have been acquired by FBS, the commercial operator of the DHFS and of these 26 are the HT Mk 1 (AS350BB) operated for tri-service training at Shawbury. The type accommodates up to five personnel and has an endurance of around two hours or range of 420 miles.

Service Training DHFS (660 Sqn: 705 NAS)

HT Mk 2

Twelve of the Squirrels have been adapted for Army training at Middle Wallop and the first conversion was

Aérospatiale Squirrel HT1

The single-engined Squirrel has been bought by FBS for use at Shawbury within the civilian-owned, military-operated Defence Helicopter Flying School (DHFS). XJ260/60 was delivered as G-BXGB and forms part of the combined basic training element of 660 Sqn/705 NAS. It was first publicly displayed at Fairford in July 1997. *(Author)*

ZJ243 (ex G-BWZS). The variant is equipped for night vision goggles, GPS, Brightstar searchlight and an under-slung load hook.

Service Training DHFS (670 Sqn)

Specification and production

Mark	Role	Engine	HP	Speed mph	Crew/ passengers	Nos
HC1	Comms	2xAllison 250-C20F	420	140	2/3	2
HT1	Trainer	Arriel 1B	640	145	1/4	26
HT2	Trainer	Arriel 1B	640	135	1/4	12

7.21 Eurocopter AS365N-2 Dauphin 2 (1996–date)

Two Dauphins operated by Bond Helicopters for the Royal Navy at Plymouth have been given the serials ZJ164 and 165. The twin-engined civil Dauphin 2 is in widespread use and in military service as the Panther. It can accommodate up to ten persons in addition to a crew of two over a range of 470 miles.

Service Communications FOST

Specification and production

Mark	Role	Engine	HP	Speed mph	Crew/ passengers	Nos
	Comms	2xArriel 1M1	783	160	2/10	2

8 – Naval fighters

The term 'fighters' is used loosely in a naval context. An arbitrary division between fighters and strike/anti-submarine warfare has had to be made in some cases in order to keep some balance between chapters and at least in part to reflect the intentions behind the original designs.

HMS *Theseus*

The Korean War demanded considerable carrier support and whereas the RAF played a limited role in the war, the Fleet Air Arm provided a carrier on station throughout from 1950 to 1953. Here Carrier Air Group 17 comprising Sea Fury FB Mk 11s of 807 NAS and Firefly FR Mk 5s of 810 NAS departs Portsmouth on board HMS *Theseus* in August 1950. Also on the deck are some Sea Furys of 736 NAS from St Merryn including 114/JB. *(Author's collection)*

January 1946

The mainstay of the Fleet Air Arm five months after the end of the war was the Seafire, mainly in later marks, and the Firefly, by now used rather in the strike role although designed as a fighter. Small numbers of Hellcats and Corsairs would remain in use for a few months yet. Of the 23 squadrons in existence most were shore-based prior to disbandment, although the Royal Navy had in commission no fewer than six fleet carriers and five light fleet carriers, only two of which, HMSs *Glory* and *Vengeance*, were at sea.

January 1950

The flying role of the Royal Naval Volunteer Reserve had been established in 1947 and of the twelve notional fighter units eight were front-line and four RNVR squadrons. The ultimate in piston-engined fighter design was in service in the form of the Sea Hornet and Sea Fury, although the Seafire was still operational with one front-line squadron in Malaya. The navalised version of the Spiteful (Chapter 2.3), the Seafang, had been abandoned after testing, given that it offered little advance over the later Seafires pending the advent of jet types. The carrier fleet comprised five fleet carriers and six light fleet carriers; HMS *Ocean* was at sea, in the Mediterranean.

July 1952

The Fleet Air Arm had entered the jet age with the introduction of the Supermarine Attacker, which was embarked on two carriers in home waters. It had entered service the previous year after a lengthy gestation, given that technologically it was little more than a jet-engined late mark Seafire. The Korean War was still raging and HMS *Ocean* was on station with a Sea Fury squadron embarked. The Seafire was still in service with one of three RNVR fighter squadrons, while there were still eight front-line fighter units. Six fleet carriers and seven light fleet carriers were in commission.

November 1956

The Fleet Air Arm had expanded slightly in the build-up to the Suez crisis and the Sea Hawk (entered service 1953) and Sea Venom (1954) were the mainstays of the service. They formed the complement of eight and four squadrons respectively on board HMSs *Albion*, *Bulwark*, *Centaur* and *Eagle*. Also in the Mediterranean was HMS *Theseus*, while a further two fleet carriers and two light fleet carriers were available. The RNVR squadrons had disbanded in March 1957.

January 1960

Great Britain still had world power pretensions and the Royal Navy operated eight fighter squadrons, usually with a carrier presence in the Far and Middle East. The Sea Hawk and Sea Venom were still in service, although their replacement by the Scimitar (1958) and Sea Vixen (1959) was well in hand. The newer types were all shore-based, while Sea Hawks and Sea Venoms served on HMS *Centaur* in the Far East. HMSs *Ark Royal*, *Eagle*, *Victorious* and *Hermes* were also in commission while HMSs *Albion* and *Bulwark* were being converted to commando carriers.

January 1965

The short-lived Scimitar, which in any event was primarily a strike aircraft, had been replaced by the Buccaneer, leaving the Sea Vixen with four squadrons. The improved Mk 2 version of the fighter was in service with 899 NAS on board HMS *Eagle* in the Far East. Two further fleet carriers and four light fleet carriers remained in commission.

January 1970

The Fleet Air Arm retained just four fighter squadrons, three equipped with the Sea Vixen FAW Mk 2 and one (892 NAS) with the Spey-powered Phantom FG Mk 1. The carrier fleet was down to six ships.

January 1975

The sole fighter unit by now was 892 NAS with the Phantom, shore-based and shortly to disband. The conventional carrier force was diminished with only HMSs *Ark Royal* and *Hermes* still in commission. The withdrawal from the Far and Middle East was well under way, but the Royal Navy had managed to secure the future of carrier-based fixed-wing aircraft by ordering three so-called 'through-deck cruisers', ostensibly for anti-submarine helicopters.

May 1982

The wisdom of maintaining a naval fighter force – albeit a very small one – was justified in 1982 when the United Kingdom decided to counter the Argentinian invasion of the Falkland Islands. A small force of Sea Harriers, which had entered service in March 1980, served in the South Atlantic aboard the last of the light fleet carriers, HMS *Hermes*, and HMS *Invincible* which had been commissioned in July 1980 as the first ASW through-deck carrier. The thirty or so Sea Harriers formed the equipment of 800, 801, 899 and the temporarily formed 809 NAS.

January 1990: January 1995

Eight years on from the Falklands campaign the Sea Harrier FRS Mk 1 remained in service with three squadrons with two carriers in commission. During Operation 'Granby' in January 1991 HMS *Ark Royal* deployed to the eastern Mediterranean with 801 NAS embarked. This unit was the first to operate in the Adriatic in support of Operation 'Grapple' and in 1994 lost an aircraft to gunfire over Serbia. By 1995 the long-serving Sea Harrier FRS Mk 1 had been succeeded by the FA Mk 2 in the HQ unit, 899 NAS, and one of the two carrier-based units, 801 NAS. Two light carriers, HMSs *Illustrious* and *Invincible*, were in commission sharing the Balkans duties, while HMS *Ark Royal* was undergoing a refit.

Carriers in commission since January 1946

Fleet Carrier

HMS *Formidable*	1946 – 1947
HMS *Indefatigable*	1946 – 8/54
HMS *Implacable*	1946 – 9/54
HMS *Illustrious*	1946 – 12/54
HMS *Indomitable*	1946 – 9/55
HMS *Victorious*	1946 – 3/68
HMS *Eagle*	10/51 – 1/72
HMS *Ark Royal*	2/55 – 2/79

Light Fleet Carriers

HMS *Colossus*	1946 – 8/46
HMS *Venerable*	1946 – 5/48
HMS *Vengeance*	1946 – 11/52
HMS *Glory*	1946 – 1958
HMS *Ocean*	1946 – 3/58
HMS *Warrior*	1/46 – 7/58
HMS *Theseus*	2/46 – 12/56
HMS *Triumph*	3/46 – 12/55
HMS *Centaur*	9/53 – 4/70
HMS *Albion* *	5/54 – 3/73
HMS *Bulwark* *	10/54 – 4/76
HMS *Hermes*	11/59 – 4/84

Light ASW carriers

HMS *Invincible*	7/80 –
HMS *Illustrious*	6/82 –
HMS *Ark Royal*	5/85 –

Helicopter carrier

HMS *Ocean*	in building 1996

* converted to commando carriers 1960

8.A   Naval fighters at 1 January 1946

United Kingdom

Type	Unit	Base
Seafire FXV	802	Ayr
	803	Nutts Corner
	805, 806	Machrihanish
Seafire FXVII	807, 809, 879	Nutts Corner
Firefly FRI	816, 822	Machrihanish
	824, 825	Burscough

Mediterranean

Type	Unit	Base
Hellcat II	892	HMS *Ocean*
Firefly FRI	1792	HMS *Ocean*

Far East

Type	Unit	Base
Seafire III	887, 894	Schofields (Australia)
Seafire FXV	801	Schofields (Australia)
Hellcat II	888	Sembawang (Malaya)
Firefly FRI	814, 837	Nowra (Australia)
	1772, 1790	Schofields (Australia)
Corsair IV	1850	HMS *Vengeance* (Far East)
	1851	Nowra (Australia)

Training

Type	Unit	Base
Corsair IV	715	St Merryn
	Fighter Leader Course/Fighter Air Combat Course (SAC)	
Seafire III, F17, 46, Harvard III, Firefly FR1	736	St Merryn
	Fighter Combat School (SNAW)	
Oxford, Harvard II, Corsair III Hellcat II, Seafire III, XV	759	Zeals
	AFS (1 NAFS)	
Harvard IIa, Seafire III	760	Henstridge
	AFS (2 NAFS)	
Seafire III, XV, XVII, Harvard III	761	Henstridge
	AFS (2 NAFS)	
Firefly NFI, Corsair III, IV, Harvard IIb, III Martinet TTI, Seafire III	794	Eglinton
	AFS (3 NAFS)	
Anson I, Firefly INF, Hellcat IINF, Harvard III	784	Drem
	Night Fighter Training	

8.B   Naval fighters at 1 January 1950

United Kingdom

Type	Unit	Base
Sea Hornet F20, PR22	801	Lee-on-Solent
Sea Hornet F20, NF21, PR22	809	Culdrose
Sea Fury FB11	802	Culdrose
	807	St Merryn
Firefly NF1, FR1	1830*	Abbotsinch
Seafire FXV, XVII	1832*	Culham
Seafire FXVII	1831*	Stretton
	1833*	Bramcote

Mediterranean

Type	Unit	Base
Sea Fury FB11	804	HMS *Glory* (Mediterranean)
Firefly NF1, FR5	812	HMS *Glory* (Mediterranean)

Far East

Type	Unit	Base
Seafire FR47	800	Sembawang (Malaya)
Firefly NF1, FR1	827	Sembawang (Malaya)

* RNVR units

Training

Type	Unit	Base
Firefly FR1, T1, Seafire F15, 17	766	Lossiemouth
	Pt I Op'l FS Course	
Seafire F115, 17, Firefly FR1, T1, 2, FR4, AS5	737	Eglinton
	Pt II Op'l FS Course	
Sea Vampire F20, Meteor T7	702	Culdrose
	Naval Jet Evaluation and Training Unit	
Martinet TT1, Seafire F17, Sea Fury FB11, Firefly FR1, T1	736	St Merryn
	Fighter Combat School (SNAW)	

Type	Unit	Base
Firefly NF1, Anson I,	792	Culdrose
Sea Hornet NF21	*Night Fighter*	
	Training Unit	
Seafire F15,17,	799	Yeovilton
Firefly FR1,T1,	*Flying Check and*	
Firebrand TF5,	*Conversion Refresher*	
Sea Fury FB11,		
Harvard T2b, 3		

8.C   Naval fighters at 1 July 1952

United Kingdom

Type	Unit	Base
Attacker F1	890	Ford
Attacker FB1	800	HMS *Triumph*
	803	HMS *Eagle*
Sea Hornet NF21	809	HMS *Indomitable*
Sea Fury FB11,T20	804	Lee-on-Solent
	1831*	Stretton
	1832*	Culham
Seafire FR47,	1833*	Bramcote
Harvard T3,		
Anson I		

Mediterranean

Type	Unit	Base
Sea Fury FB11,T20	801	Hal Far (Malta)
	807, 898	Kasfareet (Egypt)
Firefly FR5	821	Hal Far (Malta)

Far East

Type	Unit	Base
Sea Fury FB11,T20	802	HMS *Ocean*
		(Korea)

* RNVR units

Training

Type	Unit	Base
Firefly FR1,T2,	766	Lossiemouth
Seafire F17,	*Pt I Op'l FS*	
Sea Fury T20		
Firebrand TF5,	759	Culdrose
Sea Hornet F20,	*1 Op'l FS (NAFS)*	
PR22		
Sea Fury FB11, T20,		
Vampire T11		
Sea Vampire F20,	702	Culdrose
Meteor T7,	*Naval Jet Evaluation*	
Vampire T11, 22	*and Training Unit*	
Attacker F1		
Seafire F17,	799	Macrihanish
Firefly FR1, T1, 2,	*Refresher Flying*	
Harvard T2B	*Training*	
Sea Fury FB11,T20	736,738	Culdrose
	Naval Air	
	Fighter School	

8.D   All naval operational units at 1 November 1956 (Suez crisis)

United Kingdom

Type	Unit	Base
Sea Hawk FGA4	898	Brawdy
Sea Venom FAW21	891	Yeovilton
Wyvern S4	831	Ford
Skyraider AEW1	849B, 849D	Culdrose
Gannet AS1	815, 820	Eglinton
Gannet AS4	824	Culdrose

Mediterranean

Type	Unit	Base
Sea Hawk FB3	802	HMS *Albion*
	895	HMS *Bulwark*
Sea Hawk FGA4, 6	810	HMS *Bulwark*
Sea Hawk FGA6	800	HMS *Albion*
	804	HMS *Bulwark*
	897, 899	HMS *Eagle*
Sea Venom FAW21	809	HMS *Bulwark*
	892, 893	HMS *Eagle*
Wyvern S4	830	HMS *Eagle*
Skyraider AEW1	849A	HMS *Eagle*
	849C	HMS *Albion*
Gannet AS1	812	HMS *Eagle*
	847	Nicosia
Whirlwind HAS22,	845	HMS *Theseus*
HAR3		

Far East

Type	Unit	Base
Whirlwind HAS21	848	Kluang/Sembawang

8.E   Naval fighters at 1 January 1960

United Kingdom

Type	Unit	Base
Sea Vixen FAW1	892	Yeovilton
Scimitar F1	800, 803, 807	Lossiemouth
Sea Venom FAW22	893, 894	Yeovilton

Far East

Type	Unit	Base
Sea Hawk FGA6	801	HMS *Centaur*
Sea Venom FAW22	891	HMS *Centaur*

Training

Type	Unit	Base
Sea Hawk FGA6,	736	Lossiemouth
Scimitar F1	*Operational Flying*	
	School (NAFSS)	
Sea Hawk FGA6,	738	Lossiemouth
Sea Venom FAW21,	*Sea Venom OFS*	
Sea Vampire T22	*(NAFSS)*	
Sea Venom FAW21,	766	Yeovilton
Sea Vixen FAW1	*All Weather*	
	Fighter Training	
Hunter T8	764	Lossiemouth
	Air Warfare	
	Instructor Training/	
	Swept wing CU	

8.F   Naval fighters at 1 January 1965

United Kingdom

Type	Unit	Base
Sea Vixen FAW1	890, 892	Yeovilton

Far East

Type	Unit	Base
Sea Vixen FAW1	893	HMS *Victorious*
Sea Vixen FAW2	899	HMS *Eagle*

Training

Type	Unit	Base
Scimitar F1	736	Lossiemouth
	Operational	
	Flying School	
	(NAFSS)	
Hunter T8,8c	759	Brawdy
	AFTC Phase I	
Hunter T8,GA11	738	Brawdy
	AFTC Phase II	

Type	Unit	Base
Sea Vixen FAW1	766 *All Weather Fighter Training*	Yeovilton
Hunter T8, 8b, 8c, GA11	764 *Air Warfare Instructor Training*	Lossiemouth

8.G   Naval fighters at 1 January 1970

United Kingdom

Type	Unit	Base
Sea Vixen FAW2	890, 893, 899	Yeovilton
Phantom FG1	892	HMS *Ark Royal* (UK waters)

Training

Type	Unit	Base
Hunter T8,GA11	738 *Phase II AFTC for ex 759 NAS pupils*	Brawdy
Sea Vixen FAW2	766 *All Weather Fighter Training*	Yeovilton
Phantom FG1	767 *Phantom CU*	Yeovilton
Hunter T8,8b,8c,GA11	764 *Air Warfare Instructor Training*	Lossiemouth

8.H   Naval fighters at 1 January 1975

Type	Unit	Base
Phantom FG1	892	Leuchars

8.I   Naval fighters at 1 May 1982

Type	Unit	Base
Sea Harrier FRS1	800	HMS *Hermes* (South Atlantic)
	801	HMS *Invincible* (South Atlantic)
	809	HMSs *Hermes*/ *Invincible*
Sea Harrier FRS1, Hunter T8M	899	Yeovilton: *HMSs Hermes*/ *Invincible*

8.J   Naval fighters at 1 January 1990

United Kingdom

Type	Unit	Base
Sea Harrier FRS1	801	Yeovilton
Sea Harrier FRS1, T4N, Hunter T8M	899 *Fixed-wing pilot training*	Yeovilton

Western Atlantic

Type	Unit	Base
Sea Harrier FRS1	800	Cecil Field (US)

8.K   Naval fighters at 1 January 1995

United Kingdom

Type	Unit	Base
Sea Harrier FA2	801	Yeovilton
Sea Harrier FA2, Harrier T4, T4N, T8	899 *Fixed-wing pilot training*	Yeovilton

Adriatic

Type	Unit	Base
Sea Harrier FRS1	800	HMS *Invincible*

8.1 Supermarine Seafire (1942–1954)

In the early years of the war naval fighters like the Fulmar traded performance for ruggedness and were no match for their land-based equivalents. After successful use of the Hurricane at sea the decision was taken to convert the Spitfire for naval use. The first tests were carried out late in 1941 with a converted Spitfire Mk VB as a result of which the decision was taken to introduce the type to naval service.

Mark IB
The Type 340 was a Spitfire Mk V conversion with four .303in machine-guns and two 20mm Hispano cannon. Some of the 166 conversions had clipped wings.

Service (post-1945) Training 748

Mark IIC
The Type 357 was similar to the Mark IB except that it was built as such from scratch and employed the C type wing generally fitted with four 20mm cannon. The variant was also equipped to carry one 250lb bomb. Some were fitted with the Merlin 32 with a four-bladed propeller for low-altitude tasks.

Service (post-1945) Training 748, 768

Mark III
The Type 358 had no RAF equivalent. Like the Mk II it had four 20mm cannon in a C type wing and the bomb load was increased to two 250lb or one 500lb bombs. However, manual wing folding was employed for the first time in the Seafire and over 1,000 were built.

Service (post-1945) Fighter 887, 894, 1832 **Training** 736, 757, 759, 760, 761, 768, 794, 799 **Trials** *700*

Mark XV
The Type 377 Mk XV was the next variant number applied as Seafire variants were now given mark numbers

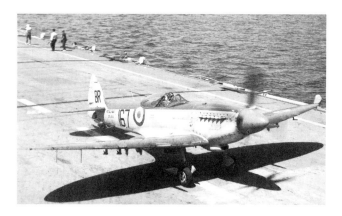

Supermarine Seafire Mk XVII

The Seafire was the standard Fleet Air Arm fighter at the end of the war together with the heavier Firefly. In front-line service the Seafire was eclipsed by the Sea Fury early on in the Korean war, but the Supermarine fighter continued in second-line service until 1954. A former trials aircraft, SX311/167 of 1833 NAS, is seen on board a fleet carrier in 1952 sporting the BR tailcode of NAS Bramcote. *(Author's collection)*

interspersed with those applied to contemporary Spitfire variants. The Mk XV was the first Seafire to be fitted with the Griffon engine, but it appeared too late to see war service. It was essentially a navalised Spitfire XII with a folding strengthened C wing with fuel tanks. Prototype was NS487 and 392 were delivered; the Mk XV entered service with 892 NAS in May 1945.

Service (post-1945) Fighter 800, 801, 802, 803, 804, 805, 806, 883, 1831, 1832, 1833 **Training** 706, 709, 718, 736, 737, 759, 761, 766, 767, 768, 780, 790, 799 **Communications** 701, 781 **Utility** 721, 728, 733, 751, 771, 773, 791 **Trials** 700, 787

Mark XVII
The Type 395 was a refined Mk XV with a clear view canopy and an extra 33 gals of fuel in the rear fuselage. The prototype (NS493) was the third Mk XV; 232 were produced and the variant was the last Seafire type to remain in naval service (764 NAS to November 1954).

Service Fighter 800, 802, 803, 805, 807, 809, 879, 883, 887, 1831, 1832, 1833 **Training** 727, 736, 737, 738, 759, 761, 764, 766, 799 **Utility** 728 **Communications** 781, 782 **Trials** 703, 746, 777, 778, 787

FR Mark 17
The Type 395 FR version comprised a limited number of Mk XVII variants fitted with two F.24 cameras (one vertical and one oblique) in place of the extra fuel tank. They were allocated to most of the units using the basic Mk XVII model.

F Mark 45
The Type 474 Mk 45 was a naval version of the RAF's Spitfire Mk 21 built to a new specification, N.7/44. The high mark number reflected a change in the system whereby naval variants were given a new potential range. The prototype, TM379, was a converted Spitfire Mk 21 with a Griffon engine driving five or six-bladed (contra-rotating) airscrews. Armament comprised four 20mm cannon and provision for one 250lb or 500lb bomb. With no provision for wing folding the type did not enter front-line service.

Service Training 709, 780 **Utility** 771 **Trials** 700, 703, 778, 787

F Mark 46
The Type 474 Mk 46 was equivalent to the Spitfire Mk 22 with a bubble hood and 24-volt electrical system. The prototype was TM383, originally a Mk 45, and just 24 were built.

Service Fighter 1832 **Training** 736, 737, 738, 767 **Communications** 781 **Utility** 771 **Trials** 778, 787

FR Mark 46
The Type 474 FR variant was the designation applied to a handful of the Mk 47 fitted with a single F.24 camera.

Service *included* **Fighter** 1832

F Mark 47
The Type 388/474 was the final Seafire variant, being a navalised version of the Spitfire Mk 24 with wing folding,

a six-blade airscrew and additional fuel. The Mk 47 served in Malaya and Korea.

Service **Fighter** 800, 804, 1832, 1833 **Training** 759 **Trials** 778, 787; ETPS

FR Mark 47
The Type 388/474 FR model was fitted with a single F.24 camera and most of the 90 Mk 47s were either built or converted to this standard.

Service *included* **Fighter** 800, 804, 1832

Specification and production

Mark	Role	Engine	HP	Weight lb	Speed mph	Nos
I	Fighter	Merlin 45/46	1470/1417	6,700	365	166*
II	Fighter	Merlin 45/46	1470/1417	7,000	333	402
III	Fighter	Merlin 55	1470	7,100	352	1,220
XV	Fighter/ FR	Griffon VI	1815	8,000	392	384
XVII	Fighter/ FR	Griffon VI	1815	8,100	392	232
F45	Fighter/ FR	Griffon 61/85	2035	9,500	446	50
F46	Fighter/ FR	Griffon 61/64	2035	9,900	446	24
F47	Fighter/ FR	Griffon 87/88	2145/2350	10,200	451	90

* Spitfire V conversions

Further reading
Spitfire – The History Morgan, E B and Shacklady E, Guild Publishing, London, 1987
Spitfire – The Story of a Famous Fighter Robertson, B, Harleyford Publications, Letchworth, 1960
Supermarine Seafire (Merlins) Profile 221 Bachelor, L, Profile Publications, Windsor, 1971

8.2 Grumman Wildcat (1940–1946)

The early versions of the US F4F-3 Grumman G-36 were bought by the British as the Martlet and three versions served in the Royal Navy between 1940 and 1943. When the United States supplied the type under lend-lease the name was changed to Wildcat, to match American nomenclature. The Martlet comprised the Mks I, II and III, all of which were out of service by 1946.

Mark IV
The Mk IV was equivalent to the F4F-4 with a single Double Wasp R-1830-86 and fitted with six .50in calibre machine guns; 220 were supplied and it served with fourteen front-line squadrons and numerous second-line units.

Service (post-1945) **Trials** 700

Mark V
The Mk V was similar in all respects to the Mark IV except that the aircraft were built by General Motors, thus conferring the US designation FM-1.

Service (post-1945) **Training** 748

Mark VI
The final Wildcat was equivalent to the FM-2 with a much taller fin and rudder and the Wright Cyclone engine. Armament was reduced to four .50in calibre guns and two 250lb bombs. The variant was delivered in quantity in mid-1944 but most were out of service and returned to the US within a year, having been superseded by the Hellcat.

Service (post-1945) **Training** 748

Specification and production

Mark	Role	Engine	HP	Weight loaded	Speed mph	Nos
I	Fighter	Cyclone G-205A	1,200	5,876	310	85
II	Fighter	Double Wasp R-1830-86	1,200	6,100	330	90
III	Fighter	Double Wasp R-1830-86	1,200	6,100	330	40
IV	Fighter	Double Wasp R-1830-86	1,200	6,100	330	220
V	Fighter	Double Wasp R-1830-86	1,200	6,100	330	312
VI	Fighter	Cyclone R-1820-56	1,350	8,271	332	370

Further reading
F4F Wildcat in Action (In Action 84) Squadron Signal Publications, Carrollton, 1984
Grumman F4F-3 Wildcat (Profile 53) Greene, F L, Profile Publications, Leatherhead, 1964

8.3 Grumman Hellcat (1944–1946)

The American Grumman G-50 F6F was the natural successor to the Wildcat, based on advice from those flying the earlier type in combat. In general the Hellcat was streamlined and fitted with a more powerful engine conferring a higher ceiling and greater speed. Although retaining the F4F's armament there was increased ammunition capacity and armour, and the narrow track undercarriage of the earlier type was abandoned for a wider track type.

Mark I
The Mk I was the equivalent of the F6F-3 with the Double Wasp engine. It was initially known as the **Gannet Mk I** in British service but as a lend-lease type the US name was soon adopted. Six .50in calibre guns were fitted.

Service (post-1945) **Training** 709

Mark II
The Mk II was fitted with a water-injected version of the Double Wasp and as such equated to the F6F-5. The cowling and windshield were modified and there was provision for 2,000lb of bombs under the fuselage. The **FR Mark II** designation was applied to some of the 930 Mk IIs supplied to the Royal Navy and fitted with an

Grumman Hellcat NF Mk II

The Hellcat NF Mk II was equivalent to the USN's F6F-5N night fighter and as seen here the radar was carried in a radome on the starboard wing. JZ823/O5B was with 892 NAS on HMS *Ocean* early in 1946. *(R C Sturtivant)*

oblique camera in the rear fuselage while retaining the original wing armament.

Service (post-1945) **Training** 706, 757, 784 **Trials** 700

NF Mark II

The night fighter variant was similar to the American F6F-5N night fighter fitted with an AN/APS-6 radar in a radome on the starboard wing. By 1946 they served in the sole remaining Hellcat fighter unit while several remained in service in training units mainly equipped with the day-fighter model.

Service (post-1945) **Night fighter** 892

PR Mark II

The PR designation applied to a few aircraft with cameras only.

Service (post-1945) **Reconnaissance** 888

Specification and production

Mark	Role	Engine	HP	Weight loaded	Speed mph	Nos
I	Fighter	Double Wasp R-2800-10	2,000	13,753	371	252
II	Fighter	Double Wasp R-2800-10W	2,000	13,750	380	856
II	Night fighter	Double Wasp R-2800-10W	2,000	13,950	365	74

8.4 Chance Vought Corsair (1943–1946)

The V-166B Corsair was a robust fighter which served from the middle of the Second World War until after the end of the Korean war. The prototype flew in 1940 and the distinctive inverted gull wing was incorporated to allow large propeller diameter combined with short undercarriage legs and a low wing fold. First deliveries to

Britain through the lend-lease scheme were made in 1943 with 1830 NAS forming in June. Armament comprised four .50in machine-guns in the wings.

The Mark I was the equivalent of the American F4U-1 fitted with the Double Wasp R-2800-8. The Mark II equated to the F4U-1A or -1D, similar to the original version but with a blown canopy. Like all successive Corsairs in RN service, wing-span was reduced by 16in to accommodate the type in small carriers. There was provision for two 1,000lb bombs and attachment points on the wings for eight 5in rockets. Both early variants were out of service by the end of 1945.

Mark III

The Mk III was basically the same as the Mk II being the F4U-1 built by Brewster as the F3A-1D. The engine incorporated water injection giving increased power at take-off.

Service (post-1945) **Training** 757, 759, 767, 794 **Trials** 700

Mark IV

The Mk IV was similar to the Goodyear-produced FG-1D, like the Mk II fitted to carry two 1,000 bombs or under-fuselage fuel tanks.

Service (post-1945) **Fighter** 1831, 1846, 1850, 1851 **Training** 706, 715

Specification and production

Mark	Role	Engine	HP	Weight loaded	Speed mph	Nos
I	Fighter	Double Wasp R-2800-8	2,000	11,800	417	95
II	Fighter	Double Wasp R-2800-8	2,000	11,800	417	510
III	Fighter	Double Wasp R-2800-8	2,250	12,100	415	430
IV	Fighter	Double Wasp R-2800-8	2,250	12,100	415	942

Chance Vought Corsair Mk IV

The inverted gull-wing Corsair served with the Fleet Air Arm in the Far East but as a lend-lease type was soon out of service after the War's end. KD725/V8K of 1850 NAS has taken the barrier on HMS *Vengeance* off Trincomalee on 18 June 1946 *(R C Sturtivant)*

Further reading
Chance Vought F4U-1 Corsair (Profile 47) Dial, J F,
    Profile Publications, Leatherhead, 1964
Chance Vought F4U-4 to F4U-7 Corsair (Profile 150)
    Dial, J F, Profile Publications, Leatherhead, 1968

8.5 Fairey Firefly (1943–1961)

The Firefly was designed to specification N.5/40 which
called for a fast two-seat fighter aircraft, also capable of
fulfilling the reconnaissance role, to replace the Fulmar.
Broadly similar in design and dimensions, the prototype
Firefly (Z1826) flew on 22 December 1941. It was fitted
with the Griffon engine and armed with four 20mm
cannon. Although designed as a fighter-reconnaissance
type, it was used in the fighter-strike role rather than as
an air superiority fighter. There appear to have been two
strands to mark numbers for the Firefly. The first was
based on an original series up to the Mk IV, while later
Mk I conversions were given Arabic mark numbers
including typically the T Mk 1.

Mark I
The initial variant saw service during the Second World
War both off Norway and in the Far East; first unit
equipped with the Firefly was 1770 NAS. The Mk I was
fitted with the Griffon IIB with a distinctive chin radiator
and it had provision for eight 60lb RPs or two 1,000lb
bombs. Several minor modifications were incorporated
on the production line including a revised cockpit canopy
and faired guns. By 1946 most had been converted to FR
Mk I standard.

Service (post-1945) Training 767

FR Mark I
The FR variant was similar to the Mk I but with the addition of AN/APS4 ASH radar fitted on a rack under the
nose; 273 aircraft were built to this standard. The **Mark
IA** designation was applied to a number of Mk I aircraft
brought up to FR Mk I standard.

Service (post-1945) Fighter 1830, 1841 **Training** 796

NF Mark I
The night fighter comprised some 140 Mk I aircraft fitted
with shrouded exhausts and AI Mk 10 radar.

Service (post-1945) Training 792

T Mark I
This was a conversion of the Mk I/FR Mk I (34 aircraft)
for training with a 12in raised instructor cockpit in place
of the observer's cockpit. Several aircraft retained their
armament.

Service   (post-1945) Training   736,   1830
Communications 781
The TT Mark I designation was applied to Mk I/FR Mk
I target tug conversions, with a windlass on the port side,
for Denmark, India and Sweden. The NF Mark II was a
new version with Mk 10 radar fitted on the wings, either
side of the fuselage. Some 37 were built, but the radar fit
was cumbersome, resulting in the simpler Mk I conversions; most NF Mk IIs were converted to Mk I standard.

T Mark 2
The Mk 2 was a weapons training conversion of the Mk
I, like the T Mk I fitted with a raised rear cockpit.
Gunsights were fitted in both cockpits.

Fairey Firefly AS Mk 6

The early Fireflys sported a chin radiator, but the Griffon 74 engined Mk 6 was clean-cowled as seen here. By the time this
photograph was taken in 1952 the AS Mk 6 had been optimised for the anti-submarine role with guns deleted but with provision
for underwing stores including rockets as seen. Four aircraft of the Channel Air Division are seen, possibly on HMS *Illustrious*,
with WB380/211FD in the foreground. *(Author's collection)*

Service (post-1945) Training 737, 764, 765, 766, 781, 782, 799, 1830, 1833, 1840, 1841, 1844 **Trials** 744 **Utility** 771.

The Mark III was a fighter version which flew in prototype form only (Z1835) in 1943. The Griffon 61 required a revised radiator and the resulting nose profile offered an unacceptable performance.

T Mark 3

The **T Mark 3** was a Mk I conversion for training observers. It was unarmed and the rear cockpit (not raised) was fitted with a drift indicator.

Service Training 796, 1830, 1833, 1840, 1841, 1844

Mark IV

The Mk IV was the first variant to be clean-cowled with a more powerful Griffon 74 engine and radiators in the wing roots. A four-bladed propeller replaced the three-bladed type of earlier versions. The wing-tips were clipped, the ASH radar was housed in a pressurised container on the starboard wing with a counterbalancing fuel tank on the port wing and a revised fin and rudder. Seventy-seven were built new and a further 43 were converted from the Mk I.

Service Fighter 810, 812, 814, 816, 825, 1830, 1840 **Training** 727, 736, 767, 799 **Communications** 781, 782 **Trials** 703, 778, 787

TT Mark 4

The TT Mk 4 was converted from the Mk IV as a target tug similar to the TT Mk 1 but with the winch under the fuselage.

Service Utility 771 **Trials** 700

FR Mark 5

The Mk 5 was an improved version of the Mk IV with various minor equipment changes and, on later aircraft, powered wing folding. The variant was a true multi-role aircraft and the designations **AS Mark 5** and **NF Mark 5** were also applied to reflect the speed with which the model could be adapted to role with different equipment in both pilot and observer cockpits. Underwing stores included depth charges and sonobuoys. This mark of Firefly served extensively throughout the Korean War. The **T Mark 5** and **TT Mark 5** designations were applied to two of each type being conversions for the RAN.

Service Fighter 804, 810 **Night fighter** 821 **Anti-submarine** 812, 814, 816, 817, 820, 825, 880, 1830, 1841, 1844 **Training** 719, 737, 796 **Communications** 781, 782 **Trials** 703, 778

AS Mark 6

The Mk 6 was a development of the FR Mk 5 solely for anti-submarine warfare. The guns were deleted and the electrical equipment changed to accommodate a wide range of underwing stores. The type entered service with 814 NAS in 1951 and served until 1956 when replaced by the Gannet. The **TT Mark 6** designation was applied to four conversions for the RAN.

Service Anti-submarine 812, 814, 817, 820, 825, 826, 1830, 1840, 1841, 1842, 1843, 1844 **Training** 719, 737, 767, 796 **Utility** 771 **Communications** 782 **Trials** 703, 744, 751

AS Mark 7

The Mk 7 was the last major variant and as such it differed from all previous marks. The Gannet was found to be too heavy for the light carriers and as an interim solution the Firefly was re-designed to accommodate two radar operators. The engine was switched to the Griffon 59 with the original chin radiator. The wings were also based on the elliptical form of the Mk I and to improve directional stability a taller fin and rudder were incorporated. There was no provision for armament or stores, the type being intended for search only.

Service Anti-submarine 814, 824 **Training** 719, 737, 750, 766, 796 **Trials** 744

T Mark 7

The trainer was similar to the AS Mk 7 but with the arrester hook deleted. The Mk 7 was not considered suitable for the original role and thus was mainly used for training.

Service Training 719, 750, 765, 796 **Trials** 744

U Mark 7

A single AS Mk 7 (WJ194) was converted for use as a drone target by having all unnecessary equipment removed. It was later converted to U Mk 8 standard.

T Mark 8

The designation was applied to six AS Mk 7 aircraft converted for chase and drone trials; all were later converted to U Mk 8 standard.

Service Trials RAE

U Mark 8

The Mk 8 were new-build aircraft from the AS Mk 7 production line. All unnecessary equipment was removed, the propeller locked for 2,600rpm and an autopilot and wing-tip camera pods fitted; 34 were built in addition to six T Mk 8 conversions.

Service Trials 728B

U Mark 9

The Mk 9 comprised 40 conversions of the AS Mk 5 to drone configuration in a similar fashion to the AS Mk 7 variant.

Service Trials 728B

Specification and production

Mark	Role	Engine	HP	Weight loaded	Speed mph	Nos
I	Fighter	Griffon IIB	1,730	14,020	316	429
FR I	Fighter/recce	Griffon IIB	1,730	14,020	312	273
IA	Fighter/recce	Griffon IIB	1,730	14,020	316	1

220

Mark	Role	Engine	HP	Weight loaded	Speed mph	Nos
NF I	Night fighter	Griffon 12	1,990	14,020	316	140 [2]
T1	Trainer	Griffon 12	1,990	14,000	300	34 [2]
TT1	Target tug	Griffon 12	1,990	14,020	316	26 [3]
NF II	Night fighter	Griffon 12	1,990	14,020	316	37 [4]
T2	Trainer	Griffon 12	1,990	14,020	316	54 [2]
III	Fighter	Griffon 61	2,035	14,900	330	1
T3	Trainer	Griffon 12	1,990	13,415	316	50 [2]
IV	Fighter/NF	Griffon 74	2,245	15,615	386	120 [5]
TT4	Target tug	Griffon 74	2,245	15,615	360	28 [6]
FR5	FR/AS/NF	Griffon 74	2,245	15,615	386	338
T5	Trainer	Griffon 74	2,245	15,615	386	2 [7]
TT5	Target tug	Griffon 74	2,245	15,615	386	2 [7]
AS6	Anti-submarine	Griffon 74	2,245	16,096	386	149 [8]
TT6	Target tug	Griffon 74	2,245	15,615	386	4 [3]
AS7	Anti-submarine	Griffon 59	2,435	15,800	300	108
T7	Trainer	Griffon 59	2,435	15,800	300	43
U7	Drone	Griffon 59	2,435	15,800	300	1 [9]
T8	Chase	Griffon 59	2,435	15,800	300	6 [9]
U8	Drone	Griffon 59	2,435	15,800	300	40 [10]
U9	Drone	Griffon 74	2,245	15,615	380	40 [11]

[1] unknown number of Mk I brought up to FR I standard locally
[2] FR I conversions
[3] export only
[4] most converted to NF I
[5] including 43 Mk I conversions
[6] Mk IV conversions
[7] FR5 conversions export only
[8] including 16 FR5 conversions
[9] AS7 conversion
[10] including 6 T8 conversions
[11] FR5 conversions

Further reading
Fairey Firefly, Harrison, W, Airlife, Shrewsbury, 1992

8.6 Supermarine Seafang (1946)

The Type 383 Seafang was designed to N.5/45 as a navalised Spiteful which itself was based on the Spitfire Mk XIV mated to a new laminar flow wing. The first step was to add a sting-type arrester hook to Spiteful RB520 and the first Seafang prototype flew in 1946. Unlike the Seafire, the Seafang had an inward retracting main undercarriage. In the event the Seafang was not put into production, since the Seafire F Mk 47 was deemed to be adequate until the first generation of jet fighters was available.

The F Mark 31 was fitted with the Griffon 61 driving a five-bladed propeller. The first of ten (VG471) was delivered to the RAE on 15 January 1946. Armament comprised four 20mm cannon and provision for two 1,000lb bombs or rockets.

The F Mark 32 had wing folding, increased fuel

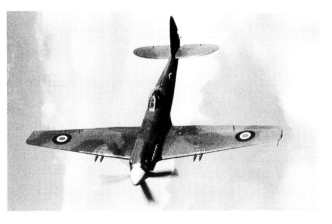

Supermarine Seafang F Mk 31

The Spitfire lineage is obvious in this fine shot of Seafang F Mk 31 which mated a late mark Spitfire fuselage and tail assembly with a new laminar flow wing with inward-retracting main undercarriage. The type did not offer sufficient improvement on the late mark Seafires and was not put into production. *(MAP)*

capacity and a Griffon 89 driving two three-bladed contra-rotating propellors. Of this variant eight were built but only two were completed (VB893 & 895) and there is doubt about whether the type flew.

Specification and production

Mark	Role	Engine	HP	Weight lb	Speed mph	Nos
F31	Fighter	Griffon 61	2,035	10,574	470	10
F32	Fighter	Griffon 89	2,350	10,694	475	8

8.7 Hawker Sea Fury (1947–1954)

The P.1022 Sea Fury originated in the Fury land-based fighter (Chapter 2.4) intended to complement the Tempest in the long-range escort role and based on it in many respects. The Fury, designed to meet specification F.6/42, was intended to be a lightweight fighter utilising the Centaurus engine, which in the event was used successfully in the Tempest Mk II. The main change was a reduced wing-span and modified fin and rudder. In the event the Fury would offer little to the RAF but the type was also designed to meet specification N.7/43 calling for a naval fighter. The prototype, SR661, flew on 21 February 1945, but with a four-bladed propeller and non-folding wings.

F Mark 10
The Mk 10 was the first Sea Fury variant, earlier mark numbers being reserved for potential RAF Fury variants. It was armed with four 20mm cannon and the first production aircraft, TF895, flew on 30 September 1946. The first unit to receive the Sea Fury was 807 NAS at Eglinton in August 1947.

Service Fighter 802, 803, 805, 807 **Training** 736, 738, 799
Communications 781 **Trials** 700, 703, 778, 787

Hawker Sea Fury FB Mk 11

The lightweight Sea Fury was the fastest single piston-engined fighter in British service but it was rejected by the RAF against the new generation of jets. It was ideal for naval use, however, especially from small carriers and in Korea the type accounted for at least one MiG-15 destroyed. VR920/122 of 738 NAS is seen landing on a carrier in 1954. *(Author's collection)*

FB Mark 11
The Mk 11 differed from the first version in having provision for underwing weapons carriage, including twelve 60lb RPs or two 1,000lb bombs. The new variant complemented the Seafire 47, which had superior performance as an interceptor, and the Mk 11 came off the production line from TF956. First unit to receive the type was 802 NAS and it remained in front-line service until 1954 when replaced by the Sea Hawk or Sea Venom.

Service Fighter 801, 802, 803, 804, 805, 806, 807, 808, 811, 898, 1831, 1832, 1833, 1834 **Training** 736, 738, 767, 799 **Communications** 781, 782 **Utility** 773 **Trials** 700, 703, 739, 744, 751, 778, 787

T Mark 20
The trainer was produced in relatively large numbers by the simple expedient of adding a second cockpit behind the original and fitting dual controls. Two cannon were removed, as was the arrester hook, and the variant was used for conversion and specialist training.

Service Training 736, 738, 759, 799, 801, 802, 809, 1830, 1831, 1832, 1833, 1834 **Communications** 781, 782 **Utility** 771 **Trials** 703, 787, RAE

Specification and production

Mark	Role	Engine	HP	Weight loaded	Speed mph	Nos
F10	Fighter	Centaurus 18	2,550	12,500	460	50
FB11	Fighter bomber	Centaurus 18	2,550	12,500	460	615
T20	Trainer	Centaurus 18	2,550	11,930	445	60

Further reading
Hawker Sea Fury, The (Profile 126) Mason, F K, Profile
  Publications, Leatherhead, 1967

8.8 de Havilland Sea Hornet (1947–1957)

The DH103 Sea Hornet was initially produced to specification N.5/44 calling for a long-range fighter for use against the Japanese. The first prototype was PX212, a converted Hornet I (Chapter 3.7) which flew on 19 April 1945. The Sea Hornet was the first twin-engined type to operate from British carriers, but it entered service too late to play any part in the Second World War.

F Mark 20
The Mk 20 was similar to the RAF's F Mk 3 but with folding wings and a fuselage camera window. The engines were the Merlin 130/131, which were handed, and armament comprised four 20mm cannon, and eight 60lb RPs or two 1,000lb bombs. Only one front-line unit was fully equipped with the variant.

Service Fighter 801, 809 Display 806 **Training** 736, 738, 759 **Utility** 728, 771 **Trials** 703, 739, 778

NF Mark 21
The night fighter was built to specification N.21/45 and fitted with an ASH radar in a thimble radome and a radar operator's cockpit in the rear fuselage. The tailplane span was increased to improve stability and the engines were the Merlin 134/135. The NF Mk 21 served with only one front-line unit, and that for only two years from completion of working-up.

Service Night fighter 809 **Training** 759, 762, 792 **Utility** 728, 771 **Trials** 703, 787

PR Mark 22
For photo-reconnaissance the armament of the F Mk 20 was removed and replaced with two F.52 cameras (day photography) or a K.19B camera for night work.

Service Photo-reconnaissance 801, 806, 1833 **Training** 738, 759 **Trials** 703, 739, 787

de Havilland Sea Hornet F Mk 20

The Sea Hornet was intended as a long-range fighter for Far East use, but in the event it was too late for wartime use. It was the Navy's first twin-engined fighter for carrier operations, but most of the 182 ordered were used in second-line units. VR851/450C is on loan to 806 NAS from 801 NAS for a North American display tour in 1948. *(R C B Ashworth via P H T Green)*

Specification and production

Mark	Role	Engine	HP	Weight lb	Speed mph	Nos
F20	Fighter	2xMerlin 130/131	2,070	18,530	467	79
NF21	Night fighter	2xMerlin 133/134	2,030	19,530	430	80
PR22	Photo-recce	2xMerlin 130/131	2,070	18,230	467	23

Further reading
de Havilland Hornet, The (Profile 174) Birtles, P J, Profile Publications, Leatherhead, 1967
Hornet File, The, Cooper, L G, Air Britain, Tonbridge, 1992

8.9 de Havilland Sea Vampire (1949–1967)

The Sea Vampire (DH100) was the first jet aircraft operated by the Royal Navy and was a navalised version of the Vampire (Chapter 3.9). The type was used in single-seat and two-seat versions.

F Mark 10
The sole Mk 10 was the third prototype Vampire Mk I, LZ551, fitted with 40% extra flaps, long travel oleos and an arrester hook. It made the first ever deck landings on HMS *Ocean* on 3 December 1945.

Service Trials 778

F Mark 20
The Mk 20 was the production version of the Sea Vampire, being a navalised FB Mk 5 with the Goblin 2 engine. The wing was strengthened and the dive brakes and flaps enlarged to reduce landing speeds. The type was generally issued to second-line units for jet familiarisation, although armed with four 20mm cannon.

Service Training 702, 759, 764, 806 **Utility** 728, 771 **Trials** 700, 703, 787

de Havilland Sea Vampire T Mk 22

The Fleet Air Arm's introduction to the jet age was with the Vampire, eighteen single-seat variants of which were bought for familiarisation duties. More common was the T Mk 22 which was used extensively for training from 1953 to 1964; the example seen at Ford in 1956 is XA126/692 of 764 NAS. (*'Buzz' Burr via author*)

F Mark 21
The Mk 21 was another trials version, probably unique in concept. Three aircraft (TG286, VG701 and VT802) were fitted with a strengthened fuselage for undercarriage-less trials on a rubberised deck. The trials were conducted at RAE Farnborough and then on HMS *Warrior* between 1949 and 1953.

Service Trials 703, 771

T Mark 22
The DH115 Mk 22 was the equivalent of the RAF's T Mk 11. It was similar in most respects, did not have an arrester hook, but did have various minor equipment changes. The type served in the training and communications roles.

Service Training 702, 718, 727, 736, 750, 759, 764, 766, 802, 806, 808, 809, 831, 890, 891, 892, 893, 1831, 1832 **Communications** 781 **Trials** 700

Specification and production

Mark	Role	Engine	Thrust lb	Weight lb	Speed mph	Nos
F10	Trials	Goblin 1	2,700	10,480	540	1*
F20	Fighter	Goblin 2	3,000	12,660	526	18
F21	Trials	Goblin 2	3,000	12,500	525	3+
T22	Trainer	Goblin 35	3,500	11,150	538	73

* F1 prototype
+ F3 conversions

Further reading
de Havilland Vampire: The Complete History, Watkins, D, Sutton Publishing, Stroud, 1996
de Havilland Vampire, Venom and Sea Vixen, Birtles, P, Ian Allan, Shepperton, 1986

8.10 Supermarine Attacker (1951–1954)

The Attacker was the Royal Navy's first operational jet fighter, although originally designed as a land-based aircraft. The design, against which specification E.10/44 was written, continued the Spitfire lineage in that it incorporated the laminar flow wing of the Spiteful. Its transitional status was confirmed by the retention of a conventional tailwheel undercarriage. The type entered service with 800 NAS in August 1951 and it remained in front-line service only until 1954 when supplanted by the Sea Hawk.

F Mark 1
The Type 392 flew in prototype, land-based form (TS409) on 27 June 1946. The first naval prototype, Type 398 TS413, was built to specification E.1/45 and flew a year later. Powered by the Nene 3, the Attacker was armed with four 20mm Hispano cannon. Service entry was with 800 NAS in August 1951.

Service Fighter 800, 803, 890 **Training** 702, 736, 767 **Trials** 787

Supermarine Attacker F Mk 1

The Attacker was a jet aircraft utilising the Spiteful laminar flow wing. It became the Royal Navy's first operational jet fighter with 800 NAS in 1951 but the aircraft shown, WA497, is on manufacturer's pre-delivery trials. (*Vickers-Armstrong Ltd*)

FB Mark 1

The Type 398 FB Mk 1 was the designation applied when wing hard points were fitted to enable the carriage of eight 60lb RPs or two 1,000lb bombs. Eight aircraft, from WA529, were built to the standard while a number of F Mk 1s was converted. In due course most of the F Mk 1 and FB Mk 1 aircraft were fitted with the dorsal fin of the FB Mk 2.

Service Fighter 800 **Training** 767 **Utility** 771 **Trials** 787

FB Mark 2

The Type 398 Mk 2 had a more powerful Nene 102, modified ailerons and a revised cockpit hood. A dorsal fin was also fitted to improve stability.

Service Fighter 800, 803, 1831, 1832, 1833, 1834 **Training** 736, 767 **Utility** 771 **Trials** 787

Specification and production

Mark	Role	Engine	Thrust lb	Weight lb	Speed mph	Nos
F1	Fighter	Nene 3	5,000	11,500	590	61
FB1	Fighter bomber	Nene 3	5,000	11,500	590	8*
FB2	Fighter bomber	Nene 102	5,100	12,300	590	84

* plus some F1 conversions

Further reading
Supermarine Attacker, Swift and Scimitar, Birtles, P, Ian Allan, London, 1992

8.11 Hawker Sea Hawk (1953–1966)

The Hawker P.1040 was Hawker's first jet aircraft which became specification N.7/46. The design began as a jet-

engined Fury (P.1035) then progressed to the P.1040 with a bifurcated jet pipe. The non-navalised prototype, VP401, was powered by the Nene 1 and flew on 2 September 1947, and although in many respects the type was less advanced than the Attacker, its development was later and slower and it eventually superseded the Attacker in service.

F Mark 1

The Mk 1 had increased wing-span and tailplane area and a revised cockpit canopy. In the course of production an acorn fairing was fitted at the junction of the tailplane and fin to alleviate buffeting. The more powerful Nene 101 was fitted and armament comprised four 20mm Hispano Mk 5 cannon. The fully navalised prototype, VP413, flew on 3 September 1948 and the Sea Hawk entered service with 806 NAS in 1953.

Service Fighter 802, 804, 806, 807, 831, 1832 **Training** 736, 738, 764, 767: ETPS **Trials** 700, 703, 787 **Communications** Brawdy SF

F Mark 2

The next variant was similar to the F Mk 1 but with powered ailerons and provision for 90-gallon wing fuel tanks. First of the new type was WF240.

Service Fighter 802, 806, 807 **Training** 736, 738, 764, 767 **Trials** 700

FB Mark 3

The first fighter-bomber reflected a production line change with the wing pylons adapted to carry two 500lb bombs.

Service Fighter 800, 801, 802, 803, 807, 811, 895, 897, 898 **Training** 736, 738, 764, 767 **Trials** 700, 703, 787

FGA Mark 4

The Mk 4 was similar to the FB Mk 3 but with provision for four 500lb bombs or up to sixteen rockets.

Hawker Sea Hawk FGA Mk 6

The Sea Hawk was obsolete by 1956 when the type was in action for the first and only time during the Suez campaign. It entered service in 1953 in fighter form and would have been no match for contemporary land-based fighters but as a ground-attack type it proved a stable weapons platform. XE401/492J of 899 NAS floats off the foredeck of HMS *Eagle* during the campaign; noteworthy are the yellow/black campaign stripes on wings and fuselage. (*Author's collection*)

Service Fighter 800, 801, 804, 806, 807, 810, 811, 895, 898 **Training** 736, 738, 764 **Trials** 700, 787 **Communications** Lossiemouth SF

FB Mark 5

The Mk 5 comprised 50 upgraded FB Mk 3 fitted with the Nene 103 from 1955. The extra 200lb of thrust conferred better low-speed performance and a slightly improved ceiling.

Service Fighter 802, 806, 897 **Training** 736 **Trials** 700

FGA Mark 6

The final variant was the Nene 103 re-engined version of the FGA Mk 4. About 40 of the earlier version were converted and in addition 86 new aircraft were built, the last coming into service early in 1956. Underwing stores included two 75gal fuel tanks.

Service Fighter 800, 801, 803, 804, 806, 810, 895, 897, 898, 899 **Training** 736, 738, 750, 766 **Trials** 700, 787

Specification and production

Mark	Role	Engine	Thrust lb	Weight lb	Speed mph	Nos
F1	Fighter	Nene 101	5,000	13,200	560	95
F2	Fighter	Nene 101	5,000	13,400	560	40
FB3	Fighter-bomber	Nene 101	5,000	15,525	560	116
FGA4	Fighter/GA	Nene 101	5,000	15,525	560	97
FB5	Fighter-bomber	Nene 103	5,200	15,990	560	50*
FGA6	Fighter/GA	Nene 103	5,200	16,153	560	86+

* FB3 conversions
+ plus about 40 FGA4 conversions

Further reading

Hawker Sea Hawk, The (Profile 71) Mason, F K, Profile Publications, Leatherhead, 1965

8.12   de Havilland Sea Venom (1954–1970)

The DH112 Sea Venom was developed from the land-based NF Mk 2 (Chapter 3.10) and was the Royal Navy's first jet all-weather fighter, produced to specification

de Havilland Sea Venom FAW Mk 21

The Sea Venom was a development of the RAF's two-seat NF Mk 2 and although intended as a night fighter, it was used operationally for ground attack at Suez. WW281/095 of 893 NAS crash-landed on HMS *Eagle* during the campaign after being hit by AAA which took out the hydraulic system. *(Author's collection)*

N.107P. The Navy used the NF Mk 2 prototype, WP227, for carrier trials and the first Sea Venom prototype was WK376 which flew on 19 April 1951.

FAW Mark 20

The first variant was originally designated NF Mk 20 and was similar to the RAF's NF Mk 2A. It was fitted with AI Mk 10 radar and armed with four 20mm cannon with provision for eight 60lb RPs or two 250lb or 500lb bombs. The Sea Venom entered service with 890 NAS in March 1954.

Service **Fighter** 808, 809, 890, 891 **Training** 766 **Communications** Merryfield SF **Trials** 700

FAW Mark 21

The Mk 21 was fitted with the slightly more powerful Ghost 104 engine, powered ailerons and had no extended tailplane outboard of the booms. It also had a clear view canopy, ejection seats and a longer stroke undercarriage. It was the equivalent of the NF Mk 3 and employed the AI Mk 21 (APS-57) radar.

Service **Fighter** 809, 890, 891, 892, 893, 894 **Training** 736, 738, 750, 766: ETPS

FAW Mark 21ECM

The ECM variant comprised six of the basic model with the guns replaced by electronic countermeasures equipment. It was used for trials and training.

Service **Trials/training** 751, 831

FAW Mark 22

The Mk 22 was fitted with the Ghost 105 which gave a better climb rate, but in other respects it was similar to the FAW Mk 21; 39 were built as new, while an unspecified number was converted from the FAW Mk 21. The Sea Venom was retired from front-line service in 1961, but it continued in second-line service to 1970.

Service **Fighter** 891, 893, 894 **Training** 750, ADS (Airwork) **Trials** 700

FAW Mark 22ECM

The second ECM variant comprised a number of FAW Mk 22 aircraft with guns replaced by ECM equipment.

Service **Trials/training** 831

Specification and production

Mark	Role	Engine	Thrust lb	Weight lb	Speed mph	Nos
FAW20	All-weather fighter	Ghost 103	4,850	14,100	630	50
FAW21	All-weather fighter	Ghost 104	4,950	15,400	630	168*
FAW22	All-weather fighter	Ghost 105	5,300	15,800	575	39+

* 6 converted to FAW21ECM; unspecified number converted to FAW22
\+ unspecified number converted to FAW22ECM

Further reading
de Havilland Vampire, Venom and Sea Vixen, Birtles, P J, Ian Allan, Shepperton, 1986

8.13   Supermarine Scimitar (1958–1966)

The Scimitar had an unusual gestation leading from a straight-winged, butterfly tail design to the operational fighter. The **Supermarine 508** was a twin-jet design around which specification N.9/47 was written. The original design was to have featured no undercarriage and hence very thin wings, but trials with the Vampire (Chapter 8.9) were not promising and the idea was dropped in favour of a tricycle undercarriage. The prototype VX133 flew on 31 August 1951 and deck-landing trials on HMS *Eagle* followed in 1952. The second prototype, VX136, was designated **Supermarine 529** and had a slightly re-designed tail with variable incidence and strakes and changed intakes. The third prototype to specification N.9/47 (VX138) was the **Supermarine 525** (Chapter 12.4). It was fundamentally different from the earlier types in having a swept wing and conventional tail arrangement and blown flaps.

F Mark 1

The Type 544 was built to specification N.113D and was broadly similar to the type 525. Armament comprised four 30mm cannon, 24 3in RPs or four 1,000lb bombs or four Bullpup ASMs or AIM-9 Sidewinders. The Scimitar entered service with 803 NAS in 1958; despite its designation as a fighter type it was the first naval aircraft capable of carrying the British tactical nuclear bomb. In most respects the type was an interim aircraft, soon replaced in service by the Buccaneer.

Service **Strike fighter** 800, 803, 804, 807 **Air refuelling** 800B **Training** 736, 764 **Utility** FRU **Trials** 700

Supermarine Scimitar F Mk 1

The Fighter designation for the Scimitar was somewhat misplaced since it was the first British naval aircraft capable of carrying a tactical nuclear bomb. It also weighed over twice as much as the Sea Hawk which it replaced. At Farnborough in 1959 XD267/199R of 807 NAS shows off an asymmetric load of fuel tanks and a single 500lb bomb. (*Author's collection*)

Specification and production

Mark	Role	Engine	Thrust lb	Weight loaded	Speed mph	Nos
508	Proto	2xAvon RA.3	6,500	30,000	640	1
529	Proto	2xAvon RA.3	6,500	30,000	640	1
525	Proto	2xAvon RA.3	6,500	30,000	670	1
F1	Fighter	2xAvon 202	11,250	34,200	710	76

8.14 de Havilland Sea Vixen (1959–1974)

The twin-boom de Havilland DH110 was developed against RAF specification F.44/46 for a night fighter and the prototype, WG236, flew on 26 September 1951. In the event the specification was met by the Gloster Javelin (Chapter 2.9) while a contemporary naval specification, N.40/46, was met by the de Havilland Sea Venom (Chapter 8.12). Naval interest in the DH110 was kept alive, however, and after a swept-wing Venom development (the DH116) was rejected work progressed on the DH110 prototypes. (In 1962 four Sea Venoms were rebuilt as Sea Vixen models – known to the FAA as Vixettes – for the Royal Tournament.) WG236 had crashed with appalling results at the Farnborough air show in 1952, but the second prototype, WG240, was used for touch and go trials on HMS *Albion* in 1954. The third prototype, XF828, flew on 20 June 1955. It had a rounded nose and an arrester hook, allowing full carrier trials on HMS *Ark Royal*, but no folding wing.

FAW Mark 1
The Mk 1 was originally designated FAW Mk 20 and was produced against specification N.139P. The first production aircraft was XJ474 which flew on 20 March 1957 and the Sea Vixen entered operational service with 892 NAS in July 1959. The Sea Vixen was the first British fighter aircraft to be designed without guns. Armament comprised four Firestreak AAMs or four Microcell rocket packs or two 1,000lb bombs and two Bullpup

de Havilland Sea Vixen FAW Mk 1

Although not taken up by the RAF, which preferred the Javelin as its all-weather/night fighter, the DH110 became the Sea Vixen in FAA service. The type equipped four front-line squadrons and nine from 890 NAS are seen here in formation in 1964, led by XJ483/248. *(Author)*

ASMs. In addition 28 51mm rockets were stored internally and two underwing fuel tanks were also carried.

Service **All-weather fighter** 890, 892, 893, 899 **Training** 700Y, 766 **Trials** RAE

FAW Mark 2
The second version incorporated provision for 2,000lb of extra fuel in slipper tanks within boom extensions projecting forward of the wing leading edge. In addition the armament was improved by the replacement of the Firestreak by the Red Top all-aspect AAM. Some 67 FAW Mk 1 aircraft were converted, and these were supplemented by a number of new-build aircraft. The new arrangements were tested on two FAW Mk 1 aircraft beginning in June 1962 and the first production FAW Mk 2, XP919, flew on 8 March 1963.

Service **All-weather fighter** 890, 892, 893, 899 **Training** 766; FRU **Trials** RAE

D Mark 3
The Mk 3 applied to three FAW Mk 2 conversions by Flight Refuelling for use as fast target drones at RAE Llanbedr. Operational equipment was removed and auto-pilot fitted; the designation U Mk 3 was also used informally.

Service **Trials** RAE

Specification and production

Mark	Role	Engine	Thrust lb	Weight lb	Speed mph	Nos
FAW1	AW fighter	Avon 208	11,230	35,000	645	119
FAW2	AW fighter	Avon 208	11,230	37,000	640	96*
D3	Drone	Avon 208	11,230	37,000	640	3+

* Including 67 FAW1 conversions
+ FAW2 conversions

Further reading
de Havilland Vampire, Venom and Sea Vixen, Birtles, P J, Ian Allan, Shepperton, 1986

8.15 BAe Sea Harrier (1980–date)

The P.1127 (Chapter 3.11) undertook sea trials on board HMS *Ark Royal* in 1963 but it was some time before the project reached fruition and then only because the Navy was denied conventional carriers. A VTOL aircraft could, however, utilise the so-called 'through-deck cruiser' which had managed to escape political oversight; thus was born the Sea Harrier. Twenty-four Sea Harriers were ordered in May 1975.

The Sea Harrier came into its own during the Falklands war when a total of 28 aircraft deployed accounted for the destruction of 28 Argentinian aircraft, most in air combat, for the loss of six aircraft (four in accidents and two to ground fire). As far as is known the Sea Harrier is one of only two types to have been involved in air-to-air

BAe Sea Harrier FRS Mk 1

Twenty-four Harriers were ordered for the Navy as the Sea Harrier based on the RAF's GR Mk 3 but with changes in materials and fuselage design, which incorporated radar in the nose. Service entry was in 1980 and this photograph shows aircraft of 899 (XZ494/106VL), 800 (XZ458/124H) and 801 (XZ493/001N) naval air squadrons in bright, pre-Falklands War, colours. *(BAe)*

combat in British service since the end of the Second World War (the other was the Sea Fury in the Korean War).

FRS Mark 1

The Mk 1 was closely based on the RAF's GR Mk 3 (Chapter 3.12) with about 90% commonality. The naval version has Blue Fox radar requiring a modified forward fuselage and better placed cockpit. As many as possible of the magnesium components were replaced by aluminium; tie-down lugs were fitted to an otherwise unchanged undercarriage and the brakes and V/STOL handling were improved. There was no prototype and the first production aircraft, XZ450, made its first flight on 20 August 1978. Armament comprised four AIM-9L AAMs plus twin 30mm cannon under-fuselage pods in the fighter role or up to 8,000lb of stores on four under-wing pylons and the two fuselage mounting points. The type joined 800 NAS in March 1980 and was replaced in front-line service by the FRS Mk 2 by 1994.

Service Fighter 800, 801, 809, 899 **Training/trials** 700A

FA Mark 2

The FA Mk 2 (also originally FRS Mk 2) is a potent upgrade of the earlier version incorporating Blue Vixen radar in a revised nose, improved avionics and provision for the carriage of AIM-120 AAMs. The first aircraft was a FRS Mk 1 conversion, ZA195, which flew on 19 September 1988. Up to 34 FRS Mk 1 airframes will be converted in addition to eighteen new-build aircraft on order.

Service Fighter 800, 801, 899

Specification and production

Mark	Role	Engine	Thrust lb	Weight lb	Speed mph	Nos
FRS1	Fighter	Pegasus 104	21,500	26,200	736	57
FA2	Fighter	Pegasus 106	21,500	26,200	736	52*

* Ordered; includes up to 34 FRS1 conversions, subject to attrition

Further reading

Harrier, Calvert, D J, Ian Allan, Shepperton, 1990
Harrier – Ski-Jump to Victory, Godden, J (ed), Brasseys, Oxford, 1983
Sea Harrier Over the Falklands, Ward, N D, Leo Cooper, London, 1992

BAe Sea Harrier FA Mk 2

The Sea Harrier proved its worth during the Falklands War and it was inevitable that there would be an updated version to exploit technological improvements. The FA Mk 2 incorporated 'Blue Vixen' radar in a modified nose and weapons changes, as seen here on ZE690/003 of 801 Sqn. Some FRS Mk 1 aircraft were converted to the new standard. *(BAe)*

9 – Naval anti-submarine and strike

See also: Buccaneer (4.12); Firefly (8.5); Lynx (10.11); Whirlwind (11.11)

This chapter concentrates on the Fleet Air Arm in the anti-shipping role, primarily anti-submarine warfare. Because roles are not invariably closely compartmentalised some naval strike types are described elsewhere as are those aircraft operated by the RAF and optimised for anti-shipping strike. The Fleet Air Arm has been poorly served by the country's politicians over many years and this is reflected in the poor levels of obsolete equipment with which it has often had to fight. It is therefore the more remarkable that the service has spawned so many developments, eagerly adapted across the Atlantic, which relied more on the initiative of its officers and men than on official support. The speed with which some equipment was designed and brought into service in the Falklands war demonstrates the potential for solving complex problems when the services and industry are freed from Treasury stifling and MoD indecision.

Fairey Firefly AS Mk 5

Although designed as a fighter and described in Chapter 8, the Firefly spent its post-war career as a strike aircraft. WB246/227O is preparing to take off from the flight deck of HMS *Ocean* in 1951. *(Author's collection)*

January 1946

In front-line service were the Firefly (eight squadrons) and Barracuda (six squadrons), generally shore-based; only two units were embarked on carriers with a number awaiting disbandment in Australia. Only one squadron flew the Firebrand which was due to replace the Barracuda. Lend-lease Avengers were shortly to be scrapped or returned to the US. The Royal Navy had in commission no fewer than six fleet carriers and five light fleet carriers, only two of which, HMSs *Glory* and *Vengeance*, were at sea.

In training and support was a number of front-line types plus a few Hellcats and Corsairs. The venerable Swordfish and its successor the Albacore survived in trials and utility roles. Not surprisingly most second-line bases were spread around the coastline of the UK, generally well away from concentrations of RAF operational airfields in the east and south of the kingdom.

July 1948

In common with other services the Fleet Air Arm had run down dramatically since the war, notwithstanding the emerging signs of trouble across the globe. There were just four operational units, three with the Firefly and one with the Firebrand, and two of these were embarked on carriers in the Far East. The Firefly AS Mk 5 optimised for anti-submarine warfare had entered service with 812 NAS while the Barracuda was to remain in the training role for some time.

January 1950

On the verge of the Korean war and as conflict spread the Fleet Air Arm increased its front-line units by adding another Firefly AS Mk 5 squadron and bringing the Barracuda back into front-line service. Training was consolidated in four units. The carrier fleet comprised five fleet carriers and six light fleet carriers; HMS *Ocean* was at sea, in the Mediterranean.

July 1952

There were now eleven front-line units with a further two reserve squadrons; the flying role of the Royal Naval Volunteer Reserve had been established in 1947. By now the Firebrand served with two units but the main anti-submarine vehicle remained the Firefly, now over ten years old and no match for the growing Soviet submarine threat. Training had been adjusted to cope with the increased demand for aircrew following the Korean war. A most significant development was the introduction of the potent Skyraider in the airborne early warning role; its AN/APS20A search radar was handed down via the Gannet to the Shackleton and remained in sevice until 1991. Six fleet carriers and seven light fleet carriers were in commission.

January 1955

There were now nine front-line units equipped with a miscellany of aircraft. The first Gannets, designed to meet the GR.17/45 requirement for an anti-submarine aircraft, had taken too long to bring into service and as an interim measure the wartime Avenger was re-introduced to the

Fleet Air Arm for several years. By 1955 the first Gannets were just in service with 826 NAS. Another milestone was the introduction of the Whirlwind helicopter which was to presage the eventual shift to an all-helicopter anti-submarine Fleet Air Arm capability. The potent Wyvern had also joined the FAA in two units, but like the Gannet, later than intended; by the time of its introduction it was obsolete in the strike role. Finally, there was new equipment in the training function in the form of the Sea Prince T Mk 1 which was one of the few types specifically designed to meet a training need and not adapted. There were now three fleet and eight light fleet carrriers in commission.

January 1960

The scope of the Fleet Air Arm during the Suez crisis is covered in Chapter 8 and shown in table 8.D. At that time the Wyvern operated in the strike role with two units while the Gannet was the main anti-submarine type serving with five squadrons. By 1960 the Gannet was making way for the Whirlwind and served with just one squadron in the Far East. The Whirlwind, in its more advanced HAS Mk 7 form, operated with three shore-based units. The RNVR squadrons had disbanded in March 1957. HMSs *Ark Royal, Centaur, Eagle, Hermes* and *Victorious* were in commission while HMSs *Albion* and *Bulwark* were being converted to commando carriers.

January 1965

The future of anti-submarine warfare seemed well-established as being helicopter-based but the Whirlwind lacked any significant search facility and was short-ranged. Its successor, the Wessex, remedied some of these problems although too large to serve on small warships and still short-ranged. The early, single-engined HAS Mk 1 was now in service with four units, including two in the Far East. Another significant change was the introduction of the Wasp, serving with 829 NAS which was to be the parent unit for the many ships' flights destined to operate the Wasp from frigates and destroyers. Another equipment change was the Gannet AEW Mk 3 which had replaced the Skyraider in the early warning role. HMSs *Ark Royal, Eagle* and *Victorious* were in commission with two light fleet and two commando carriers.

January 1970

The more capable Wessex HAS Mk 3 had replaced the first variant with four front-line and two training units. By now several squadrons provided detachments for a range of warships including the cruisers HMS *Blake* and *Tiger* and Royal fleet auxiliaries. This wider use of a variety of ships as ASW platforms compensated for the reduction in the carrier fleet to six.

January 1975

With the introduction of the Sea King the Fleet Air Arm had a versatile aircraft with the ability to hunt and kill submarines at long range from the host carrier. Five units were equipped with the type, one in the Far East. With the withdrawal from this theatre the carrier fleet was further run down with just HMSs *Ark Royal, Bulwark* and

Hermes available. On the training front, the Sea Prince was being replaced by the Jetstream T Mk 1 for observer training.

May 1982

The Argentinian invasion of the Falklands demonstrated how seriously the Fleet Air Arm had been run down. Fortunately small carriers – 'through-deck cruisers' – had been built, with one, HMS *Invincible*, on hand to complement HMS *Hermes*, the sole remaining conventional carrier. The use of helicopters in the anti-submarine role was also propitious and by 1982 there were three types in front-line service with the Wessex still operating in the training role. The tragedy of the Falklands war was the absence of any airborne radar cover which led to the loss of six ships from air attack with serious damage to many more.

The way in which the anti-submarine helicopters were deployed in the South Atlantic gives a useful indication of their use and versatility. The Wasp, which lacked its own search capability, served with 829 NAS based at Portland. Twenty were based on Type 12, Type 21 or Leander class frigates, survey vessels and the ice-patrol ship HMS *Endurance*. The Lynx HAS Mk 2 was replacing the Wasp and was in service with 815 NAS at Yeovilton with 23 on ships' flights on Type 42 destroyers and Type 21, Type 22 (two Lynx) or Leander class frigates. The Sea King HAS Mk 5 served with 820 NAS aboard HMS *Invincible* and 826 NAS on HMS *Hermes*. The Sea King HAS Mk 2/2A served with 824 NAS based at Culdrose and with flights on RFA *Olmeda*, RFA *Fort Grange* and Gibraltar. No 814 and 815 NAS both continued to operate from UK shore bases. Finally, two Wessex HAS Mk 3 of 737 NAS were embarked on the County class destroyers HMSs *Antrim* and *Glamorgan*.

January 1990

The Sea King had continued to be improved with the HAS Mk 5 being replaced by the HAS Mk 6, almost entirely through a conversion programme. Five Sea King units now operated in the UK, deployed as necessary on carriers or other heavier vessels. The Wasp had been completely superseded by the Lynx with two squadrons operating to parent a large number of the smaller ships' flights. In the light of the lack of airborne early warning highlighted in the Falklands war, eleven HAS Mk 2A Sea Kings were cleverly adapted in record time to carry a Searchwater radar with 125-mile range at 10,000ft, and these served with 849 NAS.

January 1995

There were now three carriers, HMSs *Ark Royal*, *Illustrious* and *Invincible*, and these regularly deployed to the Adriatic in connection with peace-keeping operations in Bosnia. With the end of the Cold War there has been a further drawdown of units and now only four Sea King and one Lynx squadrons remain in service. The Sea Kings are due to be replaced by the Merlin from the turn of the century and the Lynx HAS Mk 3 will be superseded by the Mk 8 variant which began to trickle into 815 NAS in 1996.

9.A Naval anti-submarine and strike at 1 January 1946

United Kingdom

Type	Unit	Base
Firefly FR1	816, 822	Machrihanish
	824, 825	Burscough
Barracuda II	826	Fearn
Barracuda TRIII	815, 821	Rattray
	860	Fearn
Firebrand TFIV	813	Ford

Mediterranean

Type	Unit	Base
Firefly INF	1792	HMS *Ocean* (Mediterranean)

Far East

Type	Unit	Base
Barracuda II	812	HMS *Vengeance* (Far East)
Barracuda II, Firefly FR1	814	Nowra (Australia)
Firefly F1, FR1	837	Nowra
Avenger III	828	Nowra
Avenger II	820	Schofields (Australia)
Firefly I	1772, 1790	Schofields

Training

Type	Unit	Base
Anson I, Firefly FR1, Martinet TT1	766 *1 Naval OTU*	Inskip
Barracuda II, TRIII, Avenger I, II, Anson I	785 *1 Naval OTU*	Crail
Barracuda TR111	744 *Anti-Submarine Training*	Eglinton
Hellcat I, Harvard IIB, Seafire XV, F45	709 *Ground Attack School*	St Merryn
Barracuda II	717 *Part I TBR Course*	Rattray
Barracuda II, Corsair III	767 *Part II TBR Course*	East Haven
Seafire III, Harvard III,	736 *TBR Air Strike Course*	St Merryn
Barracuda II, III	735 *ASV Training*	Burscough
Anson I, Firefly F1, FR1, Avenger II, Barracuda II	783 *ASV Radar Training*	Arbroath
Barracuda II	753 *Observer School*	Rattray

9.B Naval anti-submarine and strike at 1 July 1948

United Kingdom

Type	Unit	Base
Firebrand TF5	813	Anthorn
Firefly FR4	814	Eglinton

Far East

Type	Unit	Base
Firefly FR1, FR4, AS5	812	HMS *Theseus*
Firefly FR1	827	HMS *Colossus*

Training

Type	Unit	Base
Harvard III, Firefly FR1, T1, Seafire III, F15, 17	766 *Part I Op'l Flying Course*	Lossiemouth
Seafire F15, Firefly FR1	767 *Part I Op'l Flying Course*	Milltown
Seafire III, Firefly FR1	741 *Part II Op'l Flying Course*	St Merryn
Barracuda III, Harvard IIB, Firefly FR1	719 *Anti-Submarine Training I*	Eglinton
Barracuda TRIII, Anson I, Oxford I	744 *Anti-Submarine Training II*	Eglinton
Harvard III, Martinet TT1, Seafire F15, F17	736 *TBR Air Strike Course*	St Merryn

9.C Naval anti-submarine and strike at 1 January 1950

United Kingdom

Type	Unit	Base
Firebrand TF5	813	Lee-on-Solent
Firefly AS5	814	Culdrose
Barracuda TR3	815	Eglinton
Firefly FR1, T1	1830*	Abbotsinch

Mediterranean

Type	Unit	Base
Firefly NF1, AS5	812	HMS *Glory*

Far East

Type	Unit	Base
Firefly FR1, NF1	827	Sembawang (Malaya)

Training

Type	Unit	Base
Firefly FR1, T1, Seafire III, F15, 17	766 *Part I Op'l Flying Course*	Lossiemouth
Seafire F15, 17, Firefly FR1, T1, 2, FR4, AS5	737 *Part II Op'l Flying Course*	Eglinton
Martinet TT1, Seafire F17	736 *TBR Air Strike Course*	St Merryn
Barracuda III, X Seafire F17	796 *Observer School*	St Merryn

* RNVR unit

9.D Naval anti-submarine and strike at 1 July 1952

United Kingdom

Type	Unit	Base
Barracuda TR3	815	Eglinton
Firefly FR4, AS5	810	St Merryn
Firefly AS6	812	Anthorn
	824	Eglinton
	814	HMS *Eagle* (Home waters)
	820, 826	HMS *Indomitable* (Home waters)
Firebrand TF5	813	Lee-on-Solent

Type	Unit	Base
Firebrand TF5	827	HMS *Eagle* (Home waters)
Skyraider AEW1	849	Culdrose (from 7/7/52)
Harvard T2B, T3, Firefly T2, AS6	1830*	Donibristle
Harvard T2B, T3, Anson I, Firefly T2, AS6	1840*	Ford

Mediterranean

Type	Unit	Base
Firefly FR5	821	Hal Far (Malta)
Firefly FR5, AS5	825	HMS *Ocean*

Training

Type	Unit	Base
Firefly AS5,6	719 *Naval Air Anti-Submarine School (NASS) (53 TAG)*	Eglinton
Firefly FR1, T1, 2, FR4, AS5	737 *NASS (53 TAG)*	Eglinton
Anson I, Barracuda TR3	750 *Observer School Pt I*	St Merryn
Firefly T3, AS6	796 *Observer School Pt II*	St Merryn
Seafire F17, Firefly FR1, T1, 2 Harvard T2b	799 *Refresher Flying Training*	Macrihanish

* RNVR units

9.E Naval anti-submarine at 1 January 1955

United Kingdom

Type	Unit	Base
Firefly AS6, Gannet AS1	826	Lee-on-Solent
Avenger AS4	824	Eglinton
Avenger AS5	814	Lee-on-Solent
	815	Culdrose
Wyvern S4	827	Ford
Skyraider AEW1	849	Culdrose
Firefly FR5, AS6, Sea Prince T1, Sea Balliol T21	1830*	Abbotsinch
Firefly AS6, T2, Sea Prince T1, Sea Balliol T21	1840*	Ford
Firefly T2, Harvard T2B, T3, Sea Prince T1	1841*	Stretton
Firefly FR5, AS6, Sea Balliol T21, Sea Prince T1	1844*	Bramcote

Mediterranean

Type	Unit	Base
Skyraider AEW1	849 B Flt	Hal Far (Malta)
	849 C Flt	HMS *Albion*
Whirlwind HAS22	845	Hal Far (Malta)
Firefly FR5	810	HMS *Glory*
Avenger AS4	820	HMS *Centaur*
Wyvern S4	813	Hal Far (Malta)

Training

Type	Unit	Base
Firefly T7	719 *Naval Air Anti-Submarine School*	Eglinton
Firefly T2,AS5	737 *NASS*	Eglinton
Sea Prince T1Firefly T7	750 *Observer School Pt I*	Culdrose
Firefly T7	796 *Observer School Pt II*	Culdrose

* RNVR units

9.F Naval anti-submarine at 1 July 1957

United Kingdom

Type	Unit	Base
Wyvern S4	813	Brawdy
	831	HMS *Ark Royal* (Home waters)
Gannet AS1, T2	815	HMS *Ark Royal* (Home waters)
	820	HMS *Bulwark* (Home waters)
Gannet AS4	824	HMS *Albion* (Home waters)
Gannet AS4, T2	814, 825	Culdrose
Whirlwind HAS22, HAR3, HAS7	845	Lee-on-Solent
Skyraider AEW1	849	Culdrose
	849 B Flt	HMS *Ark Royal* (Home waters)
	849 C Flt	HMS *Albion* (Home waters)
	849 D Flt	HMS *Bulwark* (Home waters)

Mediterranean

Type	Unit	Base
Gannet AS1	847	Nicosia

Training

Type	Unit	Base
Gannet AS1, T2	719,737 *Naval Air Anti-Submarine School*	Eglinton
Firefly T2, 7, Oxford T2	765 *Piston Engine Pilot Pool*	Culdrose
Sea Prince T1	750 *Observer and Air Signal School Pt I*	Culdrose
Firefly T7	796 *Observer and Air Signal School Pt II*	Culdrose

9.G Naval anti-submarine at 1 January 1960

United Kingdom

Type	Unit	Base
Whirlwind HAS7	815	Culdrose
	820, 824	Portland
Skyraider AEW1, Gannet AS4	849	Culdrose
	849 A Flt	Culdrose

Type	Unit	Base
	849 B Flt	Culdrose
	849 C Flt	Culdrose
	849 D Flt	Culdrose

Far East

Type	Unit	Base
Gannet AS4	810	HMS *Centaur*

Training

Type	Unit	Base
Whirlwind HAS3, 7	737 *Naval Air Anti-Submarine School*	Portland
Sea Prince T1	750 *Observer and Air Signal School*	Hal Far (Malta)

9.H Naval anti-submarine at 1 January 1965

United Kingdom

Type	Unit	Base
Wessex HAS1	815	Culdrose
	819	Ballykelly
Wasp HAS1, Whirlwind HAS7, Wessex HAS1	829	Portland
Gannet AEW3, T4, COD4, T5	849	Brawdy
Gannet AEW3	849 B Flt	Brawdy
	849 C Flt	Brawdy

Far East

Type	Unit	Base
Wessex HAS1	814	HMS *Victorious*
	820	HMS *Eagle*
Gannet AEW3	849 A Flt	HMS *Victorious*
	849 D Flt	HMS *Eagle*

Training

Type	Unit	Base
Wessex HAS1, Wasp HAS1	706 *Advanced Helicopter Training*	Culdrose
Wessex HAS1	737 *Anti-Submarine School*	Portland
Sea Prince T1, Sea Vampire T22, Sea Venom FAW22	750 *Observer and Air Signal School*	Hal Far (Malta)

9.I Naval anti-submarine at 1 January 1970

United Kingdom

Type	Unit	Base
Wessex HAS3	814, 820, 826	Culdrose
	819	Ballykelly
Wasp HAS1, Whirlwind HAR9, Wessex HAS1, HAS3	829	Portland
Gannet AEW3, COD4, T5	849	Brawdy
	849 A Flt	Brawdy
	849 B Flt	Brawdy
	849 D Flt	Brawdy

Training

Type	Unit	Base
Wessex HAS1,HAS3	706 *Advanced Helicopter Training*	Culdrose
Wessex HAS1, HAS3	737 *Anti-Submarine School*	Portland
Sea Prince T1, Sea Venom FAW22	750 *Observer and Air Signal School*	Lossiemouth

9.J   Naval anti-submarine at 1 January 1975

United Kingdom

Type	Unit	Base
Sea King HAS1	814	HMS *Hermes* (Home waters)
	819	Prestwick
	824	Culdrose
	826	HMS *Tiger* (Home waters)
Wasp HAS1, Wessex HU5	829	Portland
Gannet AEW3, COD4, T5	849	Lossiemouth
	849 B Flt	Lossiemouth

Far East

Type	Unit	Base
Sea King HAS1	820	Kai Tak (Hong Kong)

Training

Type	Unit	Base
Wasp HAS1, Sea King HAS1	706 *Advanced Helicopter Training*	Culdrose
Sea King HAS1, Wessex HAS1, HAS3	737 *Anti-Submarine School*	Portland
Sea Prince T1, Jetstream T1	750 *Observer and Air Signal School*	Culdrose

9.K   Naval anti-submarine at 1 May 1982

United Kingdom

Type	Unit	Base
Sea King HAS2/2A	814	Culdrose
	819	Prestwick
	825 HQ	Culdrose
Sea King HAS2/2A, HAS5	824 HQ	Culdrose
Lynx HAS2	815 HQ *parenting ships' flights*	Yeovilton
Wasp HAS1	829 HQ *parenting ships' flights*	Portland

South Atlantic

Type	Unit	Base
Sea King HAS2/2A	825 dets	SS *Queen Elizabeth II*, Atlantic *Causeway*, RFA *Engadine*
Sea King HAS5	820	HMS *Invincible*
Sea King HAS2/2A, HAS5	824 A Flt	RFA *Olmeda*
	826	HMS *Hermes*
Lynx HAS2	815	various ships' flts
Wasp HAS1	829	various ships' flts

Type	Unit	Base
Wessex HAS3	737	HMS *Antrim*, *Glamorgan*

Training

Type	Unit	Base
Lynx HAS2	702 *Lynx OCU*	Yeovilton
Sea King HAS2, 2A, HAR3, HAS5	706 *Advanced Helicopter Training*	Culdrose
Wessex HAS3	737 *Anti-Submarine School*	Portland
Jetstream T1, T2	750 *Observer and Air Signal School*	Culdrose

9.L   Naval anti-submarine at 1 January 1990

United Kingdom

Type	Unit	Base
Sea King HAS5	810	Culdrose (RFA *Argus*)
	820	Culdrose (HMS *Ark Royal*)
	826 B Flt	Culdrose (RFA *Tidespring*)
	826 C Flt	Culdrose (RFA *Olmeda*)
Sea King HAS6	819	Prestwick
Lynx HAS3	815, 829 *parenting ships' flights*	Portland
Sea King AEW2A	849 HQ	Culdrose

West Atlantic

Type	Unit	Base
Sea King HAS5	814	HMS *Invincible*

Training

Type	Unit	Base
Lynx HAS3	702 *ASW Conversion*	Portland
Sea King HAS5	706 *ASW Training*	Culdrose
Jetstream T2, T3	750 *Observer Training*	Culdrose

9.M   Naval anti-submarine at 1 January 1995

United Kingdom

Type	Unit	Base
Sea King HAS6	810, 820	Culdrose
Sea King HAS6	820	HMS *Illustrious*
	819	Prestwick
Lynx HAS3S, 3CTS, 3GM	815	Portland
Sea King AEW2A	849 HQ	Culdrose
Sea King AEW2A	849 B Flt	HMS *Illustrious*

Adriatic

Type	Unit	Base
Sea King HAS5, 6	814	HMS *Invincible*
Sea King AEW2A	849 A Flt	HMS *Invincible*

Training

Type	Unit	Base
Lynx HAS3S, 3CTS	705	Portland
Sea King HAS5, 6	706	Culdrose
Jetstream T2	750	Culdrose

9.1 Fairey Swordfish (1936–1946)

The Swordfish was one of the truly great aircraft of the Second World War. It was remarkably robust and had its origins in the private-venture Fairey TSR.I biplane torpedo-bomber. After the prototype crashed in 1933 a revised model, the TSR.II, was built to specification S.15/33 and the prototype, K4190, flew on 17 April 1934.

Mark I
The first Swordfish variant to specification S.38/34 was powered by a single Pegasus III.M3 engine driving a three-blade propeller. It had an open cockpit and fixed undercarriage, easily interchangeable with floats, and was armed with a Vickers .303in machine-gun firing forward and a Lewis or Vickers gun in the aft cockpit. An 18in torpedo or 1,500lb mine was carried under the fuselage or up to 1,500lb of bombs, a maximum of 500lbs being carried on wing points. The Swordfish entered service with 825 NAS in 1936 and it served with distinction in all theatres apart from the Pacific.

Service (post-1945) Fleet requirements 728

Mark II
The second variant was initially distinguished only by having the lower mainplanes stressed to launch eight 60lb rocket projectiles. Later, the Pegasus XXX was fitted to some aircraft.

Service (post-1945) Air-sea rescue 1700

Mark III
The Mark III had provision for an ASV Mk X radar scanner beneath the forward fuselage which inhibited the carriage of a torpedo. These operated from the smaller carriers in the Atlantic.

Service (post-1945) Trials ATDU.
A small number of early versions was fitted with an enclosed canopy for use in Canada and designated Mark IV.

Specification and production

Mark	Role	Engine	HP	Speed mph	Weight lbs	Nos
I	ASW	Pegasus IIIM.3	690	139	7,720	992
II	ASW	Pegasus XXX	750	139	7,580	1080
III	ASW	Pegasus XXX	750	139	7,580	320
IV	ASW	Pegasus XXX	750	139	7,580	*

* small number of earlier mark conversions

Further reading
Fairey Swordfish Mks I-IV (Profile 212) Stott, I G, Profile Publications, Windsor, 1972

Swordfish Special, Harrison, W A, Ian Allan, Shepperton, 1977

Fairey Swordfish

The biplane Swordfish was remarkably robust and performed well from the attack at Taranto to cover of the D-Day invasion. It remained on second-line tasks for some years after the war and LS326, seen here in preserved state, was flown as a hack by the Fairey Aviation Company before transfer to the FAA. *(Author)*

9.2 Fairey Albacore (1940–1946)

The Albacore was designed as a Swordfish successor to specification S.41/36. The prototype, L7074, flew on 12 December 1938 and service entry was with 826 NAS in March 1940.

Mark I

Unlike the Swordfish the Albacore was a single-bay biplane with a number of improvements for the crew of three and a more powerful engine. One forward-firing and one or two rear-firing machine-guns were fitted and up to 2,000lb of bombs under the wings or a single torpedo were carried. However, the later type was far less agile and was withdrawn from service before the Swordfish.

Service (post-1945) Trials 700 **Utility** Anti-locust Flt, Eastleigh

---

Specification and production

Mark	Role	Engine	HP	Speed mph	Weight lb	Nos
I	ASW	Taurus II/XII	1,065/ 1,130	161	10,460	800

Fairey Albacore Mk I

The Albacore was intended as a Swordfish replacement but was withdrawn from front-line service before its predecessor. Several were still around on miscellaneous duties in early 1946. *(MAP)*

9.3 Fairey Barracuda (1943–1953)

The Barracuda was a pre-war design to specification S.24/37 intended to replace the then unbuilt Albacore as a torpedo-bomber-reconnaissance design. Fairey's solution was the Type 100 which was a shoulder-wing monoplane with large complex flaps and accommodating a crew of three under a long glasshouse canopy. The Barracuda was one of the least attractive of aircraft which reflected the functionality of the design. Armament comprised one or two rear-mounted .303in machine-guns

in the telegrapher air gunner's cockpit and provision was made for a single torpedo or 1,500lb of bombs, depth charges or mines.

The prototype, P1767, flew on 7 December 1940, development having been delayed by the cancellation of the intended Rolls-Royce X engine and its replacement by the Merlin. The Mark I entered service with 827 NAS but it was built in limited numbers and was out of service by 1946.

Mark II

The Mark II differed from the Mk I only in having a slightly more powerful Merlin engine driving a four-bladed propeller compared with the three-bladed unit of the original version. In service the Barracuda proved difficult to fly and early casualties included aircrew who were used to the more forgiving characteristics of slow biplanes.

Service (post-1945) Strike 812, 814, 826, 827 **Training** 717, 735, 753, 767, 783, 785 **Trials** 700, 703 **Utility** Gosport SF

TR Mark III

The ASV IIN radar of the Mks I and II employed fixed *yagi* aerials on the upper surfaces of the wings. The Mk III had a new radar, the Mk X, which required the fitting of a radome under the rear fuselage. These aircraft were intended for the anti-submarine role on escort carriers and torpedoes were generally not carried.

Service (post-1945) Strike 815, 821, 860 **Training** 706, 719, 735, 750, 783, 785, 796, 799 **Trials** 700, 703, 737X, 744 **Utility** HMSs *Implacable, Indomitable, Theseus, Vengeance*; 5 FP

Mark V

Early in the career of the Barracuda it had been appreciated that with the Merlin the aircraft was under-powered. The preferred option was the Sabre but supplies were not available so the Griffon was fitted instead. The Mk IV did not proceed beyond prototype stage, retaining the features of the Mk II. However the definitive Barracuda had a larger, triangular fin and extended wings with squared-off tips. The rear mounted guns were deleted but a single forward-firing .50in machine-gun was fitted. Only two underwing bomb racks were retained and the fuselage

Fairey Barracuda Mk III

The Barracuda was one of the most functional of aircraft, designed as a torpedo-bomber to replace the Albacore. Early marks were fitted with the Merlin engine with a large chin radiator as on this Mk III, RJ797/300GN from 815 NAS Eglinton seen in 1946. *(R C Sturtivant)*

ordnance point was stressed to allow carriage of up to 2,000lb. The variant was not available until after the war and saw only second-line service.

Service (post-1945) Training 783 **Utility** HMSs *Illustrious, Implacable*

Specification and production

Mark	Role	Engine	HP	Speed mph	Weight lb	Nos
I	Anti-shipping	Merlin 30	1,260	221	12,064	30
II	Anti-shipping	Merlin 32	1,640	228	12,600	1,688
III	Anti-shipping	Merlin 30	1,640	225	12,895	852
IV	Anti-shipping	Griffon 37	2,020	250	12,064	7*
V	Anti-shipping	Griffon 37	2,020	256	12,064	30

* Prototypes leading to Mk V, all converted Mk II

Further reading
Fairey Barracuda Mks I-V (Profile 240) Brown, D, Profile Publications, Leatherhead, 1973

9.4 Grumman Avenger (1943–1960)

The Grumman G-40 TBF-1 Avenger first flew on 1 August 1941 and it was supplied to the Fleet Air Arm under lend-lease arrangements from 1943. It was a large, rotund, single-engined torpedo-bomber with a crew of three, originally named Tarpon in Fleet Air Arm service.

TR Mark I
The first version supplied was equivalent to the USN's TBF-1B and -1C. It was powered by a single 1,850hp Wright Cyclone R-2600-8 engine and armament included two .50in guns in the wings plus one in a dorsal turret and a .30in gun in a ventral position. Up to 2,000lb of

Grumman Avenger AS Mk 5

The chunky Grumman torpedo-bomber first flew with the Fleet Air Arm in 1943 under lend-lease arrangements. A number remained in service after the War with two anti-submarine squadrons plus second line units. Much later, in 1953, 70 TBM-4 variants were supplied through MDAP to supplement the Firefly. XB389/382B and XB374/381B of the Ship's Flight of HMS *Bulwark* are seen in Suez markings at Hal Far in 1957. *(Author's collection)*

ordnance could be carried in the bomb-bay which accommodated a single torpedo.

Service (post-1945) Training 785

TR Mark II
General Motors was contracted to build the Avenger and aircraft from this source, while similar to the Grumman-built machines, were designated TBM-1. As supplied to Britain (TBM-1C) they were designated Mark II although indistinguishable from the Mk I.

Service (post-1945) Anti-submarine 820 **Training** 783, 785 **Trials** 703, 778 **Utility** 782

TR Mark III
Some TBM-3 and -3E aircraft with the uprated R-2600-20 engine were delivered towards the end of the war. Apart from improved performance there were no external changes.

Service (post-1945) Anti-submarine 828 **Training** 706 **Trials** 703, 708, 778, 787 **Utility** 4 FP

AS Mark 4
A batch of 70 TBM-4 with strengthened airframe was ordered as the Mk IV, but in the event they were not delivered. Quite remarkably, some years after the last of the wartime Avengers had been scrapped, a further batch was supplied under the Mutual Defence Aid Programme (MDAP) to complement the Firefly pending the (delayed) introduction of the Gannet. The Mk 4 was basically similar to the TBM-3C and -3E variants but with British electronics and radar in a radome under the right wing. Alterations were made to the bomb-bay to cater for British weapons and the guns were removed and in many cases the turrets. All were supplied in midnight blue finish and service entry was with 815 NAS in May 1953.

Service Anti-submarine 814, 815, 820, 824 **Training** 738, 751, 767 **Trials** 703

AS Mark 5
In service a number of changes was made, including provision for underwing bomb racks. An unspecified number of aircraft was designated AS Mk 5.

Service Anti-submarine 814, 815, 1830, 1841, 1844 **Training** 744

TS Mark 5
Four AS Mk 5 aircraft were converted for trials with the Orange Harvest ECM equipment and given the TS designation.

Service Trials 745

AS Mark 6
Four earlier versions of the Avenger were converted with a range of electronic equipment for electronic warfare tasks at RAF Watton.

Service Electronic warfare 831

Specification and production

Mark	Role	Engine	HP	Speed mph	Weight lb	Nos
I	ASW	R-2600-8	1,700	271	15,535	402
II	ASW	R-2600-8	1,700	271	15,535	334
III	ASW	R-2600-20	1,900	276	17,895	222
AS4	ASW	R-2600-8	1,700	278	15,535	)
AS5	ASW	R-2600-8	1,700	278	15,535	)100
TS5	EW	R-2600-8	1,700	278	15,535	4*
AS6	ASW	R-2600-8	1,700	278	15,535	4*

* AS4/AS5 conversions

9.5 Blackburn Firebrand (1943–1953)

The Blackburn B-37 Firebrand was originally designed to specification N.11/40 as an interceptor fighter. The prototype, DD804, was powered by a Sabre engine and flew for the first time on 27 February 1942. The Mark I was produced in small numbers but was no match for the contemporary Seafire. Thus the Mark II was fitted with a widened wing centre section to enable the carriage of a torpedo. Like the Mk I it did not enter service.

Mark III

Due to a shortage of Sabre engines the Firebrand was fitted with a Centaurus radial driving a four-bladed propellor as the Mk III built to specification S.8/43 (Blackburn B-45). A small number was built and used for trials duties, while some were converted to Mk IV standard.

Service (post-1945) Trials 700, 703; ATDU

TF Mark IV

The Mk III suffered from directional control problems and the solution, applied in the Mk IV, was to fit an enlarged fin and rudder. Wing dive brakes were also fitted and armament comprised four 20mm Hispano cannon. In addition to a single torpedo two 500lb bombs and rockets could be carried under the wings. The Firebrand was too late to see service in the war and the first front-line unit, 813 NAS, formed at Ford in September 1945.

Service (post-1945) Anti-shipping 813 Training 736 Trials 703, 778; ATDU

TF Mark 5

Further improvements were made in respect of control and the fitting of revised elevators and longer-span aileron tabs led to the TF Mk 5. The **TF Mark 5A** had powered ailerons and a number of the base model were brought up to this standard.

Service Anti-shipping 813, 827 **Training** 759, 767, 799 **Trials** 703, 787; ATDU

Blackburn Firebrand TF Mk IV

Originally intended as an interceptor, the Firebrand was no match for the Seafire, so the type was developed as a torpedo-fighter. Service entry was post-war and the powerful lines of the type are clear in this fine shot of EK726 in March 1948. *(P H T Green collection)*

Specification and production

Mark	Role	Engine	HP	Speed mph	Weight lb	Nos
I	Fighter	Sabre III	2,305	344	14,990	12
II	Torpedo fighter	Sabre III	2,305	344	14,990	12
III	Torpedo fighter	Centaurus IX	2,500	340	16,000	25
IV	Torpedo fighter	Centaurus IX	2,500	342	16,227	145*
TF5	Torpedo fighter	Centaurus IX	2,500	342	16,227	150+

* including 5 Mk III conversions
+ plus about 40 Mk IV conversions

9.6   Fairey Spearfish (1945–1952)

The Spearfish was designed to specification O.5/43 as a replacement for the Barracuda torpedo fighter. The aircraft was powered by a single Centaurus engine driving a five-bladed propeller. Stores were carried in a bomb-bay and could include a single torpedo or 2,000lb of bombs or mines. Armament comprised two .5in Browning guns in the wings and two more in a remotely controlled dorsal barbette while sixteen RPs could be carried under the wings. ASV radar would be contained in a retractable 'dustbin' aft of the bomb-bay.

The first prototype (RA356) flew on 5 July 1945. Five aircraft were completed (four of which flew) before the end of the war with Japan determined the programme. Although not especially fast, with a wing-span exceeding 60ft the Spearfish was one of the largest single-engined aircraft designed for carrier operations. Several were used for trials for some years after the war.

Service (post-1945)   Trials CTU

Specification and production

Mark	Role	Engine	HP	Speed mph	Weight lb	Nos
I	Torpedo fighter	Centaurus 57	2,585	292	22,083	5

Fairey Spearfish Mk I

When it was built, as a replacement for the Barracuda, the Spearfish was among the heaviest and largest single-engined aircraft ever constructed. The war with Japan ended before the type was fully assessed and orders were cancelled. RN241 was the second prototype; several of the prototypes were flown on trials tasks. *(MAP)*

9.7   Blackburn Firecrest (1948–1953)

The Blackburn B-48 strike aircraft was designed to specification S.28/43 as a Firebrand replacement. The design was clearly based on the Firebrand fuselage but with a completely new inverted gull wing. No guns were fitted to the prototypes but there was provision for a single torpedo plus underwing bombs or rocket projectiles.

Given the SBAC designation YA.1 the prototype, RT651, flew on 1 April 1947 and two further airframes followed. In the event the type was not ordered, the need being met by the Wyvern, but the third prototype was used for a range of trials at the A&AEE.

Specification and production

Mark	Role	Engine	HP	Speed mph	Weight lb	Nos
	Strike	Centaurus 59	2,875	380	15,280	3

Blackburn Firecrest

The Firecrest was a Firebrand replacement built around the latter's fuselage but with a completely new wing as seen on this photograph of the third prototype VF172. In the event the type was not ordered, the Wyvern being preferred. *(P H T Green collection)*

9.8   Blackburn YA.7, YA.8 and YB.1 (1949–1950)

In common with Short Brothers (SB.3) and Fairey Aviation (Gannet) Blackburn responded to specification GR.17/45 for a two-seat anti-submarine aircraft capable of operating from small carriers. Their design, given the SBAC designation YA.7, was broadly similar to that of the Gannet but through initial shortage of the intended engine, the Double Mamba, the type was fitted temporarily with a Griffon 56 driving contra-rotating propellers. In this form the prototype, WB781, flew on 20 September 1949.

The second prototype, designated YA.8, was WB788 and it flew on 3 May 1950. It incorporated a number of changes including provision for a crew of three, slight sweepback of the wing and an enlarged fin and rudder to improve directional stability.

The first Double Mamba-powered prototype was WB797 which, as the YB.1, flew on 19 July 1950. Although slightly faster than the Gannet the Blackburn design was not selected for production.

Service Trials 703

Specification and production

Mark	Role	Engine	HP	Speed mph	Weight lb	Nos
YA.7	ASW	Griffon 56	2,000	300	13,000	1
YA.8	ASW	Griffon 56	2,000	300	13,000	1
YB.1	ASW	Double Mamba	2,950	320	13,090	1

Blackburn YA.7

The YA.7 was the first of three aircraft designed to the same specification as the successful Gannet. Due to shortages of the intended Double Mamba turboprop engine the type was initially fitted with the Merlin, driving contra-rotating propellers as seen here. WB781 flew on 20 September 1949. *(MAP)*

9.9 Douglas Skyraider (1951–1960)

The Douglas AD-1 Skyraider was one of the most successful military aircraft of all time. It was designed as a successor to the Dauntless dive-bomber as a single-seat attack aircraft with an ordnance load of 1,000lb. In fact it carried up to 10,500lb and 3,180 were built in a number of different versions over a twelve-year period.

AEW Mark 1

With its huge carrying capacity the Skyraider was ideal as a radar picket and from the AD-3W variant it was fitted with a bulbous under-fuselage radome. In the AD-4W version the radar was the AN/APS20A search radar and to compensate for the bulk of the radome finlets were fitted. A crew of three – a pilot and two observers – was carried. Fifty were supplied to the Royal Navy under the Mutual Defence Aid Programme. Service entry was with 778 NAS in 1951 and the Skyraider remained in service until superseded by the Gannet AEW Mk 3 in 1960.

Service AEW 849 Training 778

Specification and production

Mark	Role	Engine	HP	Speed mph	Weight lb	Nos
AEW1	AEW	R-3350-26WA	3,300	350	17,311	50

Further reading
Douglas Skyraider (Profile 60) Gann, H, Profile Publications, Leatherhead, 1965

Douglas Skyraider AEW Mk 1

The hugely powerful Douglas AD-1 was an ideal vehicle for carting heavy airborne radars around the skies. Fifty were supplied to the Fleet Air Arm under MDAP to serve as radar pickets. Seen departing HMS *Albion* during the Suez campaign is WV178/424Z of C Flight, 849 NAS. *(Author's collection)*

9.10   Westland Wyvern (1952–1958)

The Wyvern was built to specification N.11/44 which was for a medium-range carrier or land-based strike fighter. For a brief time there was RAF interest in the Westland proposal for specification F.13/44 but this was soon dropped in favour of jet fighters.

TF Mark 1
The Westland W.34 was designed to be powered by the ultimate Rolls-Royce piston engine, the 24-cylinder Eagle, which delivered 2,690hp driving a large eight-blade contra-rotating propeller unit. The first of six prototypes, TS371, flew on 12 December 1946 and it was soon followed by the second TS375. Both were basic, non-navalised aircraft. Although a production order was placed for 20 pre-production aircraft to specification F.17/46 only seven were produced and, with the prototypes, they served for trials work.

Service Trials AAEE; RAE

TF Mark 2
Late in 1946 the Eagle engine was cancelled in favour of turbojet and turboprop engine development. Accordingly Westland determined to switch to a turboprop engine and two, the Rolls-Royce Clyde and Armstrong-Siddeley Python, were chosen for comparative assessment in the TF Mk 2 (Westland W.35) to specification N12/45. The former was cancelled after the first prototype, VP120, flew on 18 January 1949. The two Python-powered prototypes (VP113 first flight 30 August 1949 and VP113) were followed by 20 production aircraft. These were used primarily for development work although seven were converted to S Mk 4 standard but without the latter's cutback cowling and finlets.

Service Trials AAEE; ATDU; RAE

T Mark 3
A sole Wyvern, VZ739, was retained by Westland and developed as the W.38 to a two-seat tandem trainer to specification T.12/48. No production order was forthcoming.

Westland Wyvern S Mk 4

The powerful Wyvern was originally built as a medium range, piston-engined, strike fighter, but when the intended Eagle engine was abandoned turboprop power was chosen in the form of the Python driving a contra-rotating propeller. VW885 is seen on delivery to 764 NAS at Ford where it later became 689FD. (*'Buzz' Burr via author*)

TF Mark 4/S Mark 4
During the course of development various problems were experienced with the engine installation. It was not until 1954 that these were fully overcome but in the meantime the first of what were ordered as the TF Mk 4, but designated S Mk 4 in service, had been delivered to 813 NAS in May 1953. The definitive version featured the Python 3 with propeller inertia controller, a larger rudder and finlets; in addition the engine cowling was cut back. The Wyvern was finally cleared for carrier operations from 1954 and during production minor changes were made, the most significant of which was a strengthened canopy with bullet-proof windscreen. Armament comprised four 20mm Hispano cannon in the wings with provision for a single torpedo, three 1,000lb bombs or sixteen 60lb RPs. After service during the Suez campaign the Wyvern was withdrawn from service in 1958.

Service Strike 813, 827, 830, 831 **Training** 764, 787; WCU **Trials** 700, 703W

S Mark 5
There was a Westland intention to fit the Wyvern with a double Napier Eland engine and tip tanks but the project was short-lived although the tanks were tested. Another abandoned proposal was the fitting of the Napier Nomad diesel engine for which purpose a TF Mk 2 prototype was delivered to Napiers.

Specification and production

Mark	Role	Engine	HP	Speed mph	Weight lb	Nos
TF1	Torpedo fighter	Eagle 22	2,690	456	21,879	13
TF2	Torpedo fighter	Clyde	4,050	440	21,100	1
TF2	Torpedo fighter	Python 1/2	4,110	445	20,732	23
T3	Trainer	Python 1	4,110	360	21,200	1
S4	Strike fighter	Python 3	4,110	380	24,500	94*
S5	Strike fighter	Eland E.141	5,000	not built		

* includes 7 TF Mk 2 conversions

Further reading
A History of the Westland Wyvern, Blackbushe Aviation Group, Camberley, 1973

9.11   Fairey Gannet (1954–1978)

The Gannet was one of three types constructed to specification GR.17/45 (the others were the Blackburn YB.1 (Chapter 9.8) and Short SB.3 (Chapter 11.9)) and it had its origins in a unique project pioneered by Faireys early in the war. A 24-cylinder P.24 Prince engine had been fitted to a Battle test-bed, each half of the engine driving one of two contra-rotating propellers. In this way twin-engined power was offered with single-engined bulk and no assymetric flight problems. Further, the aircraft could be flown economically on half an engine with full power

Fairey Gannet AS Mk 1

Early in the War Faireys had proposed a coupled piston engine driving a single set of contra-rotating propellers. The idea led to the Gannet which was the successful contender for specification GR.17/45. XA339/878 belonged to the Channel Air Division (1840/1842 NASs) when seen here at Ford in 1956. *('Buzz' Burr via author)*

being engaged when necessary. The Fairey Q, later known as the Fairey 17 and then the Gannet, was designed originally to take a Rolls-Royce Tweed turbine, and when that was cancelled the Double Mamba.

AS Mark 1

The Fairey Q was a two-seat anti-submarine aircraft and the first of three prototypes, VR546, flew on 19 September 1949. In the third prototype a third seat was installed, finlets fitted, the ASV radar 'dustbin' moved further back and the bomb-bay lengthened. No armament was fitted but the bomb-bay accommodated two torpedoes or mines and depth charges and eight 60lb RPs could be fitted under the inner wing sections. The first production aircraft was WN339 which flew on 9 June 1953 and the type entered service with 826 NAS in January 1955.

Service **Anti-submarine** 812, 815, 820, 824, 825, 826, 1840, 1842 **Anti-smuggling** 847 **Training** 719, 737, 796, 831: ETPS **Trials** 700, 703, 703X, 744

T Mark 2

To ease transition to the Gannet a trainer version was ordered, the prototype (WN365, a converted AS Mk 1) flying on 16 August 1954. A second set of controls was fitted in the forward observer's cockpit and a periscope enabled the instructor to monitor events. Most operational units were equipped with one or two of the trainers.

Service **Training** 719, 737, 796, 812, 815, 820, 824, 825, 1840, 1842 **Utility** 728 **Communications** Abbotsinch, Anthorn, Eglinton, Ford, Yeovilton SF **Trials** 700

AEW Mark 3

Early in the development of the Gannet it had been

intended to design an early-warning variant but it was not flown until some time after the AS Mk 4. The AEW variant was significantly different from other models. The more powerful Double Mamba 112 was fitted further forward and the exhausts shortened to exit under the wing leading edge. A large radome housed the AN/APS radar retrieved from the Skyraider and a single cockpit housed the pilot, the observers being completely enclosed. To counter the bulk of the radome the fin and rudder were completely re-designed and the undercarriage was lengthened to provide adequate clearance. The AEW Mk 3 joined 849 NAS in 1960 and served until 1978.

Service AEW 849 **Trials** 700G: RRE

Fairey Gannet AEW Mk 3

The Mk 3 Gannet replaced the Skyraider as a radar picket and employed the more powerful Double Mamba 112 of 3,875 hp. XL500/LM shows the radome holding the AN/APS20A inherited from the Skyraider (and later passed on to the Shackleton!) and the revised fuselage and fin. *(Author)*

AS Mark 4

During development of the Gannet the weight had inevitably increased and the initial variant was under-powered. This was resolved by fitting the more powerful Double Mamba 101. The prototype was WN372 which flew on 12 March 1956 and service entry was with 824 NAS just five months later. The Gannet was to be the last fixed-wing anti-submarine aircraft, being succeeded by the Whirlwind helicopter.

Service Anti-submarine 810, 814, 815, 824, 825 **Anti-smuggling** 847 **Utility** 849; Yeovilton SF **Trials** 700

COD Mark 4

Five AS Mk 4 aircraft were stripped of radar equipment for use as carrier onboard delivery use mainly by 849 NAS.

Service Communications 849; HMSs *Ark Royal, Eagle, Hermes, Victorious*

ECM Mark 4

At least one AS Mk 4, WN464, was given the designation ECM Mk 4 after various electronics equipment installations. It served with 831 NAS in the electronic warfare role.

Service Trials 831

T Mark 5

The final eight trainers on the production line were fitted with the Double Mamba 101 and became the T Mk 5.

Service Training 719, 737, 849 **Communications** Abbotsinch, Culdrose SF

ECM Mark 6

At least six AS Mk 4 aircraft were given a range of special electronic equipment for use with 831 NAS on trials duties.

Service Trials 831

Specification and production

Mark	Role	Engine	HP	Speed mph	Weight lb	Nos
AS1	Anti-submarine	Double Mamba 100	2,950	310	19,600	172
T2	Trainer	Double Mamba 100	2,950	310	19,600	34
AEW3	AEW	Double Mamba 112	3,875	250	25,000	44
AS4	Anti-submarine	Double Mamba 101	3,035	299	23,446	90
COD4	Communications	Double Mamba 101	3,035	299	23,446	5*
ECM4	EW	Double Mamba 101	3,035	299	23,446	1*
T5	Trainer	Double Mamba 101	3,035	299	23,446	8
ECM6	EW	Double Mamba 101	3,035	299	23,446	6*

* AS4 conversions

Further reading
Gannet, Fiddler, B P, Picton Publishing, Chippenham, 1990

9.12 Westland Wessex (1961–date)

The Wessex started life as the piston-engined Sikorsky S-58 which in USN service was the HSS-1, HUS-1 or H-34A. Westland acquired a licence for development and production in 1956 and an HSS-1 was imported in 1957. It flew initially with the temporary marks G-17-1 with the 1,525hp R-1820-84 piston engine but made its first flight shortly after, on 17 May 1957, as XL722 with the less powerful, but significantly lighter, Napier Gazelle NGII turboshaft of 1,100hp.

HAS Mark 1

The Wessex design was ideal for its initial British role as an airborne anti-submarine platform. It was robust with plenty of room for crew and equipment. The Westland-built prototype was XL727 which flew on 20 June 1958 with an uprated Gazelle and autostabilisation. Service entry was with 815 NAS in 1961 after trials with 700H NAS. Weapons included two Mk 44 torpedoes or two Mk 11 depth charges, all carried externally; however, range was limited with armament carried. A new flight control system relieved the pilot of much of the work involved in hovering precisely at low levels during sonar operations. Twelve of the total produced were built without ASW equipment for use as commando transports and a number of anti-submarine variants later had their equipment removed as attrition replacements. As such they could carry up to sixteen troops plus two SS-11 missiles or rockets or GPMG.

Service Anti-submarine 814, 815, 819, 820, 826, 829 **SAR** 771, 772; HMSs *Ark Royal, Eagle, Hermes* **Transport** 845 **Utility** Yeovilton SF **Training** 706, 737 **Trials** 700H

HC Mark 2

Westland developed the potential of the Wessex by installing a pair of Gnome turboshafts to meet an RAF need for a utility helicopter. The airframe was strengthened and the first prototype, converted HAS Mk 1 XM299, flew on 18 January 1962. The new variant had a new nose profile and single large exhausts on each side of the forward fuselage. It carried sixteen troops or 4,000lb underslung and could be fitted with a range of weapons including SS-11 anti-tank missiles. The Wessex entered RAF service with 18 Sqn in 1964 and remains in service at the time of writing.

Service Utility 18, 28, 60, 72, 78, 84, 103 **SAR** 22; 84, Muharraq SARF **Training** CFS; ETPS; 2 FTS; HOCF; 240 OCU; SARTU; SRCU; WTF **Utility** Odiham SF **Trials** RAE

HAR Mark 2

Twelve HC Mk 2 aircraft were converted for search and rescue tasks by fitting a winch above the starboard door. They were used for relatively short-range tasks in the UK.

Service SAR 22

Westland Wessex HC Mk 2

Although initially built in the anti-submarine role, the Wessex served extensively with the RAF as a light transport/utility helicopter. XR499/AW of 72 Sqn prepares to lift a 105mm Pak Howitzer of 47 Light Regt RA in 1974. *(Crown copyright)*

HAS Mark 3

The next variant for the Royal Navy was fitted with an uprated Gazelle engine and an Ekco radar on the fuselage decking behind an extended fairing behind the rotor head. A protruding pitot head supported a more advanced automatic flight control system which enabled all phases of the anti-submarine search to be conducted automatically. To support longer flight times air refuelling from ships without landing platforms was also developed; however, range remained a problem not resolved in Royal Navy service until the introduction of the Sea King.

Service Anti-submarine 814, 819, 820, 826, 829 **Training** 706, 737 **Trials** 700H

HCC Mark 4

Two specially fitted Wessex Mk 2 aircraft were acquired for the Queen's Flight for VVIP transport. Externally they are distinguished by their distinctive red and blue livery.

Service Communications QF

HU Mark 5

Experience with the Mk 1 aircraft in commando use with 845 NAS, especially in Borneo, proved the value of the type as a troop carrier, but for reliability two engines coupled with an improved transmission were considered essential. A hundred were built and they served in Aden, Borneo, Cyprus, the Falklands and Northern Ireland with distinction, having first operated with 848 NAS in 1964. Six were transferred to the RAF for use in Cyprus.

Service Utility 781, 829, 845, 846, 847, 848; Lee-on-Solent SF **SAR** 771, 772; 84 **Training** 707 **Trials** 700V

Specification and production

Mark	Role	Engine		HP	Speed mph	Weight lb	Nos
HAS1	Anti-submarine	1xGazelle	161	1,450	121	12,600	140
HC2	Utility	2xGnome	110	1,350	132	13,500	71
HAR2	SAR	2xGnome	110	1,350	132	13,500	12*
HAS3	Anti-submarine	1xGazelle	165	1,600	120	13,600	47+
HCC4	Communications	2xGnome	110	1,350	132	13,500	2
HU5	Utility	2xGnome		1,350	132	13,500	100

* HC2 conversions
+ including 44 HAS1 conversions

Further reading
Wessex, Allen, P, Airlife, Shrewsbury, 1988

9.13   Westland Wasp (1963–1988)

The Wasp had its origins in the Westland P.531 Skeeter successor for the Army, later to be named Scout (Chapter 10.8), and which flew in 1958. Trials of the new type were conducted by the Army and Navy, the latter ordering three P-531-0/N prototypes; after assessment of these the improved P.531-2 was built, by now named Sprite by the manufacturer, and with the Nimbus engine, skid undercarriage and a changed body. The Royal Navy ordered the type as the Wasp in autumn 1961; the main difference from the Scout was the fitting of four castoring wheels in place of the skid undercarriage.

HAS Mark 1
The first pre-production machine, XS463, flew on 28 October 1962 and the type joined 829 NAS in March 1964. The Wasp was bought for use as an extension of the anti-submarine frigate and was cleared for use from the small stern platforms of these warships. The first unit was to be the parent organisation for the small ship flights and as such had a large number of helicopters on charge. The Wasp did not have any form of detection equipment but acted as the 'killer' element of various hunter/killer combinations. The 'hunter' element might include the host ship, the larger Wessex or land-based Shackleton. The Wasp's weapons included two Mk 44 torpedoes or two Mk 11 depth charges or the AS-12M missile. After service in Borneo and the Falklands the type was replaced by the Lynx in 1988.

Service **Anti-submarine** 829 **Utility** 845, 848 **Training** 705, 706 **Trials** 700W, 703, 771

Westland Wasp HAS Mk 1

The Wasp started life as a Skeeter successor which became the Scout in Army service and the Wasp with the FAA. The type was flown from the stern platforms of anti-submarine frigates and also operated from auxiliaries. XT432/HT operated from HMS *Hydra* during the Falklands war in the casevac role *(Crown copyright)*

Production and specification

Mark	Role	Engine	HP	Speed mph	Weight lb	Nos
HAS1	ASW	Nimbus 503	710	120	5,500	98

9.14   Westland Sea King (1969–date)

The Sea King was the fourth of the Sikorsky designs developed and built under licence by Westland. The S-61 flew on 11 March 1959 and in US service became the H-3 series. The type featured a sealed boat hull enabling security and recovery in the event of ditching, but not for operations from water. Four examples were shipped to the UK to act as pattern and development aircraft and the first of these, SH-3D G-ATYU (later XV370), flew at Avonmouth docks on 11 October 1966 shortly after the type had entered US service.

HAS Mark 1
The initial naval variant was built to specification HAS.261 and the first, XV642, flew on 7 May 1969. The Sea King was a medium-range hunter/killer capable of flying from larger ships, although it was later cleared for use from some frigates. Search equipment included Plessey Type 195 sonar, Marconi AD580 Doppler and Ekco AW391 radar in a thimble housing on the fuselage decking. Winches were retained for rescue and Louis Newmark Mk 31 automatic flight control system was fitted. Weapons included four Mk 44 torpedoes or Mk 11 depth charges or a single nuclear depth bomb. The Sea King joined 706 NAS for training in 1969 and the first operational unit was 824 NAS in February 1970.

Service **Anti-submarine** 814, 819, 820, 824, 826 **Training** 706, 737; ETPS **Trials** 700S; RAE/DRA

HAS Mark 2/2A
The next variant was the result of developments for the Australian Navy incorporating more powerful Gnome engines and a matching transmission improvement. A six-bladed tail rotor replaced the five-bladed type of the HAS Mk1 and various equipment changes were made including Plessey 2069 sonar and Racal Decca 71 Doppler. Other changes included an intake guard to prevent ice ingestion and on some aircraft provision for the Dowty SSQ904 passive sonobuoy. Some machines were designated **Mk 2A** but there is uncertainty as to the distinction. Twenty-one were built new and most of the HAS Mk 1 aircraft were converted to the standard.

Service **Anti-submarine** 814, 819, 820, 824, 826 **Utility** 825 **Training** 706

AEW Mark 2A
The disastrous situation in the South Atlantic in 1982 where British ships were exposed to Argentine air attack with no airborne early warning led to an immediate need for some form of cover. The response, managed in a remarkable eleven weeks, was to fit Sea King HAS Mk2A airframes with the Thorn EMI Searchwater radar in an inflatable and semi-retractable Kevlar radome attached

Westland Sea King HAR Mk 3

The Sea King was developed by Westland from the Sikorsky S-61 as a submarine hunter/killer. It was developed as a robust search and rescue vehicle, XZ590 being loaned from the Navy to RAF Valley in 1978 for trials. *(Crown copyright)*

to the starboard fuselage. The variant also had 'Orange Crop' ESM, new IFF and a Ferranti INS.

Service **Early warning** 824, 849

HAR Mark 3
The RAF ordered the Sea King to replace and complement its Whirlwind and Wessex search and rescue fleet. For the purpose the rear bulkhead was moved back to accommodate up to 26 survivors and extra tankage was installed. A long-reach winch was also fitted and extra observation windows provided. The radio fit was designed to enable direct communications with a range of services and a Smiths Industries AFCS was also fitted. Six machines were given extra equipment including the ARI 18228 RWR for use in the Falklands where they operate in a grey finish.

Service **SAR** 22, 78, 202; 1564 Flt **Training** RAFSKTU: 706 NAS

HAR Mark 3A
In 1992 six new HAR Sea Kings were ordered to replace the remaining Wessex in service. Externally the new variant is distinguished only by several additional blade

aerials but the avionics fit is almost completely new, including the communications equipment, colour search radar, Smiths-Newmark FCS and Decca 91 Doppler.

Westland Sea King HC Mk 4

For Marine Commando movement the Sea King HC Mk 4 was chosen to complement the Wessex. The training squadron was 707 NAS whose aircraft included ZA299/ZD photographed at Yeovilton in 1984. *(Author)*

Service SAR 22 **Training** SKOCU

HC Mark 4

The Commando was a private-venture development of the Sea King intended typically in the utility and especially troop transport role. In due course the type was ordered for the Royal Navy as the Sea King HC Mk 4 to replace the Wessex with the Commando units. The under-carriage was changed from the retractable-into-sponsons type of other variants to a fixed unit. The radar is deleted and the extra windows of the HAR Mk 3 retained. Night vision goggles may be used with cockpit lighting altered accordingly and except in the search and rescue role the AFCS is disabled. The first, ZA290, flew on 26 September 1979 joining 846 NAS shortly after. Through use in a succession of war zones including the Falklands, the Gulf, northern Iraq and Bosnia, many equipment changes have been incorporated including armoured crew seats, GPS, jammers, chaff/flare dispensers, floodlight and Kevlar floor armour. Provision has also been made for a door-mounted FN-Herstal .50 calibre machine-gun to be fitted.

Service Utility 845, 846, 848 SAR 772 **Training** 707 **Trials** RAE/DTEO

Mark 4X

Two Mark 4 aircraft were supplied to the RAE for a wide range of trials and research work, including tests of avionics and other equipment for the EH101.

Service Trials RAE/DRA

HAS Mark 5

The Navy's ASW Sea Kings were subject to continuous improvement. In the Mk 5 the most significant change was the MEL Sea Searcher radar with almost twice the range of the earlier type housed in a larger radome. The data from a new dipping sonar and sonobuoys were processed through a GEC-Marconi AQS902 system which could, in addition, handle data from sonobuoys dropped by other vehicles including the Nimrod. Orange Crop ESM was also fitted. The first was a converted HAS Mk 2, XZ916, which flew on 1 August 1980, and although some new-build helicopters were produced most were HAS Mk 2 conversions.

Service ASW 810, 814, 819, 820, 824, 826 **Training** 706

HAR Mark 5

771 NAS equipped with modified HAS Mk 5 aircraft for use in the search and rescue role. The ASW avionics was removed but the MEL radar retained and eight aircraft were converted.

Service SAR 771

HAS Mark 6

Improvements in electronics technology led to the next Navy variant, the HAS Mk 6. New GEC Avionics AQS-902G-DS digital sonar handled dunking to 700ft and a new radar display eased workload. Further changes included a better MAD system, IFF, Orange Reaper ESM and secure speech communications while composite main rotors were fitted together with emergency gearbox lubrication system. Externally the only new feature was

an additional blade aerial under the forward fuselage. The first of 73 HAS Mk 5 conversions, XZ581, flew on 15 December 1987 and in addition there were six new-build aircraft.

Service Anti-submarine 810, 814, 819, 820, 824 **Training** 706 **Trials** SK OEU

AEW Mark 7

At least three new airframes have been earmarked to replace the ageing AEW Mk2A being ZD636, ZE418 and ZE420.

Specification and production

Mark	Role	Engine	HP	Speed mph	Weight lb	Nos
HAS1	Anti-submarine	2xGnome 1400	1,250	126	20,500	60*
HAS2/A	Anti-submarine	2xGnome 1400-1	1,250	126	21,000	68+
AEW2	AEW	2xGnome 1400-1	1,250	103	21,000	11~
HAR3	SAR	2xGnome 1400-1	1,250	143	21,400	19
HAR3A	SAR	2xGnome 1400-1	1,250	143	21,400	6
HC4	Utility	2xGnome 1400-1	1,250	126	21,500	40
4X	Trials	2xGnome 1400-1	1,250	126	21,000	2
HAS5	Anti-submarine	2xGnome 1400-1	1,250	126	21,000	86#
HAR5	SAR	2xGnome 1400-1	1,250	126	21,000	8>
HAS6	Anti-submarine	2xGnome 1400-1	1,250	126	20,500	84^
AEW7	AEW	2xGnome 1400-1	1,250			3$

* including four Sikorsky-built pattern aircraft
+ including 47 HAS1 conversions
~ HAS2A conversions
# including 56 HAS1, HAS2/2A conversions
> HAS5 conversions
^ including 80 HAS5 conversions
$ at August 1996

Further reading

Westland Sea King, World Air Power Journal volume 25, London, 1995
Westland Sea King, Chartres, J, Ian Allan, London, 1984

9.15 EH Industries Merlin (1996–date)

Planning for a Sea King replacement began in 1977 and in 1979 a joint Anglo-Italian company was set up to progress work on a design. By 1985 a mock-up was completed and the first pre-production aircraft, PP1/ZF641, flew on 9 October 1987. The EH-101 project was unusual in that it was developed from the outset to cover military and civil markets. PP2 was the first Italian aircraft followed by PP3/G-EHIL/ZH647. PP4/ZF644 was the first British naval trials machine, followed by PP5/ZF649. A total of nine pre-production aircraft served the development programme in Italy and the United Kingdom. The pre-production aircraft were powered by the General Electric T700-GE-401 turboshaft of 1,600hp and the EH-101 has an advanced five-bladed composite main rotor.

HM Mark 1
The production Merlin is powered by the Rolls-Royce-Turbomeca RTM322 turboshaft of 2,312hp and is fitted with the Ferranti Blue Kestrel radar, 'Orange Reaper' ESM, AQS-930 acoustic processing, sonobuoys and Ferranti-Thomson Sonar Systems AQS950 dipping sonar. Weapons include four Stingray torpedoes. The Merlin is optimised for operation from the Type 23 Duke class frigates but it will also be embarked on the light carriers. It is due to enter service in 1999, 44 (ZH821-864) having been ordered.

Service Anti-submarine

HM Mark 2
The designation has been reserved for a naval upgrade of the HM Mk 1 and may include additional airframes.

Service Anti-submarine

HC Mark 3
The Merlin has been ordered for the RAF as a battlefield support helicopter to replace the Puma. It will be broadly similar to the naval variants in respect of rotors, engine and transmission but will feature a rear loading ramp door and completely changed avionics. Twenty-two have been ordered and service entry will be around 2000.

Service Transport

Specification and production

Mark	Role	Engine	HP	Speed mph	Weight lb	Nos
HM1	Anti-submarine	3xRTM322	2,102	184	32,180	44
HM2	Anti-submarine	3xRTM322	2,100	184	29,500	*
HC3	Transport	3xRTM322	2,100	184	29,500	22

* HM1 conversions but may include new airframes

EH Industries Merlin HAS Mk 1

Planning for the Sea King replacement started in 1977 and twenty years later the Merlin is still some way off service entry. The 'Blue Kestrel' radar is evident on ZF649, trials machine PP5, seen here overflying HMS *Norfolk*. (*Westland Helicopters Ltd*)

10 – Army Aviation

See also: Islander (7.19); Sycamore (7.10)

Given that the primary readership of this book will probably be more familiar with RAF than Army structure it may be worth introducing this chapter by outlining (simply) Army organisation. At the highest level is an Army under which may be **Corps** or **Command** within which are **Divisions** (10,000 – Major-General) generally comprising two **Brigades** (2,500 – Brigadier) which might be infantry or armoured and containing **Battalions** (600 – Lt-Col) (two infantry and one armoured regt or one infantry and two armoured regts respectively) which in

Auster AOP Mk 6

For many years the Auster was synonymous with Army flying. The AOP Mk 6 first flew in 1945 and it remained in service until about 1965. VF573/TS-E of 657 Sqn is photographed at Cranwell in 1949 (*R C B Ashworth via P H T Green*)

turn comprise **Companies** (100 – Major), themselves broken down into **Platoons**.

The term 'Regiment' may be applied to a group of units bearing the same badge which may form a number of battalions, perhaps serving in different brigades, or regiments, typically the somewhat confusing sub-structure within the Royal Tank Regiment. Various specialised corps have their own structures, sub-divisions of which may be attached to main fighting units, usually at battalion level or above. In cavalry regiments sub-divisions include **squadrons** and **troops**, while artillery is distributed in **batteries**.

January 1946

At the end of the war army flying was confined to two distinct functions: glider piloting and artillery spotting. However, starting in Italy in 1944 the Army had developed a workable forward air control function. By 1946 there were ten air observation post squadrons all flying the Auster IV and/or V. Training was undertaken by 43 OTU at Andover, which also operated the first helicopters in British service, the Hoverfly. Although the Glider Pilot Regiment remained in being it had no aircraft formations, but pilots flew in Palestine on Austers.

The structure and nature of the AOP units was unique. The squadrons were within RAF command with RAF ground staff but Army (usually Royal Artillery) pilots working outside RAF control. During the war the squadrons had operated as relatively independent lettered flights flying from any available small field or strip and constantly on the move, staying close to their gunners. With no effective higher command structure, there was no focus for Army flying and after the war attempts were made by the Army to establish a separate Air Corps, but with no success against tough resistance from the RAF. By now the Army also saw the value of the aircraft for short-range, small field communications duties.

July 1947

The number of squadrons had reduced considerably but the flight system had been introduced on a more formal numerical basis from 1 January 1947 with the introduction of flights in the 1900 series. There were four squadrons, one each in the UK, Germany, the Middle East and the Far East, with a further squadron in India about to disband. This pattern was to remain until 1957. In terms of equipment the Auster Mk 5 was being replaced by the more powerful AOP Mk 6.

July 1952

Little had changed with the regular units since 1947 except that an independent flight had been established at Hong Kong supporting the garrison there. Through the spring and summer of 1949 twenty new flights in five RAuxAF squadrons were formed in the UK within Reserve Command with the Auster 5, 6 and 7. Aircrew comprised a few regular and mainly TA army pilots.

Although there was little in the way of equipment changes, the Sycamore had been introduced in 1906 Flt, ostensibly for AOP tasks pending delivery of the troubled Skeeter, but in general used for communications tasks. In Malaya the flights of 656 Sqn were heavily engaged on reconnaissance work in Operation 'Firedog'. Two flights were operational in Korea, one having been specially formed for passenger recce and liaison and flying the Auster AOP Mk 6, and a single L-19 on long-term loan from the US Army.

July and December 1957

The final version of the Auster, the AOP Mk 9, had been introduced into service in Germany and Malaya and nearer home the Joint Experimental Helicopter Unit (JEHU) had been established at Middle Wallop to investigate the Army's needs for helicopter support. The unit's aircraft had served operationally at Suez in Operation 'Musketeer'. The Skeeter helicopter had entered service, although it would prove of no value outside Europe. The busiest theatre for the Army was Malaya where Operation 'Firedog' was drawing to a close. Early in 1957 the RAuxAF units had disbanded. The decision had been taken in 1956 to enable the Army to form its own Air Corps for AOP and liaison tasks only and with a limit on the all-up weight of the types it could use of 4,000lb. A date for formation was set at 1 September 1957 by which time Army ground crew and support staff would need to be in place.

The structure was to be changed, initially by creating new flights using the last two digits of the RAF 1900 series flights. Over subsequent years there were to be several significant structural changes based in part on two sets of tensions. One tension was between the needs of BAOR, which was essentially heavily armoured and gunned, and the 'out of area' army fighting various low-level wars and operations across the world. The other tension was between the new corps and the regiments which would have to provide the manpower.

December 1962

The first significant re-organisation had been implemented. It was intended at the outset to have two forms of flight, recce and liaison, each of three fixed-wing aircraft and three helicopters. The recce flights were to support Brigade group with AOP and general recce while liaison flights were to run people around and provide some casevac. Independent flights were to perform both tasks at higher level. There was intended to be a Wing HQ in each theatre, with (purely administrative) squadrons at divisional level and flights attached to brigades.

Theatre wings were 1 Germany (652, 654, 655 Sqns), 2 United Kingdom (651 Sqn), 3 Cyprus (653 Sqn) and 4 Far East (656 Sqn). Direct reporting flights operated in the UK and Germany with independent flights in Kenya and Hong Kong. In terms of equipment the Auster AOP Mk 6 had given way to the AOP Mk 9 completely and helicopters were widely in use in BAOR including the newly purchased Alouette, bought pending delivery of the delayed Scout. The Beaver was also now in use, the first type to exceed the 4,000lb Army weight 'limit'.

Notwithstanding the end of Operation 'Firedog' in Malaya the AAC maintained a significant presence in Malaya and the troubles in Aden, as well as Cyprus, spread the units deployed in the Middle East. Against these demands BAOR could still demand nine flights supporting Army, Corps and Divisional levels. As an indication of things to come there was a new style flight at Aldergrove, Northern Ireland, manned by 4 Royal Tank Regiment.

January 1967

Manpower problems dating from the 1950s, coupled with the availability of relatively low-cost helicopters including the Skeeter and the later Sioux, of which over 250 were bought, led to the 'integration' scheme. From 11 November 1964 field units manned and operated their own organic air platoons or troops or sometimes squadrons. The order of battle for 1967 clearly highlights the extent of the scheme with no fewer than nine flights supporting 1 Division alone. The organic flights were not confined to Europe; they were widely deployed in Aden and Malaya.

January 1972

'Re-centralisation' of the AAC was inevitable for at least three reasons. There were threats that the RAF would force absorption of the Army's aircraft to provide greater economy. Then there was the lack of overall direction, leadership and thus, for example, tactics, and finally there was the increasing cost – and thus fewer numbers – of new equipment. The Scout had completely replaced the Skeeter in service by now and it was widely deployed abroad.

Newly formed or re-formed squadrons supported two divisions in the UK and three in Germany and there was usually at least one in Ulster on 'roulement' together with based units. To all intents the British had withdrawn from the Far East and Aden, although a flight of Beavers remained in Laos detached from Seletar. In Canada a flight of Beavers also supported the British Army Training Unit Suffield (BATUS). The Royal Marines also now had their own aircraft in 3 Commando Brigade Air Squadron, formed in Malaya but by now home-based.

January 1977

The organisation pattern remained little changed but new equipment pointed the way to future structural change based on newly emerging roles. The Gazelle was in wide-spread service complementing the Scout, and the potent Lynx had just joined 654 Sqn in BAOR. All three helicopters were to be armed over the next few years turning the AAC from a support corps to a fighting arm, primarily in the anti-tank role.

June 1982

Yet another re-organisation had been implemented with, in BAOR, squadrons operating in regiments with the Gazelle or Lynx for recce and attack respectively. Northern Ireland Regiment had formed and commitments abroad included Cyprus, Brunei, Belize and the Falklands where the Gazelle had not fared well. Both 656 Sqn and 3 CBAS had been sent south and had a hard and short war; within days of the recovery of Stanley personnel and aircraft of 3 CBAS were embarked on several ships for return to the UK. A detailed, but important, development was a detachment

of 658 Sqn to Hereford, home of the Special Air Service (SAS).

January 1987

By now the Scout was in limited service but significantly it operated with a TA unit, 666 Sqn, at Netheravon. The structure remained largely intact but the Lynx was now in service in the UK as well as Germany. Equipment changes were confined to the use of four A109A helicopters, two of which had been captured from the Argentine Army in the Falklands and sometimes seen in civil colour schemes.

January 1992

The run-down from Germany was now signalled, but although there were no withdrawals 9 Regiment had formed at Dishforth in the UK. The more powerful Lynx AH Mk 7 was in widespread service as AH Mk 1 airframes were modified. The second generation Lynx, the wheeled AH Mk 9, was also just entering service with 673 Sqn in 9 Regiment.

January 1997

The withdrawal from Germany was now well advanced with 3 and 4 Regiments now based in the UK at Wattisham. 664 Sqn had left Germany while 7 Flt at Berlin had disbanded, the number being transferred to the Brunei detachment. The Scout had soldiered on until 1994 to be replaced in Brunei by the Bell 212, while perhaps one of the most dramatic changes was flagged in 1995 with the order of the McDonnell Douglas Longbow Apache attack helicopter.

Army abbreviations

General abbreviations are dealt with in Appendix I, but for ease of reference Army unit short forms are set out below.

Term	Meaning
AAC	Army Air Corps
AB	Armoured Brigade
AFWF	Advanced Fixed Wing Flight
AOPS	Air Observations Post School
AP	Air Platoon
ARWF/S	Advanced Rotary Wing Flight/Squadron
AT	Air Troop
BAE	British Antarctic Expedition
BATUS	British Army Training Unit Suffield
BCF	Beaver Conversion Flight
BFWF	Basic Fixed Wing Flight
BRWF	Basic Rotary Wing Flight
CBAS	Commando Brigade Air Squadron
Div	Division
DG	Dragoon Guards
D&TS	Development and Trials Squadron
Eng	Engineer
Flt	Flight
FWTF	Fixed Wing Training Flight
GH	Green Howards
GR	Gurkha Regiment
H	Hussars
HKAAF	Hong Kong Auxiliary Air Force
IB	Infantry Brigade

IDG	Inniskilling Dragoon Guards
IG	Irish Guards
KOBR	King's Own Border Regiment
L	Lancers
LAS	Light Aircraft School
LG	Life Guards
MELF	Middle East Land Forces
NI	Northern Ireland
QDG	Queen's Dragoon Guards
QRIH	Queen's Royal Irish Hussars
RA	Royal Artillery
RAC	Royal Armoured Corps
RGJ	Royal Green Jackets
RHA	Royal Horse Artillery
RMC	Royal Marine Commando
RNF	Royal Northumberland Fusiliers
RSG	Royal Scots Greys
RTR	Royal Tank Regiment
RWCF	Rotary Wing Conversion Flight
SG	Scots Guards
UNFICYP	United Nations Forces In CYPrus

10.A   Army flying at 1 January 1946

Fighter Command, 12 Group

Type	Unit	Base
Auster V	657	Rollestone Camp

BAFO

Type	Unit	Base
Auster IV, V	652	Hoya
	660	Kiel/Holtenau
	664	Rostrup

Middle East Air Force

Desert Air Force

Type	Unit	Base
Auster IV, V	654	Ronchi (Italy)
	663	Monza (Italy)

AHQ Levant

Type	Unit	Base
Auster V	651	Ismailia (Egypt)
	651 (det)	Haifa (Palestine)

ACSEA

Type	Unit	Base
Auster V	656	Kuala Lumpur
	658, 659	Dhubalia

Training and Development

11 Group

Type	Unit	Base
Auster V	Sch Air Support	Old Sarum
Auster III, IV, V, Hoverfly I	43 OTU	Andover

225 Group, ACSEA

Auster	1587 Ref Flt	Deolali (India)

10.B   Army flying at 1 July 1947

United Kingdom 657 Sqn

Type	Unit	Base
Auster 5	1900 Flt	Andover
Hoverfly II, Auster AOP4, AOP5, AOP6	1901 Flt	Andover

BAFO 652 Sqn

Auster AOP6	1902, 1903, 1904 Flt	Celle

MED/ME Middle East (651 Sqn Palestine)

Type	Unit	Base
Auster AOP6	1906, 1907, 1908 Flt	Quastina
	1909 Flt	Ramat David

ACFE

Type	Unit	Base
Auster AOP6	1914 Flt (656 Sqn)	Kuala Lumpur (Malaya)
	659	Lahore (India)

Training and development

Type	Unit	Base
Auster AOP5, AOP6, T7, Hoverfly II	43 OTU	Andover

10.C   Army flying at 1 July 1952

Fighter Command (81 Group) 657 Sqn

Type	Unit	Base
Auster AOP6, T7	1900 Flt	det El Adem
Hiller HT1, Sycamore HC11, Dragonfly HC4	1906 Flt	Middle Wallop
Auster AOP6, T7	1912 Flt	Middle Wallop

Home Command

61 Group 661 Sqn Kenley

Type	Unit	Base
Auster AOP6, T7	1957, 1960 Flts	Kenley
	1958 Flt	Hendon
	1959, 1961 Flts	Henlow

62 Group 662 Sqn Colerne

Auster AOP6, T7	1956, 1963 Flts	Colerne
	1962 Flt	Middle Wallop

63 Group 663 Sqn Hooton Park

Auster AOP6, T7	1953, 1955 Flts	Hooton Park
	1951 Flt	Ringway
	1952 Flt	Llandow
	1954 Flt	Wolverhampton

64 Group 664 Sqn Hucknall

Auster AOP6, T7	1970 Flt	Hucknall
	1964 Flt	Yeadon
	1965 Flt	Ouston
	1969 Flt	Desford

66 Group 666 Sqn Perth (Scone)

Auster AOP6, T7	1966 Flt	Scone
	1967 Flt	Dyce
	1968 Flt	Turnhouse

BAFO 652 Sqn Detmold

Auster AOP6, T7	1901, 1904, 1905, 1909 Flt	Detmold

Middle East Air Force 651 Sqn Ismailia

Auster AOP6, T7	1908 Flt	Ismailia (Egypt)
	1910 Flt	Asmara (Ethiopia)
	1900 Flt det	El Adem (Libya)

Far East Air Force

AHQ Hong Kong

Type	Unit	Base
Auster AOP6, T7	1903 Flt	Fort George
Auster AOP6, L-19	1913 Flt	Fort George
Auster AOP6	1 Comm Div LLF	Iwakuni (Japan)

AHQ Malaya 656 Sqn Kuala Lumpur

Auster AOP6, T7	1902 Flt	Benta
	1907 Flt	Sembawang

Type	Unit	Base
	1911 Flt	Seremban
	1914 Flt	Taiping

Training and Development (81 Group Fighter Command)

Type	Unit	Base
Auster AOP6, T7, Tiger Moth, Chipmunk T10	AOP School	Middle Wallop

10.D   Army flying at 1 July 1957

Fighter Command (11 Group) 651 Sqn

Type	Unit	Base
Auster AOP6	1903 Flt	Feltwell
	1913 Flt	Aldergrove
Hiller HT1, Sycamore HC11, Chipmunk T10, Skeeter AOP6, 10, Auster T7	1906 Flt	Middle Wallop

BAFO 652 Sqn

Type	Unit	Base
Auster AOP9	1901, 1904, 1905, 1909 Flt	Detmold
Auster AOP9, Chipmunk T10	1912 Flt	Wildenrath

Middle East Air Force

Type	Unit	Base
Auster AOP6, T7	1908 Flt	Ismailia (Egypt)
	1910, 1915 Flts	Kermia (Cyprus

Far East Air Force Hong Kong

AHQ Malaya 656 Sqn

Type	Unit	Base
Auster AOP9	1902 Flt	Ipoh
	1907 Flt	Taiping
	1911 Flt	Sembawang
	1914 Flt	Port Dickson
Auster AOP9	1900 Flt	Sha Tin (Hong Kong)

Training and Development Flying Training Command

Type	Unit	Base
Auster AOP6, AOP9, T7, Tiger Moth, Chipmunk T10	AOP School	Middle Wallop

10.E   Army flying at 1 December 1957

Army Air Corps

United Kingdom (651 Light Aircraft Sqn)

Type	Unit	Base
Auster AOP6	3 Flt	Feltwell
	13 Flt	Aldergrove

Germany (652 Sqn)

Type	Unit	Base
Auster AOP9	1, 4, 5, 9 Flt	Detmold

Malaya (656 Sqn)

Type	Unit	Base
Auster AOP9	2 Flt	Ipoh
	7 Flt	Taiping
	11 Flt	Sembawang
	14 Flt	Port Dickson

Independent Flights

Type	Unit	Base
Skeeter AOP10, Auster T7, Chipmunk T10	6 Flt	Middle Wallop
Auster AOP6, T7	8 Flt	Libya
	10, 15 Flt	Kermia (Cyprus)
	20 Flt	Sha Tin (Hong Kong)
Auster AOP9, Chipmunk T10	12 Flt	Wildenrath (Germany)

Training and development

Type	Unit	Base
Auster AOP6, AOP9, T7, Tiger Moth, Chipmunk T10	LAS	Middle Wallop

10.F Army flying at 1 December 1962

United Kingdom

Direct reporting

Type	Unit	Base
Skeeter AOP12, Auster AOP9, Chipmunk T10	6 Flt	Middle Wallop

2 Wing 651 Sqn (supporting 3 Division)

Type	Unit	Base
Auster AOP9	3 Flt	Middle Wallop
Auster AOP9, Beaver AL1	19 Flt	Middle Wallop
Skeeter AOP12	2 RTR	Aldergrove

Germany BAOR 1 Wing

Type	Unit	Base
Alouette AH2, Beaver AL1	12 Flt (HQ)	Wildenrath
Alouette AH2, Beaver AL1	18 Flt (1 (BR) Corps)	Detmold

652 Sqn (supporting 1 Division)

Type	Unit	Base
Skeeter AOP12	1, 9 Flts	Detmold

654 Sqn (supporting 2 Division)

Type	Unit	Base
Skeeter AOP12	4 Flt, 22 Flt (QDG)	Hildesheim
Auster AOP9	5, 17 Flt	Hildesheim

655 Sqn (supporting 4 Division)

Type	Unit	Base
Skeeter AOP12	23 Flt	Detmold
Alouette AH2	24 Flt	Detmold

Middle East

Cyprus

Type	Unit	Base
Auster AOP9, Alouette AH2	10 Flt	Dhekelia
Auster AOP9	21 Flt	Kermia

Aden (653 Sqn)

Type	Unit	Base
Auster AOP9	13 Flt	Falaise
Auster AOP9, Beaver AL1	15 Flt	Falaise

Malaya (656 Sqn)

Type	Unit	Base
Auster AOP9	2, 7 Flt, 16 Flt/QRIH	Kluang
	7 Flt det	Brunei
Beaver AL1	11 Flt	Kluang
Beaver AL1, Auster AOP9	14 Flt	Brunei

Independent Flights

Type	Unit	Base
Alouette AH2, Beaver AL1	8 Flt	Wilson Field (Kenya)
Auster AOP9	20 Flt	Sha Tin (Hong Kong)

Training and development

Type	Unit	Base
Auster AOP6, AOP9, T7, Skeeter AOP10, Chipmunk T10	LAS	Middle Wallop

10.G   Army flying at 1 January 1967

United Kingdom

Direct reporting

Type	Unit	Base
Scout AH1	6 Flt	Middle Wallop

2 Wing 651 Sqn (supporting 3 Division)

Type	Unit	Base
Scout AH1	19 Flt (Div HQ)	Netheravon
	3 Flt (5 Inf Bde)	Netheravon
	21 Flt (16 Para Bde)	Netheravon
	10 Flt (51 Gurkha Bde)	Netheravon
Sioux AH1	4/7 DG AT	Aldergrove

Germany BAOR 1 Wing

Type	Unit	Base
Alouette AH2, Beaver AL1	12 Flt (HQ)	Wildenrath
	18 Flt (1 (BR) Corps)	Detmold

1 Division Aviation (652 Sqn) Detmold

Type	Unit	Base
Alouette AH2	26 Flt (Div Flt)	Verden
Sioux AH1	1 Eng AT	Verden
Skeeter AOP12	9 Flt (7 Arm Bde)	Soltau
	2 RTR AT (7 AB)	Bergen-Hohne
	3 RTR AT (7 AB)	Fallingbostel
	26 Fd Regt RA AT (7 AB)	Bergen-Hohne
	17 Flt (11 Inf Bde)	Minden
Sioux AH1	SG AT (11 IB)	Fallingbostel
Skeeter AOP12	4 Fd Regt RA AT(11 IB)	Münsterlager

2 Division Aviation (654 Sqn) Hildesheim

Type	Unit	Base
Alouette AH2	27 Flt (Div Flt)	Ostkilver
Sioux AH1	2 Eng AT	Bünde
Skeeter AOP12	4 Flt (6 Inf Bde)	Münster
	15/19 H AS (6 IB)	Münster
Sioux AH1	2 Fd Regt RA AT(6 IB)	Münster
Skeeter AOP12	5 Flt (12 Inf Bde)	Osnabruck
	9/12 L AS (12 IB)	Osnabruck
	5 Fd Regt AT (12 IB)	Gütersloh

4 Division Aviation (655 Sqn) Detmold (in process of building up)

Type	Unit	Base
Alouette AH2	24 Flt (Div Flt)	Herford
Skeeter AOP12	23 Flt (4 Gds Bde)	Iserlohn
	1 Flt (20 Arm Bde)	Detmold
	17/21 L AT (20 AB)	Sennelager

The intended, but not always achieved, light aircraft/helicopter unit structure for BAOR was: Army HQ Flight; Corps HQ Flight; Divisional HQ Flight; Divisional Engineer Troop; Brigade HQ Flight; one or two Brigade RAC Troops; one RA AOP Troop.

Cyprus

Type	Unit	Base
Alouette AH2	16 Flt	Dhekelia

Middle East Land Forces 3 Wing

Aden Falaise Camp (653 Sqn)

Type	Unit	Base
Sioux AH1	MELF AT	Falaise
Scout AH1, Alouette AH1	8 Flt	Habilayn
Beaver AL1	13 Flt	Habilayn
Sioux AH1	15 Flt	Falaise
	1 RNF AP	Falaise
	QDG AS	Falaise
	RAC/RA AT	Khormaksar
	1 Fd Regt RHA AT	Falaise
	45 RMC AP	Khormaksar

Far East Land Forces 4 Wing

17 Division (656 Sqn) Seremban

Type	Unit	Base
Scout AH1	2 Flt (Div Flt)	Seremban
	LG AS	Seremban
	7 Flt	Terendak
	2/7 GR AP	Terendak
	11 Flt	Kluang
	2/6 GR AP	Kluang
	14 Flt	Sembawang
	1 IG AP	Sembawang
	2 GR AP	Seria
	20 Flt	Kai Tak
	40 Lt Regt RA AT	Terendak
	45 Lt Regt RA AT	Kluang
	49 Lt Regt RA AT	Sembawang

3 CBAS AS

Type	Unit	Base
Sioux AH1	40 RMC AP	Ulu Tiram
	41 RMC AP	?
	42 RMC AP	?
	95 Commando Lt Regt AT	Sembawang

10.H   Army flying at 1 January 1972

United Kingdom (2 Wing Netheravon)

7 Division Aviation Regiment

Type	Unit	Base
Alouette AH2, Beaver AL1	6 Flt	Netheravon
Beaver AL1	15 Flt	Topcliffe

Type	Unit	Base
Beaver AL1	132 Flt	Netheravon
Scout AH1, Sioux AH1	664, 657	Long Kesh
Sioux AH1	4/7 RDG AT	Omagh

3 Division Aviation Regiment

Scout AH1	653, 663	Netheravon
	665	Colchester
	666	Topcliffe

Royal Marines

Scout AH1	3 CBAS	Plymouth

Germany

Type	Unit	Base
Sioux AH1	7 Flt	Berlin

1 Wing BAOR

Scout AH1, Sioux AH1, Beaver AL1	655	Detmold
Scout AH1, Beaver AL1	669	Wildenrath

1 Division Aviation Regiment

Scout AH1	651	Verden
	658	Soltau

2 Division Aviation Regiment

Scout AH1, Sioux AH1	652	Bünde
	659	Detmold
	660	Münster

4 Division Aviation Regiment

Scout AH1	654	Minden
Scout AH1, Sioux AH1	661	Herford
	662	Minden
Beaver AL1	BATUS	Suffield (Canada)

Near East

Type	Unit	Base
Alouette AH2	12, 16 Ind Flt	Cyprus

Far East

Beaver AL1	30 Flt	Seletar
	30 Flt det	Laos
Scout AH1	656	Sek Kong (Hong Kong)

Training and development

Type	Unit	Base
Auster AOP9	AFWF	Middle Wallop
Scout AH1	ARWF	Middle Wallop

10.I Army flying at 1 January 1977

United Kingdom

Type	Unit	Base
Gazelle AH1	2 Flt	Netheravon
	3 Flt	Omagh
Gazelle AH1, Beaver AL1	6 Flt	Netheravon
Scout AH1	8 Flt	Netheravon
Scout AH1, Gazelle AH1	655	Topcliffe
	656	Farnborough
	657	Colchester
Scout AH1	658	Netheravon

Royal Marines

Scout AH1, Gazelle AH1	3 CBAS	Coypool

Germany BAOR

Type	Unit	Base
Gazelle AH1	12 Flt	Wildenrath
	7 Flt	Berlin

1 British Corps

1 Division

Type	Unit	Base
Scout AH1	651	Verden
Scout AH1, Lynx AH1	654	Minden
Gazelle AH1	663	Soest

2 Division

Scout AH1	652	Büde
	659	Detmold
Gazelle AH1	662	Münster

4 Division

Scout AH1	653	Herford
Gazelle AH1	661, 664, 669	Detmold
Beaver AL1	BATUS	Suffield (Canada)

Cyprus

Type	Unit	Base
Alouette AH2	16 Flt	Dhekelia (Cyprus)
	UNFICYP	Nicosia

Hong Kong

Type	Unit	Base
Scout AH1	11 Flt	Sek Kong (Hong Kong)
	11 Flt det	Brunei

Training and development

Type	Unit	Base
Chipmunk T10	BFW	Middle Wallop
Beaver AL1	BCF	Middle Wallop
Scout AH1, Gazelle AH1, Lynx AH1	RWCF	Middle Wallop

10.J Army flying at 16 June 1982

United Kingdom Land Forces

Type	Unit	Base
Scout AH1, Gazelle AH1	657	Oakington

Northern Ireland Regiment

Scout AH1	655	Omagh
Gazelle AH1	655	Aldergrove
Beaver AL1	Beaver Flt	Aldergrove

7 Regiment

Scout AH1, Gazelle AH1	658	Netheravon
Scout AH1	658 det	Hereford
Gazelle AH1	2 Flt	Netheravon
	3 Flt	Topcliffe

Germany BAOR

Type	Unit	Base
Gazelle AH1	12 Flt	Wildenrath
	7 Flt	Berlin Gatow

1 Regiment (supporting 1 Arm Div) Hildesheim

Lynx AH1	651	Hildesheim
Gazelle AH1	661	Hildesheim

2 Regiment (supporting 2 Arm Div) Münster

Lynx AH1	652	Bünde
Gazelle AH1	662	Münster

3 Regiment (supporting 3 Arm Div) Soest

Lynx AH1	653	Soest
Gazelle AH1	663	Soest

4 Regiment (supporting 4 Arm Div) Detmold

Lynx AH1	654	Detmold
Gazelle AH1	664	Minden

9 Regiment (supporting HQ 1(BR) Corps) Detmold

Type	Unit	Base
Lynx AH1	659	Detmold
Gazelle AH1	669	Detmold
Beaver AL1, Gazelle AH1	BATUS	Suffield (Canada)

Middle East, Far East and South America

Type	Unit	Base
Alouette AH2	16 Flt	Dhekelia
	UNFICYP	Nicosia
Scout AH1	660	Sek Kong (Hong Kong)
	660 det	Seria (Brunei)
Gazelle AH1	AAC Flt	Belize
Scout AH1, Gazelle AH1	656	Port Stanley (Falklands)

Royal Marines

Type	Unit	Base
Scout AH1, Gazelle AH1	3 CBAS	Port Stanley (Falklands)

Training and development

Type	Unit	Base
Chipmunk T10	BFWF	Middle Wallop
Chipmunk T10, Auster AOP9, Beaver AL1	AFWF	Middle Wallop
Scout AH1, Gazelle AH1, Lynx AH1	RWCF	Middle Wallop
Gazelle AH1	BRWF	Middle Wallop
	ARWS	Middle Wallop

10.K Army flying at 1 January 1987

United Kingdom Land Forces

7 Regt

Type	Unit	Base
Gazelle AH1	2 Flt	Netheravon
	3 Flt	Topcliffe
A109A	7 Regt HQ Flt	Netheravon
Scout AH1	666(TA)	Netheravon
Gazelle AH1, Scout AH1	658	Netheravon
Gazelle AH1, Lynx AH1	656	Netheravon
	657	Oakington

Northern Ireland

Type	Unit	Base
Beaver AL1	Beaver Flt (NI Regt)	Aldergrove
Gazelle AH1 Lynx AH1	655, 665	Aldergrove
Gazelle AH1	655 det	Ballykelly

Royal Marines

Type	Unit	Base
Gazelle AH1, Lynx AH1	3 CBAS	Yeovilton

Germany (BAOR)

1 (BR) Corps

Type	Unit	Base
Gazelle AH1	12 Flt	Wildenrath
	7 Flt	Gatow
	664	Minden/Detmold
	29 Flt BATUS	Suffield (Canada)

1 Regt

Type	Unit	Base
Gazelle AH1	661	Hildesheim
Gazelle AH1, Lynx AH1	651, 652	Hildesheim

3 Regt

Type	Unit	Base
Gazelle AH1	653	Soest
Gazelle AH1, Lynx AH1	662, 663	Soest

4 Regt

Type	Unit	Base
Gazelle AH1, Lynx AH1	654, 659, 669	Detmold

Middle East, Far East and South America

Type	Unit	Base
Alouette AH2	UNFICYP	Nicosia (Cyprus)
	16 Flt	Dhekelia (Cyprus)
Scout AH1	660	Sek Kong (Hong Kong)
	660 det	Seria (Brunei)
Gazelle AH1	25 Flt	Belize
Scout AH1, Gazelle AH1	Air Garrison	Port Stanley (Falklands)

Training and development

Type	Unit	Base
Chipmunk T10, Beaver AL1	FWTF	Middle Wallop
Gazelle AH1	BRWS	Middle Wallop
Gazelle AH1, Lynx AH1	ARWS	Middle Wallop
Scout AH1, Gazelle AH1, Lynx AH1	D&TS	Middle Wallop

10.L Army flying at 1 January 1992

United Kingdom Land Forces

7 Regt

Type	Unit	Base
Gazelle AH1	2 Flt	Netheravon
A109A	8 Flt	Netheravon
Scout AH1	666(TA)	Netheravon
Gazelle AH1, Scout AH1	658	Netheravon
Gazelle AH1, Lynx AH1	656	Netheravon

9 Regt

Type	Unit	Base
Gazelle AH1	3 Flt	Dishforth
Gazelle AH1, Lynx AH1, 7	657	Dishforth
Lynx AH9	673	Dishforth

5 Regt Northern Ireland

Islander AL1	1 Flt	Aldergrove
Gazelle AH1, Lynx AH7	655, 665	Aldergrove
Gazelle AH1	655 det	Ballykelly

Royal Marines

Gazelle AH1, Lynx AH7	3 CBAS	Yeovilton

Germany (BAOR)

1 (BR) Corps

Type	Unit	Base
Gazelle AH1, Lynx AH7	664	Minden/Detmold
Gazelle AH1	12 Flt	Wildenrath
	7 Flt	Berlin Gatow
	29 Flt BATUS	Suffield (Canada)

1 Regt

Gazelle AH1, Lynx AH1	661	Hildesheim
Gazelle AH1, Lynx AH1, 7	651, 652	Hildesheim

3 Regt

Gazelle AH1, Lynx AH1	662	Soest
Gazelle AH1, Lynx AH1, 7	653, 663	Soest

4 Regt

Type	Unit	Base
Gazelle AH1, Lynx AH7	654, 659, 669	Detmold

Middle East, Far East and South America

Type	Unit	Base
Alouette AH2	UNFICYP 16 Flt	Nicosia (Cyprus) Dhekelia (Cyprus)
Scout AH1	660	Sek Kong (Hong Kong)
	660 det	Seria (Brunei)
Gazelle AH1	25 Flt	Belize

Training and development

Type	Unit	Base
Chipmunk T10, Beaver AL1	FWTF	Middle Wallop
Islander AL1	Islander TF	Middle Wallop
Gazelle AH1	670 (BRWS)	Middle Wallop
Gazelle AH1, Lynx AH1, 7	671 (ARWS)	Middle Wallop
Gazelle AH1, Lynx AH7	667 (D&TS)	Middle Wallop

10.M   Army flying at 1 January 1997

United Kingdom Land Forces

3 Regt

Type	Unit	Base
Gazelle AH1, Lynx AH7	662, 663	Wattisham
Gazelle AH1, Lynx AH9	653	Wattisham

4 Regt

Type	Unit	Base
Gazelle AH1, Lynx AH7	654, 669	Wattisham
Gazelle AH1, Lynx AH9	659	Wattisham

7 Regt

Type	Unit	Base
A109A	8 Flt	Netheravon
Gazelle AH1	666(TA), 658	Netheravon

9 Regt

Type	Unit	Base
Gazelle AH1, Lynx AH7	656, 657, 664	Dishforth

5 Regt Northern Ireland

Islander AL1	1 Flt	Aldergrove
Lynx AH7	655	Ballykelly
Gazelle AH1, Lynx AH7	665	Aldergrove

Territorial Army

Gazelle AH1	2 Flt	Netheravon
	3 Flt	Turnhouse
	6 Flt	Shawbury

Royal Marines

Gazelle AH1, Lynx AH7	847	Yeovilton

Germany (BAOR)

1 (BR) Corps

Type	Unit	Base
Gazelle AH1	12 Flt	Laarbruch
	29 Flt BATUS	Suffield (Canada)

1 Regt

Gazelle AH1, Lynx AH7	651, 652, 661	Gütersloh

Middle East, Far East and South America

Type	Unit	Base
Gazelle AH1	UNFICYP 16 Flt	Nicosia (Cyprus) Dhekelia (Cyprus)
Bell 212	7 Flt	Seria (Brunei)

Training and development

Type	Unit	Base
Chipmunk T10	BFWTF	Middle Wallop
Islander AL1	AFWTF	Middle Wallop
Gazelle AH1	670 (BRWS)	Middle Wallop
Lynx AH7	671 (ARWS)	Middle Wallop
Gazelle AH1, Lynx AH7	667 (D&TS)	Middle Wallop

10.1   Auster (1941–1965)

The Auster is unusual in that the manufacturer in due course adopted the type name of the first version in military service and the name was then used as the type name through numerous marks which included completely new designs. (*Auster* is the South Wind.) Taylorcraft Aeroplanes (England) was formed to produce the American Taylorcraft light aircraft design under licence.

Mark I

The Type D went into service powered by a 55hp engine. It was out of front-line service by 1946 but several were operated by second-line units in the FAA.

Service (post-1945) Utility 790 NAS

The Mark II (Type F) was in effect the Mk III prototype; only two were produced.

Mark III

The Type E was much improved and powered by the Gipsy Major engine. The type (serials from MZ100) served mainly throughout North Africa and Europe, but it was largely out of service by 1946.

Service   (post-1945) Training   43   OTU **Communications** 657; AHQ Malaya CF

Mark IV

The Type G was broadly similar to the Mk III but with a re-designed rear fuselage to provide better rearward vision and the Lycoming O-290 engine, which gave a shorter, squatter, nose profile. First aircraft was MS934.

Service   (post-1945) Training   43   OTU **Communications** 657; AHQ Malaya CF

Mark V

The Type J incorporated several improvements on the Mk IV, notably an elevator trim tab and blind flying panel.

Service (post-1945) Air Observation 652, 653, 654, 656, 657, 658, 659, 660, 661, 662, 663, 664; 1901, 1902,

Auster Mk V

The Auster was the first fixed-wing aircraft in Army service, used in all theatres during the war for artillery spotting and forward air control. Post-war the Mk V served extensively both as an AOP platform and in communications. TW373 was with the British Commonwealth Air Communications Squadron at Iwakuni in Japan in 1947. *(Author's collection)*

1903, 1904, 1906, 1907, 1908, 1909, 1910, 1911, 1914, 1951, 1952, 1953, 1954, 1956, 1957, 1958, 1960, 1961, 1963, 1964, 1965, 1966, 1967, 1968, 1969, 1970 Flts **Training** 43 OTU; 227 OCU; AOPS; LAS; 21, 22, 29 EFTS; CFS **Communications** 1, 27, 129, 247, 252, 293, 294, 317; 1315 Flt; 2, 12, 19, 38, 47, 61, 62, 66, 83, 84, 85 GCF; 2 GCS; BAFO CW; 2 TAFCS; BCACS; FECS; 1, 3 FP; HCCS; RAF Film Unit; Aqir, Bückeburg, Brize Norton, Chivenor, Lydda, Marham, Turnhouse, West Malling SF; CF Austria, Italy; CS Malaya: 790, 1831, 1832 NAS Trials AFEE; CBE; CFE; SAW; SCO; ETPS; TCDU

AOP Mark 6

The Type K was a further development of the Taylorcraft, the prototype of which, TJ707, flew on 1 May 1945. It had a completely different nose again, this time housing the Gipsy Major 7 engine of 145hp with an electric self-starter. Fuel load was increased, the blind flying panel was replaced, and the undercarriage lengthened. The most significant change was the addition of auxiliary flaps which reduced the take-off and landing run. The type entered service with 657 Sqn in June 1946.

Service Air Observation 651, 652, 653, 654, 656, 657, 661, 662, 663, 664, 666; 1340, 1900, 1901, 1902, 1903, 1904, 1905, 1908, 1909, 1910, 1912, 1913, 1915, 1954, 1958, 1961, 1966, 1967 Flts; 8, 10, 12, 15 Army Flts **Training** 43 OTU; 227 OCU; AOPS; LAS; CFS **Communications** 267; 1311 Flt; 61, 62, 81 GCF; APSF; Brit Antarctic Flt; FCCS; FECS; 3 FP; HKAAF; MEAFCF; Palestine Truce Observation Flt; Abu Sueir, Aden, Amman, Eastleigh, El Adem, Fayid, Hassani, Horsham St Faith, Iwakuni, Nicosia, Leuchars, Linton-on-Ouse, Odiham, Turnhouse, Wattisham, West Malling SF; AA Hague Trials AFEE; ETPS; MAEE; Light Comms Trials Flt

T Mark 7

The Type Q was a dual control version of the AOP Mk 6, the first of which was VF665. Two were supplied to the Trans Antarctic Expedition as the C4 and the prototype was later modified in 1961 as the Marshall MA.4 with high-lift wings (Chapter 12.7). The T Mk 7 served in small numbers with most operational AOP Mk 6 units.

Service Training 28, 651, 652, 656, 657, 661, 662, 663, 664, 666, 667; 1900, 1903, 1907, 1908, 1910, 1912, 1913 Flts; 227 OCU; AOPS; LAS; 2 FTS; 1 CWDiv; FECS; HCEU; HKAAF **Communications** BAE.

The **AOP Mark 8** designation was not used and may have been intended for one of two aircraft designed and flown before the Mk 9. The **Type N** was produced to specification A.2/45 which called for an aircraft capable of taking more equipment than the AOP Mk 6 and which could be easily dismantled. Two machines were completed and the first (VL522) flew on 28 April 1948. The **Type S** was a light observation project powered by the Blackburn Bombardier engine, the prototype of which, WJ316, flew in September 1950. It was not taken into service but after much development flying led to the AOP Mk 9.

Service (Type N) Trials/communications 227 OCU; LAS

Auster AOP Mk 9

Auster Aircraft Ltd took its name from the first Taylorcraft type produced for the Army and successive marks incorporated major changes which would normally have resulted in name rather than just designation change. WZ670 is a Mk 9 which used the Bombardier engine. *(Auster Aircraft Ltd)*

AOP Mark 9

The Type B5 was the final operational fixed-wing recce aircraft flown by the Army. The type was unusual in not being developed from a civil design and it incorporated a number of improvements on the Mk 6 including better instrumentation. It was relatively light although the hydraulic flaps were slower to respond than the manual ones of the earlier types. The prototype, WZ662, flew on 19 March 1954 and it entered service operationally with 656 Sqn in Malaya.

Service Air Observation 651, 652, 653, 654, 656, 657; 1900, 1901, 1902, 1903, 1906, 1907, 1911, 1912, 1914 Flts; 2, 3, 5, 6, 7, 8, 10, 11, 12, 13, 14, 16, 18, 20, 21 Army Flts; 1/10 GR, LG, 14/20 H, 5 IDG, QDG, QRIH, RA, 3 RGJ, 4 RTR Air Plats; 1 Comm Div LL, 2 Wing Av, 2 Div Av Sections **Training** LAS; AFWF **Communications** 38 GCF; SF West Raynham **Trials** BCS; RAE **Insect spraying** 160 Wing, Christmas Island

T Mark 10

The designation applied to ten AOP Mk 6 aircraft converted to T Mk 7 standard with minor variations.

Service see T Mk 7

AOP Mark 11

The Type E3 was essentially a Mk 9 with a 260hp Continental engine and spatted wheels. The only airframe was XP254, a Mk 9 conversion, but the type did not go into production since helicopters proved more versatile at meeting the Army's needs.

The **Type B4** ambulance/freighter merits mention since it was extensively tested in military marks as XA177. It did not meet any Army need and reverted to civil markings.

Specification and production

Mark	Role	Engine	HP	Weight lb	Speed mph	Nos
I	AOP	Cirrus Minor	90	1,400	86	100
II	AOP	Gipsy Major	130	1,700	126	2
III	AOP	Gipsy Major	130	1,700	126	469
IV	AOP	Lycoming O-290	130	1,920	130	255
V	AOP	Lycoming O-290	130	1,920	130	790
6	AOP	Gipsy Major 7	145	2,160	124	312
7	Trainer	Gipsy Major 7	145	2,200	104	83
N	AOP	Gipsy Queen 34	240	3,365	125	2
S	AOP	Bombardier	180	2,300	125	1
B4	Freighter	Bombardier 702	180	2,600	100	1
9	AOP	Bombardier 203	180	2,550	125	131
10	Trainer	Gipsy Major 7	145	2,200	104	10*
11	AOP	Continental O.470	260	2,550	135	1~

* AOP6 conversions
~ AOP9 conversion

Further reading
Auster Aircraft, Ellison, N H & Macdemitria, R O, Air Britain (Monograph 4), Leicester, 1965

10.2 Sikorsky Hoverfly (1944–1951)

The American R-4 was the first helicopter to be put into series production having been developed from the VS-300. Britain had given early support to the development of the Sikorsky type and at an early date it was evaluated by an RAF pilot. As a result an initial order was placed for seven YR-4A aircraft (FT833-9), two of which were

Sikorsky Hoverfly Mk I

Until 1957 the RAF operated the Army's aircraft with aircrew alone provided by the Army, either Royal Artillery or Glider Pilot Regt. The Sikorsky R-4 Hoverfly was evaluated for Army use during 1944 and operated by 43 OTU at Andover. Preserved KK915/E is pictured at Abingdon in 1968. *(Author)*

delivered as such while the remainder were modified to full YR-4B standard.

Mark I
The VS-316A was the equivalent of the R-4B and 45 were purchased. The first travelled to the UK on the SS *Daghestan* in January 1944, and experience on the convoy confirmed that the new type would have limited operational value, especially in the intended ASW role. On arrival in the UK they went to 529 Sqn for radar calibration tests. The type was used both by the RAF and Navy (as the Gadfly) for training and trials tasks and for communications duties.

Service (post-1945) Training HTF/HTS; 43 OTU **Trials** AFEE; ASWDU; RAE; TCDU; TFU: 703, 771 NAS **Communications** King's Flight: 705 NAS; Gosport SF

Mark II
The VS-316B was a much streamlined variant of the R-4 with a more powerful Franklin engine and cleaner monocoque boom compared to the fabric-covered steel tube frame of the original. In USN service it was designated R-6. Reliability was low and the type saw limited service at a time when there was little enthusiasm for the helicopter in either the RAF or the FAA.

Service Training, utility and trials 1901/1906 Flts (657 Sqn); AFEE: 705, 771 NAS; Eglinton SF

Specification and production

Mark	Role	Engine	HP	Speed mph	Weight lb	Nos
I	Utility	Warner R-500-1	180	75	2,535	52*
II	Utility	Franklin O-405	245	100	2,600	43

* including two YR-4A, five YR-4B

10.3 Cessna L-19 Bird Dog (1952–1954)

The main RAF contribution to the Korean War was in the form of the Auster Mk 6 aircraft of 1903 and 1913 Flights. The latter unit broke new ground in the Army for, flown by ex Glider Pilot Regiment pilots, it had an *explicit* communications and liaison function. For the purpose the Auster was not always suitable and the American Army loaned a sole L-19, 14754, to 1913 Flight for over two years. The aircraft was not given a British serial, but it was marked with roundels.

Service Communications *1913 Flt*

Specification and production

Mark	Role	Engine	HP	Speed mph	Weight lb	Nos
L-19A	Observation	Continental O-470	213	135	2,200	1

10.4 Saro Skeeter (1958–1969)

The Skeeter had a long and complicated gestation period. (To avoid confusion it should be noted that the mark numbers listed in the text, except where obvious, are the manufacturer's.) It started life as the Cierva W.14 Sceptre, the prototype Mk 1 (G-AJCJ) flying on 10 October 1948 with a 110hp Jameson FF-1 engine. The machine was underpowered and the Mk 2, G-ALUF, which flew a year later, employed the 145hp Gipsy 10. By now the military was taking an interest and the Mk 3 was built to specification A.13/49. Saro had bought Cierva, applying the type number P.501 and the name Skeeter, and the first flight of WF112 was on 3 October 1951, the aircraft being fitted with the Gipsy Major 8 engine. Two were built and WF112 was later fitted with the Bombardier engine (as the Mk 3b) but the type remained underpowered and suffered from resonance problems.

Saro Skeeter AOP Mk 10

After prolonged development the Skeeter eventually joined the Army in 1957, nine years after the first variant flew. It really pioneered light helicopter application with the Army, although unsuitable for use in tropical climates. XK481 was one of three development aircraft which flew with 1906 Flt. *(Author)*

The sole Mk 4 (WF114) also used the Bombardier engine and after flying on 15 April 1952 it was employed on trials to solve the continuing resonance problems. The first relatively successful variant was the Mk 5 which incorporated various minor modifications. G-AMTZ which flew in May 1953, was used by the CFS for trials as XG303. The Mk 6 was based on the Mk 5 with a Gipsy Major 200 engine and the first machine was the converted Mk 5 prototype. Three new-build aircraft were also built and these all served in military marks (XJ355, XK773, 964) for trials with the CFS.

AOP Mark 10
The Mark 10 was based on the manufacturer's Mk 6 and constructed to specification H.126. Three were produced fitted with two seats, HF radio and optional dual control.

Service Trials and training 1906/6 Flt: CFS

HT Mark 11
The Mark 11 comprised a single machine, XK479, also built to Mk 6 standard but with a cyclic bias trim switch on both control columns.

Service Trials and training CFS.
The next manufacturer's model was the Mk 7, a converted Mk 6 which flew on 13 April 1957. A more powerful Gipsy Major was fitted and this proved the pre-production standard for the next military version. The Mk 8 differed in detail only.

AOP Mark 12
The P.502 was the definitive production variant built to specification H.163/P2. By the time of first deliveries in 1958 the Army had its own independent air arm and the Skeeter saw extensive service in Europe. It was not suited to use in hotter climates and although of limited range and payload it launched the Army into operational helicopter flying. In later life a number of aircraft served with the RAF as fire crash rescue support.

Service Observation and liaison 651, 652, 654, 655; 1, 4, 5, 9, 12, 13, 17, 22, 23, 24, 26, 27 Flts; 4, 5, 18, 19, 26 Fld Regt, QRIH, 17/21 L Air Troops; 2, 3, 4 RTR, 9/12 L, 15/19 H, QDG Air Sqns **Training** HTF; AACC; ETPS **Rescue** Chivenor, Finningley, Leuchars, Manston, Waddington, Wyton.

HT Mark 13
The Mark 13 comprised just three aircraft similar to the AOP Mk 12 but with minor modifications for RAF use.

Service Training CFS

Specification and production

Variant/ Mark	Role	Engine	HP	Speed mph	Weight lb	Nos
1	Utility	Jameson FF-1	110	80	1,210	1
2	Utility	Gipsy 10	145	95	1,800	1
3	Utility	Gipsy Major 8	130	95	2,100	2
4	Utility	Bombardier	180	97	2,200	1
5	Utility	Bombardier	180	97	2,200	1
6	Utility	Gipsy Major 200	200	107	2,200	4*
7	Utility	Gipsy Major	215	103	2,300	1
8	Utility	Gipsy Major	215	103	2,300	1
AOP10	Trials	Gipsy Major 200	200	107	2,200	3
HT11	Trainer	Gipsy Major 200	200	107	2,200	1
AOP12	Obs	Gipsy Major	215	103	2,300	64
HT13	Trainer	Gipsy Major	215	103	2,300	3

* included 1 Mk 5 conversion

10.5 Fairey Ultra-light (1955)

The War Office and Air Ministry in 1953 expressed an interest in a light reconnaissance helicopter for Army use against which specification H.144T was written. Fairey won the contract for four prototypes, the first of which, XJ924, flew on 14 August 1955. The Ultra-light was extremely small – the specification required that the type could be transported on a standard three-ton truck – and it was powered by a Palouste providing rotor tip drive.

Trials continued over several years and even after the War Office lost interest the manufacturer continued to demonstrate the helicopter in a range of military settings including conducting over 70 landings on HMS *Grenville*.

Specification and production

Mark	Role	Engine	Thrust	Speed mph	Weight lb	Nos
	Utility	Palouste	2 lb/sec	95	1,800	4+2 civil

10.6 Sud Est Aviation Alouette (1961–1988)

Early in its existence as a separate force the Army Air Corps recognised the limitations of the piston-engined Skeeter helicopter, especially in hot climates, and looked elsewhere for an interim machine pending development of the Scout. The selected helicopter was the SE3130B Alouette II, already an established type, and it entered service without problem.

AH Mark 2
The Mark 2 designation was the only one used, presumably to reflect the fact that the type was the

Sud Est Aviation Alouette AH Mk 2

Limitations in the use of the Skeeter in warmer climates led to the purchase of the French Alouette. In service from 1961 to 1988 the type was extremely reliable. XR379 operated with 6 Flt in 1976 at Netheravon. *(MAP)*

manufacturer's Mark II. Seventeen were ordered and they saw service widely in Europe, the West Indies, Kenya and Cyprus. The Alouette entered service in 1961 and was finally withdrawn late in 1988 from 16 Flt in Cyprus. Like the Skeeter, which it complemented, it was unarmed but having a turbine engine was more versatile.

Service Liaison 652, 653, 655, 657, 667; 6, 8, 9, 10, 12, 14, 16, 18, 24, 25, 26, 27, 31, 131 Flts; UNFICYP

Specification and production

Mark	Role	Engine	HP	Speed mph	Weight lb	Nos
AH2	Liaison	Artouste IIC6	360	115	3,527	17

10.7 de Havilland Canada Beaver (1961–1988)

Once the need for liaison flying, as opposed to artillery spotting, was acknowledged the search began for a type suitable for a number of short-range utility duties. From 1952 a DHC.2 Beaver Srs 1, G-AMVU, was evaluated by the RAF as XH455 and by 1954 it was joined by a Srs 2 aircraft G-ANAR/XH463. The Beaver had flown originally in 1947. As the time drew near for the Army to assume responsibility for its own flying, decisions about a utility aircraft were deferred, especially given the 4,000lb weight limit initially determined for Army aircraft.

AL Mark 1

The Beaver was eventually ordered against specification GSOR 342. Deliveries of 42 aircraft (plus four for Oman with British serials) began in late 1961. The Beaver could accommodate four passengers in addition to a crew of two over a range of up to 700 miles. Underwing racks allowed supplies or markers to be dropped. First deliveries, after the AAC Centre, were to 15 Flight in the Middle East and the Beaver was finally retired (in Northern Ireland) in 1989.

Service Liaison 655, 667, 668; 6, 8, 11, 12, 13, 14, 15, 18, 19, 30, 31, 130, 131, 132 Flts; Beaver Flt NI (7 Regt); BATUS; Laos Embassy **Training** AFWF

Specification and production

Mark	Role	Engine	HP	Speed mph	Weight lb	Nos
AL1	Liaison	Wasp R985	450	160	5,100	42*

* plus two aircraft evaluated between 1952 and 1958 and four ordered for Oman

10.8 Westland Scout (1962–1994)

Saro began design work on a successor to the Skeeter in 1957 and the prototype P-531, G-APNU, flew on 20 July 1958. The new type was powered by the Turbomeca

de Havilland Beaver AL Mk 1

By the time the Beaver joined the now independent Army Air Corps, the Service was committed to light transport and liaison as well as reconnaissance and artillery spotting. XV268 is in dark green/black camouflage in 1985 when it was with the Beaver Training Flight. *(Author)*

Westland Wasp AH Mk 1

The Wasp was a Skeeter replacement powered by a 685hp Nimbus engine and capable of carrying five including the pilot. The type was the first Army helicopter to be missile-armed as seen here; XR629 of 657 Sqn carries four SS-11 anti-tank missiles. *(Author)*

Turmo 600 turbine engine, built under licence by Blackburn. Both the Navy and Army were interested and an early development, the P.531-2, by now named Sprite by the manufacturer, featured the Nimbus engine, skid undercarriage and a changed body. When Westland absorbed Saro the type was re-named Scout.

AH Mark 1

The Scout started life as G-APVL powered by a Turmo engine which flew on 9 August 1959. Eight pre-production aircraft were ordered, the first, XP165, flying on 29 August 1960. Development of the engine caused delays with service entry, resulting in a limited Alouette purchase. The Scout carried five people including the pilot, could take a 7.62mm GPMG and from 1970 was equipped with four SS-11 anti-tank missiles making it the first formally armed aircraft flown by the Army. The Scout was withdrawn from use in 1994 after over 30 years of service in Aden, Borneo, Germany and the Falklands.

Westland (Agusta-Bell) Sioux AH Mk 1

In 1964 the decision was taken to introduce a unit light aircraft and a number of types was evaluated. The Bell 47 was selected and ordered in large numbers, especially for use with air troops. Three 'clockwork mice' of 666 Sqn are seen over the Ulster countryside in 1973. *(Crown copyright)*

Service Utility 651, 652, 653, 654, 655, 656, 657, 658, 659, 660, 661, 663, 664, 665, 666; 2, 3, 6, 7, 8, 9, 10, 11, 13, 14, 15, 17, 19, 21, 26, 27, 31, 131 Flts; 3 CBAS **Training** ARWF; ETPS **Trials** *ATF*

Specification and production

Mark	Role	Engine	HP	Speed mph	Weight lb	Nos
AH1	Utility	Nimbus 101	685	131	5,300	148*

* included 8 pre-production and one prototype brought into service

10.9 Westland (Agusta-Bell) Sioux (1965–1974)

The intended Skeeter replacement, the Scout, was delayed entering service and although the Alouette had been ordered in small numbers to bridge the gap, especially in hotter climates, there was an urgent need for a simple helicopter for the Unit Light Aircraft role. The intention was to provide units at battalion level with their own organic airborne observation and liaison capability, a need partly dictated by a shortage of pilots coming forward from line regiments. In 1964 the twenty-year-old Bell 47G was evaluated against the Brantly B.2A, Hiller UH-12E and Hughes 269A. Some 200 of the Bell 47G-3B1 were ordered against specification H.240 with the first 50 being delivered from Agusta and the remainder built by Westland under licence, but in the event many more were supplied.

AH Mark 1
The Mark 1 was broadly similar to the US Army OH-13S. It went first to the School of Army Aviation at Middle Wallop and the first operational machines went to air troops in the Far East. The Sioux carried a pilot and observer and it saw active service in Aden and Borneo. Although unarmed, it was sometimes fitted with a 7.62mm GPMG. It was eventually replaced by the Gazelle by which time the organic flights had been disbanded.

Service **Liaison** 652, 653, 654, 655, 656, 657, 658, 659, 660, 661, 662, 663, 664, 665, 666, 667; 1, 2, 4, 5, 6, 7, 13, 11, 16, 17, 18, 20, 23 UNFICYP Flts; LG, QDG, 5 IDG, 9/12 L, 16/5 L, 17/21 L, 10H, 4/7 RDG, RAC Air Sqns; 1,2, 4 Eng, 14/20H, 15/19H, 17/20 L, MELF, 1, 2, 4, 5, 6, 19, 25 Fld Regts RA, 14, 40, 45, 49 Lt Regts RA, 29, 95 (Commando) Lt Regts RA, 1, 3 RHA, RAC/RA, RSG, 1, 2, 3, 4 RTR, SG, Air Troops; GH, 2/2 GR; 2/6 GR, 2/7 GR, 10 GR, 1 IG, KOBR, 2, 7 Para, 1, 2 RA, 40, 41, 42, 45 RMC, 1 RNF Air Platoons; **Training** ARWF: CFS

HT Mark 2
The Mark 2 was similar in all respects to the Army version; fifteen were supplied to the RAF for training to replace the Sycamore.

Service **Training** CFS.
The **Model 47G-4A** merits mention since Westland

provided sixteen of the more powerful variant to civilian contractors Bristows to use to train Army pilots at Middle Wallop.

Specification and production

Mark	Role	Engine	HP	Speed mph	Weight lb	Nos
AH1	Liaison	Lycoming TVO-435	200	105	2,950	266
HT2	Trainer	Lycoming TVO-435	200	105	2,950	15
47G-4A	Trainer	Lycoming VO-540	270	105	2,950	16

10.10 Aérospatiale Gazelle (1974–date)

The SA341 Gazelle was French-designed and came into British service as a result of the Anglo-French agreement to collaborate on helicopter development and acquisition. The original prototype flew on 7 April 1967 and the type was ordered in large numbers for all four British services (including the Royal Marines) with only very minor differences between variants. The Gazelle was significant in having a semi-rigid main rotor and shrouded tail rotor (or fenestron).

AH Mark 1
The Army variant (SA341B) carried five including the pilot and it was armed with TOW anti-tank missiles and the 7.62mm GPMG. The first production aircraft, XW842, flew on 31 January 1972 and the Gazelle entered service with 660 Sqn at Soest in May 1974 and in Germany it acted as reconnaissance for heavily armed Lynx helicopters. The Gazelle saw service in the Falklands, Belize and the Gulf.

Service Utility 651, 652, 653, 654, 655, 656, 657, 658, 659, 661, 662, 663, 664, 669; 2, 3, 6, 7, 12, 16, 25, 29 Flts; Falkland Islands garrison; 3 CBAS; BATUS **Training** RWF/BTS; ARWS

Aérospatiale Gazelle AH Mk 1

The Gazelle was one of three types within the Anglo-French agreement to collaborate on helicopter types. It is a compact five-seater with shrouded tail rotor. XZ309 is in the latest Army colours flying with 6(TA) Flt based at Shawbury. (*Westland Helicopters Ltd*)

HT Mark 2

The SA341C was bought for the Royal Navy solely for the training role. It is similar in all details to the Army variant.

Service Training 705 NAS: 2 FTS; ETPS

HT Mark 3

The SA341D was the RAF training version of which 29 were delivered mainly for 2 FTS. Later several were delivered to the RAF's Chinook squadrons for route reconnoitring and (relatively) inexpensive training.

Service Training 2 FTS; CFS; 7, 18 Sqns; ETPS

HCC Mark 4

The SA341E comprised four aircraft equipped as fast VIP transport carrying three passengers and two crew. Flotation equipment was added to the skids and IR decoy flares were fitted.

Service Communications 32

Specification and production

Mark	Role	Engine	HP	Speed mph	Weight lb	Nos
AH1	Utility	Astazou IIIN2	643	165	4,189	212
HT2	Trainer	Astazou IIIN2	643	165	4,189	40
HT3	Trainer	Astazou IIIN2	643	165	4,189	29
HCC4	Comms	Astazou IIIN2	643	165	4,189	4*

* 1 new build, 3 HT3 conversions

10.11 Westland Lynx (1978–date)

The Lynx was the third of the helicopters involved in the Anglo-French collaboration agreement of 1968 (the others were the Gazelle and Puma) and it was the only one

Westland Lynx HAS Mk 8

Westland had design lead of the Anglo-French Lynx – is it churlish to wonder whether that accounts for a paltry French order for fourteen aircraft? The type replaced the Wasp with the Fleet Air Arm, and the latest version with improved main rotors, the HAS Mk 8 (XZ236), joined 815 NAS from 1995. *(Westland Helicopters Ltd)*

in which Westland had design lead. The WG.13 design was intended for civil and general naval use and the prototype, XW835, flew on 21 March 1971. The Lynx was extremely robust and was fitted with a rigid rotor driven by a pair of Gem turboshafts; its versatility soon led to British Army orders, but French interest was confined to around fourteen for the Aéronavale. The company demonstrator G-LYNX/ZB500 was developed and in a hybrid form, with advanced rotors, secured the world helicopter speed record of 249.09mph on 11 August 1986, a record which still stands at the time of writing.

AH Mark 1

The Mark 1 was built for the British Army to GSOR 3335 to fulfil a number of roles. These included troop transport (twelve troops), logistic support (2,000lb internally; 3,000lb externally), armed escort, anti-tank strike, casevac, search and rescue, reconnaissance and command post. The first production aircraft, XZ170, flew on 11 February 1977 and the Lynx joined BAOR squadrons from August 1978 and from 1980 the TOW ATM was fitted (eight missiles). The **AH Mark 1GT** designation was applied to some machines taken to Mk 7 standard but retaining AH1 avionics.

Service Utility 651, 652, 653, 654, 656, 657, 659, 661, 662, 663, 671 **Training** ARWF

HAS Mark 2

The Mark 2 was the first naval version built for the Fleet Air Arm and Aéronavale for the ship-borne anti-submarine warfare role. It had a fixed castoring undercarriage, folding tail, Seaspray search radar and carried four Sea Skua ASMs, two Mk 46 or Stingray torpedoes or two Mk 11 depth charges. Prototype was XZ227 which flew on 10 February 1976 and service entry was with 700L NAS in September 1976.

Service ASW 815, 829 **Training** 702 **Trials** 700L

HAS Mark 3

The next naval version had the more powerful Gem 41 engine but was otherwise similar to the HAS Mk 2, some of which were re-built to HAS Mk 3 standard. Two helicopters were downgraded for use on HMS *Endurance* as the **HAS Mk 3ICE**. In the Gulf War eighteen aircraft were fitted with improved cooling, an IR jammer and ALQ-167 ECM system as the **HAS Mk 3GM**.

Service ASW/SAR 815, 829 **Training** 702

HAS Mark 3S and HAS Mark 3CTS

These two sub-variants represented stages in the conversion of Mk 3 aircraft to Mk 8 configuration. The former included at least 55 airframes fitted with Orange Crop ESM and GEC Marconi AD 3400 radios. The CTS aircraft were in addition fitted with Racal 4000 central tactical system and flotation bags on the sponsons.

Service ASW/SAR 815, 829 **Training** 702.
The **Mark 4** comprised fourteen aircraft for the Aéronavale.

AH Mark 5

The intended Mark 5 was very much an interim type fitted with the Gem 41-1 engine but otherwise similar to the AH Mk 1. By the time the first (ZE375) had flown on 23 February 1985 it had been decided to incorporate further improvements and the remainder of the batch was completed to AH Mk 7 standard, although a further aircraft, designated **Mark 5X**, was delivered to the RAE.

Service Trials RAE.
The **AH Mark 6** was an intended version of the AH Mk 5 fitted with a wheeled undercarriage, but it was not developed.

AH Mark 7

The Mark 7 was similar to the AH Mk 5 but with a larger tail rotor working clockwise. Like many later AH Mk 1 aircraft the type was fitted with a TOW sight on the cabin and a large IR suppression shroud on the exhaust. Many AH Mk 1 machines were converted to AH Mk 7 standard. When 3 CBAS gave up its Gazelles and transferred its remaining Lynx to 847 NAS it was reported that the **HAS Mark 7** designation would apply.

Service Utility 651, 652, 653, 654, 655, 657, 659, 663, 664, 665, 667, 669, 671, 672; 3 CBAS **Troop carrier** 847 **Training** ARWF; ETPS

HAS Mark 8

The definitive naval variant was the first of the 'Super Lynx' variants fitted with the much improved British Experimental Rotor Programme (BERP) main rotors driven by two Gem 42-1 engines. The reverse tail rotor was employed and improved avionics including the Racal 4000 CTS, MIR-2 ESM together with the GEC Sensors Sea Owl thermal imaging system. ZD267 was the first machine brought up to full HAS Mk 8 standard and 65 HAS Mk 3 airframes are being converted to Mk 8 standard. Some Mk 8 helicopters optimised for attack are designated **HMA Mark 8**.

Service ASW/SAR 815

Westland Lynx AH Mk 9

The latest version of the Lynx for the Army is singularly different from earlier versions having a tricycle undercarriage rather than skids. XZ170 was built as a Mk 1 and was the first conversion to the transport/command post model with more powerful engine and improved main rotors. (*Westland Helicopters Ltd*)

AH Mark 9

The Mark 9 was, in the broadest sense, the Army equivalent of the HAS Mk 8 incorporating BERP main rotors and the Gem 42-1 engine. But perhaps the most significant external change is the provision of a fixed tricycle undercarriage instead of skids. It is intended as an unarmed troop carrier and command post and incorporates improved avionics.

Service Utility 653, 659, 664, 672, 673

Specification and production

Mark	Role	Engine	HP	Speed mph	Weight lb	Nos
AH1	Utility	2xGem 2	900	160	9,600	160
HAS2	ASW/SAR	2xGem 2	900	144	9,750	60
HAS3	ASW/SAR	2xGem 41	1,120	144	10,750	31*
Mk 4	ASW	2xGem 41	1,120	144	9,500	14~
AH5	Utility	2xGem 41	1,120	160	10,000	2
AH6	Utility	2xGem 41	1,120	160	9,600	–
AH7	Utility	2xGem 41	1,120	160	10,750	120#
HAS8	ASW/SAR	2xGem 42	1,120	144	11,300	65+
AH9	Utility	2xGem 42	1,120	160	11,300	24^

*   plus HAS2 conversions
~   for Aéronavale
#   13 new build, 107 AH Mk 1 conversions
+   HAS3 conversions
^   16 new build, 8 AH7 conversions

10.12   Agusta A 109A Hirondu

On recapturing the Falkland Islands the British services recovered two intact A 109A helicopters from the Argentine Army, AE-331 and 334. These were brought to the UK and after exhibition returned to flying condition as ZE410 and 411.

The **A 109A** is twin-engined and carries a payload of 1,980lb or 6/7 passengers. The two captured aircraft were delivered to a detached flight of 7 Regt at Hereford together with two machines bought in the UK. The unit later became 8 Flt and it is understood to work with the SAS who may also have had access to a civilian-registered A 109.

Service Communications 8 Flt

Specification and production

Mark	Role	Engine	HP	Speed mph	Weight lb	Nos
A109A	Transport	2xAllison 250-C20B	420	193	5,732	4*

*   2 captured, 2 bought

10.13   Bell 212, UH-1 and Griffin (1994–date)

To replace the Scout in the Far East (Brunei) three civil **Bell 212s** were ordered for C Flight 660 Sqn (later 7 Flight) in 1994. The type is equivalent to the US UH-1N and can accommodate fourteen troops over a range of 250 miles.

Service Utility 7 Flt.
An earlier version of the ubiquitous 'Huey', the **UH-1H**, had been flown briefly by the British in the Falklands in the shape of captured Argentine examples including AE-409 (656 Sqn), AE–413 (5 Brigade), AE-422 (820, 825 NAS) and AE-424 (820 NAS).

In 1996 all basic military helicopter aircrew training was put to commercial tender, the successful bidder being FBS who were awarded a ten year contract. The Squirrel (Chapter 7.20) was selected for basic training replacing the Gazelle, while the **Bell 214EP Griffin HT Mk 1** was chosen to replace the Wessex. The 214 carries up to fifteen and is powered by a Pratt & Whitney Twin Pac turbine delivering 1,800 hp.

Service Training DHFS (60(R) Sqn); SARTU

Agusta A 109A Hirondu

Two A 109s were captured from the Argentine Army during the Falklands War and returned to the United Kingdom for exhibition. Two further examples were bought and the aircraft served with 8 Flt allegedly in support of the SAS. ZE411 was originally AE-334 with the Argentine Army. *(MAP)*

Bell UH-1H

The Army flies three Bell 212 helicopters with 7 Flt in Brunei. However, it also very briefly gained experience on the type when captured Bell UH-1H machines were flown immediately after the Falklands War. AE-422, seen here at Yeovilton in 1982, was actually flown by 820 and 825 NAS crews. *(Author)*

Griffin HT1

Seen here in stunning Welsh mountain scenery is the first Bell 214EP Griffin HT1 of the DHFS at Shawbury. ZJ234/S originally joined the school in April 1997 as G-BWZR after spending some time at Boscombe Down and is one of nine operated for the RAF, six at Shawbury and three at RAF Valley for air-sea rescue training. The Griffin is operated under contract by FBS as 60(R) Sqn RAF. (*David Dare Jones, RAF Shawbury*)

Specification and production

Mark	Role	Engine	HP	Speed mph	Weight lb	Nos
212	Utility	PW T400-CP	1,290	161	11,200	3
UH -1H		Lycoming T53	1,400	130	9,500	4*
Griffin HT1		PT6T-3D	1,800	161	11,900	12

* Captured machines from Argentine forces

10.14　McDonnell Douglas Apache (ordered)

The AH-64D Longbow Apache was ordered in 1995 to meet Army requirement SR(A)428. The original need for 127 airframes has been reduced to 67 and the first are expected to enter service in 1998. Most will be built by Westland and they will be fitted with two Rolls-Royce RTM322 turboshafts to enable commonality with the EH101/Merlin. Armament includes provision for sixteen AGM-114A Hellfire ATMs and a fixed M230 30mm chaingun in a remote under-fuselage turret.

With the Apache the original aircraft weight limit of 4,000lb imposed on the Army Air Corps in 1957 will have increased in 40 years fivefold to over 20,000lb.

Specification and production

Mark	Role	Engine	HP	Speed mph	Weight lb	Nos
AH-64D	Attack	2xRTM322	2,100	225	21,000	67

10.15　Types used for evaluation

Throughout the period covered in this book the Army has used a variety of types in military markings for evaluation. These do not merit separate entries except where, like the Skeeter, the evaluation related to pre-service entry of the type in question. Catalogued are the types used for evaluation, usually by 1906 Flt or the AAC Centre.

The **Heston JC.6** was built to specification A.2/45 as an air observation platform. It was a twin-boom, two-seat design powered by a single Gipsy Queen 33 engine driving a pusher propeller. The prototype, VL529, flew in 1947 but after trials with A&AEE the type was dropped, not in favour of the Auster Type N (Chapter 10.1), but the later Auster AOP Mk 9.

The **ML Utility** was a forerunner of the microlight using an inflatable wing designed and built by R&DE Cardington. Three examples were tested from 1957 for

McDonnell Douglas Apache

Sixty-seven potent Longbow Apache attack helicopters have been ordered by the Army for service entry in 1998. Most will be built by Westland and will feature the RTM322 turboshaft engines to ensure commonality with the EH101 Merlin. *(Westland Helicopters Ltd)*

ML Utility Mk 1

Three examples of the unusual inflatable-wing Utility were tested over a four-year period but eventually it was decided that the type was not robust enough for the intended application. XK776 was a Mk 1 aircraft with the Walter Mikron engine. *(MAP)*

Dornier Do 27

The Pioneer and Do 27 were both evaluated for the liaison role for which the Beaver was ultimately selected. PA+110 of the Heer (German Army) is seen at Middle Wallop in 1965. *(Author)*

possible use by officers at company commander level for observation. The type needed calm weather and trials were eventually abandoned in 1961 after a number of wing designs had been tried. The two Mark 1 aircraft XK776 and XK784 were powered by the Walter Mikron engine while the Mark 2 (XK781) was powered by a JAP J.99.

Edgar Percival EP.9

As the Lancashire Prospector the EP.9 was evaluated against the Beaver in 1958. G-ARDG, seen here in crop-spraying mode at Farnborough, was subsequently acquired by the Museum of Army Flying. *(Author)*

The **Edgar Percival EP.9** (later Lancashire Prospector) was evaluated against the Beaver in 1958. Two aircraft were bought and tested, XM797 and XM819, but the view was taken that an aircraft was required with a reliable pedigree from an established supplier. The type continued with the AAC at Middle Wallop until 1961 when the Beaver entered service.

In addition to the EP.9 the **Do.27** (borrowed) and **Pioneer** (Chapter 7.13) XE512 were also evaluated for the liaison role fulfilled by the Beaver; the Pioneer had also been earlier evaluated in 1954 by the Army (Srs 2 XH469), again with the Beaver and without conclusion.

With the need for a unit light helicopter, potentially for organic use, the **Hughes 269A, Hiller UH-12E** and **Brantly B2A** were assessed against the Bell 47 which in the event

was ordered in large numbers. The trials were conducted in 1962 and 1963 by the A&AEE in the UK and in Libya. Two Hughes were used, sponsored by Westland; they were G-ASBL/XS349 (later XS684) and G-ASBD/XS685. The Brantlys, sponsored by BEAS, comprised three helicopters G-ASHK/XS681, G-ASEH/XS682 and G-ASHJ/XS683. The Hillers are believed to have been lent by the Fleet Air Arm.

Three **Beagle Wallis Wa.116** autogiros were evaluated for local reconnaissance and liaison during 1962 to 1963 as XR942-4 (G-ARZA-C). The type was not considered sufficiently robust for military use.

The **Powerchute Raider** is unique in British military service and is included for the sake of completeness. It is a powered parachute comprising a lightweight wheeled frame with seat and 35hp engine behind hanging under an eleven-cell 35ft paraglider (parafoil). The type was displayed at the Farnborough air show in 1988 and shortly after one was given the serial ZG879 allocated to the RAE. By 1995 it was at Hereford and may have been evaluated by, or accessible to, the SAS. Significant numbers of similar equipment are held by the US Army.

Hiller UH-12

The unit light helicopter requirement was to result in a large order for a type which would be used globally. Four types were evaluated, including the Hiller 360/UH-12 seen here in civil guise as G-APJN which was operated by Bristow Helicopters who had a contract for the basic training of Army pilots. *(Author)*

11 – Utility aircraft

See also: Andover (6.18); Anson (7.2); Argosy (6.15); Auster (10.1); Beaufighter (3.2); Brigand (3.8); Canberra (4.7); Dakota (6.3); Gazelle (10.10); Halifax (6.2); Hastings (6.8); Harvard (1.5); Hawk (1.25); Hudson (5.3); Hurricane (3.1); Lancaster (4.3); Lynx (10.11); Meteor (2.5); Mosquito (3.4); Sea King (9.14); Sea Otter (5.2); Skeeter (10.4); Spitfire (2.1); Sycamore (7.10); Tempest (2.2); Vampire (3.9); Varsity (1.13); Walrus (5.1); Wessex 9.12

All services, but especially the Navy and RAF, have requirements for aircraft for a variety of support tasks, typically including target facilities and rescue. In most cases obsolete aircraft or variants of types designed for other purposes were used, although occasionally a need was met by a purpose-built type.

In this chapter three key areas are considered – target facilities, air rescue and calibration – with miscellaneous units, which do not logically fit elsewhere, also included. In addition some of the various test and trials units are recorded for the sake of completeness.

January 1946

Fighter Command provided most of the RAF's target units, equipped with the Spitfire for high-speed tasks and the Vengeance and Martinet for slower towing duties. There were nine squadrons, most of them raised towards the end of the war. Of particular note was the Pilotless Aircraft Unit, still equipped with a handful of drones in Wales. The Fleet Air Arm also used the Vengeance and Martinet extensively, together with a miscellany of other

Bristol Beaufighter TT Mk 10

The Beaufighter served as a target tug for many years after the war, the last being retired in Singapore in 1960. For the task the radar was removed and a winch fitted on the fuselage; it can just be made out forward of the roundel. In addition to trainer bands the underside of the aircraft was painted with 'Oxydol' black and yellow stripes. RD788 operated with 695 and 34 squadrons and 5 CAACU before ending its days on the inventory of the Malta Communications and Target Towing Squadron. *(Author's collection)*

types including the first helicopter in service use, the Hoverfly.

Great store had always been set on the ability of the Royal Air Force to recover downed airmen speedily. Much of the air war was fought over the sea and air-sea rescue units were spread across the United Kingdom and Middle East. In the Far East they were based only around the Indian sub-continent, the maritime patrol Sunderlands taking on the role further afield in that theatre. The Wellington, Warwick and Liberator were the main types involved in medium-to long-range search with the rescue element comprising air-dropped lifeboats. For shorter-range duties, the Walrus was still in service, supplemented by the Sea Otter. In general squadrons were dispersed in flights. The Fleet Air Arm also operated flights abroad, equipped with the Sea Otter, Walrus and the venerable Swordfish.

There were two insect-control flights, one in Burma and one in Kenya, with 1340 Flt supporting smoke and gas trials in India. Most of the various test and trials units are described in the relevant chapters. However, the RAE strictly belongs in the utility category flying a large number of types at Farnborough, where it remained for some years. The Search and Rescue Training Unit at Calshot supported the development of rescue techniques.

July 1948

The RAF target units had reduced considerably as the demand for their services diminished. The types used were still the Spitfire Mk 16 and Martinet. The Fleet Air Arm now used the Mosquito extensively with a range of lesser types, in the UK and Malta, to serve the needs of the Fleet in the Mediterranean. An anomaly was the disappearance – for a time at least – of the air-sea rescue units. An unusual unit was the Visual Inter-Service Training and Research Unit at Keevil which served to support camouflage and related trials.

January 1950

The original target facilities squadrons changed their numbers to preserve older unit identities and to reflect the army co-operation role. They were still equipped with the Spitfire Mk 16 and Martinet, and also with redundant and converted Tempests and Beaufighters. A major armament practice camp had been established at Acklington in Northumberland, with another, smaller, such unit at Butterworth in Malaya. The major Fleet Air Arm target unit, 728 NAS, was in Malta, equipped with, among other types, the target version of the Mosquito.

July 1952

The operational army co-operation squadrons had been disbanded, their roles taken over by civilian anti-aircraft co-operation units (CAACU). The needs of the RAF for air gunnery support were met by the Acklington Armaments Practice Station. There was a second station at Sylt to serve the needs of the RAF in Germany with camps in Cyprus and Malaya. The civilianisation of second-line units extended to the Fleet Air Arm where the Air Direction School was managed by Airwork, while an ever-increasing number and variety of types was operated by 728 NAS in Malta where the RAF also now had a

target facilities flight. Among types in use by the Navy was the Sturgeon – flawed as a twin-engined bomber but useful for target duties.

A most significant development was the resurrection of the rescue units, now equipped with helicopters. The Coastal Command Development Unit at St Mawgan was to pioneer the use of the helicopter for off-shore rescue, while the RAF was using Dragonflys in Malaya for casualty evacuation in difficult circumstances. From using destroyers for carrier plane-guard duties the Navy was turning to helicopters as a faster and more cost-effective option.

As an indication of the speed of developments in technology during this period, the Fleet Air Arm had commissioned a number of trials units, in several cases physically alongside RAF units with similar functions.

January 1955

One of the CAACUs had disbanded while the Vampire was coming into service for target work to replace the ageing Spitfire whose days were now numbered. The European APCs still operated the Tempest and Mosquito while the Beaufighter remained in use in Cyprus and Malaya. A new facilities unit, 288 Sqn, had formed with the Balliol to provide targets for navigators in training with 228 OCU.

On the rescue front Fighter Command had assumed responsibility for a helicopter-based unit, 275 Sqn, equipped with the Sycamore (with other types for communications and training) and detached to bases around the country from Thornaby. In Malaya the Casualty Evacuation Flight (CEF) had been formed into 194 Sqn.

Within 90 Group two units had formed from the Central Signals Establishment (CSE) at Watton for radar calibration tasks. In general the various trials units continued their work, although the Telecommunications Flying Unit (TFU) had become the Radio Research Flying Unit (RRFU).

July 1957

Few changes had taken place in the target facilities units, although the Spitfire had been retired in favour of the Vampire. The APC at Acklington had disbanded while that at Sylt had just a year or so to go. The Fleet Air Arm 728 NAS in Malta had now become more of a trials unit. While 275 Sqn continued to operate its Sycamores, Coastal Command had formed 22 Sqn with the Whirlwind, mainly in the south. A utility helicopter squadron, 284, had formed to support ground forces in Cyprus.

Such was the demand for trials work that a regular Canberra unit, 100 Sqn, had been detached to the Bomber Command Development Unit to carry out a variety of tasks.

July 1960

The CAACUs had now merged into just one, based at Exeter with the Vampire and the Hunter. The Canberra Mk 11 was used as a target by 228 OCU while Meteors served with the TTF in Malta and 1574 Flt in Malaya. The Fleet Air Arm had contracted much of its target work to

Airwork in the UK and in Malta 728 NAS now operated Firefly and Meteor drones.

Fighter Command had formed a second rescue unit in Northern Ireland and 228 Sqn had taken over the role of 275 Sqn, operating the Whirlwind in addition to the Sycamore. Changes further afield also involved unit number changes. No 284 Sqn in Cyprus became 103, while 194 Sqn in Malaya was replaced by 110 Sqn with the Whirlwind and Sycamore. In the Fleet Air Arm the ships' flights had equipped with the Dragonfly Mk 5. The calibration units had also exchanged numbers. Low-level 116 Sqn had moved to Tangmere becoming 115 Sqn, while the high-level Canberra 527 Sqn also made the move becoming 245 Sqn.

January 1965

The Canberra element of 228 OCU had become a separate numbered unit, 85 Squadron, based at Binbrook and also operating the Meteor. No 1574 Flt at Changi also operated the Meteor. Fighter Command had disbanded its rescue units and the function had become the responsibility of Coastal Command which had formed a second squadron – 202 – in the north of England. Both this unit and 22 Sqn were equipped with the much more capable turbine-engined Whirlwind Mk 10 which also equipped 103 Sqn in Seletar. Although the emergency in Malaya had ended there was still the need for support for the Army in the region. Two utility flights had formed for local search and rescue tasks in Cyprus and Libya. In the Navy the ships' and stations' flights had switched from the Dragonfly to the Whirlwind which also served with the shore-based 771 NAS which had a secondary SAR role.

January 1970

The long-serving 728 NAS at Malta had finally disbanded leaving the Navy with the Air Direction Training Unit (ATDU) at Yeovilton and the Fleet Requirements Unit (FRU) at Hurn, both operated by Airwork. The RAF retained its civilian army co-operation unit at Exeter and 85 Sqn, but for high-speed targets for the Lightning interceptors each Lightning base operated a target facilities flight with redundant Mk 1 or Mk 1A aircraft.

In relation to search and rescue the RAF situation was static while the Fleet Air Arm had introduced the Wessex into service on its carriers. For high-level radar calibration 245 Sqn had become 98 Sqn, now equipped with the Canberra E Mk 15.

January 1975

There had now been changes in the target units with the Canberra operating with all RAF units. There were three conventional target units, 7 Sqn at St Mawgan and 85 and 100 Sqn at West Raynham. In addition the electronic warfare training unit, 360 Sqn, was equipped with the new and bulbous Mk 17 Canberra. The Cyprus TTF was also equipped with the Canberra. Elsewhere in the Middle East the two utility flights had disbanded but 84 Sqn, which had long service in the Middle East, had formed with the Whirlwind Mk 10 at Akrotiri. The Fleet Air Arm now had a sole support unit in the form of the Fleet Requirements and Air Direction Training Unit

(FRADTU) with the Hunter and ubiquitous Canberra.

The domestic SAR structure had settled at 22 and 202 Sqns in the RAF while in the Fleet Air Arm 771 had given place to 772 NAS and 707 NAS at Yeovilton also had a secondary SAR role. For calibration the Argosy E Mk 1 had succeeded the Varsity with 115 Sqn.

January 1980

The target facilities units were little changed now except that 85 Sqn had disbanded. Search and rescue arrangements were improved with partial re-equipment of 22 and 202 Sqns. The former operated the shorter-range end of the spectrum with the Whirlwind and Wessex while 202 Sqn had the Sea King Mk 3. In addition three Fleet Air Arm helicopter units along the south coast had support SAR roles. Calibration was confined to 115 Sqn, now with redundant Andovers converted to the role.

January 1985

100 Sqn operated a range of Canberras at Wyton, which complemented the Mk 17 version with 360 Sqn for electronic warfare training. The Wessex Mk 2 had fully replaced the Whirlwind with 22 Sqn and the Mk 5 variant had replaced it with 84 Sqn in Cyprus. In the aftermath of the Falklands war 1564 Flt was based at Navy Point with the Sea King while Navy Wessex of 845 Sqn provided SAR on Ascension. In Scotland 819 NAS, an operational anti-submarine unit, added its Sea Kings to the SAR service.

January 1990

Few changes had taken place in five years, although on the Falklands 1564 Flt had disbanded into 78 Sqn.

January 1995

The most obvious sign of change in the second-line units was the replacement of military units by civilian contract services. The Hawk now served with 100 Sqn at Finningley and with FRADU at Yeovilton (under contract). FR Aviation operated Falcons from Hurn and Teesside for electronic warfare training following the disbandment of 360 Sqn. The balance of the 115 Sqn Andovers had transferred to Hunting Aviation Services based at East Midlands airport for calibration support. The Sea King was now in wider use in the air-sea rescue role, although 78 Sqn in the Falklands had disbanded.

11.A   Utility and trials at 1 January 1946

Target facilities

Fighter Command

11 Group

Type	Unit	Base
Spitfire XVI, Oxford I, Vengeance TTIV	567	West Malling
Spitfire XVI, Harvard, Vengeance TTIV	587	Weston Zoyland
Spitfire XVI, Vengeance TTIV	595	Aberporth

Type	Unit	Base
Spitfire XVI, Martinet I, Vengeance TTIV	691	Exeter
Queen Bee, Queen Martinet	PAU	Manorbier

12 Group

Type	Unit	Base
Spitfire XVI, Oxford II	287	Spilsby (2 APS)
Spitfire IX, Vengeance II	288	Hutton Cranswick
Spitfire XVI, Oxford, Vengeance TTIV	577	Castle Bromwich
Spitfire XVI, Vengeance TTIV	631	Llanbedr
	695	Horsham St Faith

13 Group

Type	Unit	Base
Spitfire XVI, Vengeance TTIV	1353 Flt	West Freugh

Coastal Command HQ Gibraltar

Type	Unit	Base
Martinet I	1500 Flt	North Front

Transport Command (38 Group)

Type	Unit	Base
Martinet I	1677 Flt	Wethersfield

ACSEA

Type	Unit	Base
Oxford, Anson I	22 ACU	Santa Cruz

Fleet Air Arm

Type	Unit	Base
Martinet TT1, Sea Otter, Wildcat IV, V, Hoverfly I, II, Mosquito XXV	771	Gosport
Anson C12	773	Lee-on-Solent
Martinet TT1, Firefly I, Wildcat V, Anson I, Mosquito XVI, XXV	772	Ayr
Baltimore IV, V, Beaufighter X, Martinet TT1, Mosquito XXV, Seafire IIC, III, Swordfish I, Walrus, Wellington XIV	728	Luqa (Malta)
Corsair IV, Vengeance TTIV,	791	Sembawang (Malaya)
Harvard T2B IV, Corsair, Defiant TT1, Seafire III, Vengeance TTIV	721	HMS *Speaker* (Far East)
Martinet TT1	723	Nowra (Australia)

Air-sea rescue

Coastal Command

RAF Northern Ireland

Type	Unit	Base
Warwick II	280 (det)	Aldergrove

16 Group

Lancaster ASR III	279	Beccles
Warwick I	280	Thornaby
	280 (det)	Thorney Island

18 Group

Warwick I	280 (det)	Tain

19 Group

Type	Unit	Base
Warwick I	280 (det)	St Eval

247 Group

Warwick I	280 (det)	Azores

Mediterranean and Middle East Air Force

AHQ Eastern Mediterranean

Type	Unit	Base
Wellington XIV	621	Mersa Matruh (Eg)

AHQ Malta

Warwick I	283	Hal Far (Malta)
	283 (det)	Elmas (Sardinia)
	283 (det)	Istres (Fr)
	283 (det)	Maison Blanche (Alg)

AHQ Italy

Walrus I, Warwick I	293	Pommigliano (It)
	293 (det)	Pisa (It)

AHQ Iraq and Persia

Walrus I, Warwick I, Auster V	294	Basrah (Iraq) dets Bahrein, Masirah, Sharjah

Allied Command South East Asia

AHQ Burma

Type	Unit	Base
Warwick I, Liberator VI, Lancaster ASR 3	1348 Flt	Agartala (India)
Warwick I, Liberator V, VI	1347 Flt	Chittagong (India)
Sea Otter I	1351 Flt	Chittagong (India)

AHQ Ceylon

Warwick I, Liberator VI	1346 Flt	Kankesanturai (Cey)

227 Group

Warwick I, Liberator VI	1349 Flt	Karachi (India)

Fleet Air Arm

Type	Unit	Base
Sea Otter I	1702	Hassani (Greece)
Swordfish II, Walrus, Sea Otter I	1700 A Flt, B Flt, C Flt	Trincomalee, Katukurunda, Sembawang
Sea Otter I, Oxford, Tiger Moth	1701	Kai Tak (Hong Kong)

Miscellaneous

Type	Unit	Base
Anson I, Baltimore IV, Albacore	AL Flt *anti-locust*	Eastleigh (Kenya)

Allied Command South East Asia

AHQ Burma

Type	Unit	Base
Auster AOP5	1354 Flt *insect control*	Pegu (Burma)
Vengeance III, Harvard IIB, Mosquito XVI, Thunderbolt II, Reliant	1340 Flt *smoke/gas trials*	Cannanore (India)

Trials and training

Technical Training Command (23 Group)

Type	Unit	Base
Various	RAE	Farnborough

Maintenance Command

Type	Unit	Base
Lancaster III	BTU	West Freugh
Halifax, Mosquito	BBU	Martlesham Heath
Wellington, Beaufighter, Anson, Oxford	SFU	Honiley

Coastal Command

16 Group

Type	Unit	Base
Martinet I, Spitfire	FATU	Langham
Sea Otter II, Beaufighter X, Mosquito VI, Spitfire V, IX, Walrus II, Anson I, Liberator VI, Warwick I Lancaster III, Wellington XIV, Sunderland V	ASWDU	Thorney Island
Swordfish III, Wellington, Beaufighter X	ATDU	Gosport

19 Group

Type	Unit	Base
Sea Otter I	SRTU	Calshot

Flying Training Command (23 Group)

Type	Unit	Base
Stirling V, Halifax III, VII, Lancaster III, York C1, Dakota, Hadrian, Hamilcar, Hotspur II, CG-13	AFEE	Beaulieu

11.B   Utility at 1 July 1948

Target facilities

Fighter Command

11 Group

Type	Unit	Base
Spitfire16, Martinet I, Vengeance TTIV	691	Exeter

12 Group

Type	Unit	Base
Spitfire 16, Martinet I	631	Llanbedr
Spitfire 16, Martinet I, Oxford, Harvard T2B	695	Horsham St Faith

Fleet Air Arm

Type	Unit	Base
Martinet TT1, Sea Otter, Seafire F15, 45, 47, Anson I, Harvard T2B, Mosquito TR33,	771	Lee-on-Solent
Mosquito PR34	772	Arbroath
Martinet TT1, Mosquito B25, Seafire F15, 17, Sea Otter 2, Expeditor C2	728	Hal Far (Malta)

Miscellaneous

Fighter Command 12 Group

Type	Unit	Base
Anson 1, C12, Auster AOP5, 6, Dakota C4	VISTRE Flt	Keevil

Trials and training

Technical Training Command (23 Group)

Type	Unit	Base
Various	RAE	Farnborough

Maintenance Command

Lancaster III	BTU	West Freugh
Halifax, Mosquito	BBU	Martlesham Heath

Coastal Command (16 Group)

Lancaster GR3, Lincoln B2, Anson 19	ASWDU	Ballykelly
Wellington, Beaufighter X, Barracuda	ATDU	Gosport

Flying Training Command (23 Group)

Stirling V, Halifax III, VII Lancaster III, York C1, Dakota	AFEE	Beaulieu

11.C   Utility at 1 January 1950

Target facilities

Fighter Command (12 Group)

Type	Unit	Base
Spitfire 16, Martinet TT1, Vampire F1 Oxford, Harvard T2B, Beaufighter TT10	20	Valley
Spitfire 16, Beaufighter TT10, Oxford	34	Horsham St Faith
Spitfire F16, Martinet TT1, Beaufighter TT10, Oxford	5	Chivenor
Spitfire F16, Beaufighter TT10, Oxford	17	Chivenor
Meteor F4, Tempest TT5, Spitfire 16	APS	Acklington

FEAF – AHQ Malaya

Type	Unit	Base
Beaufighter TT10	27 APC	Butterworth

Fleet Air Arm

Type	Unit	Base
Seafire F17, Sea Otter 2, Expeditor C2, Mosquito PR16, TT39	728	Hal Far

Miscellaneous

Fighter Command (12 Group)

Type	Unit	Base
Anson 1, C12, Auster AOP5, 6, Dakota C4	VISTRE Flt	Netheravon

Maintenance Command (41 Group)

Type	Unit	Base
Various	AAEE	Boscombe Down
Various	AFEE	Beaulieu
Various	TFU	Defford
Sunderland GR5	MAEE	Felixstowe
Barracuda	ATDU	Gosport
Lincoln II, Mosquito	BTU	West Freugh
Lancaster	BBU	Martlesham Heath

Fleet Air Arm

Mosquito PR16, TR33, PR34, TT39, Anson I, Seafire F15, 45	771	Lee-on-Solent
Dominie, Sea Fury F10, Firefly FR1	SLAW	Old Sarum

11.D   Utility at 1 July 1952

Target and air gunnery

Fighter Command

11 Group

Type	Unit	Base
Spitfire 16, Oxford	CRS	Middle Wallop

81 Group

Tempest TT5, Mosquito TT35, Vampire FB5	APS	Acklington

Home Command

61 Group

Type	Unit	Base
Spitfire LF16, Beaufighter TT10	1 CAACU	Hornchurch
Spitfire LF16, Beaufighter TT10	2 CAACU	Little Snoring

62 Group

Spitfire LF16, F21, Beaufighter TT10	3 CAACU	Exeter

63 Group

Vampire FB5, Spitfire, Beaufighter TT10	5 CAACU	Llanbedr

66 Group

Spitfire 16, Anson T21	4 CAACU	Llandow

2 TAF – 2 Group

Tempest TT5	APS	Sylt

MEAF

AHQ Malta

Meteor T7	TTF	Ta Kali

205 Group

Beaufighter TT10, Meteor T7	APC	Nicosia

FEAF – AHQ Malaya

Type	Unit	Base
Beaufighter TT10	27 APC	Butterworth
Meteor F8	TTF	Changi

Fleet Air Arm

Type	Unit	Base
Anson I, Mosquito PR16, Sea Hornet NF21, Meteor T7, Sea Vampire F20, Sturgeon TT2, Firefly FR1, T2, TT4, TT5, AS6	771	Lee-on-Solent
Sea Otter 2, Expeditor C2, Mosquito PR16, Sea Hornet FR20, Sea Vampire F20, Sturgeon TT2	728	Hal Far
Auster AOP5, Mosquito T3, TR33	Airwork *Air direction school support*	St Davids

Rescue

Coastal Command 18 Group

Type	Unit	Base
Sycamore HR12	CCDU	St Mawgan

FEAF (230 Group)

Dragonfly	CEF	Changi

Fleet Air Arm

Dragonfly HR1	SF	HMS *Indomitable*
	SF	HMS *Ocean*
Dragonfly HR3	SF	HMS *Campania*

Trials

Maintenance Command (41 Group)

Type	Unit	Base
Various	TFU	Defford
Various	AAEE	Boscombe Down
Sunderland MR5	MAEE	Felixstowe
Canberra B2	AIEU	Martlesham Heath
Canberra B2	BCIRE	Scampton
Lincoln II, Canberra B2	BTU	West Freugh

Fleet Air Arm

Type	Unit	Base
Barracuda III, Anson I, Dominie I, Firefly AS5	744 *AS trials*	Eglinton
Mosquito FB6, PR32, TR33, Sea Fury FB11	751 *Signals trials*	Watton
Skyraider AEW1	778 *AEW trials*	Culdrose
Sea Fury FB11, Vampire FB5	787 *NAFDU*	West Raynham

11.E   Utility at 1 January 1955

Target and air gunnery

Fighter Command

11 Group

Type	Unit	Base
Balliol T2	288	Middle Wallop
Provost T1, Oxford, Meteor F8	CFCCU	Woodvale

81 Group

Tempest TT5, Mosquito	2 APC	Acklington

Home Command

61 Group

Type	Unit	Base
Spitfire LF16, Chipmunk, Anson C19	1 CAACU	Hornchurch
Vampire FB5, FB9, T11 Meteor T7	2 CAACU	Langham

62 Group

Type	Unit	Base
Spitfire LF16, Beaufighter TT10, Vampire FB5	3/4 CAACU	Exeter

63 Group

Type	Unit	Base
Spitfire LF16, Beaufighter TT10, Vampire FB5	5 CAACU	Llanbedr

2 TAF – 2 Group

Tempest TT5, Mosquito	APS	Sylt

MEAF

AHQ Malta

Type	Unit	Base
Meteor T7	TTF	Ta Kali

205 Group

Beaufighter TT10, Meteor T7	APC	Nicosia

FEAF – AHQ Malaya

Type	Unit	Base
Beaufighter TT10	27 APC	Butterworth
Meteor F8	TTF	Changi

Fleet Air Arm

Type	Unit	Base
Anson I, Firefly TT4, Sea Vampire F20	771	Lee-on-Solent
Sea Hornet F20, NF21	FRU (Airwork)	Hurn
Mosquito T3, Sea Hornet NF21, Meteor T7	Airwork *Air direction school support*	St Davids
Dragonfly HR3, Expeditor C2, Sea Hornet FR20, Sturgeon TT2, 3, Sea Vampire F20	728	Hal Far

Rescue

Fighter Command (12 Group)

Type	Unit	Base
Sycamore HR14, Hiller HTE-2, Chipmunk T10 Anson C21	275	Thornaby dets, Aldergrove, Chivenor, Horsham St Faith, Leconfield Leuchars, North Coates

FEAF (230 Group)

Dragonfly HR14	194	Kuala Lumpur

Fleet Air Arm

Dragonfly HR3	SF	HMSs *Albion, Bulwark, Centaur, Eagle*
Hiller HT1	SF	HMS *Vidal*

Calibration

90 Group

Type	Unit	Base
Anson C19, Varsity T1	116	Watton
Canberra B2, Meteor NF11, 14, Varsity T1	527	Watton

Trials and training

Maintenance Command (41 Group)

Type	Unit	Base
Meteor NF11	RRFU	Defford
	AAEE	Boscombe Down
Sunderland MR5	MAEE	Felixstowe
	AIEU	Martlesham Heath
	ATDU	Gosport
Lincoln B2	BTU	West Freugh

Fleet Air Arm

Type	Unit	Base
Firefly AS6, Sea Fury FB11, Gannet AS1, Sea Hawk F1	703 *Trials*	Ford
Firefly AS6, Sea Fury FB11	744 *NASWDU*	St Mawgan
Firefly AS6, Sea Fury FB11, Anson I, Avenger AS4	751 *Radio warfare trials*	Watton
Sea Hawk FB3, FGA4, Dominie I	787 *NAFDU*	West Raynham

11.F   Utility at 1 July 1957

Target and air gunnery

Fighter Command (11 Group)

Type	Unit	Base
Balliol T2	288	Middle Wallop
Anson 21	1 CFCCU	Scone
	2 CFCCU	Usworth
	3 CFCCU	Sydenham

Home Command

61 Group

Type	Unit	Base
Vampire FB5, FB9, T11 Meteor T7	2 CAACU	Langham

62 Group

Type	Unit	Base
Beaufighter TT10, Vampire FB5	3/4 CAACU	Exeter

63 Group

Type	Unit	Base
Beaufighter TT10, Vampire FB5	5 CAACU	Llanbedr

2 TAF (2 Group)

Tempest TT5, Mosquito	APS	Sylt

MEAF

Type	Unit	Base
Beaufighter TT10, Meteor T7, F8	TTF	Ta Kali
Beaufighter TT10, Meteor T7	APC	Nicosia

FEAF – AHQ Malaya

Type	Unit	Base
Beaufighter TT10	27 APC	Butterworth
Meteor F8	TTF	Changi

Fleet Air Arm

Type	Unit	Base
Meteor T7, Sea Venom FAW20, 21	Airwork *Air direction school support*	St Davids
Sea Fury FB11, Sea Hawk F1	FRU (Airwork)	Hurn
Expeditor C2, Dragonfly HAR3, Gannet T2, Sea Devon C20, Whirlwind HAR3, Sturgeon TT3	728	Hal Far

Rescue

Fighter Command (12 Group)

Type	Unit	Base
Sycamore HR14, Hiller HTE-2, Chipmunk T10, Anson C21	275	Thornaby dets, Aldergrove, Chivenor, Horsham St Faith, Leconfield Leuchars, North Coates

Coastal Command (18 Group)

Type	Unit	Base
Whirlwind HAR2	22	Thorney Island dets Felixstowe, Martlesham Heath, Valley

MEAF

Type	Unit	Base
Sycamore HR14, Whirlwind HAR2	284	Nicosia

FEAF (230 Group)

Type	Unit	Base
Dragonfly HR14	194	Kuala Lumpur

Calibration

Signals Command

Type	Unit	Base
Anson C19, Varsity T1	116	Watton
Canberra B2	527	Watton

Trials and training

Bomber Command (1 Group)

Type	Unit	Base
Canberra B2, B6, PR7, B(I)8	100 BCDU	Wittering

Maintenance Command (41 Group)

Type	Unit	Base
Various	RAE	Farnborough, Bedford
	RRFU	Defford
	AAEE	Boscombe Down
	BCBS	Lindholme
Hastings	BCDU	Wittering
Valiant B1, Canberra B2, T4		
Canberra B6	BTU	West Freugh
Brigand TF1, Canberra B6, Dragonfly HAR3	ATDU	Culdrose
Canberra PR3, Hunter F4, Meteor T7	RAE	Llanbedr

11.G Utility at 1 July 1960

Target and air gunnery

Fighter Command (11 Group)

Type	Unit	Base
Vampire FB5, T11, Hunter F4, T7	3/4 CAACU	Exeter

61 Group

Type	Unit	Base
Vampire FB5, Meteor T7, TT8	5 CAACU	Woodvale
Canberra T11	228 OCU	Leeming
Anson 21	1 CFCCU	Scone
	2 CFCCU	Usworth

MEAF

Type	Unit	Base
Meteor T7, F8, Devon C1	TTF	Ta Kali

FEAF – AHQ Malaya

Type	Unit	Base
Meteor T7, F8	1574 Flt	Changi

Fleet Air Arm

Type	Unit	Base
Sea Venom FAW21, Sea Vampire T22	Airwork *Air direction school support*	Brawdy
Sea Fury FB11, Sea Hawk FB5, Meteor TT20, Dragonfly HR3	FRU (Airwork)	Hurn
Meteor T7, U15, TT20, Sea Devon C20, Firefly U9, U8	728	Hal Far (Malta)

Rescue

Fighter Command (12 Group)

Type	Unit	Base
Sycamore HR14, Whirlwind HAR2, 4	228	Leconfield dets, Acklington, Horsham St Faith, Leuchars
Sycamore HR14	118	Aldergrove

Coastal Command (18 Group)

Type	Unit	Base
Whirlwind HAR2	22	St Mawgan dets Chivenor, Coltishall, Felixstowe, Manston, Tangmere, Thorney Island, Valley

MEAF

Type	Unit	Base
Sycamore HR14, Whirlwind HAR2	103	Nicosia, det El Adem

FEAF

Type	Unit	Base
Sycamore HR14, Whirlwind HAR4	110	Butterworth

Fleet Air Arm

Type	Unit	Base
Dragonfly HR5	SF	HMSs *Ark Royal, Centaur Victorious, Vidal*

Calibration

Signals Command

Type	Unit	Base
Varsity T1	115	Tangmere
Canberra B2	245	Tangmere

Trials and training

Maintenance Command (41 Group)

Type	Unit	Base
Various	RAE	Farnborough, Bedford
	AAEE	Boscombe Down
Canberra	RRFU	Pershore
Canberra B6, Whirlwind HAR2	ATDU	Culdrose
Canberra B2	BCTU	West Freugh
Meteor T7, D16, TT20	RAE	Llanbedr
Sea Balliol T21	JWE	Old Sarum

11.H Utility at 1 January 1965

Target and air gunnery

Fighter Command

Type	Unit	Base
Vampire T11, Hunter F4, T7, Meteor TT20	3/4 CAACU	Exeter
Vampire FB5, Meteor T7, TT8	5 CAACU	Woodvale
Canberra B2, T11, Meteor F(TT)8	85	Binbrook

FEAF – AHQ Malaya

Type	Unit	Base
Meteor F8, TT20	1574 Flt	Changi

Fleet Air Arm

Type	Unit	Base
Sea Venom FAW21, Sea Vampire T22	Airwork *Air direction training*	Yeovilton
Sea Hawk FGA6, Meteor TT20	FRU (Airwork)	Hurn
Meteor T7, TT20, Heron C2, Whirlwind HAS22	728	Hal Far (Malta)

Rescue

Coastal Command (18 Group)

Type	Unit	Base
Whirlwind HAR10	22	St Mawgan dets Chivenor, Manston, Thorney Island, Valley
	202	Leconfield dets, Acklington, Coltishall, Leuchars, Ouston

MEAF

Type	Unit	Base
Sycamore HR14, Whirlwind HAR2	1563 Flt	Nicosia
	1564 Flt	El Adem

FEAF

Type	Unit	Base
Whirlwind HAR10	103	Seletar

Fleet Air Arm (Ships' or station flights)

Type	Unit	Base
Whirlwind HAS7		HMSs *Ark Royal, Centaur,* Brawdy, Culdrose, Lossiemouth, Yeovilton
	771	Portland

Calibration

Signals Command (90 Group)

Type	Unit	Base
Varsity T1	115	Watton
Canberra B2	245	Watton

Trials and Training

Type	Unit	Base
Various	RAE	Farnborough, Bedford
	AAEE	Boscombe Down

11.I Utility at 1 January 1970

Target and air gunnery

Fighter Command (11 Group)

Type	Unit	Base
Vampire T11, Meteor TT20	3/4 CAACU	Exeter
Vampire FB5, Meteor T7, TT8	5 CAACU	Woodvale
Canberra B2, T19, Meteor F(TT)8	85	Binbrook
Lightning F1, F1A	TTF	Binbrook
	TTF	Leuchars
Lightning F1, F1A, Chipmunk T10	TTF	Wattisham

MEAF

Type	Unit	Base
Canberra B2	TTF	Akrotiri

FEAF

Type	Unit	Base
Meteor F8, TT20	1574 Flt	Changi

Fleet Air Arm

Type	Unit	Base
Sea Venom FAW21,	ADTU Airwork	Yeovilton
Sea Vampire T22	*Air direction training*	
Meteor T7, TT20, Hunter T8, T8C, Scimitar F1, Canberra B2, T4, TT18	FRU (Airwork)	Hurn

Rescue

Coastal Command (18 Group)

Type	Unit	Base
Whirlwind HAR10	22	St Mawgan dets Chivenor, Felixstowe, Manston, Thorney Island, Valley
	202	Leconfield dets, Acklington, Coltishall, Leuchars, Ouston

MEAF

Type	Unit	Base
Sycamore HR14, Whirlwind HAR2	1563 Flt	Nicosia
	1564 Flt	El Adem

FEAF

Type	Unit	Base
Whirlwind HAR10	103	Changi

Fleet Air Arm (Ships' or station flights)

Type	Unit	Base
Wessex HAS1	SF	HMSs *Eagle, Hermes*
Whirlwind HAR9	SF	Brawdy, Culdrose, Lossiemouth
Whirlwind HAS7	SF	Yeovilton
Whirlwind HAS7	771	Portland

Calibration

Signals Command (90 Group)

Type	Unit	Base
Varsity T1, Argosy E1	115	Cottesmore
Canberra E15	98	Cottesmore

Trials and training

Type	Unit	Base
Various	RAE AAEE	Farnborough, Bedford, Boscombe Down
Meteor T7, D16, TT20	RAE	Llanbedr

11.J   Utility at 1 January 1975

Target and air gunnery

Fighter Command

Type	Unit	Base
Canberra B2, TT18	7	St Mawgan
Canberra B2, T19	85, 100	West Raynham
Canberra T17	360	Cottesmore

MEAF

Type	Unit	Base
Canberra B2	TTF	Akrotiri

Fleet Air Arm

Type	Unit	Base
Hunter T8C, GA/PR11, Canberra T4, TT18, T22	FRADTU *Airwork*	Yeovilton

Rescue

Coastal Command (18 Group)

Type	Unit	Base
Whirlwind HAR10	22	Thorney Island dets Brawdy, Chivenor, Valley
	202	Leconfield dets, Acklington, Coltishall, Leuchars, Ouston

MEAF

Type	Unit	Base
Whirlwind HAR10	84	Akrotiri

Fleet Air Arm

Type	Unit	Base
Wessex HAS1	772	Portland HMSs *Ark Royal, Eagle*
Whirlwind HAR9	SF	Culdrose
Wessex HU5	707	Yeovilton

Calibration

Signals Command 90 Group

Type	Unit	Base
Argosy E1	115	Cottesmore
Canberra B2, E15	98	Cottesmore

Trials and training

Type	Unit	Base
Various	AAEE RAE	Boscombe Down Farnborough, Bedford
Buccaneer S2, Canberra B2, Viscount	RRE	Pershore
Canberra B6, Whirlwind HAR2	ATDU	Culdrose
Canberra B2	BCTU	West Freugh
Meteor T7, D16, TT20	RAE	Llanbedr

11.K   Utility at 1 January 1980

Target and air gunnery

Strike Command (18 Group)

Type	Unit	Base
Canberra TT18	7	St Mawgan
Canberra B2, E15, T19	100	Marham
Canberra T17	360	Wyton

Fleet Air Arm

Type	Unit	Base
Hunter T8C, GA/PR11, Canberra T4, TT18, T22	FRADTU *Airwork*	Yeovilton

Rescue

Strike Command (18 Group)

Type	Unit	Base
Whirlwind HAR10, Wessex HC2	22	Finningley dets Brawdy, Chivenor, Leconfield, Manston, Valley
Sea King HAR3	202	Finningley dets Boulmer, Brawdy, Coltishall, Leconfield, Lossiemouth

MEAF

Type	Unit	Base
Whirlwind HAR10	84	Akrotiri

Fleet Air Arm (Training units providing station SAR)

Type	Unit	Base
Wessex HU5	771	Culdrose
	772	Portland
	707	Yeovilton

Calibration

Signals Command (1 Group)

Type	Unit	Base
Andover C1, E3	115	Brize Norton

Trials and training

Type	Unit	Base
Various	RAE	Farnborough, Bedford
	AAEE	Boscombe Down
Canberra B6, Whirlwind HAR2	ATDU	Culdrose
Canberra B2	BCTU	West Freugh

11.L Utility at 1 January 1985

Target and air gunnery

Strike Command (18 Group)

Type	Unit	Base
Canberra B2, T4, E15, TT18	100	Wyton
Canberra T17	360	Wyton

Fleet Air Arm

Type	Unit	Base
Hunter T8C, GA/PR11, Canberra T4, TT18, T22	FRADTU Airwork	Yeovilton

Rescue

Strike Command (18 Group)

Type	Unit	Base
Wessex HC2	22	Finningley dets Chivenor, Coltishall, Leconfield, Manston, Valley
Sea King HAR3	202	Finningley dets Boulmer, Brawdy, Lossiemouth

MEAF

Type	Unit	Base
Wessex HU5	84	Akrotiri

Falklands

Type	Unit	Base
Sea King HAR3	1564 Flt	Navy Point

Fleet Air Arm (Training units providing station SAR)

Type	Unit	Base
Wessex HU5	771	Culdrose
	772	Portland
	707	Yeovilton
	det 845	Ascension
Sea King HAS2A	819	Prestwick

Calibration

Strike Command (1 Group)

Type	Unit	Base
Andover C1, E3, E3A	115	Benson

Trials and training

Type	Unit	Base
Sea King HAR3	SKTF	Culdrose
Wessex HC2	SATF	Valley
Various	AAEE	Boscombe Down
Hunter T7, Jaguar T2	IAM	Farnborough
Various	RAE	Bedford, Farnborough
Meteor D14, D16, Hawk T1	RAE	Llanbedr
Andover C1, Buccaneer S2	RAE	West Freugh

11.M Utility at 1 January 1990

Target and air gunnery

Strike Command (18 Group)

Type	Unit	Base
Canberra B2, T4, E15, TT18	100	Wyton
Canberra T17, T17A	360	Wyton

Fleet Air Arm

Type	Unit	Base
Hunter T8C, GA/PR11, Canberra T4, TT18, T22	FRADTU Airwork	Yeovilton

Rescue

Strike Command (18 Group)

Type	Unit	Base
Wessex HC2	22	Finningley dets Chivenor, Coltishall, Leuchars
Sea King HAR3	202	Finningley dets Boulmer, Brawdy, Leconfield, Lossiemouth, Manston

MEAF

Type	Unit	Base
Wessex HU5C	84	Akrotiri

Falklands

Type	Unit	Base
Sea King HAR3	78	Mount Pleasant

Fleet Air Arm (Training units providing station SAR)

Type	Unit	Base
Wessex HU5	771	Culdrose
	772	Portland
	707	Yeovilton
	det 845	Ascension
Sea King HAS2A	819	Prestwick

Calibration

Strike Command (1 Group)

Type	Unit	Base
Andover C1, E3, E3A	115	Benson

Trials and training

Type	Unit	Base
Sea King HAR3	SKTF	Culdrose
Wessex HC2	SATF	Valley
Various	AAEE	Boscombe Down
Harrier GR7, Tornado GR1	SOEU	Boscombe Down
Hunter T7, Jaguar T2	IAM	Farnborough
Various	RAE	Bedford, Farnborough
Meteor D14, D16, Hawk T1	RAE	Llanbedr
Andover C1, Buccaneer S2	RAE	West Freugh

11.N   Utility at 1 January 1995

Target facilities

Type	Unit	Base
Hawk T1, T1A	100	Finningley
Falcon 20	FR Aviation	Hurn, Teesside

Fleet Air Arm

Type	Unit	Base
Hawk T1, T1A	FRADU	Yeovilton

Rescue

Type	Unit	Base
Sea King HAR3	22 HQ	St Mawgan
	22 A Flt	Chivenor
	22 B Flt	Wattisham
Wessex HC2	22 C Flt	Valley
	202 HQ	Boulmer
Sea King HAR3	202 A Flt	Boulmer
	202 D Flt	Lossiemouth
	202 E Flt	Leconfield
Wessex HC2	SRTU	Valley
Sea King HAR3	SKTU	St Mawgan

Fleet Air Arm

Type	Unit	Base
Sea King HC4	772	Portland

Calibration

Type	Unit	Base
Andover E3	Hunting Av'n Services	East Midlands

Trials and training

Type	Unit	Base
Various	AAEE	Boscombe Down
Various	DRA	Boscombe Down
Harrier T4,GR7, Jaguar T2A, Tornado GR1,GR1A, GR1B	SAOEU	Boscombe Down
Tornado F3	Tornado F3 OEU	Coningsby
Canberra B2, Hawk T1	TEE	Llanbedr
Devon C2	TEE	West Freugh

11.1 de Havilland Queen Bee (1936–1947)

The Queen Bee was a radio-controlled target aircraft externally similar to the DH.82A Tiger Moth (Chapter 1.2) but with many significant differences.

Mark I

The DH.82B Queen Bee had, unlike the Tiger Moth, a fuselage built of spruce and ply and the engine was the Gipsy Major; many were fitted with floats. The prototype flew in 1935 to specification 18/33 and no fewer than 380 were built for use by Anti-Aircraft Co-operation Units as targets. Although out of operational use by 1946, some were apparently retained and used for trials until early 1947.

Service (post-1945) Trials PAU

Specification and production

Mark	Role	Engine	HP	Speed mph	Weight lb	Nos
I	Drone	Gipsy Major I	130	104	1,825	380

11.2 Armstrong Whitworth Whitley (1937–1946)

The Whitley was the RAF's first twin-engined monoplane bomber, entering service with 10 Sqn in March 1937. It served in the early part of the war as a night bomber, later serving with Coastal Command. Early versions were long out of service by the end of the war. In summary the early versions were the bomber **Mark I** (Tiger IX engines), **Mark II** (Tiger VIII), **Mark III** (changed turret), **Mark IV** (Merlin IV) and **Mark VI** (Twin Wasp engine – not built).

Mark V

The AW.38/207 was fitted with two Merlin X engines and had a longer fuselage than earlier versions. A number had been converted as glider tugs and a few remained in service for training into 1946.

Service (post-1945) Training 21 HGTS

Mark VII

The AW.38/217 was the general reconnaissance version used by Coastal Command. Although obsolete by 1946

Armstrong Whitworth Whitley Mk VII

The Whitley was highly vulnerable in its bomber role at the War's outset. Remarkably in 1946 several were still in service including this Mk VII with 734 NAS at Hinstock. *(M Brown via R C Sturtivant)*

several were to remain in use for a few months by the Fleet Air Arm for (pilot) engine handling training.

Service (post-1945) Training 734 NAS

Specification and production

Mark	Role	Engine	HP	Speed mph	Weight lb	Nos
I	Bomber	2xTiger IX	795	205	22,100	34
II	Bomber	2xTiger VIII	845	209	22,290	46
III	Bomber	2xTiger VIII	845	209	22,290	80
IV	Bomber	2xMerlin IV	1,030	215	25,000	40
V	Glider tug	2xMerlin X	1,075	222	28,200	1,466
VI	Bomber	2xWasp	not built			
VII	Training	2xMerlin X	1,075	225	33,500	146*

* plus an unspecified number of Mk V conversions

11.3 Miles Master (1939–1950)

To provide transition from basic trainers to the new, fast monoplane fighters like the Spitfire and Hurricane the RAF needed a fast monoplane trainer. Miles had identified the need with the fast private-venture Kestrel and was ready to meet specifications T.6/36 and 16/38 with the less powerful Kestrel XXX engine. The Mark I (M9B) was a tandem trainer looking very much like a slightly distorted Hurricane and, although built in large numbers, was out of service by 1946.

Mark II

The Miles M19 was powered by a Mercury XX radial engine with left-hand airscrew and first flew in November 1939 (N7422). Although still operating as a trainer in early 1946 the type was used mainly as a glider tug to replace the ageing biplane types in the glider training schools as the **GT Mk II**. This variant had the Mercury 30 engine with a spinner on the propeller; as such the Mk II remained in service until 1949.

Service (post-1945) Training EFS; 3 GTS; 10 OTU; 5 (P)AFU

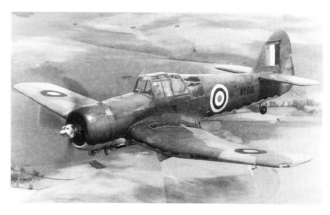

Miles Master Mk III

Designed as an advanced trainer, the Master was confined to a range of utility roles by 1946. The Mk III with Wasp engine was latterly used as a glider tug with 1 and 3 GTS. *(MAP)*

Mark III

The Miles M27 was the final version with the Wasp Junior engine and right-hand airscrews; the prototype flew in 1940 and the variant remained in service for a few months into 1946 for training and utility purposes.

Service (post-1945) **Training** 587; 10 AGS; 1, 3 GTS; 17, 26, 80 OTU; 5(P)AFU

Specification and production

Mark	Role	Engine	HP	Speed mph	Weight lb	Nos
I	Trainer	Kestrel XXX	715	226	5,573	900
II	Trainer	Mercury XX	870	230	5,570	1,747
GT II	Glider tug	Mercury 30	870	230	5,570	*
III	Trainer	Wasp Junior	825	232	5,570	602

*   unknown number of Mk II conversions

11.4   Boulton Paul Defiant (1939–1946)

The P82 Defiant was originally built as a fighter for the RAF to specification F.9/35, but with four-gun armament limited to a turret it suffered badly as a day fighter. It was soon confined to night fighting. The Mark I was the fighter version powered by a Merlin III; it was out of service by 1946, but after being phased out of front-line service it operated for a time in the ASR role.

TT Mark I

The target tug was actually based on the **Mark II** fighter, powered by the Merlin XX. The turret was removed and replaced by a faired observer's canopy, a drogue box was fitted beneath the rear fuselage and a windmill for winch power behind the cockpit. The prototype, DR863, flew on 31 January 1941.

Service (post-1945) **Target tug** 733 NAS

Boulton Paul Defiant TT Mk III

The Defiant was originally fitted with a turret but as a day fighter it suffered badly. 150 Mk I aircraft were converted for the target-towing role and N3488 was the prototype. The turret was replaced by an observer's cockpit and a winch fitted on the fuselage side with drogue stowage under the fuselage. *(MAP)*

TT Mark III

The Mark III was the next operational variant; there was an intended **TT Mark II** which would have employed a Merlin 24 engine to boost speed but it was not built. In the event there was a surplus of Mk I aircraft for conversion to TT Mk III standard which was, apart from the engine, similar to the TT Mk I.

Service (post-1945) **Target tug** 721 NAS

Specification and production

Mark	Role	Engine	HP	Speed mph	Weight lb	Nos
I	Fighter	Merlin III	1,030	303	8,350	713
TTI	Target tug	Merlin XX	1,260	250	8,250	140
II	Fighter	Merlin XX	1,260	315	8,600	207
TTII	Target tug	Merlin 24	1,620	not built		
TTIII	Target tug	Merlin III	1,030	250	8,227	150*

*   Mk I conversions

11.5   Miles Martinet (1942–1950)

The Martinet was unique in being the only purpose-designed target tug; previous types used in the role had been obsolescent or converted from other roles.

TT Mark I

The Miles M25 was built to specification 12/41 and the prototype (LR241), based on the Master trainer, flew on 24 April 1942. The nose was longer than that of the trainer to compensate for the weight of the towing gear in the rear fuselage. As an indication of the demand for training no fewer than 1,700 Martinets were built and the type served for some years after the war.

Service (post-1945) **Target tug** 5, 17, 20, 34, 631, 691, 695; 11 AGS; APS Acklington; 226, 228 OCU; 10, 26, 54 OTU; Gibraltar, Horsham St Faith, Leconfield SF; 723, 728, 771, 773, 794 NAS

Queen Martinet

The Miles M50 was a radio-controlled variant built to specification Q.10/43 to replace the DH82B Queen Bee. Compared to its predecessor it was built in limited numbers and was soon withdrawn from use.

Service (post-1945) **Drone** PAU; 773 NAS

Specification and production

Mark	Role	Engine	HP	Speed mph	Weight lb	Nos
TTI	Target tug	Mercury XX	870	240	6,750	1,700
Queen Martinet	Drone	Mercury XX	870	240	6,500	87*

*   includes 18 Martinet conversions

Miles Martinet TT Mk I

The Martinet was unique since it was the first RAF aircraft designed at the outset as a target tug. It was based on the Master and remained in service until about 1952 when replaced by the faster Tempest. HN884/6D-K is seen over Cardigan Bay in 1949 while operating with 20 Sqn based at Llanbedr. *(K W T Pugh via A S Thomas)*

11.6 Armstrong Whitworth Albemarle (1942–1946)

The AW.41 Albemarle started life as a reconnaissance bomber built to a pre-war specification B.18/38 and was distinctive for being the first British aircraft in RAF service to be fitted with a tricycle undercarriage. The prototype, P1360, flew on 18 March 1940. Delays in production and delivery resulted in the Albemarle being obsolete in its original role so later versions were completed as glider tugs or special transports.

The **Mark I** was fitted with two Hercules engines and flew in bomber (B), special transport (ST) and glider tug (GT) forms. The **Mark II** was equipped for carrying ten paratroops, while the **Mark III** was intended to be powered by the Merlin, but in the event was not built. The **GT Mark IV** was powered by the Wright Cyclone engine and the **ST Mark V** was similar to the Mk II but with fuel jettison capability. All of these variants were withdrawn from service before 1946.

GT Mark VI
The Mark VI was similar to the Mk V but with a large freight door in the fuselage; some had the dorsal turret removed. The type was in use for a few months into 1946 for training purposes.

Service (post-1945) Training 38 Grp ORTU; 21 HGCU

Specification and production

Mark	Role	Engine	HP	Speed mph	Weight lb	Nos
BI	Bomber	2xHercules XI	1,590	265	35,000	32
GTI	Glider tug	2xHercules XI	1,590	265	35,000	90
STI	Transport	2xHercules XI	1,590	265	35,000	78
II	Tug/transport	2xHercules XI	1,590	265	35,000	100
III	Bomber	2xMerlin	Not built			
GTIV	Glider tug	2xGR-2600-ASB	1,600	265	35,000	1
STV	Transport	2xHercules XI	1,590	265	35,000	49
STVI	Transport	2xHercules XI	1,590	265	35,000	133
GTVI	Glider tug	2xHercules XI	1,590	265	35,000	117

11.7 Vultee Vengeance (1942–1947)

The Vengeance Model 72 was initially bought by the RAF from the United States as a dive-bomber. The first variant was the **Mark I** of which 200 were bought and a further 200 (from Northrop) supplied under lend-lease. These aircraft featured a single rear-firing machine-gun and in due course became the A-31A in US service. All were out of service by 1946.

Mark II
The Mark II was similar to the Mk I but with the addition

Vultee Vengeance Mk II

Judging from the cars in the background, this shot of AF745 was taken in the United States prior to delivery to the RAF. It was supplied as a dive-bomber and operated as such mainly in the Far East, but some were retained as target tugs into 1947. *(MAP)*

Miles Monitor TT Mk II

The RAF cancelled its order for the high speed Monitor target tug with the cessation of hostilities. However, twenty completed examples were take over by the Royal Navy which operated them with the FRU briefly into 1946. *(MAP)*

of a second machine-gun in the rear cockpit. A large number of the 500 ordered or supplied under lend-lease was diverted to US or Australian service but a few remained in RAF use after the war.

Service (post-1945) Utility 288: 733 NAS.
The Mark III (V-72/A-31C) was externally similar to the Mark II and of the 100 supplied none remained in service by 1946.

TT Mark IV
The Mark IV had originally been supplied as a dive-bomber with more powerful R-2600-8 engines with a large air intake under the nose and a slightly re-designed wing incorporating a further two .50in MGs. None remained in service as such but many were converted to target tug status in which role they flew until at least 1947.

Service (post-1945) Target tug/general hack 567, 577, 587, 595, 631, 691, 695; 1353 Flt: 721, 791 NAS

Specification and Production

Mark	Role	Engine	HP	Speed mph	Weight lb	Nos
I	Dive-bomber	R-2600-A5B-5	1,600	275	14,300	400
II	Dive-bomber	R-2600-A5B-5	1,600	275	14,300	500
III	Dive-bomber	R-2600-A5B-5	1,600	275	14,300	100
IV	Target tug	R-2600-13	1,700	275	11,865	562*

* data for TT Mk IV, numbers are total for Mk IV deliveries

11.8 Miles Monitor (1945–1948)

The Monitor was designed as a high-speed twin-engined target tug for the RAF to specification Q.9/42 and the first of three prototypes of the intended Mark I (NF900) flew

on 5 April 1944. Although 600 were ordered, with the end of the war the requirement diminished and was met by obsolete combat types.

TT Mark II
The Miles M.33 comprised the residue of the 20 airframes completed when the RAF order was cancelled. They were fitted with the Miles dorsal cupola rather than the Beaufighter-type blister of the original and had hydraulic airbrakes. Not only was the Monitor intended to fly fast mock attacks on warships, it also towed a target of up to 32ft wingspan at 300mph.

Service Target tug FRU (728 NAS)

Specification and Production

Mark	Role	Engine	HP	Speed mph	Weight lb	Nos
I	Target tug	2xR-2600-31	1,750	360	21,000	3
II	Target tug	2xR-2600-31	1,750	360	21,056	20

11.9 Short Sturgeon (1951–1958)

The Sturgeon was designed during the war as a twin-engined fast reconnaissance bomber for the Fleet Air Arm to specification S.11/43. In the event, for whatever reason, it did not serve in its intended role. The S Mark 1 (SA.1) was a sleek short-nosed machine which flew on 7 June 1946 (RK787). The requirement for the type was aborted at the same time.

TT Mark 2
The Short SA.2 was built to specification Q.1/46 as a dedicated fast target and target tug capable of operating from carriers. The nose was lengthened to accommodate photographic equipment and like the Mk 1 the variant employed two Merlin 140S engines driving contra-rotating propellers. The prototype (VR363) flew on 1 September 1949 and the first production aircraft, TS475, on 8 August 1950.

Short Sturgeon TT Mk 2

The twin Merlin-engined Sturgeon was built as a fast reconnaissance bomber for the FAA but it was not put into production as such. In Mk 2 form it was fitted with a lengthened nose to accommodate camera equipment and the twenty examples completed served as targets/target tugs from 1951 to 1956. TS476 of 728 NAS demonstrates the type's deck-landing capability. *(P H T Green collection)*

Service Target facilities 703, 728, 771 NAS

TT Mark 3
The SB.9 comprised five Mk 2 aircraft converted for purely shore-based operation. Without the long nose, the variant reverted to the original profile and with all carrier-related equipment deleted and wing folding being unnecessary, it was significantly faster than the Mk 2.

Service Target facilities 728 NAS

SB.3
The final Sturgeon was the grotesque SB.3 anti-submarine prototype built to the same specification (M.6/49) that the Gannet met. The nose profile was changed to accommodate a deep radar. The sole SB.3 (WF632) employed twin Mamba turboprop engines but unlike the

Gannet, whose engines were coupled, the SB.3 could not fly on a single engine for any period.

Specification and production

Mark	Role	Engine	HP	Speed mph	Weight lb	Nos
1	Strike	2xMerlin 140S	1,660	430	23,000	1
TT2	Target tug	2xMerlin 140S	1,660	370	22,350	25
TT3	Target tug	2xMerlin 140S	1,660	390	21,750	5*
SB.3	Anti-submarine	2xMamba ASMa.3	1,475	290	23,500	1+

* TT2 conversions
+ TT2 prototype conversion

11.10 Westland Dragonfly (1950–1963)

Westland acquired manufacturing rights for the American Sikorsky S-51 in 1947 after initial military experience with the Hoverfly (Chapter 10.2) highlighted the potential of the helicopter. In fact the S-51 was a four-seat commercial development of the R-5 first flown in 1946. The first British-built Dragonfly Mk 1A, G-AKTW, flew on 5 October 1948 and work was put in hand to produce speculatively, by hand, a further 30 examples.

HR Mark 1
The Mark 1 was ordered for the Royal Navy for assessment and trials. The first was VX595 which flew on 22 June 1949 and the type entered service in January 1950, soon being engaged on deck-landing trials. Several later served as plane-guards on carriers.

Service SAR HMSs *Glory, Indomitable, Ocean, Sydney, Vidal* Trials 700, 705 NAS: NGTE

HC Mark 2
This was the first version supplied to the RAF to meet an urgent need for casualty evacuation in Malaya where Operation 'Firedog' against communist terrorists was

Short SB.3

If the Sturgeon was un-pretty to begin with the SB.3 development was positively grotesque. It was produced to the specification for which the Gannet was selected and Mamba turboprops were fitted with the nose profile changed to accommodate ASV radar as seen on the sole conversion WF632. *(MAP)*

Westland/Sikorsky Dragonfly HR Mk 3

The Sikorsky S-51 was built speculatively under licence by Westland and eventually a total of 79 was bought for the RAF and FAA. The Navy used the type for trials, training and plane-guard duties. WN493/534 operated in the training role with 705 NAS at Lee-on-Solent when this photograph was taken in 1956. *(Author's collection)*

underway. Three aircraft were built, the first being a converted civil aircraft G-ALMC/WF308, and like the HR Mk 1 it had a three-blade wood and fabric composite rotor. In service the RAF Dragonflys formed the world's first helicopter rescue unit and the first airlift took place on 19 June 1950. After initial trials a single pannier was designed for carrying one casualty.

Service **Casualty evacuation** 194; FEAF CEF

HR Mark 3
The Mark 3 was similar to the HR Mk 1 but with a metal three-blade rotor and hydraulic controls to ease pilot workload; 50 were bought for plane guard duties on carriers and ship-to-shore communications. Range was short but the type was more effective than the traditional destroyer escort.

Service SAR HMSs *Albion, Ark Royal, Bulwark, Campania, Centaur, Eagle, Glory, Illustrious, Indomitable, Ocean, Sydney, Theseus, Warrior* **Trials/training** 705, 728 NAS **Communications** 744; Anthorn, Brawdy, Culdrose, Eglinton, Ford, Hal Far, Lossiemouth, St Merryn, Yeovilton SF

HC Mark 4
The Mark 4 enjoyed the same improvements as the naval HR Mk 3 and it quickly joined the HC Mk 2 machines in Malaya. Three served in the training role and one of these was later with the Queen's Flight.

Service **Casualty evacuation/utility** 194; Gütersloh **Training** CFS(H) **Communications** QF

HR Mark 5
The Mark 5 comprised some 25 HR Mk 1 and Mk 3 conversions with slightly increased power and better instrumentation.

Service SAR 701; HMSs *Ark Royal, Centaur, Eagle, Hermes, Victorious* **Training** 705, 727 **Communications** Brawdy, Culdrose, Ford, Hal Far, Lossiemouth, Portland, Yeovilton SF **Trials** 771; JWE

Since alternate mark numbers were allocated to naval and RAF variants there is no evidence of a Mark 6 but the HR Mark 7 was an intended conversion of naval machines to civil Widgeon standard with an enlarged cabin seating five. In the event the need was met by the Whirlwind.

Specification and production

Mark	Role	Engine	HP	Speed mph	Weight lb	Nos
HR1	Utility	Leonides 50	520	92	5,870	14*
HC2	Casevac	Leonides 524/1	540	95	5,870	3
HR3	SAR	Leonides 50	520	92	5,870	50
HC4	Utility	Leonides 524/1	540	95	5,870	12
HR5	SAR	Leonides 52	540	95	5,870	25+
HR7	SAR	Leonides 52	540	not built		

* 1 taken on by RAF as HC Mk 2, 1 for MoS
+ HR1/3 conversions

11.11   Westland Whirlwind (1952–1982)

The Sikorsky S-55 was a larger helicopter than its predecessor the S-51 and it was the second type for which Westland acquired a licence in November 1950. The American prototype flew on 7 November 1949 and it entered US service in 1951. Initial deliveries to British services were of US-built machines supplied through the Mutual Defence Aid Plan (MDAP) and they were given high mark numbers starting with 21.

The Whirlwind, as the S-55 became in British service, was produced in three series in the UK. Series 1 aircraft had American Wasp or Cyclone engines, Series 2 aircraft the Leonides Major and Series 3 aircraft the Gnome turbine. Although for the times a large helicopter, the Whirlwind suffered from its small payload which was not satisfactorily addressed until the Gnome-powered aircraft came into service. It also lacked automatic flight control systems making night and adverse weather flying difficult. One pattern aircraft was supplied, WW339, later re-serialled XA842.

HAR Mark 21
The Mark 21 was the first supplied under MDAP and was powered by an R-1340-40 engine. It was similar to the USMC HRS-2 and ten were supplied starting with WV189; they were dispatched almost immediately to Malaya where they served within 303 Wing in the troop transport role carrying up to ten passengers.

Service **Transport** 848

HAS Mark 22
The Mark 22 was powered by the R-1300-3 Cyclone engine and was equivalent to the USN HO4S-3. It was equipped with a US AN/AQS-4 dunking sonar. Fifteen were supplied starting WV199 and they were used extensively for trials and SAR attached to a range of training and fleet requirements units.

Service **Utility** 705, 728, 737, 771; Eglinton, Hal Far SF **Communications** 781 **Transport** 845, 848 **Trials** 701, 706: RAE

Westland/Sikorsky Whirlwind HAR Mk 1

The Sikorsky S-55 was first supplied to the Royal Navy under MDAP from 1952. The first licence-built variant was the HAR Mk 1 of which 10 were built and used in the utility and trials roles. XA864 was the third production machine. *(Author)*

HAR Mark 1

The Mark 1 was the first Westland-built variant fitted with the R-1340-40. The first of ten delivered was XA862 which flew on 15 August 1953. The variant was mainly used for trials and then SAR duties, although it also supplemented the HAR Mk 21 in Malaya.

Service Utility 705, 771, 781, 829; HMS *Protector* **Trials** 700, 701; RAE **Transport** 848

HAR Mark 2

The Mark 2 was the RAF Wasp variant and like the Navy's HAR Mk 1 it was significantly under-powered. This was due to weight increases through the use of thicker gauge metal and other changes in construction. Serials were out of sequence due to the original XDxxx range being allocated to Sabres and the first, XD798/XJ429, flew on 14 January 1955; first deliveries were for air-sea rescue with 22 Sqn in February 1955.

Service SAR 22, 217, 228, 284; 1360 Flt; ISF Cyprus **Transport** 225, JEHU **Communications** QF **Training** ETPS

HAR Mark 3

The Mark 3 was the Royal Navy's attempt to improve the disappointing performance of the Whirlwind by fitting the Cyclone R-1300-3 of the HAS Mk 22. Unfortunately the added weight of the engine balanced any improvement and the type still operated with limitations on payload and range. Fitted permanently with a rescue winch the variant served mainly on plane-guard duties and trials. The prototype was XJ393 which flew on 28 June 1955, and service entry was with 845 NAS in November 1955.

Service Utility 705, 728, 737, 771, 781, 815; HMSs *Albion, Ark Royal, Bulwark, Eagle, Warrior* **Trials** 700, 701; JWE **Transport** 845 **Communications** Lee-on-Solent SF

HAR Mark 4

The Mark 4 was an attempt to improve on the performance of the HAR Mk 2 by the installation of the R-1340-57 with more powerful supercharger. In other respects the variant was similar to the HAR Mk 2 and the variant went first to units in Malaya.

Service SAR 22, 217, 228, 275; 1362 Flt; SAR Flt Aden **Transport** 110, 155, 225 **Training** CFS **Trials** RRE

HAR Mark 5

This was the first variant to be fitted with the British Leonides Major engine and a drooped tail cone to give greater rotor clearance. The first of two development

Westland Whirlwind HAR Mk 10

The Whirlwind was developed by Westland from the HAR Mk 9 and was fitted with the Gnome turbine engine in a re-designed nose. XP329/V of 84 Sqn Akrotiri is seen in UN peacekeeping role over Cyprus. (*Rolls-Royce*)

aircraft was XJ396 which flew on 28 August 1958, but the model did not go into production.

Service **Trials** RAE.
The HC Mark 6 was an intended turbine-engined variant with a coupled Turmo of 900hp. Although an HAR Mk 3 airframe, XJ445, was set aside for the conversion it was not completed as such.

HAS Mark 7
The Mark 7 featured a Leonides Major 755 engine and like successive variants had a drooped tail cone. The HAS Mk 7 was the first British helicopter designed specifically for the anti-submarine role and it employed a range of ASW equipment including an anglicised AN/AQS-4 sonar, radar and provision for a single Mk 30 torpedo. It could also carry a small hand winch. A combination of engine problems and weight restrictions led to later use in the commando carrying and utility roles. The prototype was XG589 which flew on 17 October 1956 and first deliveries were to 820 NAS in January 1958.

Service **ASW** 814, 815, 820, 824, 825, 829 **Utility** 737, 771, 781; HMSs *Albion, Ark Royal, Centaur, Eagle, Hermes*; Brawdy, Culdrose, Eglinton, Hal Far, Lossiemouth, Yeovilton SF **Transport** 845, 846, 847, 848 **Training** 705, 719 **Trials** 700, 701; JWE: RAE

HCC Mark 8
The VIP communications variant was based on the HAR Mk 5 but with dual controls and sound-proofing. Given its role as a VIP transport with the Queen's Flight external folding steps were fitted and the cabin windows enlarged. The first of three was XN126 which flew on 2 May 1959.

Service **Communications** QF **Utility** 22, 225: CFS

HAR Mark 9
The Mark 9 comprised some HAS Mk 7 conversions to the equivalent of the RAF HAR Mk 10 with the Gnome turbine. This engine, in General Electric T-58 form, had first been fitted and flown in a Whirlwind on 28 February 1959 following which the RAF variant was produced but the Royal Navy did not receive its first uprated machines until 1965; they served in the Antarctic and for SAR duties.

Service **Utility** 829 (HMSs *Protector, Endeavour*); HMS *Hermes;* Brawdy, Culdrose, Lee-on-Solent, Lossiemouth SAR Flts

HAR Mark 10
This was the RAF's major utility variant with the Gnome turbine engine which weighed much less than the piston engines while being much more powerful. The nose was extended to accommodate the new engine. The result was much better performance and payload and the variant was the first to be tested to carry four SS.11 ASMs. The first of 68 new-build HAR Mk 10s, XP299, flew on 28 March 1961 and first deliveries were to 225 Sqn in the tactical support role from November 1961.

Service **SAR** 22, 103, 202, 228; 1310, 1563, 1564 Flts; Akrotiri, Khormaksar SAR Flts **Utility** 28, 84, 110, 225,

230 **Communications** 21, 32; QF **Training** CFS; ETPS; 2 FTS **Trials**. RAE.
There was no Mark 11 which would have been reserved for a naval variant.

HCC Mark 12
The Mark 12 comprised just two Gnome-powered HAR Mk 10s fitted to VIP transport standard for use by the Queen's Flight. The first was XR486.

Service **Communications** QF

Specification and production

Mark	Role	Engine	HP	Speed mph	Weight lb	Nos
HAR21	Utility	Wasp R-1340	600	101	7,900	10
HAS22	Utility	Cyclone R-1300	700	98	7,900	15
HAR1	Utility	Wasp R-1340-40	600	97	8,000	10
HAR2	Utility	Wasp R-1340-40	600	98	7,800	33
HAR3	Utility	Cyclone R-1300	700	98	7,700	26
HAR4	Utility	Wasp R-1340-57	600	98	7,800	30
HAR5	Utility	Leonides Major 155	750	105	7,800	2
HC6	Utility	Coupled Turmo	900	not built		
HAS7	ASW	Leonides Major 155	750	109	7,800	145*
HCC8	Comms	Leonides Major 155	750	110	7.900	3+
HAR9	Utility	Gnome 101	1,050	104	8,000	17#
HAR10	Utility	Gnome 101	1,050	92	8,000	114~
HCC12	Comms	Gnome 101	1,050	92	8,000	2

*   plus an unspecified number of HAR3 conversions
\+   including 1 HAR4 conversion
\#   HAR5 conversions
~   including 46 HAR Mk 2/4 conversions

11.12   Civil contract types (1987–date)

As the process of competitive tendering has taken hold in the armed services, the number of types engaged on

Dassault Falcon 20E

In 1994 Flight Refuelling Aviation Ltd took over responsibility for electronic warfare training from 360 Sqn using Falcon 20 aircraft with a variety of underwing jammers. G-FRAJ is seen overflying RAF Waddington in 1993. *(Author)*

supporting second-line tasks has increased. Two very different types are involved in utility tasks.

Dassault Falcon 20

Flight Refuelling operates five versions of the twin-jet Falcon, the 20C, DC, E, EC and F from Hurn and latterly Teesside. Originally registered in the United States, by 1988 the aircraft were beginning to transfer to British civil markings during which time FR handled a contract with the Fleet Air Arm for fleet requirements tasks. In 1994 the firm took over electronic warfare training from 360 Sqn. The aircraft can accommodate up to nine passengers or freight and in various forms is equipped for radar and radio jamming and target towing. It is understood that FR also uses the type on other government contracts.

Service **Target facilities** FR

Short Skyvan 3M

In 1995 Hunting Aviation Ltd won a contract for parachute training support when the Army finally stopped using tethered barrage balloons. Two Skyvans are involved, one using Weston-on-the-Green and the other operating country-wide as required. The Skyvans accommodate up to fourteen parachutists.

Service **Parachute training** Hunting Aviation

Specification and production

Mark	Role	Engine	HP/ thrust	Speed mph	Weight lb	Nos
Falcon	Utility	2xGarrett ATF3	/5,200	540	32,000	20
Skyvan 3M	Utility	2xGarrett TPE.331	715/	210	14,500	2

12 – Research aircraft, cancelled projects and other vehicles in military marks

This final chapter is quite different from the others. It is a reminder of the innovative and technological richness of the British aviation industry, of the bravery of test crews, and of little-known aspects of military aviation in the post-war years. It represents all that is best and worst about British technology and politics. Unworkable aircraft and those with great potential are described, while the cost to the taxpayer and the military of cancelled projects can only be guessed at. The price of many of the types described in this chapter is much greater than financial investment: so many pilots lost their lives testing their aircraft to the limits, and wherever possible the author has noted their contributions.

A very wide range of machines, including drones and hovercraft, was allocated British military serials and these items are placed in sections. Deciding where to place them has been difficult because some have served more than one function. Hopefully the reader will detect some logic. There are no unit tables, for obvious reasons. None of the types featured in this section served with operational units, although many have been evaluated by the Royal Aircraft Establishment or the Aircraft and Armament Experimental Establishment.

Just some of the types involved in the development of the Concorde are included giving some clues as to the cost of developing a truly great aircraft – but one which never flew in military marks itself.

Finally, there is a touch of mystery in the way some apparently innocuous types have received military serials in the days before the present relaxation of security. It is easy to forget that up to 1956, at least, cameras were forbidden at RAF open days and magazines were prohibited from reporting lists of units, serial blocks, production or full performance data.

This final chapter, then, is a *pot pourri* to dip into and hopefully to stimulate wider reading or research into often overlooked territory.

12.1 Tailless aircraft

A Tailless Aircraft Advisory Committee had been established in 1943 to press forward with research on what was perceived to be the most promising layout for fast aircraft. Work was carried out at the low end of the spectrum with gliders and at the faster end through the de Havilland 108 Swallow.

Research on tailless aircraft had begun in the early years of flight but in Britain the work of J W Dunne was developed by Geoffrey Hill with the Westland-Hill Pterodactyl which flew in 1924 in glider form. There followed a number of powered versions.

Two types were tested during the war and were still just flying early in 1946. The **Handley Page HP.75 Manx** had a span of 39ft 10in and was powered by two Gipsy Major II engines of 140hp. Class B registration H0222 was applied. The **Baynes Bat Carrier Wing** was a 'model' glider, built by Slingsby and with a 33ft 4in wing-span. Given the serial RA809 it was intended to prove the concept of towing a tank under a 100ft wing-span glider.

General Aircraft GAL56 and GAL61

To test the low end of the speed range of flying wings a series of gliders was commissioned from General Aircraft Limited. Six gliders were originally intended but the order was reduced to three which for most of their lives were tested for the RAE by GAL pilots and observers. These three, all designated **GAL 56**, comprised a short fuselage with accommodation for pilot and engineer, a swept wing of between 45 and 51ft span with wing-tip fin and rudders. The first, GAL56/01 TS507, had a medium V wing of

General Aircraft GAL56/01

Three flying wing gliders were built to test the low end of the speed range. TS507 was the first with a medium V wing; in February 1948 it crashed killing the pilot, Robert Kronfeld.
(*P H T Green collection*)

28.4° sweep. It flew at Farnborough on 13 November 1944 and was used for a series of trials until 12 February 1948 when the glider crashed after spinning, killing the pilot, the well-known glider expert Robert Kronfeld.

The second aircraft was GAL56/04 TS510D with a complex wing of straight centre section and swept outer section described as a medium U. It first flew on 27 February 1946 finally being scrapped early in 1950. The third GAL56/03 was TS513B, the so-called maximum V glider with a swept wing of 36.4° sweep. It flew on 30 May 1946 and like TS510D it ended its days being scrapped at the Airborne Forces Experimental Establishment at Beaulieu in 1950.

The **GAL61**, TS515, was a different design. It had no fuselage nacelle, featuring a raised cockpit in the wing centre section with provision for an observer lying prone in the wing. It also lacked end-plate fin and rudders. These tailless gliders were extremely difficult to fly and in the light of the accident to GAL56/01 the programme was terminated without the GAL61 flying.

de Havilland DH.108 Swallow

The DH.108 was a single-seat research aircraft built to specification E.18/45 and intended to provide data for the Comet airliner and DH.110 fighter. The type was based on a standard Vampire fuselage, with a Goblin 2 engine, but with a new 43° swept wing and single fin and rudder. Elevons, outboard of the flaps, combined the functions of ailerons and elevators.

The first prototype, TG283, flew at Woodbridge, with its long runway, on 15 May 1946. After a number of flights it crashed at Hartley Wintney in May 1950, killing the pilot Sqn Ldr G.E.C. Genders. The second machine, TG306, was intended to assess the high-speed characteristics of the design and sweep was increased to 45°. The first flight was in June 1946, but the aircraft broke up on 27 September that year over the Thames estuary flying at a speed in excess of Mach 0.9. Geoffrey de Havilland, the son of the company founder, was killed.

A third Swallow, VW120, was first flown on 24 July 1947 with a revised cockpit. After setting a new speed record it exceeded the speed of sound on 9 September 1948 flown by John Derry – the first time the barrier had been broken in Britain. Like the other machines it was destroyed in a crash in 1950 while flying fast.

Armstrong Whitworth AW52G and AW52

Through being involved in laminar-flow wing development Armstrong Whitworth was keen to put its experience to practical application and proposed a jet-powered four-engined 120ft-span laminar flow flying wing bomber. The design was to be evaluated through the use of a 1/3 scale glider. The end of the war brought an end to the project but not before work had started on the **AW52G** glider. It was completed as RG324 and first flew at Bitteswell, towed behind a Whitley, on 2 March 1945. Like the GAL gliders it went to AFEE then to the AAEE until 1953.

Armstrong Whitworth, after cancellation of the bomber project, maintained its interest in a large flying wing and was eventually given a contract to produce two large prototypes to specification E.9/44 as the **AW52**. To give some point to the project beyond research the type was designed to carry 4,000lb of mail. The first Nene-powered aircraft, TS363, flew on 13 November 1947 and

Armstrong Whitworth AW52

Although an intended 120ft span flying wing bomber was abandoned, Armstrong Whitworth did produce the smaller AW52, two examples of which were built and tested. TS363 is seen at Farnborough in 1948. (*P H T Green collection*)

eventually achieved speeds of around 500mph. It crashed on 30 May 1949 through control problems and the pilot, John Lancaster, made the first emergency ejection in Britain.

The second AW52, TS368, was powered by the Derwent and it flew on 1 September 1948, later flying on trials with the RAE until May 1954 when it was scrapped.

Captured German aircraft

In the aftermath of the war various aircraft were recovered by the Allies and tested before being scrapped or placed in store. Two in particular related to the flying wing 'programme' and were held on charge by the RAE. Between them they reflected the work of the foremost German designers, Alexander Lippisch and the Horten brothers. The latter had been working on a range of powered and unpowered flying wings and one glider, the **Horten HoIV**, with a high-aspect ratio (21.8) gently swept wing was taken to Farnborough where it was accorded the serial VP543 and tested by the RAE. It was later sold in the United States. A second HoIV was used in Germany by BAFO Gliding Club until around 1950. A

Messerschmitt Me 163B Komet

The rocket-powered Komet was operational during the War and a number of captured examples of the tailless aircraft was tested in the United Kingdom. Some survive including 191904/25 of JG400 which was given the Air Ministry number AM219. (*Author*)

number of Hortens of various types went direct to the United States where flying wing developments were being pioneered by Northrop.

The rocket-powered **Me163B Komet** designed by Lippisch was retrieved in large numbers, no fewer than 24 examples being given British serials, mostly in the AM range. One or two were used for tests but most were soon scrapped or placed in museums (at least seven survive). VF241 was secured before the end of hostilities and was flown by the RAE between 1945 and 1947 as a glider, towed by a Spitfire, usually from Wisley.

Short SB.1 and SB.4 Sherpa

Short's involvement in tailless research was stimulated through Geoffrey Hill of Pterodactyl fame. A particular concern with swept wings was distortion at speed, starting from the tips, and the **SB.1** glider was designed to test what amounted to rotating wing-tip controls. With the Class B marks G-14-5 it first flew from Aldergrove under winch tow on 14 July 1951. After several flights it crashed in the wake of the tow aircraft and the wings were recovered as the basis for a powered aircraft.

The **SB.4**, G-14-1, was powered by two Turbomeca Palas turbojets and it flew on 4 October 1953. Although valuable data were obtained conventional wing design had improved and the Sherpa finished its days at Cranfield, eventually being preserved with the IWM at Duxford.

Specification and production

Type	Engine	HP/thrust	Speed mph	Weight lb	Nos
HP.75 Manx	2xGipsy Major 2	140/	145	4,100	1
Baynes Bat	none		n/a	963	1
GAL56/01 TS507	none		n/a	4,200	1
GAL56/03 TS513B	none		n/a	5,000	1
GAL56/04 TS510D	none		n/a	5,600	1
GAL61	none		n/a	c5,000	1
DH108 TG283	1xGoblin 2	/3,000	280	8,800	1
DH108 TG306	1xGoblin 3	/3,300	640	8,960	1
DH108 VW120	1xGoblin 4	/3,750	640	8,800	1
AW52G	none		n/a	n/k	1
AW52 TS683	2xNene 2	/5,000	500	34,154	1
AW52 TS688	2xDerwent 5	/3,500	450	33,305	1
HoIV	none		n/a	c2,000	2*
Me163B	1xHWK-109	/3,300	559	8,707	24*
SB.1	none		n/a	c3,000	1
SB.4	2xPalas	/353	170	3,268	1

* only relates to numbers in British marks and usage

12.2 Deltas

After the war, and with the benefit of access to German research, there was interest in the delta wing as the solution to problems of transonic flight. A number of contracts was issued for research aircraft.

Boulton Paul P.111a

The P.111 was designed to investigate the performance of delta wings at transonic speeds. It is preserved at the Midland Air Museum, Coventry, where it was photographed in 1988. *(Author)*

Boulton Paul P.111 and P.120

Specification E.27/46 was issued for investigation of delta wings at transonic speeds. Boulton Paul produced the **P.111**, VT935, powered by a single Nene RN2 which first flew on 6 October 1950. It was very compact and had an exceptionally thin 45° delta wing and triangular fin and rudder, with wing and fin-tips removable for comparative trials; thus the wing-span could be adjusted between 25ft 8in and 33ft 6in. The aircraft was flown on company-based trials which identified high sensitivity and unduly high landing speed. Late in 1951 a landing accident led to an extensive re-build.

The design was changed on the second aircraft, VT951. Designated the **P.120**, it now featured horizontal tail surfaces atop a revised fin and rudder. It flew from

Fairey Delta 1

The tubby FD.1 had a wingspan of just 19.5ft and was built to test the performance of small deltas in association with vertical ship-based launch. It was used for trials from 1951 to 1956. *(MAP)*

Boscombe Down on 6 August 1952 but crashed on the 29th of the month after 20 flights as a result of loss of the port elevon through wing flutter.

The P.111 was re-built as the P.111a with alterations to the undercarriage doors and air brakes to reduce landing speed. A long pitot head was fitted in the intake and the anti-spin parachute modified to act as a braking aid. In its new guise the P.111a flew on 2 July 1953 and soon transferred to the RAE where it served until 1958. It is preserved at Coventry.

Fairey FD.1

Fairey, with its close association with naval flying, had considered the possibility of a vertically launched delta-wing fighter for use from ships. Specification E.10/47 sought a delta-winged research aircraft to investigate the possibilities of the configuration and Fairey responded with the FD.1. Initially 40 10ft span models were constructed and flown from Aberporth, then from a tank-landing craft in Cardigan Bay and latterly Woomera. Power for these models was from a single Beta 1 engine of 1,800lb thrust with two 600lb thrust rockets for initial boost. The first successful launch was on 1 May 1949.

The FD.1 proper was extremely small with a span of 19ft 6in and it featured a broad delta wing and small delta tailplane on top of the fin. Powered by a single Derwent engine without the intended booster rockets the only one of three ordered to be built, VX350, flew on 12 March 1951. By now interest in a VTO fighter was diminished but the aircraft was used for trials until 1956 when its undercarriage was torn off in an emergency landing.

Avro 707

In support of the decision to build the Avro 698, later Vulcan (Chapter 4.10), against specification B.35/46 it

Avro 707C

Five diminutive 707 deltas were produced by Avro to support development of the Vulcan bomber. WZ744, a two-seat 'trainer', flew on 1 July 1953. *(P H T Green collection)*

was decided to accelerate development through the use of 1/3 scale models. Two low-speed aircraft (707B) were ordered under specification E.15/48 and one high-speed aircraft (707A) to E.10/49. A second order called for a further 707A and a two-seat trainer to become the 707C.

The first **707** was VX784 with a split dorsal air intake for its Derwent engine and fin with extended strake. It first flew 4 September 1949 but crashed on 30 September killing pilot Eric Esler.

The next aircraft was **707B** VX790 which was similar to the prototype but with a 12ft longer fuselage and revised dorsal intake. It flew on 6 September 1950 and eventually joined the RAE fleet at Bedford where it was struck off charge in 1957.

Avro **707A** WD280 had wing root intakes similar to those fitted to the Type 698 and a longer dorsal fin. In due course it was fitted with a cranked wing which was transferred to the Vulcan and later sent to Australia where it flew from 1956 to 1967, presently being preserved in Melbourne. The second aircraft was WZ736 which flew from Waddington on 20 February 1953; neither this aircraft nor the sole trainer were much involved in Vulcan development but they flew on trials duties until 1967, with the RAE. It is preserved at Manchester.

The **707C** had side-by-side seating and the wing root intakes of the 707A. The only example was WZ744 which flew on 1 July 1953; it is now preserved at Cosford.

Armstrong Whitworth AW58

Armstrong Whitworth received a contract against specification E.16/49 for a design study for a Mach 1.2 aircraft in 1958 and their response was an advanced 59° swept wing design. Serials WD466 and 472 were allocated but in due course the project was cancelled. The company was invited to propose a revised delta design but that was also cancelled before construction had begun.

Fairey FD.2 and BAC 221

An advanced design was commissioned from Fairey to meet specification ER.103 for a delta-winged aircraft for transonic and supersonic research. Two aircraft were ordered with the serials WG774 and WG 777. The wing had a straight leading edge with 60° sweep and power was a single re-heated Avon R.A.16. An unusual feature, lent in due course to Concorde, was a drooping nose to enable the pilot to see ahead on the ground. WG774 was completed in 1954 and the first flight was from Boscombe Down on 6 October 1954. By late 1955 Mach 1.1 had been achieved and on 10 March 1956 Peter Twiss established a new world air speed record at 1,132mph. The second aircraft flew on 15 February 1956 and after serving with the RAE at Bedford it was retired in 1967, now being preserved at Cosford.

In 1959 specification ER.193D was issued for a high speed research aircraft to test the intended ogival wing of the Concorde. BAC took WG774 from Bedford and converted it to the intended configuration with revised wing and extended fuselage. It flew on 1 May 1964 at Filton and was retired in 1974 having provided invaluable data on the high-speed performance of the wing. It is preserved at Yeovilton.

Handley Page H.P.115

The Supersonic Transport Advisory Committee was formed in 1956 and among its early tasks was the identification of potential design problems with a slender delta wing and the means of examining them. Specification ER.197D resulted in the H.P.115, the sole example of which, XP841, flew on 17 August 1961 at RAE Bedford. It had a narrow delta wing of 74.7° sweep and 20ft span while overall length was 50ft. The single Viper engine was mounted in a nacelle above the rear fuselage and the aircraft had a fixed undercarriage. The aircraft provided

Fairey FD.2

The FD.2 was built to research the delta wing at transonic and supersonic speeds. WG774 was completed in 1954 and on 10 March 1956 Peter Twiss set a new world speed record in the aircraft of 1,132mph. It was later converted as the BAC221 to support the Concorde development programme. *(MAP)*

a considerable amount of invaluable data for the Concorde programme over the next four years and it was finally retired in 1974, currently being preserved at Yeovilton.

Specification and production

Mark	Engine	Thrust lb	Speed mph	Weight lb	Nos
BP111	Nene 3	5,100	650	9,600	1
BP120	Nene 3	5,100	600	12,580	1
FD.1	Derwent 8	3,600	365	6,800	1
Avro 707	Derwent 5	3,500		8,600	1
Avro 707A	Derwent 5	3,500		9,800	2
Avro 707B	Derwent 8	3,600		9,500	1
Avro 707C	Derwent 8	3,600		10,000	1
AW58	Sapphire	10,000	M1.5	13,200	-
FD.2	Avon RA14	12,000	1,132		2
BAC 221	Avon RA28	10,050	M1.6		1*
HP115	Viper BSV.9	1,900			1

* F.D.2 conversion

12.3 Manned models

Although the United Kingdom was well served by research establishments there were limits to which laboratory tests could simulate performance of aircraft with novel power and design configurations. Through the first decade or so after the end of the war it was not uncommon for manned 'models' to be secured in order to assess aspects of performance. In addition to the types described below models were built for the DH.110 (DH.108, Ch 12.1), Vulcan (Avro 707, Ch 12.2) and Concorde (H.P.115 and BAC 221, Ch 12.2).

Short SB.5

In 1948 English Electric was contracted to design a supersonic aircraft with highly swept wings. Wind tunnel tests were conducted and in 1949 specification F.23/49 was issued for a day fighter with supersonic performance. The original design incorporated highly swept wings and a low-set tailplane, about which characteristics there was

Short SB.5

While the Avro 707 supported the Vulcan programme, so many features of what was to become the English Electric Lightning were tested on the Short SB.5 'model'. The wings could be set, on the ground, at various angles, while the tailplane was also shifted in position. WG768 flew with the ETPS for some time coded '28' in which guise it is preserved at RAF Cosford. (*Author*)

some official concern. Apart from investment in a new wind tunnel by English Electric, it was also decided to build a flying model to test wing sweep and tailplane setting, especially at low speeds. Thus the Short SB.5 (WG768) with fixed undercarriage and powered by a Derwent engine flew on 2 December 1952. The wings could be swept (on the ground) to 50°, 60° and 69° and the tailplane position could be moved from fin-tip to lower fuselage.

As a result of tests on the SB.5 the design was set with 60° wing sweep and with a low-set tailplane. Three prototype P1A aircraft (Chapter 2.10) were ordered and the first (WG760) flew on 4 August 1954. On its third flight on 11 August 1954 WG760 became the first British aircraft to exceed Mach 1 in level flight. In 1958 the SB.5 was fitted with an Orpheus B.Or.3 of 4,850lb thrust for further research at Bedford with the wing set at 69° sweep. It was retired in 1968 and is preserved at Cosford.

Handley Page H.P.88/Supermarine 521

The Handley Page H.P.80 (later Victor, Chapter 4.11) response to specification B.35/46 incorporated wings of an unusual crescent design and it was decided to test the shape and the horizontal tail surfaces on a 2/5 scale model. An existing fuselage was used, that of the Supermarine Attacker with some Swift elements, and the wings were designed under sub-contract by Blackburn. The resulting aircraft was unusual if not unique in having three designations: Handley Page H.P.88, Supermarine Type 521 and Blackburn YB.2!

Two aircraft were ordered with serials VX330 and 337 but only the first was built. It flew on 21 June 1951 from Carnaby and had made several dozen flights when it crashed on 26 August 1951 killing the Handley Page test pilot Douglas Broomfield. The H.P.88 had contributed to the Victor programme and its loss had no adverse effect on it.

Vickers Wild Goose and Swallow

Dr Barnes Wallis had been a foremost proponent of variable sweep wings for aircraft needing to fly fast. Thus the wings could be extended to provide optimal configuration for take-off or landing and swept for high-speed flight. Barnes Wallis tested several models at Brooklands and a manned aircraft was under construction by Heston Aircraft Company when the project was stopped in favour of unmanned models. A contract was secured by Vickers for twelve variable sweep **Wild Goose** models with serials XA197-202 and XA947-952. These were radio-controlled and of unusual design with the wings set well back and no tailplane, being powered by a single HTP rocket. It was flown by the RAE from the disused airfield at Predannack in Cornwall, being launched at about 100mph from a trolley.

These tests were extremely successful and a supersonic model followed in the form of the **Swallow**. The design was quite different being a slender delta from nose to tail – rather like an arrow-head but with the wing break at about half the length. Span was 30ft and the Swallow was powered by two HTP engines. Ten were ordered with serials XK831-835 and XK850-854 and the first flight, on which the model was lost, took place on 18 November 1955 at Predannack. The programme was terminated in 1957.

Specification and production

Type	Engine	Thrust lb	Speed mph	Weight lb	Nos
SB.5	1xDerwent 8	3,600	311	12,000	1
HP88	1xNene 3	5,100	475	14,460	1
Wild Goose	1xHTP	c200			12
Swallow	2xHTP	c750			10

12.4 Jets and rockets

With the advent of the jet engine a number of projects was started, sometimes as private ventures, more usually as a response to a formal specification. There was not necessarily an intention to proceed to production but neither were the types listed below purely intended for research.

Gloster GA.1 Ace and GA.2

The single-engined Gloster G.42 was built to specification E.1/44 which called for a small fighter with two cannon and a maximum speed of 485mph. The original specification had been E.5/42 which would be powered by a Halford engine; serials NN648, 651 and 655 were allocated. The later specification was based around the Nene engine and serials SM801, 805 and 809 were now allocated to what was due to become the **GA.1**.

In due course work was abandoned on the first two aircraft and the third, now designated **GA.2**, was completed and transported by road to Boscombe Down; en route it was wrecked in a road accident. A further three GA.2 aircraft had been ordered as TX145, 148 and 150 followed by two orders for 20 aircraft each, serialled VP601-620 and VR164-183. TX145 made the first flight of the type on 9 March 1948 with a low-set tailplane. TX148 flew with a higher tailplane which was later fitted to the Meteor Mk 8. The third prototype was due to be fitted with the Ghost engine as the **GA.3** but it was not completed. The Meteor met all likely needs against which

the aircraft had been built and the pre-production orders were cancelled. The two completed aircraft went to the RAE where they were used until 1951.

Saunders-Roe SR.A/1

The idea of a small jet-powered flying-boat fighter originated in the need to pursue an island-hopping campaign against the Japanese and specification E.6/44 was issued to Saunders-Roe. Three prototypes were ordered, serials TG263, 267 and 271, and the first flew from Cowes on 16 July 1947. The aircraft was relatively large with a high straight wing with cleanly retracting underwing floats. Four 20mm cannon were located on the upper nose. Two Metrovick Vickers F.2/4A Beryl turbojets were fitted, with the intake in the nose and the exhausts behind the wing trailing edges.

TG267 and TG271 flew with uprated engines and the latter reached 516mph. Given the end of the war and thus the original need, the SR.A/1 remained experimental. The first aircraft survived to be preserved at Duxford while the other two aircraft were destroyed in 1949, one killing the pilot, Sqn Ldr K A Major.

Supermarine straight-wing designs – Types 392, 508, 529

Specification E.10/44 resulted in the **Type 392** laminar flow wing design based on the Spiteful wing and powered by the Nene. The prototype was TS409 which flew on 27 July 1946 and it was joined by TS412 on 17 June 1947. There was no RAF interest but the design was developed as the Type 398 Attacker (Chapter 8.10) for the Royal Navy.

The **Type 508** was a twin-jet design with butterfly tail around which specification N.9/47 was written. The engines were mounted side-by-side on the fuselage with cheek intakes below the cockpit and the exhausts behind the wing trailing edge. The original design was to have featured no undercarriage and hence very thin wings, but

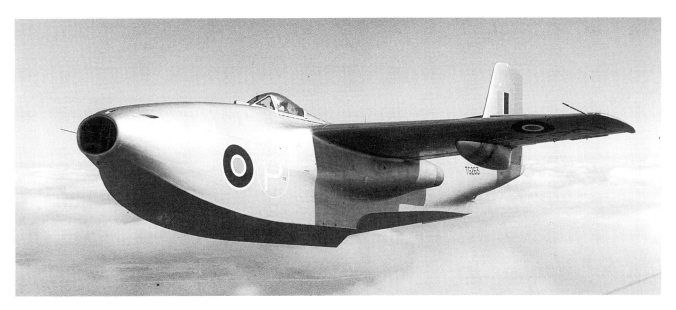

Saunders Roe SR.A/1

The SR.A/1 was unique in British aviation history in being the only jet-powered flying boat to take to the air. It was originally proposed as a fighter operating against the Japanese but it was completed too late and only served as a trials type. Three were produced, but only the first aircraft, TG263 seen here, has survived. *(Author's collection)*

Supermarine Type 517

Both Supermarine and Hawker built and flew a series of fighter types from the late 1940s almost using the air as a drawing board. Supermarine Type 517 (VV106) was based on an Attacker fuselage but with swept wings and arrester hook. In due course, through the types 528 and 535, it led to the Swift fighter. *(Author)*

trials with the Vampire were not promising and the idea was dropped in favour of a tricycle undercarriage. The prototype, VX133, flew on 31 August 1951 and deck-landing trials on HMS *Eagle* followed in 1952. The second prototype, VX136, was designated **Type 529** and had a slightly re-designed tail with variable incidence and strakes and changed intakes. Through the Type 525 the aircraft became the Scimitar.

Supermarine swept-wing designs – Types 510, 517, 525, 528, 535

The Supermarine **Type 510** (VV106) was intended as a high-speed fighter built to specification E.38/46; it flew on 29 December 1948. It had swept wings and tail combined with an Attacker fuselage and incorporating the latter's tailwheel undercarriage. In due course it was fitted with an arrester hook and as the **Supermarine 517** made carrier deck landings on HMS *Illustrious*. It is preserved at Wroughton. The second prototype (VV119) was designated **Type 528** and its first flight was on 27 March 1950.

It was later fitted with an afterburning Nene engine, a lengthened nose and tricycle undercarriage as the **Type 535**. From there it was developed to the unsuccessful Swift fighter (Chapter 2.7).

The **Type 525** was a swept-wing development of the straight-winged Type 529. It featured a conventional tail assembly and to help with handling at relatively high landing speeds included blown-flaps. It led to the Scimitar naval strike aircraft (Chapter 8.13).

Hawker straight-wing designs – P1040, P1072

The Hawker **P1040** was the company's first jet design which became specification N.7/46. The type began as a jet-engined Fury (P.1035) then progressed to the P1040 with a bifurcated jet pipe. The non-navalised prototype, VP401, was powered by the Nene 1 and flew on 2 September 1947, and although in many respects the type was less advanced than the Attacker, its development was later and slower and it eventually superseded the Attacker in service as the Sea Hawk (Chapter 8.11).

The **P1072** was an additional P1040 prototype, fitted with a Snarler rocket in addition to the Nene. It first flew on 16 November 1950 under turbojet power only and it first flight with rocket assistance was on 20 November. Although the combination worked well it was relatively complex and improvements in afterburner design made the concept of such a mixed power arrangement unneccesary.

Hawker swept-wing designs – P1052, P1081

Specification E.38/46 was issued against the **P1052** which was a swept-wing version of the P1040 retaining all the characteristics of the original apart from the wing. Two prototypes were ordered and the first, VX272, flew on 19 November 1948 from Boscombe Down and it flew on trials until 1953 by which time it had been fitted with a swept tailplane. The second aircraft was destined to become the sole P1081.

Hawker P.1052

A glance at the Sea Hawk confirms the origins of the P.1052 (VX272 in this photograph) which was in effect a swept-wing version of the naval fighter. The developed P.1081, with tail exhaust, led to the Hunter. *(Author)*

The **P1081** was fully re-designed with swept tail surfaces and the jet exhaust through the rear of the fuselage. The second P1052, VX279, was re-built and flew on 19 June 1950. It crashed on 3 April 1951 flying from Farnborough killing the pilot Sqn Ldr T S Wade. Experience with the P1081 supported the development of the Hunter (Chapter 2.8).

SARO S.R.53

In the light of experience of the German Me163B Komet (Chapter 12.1) the decision was taken to issue specifications for a rocket-powered interceptor. The main problem with the rocket was its thirst and thus the short practical range of aircraft powered in this way; the Me163B climbed to 40,000ft in just two minutes before fuel was expended. Specification F.137D was addressed by Avro (Type 720 Ch 12.9) while Saunders-Roe responded to specification F.138D.

The S.R.53 was a delta-wing design with a T-tail and small intakes on the fuselage just to the rear of the cockpit for the Viper engine of 1,750lb thrust. For fast acceleration an 8,000lb thrust Spectre rocket was fitted. The first of two prototypes, XD145, flew on 16 May 1957 from Boscombe Down piloted by Sqn Ldr J S Booth, who was killed in the second aircraft, XD151, when it crashed on 5 June 1958. The S.R.53 reached Mach 1.33 in level flight and climbed to 50,000ft in two minutes but the type and its intended successor the S.R.177 were casualties of the 1957 Defence White Paper and work stopped in late 1958. XD145 is preserved at Cosford.

Specification and production

Mark	Engine	Thrust lb	Speed mph	Weight lb	Nos
Gloster GA.1	1xNene	4,500	not built		
Gloster GA.2	1xNene 2	5,000	620	11,470	2
SR.A/1 TG263	2xBeryl MVB.1	3,300	460	16,255	1
SR.A/1 TG267	2xBeryl MVB.1	3,500	480	16,225	1
SR.A/1 TG271	2xBeryl MVB.2	3,850	516	16,225	1
Supermarine 392	1xNene 1	5,000	590	11,500	3
Supermarine 508	2xAvon RA.3	6,500	600	c25,000	1
Supermarine 529	2xAvon RA.3	6,500	600	c25,000	1
Supermarine 510	1xNene 102	5,000	630	12,790	1
Supermarine 517	1xNene102	5,000	630	12,790	1*
Supermarine 528	1xNene 102	5,000	630	13,000	1
Supermarine 535	1xNene 102	5,000	640	13,000	1+
Supermarine 525	2xAvon RA.3	6,500	670	c25,000	1
Hawker P1040	1xNene 102	5,000	540	15,000	3
Hawker P1072	1xNene 102 + 1xSnarler	5,000 2,000	630	14,050	1
Hawker P1052	1xNene 102	5,000	670	13,488	2
Hawker P1081	1xNene 102	5,000	685	14,480	1#
SR.53	1xViper Mk 102 + 1xSpectre	1,750 8,000	M2.2	18,400	2

* Type 510 conversion
+ Type 528 conversion
\# P1052 conversion

Saro S.R.53

Interest in a rocket-powered fighter was stimulated by experience of the Me163B Komet, but the main problem was short flight duration. In the S.R.53 the solution was to match the Spectre rocket with a Viper 102 jet and in this format the type could reach 50,000ft in two minutes with a top speed of M1.33 in level flight. XD145 flew in May 1957 but the programme was scrapped the next year. *(R C B Ashworth via P H T Green)*

12.5 Helicopters

Early British experience with rotorcraft was largely confined to autogiros which had served a useful purpose with 529 Sqn on calibration duties during the war. However, the first practical helicopter, the Sikorsky R-4, had been imported from the United States and there was renewed interest in the type. Specifications had been issued during the war and a number of interesting types was produced as a result.

Cierva W.9

G&J Weir Ltd had been involved in helicopter design at the outbreak of the war with the W.5 and W.6 and as a result of pressure had succeeded in securing specification E.16/43 which was issued to the Cierva company in which Weir had a stake. The W.9 was the result, the first of two intended machines, PX203, flying in late 1944 or early 1945 from Henley-on-Thames.

The design was basic and in its life it went through numerous changes. In principle it comprised a glazed cockpit area, a conical tubular fuselage and an upright fin. The Gipsy Six engine drove a three-bladed rotor with exhaust bled through a vent in the tail in lieu of a tail rotor, a remarkable advance at the time. The second machine was not built and the sole W.9 was damaged beyond repair in January 1948.

Fairey Gyrodyne, Jet Gyrodyne and Rotodyne

The FB.1 **Gyrodyne** was a pre-war design resurrected in 1946 when specification E.4/46 was issued. It comprised a tubby fuselage with stub wings, a single rotor and a tailplane with twin fins and rudders. Power was provided by a 515hp Leonides engine driving the main three-blade rotor and a propeller on the starboard wing to counter yaw. Possible Army needs were covered by specification A.7/47 and serials VW796-7 were allocated. A further specification, E.16/47, was issued with an order for one aircraft, VX591.

In the event the first Gyrodyne was registered G-AIKF and as such it flew on 7 December 1947. On 28 June 1948 it established a speed record for helicopters of 123.4mph

Fairey Jet Gyrodyne

The Gyrodyne was first built in 1947 powered by a Leonides driving a three-blade main rotor and with a propeller on one wing to counter yaw. It was rebuilt as XJ389 with the engine supporting pressure jets at the rotor tips as seen here. Once off the ground power was transferred to the pusher propellers for forward flight. (*P Pountney via P H T Green*)

but on 17 April 1949 it crashed, killing the crew, including pilot F.H. Dixon, while preparing for a further record attempt. A second Gyrodyne, G-AJJP, was also built but was grounded in 1949.

From about 1947 there had been interest in a large transport helicopter from several quarters and Fairey secured specification RH.124D which included provision for a test 'model'. Serial XD759 was allocated but it had to be changed to XJ389 through having been duplicated. The test vehicle was the second Gyrodyne re-built with a large twin-bladed propeller with pressure-jets at the blade tips as the **Jet Gyrodyne**. These were driven from the Leonides engine which also powered pusher propellers on each stub wing-tip. In take-off and landing maximum power was applied to the main rotors but as the machine lifted power was transferred to the propellers for maximum forward speed and the rotor left to auto-rotate. The first free flight was made in January 1954 with transitional flight in March 1955. Flight testing was largely complete by 1957 when the Rotodyne flew and the aircraft survived to be preserved at Cosford.

Gyrodynes, with engine(s) for forward propulsion and rotor-tip power for vertical take-off, were of continuing interest after the war with the Gyrodyne and Jetcopter. Jet-driven rotors, as described above, offered considerable weight and complexity reduction and Faireys were interested in development. Over a number of years the company refined ideas for a passenger-carrying aircraft capable of operating commercially. Eventually the design firmed up as the 40-plus passenger **Rotodyne** to meet the BEA requirement for a 'bus' to transfer passengers between city centres. Specification RH.142D was issued with serial XE521 and a second machine, XH249, was envisaged to meet an Army need described in OR.334. In the event the latter, the Rotodyne Z, was not built.

The Rotodyne was completed in 1957 and, powered by two Napier Eland engines, it first flew untethered on 6 November of that year. A large 58ft 8in fuselage was surmounted by the rotor head carrying a four-bladed rotor. Shoulder wings of 46ft 4in span set about half-way along the fuselage carried the two engines driving conventional propellers and a large tailplane, also set atop the rear fuselage, was fitted with twin fins and rudders. Transitional flights were conducted between April and October of 1958 and development proceeded with remarkably little in the way of problems for such a complex project. Consolidation in the aircraft industry combined with defence cuts and noise problems led to the Rotodyne being scrapped in May 1962.

Bevan Brothers E.1/48 Jetcopter

As early as 1928 the Air Ministry had ordered a form of autogyro, the Helicogyre, from the Italian designer Isacco. While similar in principle to an autogiro, the type featured small engines attached to the rotor blades. It was not successful and Isacco worked on other projects until after the war when he came to England from France to work with Bevan Brothers on specification E.1/48. This provided for a jet-powered version of the Helicogyre, the Jetcopter. Three captured **Focke-Achgelis Fa 330** rotor-kites were brought to the UK with the serials VX259, 266 and 850 to provide the basis of the new helicopter. In the event the project was abandoned in 1951. (The Fa 330 was extensively tested until about 1950, primarily at the AFEE.)

Fairey Rotodyne

Experience with the Jet Gyrodyne led to the much larger Rotodyne which was proposed to BEA for passenger transfer from airport to city centre. Powered by two Eland turboprops the Rotodyne would have carried 40 passengers. XE521 was the sole prototype. *(MAP)*

Cierva W.11 Air Horse

The W.11 was intended to meet a range of needs including crop-spraying and transport and in 1946 specification E.19/46 was issued to cover the procurement of a prototype; later a second machine was ordered. It was a large machine with three rotors, one at the front and one on each side, all powered by a single Merlin engine. The fuselage was of box section and was nearly 90ft long, with overall width of 95ft. Twin fins and rudders were set on the end of short tailplanes and the helicopter featured a simple long-stroke undercarriage. With its rotors set on outriggers, the design may well have been influenced by the **Focke-Achgelis Fa 223E** which had been evaluated at AFEE late in 1945 as VM479.

First untethered flight of VZ-724/G-ALCV was on 8 December 1948 at an all-up weight of 14,600lb and progress was steady, with the second aircraft, WA555/G-ACLW, ready for trials by October 1948. VZ-724 was destroyed on 13 June 1950 with the loss of the crew of three and when Saunders-Roe took over Cierva in 1951 the project was abandoned.

Bristol 173

The Type 173 was essentially a civil project for a ten-seat helicopter for which specification E.4/47 was issued. The Bristol proposal was for a tandem-rotor machine with high commonality with the smaller Type 171 (later Sycamore, Chapter 7.10). A long, slender fuselage was fitted with a fixed four-wheel undercarriage and sharply

upswept tailplane. The first Type 173 flew on 3 January 1952 as G-ALBN and later, in 1953, it was allocated the serial XF785 for deck-landing trials. The second prototype was G-AMJI/XH379 with revised tailpane which was also engaged on service trials. Serial XG354 was allocated to an airframe used as a ground test-rig.

Three series 3 aircraft were ordered with the Leonides Major driving four-bladed rotors and with a taller rear pylon. They were XE286-8 (G-AMYF-H) but only the first had begun ground running in November 1956 when work on the type was stopped. The RAF remained interested in the design and this led to the Type 192 Belvedere (Ch 6.14)

Percival P.74

Rotor-tip drive through jet exhaust was seen as being a solution to problems of torque and the weight of engine and transmission involved in driving a conventional helicopter with tail rotor. Hunting teamed with neighbours Napier to build the P.74 to specification EH.125D to be powered by two 750hp Oryx engines. The shape approximated that of a barrage balloon with windows and a three-bladed rotor and the serial XK889 was allocated. After many delays through the need to make adjustments to the design – including fitting a tail rotor – the aircraft was rolled out in May 1956. Attempts to lift it from the ground were fruitless and although the manufacturers re-designed the aircraft the project was abandoned in 1957.

Specification and production

Type	Engine	HP	Speed mph	Weight lb	Nos
Cierva W.9	Gipsy Six	205	115	2,647	1
Gyrodyne	Leonides 55	515	123	4,800	2
Jet Gyrodyne	Leonides 54	515		6,000	1*
Rotodyne	2xEland 3	3,150	190		1
Cierva W.11	Merlin 32	1,620	140	7,500	2
Bristol 173	2xLeonides 1M	550	115	10,600	2
Bristol 173 srs 3	2xLeonides Major	870	115	13,500	1
P.74	2xOryx	750	n/a	?	1

* Gyrodyne conversion

12.6 Vertical Take-Off and Landing (VTOL)

The limited speed of the helicopter led to a search for forms of vertical take-off and landing which offered more scope for combat applications. In due course the arguments revolved around two formats: separate engines for lift and forward propulsion and vectored thrust as later used on the Harrier family. Development of the latter is covered elsewhere (Ch. 3.12) but there were two important dual engine projects in the UK.

Rolls-Royce Thrust Measuring Rig ('Flying Bedstead')

The TMR was a rig only, made of tubular steel and comprising two opposed Nene 101 engines with most of the thrust directed immediately downwards but with 9% of the power being bled off to puffer pipes projecting fore and aft. The first of two rigs, without serial but later XJ314, flew on 9 July 1953 tethered and on 3 August 1954 free and 224 tethered and 16 free flights had been completed by December 1954. It went to the RAE where it eventually crashed on 16 September 1957.

The second rig, XK426, flew on 12 November 1956 but it crashed on 27 November 1957 on a tethered flight after hitting the gantry and killing the pilot, Wg Cdr H. G. F. Larson. The TMR had a design thrust-to-weight ratio of 1.25:1 but the actual figure was slightly less with fuel for about fifteen minutes' 'flight'.

Short SC.1

In 1952 specification ER.143D was issued for a relatively conventional aircraft capable of vertical and horizontal flight and in 1954 Short Bros was awarded a contract for the manufacture of two prototypes XG900 and 905. The shape was to be a delta with a fixed undercarriage, vertical tail surfaces only and a tubby fuselage accommodating five RB.108 engines each of 2,000lb thrust and a power to weight ratio of 8:1. Four of the engines were clustered vertically, but with some degree of fore and aft movement to provide lift, while a single engine was fitted at the rear for forward power.

XG900 was completed and shipped to Boscombe Down for initial trials on 2 April 1957 with only the propulsion engine fitted while XG905 was fully fitted by September when the lift motors were run. The first teth-

Short SC.1

Early thoughts on VTOL design were based around a mix of high thrust/weight ratio lift engines and separate engine(s) for forward flight. The first test design was the SC.1 and seen here is XG900 at the hover at Farnborough in 1960. *(Author)*

ered hovering flight was on 23 May 1958 and the first free flight on 25 October. Both aircraft went to the RAE at Bedford in due course but not before XG905 had crashed, killing the pilot, J R Green, but being re-built. Although vectored thrust had overtaken the dual engine approach in Britain the two aircraft remained on trials tasks until retired in 1971, one being preserved in Ulster and the other at Yeovilton.

Specification and production

Type	Engine	Thrust lb	Speed mph	Weight lb	Nos
R-R TMR	2xNene 101	5,100	n/a	7,500	2
Short SC.1	5xRB.108	2,010	n/a	8,050	2

12.7 General research

Numerous types in this chapter have been used to examine specific problems but usually in a wider context or as by-products or after the original need had been addressed. The types described in the section are a miscellany built for a wide range of research.

Youngman-Baynes HL.1

An innovative high-lift wing designed by R T Youngman was wedded to a re-designed Proctor Mk IV fuselage to evaluate fullspan slotted flaps. As VT789 the type was designated P.46 and flew on 5 February 1948 conferring excellent low-speed lift. It was evaluated by RAE and later sold to the designer as G-AMBL.

Reid & Sigrist RS.4 Bobsleigh

The RS.3 Desford was a twin-engined monoplane with fixed undercarriage built as a trainer, although only one was made, G-AGOS. It was bought by the Ministry of Supply for prone pilot research in 1948, it being believed that fast jets would require a very low frontal profile. The nose was lengthened and glazed and provision made for a pilot lying prone while retaining the original cockpit; the name was changed to Bobsleigh to reflect the driving position. The first flight, as VZ728, was made on 13 June 1951 and tests were conducted over several years until the aircraft reverted to the civil register in 1956. The Bobsleigh is preserved at East Fortune. Research continued later on a specially adapted Meteor 8, WK935, which flew on 10 February 1954 with the Institute of Aviation Medicine. It was retired after a year and is preserved at Cosford.

Marshalls MA.4

An Auster T Mk 7, VF665, was modified by Marshalls to specification ER.184D to enable Cambridge University to explore boundary-layer control by suction. For this purpose a revised wing, stronger undercarriage and enlarged fin and rudder were fitted together with a small turbine to provide the suction through wing perforations. Lift was greatly improved and the MA.4 flew from early

1959 until it was lost in a crash on 8 March 1966.

Avro Type 706 Ashton

Experience with the Tudor Mk 8 (Ch 12.11; 12.12) highlighted the problems of a tailwheel configuration for jet-engined aircraft. The Type 706 Ashton was in essence a Tudor development with nosewheel undercarriage. Six were ordered by the MoS in four configurations solely as research vehicles. The Mark 1, WB490, was based on Tudor 2 TS896/G-AJJV and featured a nose probe; it flew on 1 September 1950 and served with the A&AEE until 1957. Mark 2 WB491 flew on 2 August 1951. Based on Tudor TS897/G-AJJW it was operated by the RAE until 1960 as an engine test-bed with a variety of engines fitted in a ventral pod under the centre fuselage section.

Three Mark 3 aircraft were built, all with shorter pressurised fuselage sections and based on Tudor 2 airframes. They were WB492 ex TS898/G-AJJX (first flight 6 July 1951), WB493 ex TS899/G-AJJY (first flight 18 December 1951) and WE670 ex TS901/G-AJKA (first flight 9 April 1952). WB492 was fitted with underwing nacelles to contain bombs and served with the RRE from 1952 to 1955 where it was fitted with a radar scanner under the centre fuselage. WB493 was used by the Bristol Aeroplane Company from 1952 to 1962 for engine test-bed work. At one time it was fitted with two Olympus engines outboard of the Nenes and as such was the only British six-jet aircraft to fly; in 1956 it secured the world altitude record of 63,668ft. WE670 was used by the A&AEE for bomb ballistics trials from 1952 and then went to Rolls-Royce as a test-bed until 1962.

The sole Mark 4 was WB494 ex TS900/G-AJJZ which flew on 18 November 1952. It had a pressurised ventral pannier for the bomb-aimer and went to the RAE for visual bombing research, then on to de Havilland for engine development until 1962.

Avro Ashton

The Ashton was essentially a jet-powered Tudor and six were ordered in different configurations as research vehicles. WB491 was a Mk 2 aircraft based on Tudor TS897 and used as an engine test-bed with the RAE. It is seen here with a Conway installed in a nacelle under the centre fuselage. *(P H T Green collection)*

Bristol 188

The Type 188 was built of stainless steel and was powered by two Gyron engines. Its purpose was to examine the effects of kinetic heating on airframes, but performance did not meet expectations. XF926 was the second of two to be built. *(P H T Green collection)*

Bristol 188

Specification ER.134T called for a research aircraft capable of flying at sustained speeds in excess of Mach 2 in order to examine the effects of kinetic heating on airframes. The Bristol design, powered by two de Havilland Gyron engines of up to 20,000lb thrust, was

Hunting H.126

A pure research vehicle, Hunting H.126 XN714 was constructed to explore the use of a jet flap with the engine exhaust ducted through the wing. It flew in the United Kingdom and US for some years from 1963 before preservation at Cosford. *(Author)*

selected and two aircraft, XF923 and XF926, were ordered. (Three further aircraft, XK429, 434 and 436, were cancelled.) The aircraft was built of stainless steel with a long, thin fuselage, high-set tailplane and with the engines mounted midway along extremely thin wings. First flight of XF923 was on 14 April 1962 and the second machine flew a year later. The programme was a failure, with speed limited to Mach 1.88 and very poor flight duration, and it ceased in 1964 with XF926 preserved at Cosford.

Hunting H.126

This pure research aircraft was built to specification ER.189D to provide a tool for exploring the use of the jet exhaust channelled through the wing trailing edge to produce a jet flap. Two airframes were ordered, XN714 and 719, but the latter was cancelled, the former flying on 26 March 1963 from RAE Bedford. The H.126 was an ungainly aircraft with a single Orpheus 805 engine, fixed undercarriage and high-set tailplane. It was flown at RAE for several years and was eventually transferred to Cosford where it is preserved.

12.8 Miscellaneous assignments

Numerous aircraft were given military marks for diplomatic or other reasons or when non-military types were bought for use by the research establishments. The types so marked are listed in serial order.

Bell P-63 Kingcobra
One of two P-63 single-engined fighters, FZ440, was still flying with the RAE on laminar wing trials until September 1948.

Westland Welkin
The P14 Welkin was designed to specification F.4/40 for a high-altitude fighter. In appearance it looked not unlike a scaled-up Whirlwind and first flight (DG558) was on 1 November 1942. The anticipated high-altitude bombing campaign did not materialise and the Spitfire Mk 9 was up to the task of intercepting high-flying German reconnaissance aircraft. The Welkin was eventually abandoned in its originally intended role. The NF Mark 2 was a two-seat variant produced against specification F.9/43 and equipped with AI Mk 8 radar and wing-mounted 20mm cannon. The prototype, PF370, flew in October 1944 but the type was not put into production, the night fighter requirement being met by the Mosquito NF Mk 30. Re-serialled WE997 the aircraft served for some years as a radar test-bed with TRE.

Bristol 170 Freighter
The Bristol 170, built to specification C.9/45, was a twin-engined, high-wing monoplane freighter with nose loading for large loads, typically cars. The prototype Mk 30, G-AGPV, became VR380 for trials with A&AEE in 1946 while G-AGUT became VR382 for use with the TRE at Defford. Mark 31 G-AINK became WH575 for winterisation trials in Canada but was damaged before delivery. It was replaced by WJ320 ex G-AINL. Finally, XJ470 was bought direct for the A&AEE.

Aircraft WB482-484 were Mark 21Es ex G-AIMI, IMO and IMR bought by the MoS for the RAAF. Later Mark 21E WW378 ex G-AHJN was also bought for the RAAF.

Bristol 170 Freighter

While one Freighter was used by the TRE for trials it is believed that XJ470 with the A&AEE was used for moving test equipment and personnel around between sites. *(MAP)*

Ercoupe 415CD
The single-engined light aircraft was evaluated by the RAE and A&AEE from 1948 to 1952. The sole example was VX147, previously G-AKFC ex NC7465H.

Brunswick Zaunkonig II
This high-wing lightplane was built at Brunswick and captured in May 1945. It was brought to the UK and as VX190 was used by the RAE from 1947 to 1949 when it became G-ALUA.

Ercoupe 415CD

Quite why the Ercoupe G-AKFC was evaluated between 1948 and 1952 is a mystery to the author. It is seen as VX147 marked '57' presumably for the King's Cup air races. *(MAP)*

Vickers Viscount
The successful Viscount airliner (specification C.8/46) was powered by four Rolls-Royce Dart turboprops and several were used for research. The prototype Type 630, G-AHRF, became VX211 for trials. The second aircraft, Type 663, was bought to specification E.4/49 and flew as VX217. It was used as a Tay test-bed before going to the TRE, then Boulton Paul Aircraft. The prototype Type 700 G-AMAV was allocated WB499.

700 series XR801 (ex G-APKK) and XR802 (ex G-ARUU) were purchased for the ETPS while 800 series XT575 (ex OE-LAG) and XT661 (ex 9G-AAV) were bought for the RRE.

Vickers Viscount Series 838

A total of six Viscounts was used for trials purposes. Series 838 VX661, seen here at Greenham Common in 1983, was used for radar trials with the Royal Radar Establishment. *(Author)*

North American B-45 Tornado
At least four 91 SRW RB-45C Tornados were flown by RAF crews from their base at Sculthorpe in 1952. Although marked with RAF roundels and fin flash, the aircraft do not appear to have had British military serials applied.

Sikorsky S-51
Sikorsky S.51 G-AJHW became WB220 for Antarctic exploration.

Auster J/5G Autocar
G-ANVN was used by the Colonial Office as XJ941 for trials with 'pest control' equipment prior to defoliation tasks in Malaya during the insurgency.

de Havilland Canada DHC-3 Otter
A single UC-1 Otter (BuAer 147574) was loaned to the 1956 Commonwealth Trans-Antarctic Expedition as XL710.

Miles M.100 Student 2
The Miles M.100 Student was built as a lightweight trainer building on the company's experience with the M.77 Sparrowjet. The sole aircraft, G-APLK, was allocated XS941 when developed in the Mark 2 version as a prospective COIN type.

Beagle D5/180 Husky
Husky G-AWSW was donated to the Air Training Corps and flew for some years with 5 AEF at Teversham as XW635.

Beagle D5/180 Husky

A sole Auster was flying in RAF marks from 1969 to 1990 in the form of Husky XW635 which was donated to the ATC. It flew with 5 AEF and is seen here at Teversham in 1984. *(Author)*

Procter Kittiwake
An example of this kit-built aircraft was completed by Royal Navy apprentices at Arbroath and latterly at Lee-on-Solent and given the serial XW784.

Piper PA-30 Twin Comanche
A sole Twin Comanche XW938 ex G-ATMT was bought for the College of Aeronautics at Cranfield.

BAC-111
Four BAC-111 airliners were bought for research use by the RAE/DRA as flying laboratories. They were series 201 XX105 (ex G-ASJD); series 402AP XX919 and series 479F ZE432 and ZE433. All remain in service at the time of writing, the latter with GEC Ferranti.

FMA IA58 Pucara
Three Argentine Pucara light attack aircraft were captured at the end of the Falklands war and were

BAC 111 Series 201

Four BAC 111 aircraft were used as flying laboratories including XX105 seen here in 1991 while with the RAE at Bedford. *(Author)*

FMA IA58 Pucara

Three Argentinian Pucara light attack aircraft were captured during the Falklands War and returned to the United Kingdom in flying condition. ZD485 is preserved at Cosford. *(Author)*

brought to the UK in flying condition. They were allocated serials ZD485-487 and evaluated before being sent to museums.

Piper PA-31 Navajo Chieftain
Three Chieftains were bought for the RAE and one for the A&AEE in 1986 for communications tasks. They were ZF520 (ex G-BLZK), ZF521 (ex N27509), ZF522 (ex N27728) and ZF622 (ex N35487). By late 1995 they were in use by DTEO at Boscombe Down or Llanbedr.

Piper PA-31 Navajo Chieftain

Four Chieftains were bought for communications tasks in 1986; ZF522 was allocated to the RAE. *(Author)*

Westland WS70 Blackhawk
A sole Blackhawk was imported by Westland for potential sales development and given the serial ZG468.

Pilatus PC-9

A sole PC-9, ZG969, has been used by BAe at Warton in association with the Saudi Arabian contract for the type. *(Author)*

Pilatus PC-9

A PC-9 ZG969 (ex HB-HQE) is operated by BAe in connection with the Saudi Arabian contract for the type in association with the Tornado contract.

Westinghouse Skyship 500

One Skyship airship ZH762 (ex G-SKSC) was bought in 1994 for surveillance trials. It was reportedly written off at Boscombe Down in May 1995, but has since been seen flying from Middle Wallop.

12.9 Cancelled projects

From time to time specifications were issued for military aircraft, serials allocated and then the project cancelled at some stage after manufacture had begun. Some of these projects, having reached an advanced stage of flight testing, are described elsewhere but cross-referenced in this section. The following are projects which fall into the category; they are listed chronologically.

GAL 55 glider

Specification TX.3/43 called for a small training glider. Three prototypes of General Aircraft's GAL 55 were ordered with serials NP671, 674 and 678. The first flew at the end of 1943 but tests were deferred until late 1945 and ran to the summer of 1946 when it was decided to abandon the project.

Miles M.52

This intended high-speed research aircraft was designed to specification E.24/43 for which serials RT133 and 136 were issued. It was a straight-wing design intended to fly at 1,000mph and reached mock-up stage by the end of the war when captured German research suggested that swept wings were essential for supersonic flight, at which stage it was cancelled.

Gloster GA.1 Ace and GA.2

This intended fighter to specification E.1/44 is described in Ch 12.4.

Hawker P.1083

An intended supersonic Hunter with 50° swept wing of thin aerofoil section was intended and serial WN470 allocated. It would have been powered by a re-heated Avon engine but was not completed.

Supermarine Type 545

This supersonic fighter was a derivative of the Swift, with nose intake for the Avon engine and a thin crescent wing. Two prototypes, XA181 and 186, were ordered to specification F.105D2 and the first was almost completed when it was cancelled.

Vickers 1000

The Vickers 1000 (VC.7) was to have been a long-range military transport powered by four Conway engines. Seven aircraft were ordered, XD662 and XH255-260. In the event the project was cancelled before the first was completed.

Hawker P.1103 and Supermarine Type 559

These unusually large aircraft were proposed to OR.329 which led to specification F.155T calling for a fighter capable of intercepting aircraft at Mach 2.0 at 60,000ft. The two types had not got beyond the drawing board when the requirement was abandoned.

Avro 720

When specification F.124T was issued in 1951 inviting industry interest in mixed powerplant fighters, Avro and Saunders-Roe responded. The former then began construction of a remarkable delta-winged fighter to specification F.137D which comprised a metal honeycomb construction. It would have been powered by a Screamer rocket engine (8,000lb thrust) and one Viper turbojet (1,750lb thrust) but it was cancelled when the first of two prototypes, XD696 and XD701, was almost complete.

Supermarine Type 556 two-seat Scimitar

A two-seat all-weather fighter development of the Scimitar with Ferranti Airpass radar was intended, but the sole aircraft, XH451, was not completed since the contract went to the Sea Vixen.

Gloster P.376 thin-wing Javelin

In 1953 Gloster was contracted to build eighteen pre-production P.376 supersonic Javelin aircraft; serials XJ836-842 and XJ877-887 were allocated. The type, to specification F.153D, was intended for long-range interception and would have been powered by two Olympus engines. It was cancelled in 1956.

Saro S.R.177

The Saro S.R.53 (Ch 12.4) led to Admiralty interest in a development powered by a Gyron engine with Spectre rocket, designated S.R.177. Nine were ordered (XL905-907 and XL920-925) but the type was another casualty of defence cuts when the prototype was nearing completion.

Hawker P.1121

Hawkers continued development of the P1103 (above) to meet OR.339, eventually met by the BAC TSR.2 (Ch 4.13). As a private venture, completed only in mock-up form, it was not allocated a serial.

Hawker P.1154

The P1154 was a supersonic development of the P1127 for the RAF and Royal Navy to specifications SR.250D and P. Work on the prototype had just begun when it was cancelled early in 1965.

Hawker-Siddeley HS.681

The 681 was cancelled in 1965 at the same time as the TSR.2 and Hawker P1154. It was to have been a Hastings and Beverley replacement to OR.351 – a four-engined transport broadly similar in configuration to the BAe 146 but with vectored thrust engines and boundary layer control. Six were ordered as XT261-266 but none was built; the need was met by the C-130 Hercules.

Grunau Baby

A very large number of German gliders and sailplanes was acquired by the British services at the end of the war. Grunau Baby '25' with no serial but marked with a roundel on the fin was operated by AHQ BAFO Gliding Club at Minderheide. *(Crown copyright)*

Slingsby T12 Kirby Gull

Three Gulls were assessed after the War by the A&AEE and then used by the Home Command Gliding Instructors School at Detling. VW912 was one of those, seen at Detling in August 1950. *(P H T Green collection)*

General Dynamics F-111

Hardly an abandoned project, the intended F-111 order to replace, in part, the cancelled TSR.2 was itself cancelled. The serials XV884-887 were allocated for four TF-111K variants while the main buy of 46 F-111Ks would have been serialled XV902-947.

12.10 Gliders and sailplanes

From the latter part of the war small training gliders were acquired, primarily for the Air Training Corps (ATC). As the war progressed numerous German gliders were impressed and assigned to RAF and Royal Navy units. Later, gliders and sailplanes were bought in small numbers for instructor, gliding association or ATC use or evaluation. The numbers and limited use of many of these types do not merit detailed description. The types involved and their numbers are as follows:

Type	Numbers	User(s)
Akaflieg Munchen Mu-13A	1	RN
BAC III	1	ATC
BAC VII	1	ATC
Dagling	1	ATC
Dart Tottenhoe	1	ATC
DFS/30 Kranich	4	RAF
DFS SG38	5	RAF
DFS Meise	1	?
Ditmar Condor	1	ATC
EoN Olympia I	2	ATC
Grunau Baby	25	RAF, RN
Horton Ho4	1	RAF
Primary nacelle	1	ATC
Schempp-Hirth Cirrus	1	AAEE
Schleicher Rhonbussard	1	RAE
Schleicher Ka.6CR	1	ETPS
Slingsby T4 Falcon III	10	ATC
Slingsby T6 Kite	4	ATC
Slingsby T9 King Kite	1	ATC
Slingsby T12 Gull	3	AAEE
Slingsby T24 TX.8/45	3	AAEE
Slingsby T34A Sky	1	ETPS
Slingsby T45 Swallow TX1	5	ACCGS
Slingsby T53B Regal TX1	1	RAF
Unknown	6	RAF, ATC

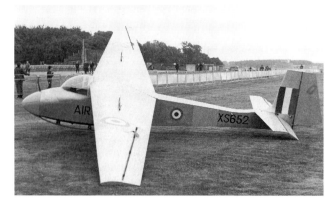

Slingsby Swallow

Small numbers of a wide variety of gliders have been taken on RAF charge since the end of the war for air cadet and recreational use. Slingsby Swallow XS652 was one of five and this example was with 662 GS in 1970. *(MAP)*

DFS/30 Kranich

Four Kranichs were given military serials but a much larger number were used without any disinguishing marks in Germany, such as this example of the mid-wing sailplane. *(Crown copyright)*

Handley Page Hermes II

The Hermes was a lengthened Hastings and when used by the MoS for trials work it was allocated serial VX234. *(MAP)*

12.11 Provisional marks

Post-war civil types were built against Ministry of Supply specifications and contracts and were allocated military serials, although these were rarely carried. The practice had ceased by about 1955 and the types involved included those listed below in serial order.

Handley Page HP.84 Hermes II
The Hermes was a four-engined airliner which was essentially a lengthened Hastings constructed to specification C.35/46. The first Mark II aircraft, G-AGUB, was also first allocated PW943 and later VX234 when it was used by the MoS for trials work.

Airspeed AS.57 Ambassador
The twin-engined Ambassador prototypes were allocated serials RT665 and 668, but flew as G-AGUA and G-AKRD. VP219-VP248 were cancelled.

Avro 688, 689 Tudor
The Tudor was a four-engined pressurised airliner designed to carry just twelve passengers across the Atlantic. **Tudor I** prototype, G-AGPF, also carried the serial TT176 and it later became VX192 with the MoS. Twelve were built and TS866-875 and VD273-278 were allocated. G-AGST/TT181 became a Tudor IV. G-AGRK/TS874 and G-AGRL/TS875 went to the MoS. The larger **Mark II** included allocations TJ161 and TJ164

Avro 689 Tudor Mk 8

The Tudor was a four-engined pressurised airliner and many were allocated military serials as described in the text. VX195 was the sole jet-powered example; compared with the Ashton it has a taller fin and rudder and tailwheel undercarriage. *(MAP)*

(both cancelled), TS884-892, TS893-902 (G-AJJS-G-AJKB), TS909-912 (G-AKTH-G-AKTK) and VD281-316, VD340-352 which later comprised a cancelled BOAC order. The second completed aircraft, G-AGRY, undertook tropical trials as VX202 but only five of this variant were completed. G-AGRZ/VZ366 and G-AGSA/VZ720 were also allocated for use with Flight Refuelling and Rolls-Royce respectively.

The **Tudor III** was a smaller aircraft based on the Mark I and for use by cabinet ministers. They were G-AIYA/VP301 and G-AJKC/VP312. Thirteen **Tudor IV** were built with Merlin 622/623 engines and an extended fuselage. At least two had serials intended for the unbuilt Mark Is, TS868 and 869. The **Mark V** was designed as a 44-seater but was, in fact, used as a tanker through the Berlin Airlift. Serials TS903 – 908 covered G-AKBY-G-AKCD. The **Tudor VII** had Hercules engines and one was built; it started life as nominal TS883 but flew as G-AGRX/VX199 with the Ministry of Supply and Aircraft Production. Finally Tudor 1 TT181 became VX195 as the sole **Mark 8** with four Nene jet engines for trials.

Vickers Type 495 Viking

This twin-engined airliner based on the Wellington was allocated TT191, 194 and 197 but not used. VP937 was applied to the prototype G-AGRV. The type later served with the RAF and for trials duties (Ch 6.9).

Vickers Viking

For trooping purposes many civil aircraft were allocated military serials during the 1950s. One such was Viking G-AHPM *Lord Rodney* of Eagle Aviation seen as XF632. *(MAP)*

Bristol Type 167 Brabazon

With a wing-span of 230ft Brabazon was the largest aircraft built in Britain. It was powered by eight Centaurus engines coupled in pairs and the prototype was allocated VX206 but flew as G-AGPW on 4 September 1949.

Armstrong Whitworth A.W.55 Apollo

The Armstrong Whitworth Apollo was built to specification C.16/46 as a DC-3 replacement. It was a sleek design with four low-profile Mamba turboprop engines and first flew as VX220 on 10 April 1949. It was later registered G-AIYN while the second prototype was VX224/G-AMCH which was used by the A&AEE and ETPS. The type was not a success.

Bristol Type 175 Britannia

The prototypes of the four-engined transport were allocated VX442 and VX454 but flew as G-ANBO and G-ALRX. The type later served with the RAF (Ch 6.13).

Vickers Type 700 Viscount

The highly successful four-engined turbo-prop airliner flew as G-AMAV but was allocated WB499. A number was taken on charge for trials work and is dealt with separately (Ch12.8).

12.12 Military charters

Through the 1950s civil aircraft were chartered for trooping, especially to the Middle East. In order to offer diplomatic protection in turbulent times such aircraft were given military serials. The following is a list of those recorded by type. In each case the last three letters of the civil registration – at the time invariably starting G-A – are given. The serials were applied to one charter only, thus some civil registrations are repeated where aircraft were used on several occasions.

Viking	**WZ**306(JFT), 311(JFS), 353(JFS), 354(IXS), 355(IXR), 356(KTU), 357(KTV), 972(HOP), 973(HON) **XD**635(HOT), 636(HOW), 637(HOR) **XF**532(JBU), 629(JBO), 630(IVO), 631(HPO), 632(HPM), 633(JCD), 638(HPB), 639(GRP), 640(GRW), 763 (HPJ), 764(HPC), 765 (HOY) **XG**349(HPM), 350(JCD), 567(KBH), 568(IVO), 895(JBO), 896(IVH) **XJ**304(JPH)
Hermes	**WZ**838(LDA), 839(LDB), 840(LDC), 841(LDF) **XD**632(KFP) **XJ**269(LDP), 276(LDX), 281(LDK), 288(LDU), 309(LDI)
DC-3	**WZ**984(GWS), 985(GZG) **XB**246(MBW) **XE**280(MRA), 281(MZD) **XF**619(MYX), 623(MYV), 645(MVC), 646(MSF), 647(MVB), 667(MSH), 746(MVL), 747(MYJ), 748(MZG), 749(MZF), 756(MPP), 757(MJU), 766(MSL), 767(MNL), 768(MSJ), 769(MSK), 791(NAE), 792(MWX)
York	**XA**191(MGK), 192(GNM) **XD**667(MUN), 668(MUU), 669(MUV), 670(GNU) **XE**304(MUN) **XF**284(MUL), 285(MUM), 919(MUS) **XG**897(MRJ), 898(NRC), 929(NSY) **XJ**264(NVO)
Tudor 2	**XF**537(GRY)
Bristol 170	**XF**662(IME), 663(IMH) **XH**385(MSA)
Tudor 1	**XF**739(GRI)

Westland SRN3

Although ground-effect vehicles rather than aircraft, hovercraft were allocated military serials. The sole SRN3, XS655, is seen beached on jacks, clearly illustrating the appearance of the machine as under power. *(MAP)*

12.13   Hovercraft

The hovercraft is a ground-effect vehicle and a variety was tested by the Army and Navy from about 1960. They were given aircraft serials, generally for trials although some, as indicated, served with the Royal Navy.

B-N Cushioncraft CC.2	XR814, XV172, XV285
British Hovercraft CC.7 Cushioncraft	XW249, XX101-102
British Hovercraft BH-7 Wellington	XW255 (RN NHTU Lee-on-Solent)
Hover-Air HA.5 Hoverhawk III	XW660 for RAE
Hovermarine HM2	XW260
Hovermarine HM2	XW555
Hovermarine Hovercat 3	XW608
Hovermarine HD.1, HD.2, HU.4	XW620-622
Vickers VA-1	XS798
Vickers VA-3 (G-15-253)	XS856, (XV336)
Westland SRN-3	XS655
Westland SRN-5 Warden	XT492-3, XW246
Westland SRN-6 Winchester	XT493, XT657,
(SRN-5 conversion)	XV614-617, XV859
	(XV615 RN Hong Kong; XV859 RN NHTU Lee-on-Solent)

GAF Jindivik

The Australian Jindivik has been in use for many years as a target, generally flying from Aberporth. A92-210 was displayed at Farnborough in 1960. *(Author)*

12.14   Target drones

From the 1960s a large number of target drones has been purchased for Army and Naval use. These are given military serials, and the types and numbers involved up to around 1985 are summarised below.

Beech SD-1 Peeping Tom	44
Government Aircraft Factories Jindivik*	2
ML Aviation ML-120D Midget	26
Northrop Chukar D Mk 1	89
Northrop Shelduck D Mk 1	963
Short MATS-B Mk 1	175
Short Skeet	225
Target Technology Ltd BTT-3 Banshee	108
Northrop Chukar D Mk 2	n/k

*   Jindiviks used in the UK from Aberporth seem to have had Australian serials in the A92-xxx range applied.

Northrop Chukar II

The Chukar has been brought in large numbers for Navy use as exemplified by Mk II ZD313. *(MAP)*

Appendix I

Abbreviations

Throughout this volume numerous abbreviations are used to spare space and avoid repetition. Such short forms are listed below with the exception of designations, which are covered in Appendix II, and Army units which are dealt with in the introduction to Chapter 10.

Term	Meaning
AA	Air Attaché
AAEE	Aircraft and Armaments Experimental Establishment
AAFCE	Allied Air Forces Central Europe
AAM	Air to Air Missile
ABTF	Air Beam Training Flight
ACCGS	Air Cadet Central Gliding School
ACSEACS	Air Command South East Asia Communications Squadron
ACU	Army Co-operation Unit
ADCS	Air Division Communications Squadron
ADLSS	Air Delivery Letter Service Squadron
ADS	Air Direction School
ADTU	Air Direction and Training Unit
AEAES	Air Electronics and Air Engineers School
AEF	Air Experience Flight
AEF	Airborne Experimental Flight
AES	Air Electronics School
AEU	Aircrew Examining Unit
AEW	Airborne Early Warning
AF	Acclimatisation Flight
AFCS	Automated Flight Control System
AFDS	Air Fighting Development Squadron (CFE)
AFEE	Airborne Forces Experimental Establishment
AFS	Advanced Flying School
AFTDU	Airborne Forces Transport Development Unit
AFTS	Advanced Flying Training School
AFWE	Allied Forces Western Europe
AFWF	Advanced Fixed Wing Flight
AGS	Air Gunnery School
AGS	Air Grading School
AI	Airborne Interception (radar)
AICF	Airborne Interception Conversion Flight
AIEU	Armament and Instrument Experimental Unit
AIS	Air Interception School
AMSDU	Air Ministry Servicing Development Unit
ANS	Air Navigation School
AOPS	Air Observer Post School
AOS	Air Observers School
AOTS	Aircrew Officers Training School
APC	Armament Practice Camp
APCS	Aden Protectorate Communications Squadron
APDU	Air Photographic Development Unit
APRF	Aden Protectorate Reconnaissance Flight
APS	Armament Practice Station
APSF	Aden Protectorate Support Flight
ARBS	Angle Rate Bombing Set
ARDU	Aircraft Repair and Development Unit
ARM	Anti-Radiation Missile
ARWCF	Advanced Rotary Wing Conversion Flight
ASDU	Air Support Development Unit
ASH	Air Service type H (radar)
ASM	Air to Surface Missile
ASR	Air-Sea Rescue
ASR	Air Staff Requirement
ASS	Air Signals School
AST	Air Service Training
ASV	Anti Surface Vessel (radar)
ASW	Anti-Submarine Warfare
ASWDU	Air/Sea Warfare Development Unit
ATA	Air Transport Auxiliary
ATC	Air Training Corps
ATDC	Air Transport Development Centre
ATDU	Aircraft Torpedo Development Unit
ATF	Andover Training Flight
ATF	Armaments Training Flight
ATM	Anti-Tank Missile
ATTDU	Air Transport Tactical Development Unit
AWC	Air Warfare Centre
AWDS	All Weather Development Squadron (CFE)
AWFCS	All Weather Fighter Combat School (CFE)
AWJRS	All Weather Jet Refresher Squadron
AWOCU	All Weather Operational Conversion Unit
AWRE	Atomic Weapons Research Establishment
AWW	All Weather Wing (CFE)
BAC	Berlin Air Command
BACF	Beam Approach Calibration Flight
BAFO	British Air Forces of Occupation
BAFOCS/W	British Air Forces of Occupation Communications Squadron/Wing
BANS	Basic Air Navigation School
BAS	Beam Approach School
BATF	Beam Approach Training Flight
BATUS	British Army Training Unit Suffield, (Canada)
BBU	Bomb Ballistics Unit
BCACS	British Commonwealth Air Communications Squadron
BCBS	Bomber Command Bombing School
BCCF/S	Bomber Command Communications Flight/Squadron
BCDU	Bomber Command Development Unit
BCF	Beam Conversion Flight
BCHU	Bomber Command Holding Unit
BCIREF	Bomber Command Instrument Rating and Examining Flight
BCIS	Bomber Command Instructors' School
BCNVTS	Bomber Command Night Vision Training School
BCOF	British Commonwealth Occupation Force (Japan)
BDTF	Bomber Defence Training Flight
BDU	Bomber Development Unit
BERP	British Experimental Rotor Programme
BFTS	Basic Flying Training School
BLEE	Blind Landing Experimental Establishment
BLEU	Blind Landing Experimental Unit
BNS	Basic Navigation School
BOAC	British Overseas Airways Corporation
BRNCAEF	Britannia Royal Naval College Air Experience Flight
BSDU	Bomber Support Development Unit
BSE	Bristol Siddeley Engines
BTU	Bombing Trials Unit

BTU	Belvedere Training Unit
BWF	Bristol Wireless Flight
CAACU	Civilian Anti-Aircraft Cooperation Unit
CAT	College of Air Training
CATCS	Central Air Traffic Control School
CATS	Central Air Traffic School
CAW	College of Air Warfare
CBAS	Commando Brigade Air Squadron
CBE	Central Bombing Establishment
CCCF	Coastal Command Communications Flight
CCDU	Coastal Command Development Unit
CCF	Check and Conversion Flight
CCF	Combined Cadet Force
CCFATU	Coastal Command Fighter Affiliation Training Unit
CCFIS	Coastal Command Flying Instructors School
CEF	Casualty Evacuation Flight
CF	Communications Flight
CFCCU	Civilian Fighter Control Cooperation Unit
CFE	Central Fighter Establishment
CFS	Central Flying School
CFS(H)	Central Flying School (Helicopter)
CGS	Central Gunnery School
CNCS	Central Navigation and Control School
CNS	Commonwealth Navigation School
CPE	Central Photographic Establishment
CRD	Controller of Research and Development
CRS	Control and Reporting School
CSDE	Central Servicing Development Establishment
CSE	Central Signals Establishment
CTTF/S	Communications and Target Towing Flight/Squadron
CTU	Combat Training Unit
CU	Conversion Unit
CVTS	Central Vision Training School
DFCS	Day Fighter Combat School (CFE)
DFLS	Day Fighter Leader School (CFE)
DME	Distance Measuring Equipment
DRA	Defence Research Agency
DTEO	Defence Test and Evaluation Organisation
DTF	Defence Training Flight
EAAS	Empire Air Armament School
EACF	East Africa Communications Flight
EANS	Empire Air Navigation School
EAS	Empire Armaments School
EASSU	Enemy Aircraft Servicing and Storage Unit
ECFS	Empire Central Flying School
ECM	Electronic Counter Measures
EFS	Empire Flying School
EFTS	Elementary Flying Training School
EGS	Elementary Gliding School
ELINT	ELectronic INTelligence
EM	Eastern Mediterranean
ERS	Empire Radio School
ESM	Electronic Support Measures
ETPS	Empire Test Pilots School
EW	Electronic Warfare
EWAU	Electronic Warfare Avionics Unit
FAA	Fleet Air Arm
FAC	Forward Air Control
FATS	Fighter Armaments Trials School
FATU	Fighter Affiliation Training Unit
FBTS	Flying Boat Training School
FCCRS	Fighter Command Control and Reporting School
FCCS	Fighter Command Communications Squadron
FCIRS	Fighter Command Instrument Rating

	Squadron
FCITS	Fighter Command Instrument Training Squadron (CFE)
FCITS	Fighter Command Instructor Training Squadron
FCMPC	Fighter Command Missile Practice Camp
FCS	Fighter Combat School
FCTTS	Fighter Command Target Towing Squadron
FCTU	Ferry Command Training Unit
FCTU	Fighter Command Trials Unit
FEAF	Far East Air Force
FECS	Far East Communications Squadron
FEFU	Far East Ferry Unit
FETS	Far East Training Squadron
FGF	Flying Grading Flight
FIS	Flying Instructors' School
FIU	Fighter Instructor's Unit
FLIR	Forward-Looking Infra-Red
Flt	Flight
FLS	Fighter Leader School (CFE)
FONA	Flag Officer Naval Aviation
FOST	Flag Officer Sea Training
FP	Ferry Pool
FPTF	Ferry Pool Training Flight
FRADU	Fleet Requirements and Air Direction Unit
FRS	Flying Refresher School
FRU	Fleet Requirements Unit
FS	Ferry Squadron
FSS	Ferry Support Squadron
FTC	Flying Training Command
FTCCF	Flying Training Command Communications Flight
FTCIS	Flying Training Command Instructor's School
FTS	Flying Training School
FTF/U	Ferry Training Flight/Unit
FU	Ferry Unit
FWF	Fixed Wing Flight
FWS	Fighter Weapons School
GCAS	Ground Controlled Approach School
GCF/S	Group Communications Flight/Squadron
GCS	Gunnery Cooperation Squadron
GFU	Germany Ferry Unit
GIF	Glider Instructor's Flight
GORTU	Group Operational Refresher Training Unit
GPEU	Glider Pilot Exercise Unit
GPMG	General Purpose Machine Gun
GPS	Global Positioning System
GPTF	Group Pilot Training Flight
Grp	Group
GS	Glider School
GSE	Glider Servicing Echelon
GTS	Glider Training School
GTPP	Group Test Pilot Pool
GWDS	Guided Weapon Development Squadron
GWTS	Guided Weapon Training Squadron
HC	Home Command
HCCS	Home Command Communications Squadron
HCEU	Home Command Examining Unit
HCGC	Home Command Gliding Centre
HCGIS	Home Command Gliding Instructors' School
HCMSU	Home Command Maintenance and Servicing Unit
HCT	Harrier Conversion Team
HCU	Harrier Conversion Unit
HCU	Heavy Conversion Unit
HDF	Helicopter Development Flight (CFS)
HDU	Helicopter Development Unit
HDU	Hose Drum Unit
HFF	Heavy Freight Flight

HFU	(Home) Ferry Unit	MF	Montforterbeek Flight
HGCU	Heavy Glider Conversion Unit	MLU	Mid Life Update
HGSU	Heavy Glider Servicing Unit	MoD	Ministry of Defence
HGTS	Heavy Glider Training Squadron	MOTU	Maritime Operational Training Unit
HOCF/U	Helicopter Operational Conversion Flight/Unit	MPC	Missile Practice Camp
		MRF	Meteorological Research Flight
HOCU	Harrier Operational Conversion Unit	MTPS	Maintenance Test Pilots School
HQFCCS	HQ Fighter Command Communications Squadron	MU	Maintenance Unit
HRF	Hastings Radar Flight	NAFDU	Naval Air Fighting Development Unit (CFE)
HTCU	Heavy Transport Conversion Unit	NAFS	Naval Air Fighting School
HTSCU	Heavy Transport Support Conversion Unit	NAS	Naval Air Squadron
HUD	Head Up Display	NASS	Naval Anti-Submarine School
		NASWDU	Naval Anti-Submarine Warfare Development Unit
IAM	Institute of Aviation Medicine		
IFF	Identification Friend or Foe	NAWCU	Night and All Weather Conversion Unit
IFTU	Intensive Flying Trials Unit	NCS	Northern Communications Squadron
ILS	Instrument Landing System	NEAF	Near East Air Force
INS	Inertial Navigation System	NECS	Near East Communications Squadron
IRBM	Internediate Range Ballistic Missile	NEICF	Netherlands East Indies Communications Flight
IRS	Instrument Rating Squadron		
IRS	Independent Reconnaissance Squadron	NFDW	Night Fighter Development Wing
ISF	Internal Security Flight	NFLS	Night Fighter Leader School
ISHTU	Inter Service Hovercraft Trials Unit	NFRU	Northern Fleet Requirements Unit
ISHU	Inter Services Hovercraft Unit	NFW	Night Fighter Wing (CFE)
ITF	Instrument Training Flight	NGTE	National Gas Turbine Establishment
ITS	Initial Training School	NHTU	Naval Helicopter Trials Unit
ITS	Initial Training Squadron	NHTU	Naval Hovercraft Trials Unit
ITW	Initial Training Wing	NICF	Northern Ireland Communications Flight
		NJETU	Naval Jet Evaluation and Training Unit
JASS	Joint Anti-Submarine School	NNFDS	Naval Night Fighter Development Squadron (CFE)
JATE	Joint Air Transport Establishment		
JCF	Jet Conversion Flight	NNFS	Naval Night Fighter School
JCU	Jet Conversion Unit	NOASS	Naval Observer and Air Signals School
JEFTS	Joint Elementary Flying Training School	NVG	Night Vision Goggles
JEHU	Joint Experimental Helicopter Unit		
JHTDU	Joint Helicopter Tactical Development Unit	OATS	Observer Air Training School
JHU	Joint Helicopter Unit	OCU	Operational Conversion Unit
JIRS	Javelin Instrument Rating Squadron	OEU	Operational Evaluation Unit
JMOTS	Joint Maritime Operational Training School	OFU	Overseas Ferry Unit
JOCU	Jaguar Operational Conversion Unit	OFTU	Operational Flying Training Unit
JSM	Joint Services Mission (Washington)	OR	Operational Requirement
JSTU	Joint Services Trials Unit (WRE)	ORTU	Operational Refresher Training Unit
JTU	Joint Trials Unit	OS	Observer School
JWE	Joint Warfare Establishment	OTU	Operational Training Unit
KF	King's Flight	(P)AFU	(Pilot) Advanced Flying Unit
		(P)RFU	(Pilot) Refresher Flying Unit
LAF	Lightning Augmentation Flight	PAU	Pilotless Aircraft Unit
LAS	Light Aircraft School	PCCS	Protectorate Command Communications Squadron (Aden)
LBS	Light Bomber School		
LCTF	Light Communications Trials Flight	PFS	Primary Flying School
LRMTS	Laser Ranging and Marked Target Seeker	PFS	Primary Flying Squadron
LRWE	Long Range Weapons Establishment	PGTS	Parachute and Glider Training School
LTF	Lightning Training Flight	PRDU	Photographic Reconnaissance Development Unit
LTW	Lyneham Transport Wing		
		PRFU	Pilot Refresher Flying Unit
MAD	Magnetic Anomaly Detector	PRU	Photographic Reconnaissance Unit
MAEE	Marine Aircraft Experimental Establishment	PTDU	Photographic Trials and Development Unit
MARU	Marine Aircraft Research Unit	PTF	Parachute Test Flight
MCCF/S	Maintenance Command Communications Flight/Squadron	PTOF	Palestine Truce Observance Flight
		PTS	Parachute Training School
MCS	Metropolitan Communications Squadron	PTU	Parachute Training Unit
MDAP	Mutual Defence Aid Plan		
MEAF	Middle East Air Force	QF	Queen's Flight
MECF/S	Middle East Communications Flight/Squadron		
		RAAF	Royal Australian Air Force
MED/ME	MEDiterranean/Middle East	RAE	Royal Aeronautical Establishment
MENVTS	Middle East Night Vision Training School	RAE	Royal Aerospace Establishment
METS	Multi Engine Training Squadron	RAECF	RAE Communications Flight
MF	Meteorological Flight	RAFC	Royal Air Force College

RAFFC	Royal Air Force Flying College
RAFGCS	Royal Air Force Germany Communications Squadron
RAFNI	Royal Air Force Northern Ireland
RAFTC	Royal Air Force Technical College
RAN	Royal Australian Navy
RATF	Radio Aids Training Flight
RATG	Rhodesian Air Training Group
RC	Reserve Command
RCCS	Reserve Command Communications Squadron
RCGIS	Reserve Command Gliding Instructor School
RCITF	Reserve Command Instructor Training Flight
REU	Radio Experimental Unit
RFS	Reserve Flying School
RFU	Refresher Flying Unit
RNEFTS	Royal Navy Elementary Flying Training School
RNVR	Royal Navy Volunteer Reserve
RNZAF	Royal New Zealand Air Force
RP	Rocket Projectile
RRE	Radar Research Establishment
RRF	Radar Reconnaissance Flight
RRFU	Radio Research Flying Unit
RS	Radio School
RSRE	Royal Signals & Radar Establishment
RWE	Radio Warfare Establishment
RWR	Radar Warning Receiver
SAAF	South African Air Force
SAC	School of Air Combat
SAM	Surface to Air Missile
SAOEU	Strike Attack Operational Evaluation Unit
SAR	Search And Rescue
SAS	Special Air Service
SATC	School of Air Traffic Control
SCBS	Strike Command Bombing School
SCDU	Strike Command Development Unit
SCS	Southern Communications Squadron
SCU	Special Conversion Unit
SEAC	South East Asia Command
SF	Station Flight
SFC	School of Flying Control
SFF	Short's Ferry Flight
SFTS	Service Flying Training School
SFU	Signals Flying Unit
SGR	School of General Reconnaissance
SHAEF	Supreme Headquarters Allied Expeditionary Forces
SIU	Signals Intelligence Unit
SKOCU	Sea King Operational Conversion Unit
SKTF	Sea King Training Flight
SMR	School of Maritime Reconnaissance
SLAIS	Specialised Low Attack Instructor's School
SLAW	School of Land and Air Warfare
SNAW	School of Naval Air Warfare
SoTT	School of Technical Training
SP	School of Photography
Sqn	Squadron
SRCU	Short Range Conversion Unit
SRF	School of Refresher Flying (RAFFC)
SRTU	Search and Rescue Training Unit
STTS	Station Target Towing Squadron
TACAN	TACtical Aid to Navigation
TAF	Tactical Air Force
TAFCS	Tactical Air Force Communications Squadron
TAG	Training Air Group (FAA)
TBR	Torpedo Bomber Reconnaissance
TCAEU	Transport Command Air Examining Unit
TCASF	Transport Command Air Support Flight

TCCF/S	Transport Command Communications Flight/Squadron
TCDF/U	Transport Command Development Flight/Unit
TCEU	Transport Command Examining Unit
TCS	Transport and Communications Squadron
TCU	Transport Conversion Unit
TDU	Tactical Development Unit
TEE	Test and Evaluation Establishment
TEU	Tactical Exercise Unit
TFF	Target Facilities Flight
TFU	Telecommunications Flying Unit
THUM	Temperature and HUMidity (Flight)
TIALD	Thermal Imaging And Laser Designator
TOW	Tube launched Optically tracked Wire guided (anti-tank missile)
TRE	Telecommunications Research Establishment
TSCU	Transport Support Conversion Unit
TSTU	Transport Support Training Unit
TTCCF/S	Technical Training Command Communications Flight/Squadron
TTF	Target Towing Flight
TTTE	Tri-national Tornado Training Establishment
TTU	Torpedo Training Unit
TWCU	Tornado Weapons Conversion Unit
TWDU	Tactical Weapons Development Unit
TWU	Tactical Weapons Unit
UAS	University Air Squadron
UHF	Ultra High Frequency
UNFICYP	United Nations Forces In CYPrus
USAAF	United States Army Air Force
USMC	United States Marine Corps
USN	United States Navy
VGS	Volunteer Gliding School
VHF	Very High Frequency
VISTRE	Visual Inter-Service Training and Research Establishment
VOR	VHF Omni-directional Range
VTF	Victor Training Flight
WACS	West Africa Communications Squadron
WCS	Western Communications Squadron
WCU	Washington Conversion Unit
WCU	Wyvern Conversion Unit
WEE	Winterisation Experimental Establishment
WRE	Weapons Research Establishment

Appendix II

Designations

Significant changes in type development – whether through new construction or conversion – usually merited a new mark number which through the war was written in Roman numerals to XIX and Arabic numerals from 20 upwards. From 1942 designatory prefix letters were used to indicate role. Then from 1947 Arabic figures became standard for all designations, although they had been in widespread but informal use as such for some time. Suffix letters were used to indicate minor changes, usually in equipment but sometimes in role.

There have been cases where the military designations have coincided with civil series numbers (DH Comet and Heron for example), presumably to avoid confusion. Indeed, in the case of the Comet the military designations alternated between the civil ones. Naval and Army variants often had designations starting at 10, 11, 20, 21 or 31 leaving earlier mark numbers available for RAF use. The Chipmunk started at Mark 10 to leave earlier designations free for Canadian use. In the unusual case of the Harrier odd numbers are for single-seat aircraft while even numbers are reserved for trainer variants. The Firefly appears to have been unique in having two sets of designations applied, one in Roman numerals and a later series in Arabic numerals.

There have also been situations where a significantly new aircraft has been developed but designated within the existing name and sequence, such as the Harrier GR Mk 5 (in US service the Harrier II). In other instances significant model changes have been made but with no change to the mark number, only to the role prefix (Sea Prince C Mk 1, T Mk 1).

Listed are post-war designations identified with examples of useage in parentheses.

Prefixes

A	Airborne Forces (Halifax)
ABR	Amphibian Boat Reconnaissance (Sea Otter)
AEW	Airborne Early Warning (Sentry)
AH	Army Helicopter (Gazelle)
AL	Army Liaison (Beaver)
AOP	Air Observation Post (Auster)
AS	Anti-Submarine (Avenger)
ASR	Air-Sea Rescue (Lancaster)
B	Bomber (Lincoln)
B(FE)	Bomber (Far East) (Lancaster)
B(I)	Bomber (Interdictor) (Canberra)
B(K)	Bomber (Tanker) (Victor)
B(PR)	Bomber (Photographic Reconnaissance) (Valiant)
BPR(K)	Bomber Photographic Reconnaissance (Tanker) (Valiant)
B(SR)	Bomber (Strategic Reconnaissance) (Victor)
B(TT)	*Bomber (Target tug) (Canberra)*
C	Transport (Beverley)
CC	Communications (Pioneer)
C(K)	Transport Tanker (VC-10)
COD	Carrier Onboard Delivery (Gannet)
C(PR)	Transport (Photo Reconnaissance) (Pembroke)
D	Drone (Sea Vixen)
E	Electronic (Argosy)
ECM	Electronic Counter Measures (Gannet)
F	Fighter (Hunter)
FA	Fighter/Attack (Sea Harrier)
F(AW)	Fighter (All Weather) (Javelin)
FAW	Fighter, All Weather (Sea Venom)
FB	Fighter Bomber (Venom)
FB(T)	*Fighter Bomber (Trainer) (Vampire)*
FG	Fighter Ground (Attack) (Phantom)
FGA	Fighter Ground Attack (Sea Hawk)
FGR	Fighter Ground-attack and Reconnaissance (Phantom)
FR	Fighter Reconnaissance (Swift)
FRS	Fighter, Reconnaissance, Strike (Sea Harrier)
F(TT)	Fighter (Target Tower) (Meteor)
GA	Ground Attack (Hunter)
GR	General Reconnaissance (to 1950) (Lancaster)
GR	Ground attack, Reconnaissance (Jaguar)
GT	Glider Tug (Master)
HAR	Helicopter Air Rescue (Wessex)
HAS	Helicopter Anti-Submarine (Wasp)
HC	Helicopter Transport (Belvedere)
HCC	Helicopter Communications (Whirlwind)
HM	Helicopter Maritime (Merlin)
HMA	Helicopter Maritime Attack (Lynx)
HR	Helicopter Rescue (Sycamore)
HT	Helicopter Trainer (Hiller)
HU	Helicopter Utility (Wessex)
ITF	*Interim Torpedo Fighter (Beaufighter)*
K	Tanker (Vulcan)
KC	Tanker, Transport (TriStar)
Met	Meteorology (Brigand)
MR	Maritime Reconnaissance (Seamew)
MRA	Maritime Reconnaissance Attack (Nimrod)
NF	Night Fighter (Meteor)
NF(T)	*Night Fighter (Trainer) (Meteor)*
PR	Photographic Reconnaissance (Mosquito)
R	Reconnaissance (Nimrod)
S	Strike (Wyvern)
SR	Strategic Reconnaissance (Vulcan)
ST	Special Transport (Albemarle)
T	Trainer (Chipmunk)
TF	Torpedo Fighter (Firebrand)
TR	Torpedo Reconnaissance (Mosquito)
TS	Trials (Avenger)
TT	Target Tower (Tempest)
TX	Trainer Glider (Prefect)
U	Unmanned (to 1956) (Firefly)
U	Utility (not used)
W	Weather (Hercules)

Suffixes

A, B, C, D	Used to denote a minor modification not meriting a fresh designation
(BS)	Blue Shadow (Canberra)
CTS	Central Tactical System (Lynx)
ECM	Electronic Countermeasures (Sea Venom)
GM	Gulf Modification (Lynx)
GT	Gulf Trials (Lynx)

ICE	Antarctic equipped (Lynx)
K	Tanker (Hercules)
K2P	*Tanker two-point (VC-10)*
LR	*Long-range (Hercules)*
(Mod)	Modification (Neptune)
MRR	Maritime Radar Reconnaissance (Vulcan)
N	Naval variant (Harrier)
P	Probe (Hercules)
PR	Photo Reconnaissance (Andover)
R	*Retrofit (Victor)*
R	Refuelling probe (Javelin)
RC	Radio Countermeasures (Canberra)
S	Secure speech radio (Lynx)
T	Trainer (usually 'two-stick') (Tornado)
W	Re-winged (Hawk)
X	Trials (Sea King)

Note – those designatory letters in italics appear to have been in informal use

Appendix III

Nicknames

In the course of service life many aircraft acquire nicknames, often alluding to some aspect of their flying characteristics or appearance or as a play on words. Names are coined by manufacturers or their staff, by enthusiasts, by groundcrew and, of course, by aircrew. Given below are some of the identified names used post-war. Surprisingly some aircraft in long term use like the Canberra, Hunter and Lightning appear to have been given little in the way of diminutives.

188 (Bristol)	Bristeel, Mayfly (or may not!)
Air Horse	Clothes Horse, Spraying Mantis
Albecore	Applecore
Albemarle	Dumbo
Andover	Budgie
Anson	Annie, Faithful Annie
Argosy	Brown Bomber, Flying Tit, Whistling Tit, Whistling Wheelbarrow
Ashton	Ashcan
Balliol	Pregnant/Sawn-off Spitfire
Barracuda	Barra, Barraweewee
Beaufighter	Beau, Flakbeau, Rockbeau, Whispering Death
Belfast	Dragmaster, Fastback
Belvedere	Flying Longhouse
Beverley	Barrack Block
Britannia	Whispering Giant
Buccaneer	Banana Bomber, Brick, Bucc
Buckmaster	Buck
Canberra	Cranberry
Catalina	Cat
Chinook	Wocka-Wocka
Chipmunk	Chippy, Flying Sardine
Dakota	Dak
Defiant	Daffy, Deffy
Dominie (DH)	Bamboo Bomber
Dominie (HS)	Jet Dragon
Expeditor	Twin Harvard
FD.1	Beast
FD.2	Delta Two
Firebrand	Brick
Freighter (Bristol)	Biffo, Frightener
GAL55	Trixie
Gannet	Dammit
Gazelle	Whistling Chicken Leg
Gliders (glassfibre modern)	Plastic V-Force
Gloster E.1/44	Gormless
Gnat	Orpheus Undershoot, Roller
Ground attack (generic)	Mud Mover
Halifax	Hali, Hallybag
Hamilcar	Jumbo
Harrier	Bonajet, Hoover, Jump Jet, Leaping Heap, SNUF (Smelly Noisy Ugly F***er)
Harvard	Pilot Maker, Window Breaker
Helicopter (generic)	Hydraulic Palm Tree
Hercules	Brownie, Chocolate Lorry, Fat Albert, Herk
Heron	Double Dove
Hoverfly	Flying Eggbeater
HPR2	Bandit
Hurricane	Hurri, Hurribird, Hurryback
Jaguar	Bomb Truck, Wheelbarrow Bomber
Javelin	Ace of Spades, Flying Flatiron, Flying Triangle, Harmonious Dragmaster
Jet aircraft (generic)	Blow Job
Jetstream	Streamer
Ju 52	Corrugated Coffin
Lancaster	Lanc, Lanky
Lightning	Fright'ning
Lincoln	Linc
Lynx	E-Type Helicopter, Larry
Lynx 9	Reliant Robin
Magister	Maggi, Yellow Peril
Meteor	Meatbox, The Reaper
Meteor 7	Phantom Diver
ML Utility	Flying Mattress
Mosquito	Balsa Bomber, Mossie, Wooden Wonder
Nimrod	Happy Hunter, Mighty Bunter, Nimjob
Oxford	Oxbox, Oxo
P111	Yellow Peril
P120	Black Widow-Maker
Phantom	Double Ugly, Tomb
Pioneer	Pin
Prentice	Clockwork Mouse
Proctor	Perce, Prog
Provost	Provo
Queen Bee	Buzzbox
SC.1	Flying Beetle
Sea Harrier	Shar
Sedbergh	Barge
Sentinel	Flying Jeep
Shackleton	Bear Hunter, Growler, Flying Spark Plugs, Magic Roundabout, Shack, Shacklebomber
Sioux	Clockwork Mouse
SM83	Porco
Spitfire	Spit
SR53	Manned Missile
SR.A/1	Squirt, Sea Jet
Stirling	Packing Case Bomber, Pulveriser
Sunderland	Sun
Swordfish	Stringbag
Tempest	Temp, Tampax
Thrust Measuring Rig	Flying Bedstead
Thunderbolt	Flying Milkbottle, Jug
Tiger Moth	Tiger, Tiggy
Tornado	Electric Jet, Fin, Flying Flicknife, Swinger
Tornado 2	Blue Circle Fighter
Tristar	Pink Pig, Timmy
Tucano	Silly Grin Aeroplane
Twin Pioneer	Double Scotch, Twin Pin
Typhoon	Bombphoon, Tiffie
Valetta	Pig
Valiant Mk 2	Black Bomber

Vampire	Flying Wheelbarrow, Kiddy Kar
VC-10	Big White Bird, Iron Duck, Skoda, Vicky Ten
Victor	Vic's Tours
Viking	Tin Wimpy
Vulcan	Aluminium Overcast, Tin Triangle
Walrus	Shagbat, Steam Pigeon
Wellington	Stickleback, Wimpy
Wessex 3	Camel
Wessex 5, Sea King 4	Jungly
Whirlwind	Iron Chicken, Whirlybird
Whitley	Flying Barndoor, Wombat
Wildcat	Peanut Special
York	Yorkie

Appendix IV

Post-war campaigns

British armed services have been involved in a number of actions since the end of the Second World War. These have included **wars, campaigns, actions**, *pre-emptive actions,* peacekeeping, humanitarian aid and miscellaneous operational tasks. Those involving aircraft are listed below in chronological order with a note of which air arms were involved. Campaigns in bold text are those in which weapons have been used. In each case the dates given are those within which British services were involved; some campaigns began prior to British involvement or continued after British disengagement.

Campaign	Air arms
Greek Civil War 1944 – 1946	**RAF**
Netherland East Indies 1945 – 1946	**Army, RAF**
Aden 1945 – 1967	**Army, FAA, RAF, RM**
French Indo-China 1945 – 1946	*RAF*
Palestine 1945 – 1948	**Army, FAA, RAF**
Somaliland 1947 – 1950	*RAF*
Egypt 1947 – 1956	*Army, RAF*
Sudan 1947 – 1948, 1955	*RAF*
Berlin Airlift (Op Plainfare) 1948 – 1949	*RAF*
Malaya (Op Firedog) 1948 – 1960	**Army, FAA, RAF**
Agent drops Ukraine 1949 – c 1952	RAF
Reconnaissance overflights 1949 – ?	**RAF**
Eritrea 1950 – 1952	**Army, RAF**
Korea 1950 – 1953	**Army, FAA, RAF**
Persian Crisis 1951	*RAF*
Kenya 1952 – 1956	**RAF**
Atomic weapons tests Monte Bello 1952	FAA, RAF
Oman 1952 – 1959	**FAA, RAF**
Hong Kong 1953, 1956	*RAF*
Cyprus 1955 – 1959	**Army, FAA, RAF**
A-bomb drop Maralinga, Australia 1956	RAF
Suez 1956 (Op Musketeer)	**Army, FAA, RAF**
H-bomb drop Christmas Island (Op Grapple) 1957	FAA, RAF
Jordan 1958	*RAF*
Maldives 1959	*RAF*
Congo support of Ghanaian UN forces 1960	RAF
Cameroons 1960 – 1961	*RAF*
Kenya, Somalia famine relief (Op Tana Flood) 1961	RAF
Berlin crisis 1961 – 1962	*RAF*
Kuwait (Op Vantage) 1961	*FAA, RAF*
Br Honduras hurricane relief (Op Sky Help) 1961	RAF
Thailand 1962	*RAF*
India 1962	*RAF*
Borneo (Op Borneo Territories) 1962 – 1966	**Army, FAA, RAF**
British Guiana 1962 – 1966	Army, FAA, RAF
Cyprus civil evacuation 1963	Army, FAA, RAF
Somalia/Kenya 1963 – 1965	*Army, RAF*
Dhofar 1964 – 1971	**RAF**
East Africa 1964	*Army, FAA, RAF*
Rhodesia 1965 – 1972	*FAA, RAF*
Anguilla 1969	*FAA, RAF*
Northern Ireland 1969 – date	**Army, RAF**
Jordan aid in civil war 1970	RAF
Pakistan flood relief (Op Burlap) 1970	RAF
Pakistan civil evacuation 1971	RAF
Iceland 1972 – 1973, 1975 – 1976	*RAF*
Nepal famine relief (Op Khana Cascade) 1973	RAF
Mali famine relief 1973	RAF
Cyprus civil evacuation 1974	RAF
Cambodia civil evacuation 1975	RAF
Angola civil evacuation	RAF
Belize 1975 – 1993	*Army, FAA, RAF*
North Sea oil-rig surveillance (Op Tapestry) 1977 – 1985	RAF
Zaire civil evacuation 1978	RAF
Iran civil evacuation 1979	RAF
Falklands (Op Corporate) 1982	**Army, FAA, RAF, RM**
Ethiopia famine relief (Op Bushell) 1984 – 1985	RAF
Colombia volcano disaster relief 1985	RAF
Antigua/Montserrat hurricane relief 1989	RAF
Gulf conflict (Op Granby) 1990 – 1991	**Army, RAF**
N Iraq (Operation Warden) 1991 – date (within Op Provide Comfort)	*RAF*
Turkey refugee relief 1991	RAF
Bangladesh hurricane relief 1991	FAA
Serbia blockade 1992	RAF
S Iraq (Op Jural) 1992 – date	*RAF*
Somalia relief 1992	RAF
Bosnia humanitarian relief (Op Cheshire) 1992 – date	RAF
Bosnia 1993 – date (inc Op Deny Flight, Op Grapple, Op Deliberate Force)	**Army, FAA, RAF**
Croatia (Op Resolute) 1995 – date	*Army, FAA, RAF*

In addition there have been numerous examples of relatively small-scale relief flights by the RAF over the years.

Appendix V

Weapons and equipment programmes

British weapons systems, in the widest sense, have been given two-word code names, apparently at random. All start with a colour which from observation appears also to be randomly chosen. Those projects maturing into operational systems usually, but not invariably, acquired more sensible names; exceptions included Blue Steel, Orange Crop and Red Top. Listed are programmes identified.

Black Arrow	Satellite launcher
Black Knight	Test rocket
Black Maria	Radar
Black Prince	Satellite launcher (Blue Streak and Black Knight)
Blue Anchor	Radar for Bloodhound II
Blue Boar	Standoff nuclear bomb (OR.1059)
Blue Danube	Nuclear bomb
Blue Devil	V-Bomber bombsight
Blue Diamond	Ground radar
Blue Diver	ECM for Vulcan
Blue Duck	ASW missile (Ikara)
Blue Envoy	SAM (Red Duster development)
Blue Falcon	Radar AA
Blue Fox	Radar AA (for Sea Harrier)
Blue Jacket	Doppler radar (for Buccaneer)
Blue Jay	AAM (Firestreak)
Blue Joker	EW radar
Blue Kestrel	Radar AA
Blue Lagoon	IR detection
Blue Moon	SSM
Blue Orchid	Doppler navigation
Blue Parrot	Radar airborne (for Buccaneer)
Blue Ranger	Blue Steel transport sorties to Australia
Blue Rapier	Tactical SSM
Blue Riband	Radar tactical
Blue Sage	Passive warning receiver
Blue Sapphire	Navigation system
Blue Shadow	Radar AA (for Canberra developed as Yellow Aster)
Blue Shield	SAM shipborne (Seaslug)
Blue Silk	Doppler radar (for Canberra post Green Satin)
Blue Sky	AAM (Fireflash)
Blue Steel	Standoff bomb (OR.1132)
Blue Streak	IRBM
Blue Study	Blind bombing system
Blue Sugar	Radio beacon
Blue Vixen	Radar (Sea Harrier Mk 2)
Blue Water	Tactical SSM
Blue Yeoman	Radar tactical (post Orange Yeoman)
Green Apple	Drift assessment
Green Archer	Ground radar
Green Bamboo	Thermonuclear weapon
Green Bottle	Homing device
Green Cheese	Anti-shipping missile
Green Flax	SAM development of Red Shoes - became Yellow Temple
Green Garland	Firestreak control
Green Garlic	Ground radar
Green Granite	Nuclear bomb (test)
Green Grass	Nuclear bomb (test)
Green Hammock	Doppler navigation
Green Light	SAM (Seacat)
Green Lizard	SAM
Green Minnow	Radiometer
Green Palm	VHF jammer (V-bombers)
Green Salad	VHF homer (for Shackleton)
Green Satin	Doppler radar (for Canberra and V-bombers)
Green Sparkler	Radar weapon
Green Thistle	IR homing incorporating Blue Lagoon and Blue Sapphire
Green Walnut	Blind bombing equipment
Green Willow	Blind firing Firestreak
Indigo Bracket	Radar jamming system
Indigo Corkscrew	Mobile radar (for Bloodhound and Thunderstreak)
Orange Blossom	ESM (for Hercules)
Orange Cocktail	Radar homing weapon
Orange Crop	ESM (for Lynx)
Orange Harvest	ECM (for Shackleton)
Orange Herald	Nuclear bomb (test)
Orange Nell	SAM
Orange Putter	Tail warning radar (for Canberra)
Orange Reaper	ESM
Orange Tartan	Navigation aid
Orange William	ATM
Orange Yeoman	Ground radar (Type 82)
Purple Granite	Nuclear bomb (test)
Red Beard	Tactical nuclear bomb (OR.1127)
Red Brick	Target illuminating radar (became Indigo Corkscrew)
Red Cabbage	Radar
Red Dean	AAM (Vickers 888)
Red Drover	Airborne radar (for Avro 730)
Red Duster	SAM (Bloodhound)
Red Eye	IR homing missile
Red Flannel	Developed H2S
Red Garter	Tail warning radar (for V-bombers)
Red Hawk	AAM (became Blue Sky)
Red Heathen	SAM study
Red Hebe	AAM (for Javelin)
Red Indian	Ground radar
Red Neck	Reconnaissance radar (for Victor)
Red Planet	Anti-tank weapon
Red Rapier	Unmanned bomber; as Blue Rapier
Red Rose	Short range ballistic missile (became Blue Water)
Red Setter	Navigation and bombing aid
Red Shoes	SAM (Thunderbird)
Red Shrimp	Radar jammer (for V-bombers)
Red Snow	Nuclear warhead (for Yellow Sun and Blue Steel)
Red Steer	ECM (for V-bombers)
Red Top	AAM (for Lightning and Sea Vixen)
Violet Banner	Homing head
Violet Club	Nuclear bomb
Violet Picture	UHF homer (for Whirlwind, Hunter and Sea Vixen)
Yellow Aster	Airborne radar (for V-bombers and Canberra)
Yellow Duckling	IR submarine detection

Yellow Fever	Ground radar
Yellow Gate	ESM system (for Nimrod)
Yellow Lemon	Doppler navigation
Yellow River	Tracking radar
Yellow Rover	Target illuminating radar (for Bloodhound)
Yellow Sun	Nuclear bomb (OR.1136) (for Vulcan)
Yellow Temple	Thunderbird SAM development
Yellow Tiger	Target illuminating radar for Thunderbird
Yellow Veil	ESM (for Lynx)

Appendix VI

Society of British Aircraft Constructors' designations

After the war the SBAC introduced an attempt at a standard format for company designations for aircraft. In the event most companies ignored the system, preferring to stick with their own. However some, notably Shorts and Blackburn, adopted the system and applied it for about ten years. Others, including Airspeed, Auster, English Electric, Fairey, Gloster and Westland have also used the system partially. Listed below are identified types referred to in the present volume.

A.1	English Electric Canberra
A.2	English Electric Canberra
A.3	English Electric Canberra
A.4	English Electric Canberra
A.6	English Electric Canberra
B.4	Auster Ambulance
B.5	Auster AOP Mk 9
E.3	Auster AOP Mk 11
FA.1	Fairey Rotodyne
FB.1	Fairey Gyrodyne
FD.1	Fairey Delta 1
FD.2	Fairey Delta 2
GA.1	Gloster E.1/44
GA.2	Gloster E.1/44
GA.3	Gloster E.1/44
GA.4	Gloster E.1/44
GA.5	Gloster Javelin
JC.6	Heston A.2/45
MA.4	Marshall experimental
P.1	English Electric Lightning
RS.3	Reid & Sigrist Desford
RS.4	Reid & Sigrist Bobsleigh
SA.1	Short Sturgeon
SA.2	Short Sturgeon
SA.4	Short Sperrin
SB.3	Short Sturgeon
SB.1	Short glider
SB.4	Short Sherpa
SB.5	Short P.1 scale model
SB.6	Short Seamew
SB.9	Short Sturgeon
SC.1	Short VTOL
SC.5	Short Belfast
SC.6	Short Canberra drone conversion
SC.7	Short Skyvan
SC.9	Short Canberra trials
VC.1	Vickers Viking
VC.2	Vickers Viscount
VC.7	Vickers 1000

VC.10	Vickers VC-10
VC.11	BAC 111
WA.4	Westland S.51
WA.8	Westland S.55
YA.1	Blackburn Firecrest
YA.7	Blackburn GR.17/45
YA.8	Blackburn GR.17/45
YB.1	Blackburn GR.17/45
YB.2	Blackburn HP.88 Model
XA.8	Airspeed Ambassador

Bibliography

Books relating to a single type are listed within the appropriate section. There are certain reference works which complement the present book and these are noted immediately below. Other general works follow with a note of magazines published in the UK which should serve to keep the reader up to date.

Companions

Action Stations (vols 1–10 and Overseas) various authors, PSL, Cambridge

Aircraft of the Royal Air Force since 1918 Thetford, O, Putnam, London, 1957, 1958, 1962, 1968, 1971, 1976, 1979, 1988, 1995

British Bomber, The Mason, F K, Putnam, London, 1994

British Fighter, The Mason, F K, Putnam, London, 1992

British Military Aircraft Serials 1878–1987 Robertson, B Midland Counties Publications, Earl Shilton, 1987

British Naval Aircraft 1912-1958 Thetford, O, Putnam, London, 1958

RAF Aircraft (volumes in serial ranges) various compilers, Air-Britain, Tonbridge

RAF Flying Training and Support Units, Sturtivant, R, Hamlin, J and Halley, J.J., Air Britain, Tonbridge, 1997

RAF Squadrons Jefford, C G, Airlife, Shrewsbury, 1988

Source Book of the RAF, The Delve, K, Airlife, Shrewsbury, 1994

Squadrons of the Fleet Air Arm Sturtivant, R, Air Britain, Tonbridge, 1984, 1996

Squadrons of the Royal Air Force Halley, J J, Air Britain, Tonbridge, 1988

General references

Air Wars and Aircraft: A Detailed Record of Air Combat, 1945 to the Present Flintham, V, Arms and Armour Press, London, 1989

Army in the Air, The: The History of the Army Air Corps Farrar-Hockley, A, Alan Sutton Publishing, Stroud, 1994

Bomber Squadrons of the RAF Moyes, P, Macdonald, London, 1964

British Prototype Aircraft Sturtivant, R, Haynes, Yeovilton, 1990

British Service Helicopters: A Pictorial History Gardner, R and Longstaff, R, Hale, London, 1985

C.F.S. Birthplace of Air Power Taylor, J W R, Putnam, London, 1958

Coastal, Support and Special squadrons of the RAF Rawlings, J D R, Janes, London, 1982

Eastward: A History of the Royal Air Force in the Far East 1945–1972 Lee, D, HMSO, London, 1984

Encyclopaedia of the Fleet Air Arm Beaver, P, PSL, Wellingborough, 1987

Fighter Squadrons of the RAF Rawlings, J D R, Macdonald, London, 1969

History of Britain's Military Training Aircraft, The Sturtivant, R, Haynes, Yeovil, 1987

Learn to Test, Test to Learn Rawlings, J D R and Sedgwick, H, Airlife, Shrewsbury, 1991

Lend-Lease Aircraft in World War II Pearcey, A, Airlife, Shrewsbury, 1996

Military Aircraft Markings March, P R, Ian Allan, London, published annually

Names With Wings Wansborough-White, G, Airlife, Shrewsbury, 1995

Per Ardua ad Astra: A Handbook of the Royal Air Force Congdon, P, Airlife, Shrewsbury, 1987

RAF Rotors Bedford, R G, SFB Publications, Huntingdon, 1996

Royal Air Force, The Armitage, M, Arms and Armour Press, London, 1993

Royal Navy Aircraft Carriers 1945–1990 Marriot, L, Ian Allan, Shepperton, 1985

Slingsby Sailplanes Simons, M, Airlife, Shrewsbury, 1996

U.S. Army Aircraft since 1947 Harding, S, Airlife, Shrewsbury, 1990

United States Military Aircraft since 1909 Swanborough, G and Bowers, P M, Putnam, London, 1963, 1971, 1989

United States Navy Aircraft since 1911 Swanborough, G, and Bowers, P M, Putnam, London, 1968, 1976, 1990

Wings in the Sun: A History of the Royal Air Force in the Mediterranean 1945–1986 Lee, D, HMSO, London, 1989

The Putnam series on specific aircraft manufacturers is also strongly recommended. It includes detailed volumes on the following: Airspeed, Armstrong Whitworth, Avro, Blackburn, Boeing, Boulton and Paul, Bristol, de Havilland, English Electric, Fairey, General Dynamics, Gloster, Grumman, Handley Page, Hawker, Lockheed, McDonnell Douglas, Miles, Saunders and Saro, Shorts, Supermarine, Vickers and Westland.

Magazines and organisations

A number of monthly (unless otherwise stated) magazines incorporate articles or news on British military aircraft, including:

Aeroplane Monthly
Air Enthusiast (quarterly)
Air Forces Monthly
Air Pictorial
Aircraft Illustrated
Flight (weekly)
Flypast
RAF Yearbook (annually)
Scale Aircraft Modelling
Wings of Fame (quarterly)
World Air Power Journal (quarterly)

There are two key enthusiast organisations which publish monthly journals. Air Britain publishes *Digest* and *Militaria*. The British Aviation Research Group (BARG) publishes *British Aviation Review* (incorporating *Roundel*).

Index

All types referred to in the book are listed below. They are invariably listed both by type name or number and separately by manufacturer. In the years covered by this book there have been numerous mergers of aircraft producers and in general the manufacturer shown is that responsible for design and initial production, rather than the eventual nominal manufacturer. Where two or more sections are shown against a type the first is the main entry and subsequent ones are incidental.